The publisher gratefully acknowledges the generous contribution to this book provided by the Simpson Humanities Endowment Fund of the University of California Press Associates.

WILLIAM
DEAN
HOWELLS

WILLIAM
DEAN
HOWELLS

A Writer's Life

SUSAN GOODMAN

CARL DAWSON

University of California Press · Berkeley Los Angeles London

University of California Press
Berkeley and Los Angeles, California

University of California Press, Ltd.
London, England

© 2005 by the Regents of the University of California

Library of Congress Cataloging-in-Publication Data

Goodman, Susan, 1951–.
William Dean Howells : a writer's life /
Susan Goodman and Carl Dawson.
p.   cm.
Includes bibliographical references and index.
ISBN 0-520-23896-6 (alk. paper)
1. Howells, William Dean, 1837–1920.
2. Novelists, American—19th century—Biography.
3. Critics—United States—Biography.
I. Dawson, Carl. II. Title.
PS2033.G66   2005
813'.4—dc22   2004026562

Manufactured in Canada
14 13 12 11 10 09 08 07 06 05
10 9 8 7 6 5 4 3 2 1

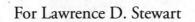
For Lawrence D. Stewart

A man remains in a measure strange to himself as long as he lives, and the very sources of novelty in his work will be within himself; he can continue to give it freshness in no other way than by knowing himself better and better.

—W. D. HOWELLS, *Literature and Life,* 1902

CONTENTS

Illustrations follow pages 196 and 324

PREFACE

What would you think of my writing my autobiography? My published reminiscences have made a beginning, and it would forestall a biography, always a false and mistaken thing.

—W. D. HOWELLS to his sister Aurelia, 1909.

Born in a hardscrabble Ohio village in 1837, William Dean Howells lived through and beyond what Mark Twain called "the greatest and worthiest of the centuries the world has seen."[1] As a young man, he faced America's cataclysm, the Civil War, and its aftermath, the years of Reconstruction. In the period that Twain and Charles Dudley Warner dubbed "the Gilded Age," he dined with robber barons like Andrew Carnegie. He protested the social injustices of the 1880s and 1890s, condemned the American imperialism that climaxed in the Spanish-American War, and died, in 1920, soon after World War I destroyed the hopes of his and the next generation.

At the opening of the twentieth century, Howells looked back forty years to measure his writing life. "If there was any one in the world who had his being more wholly in literature than I had in 1860," he wrote, "I am sure I would not have known where to find him."[2] That year, with a handful of poems and a campaign biography of Abraham Lincoln to his credit, the twenty-three-year-old made a pilgrimage to New England, the mecca of his literary dreams. In Concord and Boston he managed to meet America's leading writers: James Russell Lowell, Nathaniel Hawthorne, Ralph Waldo Emerson, and Oliver Wendell Holmes. During a dinner at the Parker House, Holmes joked about an apostolic succession, and he proved to be clairvoyant.

Howells' career is itself the stuff of fiction. The Lincoln biography, written in a week, earned him a consulship to Venice during the Civil War. The city served as the young man's university and introduced him to a world far removed from small-town Ohio. Venice furnished him with enough material about books and art to convince the powers of literary Boston to promote his career. The time came when Howells could return these favors, when he helped his own mentors and aspiring writers made their way to Boston and New York to visit him.

As editor of the *Atlantic Monthly* and later as a columnist for *Harper's Monthly,* Howells swayed the tastes and values of a growing middle-class readership, leaving his stamp on American culture. He himself published well over a hundred books. Although he lived as a self-conscious *American,* Howells' sense of that word varies throughout his works, which is to say that its defining lies at the heart of all he wrote. Anyone who wants to "trace American 'society' in its formative process," advised his friend and rival, Thomas Wentworth Higginson, "must go to Howells . . . he alone shows you the essential forces in action."[3] Howells wanted American literature to be less provincial, a national phenomenon rather than the property of New Englanders, yet he began his campaign in the *Atlantic,* New England's (and the nation's) premier magazine. More paradoxically, his vision of American literature led him to introduce readers to the works of Thomas Hardy, Ivan Turgenev, Émile Zola, and Leo Tolstoy, whom he held up as models to his compatriots. At the same time, Howells championed Henry James as an American writer when others dismissed him as unreadable or un-American for living abroad.

Howells was, as Mark Twain liked to call him, "the Boss." As a magazine editor he brokered reputations, promoted the careers of regional writers (many of them women), and introduced the reading public to the writings of African Americans like Charles Chesnutt and Paul Laurence Dunbar. He was at once a diplomatic "boss," a shrewd businessman, a political radical, and a writer whose imagination changed the standards of American fiction. Howells delighted in a story told by the sculptor Augustus Saint-Gaudens, a personal friend, who captured his mix of visionary and practical qualities in an extraordinary dream. As Howells retold it, "We were on shipboard together, and a dialogue rose between the passengers as to the distance of a certain brilliant planet in the sky. Some said it was millions of miles away, but I held that it was very near; and he [Saint-Gaudens] related that I went down to my stateroom and came up with a shotgun, which I fired at the star. It came fluttering down, and I said 'There! You see?'"[4] Howells, who wrote about his own dreams and saw the dreamworld as both revealing and amoral, would not have blamed Saint-Gaudens for imagining him a bigamist or criminal. It delighted him to be seen reaching higher and shooting bigger game than Theodore Roosevelt.

No one wields such power without considering what to leave behind for later generations, or for the untrustworthy biographers. As a writer of memoirs, autobiographical novels, and biographies, Howells understood the strategies—and the pitfalls—of writing lives as only a fellow conspirator can. When barely out of his teens, he urged one of his sisters not to throw away his letters. He intended to be famous and anticipated that a biographer would eventually find his papers useful. Toward the end of his life, he carefully selected and edited hundreds of letters and arranged for them to be typed. He did not want to stop books about himself so much as control the stories they told. The sheer volume of his gathered materials—records of royalty payments, engagements, and addresses, as well as journals, notebooks, and newspaper clippings—creates the misleading impression of an open legacy. Rather, Howells worked to keep posterity honest, or at least in check, by setting limits to our knowing. He was well aware that his own accounts—"reminiscences" of Venice or frontier Ohio, his meetings with Longfellow and Emerson, and the long friendships with James and Twain—would provide grist for future writers.

The orchestrated record he left behind reflects the quirks and paradoxes of his temperament. At once proud of his work and ashamed of his egotism, he cultivated a trait he admired in his father, William Cooper Howells. "The unfriendly eye always loses what is best in a prospect," the son explains in homage, "and his . . . eye was never unfriendly. He did not deceive himself concerning the past. He found it was often rude, and hard, and coarse; but, under the rough and sordid aspect, he was aware of the warm heart of humanity in which, quite as much as in the brain, all civility lies."[5] As civil as his father, though more cynical—he reveled in Mark Twain's iconoclasm—Howells chose to emphasize moments of joy and healing, not because he shied away from the suffering around him, but because he found no alternative to living with his conscience and facing the inevitable. Few writers have been more aware of human failings or more courageous. Almost alone among America's writers, he spoke out against the infamous Haymarket trials of 1886, which reflected widespread disquiet and brought about the hanging of innocent men. In the aftermath of Haymarket he chose to believe, perhaps pretend, that in the best of all possible worlds people could be good and happy. He knew that they were rarely either.

For the biographer, Howells proves a wily subject. In this book, we have tried to go beyond the fictions he himself created about his life and the fictions that have grown up since: the boy of his memoirs (a boy like any boy, only better); the sophisticated editor in his easy chair; the timid and emotionally scarred writer; the benevolent dean of letters. These characters have obscured Howells from his public and occasionally from himself. Mark Twain knew a more complex man. In a letter to their mutual friend Thomas Bailey Aldrich, he sent a photograph of Howells with his own description.

> Howells [is] looking—but I enclose his newest photo; it will tell you his condition. He thinks it a libel, I think it flatters. The thing that gravels *him* is, that the camera caught his private aspect, not giving him time to arrange his public one. I have never seen such a difference between the real man & the artificial. Compare this one with the imposter which he works into book-advertisements. They say, Notice this smile; observe this benignity; God be with you Dear People, come to your Howells when you are in trouble, Howells is your friend. This one says, Bile! give me more bile; fry me an optimist for breakfast.[6]

Despite this shrewd unmasking—Twain was an intimate friend—the simplistic portrayals persist, as do the grudging estimates of Howells' novels, essays, and books on places, beginning with *Venetian Life*. A few of his comments about the American temperament or the workings of fiction have defined this many-sided writer who, as Mark Twain recognized, published works that rivaled, and perhaps at times surpassed, his own. *Indian Summer, A Hazard of New Fortunes, The Rise of Silas Lapham,* and at least half a dozen others deserve a closer look by a new generation. These and his autobiographies, *Years of My Youth* and *Literary Friends and Acquaintance,* fry the simple optimist for breakfast.

We take comfort in another Twain comment—that, whatever anyone's deceptions, "the remorseless truth *is* there, between the lines"—while remembering Howells' warning to Twain, that no one can speak "the black heart's truth."[7] Howells liked to believe himself devoted to the truth, knowing very well that any historical account selects, stretches, and misses the truth. Biographers enter the spaces between the lines, make words into deeds, and reach for the nuances of a vanished world, in the hope—as Joseph Conrad once wrote—of shedding a little light. We have reimagined Howells where he lived and worked, in places as distant as Venice, Italy, and Kittery Point, Maine, and in Boston and New York, the centers of his professional life. We talk about the men and women he called "literary friends and acquaintance"; about the culture of publishing houses and magazines; about topics from political radicalism to Spanish novelists to moving pictures; and about Howells' later years, rich with new companions and causes and, as always, rich in books. We begin the story with his ancestors, the Welsh grandparents who came in search of a new life, making their way through the Cumberland Gap to the frontier of Ohio. But first a word about the making of this book.

Looking back on his life, Howells decided that autobiography could scarcely be kept from becoming biography—so much is human personality a reflection of family, friends, and historical conditions. He considered any life a kind of palimpsest, a layering of multiple lives and labor, and the same might be said about this biography. It has of course grown from its authors' collaboration, but also with the help of many others. We are deeply grateful to Howells' grandson, William White Howells, and his wife, Muriel Howells, for sharing with us documents and family memories. A gracious and gifted woman, Mrs. Howells died during the writing of this book.

No one can write about Howells without acknowledging Edwin H. Cady's landmark two-volume biography, *The Road to Realism* and *The Realist at War*. Cady's scholarship led the way for other biographers, including Kenneth S. Lynn in the mid-1970s *(William Dean Howells: An American Life)* and, more recently, John W. Crowley *(The Black Heart's Truth, The Mask of Fiction,* and *The Dean of American Letters)*. For studies that focus on specific topics or periods of Howells' career, we are much indebted to Thomas Wortham *(The Early Prose Writings of William Dean Howells, 1853–1861)*, Rodney D. Olsen *(Dancing in Chains: The Youth of William Dean Howells)*, James L. Woodress *(Howells and Italy)*, James W. Simpson *(Editor's Study)*, Ulrich Halfman *(Interviews with William Dean Howells)*, Walter J. Meserve *(The Complete Plays of William Dean Howells)*, Elsa Nettels *(Language, Race, and Social Class in Howells' America)*, George Arms, Mary Bess Whidden, and Gary Scharnhorst *(Staging Howells: Plays and Correspondence with Lawrence Barrett)*, Ellery Sedgwick *(The Atlantic Monthly, 1857–1909; Yankee Humanism at High Tide and Ebb)*, Clara M. Kirk *(W. D. Howells, Traveler from Altruria* and *W. D. Howells and Art in His Time)*, James L. Dean *(Howells' Travels toward Art)*, Kermit Vanderbilt *(The Achievement of William Dean Howells)*, James Doyle for his study of Howells' sister and brother-in-law *(Annie Howells and Achille Fréchette)*, Polly H. Howells for her work on Mildred Howells and her father, and Louis Budd for his groundbreaking articles on Howells' politics. Among Howells' most sympathetic readers are the novelists John Updike and Gore Vidal and Adam Gopnik, who appreciate both the appeal of his fiction and how it works.

An editor himself, Howells has attracted the attention of outstanding editors, including, first, his daughter Mildred (the compiler of *Life in Letters*).

We could not have written this book without the benefit of the Indiana Edition of his work and its architects: Don L. Cook, James Woodress, David J. Nordloh, Thomas Wortham, Ronald Gottesman, Donald Pizer, Martha Banta, Richard H. Ballinger, Christoph K. Lohmann, William C. Fischer, John K. Reeves, Jerry Herron, Robert C. Leitz III, Eugene Pattison, Robert D. Schildgen, Jonathan Thomas, George C. Carrington Jr., Scott Bennett, David Burrows, Everett Carter, James P. Elliott, David Kleinman, Ulrich Halfman, J. Albert Robbins, and of course Edwin H. Cady, George Arms, and William M. Gibson. In addition to the six volumes of Howells' letters published in this edition, we have relied on Michael Anesko's superb volume, *Letters, Fictions, Lives: Henry James and William Dean Howells,* as well as the classic *Mark Twain–Howells Letters,* edited by Henry Nash Smith and William M. Gibson, with the assistance of Frederick Anderson; and *If Not Literature: Letters of Elinor Mead Howells,* edited by Ginette de B. Merrill and George Arms. The bibliographies compiled by William M. Gibson and George Arms and Clayton L. Eichelberger have been especially helpful.

For his generous advice, critical reading, and knowledge of Howells' contemporaries, we give special thanks to Jerome Loving. The conference he organized on biography in 2001 brought us together with other writers whose work has inspirited our own—Ed Folsom, Scott Donaldson, Wilfred Samuels, Jeanne Campbell, and Jay Martin—as well as Linda Wagner-Martin and Robert D. Richardson, whose readings of our manuscript have been invaluable. June Hanson helped us with genealogy. Joel Fruchtman read drafts of early chapters. Gary Scharnhorst drew our attention to articles about Howells and kindly passed on to us offprints that belonged to George Arms. Polly Howells, in addition to her research on the Howells family, generously shared with us family documents and photographs.

We are grateful for the support of the dean of our college, Mark Huddleston; our department chairs, Jerry Beasley and Stephen Bernhardt; and the university's director of research, Fraser Russell. Sabbaticals and General University Research Grants from the University of Delaware and fellowships from the John Simon Guggenheim Memorial Foundation, Harvard University's Houghton Library, and the University of New England made research possible from Maine to California.

We have relied shamelessly on kind archivists and librarians. Laura L. McFadden opened the Herrick Memorial Library, Alfred University, at off-hours and guided us through the collection. Roger Stoddard got us started at the Houghton Library and kindly brought us books from Howells' library in Kittery Point. Thomas P. Ford prepared some of the photographs used in this book and, with Emily Walhout, helped us find stray sources. Mona Noureldin and Stephen Tabor offered friendly help at the Huntington Library. Kathleen Kienholz, at the American Academy of Arts and Letters, graciously organized and copied correspondence for us. We appreciate the expertise of Fred Bauman and Alice Birney, Library of Congress; L. Gayle Cooper, Heather Moore, Regina Rush, Bradley J. Daigle, Kathryn Morgan, Michael Plunkett, Margaret Down Hrabe, and Edward Gaynor, Alderman Library, University of Virginia; Robinson Gomez, New York Public Library; Therese Marcy and Jerry Carbone, Brattleboro Public Library; Christine Nelson, Morgan Library; Kara McClurken, Smith College; Nancy Shawcross, Van Pelt Library, University of Pennsylvania; Susan Anderson, American Antiquarian Society; Paul Page and Claire McCann, Margaret I. King Library, University of Kentucky; Ellen H. Fladger and Julianna Spallholz, Union College; Peter Knapp, Watkinson Library, Trinity College; John Ahouse, Claude Zachary, and Susan K. Hikida, Edward L. Doheny Jr. Memorial Library, University of Southern California; F. Michael Angelo, Thomas Jefferson University; Nan Card and Barbara Path, Rutherford B. Hayes Library; Janet H. Stuckey, King Library, Miami University; Sally M. Kuisel, National Archives and Records Administration; Patricia Willis and John Monahan, Beinecke Library, Yale University; and, for assistance with this and other projects, Deborah Watson and Valerie Harper, Diamond Library, University of New Hampshire. We wish to recognize the Massachusetts Historical Society, Boston; the Bancroft Library, University of California, Berkeley; the San Diego Public Library; Strawbery Banke Museum and the Athenaeum, Portsmouth, New Hampshire; the British Library; the Butler Library, Columbia University; Amherst College; the Columbus Historical Society; the Cincinnati Historical Society; and the Lane Library, Hamilton, Ohio. We have of course relied daily on the Morris Library at the University of Delaware; our thanks to the library staff—especially Iris Snyder, Anne Pfaelzer de Ortiz, Julia Hamm, and Linda Stein—and to Timothy Murray, head of special collections, and Susan Brynteson, director of libraries

Colleagues at the University of Delaware and beyond, including Ronald Martin, Richard Zipser, Don Mell, Jeanne Walker, Maureen Murphy, Jackson Bryer, and the late and much-missed Michael DePorte, encouraged our work. Our friend Leo Lemay made available his unbounded knowledge of American literature, and Wayne Craven his of American art. Special thanks go to Tim Dekker, Meredith Wunderlich, Joel Worden, Lejla Kucukalic,

Christine Bayles Kortsch, Melissa Sullivan, and Devin Harner, students at the University of Delaware whose research supported our own. These acknowledgments would not be complete without recognizing Lawrence D. Stewart, who listened most patiently to our talk about Howells and to whom we dedicate this book.

CHRONOLOGY OF HOWELLS'
LIFE AND WORK

1831–1837   WILLIAM COOPER HOWELLS (1807–1894), the son of Welsh immigrants, JOSEPH AND ANNE HOWELLS, marries MARY DEAN (1812–1868), from Lisbon, Ohio, in 1831. A jack-of-all-trades, William becomes an itinerant printer and publisher. Their first child is JOSEPH (JOE) HOWELLS (1832–1912).

1837   WILLIAM DEAN HOWELLS (WILL) is born on March 1 in Martinsville (now Martins Ferry), Ohio. Howells' six younger siblings are VICTORIA (VIC) (1838–1886); SAMUEL (SAM) (1840–1925), the family black sheep; AURELIA (1842–1931); ANNE (ANNIE) (1844–1938); JOHN (JOHNNY) (1846–1864); and the mentally disabled HENRY (1852–1908).

1840–1850   Lives in Hamilton, Ohio, where his father owns and edits the *Hamilton Intelligencer;* Will sets type. After William loses the paper for political reasons in 1848, he takes over the *Dayton Transcript* in 1849. The paper fails, and the family, deeply in debt, begins a short-lived utopian experiment in self-sufficiency at nearby Eureka Mills, Ohio.

1851–1852   Moves to Columbus while his father works as a legislative reporter for the *Ohio State Journal,* which publishes Howells' first poem. William Cooper Howells accepts the editorship of the *Ashtabula Sentinel,* and the family moves briefly to Ashtabula, Ohio, on Lake Erie, before settling in Jefferson, the county seat.

1854–1855	Suffers major breakdown and struggles with various ailments for several years.
1856–1857	William Cooper Howells elected clerk of Ohio House of Representatives. Will begins career as a newspaperman, contributing to Ohio papers and writing a column for the *Cincinnati Gazette*.
1858	Writes for the *Ohio State Journal* and is offered the job of city editor (reporter) of the *Cincinnati Gazette*. Leaves after a few weeks. Publishes reviews, poems, stories, and translations.
1860	Makes his pilgrimage to Boston and Concord. Meets James Russell Lowell, Oliver Wendell Holmes, Henry Wadsworth Longfellow, Ralph Waldo Emerson, Nathaniel Hawthorne, and Henry David Thoreau; in New York, meets Walt Whitman. ELINOR MEAD (1837–1910), Howells' future wife, visits relatives in Columbus. Howells courts her without proposing. Publishes *Poems of Two Friends* with James John Piatt (1860 [1859]) and *Lives and Speeches of Abraham Lincoln and Hannibal Hamlin,* a campaign biography.
1861–1864	Awarded the consulship at Venice. LARKIN MEAD, a sculptor, accompanies his sister Elinor to Paris, where she and Howells marry on Christmas Eve, 1862. Elinor's sister, MARY MEAD, later joins them in Venice. Howells writes articles on Venice that are published in the *Boston Daily Advertiser* and later revised and collected as *Venetian Life*. The Howellses' first child, WINIFRED HOWELLS (1863–1889), is born on December 17, 1863. Howells' brother Johnny dies of spotted fever at boarding school in 1864.
1865–1866	Returns to the United States in July 1865. Works for E. L. Godkin's *Nation* in New York and writes for various papers.
1866–1870	James T. Fields hires Howells as assistant editor of the *Atlantic Monthly*. Howells moves to Sacramento Street,

Cambridge, Massachusetts. Begins lifelong friendships with William and Henry James and Mark Twain. Mother dies in 1868. Son, JOHN MEAD HOWELLS (1868–1959), born on August 14, 1868. Lectures at Harvard in 1870. Publishes *Venetian Life* (1866) and *Italian Journeys* (1867).

1871–1881   On July 1, 1871, assumes editorship of the *Atlantic Monthly*. Builds house on Concord Street, Cambridge, where MILDRED (PILLA) HOWELLS (1872–1966), is born on September 26, 1872. Begins writing popular series of Christmas farces and comedies. Moves to Belmont, Massachusetts (1878–1881), and builds a new house, Redtop, designed by WILLIAM MEAD, Elinor's brother.
Publishes *Suburban Sketches* (1871 [1870]); *Their Wedding Journey* (1872 [1871]); *A Chance Acquaintance* (1873); *A Foregone Conclusion* (1875 [1874]); *Sketch of the Life and Character of Rutherford B. Hayes*, a campaign biography (1876); *The Parlor Car* (1876); *Out of the Question*, farces (1877); *A Counterfeit Presentiment* (1877); *The Lady of the Aroostook* (1879); *The Undiscovered Country* (1880); *A Fearful Responsibility, and Other Stories* (1881); *Dr. Breen's Practice* (1881).

1881–1884   Resigns from the *Atlantic* to write novels. Concerned about Winifred's health, spends year in Europe in 1882–1883. *Century* publishes his controversial essay on Henry James (November 1882). Declines professorship at Johns Hopkins University. Returns to Boston in 1883 and moves to 302 Beacon Street in 1884.
Publishes *A Modern Instance: A Novel* (1882); *A Woman's Reason* (1883); *A Little Girl among the Old Masters* (1884 [1883]).

1885–1886   After James R. Osgood & Company fails, signs contract with Harper & Brothers; agrees to provide a book a year and the Editor's Study, a column for *Harper's Monthly*. Reads Tolstoy (spring 1885) and is drawn to socialism. Declines Smith professorship at Harvard previously held by Longfellow and Lowell. Stays at the White House as the guest of RUTHERFORD B. HAYES (1886). Sister Victoria dies of malaria (1886). Disturbed by events surrounding Chicago's Haymarket "riot" (1886–1887).

Publishes *The Rise of Silas Lapham* (1885); *Tuscan Cities* (1886 [1885]); *Indian Summer* (1886).

1887–1889   Writes public letter seeking clemency for the convicted anarchists. Moves to New York. Seeks cure for Winifred, who is treated by S. Weir Mitchell, the famous nerve specialist. Winifred dies on March 3, 1889.

Publishes *The Minister's Charge* (1887 [1866]); *April Hopes* (1888 [1887]); *A Sea-Change, or Love's Stowaway* (1888); *Annie Kilburn* (1889 [1888]).

1890–1891   Returns to Boston for a year, then goes back to New York. Protests American imperialism and the Spanish-American War.

Publishes *A Hazard of New Fortunes* (1890 [1889]); *The Shadow of a Dream* (1890); *A Boy's Town* (1890); *Winifred Howells,* a privately printed memorial (1891); *Criticism and Fiction* (1891); *An Imperative Duty* (1892 [1891]).

1892–1894   Allows his Harper's contract to expire. Briefly edits, with the socialist entrepreneur John Brisben Walker, the *Cosmopolitan* (December 1891–June 1892). Visits son in Paris and is called home because of his father's health. William Cooper Howells dies in 1894.

Publishes *The Quality of Mercy* (1892); *Christmas Every Day and Other Stories Told for Children* (1893 [1892]); *The World of Chance* (1893); *My Year in a Log Cabin* (1893); *The Coast of Bohemia* (1893); *A Traveler from Altruria* (1894). Edits his father's memoir, *Recollections of Life in Ohio from 1813–1840* (1895).

1895–1898   Begins contributing Life and Letters column to *Harper's Weekly* (30 March 1895–26 February 1898). Takes cure for multiple ailments in Carlsbad, Bohemia (1897).

Publishes *My Literary Passions* (1895); *Stops of Various Quills* (1895); *Impressions and Experiences* (1896); *The Landlord at Lion's Head* (1897); *Stories of Ohio* (1897); *The Story of a Play* (1898). Writes American Letter column for *Literature* (14 May 1898–10 November 1899).

1899–1900　Lecture tour of the Midwest. Harper & Brothers goes into temporary receivership; Colonel George Harvey takes over. Begins the Editor's Easy Chair column for *Harper's Monthly*.
Publishes *Ragged Lady* (1899); *Their Silver Wedding Journey* (1899); *Literary Friends and Acquaintance* (1900).

1902–1906　Buys summer house in Kittery Point, Maine (1902). Awarded honorary degree from Oxford University (1904). Publishes *The Kentons* (1902); *Literature and Life* (1902); *Questionable Shapes* (1903); *Letters Home* (1903); *The Son of Royal Langbrith* (1904); *London Films* (1906 [1905]); *Certain Delightful English Towns* (1906).

1907–1909　Elected first president of the American Academy of Arts and Letters (1908); serves until his death. Travels in Italy (1908) and through England, Wales, and the Continent (1909).
Publishes *Through the Eye of the Needle* (1907); *Between the Dark and the Daylight* (1907); *The Whole Family*, a collaborative novel (1908); *Roman Holidays and Others* (1908); *Seven English Cities* (1909).

1910　Mark Twain dies on April 21, Elinor Mead Howells on May 6.
Publishes *My Mark Twain; Reminiscences and Criticisms* (1910).

1911　Travels to Bermuda, then Spain, where he meets the novelist Armando Palacio Valdés. Harper's begins Library Edition of his work but publishes only six of the projected thirty-five volumes.

1912–1920   Supports the Allies during the First World War. Henry
             James dies in 1916.
             Publishes *New Leaf Mills* (1913); *Familiar Spanish Travels*
             (1913); *The Leatherwood God* (1916); *Years of My Youth*
             (1916).

1920   Dies of pneumonia on May 11, at the age of eighty-three.

1

PARALLEL LIVES

> Through the whole time when a boy is becoming a man his auto-
> biography can scarcely be kept from becoming the record of his family
> and his world.
>
> —W. D. HOWELLS, *Years of My Youth,* 1916

IN JUNE 1871, the month before his appointment as editor of the *At-lantic Monthly,* William Dean Howells went back to Ohio. His father wanted company on a visit to the old family home near Steubenville. For William Cooper Howells the trip was nostalgic; for his son, who hesitated to go, something more—not just an unwelcome expense but also a reminder of where he had begun and who he was. Already by his mid-thirties a for-mer United States consul at Venice and a successful writer, critic, and edi-tor, he somehow feared meeting the man he might have become.

At half past eight in the morning, he caught the express train from Boston, which brought him to Albany by three, Rochester by ten, and Buffalo by midnight. His route retraced that of Basil and Isabel March, the fictional newlyweds in his first novel, *Their Wedding Journey* (to be published the following year). As on any journey, he used the opportunity to gather new material or check what he had written. At Albany he moved to the draw-ing-room car for a better view of the Mohawk Valley, which he thought he had accurately described. Entering into conversation with a fellow traveler, he sketched the young man as he would a character in a novel, every detail fixed in his memory and spelled out in letters home. "How confidential people become in travelling," he wrote. "We became fast friends before we reached Syracuse."[1] When the train passed Oneida, his companion talked about the community founded there in 1848 and about John Noyes, its leader. Howells, knowing far more about Oneida than his informant—Noyes was his wife's uncle—feigned ignorance to avoid an embarrassing subject. To many of his contemporaries, Noyes' practice of "complex" or communal marriage smacked of formalized adultery.

At the Buffalo train station, Howells watched a newly married couple absorbed in themselves, the bride eating a sandwich as big as his two hands. After a great deal of "playful scuffling," she fell asleep with her husband's stockinged feet in her face.[2] Both in life and in fiction, marriages intrigued Howells. *Their Wedding Journey*, a story of representative Americans in motion, describes the behavior of couples from different classes, the intimacies of affection, the silences of love strained or tested. Now, as on any return home, he reflected on his parents' hard life together and his own nine-year marriage to Elinor Mead Howells.

Howells' journey to meet his father took a whole day, including the ride from Ashtabula station to Jefferson, in the northeast corner of Ohio. He was touched by the courtesy a fire-insurance agent paid him as a literary man—a detail he probably let slip in his easy, self-deprecating manner—and there may have been other pleasant surprises. None, however, could quell the expected but no less devastating anxiety that grew with each mile. By the time he arrived at the family home in Jefferson, he could scarcely "locate or identify" himself except by profession, as if his very self were in peril. "I tho't I ws going crazy," he wrote to his wife Elinor, "though I knew pretty well what I ws about, too."[3] The "going crazy" belonged with these journeys. Homesick as he so often was, and deeply attached to his family, the return to Jefferson brought back the specters of childhood, with their reminder that his home lay elsewhere. In the Ohio River country, he wrote, "I find myself more of a stranger than I would anywhere else in the world."[4]

The day after his arrival, Howells and his father set off on a roundabout route to Steubenville, not far from Wheeling, West Virginia. They rented a buggy and drove nearly thirty miles through the afternoon and twilight to spend the night in Orwell. Howells, who filled ledgers with his observations—most to be crossed out when he used them in books—made a quick note about "a bare-legged girl driving home her cows."[5] The next day father and son visited General James Garfield at his home in Hiram. His father had known Garfield before the Civil War as a state senator, then as a repre-sentative to Congress, elected in 1862 while on active duty. Rising through the ranks, Garfield fought bravely at Shiloh and, as chief of General Rose-crans' staff, earned distinction at Chickamauga. Like William Cooper How-ells, Garfield grew up in poverty and embraced the principles of a splinter religious sect—in his case the Disciples of Christ—which had provided his schooling.

It made sense that Garfield, an imposing speaker and fervent antislavery man, would be tapped by the radical wing of the Republican party and that Howells' father, no less fervent, supported him. Throughout his career, Garfield relied on the senior Howells' backing (and that of his paper, the *Ashtabula Sentinel*) for getting out the vote and promoting his ideas. In those days of frontier America, it was not uncommon to know and befriend politi-cians from one's own state or region, men like Garfield, who did favors for both William Cooper and William Dean Howells. While Garfield's pa-tronage to the Howells family suggests a relationship of quid pro quo, it rested on mutual affection and respect that lasted until Garfield's assassi-nation. After reading *Their Wedding Journey*, Garfield thanked one of How-ells' sisters, "first of all, for having a brother Will . . . and second, . . . for the pleasure his book is giving us and, finally, . . . all the family for being our friends."[6]

Reluctant as he had been to come to Ohio, Howells entered Garfield's house with an enormous sense of relief, as if civilization greeted him "at the door and at the table." His later recollection captures the place, the mo-ment, and the sense he had of his life.

> I stopped with my father over a night at his house in Hiram, Ohio, where we found him home from Congress for the summer. I was then living in Cambridge, in the fullness of my content with my literary circumstance, and as we were sitting with the Garfield family on the veranda that overlooked their lawn I was beginning to speak of the famous poets I knew when Gar-field stopped me with "Just a minute!" He ran down into the grassy space, first to one fence and then to the other at the sides, and waved a wild arm of invitation to the neighbors who were also sitting on their back porches. "Come over here!" he shouted. "He's telling about Holmes, and Longfellow, and Lowell, and Whittier!" and at his bidding dim forms began to mount the fences and follow him up to his veranda. "Now go on!" he called to me, when we were all seated, and I went on, while the whippoorwills whirred and whistled round, and the hours drew toward midnight.[7]

Father and son stayed up late with the future president of the United States talking politics and books. The following morning, they returned through Ashtabula to continue by train and rented wagon to Steubenville, arriving in the late afternoon and lingering until nightfall. Red clover covered the site of the old homestead, and, before they left, the two gathered and pressed clover blossom to commemorate the visit. After an absence of fifty years, his father felt a childlike joy, remembering every detail, every twist and turn of the road. Howells could not separate the loveliness of its views from the desolation. If he avoided the ghost of what he might have become, he tasted the despair that in his early manhood had laid him low. It did not help to have been born in this "queer Ohio country": the familiar loneliness returned, and the sense, to quote one of his favorite poets, that "love and fame to nothingness do sink."[8]

Howells found no remedy for the unfilled duty owed his father or for bittersweet reunions, but he could escape (and did as soon as possible) to his busy life in Cambridge, to his wife and children, house building, friendships, and work. Shortly after his return he took over the *Atlantic Monthly*. In the years to follow he would join the editorial staff at Harper & Brothers and write novels such as *A Modern Instance* and *The Rise of Silas Lapham*, pursuing a writer's career as vigorously as any industrialist built his railroads or rolled his steel.[9]

So many nineteenth-century American lives—at least men's lives—mirror the plots of fiction, in which boys rise from rags to riches or light out for the territories. Abraham Lincoln's is such a story, as is James Garfield's, though the wilderness they confronted lay in the strife and conflicts of their nation. Howells' life also conforms to and escapes these conventions. As a ten-year-old boy he set type in his father's print shop; at thirteen he lived in a log cabin in the Ohio backwoods. He chose to go east rather than west from Ohio, and he later declined an offer from yet another United States president, Rutherford B. Hayes, to tour California. He *became* rather than joined the Eastern literary establishment, and he died in New York a relatively wealthy man, having learned, like Garfield and Lincoln, that regions east of the Appalachians could be as perilous as those beyond the Rockies.

The troops of writers to follow Howells—the Dreisers and Hemingways—liked to think of themselves as literary changelings or geniuses working in isolation. Edith Wharton called herself "a self-made man" and, except for the bad manners, might have added "self-made genius." Not Howells. He objected even to the word *genius* because it minimized the role of craftsmanship and hard work, reducing a writer—or a general like Ulysses S. Grant—to a freak of nature rather than the product of his own dreams, labor, and luck. Proud of a rich family history, he attributed his success as much to others as to himself.

It is hard to know the child's own earliest recollections from the things
it has been told of itself by those with whom its life began.

—W. D. HOWELLS, *Years of My Youth,* 1916

Toward the end of his life, William Cooper Howells (1807–94) wrote *Recollections of Life in Ohio,* a spirited account of his family's origins and growing up in rural Ohio. His son, who had encouraged the project, finished the manuscript and, after William died, arranged for its publication with an introduction of his own. The chronicle of his father's young life reads like a history of nineteenth-century uprooting. By 1813, engineers were laying the Cumberland road, but routes over and beyond the Alleghenies remained rough when not outright impassable. People like William's parents traveled in caravans of "road wagons," drawn by five or six horses, each capable of hauling seven thousand pounds of passengers and freight. William remembered their own jammed with clothing, cooking utensils, and books. His mother, Anne, and his younger siblings arranged themselves inside the wagon while his father, Joseph, rode alongside on horseback. As the eldest boy, William trailed on the pony or sat atop the load of piled bedding.

Their route passed through Charles Town, Virginia (now West Virginia), where John Brown, the leader of the Harpers Ferry raid, would meet his end on the gallows nearly fifty years later. There William realized why his Quaker family opposed any kind of inequality. A whipping post he saw became his emblem of slavery, the issue that divided Ohioans as it did the nation and made William and his son William Dean, peace lovers both, sympathetic to John Brown. As a young man, Howells half-joked that he hoped to find "a very small pro-slavery orphan boy" and beat him.[10]

For the last stages of their journey west, William's parents booked passage on a flatboat bound for Pittsburgh, then a keelboat to Warrenton, Ohio. They journeyed the last three miles in a cart sent down from Steer's Mill, the site of his father's employment. The son of a woolens manufacturer from Hay-on-Wye in Wales, Joseph had come to the United States at a time when England protected its woolen industry by banning both the sale of equipment and the emigration of skilled workmen to foreign countries. Joseph dodged the law by listing himself as a man of leisure, a "gentleman" without occupation; but whatever skills he brought to the New World did him little good. Even before English woolens swamped the American market after the War of 1812, his fortune in wool had become another lost hope. As an omen of things to come, Steer's Mill had just burned down, taking with it his chance of a partnership.

It needs an unsentimental novelist, perhaps Howells' friend Hamlin Garland, to tell the story of a man like Joseph Howells, whose ambitions led to failure and frustration, to sorting wool in another man's factory while his family lived miserably and his wife despaired. Each year brought another unwelcome change, the worst of which may have been Joseph's conversion from Quaker to Methodist. The new religion transformed a previously taciturn man into a ranter whose religious ecstasies left him insensible for hours. Neighbors joked that whenever Joseph saw an ominous cloud in the sky, he donned his ascension robes in readiness for eternity.[11] Howells' fascination with the story of Joseph C. Dylks, the false prophet fictionalized in his late novel *The Leatherwood God,* owes much to his grandfather's charismatic transformation.

Joseph's affairs grew desperate through the winter of 1819. Borrowing six hundred dollars, he uprooted his family to the first of several worn-out farms, this one five miles from Steubenville. Picking the red clover there fifty years later, Howells marveled at its unsuitability for an underfed and growing family. Only an enthusiast would drag his wife and children into such isolation, Howells wrote his wife in Boston. "It must have made life cruelly hard for grandmother."[12] The move put an end to the children's public education, and since Joseph worked during the week in Steubenville, much of the daily labor fell to William, who—among his never-ending chores—cut cordwood with a small, unsharpened saw and split it with a five-pound ax before dragging it uphill to their cabin. Like so many of their neighbors, the family lived hand to mouth, mostly on what they could produce themselves, subsisting on salt pork, bread, beans, and hominy. Why Joseph dreamed of farming, his son never understood. Every effort to increase the family's income dragged them further into poverty. Newly planted fruit trees succumbed to an early frost. Animals repaid less than their price and keep. Had his father been given a farm "ready-stocked," William wrote, "he would scarcely have been able to live on it."[13] Sometime in 1838 it occurred to Joseph himself that he had gained no advantage from farming. That year he moved across Ohio to Hamilton, north of Cincinnati, to run a combined drugstore and bookstore. Partly because one of his sons had become a local physician, another a dentist, this enterprise brought him better fortune.

By training and temperament an optimist, William Cooper Howells persisted in seeing the brighter side of his childhood. He described Ohio in summer as Edenic, a land where small boys feasted on fruit ripening in abandoned orchards, wild rabbits leapt into cooking pots, and whip-poor-wills sang like nightingales in the starlight. "Entering upon the voyage of life," he wrote, "we are to seek the best opportunities, and failing to find the best, to improve the second best."[14] In its charitable reminiscing, *Recollections* anticipates the tone of Howells' own autobiography, *Years of My Youth*. Most families have goals passed on from generation to generation, whether better schooling for children, ambition for political office, or the accumulation of wealth. The Howells family aimed at wealth and upward movement and liked to remember Joseph's father packing a barrel of silver, sailing to the Americas, conferring with George Washington, and marketing his good, plain flannel before returning to Wales. They also valued a type of stoicism, a determination to downplay their hardships and make the best of misfortune. "We are here on the conditions which were made without our consent in the beginning," Howells would tell his sister Aurelia, "and we must bear our lot, quite as if we had chosen it. We did not make our bed, but, as the proverb has it in the case of those who do, we must lie in it."[15]

The story of William Cooper Howells differs from Joseph's more in tone than in broad outline. William's children regarded him with the same exasperation and feigned amusement that he felt for his father. To his brothers and sisters, Howells himself indulged an occasional criticism. "Father was what God made him," he told his brother Joe, "and on the whole the best man I have known, but of course he was trying."[16] *Maddening* might have been a better word. William had enormous energy and ingenuity, and, like Joseph before him, tried any number of ways to make a living or a quick dollar. Loving his father as he did, and eager to see him independent, Howells knew better than to invest in "any of his patent sixteen-bladed, corkscrew-attachment" inventions.[17]

William moved from newspaper to newspaper as his father moved from farm to farm. Yet William's failings tell only a small part of his story. The boy who sat next to Lincoln's secretary of war, Edwin Stanton, in school and worked closely with powerful Ohio politicians before the Civil War went on to serve a term in the Ohio state legislature and won appointment to American consulships in Quebec City and Toronto. William's short history with the *Scioto Gazette*, from the fall of 1833 to the spring of 1834, testifies to the power wielded even by small-town Western editors. The paper belonged to a Swedenborgian named B. O. Carpenter, who introduced William to the teachings of the Swedish theologian and the principles of the Whig party. William in turn persuaded Carpenter to support William Henry Harrison for president in 1836, on the assumption that Harrison secretly opposed slavery. When other papers reprinted the *Scioto Gazette*'s editorial endorsement, backers of Harrison staged a mass meeting in Cincinnati to promote him as the Log-Cabin candidate—a bizarre irony given Harrison's patrician Southern heritage. Despite the mysteries about his political views, Harrison proved such a spellbinding orator that reporters counted the acres rather than numbers of people who gathered to hear him stump. Though he lost the 1836 election, five years later Harrison became the ninth president of the United States—and the first to die in office, collapsing from pneumonia one month after his inaugural address.

It might be said that William Cooper Howells and the state of Ohio came into their own in the same years. During the first quarter of the nineteenth century, Ohio had grown in population more than any other state, from 42,000 in 1800 to 800,000 in 1826.[18] By 1850 it would rank third in population, a position it held until 1890.[19] With the completion of the Erie Canal in 1825, the West had begun to feel its commercial power. By the time William turned twenty-two, Andrew Jackson's presidency had inaugurated a new era, symbolized perhaps by the western reach of the Baltimore and Ohio Railroad, which bound the eastern states to the rapidly developing new territories.

In William's day even small towns tended to have one or two newspapers for reporting on the fortunes of local businesses and on political and religious contests. Within decades, America witnessed the rise of New England Transcendentalism, Unitarianism, Universalism, the growth of Catholicism from immigration, the Presbyterian disruption of 1837, the Methodist and Baptist schisms over slavery, and, among dozens of feuding sects, the Campbellite Disciples of Christ, embraced by James Garfield and directed by one of William's employers, Alexander Campbell. William worked only briefly for Campbell. Without capital—he never had capital—he tried to build his own press and fashioned balls of buckskin stuffed with wool for inking the type. In December 1828 he published his first issue of *The Gleaner*, "a monthly periodical devoted to literature and miscellaneous selections: price one dollar a year in advance."[20] It lasted a year, twice as long as the average paper. Papers like William's sprang up as fast as mushrooms, wrote one contemporary, before the arrival of a killing frost "in the form of bills due and debts unpaid."[21] In 1829 William and a partner, S. R. Jones, proposed a semimonthly paper, *The African Liberator,* to advocate the emancipation of "the oppressed and degraded sons of Africa, from their present state of bondage, to that freedom guaranteed them by Heaven, in the common right of man." When this project failed to materialize, he launched, with the support of spiritualist and reformist followers of Robert Dale Owen (son of the capitalist architect of British socialism), the *Electric Observer and Workingman's Advocate.* That folded within six months. His next scheme, the printing of an anti-Catholic diatribe—*The Rise, Progress and Downfall of the Aristocracy*—drove him out of business and out of Wheeling, West Virginia, but not before he had met Mary Dean (1812–68) and married her (on July 10, 1831).

A native of New Lisbon, Ohio, Mary Dean was the eldest of eleven children from a family with German roots in the disputed territory of Alsace.[22] Her early portraits show a bright-eyed, pretty woman smiling happily, the later ones a dour-looking woman with heavy brows and a pronounced chin looking grimly at the camera. "I wish I could recall her," Howells wrote, "in the youth which must have been hers when I began to be conscious of her as a personality; I know that she had thick brown Irish hair and blue eyes, and high German cheekbones, and as a girl she would have had such beauty as often goes with a certain irregularity of feature."[23] He thought he inherited from his parents a poetic mix of Celtic and German blood.

With her new husband, Mary made literature into a religion. William illustrated and colored a "wreath book" composed of her favorite poems. In the evenings, he read or quoted to her from Shakespeare or the still-popular William Cowper, and she sang to him the songs of Robert Burns. Howells remembered her retaining "a rich sense in words like that which marked her taste in soft stuffs and bright colors."[24] The little that has survived to give a direct sense of Mary's voice or personality suggests a feisty, intelligent woman who worried about her children and shared their ambitions. Consenting bravely to one daughter's going to New Orleans, she felt immediate pangs about the boat's blowing up or burning and the girl facing a lynch mob as an antislavery Northerner. "That would . . . be the case if I were to go," she wrote with her eccentric spelling, "for my republican principals would be sure to show themselves on every occasion."[25] Writing to her daughters, she could be humorous, ironical, and, surprisingly, more worldly than the romanticized woman of family tradition. It made her feel "real 'fighty'" to see John Brown Jr. wearing revolvers when he came into her house: "He took his belt off and laid it on the table. & I saw he had a bowie knife in it. He told us some of his and his Father's exploits in Kansas."[26] Mary's objections may have been either to the guns themselves or Brown's need to carry them. She did not object to the man or his deeds.

Given a dreamer for a husband and eight children to be kept clean, fed, and out of mischief, Mary had to be practical. She agreed with her husband's contradictory views about the equally important but distinct "spheres of actions and duties," in which girls did the indoor work, boys the outdoor—except milking, a designated "feminine" responsibility.[27] *Improve* seems to have been their household word. "It is your duty to improve every advantage you have," she told her eldest daughter, who was visiting relatives in Pittsburgh. "I want you to see and hear every thing that will have a tendency to elevate and improve your mind read all the good and useful books you can get . . . if your cousin Lizzie can help you any in your music I hope you will improve the chance for when you get home again the chances will be poor enough."[28] Mary instilled in her children a scale of values associated with the so-called better classes and held them to ever-rising standards. Highly strung, she had ways of making them conscious of her displeasure and eager to make amends for real or imagined wrongs. Howells, who as a young boy once threw a rose to startle her, recalled the moment with words that might have been written by D. H. Lawrence. "When she looked around and saw me offering to run away, she whirled on me and made me suffer for her fright. . . . She could not forgive me at once, and my heart remained sore, for my love of her was as passionate as the temper I had from her."[29] It was she who held him accountable and she who had to be pleased. Howells would assert that Mary loved all her children equally. "What a great heart" she had, he told his sisters. "We were all alike to her; she was the home in which we were all equal and dear."[30] Elsewhere, however, he made it clear that she favored Joe, her firstborn son. The sisters might have claimed that she favored the boys over the girls. When he forgot his mother's hardships, Howells recalled her frolicking with her children on the grass or in a rare moment free from work. Writing half a century later, he describes her standing with his father, looking "at her boys in the river. One such evening I recall, and how sad our gay voices were in the dim, dewy air."[31] In that vision of himself watching his parents as they watch him (and he in memory watching them all), he suggests both the boyhood yearning for inclusion and the pathos of time past.

His mother's failings he blamed largely on his father: "I suppose a woman is always bewildered when a man comes short of the perfection which would be the logic of him in her mind."[32] During their first two years of marriage William changed jobs five times, each job requiring another move, another difficult beginning.[33] In 1835, he brought his wife and three-year-old Joe to the family farm about six miles from Chillicothe, not far from where he had once lived as a boy. They stayed a few months, while William recovered from influenza and toyed with the idea of becoming a doctor. Still without income, they moved to Martinsville (later called Martins Ferry), on the Ohio River across from Wheeling. Although by now the National Pike had been extended through Belmont County, Martinsville itself remained little more than an isolated settlement. William made a living by painting houses; when time permitted he worked on his own, which amounted to two cramped rooms connected by a passage and a lean-to kitchen.

In this makeshift house, on March 1, 1837, Mary gave birth to their second son, William Dean Howells. They would call him Will.

At that time the American frontier lay not far beyond the confluence of the Mississippi and the Ohio Rivers. Will Howells was born both a Westerner and a Northerner, in a state separated by the Ohio from neighboring slave states. That year, on his last day as president, Andrew Jackson recognized the Republic of Texas. In Cambridge, Massachusetts, Ralph Waldo Emerson made his famous "American Scholar" address (and P. T. Barnum began his career in New York City by exhibiting Joyce Heth, a black woman who, he claimed, had nursed George Washington). It was a bad financial time for the nation, which saw the failure of hundreds of banks and businesses in what came to be known as the Panic of 1837, an economic catastrophe that lasted seven more years.

It was a worse time for the Howells family. As daunting as it must have been to bring children into what seemed almost certain poverty, Mary had another baby in July of the following year, a daughter they named Victoria, soon nicknamed Vic (1838–86). She had five more children in rapid succession: Sam (1840–1925), Aurelia (1842–1931), Anne (1844–1938), John (1846–64), and finally Henry (1852–1908), whose mental infirmity would keep him a child his entire life.

In 1840, cries of "Tippecanoe and Tyler too" launched William Henry Harrison into the presidency, and William Cooper Howells moved once again, this time more luckily, to take over the *Hamilton Intelligencer*. The family would remain in Hamilton—now also home to William's father and two brothers—for nearly a decade. Will Howells, three years old when they arrived, looked back to this "boy's town," situated on the banks of the Great Miami River, as the "gladdest" place of his childhood.[34] For him,

Hamilton meant the river, its banks lined with barrels of whiskey and pork houses, where he and his friends caught fish, swam, and smoked their first smokewood "cigars." In the spring, when the river rose, its waters yellow with boiling currents smoothing into "oily eddies," he watched debris drift by, bits and pieces of people's lives and property; he saw logs, fencing, chicken coops, and once a stable, followed by "swollen bodies of horses and cattle."[35] These years gave him, if not quite a sense of belonging, at least one of self and security. Long afterward, in Venice, Boston, or New York, he would break in every new pen by writing, "W. D. Howells, Hamilton, Butler County, Ohio."[36]

To the chagrin of his Methodist father, William had baptized his children in the Swedenborgian New Church of Jerusalem. His lessons about the struggle between good and evil and every person's responsibility to godliness did not stop his Sunday afternoon quarrels with Joseph over the "true religion." Mary, who had converted to and lapsed from an evangelical sect of Methodism, found herself caught between her husband and father-in-law. William held his children to a strict standard. "We were made to feel that wicked words were of the quality of wicked deeds," Howells writes, "and that when they came out of our mouths they depraved us, unless we took them back. I have not forgotten, with any detail of the time and place, a transgression of this sort. . . . My mother had got supper, and my father was, as he often was, late for it, and while we waited impatiently for him, I came out with the shocking wish that he was dead."[37] William survived the curse and, true to his beliefs, pardoned his son, who acknowledged the transgression but still lived in fear of letting loose the evil spirits.

Howells remembered being taught that when the children teased one another "there was nothing the fiends so much delighted in as teasing. When they were angry and revengeful, they were told that . . . the good angels could not come near them if they wished while they were in that state."[38] Howells grew skeptical about Swedenborg's doctrine of correspondence, central to the thinking of American transcendentalists like Emerson, but not its social extension. Urged as a boy to work in the spirit of Christ and to see this world as probationary, he would grow up to cast his lot with visionary, socialist reformers.

In religion as in politics, William Cooper Howells stood apart from his Hamilton neighbors. Most of the town's inhabitants had crossed over from Kentucky or Virginia, and to them William might as well have been a Yankee. He was down-to-earth but an intellectual, religious but a Swedenborgian, a laborer and a man of business who employed three journeymen, a boy apprentice, and several girl compositors—a practice commonly decried for lowering wages and morals. Caught between rival values, he tempered his antislavery rhetoric in the *Intelligencer* and warned against radical socialist theories. As the editor of a religious paper, *The Retina,* from July 1843 to July 1844, he argued a socialist agenda by which labor should be divided according to talents and natural inclinations.[39] Expecting with his usual optimism that the New Church would adopt *The Retina* (hopelessly subtitled "The Tablet whereon Truth's Rays Impress the Images of Thought") as its official publication, William took a four-month break from the *Intelligencer.* When he found New Churchers no improvement on previous readers, who preferred scandal to political lectures and exegeses of religious texts, he returned to work on the newspaper.

William transformed what had been a collection of front-page advertisements and political endorsements into a paper addressing local and international news, fiction, and poetry. Its masthead announced in bold letters that "REPUBLICS ARE ONLY SAFE WHEN BOTH PEOPLE AND OFFICERS ARE CONTROLLED BY CONSTITUTIONS AND LAWS." His transition to editor and proprietor went smoothly except for complaints by local merchants about unfair monopoly. Now and for decades to come, the family business operated as a family store purveying stationery and sundries. What William didn't sell, his father did. Anyone glancing through the *Intelligencer* would assume that patent medicines for baldness, liver ailments, and dyspepsia could be bought nowhere but at Joseph Howells' drugstore. As soon as his sons had the necessary dexterity, William put them to work in the shop, first folding papers, then setting type. Except for his own tutoring—and what they read in books—he gave them little education. Resenting his father as an exacting boss, Howells felt closer to his mother. Still, he liked the chatter of the printers and the press they worked. He could remember not knowing how to read; setting type he had known forever.

William might have stayed permanently in Hamilton if he had not lost the paper to politics. In democratic Butler County, which approved the annexation of Texas and California, William's affiliation with the Whigs placed him in jeopardy; then he alienated his Whig base by disapproving of Zachary Taylor as a former slaveholder. William believed Taylor's advances to be an obvious ploy for increasing slaveholding territory and lifting himself into the presidency. He may have been right, but once the "immoral" Mexican-American War started in May 1846, he felt obliged to support American soldiers while protesting his country's policies. To fellow Whigs, William appeared at best indecisive, at worst a turncoat. Taylor, in the meantime, won praise as commander of the U.S. Army along the Texas border and came home a hero.

Since William had made enemies with *The Retina,* a fringe publication at best, and had become the target of a rival paper, even he accepted the inevitable. With Taylor elected as the twelfth president of the United States, William sold the *Intelligencer* to a new proprietor, who vowed that the paper would resume its proper role of advancing "Whig men and Whig measures."[40] Later when Taylor declared for the admission of California and New Mexico as free states and opposed the compromise proposals of a fellow Whig—the powerful Henry Clay—William returned to the party.

Whether because of his conscience or because he lacked the skills to succeed, William and his family found themselves once again homeless and nearly destitute. After casting about for work, he relocated in Dayton, the home of his younger brother Israel, and on May 17, 1849, published the first issue of the *Dayton Transcript.* The following year rivaled any for unhappiness. Whatever the hardships of Hamilton might have been, Mary missed her friends, along with the gossip, teas, and quilting parties. Howells, at twelve, continued as a child laborer. Townspeople remembered him as "an awkward and countrified youth, timid and quiet."[41] He rose in the morning between four and five to deliver papers; in the evenings he worked until eleven putting into type the new telegraphic dispatches that transformed the role of newspapers. In between, he set (as the *Transcript* announced on June 15, 1850), 9,500 ems, or four columns of the day's paper. His father and brother Joe worked even harder. The shop itself had walls spattered with ink and a floor carpeted with waste paper. William, who did everything he could to save money, plumbed his own gas pipes, which leaked and made everyone ill.

Once again the family shifted from house to house, rather like the families of Charles Dickens and James Joyce, settling for ever-smaller and meaner lodgings to reduce expenses. Howells could not help comparing his mother's modest parlor, decorated with scattered books, with his aunt's, which boasted upholstered chairs, lace curtains, and a piano. If he later satirized such middle-class trimmings—"Jamescracks," he called them in *A Hazard of New Fortunes*—he now yearned for the unassailable respectability that came with money.

Dayton, with the "airs of a city," boasted performances of light comedy and Negro dancing, popular lectures on phrenology, a Swiss bellringer's "positively last" concert, and traveling art shows. Howells began his lifelong interest in art thanks to Claude-Marie Dubufe's painting *Adam and Eve in a*

State of Innocence. "The large canvas was lighted up so as to throw the life-size figures into strong relief," which spectators viewed through a pasteboard "binocle." What he saw came as a shock of recognition. "If that was the way our first parents looked before the Fall, and the Bible said it was, there was nothing to be urged against it, but . . . a boy might well shrink ashamed, with a feeling that the taste of Eden was improved by the Fall."[42] In the same hall he attended the theater, for the actors in large part paid their printer with promises and free tickets. "As nearly as I can make out," Howells would write, "I was thus enabled to go every night to the theater, in a passion for it which remains with me ardent still."[43] Farces and melodramas with names like *Barbarossa* and *The Miser of Marseilles,* as well as productions of *Macbeth, Hamlet,* and *Richard III,* became early models for his own plays.

Since the theater drew large audiences, Howells' father thought to make money with a play of his own—an extravaganza about the War of 1812 based on the military exploits of his hero, William Henry Harrison. But neither the play, which folded after one performance, nor any other strategy could keep food on the table or the troubled paper afloat. The family circumstances worsened in the summer, when a cholera epidemic killed more than two hundred of the town's inhabitants and President Taylor declared a day of fasting to purge the nation's sins. Will Howells might have thought Dayton and his own family had been singled out for special punishment. He watched the victims of cholera passing in a steady stream of caskets by his front door, "three and four, five and six, ten and twelve a day," each a reminder of his own mortality. In his imagination he contracted cholera, pneumonia, or any of the prevailing diseases and would soon be mourned by his family. He did come down with a mild attack of cholera and "lay in the Valley of the Shadow of Death while it lasted."[44] He also suffered from rheumatic fever and recalled with rare bitterness his father's refusing to buy him an undershirt until after he had taken sick. As an old man, he asked Joe, "What could poor father have been thinking?"[45] William was of course thinking about money.

In August 1850, the end of William's employment came almost as a relief. Joe proudly remembered his father's thumbing his nose at tragedy by locking the office and going for a swim. After the collapse of the *Transcript,* William looked for work, and his oldest sons earned their keep in a German print shop. That fall, Israel Howells helped finance a bold proposal for communal living that would rescue William and bring together four of the brothers. Like so many utopian communities, this one proved a naive undertaking. William, as he editorialized in the *Transcript,* believed that family homesteads give "birth to an affection for home and its associations, and elicit a new and more intimate patriotic relation to the State."[46] To what extent his brothers shared his dream of self-sufficiency and fellowship remains unclear, as in fact did the idea for the community itself. None of the brothers considered practicalities like living arrangements, the establishment of a communal laundry or kitchen, the care and education of children, the roles of individual members, a system of management, or the distribution of (never-realized) profits. William might have found a working model in a local agency like the Ashtabula County Western Emigrant Association, except that well-planned communities foundered as often as the unplanned.

Originally, the scheme called for William and his family to prepare the way for the larger group to resettle along the Little Miami River, about twelve miles east of Dayton, on the site of the Eureka Mills. Purchased for $3,100, the property consisted of sixty acres, deeded to William's brothers Israel and Joseph. The cabin's logs had at least been plastered with mortar; the chimney was of stone and the floor of new oak planking—*hard,* as Howells knew from sleeping on it. The previous owner had squirted tobacco juice on the walls, which William papered with newsprint both to cover the stains and to keep out drafts. The children soon discovered that few of the torn and pasted stories had an ending, and the wind came through as before. Writing about the experience in *My Year in a Log Cabin,* Howells remembered jumping out of bed on winter mornings into snow that had drifted silently into the house. In *New Leaf Mills,* his fictionalized account of the experience, he described the property and its setting: the "huge gristmill, gray and weather-beaten" fronting on "an acre of open space, with the hitching-rail for the farmers' horses in the middle." On the western hillside, blue smoke curled from outlying cabins. To the east, a road wound in and out of trees until it disappeared between "the mill-races and the river."[47] North and south, the woods gave way to a hundred acres of standing corn, and, farther away still, to virgin forest.

Once William restored the grist- and sawmills on the property, his brothers planned to join them and to convert the mills to the production of paper. No one seemed concerned, as Howells wrote, that his father had never run either a sawmill or a gristmill, "much less evoke a paper-mill from them."[48] Neither had he come close to being self-sufficient. And however unfitted he might have been himself, William got no help from his brothers, who doomed the enterprise by making excuses and begging off work.

If her husband envisioned a republic founded along the lines of Ralph Waldo Emerson's creed of good manners, lucrative labor, and intellectual endeavor, for Mary Howells nothing could have been farther removed from those ideals than Eureka Mills. By comparison even Dayton had its social and practical advantages. In this "barbarous" community Mary's life stopped, and the children, who soon exhausted the offerings of the log-hut schoolhouse two miles away, needed a new start. Here, as elsewhere, money ruled as the means to land, horses, and new machinery—not to mention such town niceties as lace curtains, old silver, and Brussels carpets—and money still eluded them. In the eyes of his family, William's trusting optimism sometimes amounted to willful obliviousness. As the mother in *New Leaf Mills* says of her husband: "He is the best man in the world. . . . He hasn't a selfish thought or a mean one. But oh, if he would only be a little more *afraid!* I wish he could have some of *my* fear. . . . If only he would lose heart a little I could have some."[49] Facing the end of his utopian dream, William managed to win appointment as local postmaster, beginning in January 1851.

What can be said, Howells asks in his autobiography, of a man whose mind does not dwell on "the things that make for prosperity"?[50] His father's career forced him to consider the paradox that a good man could work hard and still fail. Although he found that he could forgive his father after accepting his failures, others neither accepted nor forgave. Alexander Dean repeatedly urged his sister to ride his paddle wheeler up the Ohio to her family while he lectured his brother-in-law about getting a salary and collecting outstanding monies—which, "to be candid . . . you know is an uphill business with you."[51] Having started as the humblest of keelboat workers and become, in turn, a pilot, captain, and steamboat owner, Alexander had no patience for another man's incompetence and believed moral scruples a luxury William could ill afford.

William's son learned as a boy that any careless or sudden move, the blinking of an eye, a blurted word, a flash of temper, could change his life forever. An early memory of a one-legged man drowning catches the perilous nature of life as he saw it. "It is all so smooth and easy," he writes, the effect of one false step, to vanish into the yellow river.[52] He came to a fuller sense of the man's drowning because he lived so much of his childhood at the edges of poverty and respectability, yet what strikes him in this account is the swiftness of the man's death and the photographic precision of his memory.

In retrospect, Howells saw himself a bewildered boy on the edge of the Ohio wilderness, frightened for his family's future, striving to make sense of his world and his jumbled feelings. In *Years of My Youth* he recalls Joe and himself being late for supper and worrying about their reception.[53] They had gone to the neighbors' to borrow a joint of meat, or was it potatoes? He no longer knew. The neighbors were out, and the boys had waited for what seemed like hours before they could sling the sack between them on a pole and point their horses toward home. It was Sunday. Will imagined his sisters helping their mother with dinner, his father selecting the evening's reading from the book of worship or returning with the younger children from a walk along the river. His mother would scold them for being late. His shoulder ached from the burden, and he began to suspect that he might be carrying more than his stronger brother. Suddenly cross and hungry, he wanted to confront Joe, who seemed to prolong their truancy, but he could not turn around for fear of spilling the load or, worse, toppling from his horse. It continued this way, the brothers riding together, Will Howells swaying to his silent recital of wrongs. At first, he did not realize that they had entered a clearing of dense grass until the chattering of cicadas caught his attention. He looked at Joe, who nodded, and together they lowered the pole and flopped on the nearest log. The shadows hung black from trees, which he remembered glowing like candles in the moonlight. He might have spoken his pent-up grievances now but said nothing. Instead he felt the hard knot inside loosening, his heart filling with a newborn sense of ease, of unfeigned sympathy, with the world and himself.

Howells grew to understand that neither personal conduct nor the vagaries of sorrow and joy could be explained by easy formulas. That recognition, which underlies his every novel, fed his sadness when he returned to Ohio and picked the clover on his father's old homestead. The place disheartened him because of William's hard past, and the family's, which he remembered as his own. It changes a boy's perspective to be asked, as he was, to ride bareback to the nearest village and buy shrouds for a neighbor's five children, all dead from influenza. He admired people like his mother and two oldest sisters, who devoted themselves to others, and he wanted something different for himself. When he came to realize that his ambition meant leaving Ohio, he would still claim the advantage of having come of age in the democratic West.

WARRING AMBITIONS

1851–1859

Our joys and pleasures are sweet to us . . . but the ghosts of our woes
and griefs we fondle to our hearts.

—W. D. HOWELLS, "A New Year's Glimpse of Memory Land," 1854

IN THE WINTER OF 1851, William Cooper Howells brought his family
from the rural misery of Eureka Mills to what they saw as urban bliss
in the booming state capital. Will Howells dated their arrival in Columbus with that of Lajos Kossuth, the flamboyant Hungarian patriot driven
from his country by the Austrian and Russian armies and seeking help for
his cause abroad. Like many Americans, Columbus residents lined the streets
to see and hear the charismatic hero. Dressed in the traditional braided coat
of the Magyars and sporting an ostrich-plumed hat, the "black-bearded,
black-haired, and black-eyed" Kossuth spoke from the steps of the unfinished State House.[1] He stood for everything the Howells family had honored since William saw his first whipping post on the journey west.

At that moment, thrilled by Kossuth's oratory and the responding "hur-
rahs" from the crowd, a young revolutionary found his idol. Swayed as much
by the man's appearance as by the performance, Will Howells imagined Kossuth as the man he wanted to be. His boyhood imitation, complete with
the feathered hat, foreshadowed his unswerving commitment to democratic

ideals in later years. If not bent on a career in literature, he might have become a political leader rather than a social commentator and writer; he hailed, after all, from a state that would send eight presidents to Washington.

Columbus opened up a new world for Will Howells. For the first time in years his family escaped pressing money worries. William, who had found temporary work as a legislative reporter for the *Ohio State Journal,* earned ten dollars a week for his letters on state politics; Joe earned three as a grocery-store clerk; and Will four as a compositor. Looking back nearly forty years later, Howells reckoned the price of "decency" at a few thousand dollars a year, a level of income William did not attain until long after the family left Columbus. While their earnings barely covered expenses, at least they now lived free from want, and William found more time to educate his children, especially his second son. Shy, awkward, and self-taught, Will Howells in 1851 had a haphazard knowledge of literature, along with Roman, Greek, and Ohio history. He showed little aptitude for arithmetic except for making ledgers of his needs and expenditures, a lifelong habit he kept in the spirit of Benjamin Franklin. At the Giles Female Academy in Hamilton, which served a broader population than its name implies, he had picked up bits of grammar and geography. He learned Spanish from a worn grammar that had belonged to a veteran of the Mexican War. "My consuming pleasures began when I had already done a day's work," he wrote in *Years of My Youth.* "I was studying four or five languages, blindly and blunderingly enough, but with a confidence at which I can even now hardly smile."[2]

Any spare time he spent "reading, reading, reading."[3] He never forgot the summer's evening when he first heard his father speak of *Don Quixote.* As William told about Sancho and Dulcinea, about Cervantes' own enslavement in Algiers and his loss of a hand in battle, Will felt the walls of the family house open to the Spanish countryside. He fancied Cervantes alive and ready to return his affection. Soon he thumbed through his own *Don Quixote,* translated by Charles Jarvis: it consisted of two small, stout volumes bound in calf, which later served as a talisman, giving strange places a bit of familiarity by its presence. Howells never wrote his proposed biography of Cervantes, although near the end of his life he undertook two last projects: a defense of his friend Henry James and an edition of an older friend, the Jarvis translation of *Don Quixote.*

As a boy, he entered so wholly into fictional worlds that he had trouble coming back. Rising before anyone else, he wrapped himself in his father's cloak and settled into a chair with a book, any book, in hand. His tastes embraced allegories and fables from medieval times, smatterings of poetry, tales of frontier life, accounts of the Caucasian steppes, and songs picked up from minstrel shows. Howells claimed never to have marked a book, and he rarely did, because to do so meant desecrating a living thing. It gave him pain "to see a book faced down or dogs-eared or broken-backed."[4] Working as a compositor gave him "living contact with literature," a term he used to include the newspaper columns he set.[5] "Printers of the day," he wrote in *Impressions and Experiences,* "had nearly all some affinity with literature . . . it was in a sort always at their fingers-ends, and they must have got some touch of it whether they would or not."[6] Country newspapers like his father's routinely printed poetry and fiction along with the editorials, news articles, gossip columns, and political diatribes. What the papers published for readers' pleasure, or as filler, young people like Howells read with the zest of their elders. This *was* literature for much of pre–Civil War America.

At a time when every village had a poet ready to commemorate public events or personal milestones, Will Howells aspired to poetry. Among his early pieces, he wrote a verse tragedy set in ancient Rome and a mock epic, "The Battle of the Cats." He knew that his present efforts bore no resemblance to what he might one day accomplish. "Oh my Diary!" he wrote at fifteen, "when I come to be a man I will take thee up, and I will look thy ill worded and worse written pages o'er and o'er as I would speak with an old friend. . . . But what is the use of lifting the thick veil that shrouds futurity, and peeping at things that may, or may not be?"[7] For all its posing, the diary set a lifelong pattern. No less than other members of his family, Howells hated to throw anything out, whether letters from friends or scraps of writing to be recycled for the magazines. Convinced that authorship had its own economy of thrift, he collected oddities of speech, jokes, anecdotes, and tidbits, which (using Ralph Waldo Emerson's metaphor) he deposited in a literary "Savings Bank." For his autobiography, *Years of My Youth,* he reached back to a diary entry from 1852 describing violent patients at a local lunatic asylum soothed like children by the cadences of verse.[8]

No one grew up in the Howells household without understanding that writing—from newspaper copy to great books—was a *business.* William, who urged his newspaper readers to give their custom to local distributors of books, assumed that people wanted to feel the weight of a book in their hands and display its engravings on their parlor tables. Books mattered for their ideas and as precious material objects. Howells, who absorbed and passed on these lessons, held firm opinions about the design of his own books, their illustrations, size, and typeface, and he took a pragmatic approach to their distribution. "The publication of a poem or a novel (which is the modern poem) is an affair of business—between the author's agent and the public," he wrote in an early review. "There is no sense of patronage received or conferred. In this country it has never been otherwise."[9] He stuck to this view throughout his career and would repeat it most famously in his 1893 essay "The Man of Letters as a Man of Business."

In a family where everyone wrote, the children knew and to varying degrees resented that Will's writing came first. He grew up the anointed child, the Jacob to Joe's Esau, except that his mother preferred Joe. William once said that "Will is so much a continuation and development of my own aspirations and efforts that he seems almost myself."[10] Without consulting his son, he published one of Will's poems in the *Ohio State Journal* in March 1852:

> Old Winter, loose thy hold on us
> And let the Spring come forth;
> And take thy frost and ice and snow
> Back to the frozen North.[11]

After seeing the poem reprinted in Cincinnati and New York newspapers, Thomas Brown, editor of the *Ohio Farmer* and a friend of William, predicted that Will Howells would make "his mark among the Poetical and Prose writers of the nineteenth century."[12] "Just think of that," he wrote in his diary, "[they] called me a poet!" Lest anyone think him arrogant, he added: "I swar it peats all."[13] Joe wasn't fooled. The family joker and unmerciful tease cut the poem out of the diary and wrote: "Thus you see the Poetry bust rite out of the young poet, like a biled tater does out of the skin."[14] They lived in a house where nothing remained private for long, and, maybe to protect himself from his prying brother, Will invented new identities. In imitation of popular pseudonyms like "Ik Marvel," he began to sign himself "Will Narlie." Only by donning "the mask of fiction," he came to believe, can a writer show "his real face or the will behind it."[15] He probably intended the pun on "will."

After the Ohio legislature adjourned on May 3, 1852, William Cooper Howells lost his job. Lacking cash but ready to barter his own and the more grudging labor of his sons, he committed to editing and buying a share in the *Ashtabula Sentinel*. His plan required the family to move by the end of June to the northeastern section of Ohio known as the Western Reserve, so named from being "reserved" or held back when Connecticut ceded to

the federal government part of what became the Northwest Territory—
and modern Ohio. The region still kept the feel of the frontier. To reach
the tiny port of Ashtabula, the Howells family traveled by way of Cleveland, where, as if for their private showing, a sun of shimmering gold sank
behind Lake Erie. "I cannot describe to you my delight on seeing the lake,"
Will Howells wrote. "Yesterday when we were there the waves were running about three feet high, and the lake was covered with white-caps, and
the shore was one continuous line of foam."[16]

The rail line from Cleveland to Ashtabula had been completed just a week
before the Howellses traveled. They stepped down from the train into an
open field. Mary, Vic, and the younger children took "the stage" (probably a public cart) to town, where they had arranged to stay at the Franklin
House. William and his three oldest sons walked under a full moon past
patches of corn and wheat, new railroad fences marking their way. Joe remembered that the evening they arrived in Ashtabula they heard of the death
of Henry Clay, the Kentucky statesman famous as the architect of the Missouri Compromise. From their first morning, William assumed the *Sentinel*'s editorial duties, Joe served as foreman, and Will, along with an apprentice boy, set the type. Sam folded papers and did any needed "rolling."
They soon brought in extra income by jobbing advertising circulars, bal-
lots, and letterheads.

The family had barely six months to adapt to Ashtabula before they and
the *Sentinel* office relocated nine miles inland to Jefferson, the county seat.
Howells recorded the muddle of yet another move: "What a time we had
getting our things arranged in Jefferson, how hard we had to work, and
how many things were broken, and spilled, and cracked."[17] In size a village,
Jefferson was home to two dominant Ohio politicians, Joshua R. Giddings
and Benjamin Wade, local and national leaders of the antislavery movement. Giddings served in the United States Congress from 1838 to 1859 before being appointed consul general to Canada during the Civil War. He
kept a law office in town, a one-room building (still intact) set apart like a
small shed. Wielding power through his personal charm, Giddings knew
every voter and could be counted on to appear at picnics or join a summer
ball game. According to Howells, he preferred rural surroundings; at home
in Jefferson between the sessions of Congress, "he liked to 'turn himself out
to grass,' . . . to put on old clothes and a straw hat, and walk barefoot through
the streets which he had known when they were forest trails."[18]

Giddings and the citizens of Jefferson expected from their newspaper editor a clear stand on slavery. A quick glance at the *Sentinel*'s affiliations—

first with the National Republican party (1832–1834), then the Whigs (1834–1848), the Free Soilers (1854), and once again the Republicans (1855–1878)—suggests some of the political vagaries of the time. In broad terms, Whigs would become Republicans, and Republicans Democrats, though they adopted roughly opposite positions from those of today's parties. William's own politics paralleled the shifts of the political parties and the paper he edited. He gave readers his stout assurance that the political character of the *Sentinel*—"No favor sways us, and no fear shall awe"—would "remain unchanged."[19] For all its political affiliations, the *Sentinel* took unswerving antislavery positions in a county that supported thirty way stations on the Underground Railroad and provided thirteen of the nineteen men who stormed the federal arsenal at Harpers Ferry.[20] Many of Jefferson's seven hundred residents belonged to the Ohio State Anti-Slavery Society, founded in 1835, which ranked second in national prominence to that of New York.

Jefferson welcomed the new editor. Here the family approached the utopian ideal of fellowship they had sought in Eureka Mills. Young men and women paired off for sleigh rides, dancing, whist (or "whisk," as they called it), and moonlight walks home. They met at debating clubs or spelling bees, at the County Fair or Fourth of July celebrations. With Jim Williams, an apprentice boarding with the family, Howells formed the closest of his new friendships. Together they read Cervantes and Shakespeare, studied Latin, Greek, and German, and contemplated a brighter future, which for Williams meant a college professorship. Citizens of Jefferson "read and talked about books, and better books than people read and talk about now," Howells remembered.[21] Outside Massachusetts, it would have been difficult to find a population of such intelligence and of "almost perfect social equality."[22] The comment includes his unspoken awareness that men like Benjamin Wade were native-born New Englanders, or—like Giddings from Pennsylvania—raised and educated in the East.

With people stopping by to gossip or occasionally to help fold and distribute their local paper, the *Sentinel* office served as a community center where citizens gathered to discuss religion, politics, and favorite writers of the day. William worked to expand the paper's appeal with squibs on the art of conversation, the ways people may have kissed in olden times, or the number of squirrels shot in a competition between Ashtabula and Jefferson marksmen (4,257). On at least one occasion, in 1854, he invited readers to the *Sentinel* office, as for a town meeting, to address troubling developments in the free territories.

If William's office functioned like a parlor, his wife's parlor answered for an office. At home William did his bookkeeping and wrote editorials amid housework and children at play. Will Howells' experience growing up belies his parents' assumption about separate spheres for men and women. Throughout his life he found the private doings of family and friends as fascinating as the greater public world, and like his father he preferred to work at home. In hundreds of later letters he commented on domestic affairs, weighing the virtues of furnace brands or begging a favorite recipe for potato cakes.

Goodwill and community support notwithstanding, newspaper publishing remained a risky trade, and even if more secure in Jefferson, the Howellses could not have been called well-off. Faced with readers dropping months or years behind in their subscriptions, William had to negotiate plans for payment, which usually came down to barter. The firewood he received in exchange for printing services did little to warm the cold and drafty *Sentinel* office. In their first Jefferson winter the compositor, who set type next to the windows, risked frostbite. Howells himself found the winter temperatures, sometimes ten to twenty below zero, unbearable after the milder climate of southern Ohio. He later marveled that the paper ever got printed, let alone paid for.

As an older man he did not romanticize his forced apprenticeship on the newspaper, his lack of schooling, or the quality of his life in Jefferson. The town's virtues, its neighborliness and size, soon emerged as limitations. Like the narrator in Sherwood Anderson's *Winesburg, Ohio,* who found small-town life suffocating, Will Howells began to imagine the ancient woods around Jefferson as his own prison wall. He felt that if people in the town guessed his real feelings, his family would lose what small means they enjoyed. Every day in "this not-to-be-sufficiently-detested village" brought its anxieties. Home itself offered little escape for a boy living with his father's employees and watching his mother, consumed by work and worry and the care of her last baby, begin to resemble an old woman by the age of forty.[23]

Do you, or does Annie, remember anything of that dreadful summer when I suffered from the fear of hydrophobia? Did father ever mention it in his later life to you? Just what summer was it? . . . I think the episode is necessary for a full realization of my life.

—W. D. HOWELLS to Aurelia H. Howells, May 23, 1915

In 1895, long after he had left Ohio, Howells wrote to his sister Aurelia that he thought he might be happier in Jefferson than Boston (he was then living in New York). His youthful sufferings too distant to torment him, he might return with a new equanimity.[24] Memory both teased and played him false. He could never return to Jefferson without reliving the summer of 1854, when he believed he might be insane. He suffered what Swedenborgians like Henry James Sr. called a "vastation," a terrifying dissolution of self that recurred at various times until his marriage in 1862, and never wholly ceased. James attributed his breakdown to an invisible and fetid presence poisoning the air he breathed. Howells attributed his to *hypochondria,* which throughout the nineteenth century signified anxiety about health as well as profound, inescapable depression, or *melancholy.* Howells' hypochondria centered on rabies or hydrophobia, which left him in terror of dogs and a host of other potential carriers.

The onset of his illness remains difficult to fix because Howells himself confused the time and shrank from reconstructing it.[25] By his best guess, his deteriorating health grew intolerable in 1854, shortly after the death of his favorite uncle, Israel. The fears had been brewing for over a decade. He could not forget the story of David Bowers, a Hamilton drayman who died a harrowing and much-publicized death from rabies. His father's *Intelligencer* recounted the poor man's ravings and convulsions, his aching thirst and loss of vision, and the water that ran like "showers of slobber from his mouth."[26] Four years old when this happened, Howells remembered every detail he overheard, including the rumor that Bowers, like a mad dog, tried to bite his wife. Several times during his boyhood, he imagined that his dog, Tip, named for Tippecanoe (and Tyler too), had contracted rabies. When he was about nine or ten, his parents returned home one day to find him cowering in a shed, afraid to move for fear of being bitten. Some time later, a dog did bite him. Convinced from reading about snakebites that he must cut out the infected flesh, but unable to bring himself to do so, he waited to meet his Maker.

The boy's fear of rabies reflected the greater fear of dying, which occupied much of his thinking. At sixteen, positive he would not survive the year, he dreaded the approach of his birthday. Believing he would die at the hour of his birth, approximately four in the morning, he woke early and came down to check the clock. His father, anticipating him, had turned the hour hand ahead to give him safe entry into his seventeenth year.

Living in Jefferson intensified Howells' growing anxieties. The town indulged in a kind of collective hypochondria, fretting (with good reason) about sanitation and outbreaks of various diseases. Its leading citizen, Joshua Giddings, openly acknowledged his fear of contracting rabies. Howells' anxiety became unmanageable when he heard a doctor remark that hydrophobia could remain dormant for seven or more years before breaking out. He never forgot "the gloomy autumnal afternoon when the thing happened, or the moment . . . certain unguarded words awoke the fear in me."[27] The ghost of the stricken David Bowers rose up, and like furies the dogs beset him. From this distance in years it may be impossible to identify his illness. Not only is the record incomplete, but the terms for assessing and describing mental infirmities have changed (often without improvement in diagnoses or cures). Generic categories for emotional disease can rarely account for individual suffering, complicated as it is by age, general health, personal and family circumstance, and, just as important in Howells' case, what might be called spiritual burdens. Everything in his Quaker-Swedenborgian background made him responsible for his behavior, even his illness and the depression that came with it.[28]

As the summer heat mounted, breeding flies and mosquitoes in the badly drained streets, Howells fell victim to incapacitating migraines. Unable to sleep and alternately frantic and paralyzed, he began to resemble one of Edgar Allan Poe's characters. According to the medical practice of the time, he would have been treated with opium to counter symptoms of malaria. In more than one passage he sounds like a recovered opium eater, a Thomas De Quincey confessing the pangs of withdrawal. "The splash of water anywhere was a sound I had to set my teeth against, lest the dreaded spasms should seize me."[29] Given the hydrophobic's difficulty swallowing, it is testimony to his anguish that he once tried to arrest his convulsive sobbing by gulping glass after glass of water.

Unable to work at the printing office that summer, Howells resented Joe, who accused him of slacking. In hindsight, he blamed his illness on "burning the candle at both ends."[30] "I cannot quite see how I found time," he remembered, "for even trying to do the things I had in hand more or less. It is perfectly clear to me that I did none of them well."[31] He knew that William's patience had a limit, that his father probably agreed with Joe. William challenged him to get better, saying that his grandfather Joseph had thought *he* would die from tuberculosis, but he had "called forth" the will and spite to prove Joseph wrong.[32] Howells understood the moral— and the appeal—of his father's story without being able to apply it.

Unlike his younger brother, Joe worked into the night, both to help pay off the mortgage their father had assumed with the *Sentinel* and to realize his mother's dream of living in a house she owned. Howells forever grudged the effort that went into purchasing the L-shaped brick house nicknamed Saints' Rest. "Unless there is an effect of our self-denial in some other world," he would write, "the purchase was as much waste as rent paid to a landlord."[33] Right as he may have been about the property, it was Joe who wasted time and money and would work for much of his life in a job he did not choose. Following his uncles, he had hoped to become a steamboat pilot, but ill health forced him off the river and into employment with his father. Not until he was an old man did Joe escape the *Ashtabula Sentinel.*

According to medical assumptions of the day, Howells suffered from hysteria, though that term generally applied to women. It was thought that hysterics failed to respond to treatment because, paradoxically, their illnesses empowered them. Hypochondria and hysteria (and later neurasthenia) freed patients from household drudgery—or, in Howells' case, that of the print shop. This was his brother's complaint writ large, and probably his father's too. William had little sympathy (as he wrote in an essay on character) "with the young man who complains that he had to work and help his father, and had no chance to learn anything more than to read and write a little, and could not improve his mind. Why it ought to have been a supreme delight to help his father."[34]

Eventually Howells' illness brought more than his newspaper labors to a halt. Writing itself became impossible. "No doubt I was secretly proud," he wrote, "to have been invalided in so great a cause," by which he meant the "most pleasant pain" of suffering for literature. "At the same time that I was so horribly afraid of dying, I could have composed an epitaph which would have moved others to tears for my untimely fate."[35] He used his enforced freedom for reading, which proved to be the one activity that let him forget himself and his family's skepticism.

In small ways, the self-deflating humor that became Howells' trademark helped him cope with the terror of what he named his "hippo." "I have the greatest antipathy to dogs of all breeds," the narrator of an early story says. "Your 'noble Newfoundland,' as they are—inappropriately, I think—termed by their admirers; your faithful St. Bernard . . . your pug-tailed, pug-nosed, and very pugnacious bull-dog; your sickly looking and snarling poodle—all, individually and collectively, I abhor. . . . I detest the whole canine race."[36] The irony is that, despite his protestations, he loved animals: he had bred rabbits and pigeons and spent countless hours attempting, without success, to make Tip pull a small wagon. After Tip he tried to harness a goat, which declined the responsibility and ate their neighbor's laundry.

Howells' hypochondria overlapped with another chronic condition, "homesickness," in his case a combination of missing home and being sick of home. Through his teenage years, his homesickness became so acute that an overnight visit to his grandparents could bring him close to panic. His family considered homesickness an honorable, even dutiful response to absence. *Not* to be homesick smacked of heartlessness. While Mary managed to make temporary dwellings into seemingly permanent "homes," she herself lived with an urgent longing for lost or unattainable places.[37] Puzzled in early years by their mother's extended visits to her family, the Howells children knew she felt depressed and referred to her absences as going "Up-the-River." Howells later associated her trips not with poverty or boredom or overwork but with an "insupportable crisis" of homesickness, a diagnosis that came firsthand.[38]

For her part, Mary Howells may have hindered her second son's independence by treating his inability to live away from home as a triumph of love.[39] As the Eureka Mills experiment neared its end, he had taken a one-week job in nearby Xenia to augment the family income. Given the choice, he would not have stayed a single night. William's fortuitous arrival and Joe's readiness to stay allowed him to go on. His near flight from Xenia came in part because he could not bear the thought that the young women staying at his boardinghouse might laugh at him.

Episodes like this recur in Howells' memoirs and make clear that his adolescent horrors of rabies or loneliness, or of private thoughts becoming deeds, overlapped with his sexual awakening. At age twelve he had developed a revulsion for a young seamstress, the former mistress of a local businessman. In "the cause of social purity," as he later joked, he refused to speak with or look at her, to eat from a dish she passed at the table, or stay in a room she entered.[40] If she noticed at all, the woman would have recognized the signs of misplaced attraction, of a boy's struggle with his feelings for a sexualized woman. The facts of life and the effects of childbirth were hard to overlook in crowded quarters and probably just as hard to deal with. Will Howells made only brief mention in his diary of his brother Henry's birth, in 1852, devoting more space to the woman who attended his mother and smoked pipefuls of foul-smelling tobacco. Almost certainly he watched the midwife come and go, heard disturbing sounds, and read anxiety on the faces of his father and sister. He knew that Vic, as the eldest daughter, had been summoned to her mother's side and warned of the "impending danger."[41] Much as Howells came to write about the relations of men and women, he remained reticent about sexuality.

Shrewd as ever, Henry James once wrote that he sensed a "depression" in Howells disconnected "from his *operative* self."[42] Twain's quip about Howells' "bile," and frying an optimist for breakfast, suggests a similar sense of the public man hiding his private self from friends, though Twain thinks of unexpressed anger, James of sorrow. For Howells some things were better left unsaid; others, like his boyhood afflictions, remained unutterable. The cooler fall weather in 1854 brought him temporary relief, as it would throughout his life, but his symptoms reappeared with the late spring heat. Long afterward he explained that it took him years to endure the sight of the word *hydrophobia:* "I shut the book or threw from me the paper where I found it in print; and even now, after sixty years, I cannot bring myself to write it or speak it without some such shutting of the heart."[43]

In the spring of 1855, Joshua Giddings' friend and political partner, "Old Ben" Wade, offered to train Howells as a lawyer, a plan that promised immediate income and a chance to whittle down the family's debt. Wade, a large, imposing man, was legendary, in Ohio and beyond, for his belligerence. When, after a long climb to power, he served as president of the U.S. Senate, he stood next in line to succeed Andrew Johnson. Preferring the devil they knew to the overbearing radical they would get, his fellow senators voted against Johnson's impeachment. After a month working for the autocratic Wade, Howells decided that he wanted to be neither a lawyer nor a politician and returned to his father's shop. At about this time a group of local farmers, recognizing his uncommon gifts, offered to pay his way through Harvard. He declined, maybe from pride or because his family needed him, but more likely because he intended to write. Shortly after his return he began to publish a serialized novel in the *Sentinel, The Independent Candidate,* which ran from the fall to the early winter of 1854. Presenting the Whig candidate as a scoundrel whom the local editor endorses for the sake of party unity, and the independent candidate as a madman, Howells exposes a world of political expediency. Even in this improbable and hastily finished story, he led the way. It took another twenty-five years before Henry Adams published his anonymous *Democracy* (1880), a novel based on corrupt officials in Washington.

At the reconvening of the Ohio legislature for the 1857 session, Howells and Vic, whom he affectionately called Sissy, returned once again to Columbus. He was to help William write a daily letter from the capital while Vic enjoyed life in the city. Their parents wanted the time to be a reward for Vic, who enjoyed few such vacations. At the Goodale House, where they boarded, she made sure that her brother and father rose with the alarm clock and ate a substantial breakfast. Howells insisted in his memoir that she kept secret, even from himself, her desire to be a writer. Evenings when they walked, she spun golden visions of *his* success. If he hoped one day to rescue her, his "kindred out of the bondage," for a better life, he would not succeed.[44] After Mary Howells died in 1868, Vic—in her father's words—became the "mother of the household."[45] There seems to have been no question that Henry's care would fall to the eldest girls—first to Vic, then to Aurelia.

At what point Mary and William acknowledged Henry's abnormalities remains unclear, though suspicions about his development may have arisen when he was two, about the time of Howells' struggle against hypochondria. Perhaps sensing that inherited defects spelled trouble for the other children, Henry's parents explained his behavior as a result of scarlet fever, a fall from a swing, or a blow to the head. In the late 1890s, when doctors used Roentgen's newly discovered X rays on Henry, the image revealed an inoperable bone spur pressing into his brain. The bone spur accounted for his pain, and perhaps more, but neither Howells nor Joe gave much credence to the X-ray. With Henry's prognosis unchanged and a remedy impossible, of what use was a belated diagnosis?

Apart from a few unstable plateaus, Henry's problems worsened with age. William Cooper Howells wrote his brother in 1888 that, at his worst, Henry had to be restrained in two adjoining rooms double-bolted from the outside. Often they found it unsafe "to go into his rooms, lest he handle us roughly."[46] As a boy he had to be kept away from visitors to spare them his outbursts or the shock of watching him dance around the parlor in (or out of) shorts. A photograph from 1856 shows a youngster older than his years, with a long slit of downturned mouth and eyes widely spaced. "How could we look into the dark blue of his lovely eyes, and see there the demon of insanity?" Vic asked. It would "make him wretched, and all of us wretched with him."[47] Because of his violence and the difficulty of finding and keeping attendants, the family later debated the benefits of a lobotomy, to which they could never consent. Once again the older brothers agreed. Joe thought a lobotomy no better than "sinking a well for oil in wild-cat territory." Howells wrote to Aurelia that they must avoid extreme measures "while father lives. . . . He is set against it, and the chances of cure, or relief even, are so small, that I could not urge him to take it."[48] The family resorted to drugging Henry with as much as forty grains—near-fatal doses—of bromide and chloral hydrate, the routine sedatives of the time.

Howells acknowledged that he owed his independence to Vic and Aurelia's servitude and to the luck of being born a boy. "There is *no* happy life for a woman," his heroine's father says in *The Undiscovered Country* (1880), "except as she is happy in suffering for those she loves, and in sacrificing herself to their pleasure, their pride and ambition."[49] Vic began to care for Henry as a young girl, and it was clear to Howells that, barring miracles, her situation would keep her from a literary life. He nevertheless encouraged Vic, Aurelia, and Annie to write as if they were the American Brontë sisters. The comparison itself must have given them pause, for the authors of *Jane Eyre, Wuthering Heights,* and *The Tenant of Wildfell Hall* took care of their talented but hapless brother. Looking back on Vic's life, Howells saw her time in Columbus as a kind of recompense; she herself saw missed opportunities and what she believed to be meager aid from the brother who had been her childhood companion. What a neighbor said of Aurelia applies to both sisters. An Ariel to her Caliban brother, she was "the most beautiful and most terrible example of self-sacrifice" he had ever known.[50]

Within a few months of Vic's return from Columbus, William followed to help Joe with the *Sentinel.* Since Howells had been writing letters signed "Jeffersonian" from material his father provided, the editor acquiesced to his continuing alone. William may have had another motive. According to the standards of the day, his son should already have been safely launched on a career. This son had his doubts. Left alone in the city and expected to provide for both his family and himself, he grew increasingly apprehensive. He had entered a world where success depended on skills he had yet to learn, from tipping to dancing. Before he left Jefferson, a friend had given him advice: be bold, be proud, and learn how to dance.

During the legislative sessions, Howells got his first taste of Columbus society. As a reporter he received invitations to lavish political receptions thrown by people who expected him to pay for his champagne and oysters with favorable newsprint. These events introduced him to the wealthy and powerful. Though many of those he met found his mix of awkwardness and erudition endearing, they saw him merely as a cub reporter describing their world for the newspaper of another city. In his first two winters in Columbus, Howells explored little of Columbus beyond the rooms and halls of its officialdom. He took up fencing and continued his studies. All the while he stored impressions and developed ideas about life made "real" in fictional books. Decades later, in *A Hazard of New Fortunes* (1890), he lets a radical German socialist summarize how a writer must approach his subject: "You have to see it, hear it, smell it, taste it, or, you forget it."[51] For the rest of his days, Howells would hear and smell and taste his Columbus experiences, things German above all. It almost broke his heart to discover that beer made him ill and that Columbus "proper" ignored its largest ethnic minority. "Germans" and "Americans" split on everything except a common "opposition to slavery."[52]

His Jeffersonian columns proved so successful that in March, within days of his twentieth birthday, he was offered the job of city editor (a title that meant "local reporter") for the *Cincinnati Gazette.* The *Gazette* had been run until 1840 by Charles Hammond, the country's leading spokesman for the Whig party. Since then the paper's circulation had fallen and lagged behind that of its main rival, the *Cincinnati Commercial,* and faced further competition from the monthlies, semimonthlies, and quarterlies sprouting in the new cultural center. Howells' position paid double his Columbus salary, or one thousand dollars a year, an enormous sum for a young man of twenty whose father supported a household on less. William once again expected his son's income to help free the family from debt.

Flattered as he was by the opportunity and by Edmund B. Babb, the man who came to offer it, Howells must have had reservations. His letters offer few details about the appointment, and in later memoirs he gives the move short shrift. One day he reported from the capital; the next he had risen to an enviable assignment on the "great Cincinnati newspaper." Yet he never formally took the job. He did some editing and contributed to a column called City Intelligence as he waited for a different position from the one he had been hired to fill. Babb offered him a bed in his dusty bachelor quarters and tried to make the young man feel at home. Roaming around the bewildering city of 160,000—ten times the population of Columbus—or following seasoned reporters on their assignments, Howells visited and revisited Cincinnati's bustling riverfront in hopes of spotting his uncles' paddle wheelers.

His sketch of Babb's devotion to journalism stands out in *Years of My Youth* for its poignant expression of competing values. Speaking of the "honor and respect" that journalism deserves, he regrets his personal distaste for the work, which can be, "for those once abandoned to it. . . . a kind of enchantment."[53] He was only briefly in Cincinnati before, to use his own phrase, his "real self" emerged. He could not bear to face "the school of reality" (a nice admission for someone closely associated with American realism) or do the job the paper offered him. Even as a novice reporter he felt the pull between scruples and professional demands, as when a respectable subscriber begged him and Babb not to report his affair with a married woman. They agreed, only to read the story the next morning on the front page of a rival paper.

For the young Howells the curse of journalism lay in confronting the sordid aspects of life and the immediacy of other people's tragedies. He felt out of place haunting the night court in search of unsavory tales about drunken, brawling couples, though he would later use such incidents to write about larger political issues for the *Nation*. Already half-aware of the links between dreams and creativity, he escaped as a young man into the world of fiction, and knew that he did. His nerves revolted at the "abhorrent contacts" with "that university of the streets."[54] A decade later, the eccentric and half-blind Lafcadio Hearn arrived in Cincinnati as a penniless nineteen-year-old to find it endlessly fascinating. He worked his way into a reporter's job, explored the Ohio wharves, the German sections of town, and the slaughterhouses, and wrote in gruesome detail about what he intuited or managed to see. Howells, his temperamental opposite, left to writers like Hearn the description of violence and social disorder. If these were the responsibilities of a city editor, he wanted none of them.

In Cincinnati Babb was his only friend. Howells later touched on his predictable loneliness in an anecdote about attractive shop girls in a restaurant. Clearly attracted and at the same time offended or frightened by their immodesty, he would come to remember them with sympathetic understanding. "I was so altogether ignorant of life, that I thought shame of them to be so boldly showing themselves in such a public place as a restaurant. I wonder what they would have thought, poor, blameless dears, of the misgivings in the soul of the censorious youth as he sat stealing glances of injurious conjecture at them while he overate himself with the food which was the only thing that could appease for a moment the hunger of his homesick heart."[55] His letters give no indication when his "homesick heart" won out over independence and a well-paid job. Writing to congratulate Joe on the birth of his first child, a son named William Dean, the proud uncle said that he liked nothing better than to wander the streets, gazing in shop windows or making up stories about fellow strangers.[56] Within ten days of his letter, he told Vic that he would be home in a week. He did not give up the Cincinnati job so much as abandon it in a panic of homesickness.

Howells came of age in a time of great change for newspapers and those who staffed them. In Jefferson, Howells had imagined the *Sentinel* going from his house to the houses of his neighbors. Now, in the cities, newspapers arrived in the daily mail or from young delivery boys racing through city boroughs. His friend Whitelaw Reid helped revolutionize journalism by installing Linotype machines, creating the first modern newspaper index, and publishing extra editions to cover breaking stories. New technology made available better, cheaper paper, and automated, steam-driven presses could print ten or twenty thousand papers an hour. Morse's telegraph patents in the 1840s soon made it possible for the fledgling Associated Press to gather news from around the country and around the world.

Journalism evolved in ways that neither Howells nor his father could have imagined when they took over the *Ashtabula Sentinel.* Newspapers from the *New York Times* to the *Cincinnati Gazette* to the *Chicago Tribune* or *Boston Transcript* hired talented journalists who built careers on daring assignments, most famously Henry Stanley's trek across Africa in search of David Livingstone. Whitelaw Reid, before his technical innovations as editor of the *New York Tribune,* began as a pioneering war correspondent. The lone reporter with Union troops at the battle of Shiloh, he revealed to the nation that Grant's officers and men had been unprepared for the Confederate charge. Reid witnessed the fighting on Missionary Ridge when the outcome at Gettysburg hung in the balance. Under threat of punishment, including prosecution for treason, he and his colleagues managed to relay news of battles or troop deployments to their readers, occasionally before Abraham Lincoln himself had been informed. Reid's bulletins made instant history; the quick copying and dissemination of, say, Matthew Brady's photographs still awaited a new technology.

Prior to the 1830s (and decades later in small towns and rural areas), the one-man paper, such as William Cooper Howells' *Sentinel,* might have standing in a community without its editor's necessarily mixing with the town's elite. The increased power and influence of journalism began to elevate editors in public esteem. By 1830, Andrew Jackson offered political patronage to editors who supported his candidacy, bringing several of them into his administrations. Later, publishers such as the socialist reformer Horace Greeley, and after him Joseph Pulitzer, wielded enormous political power by speaking directly to the voting public. Reporters, too, climbed the social ladder and considered themselves professionals. Among Howells' friends, Whitelaw Reid and George William Curtis enjoyed distinguished newspaper careers and became ambassadors to France and England. At one time Reid earned $6,000 a year (over $100,000 in today's currency) as managing editor of the *New York Tribune.* Mark Twain wrote for newspapers and owned one himself. Even a disillusioned journalist like Henry Adams described the press as "an inferior pulpit" but "still the nearest approach to a literary career for the literary survivor of a wrecked education."[57] No less than Twain or Adams, Howells dreamed of a literary life. In the library of the Ohio State Senate, he had contemplated the rows of leather-bound books and envisioned a domestic equivalent: a gentleman's study paneled in mahogany with a hand-carved mantel and an Aubusson carpet.

Looking back on his newspaper work, he called himself "passionately a journalist well after I began author," and, if he lost that passion as he aged, he never stopped being a journalist in a broad sense of the word.[58] Journalism shaped his literary principles: the importance of honest, clear prose and defining detail in the portrayal of ordinary men and women. His stint with the *Cincinnati Gazette* served as a watershed: not his last chance to commit himself to journalism, but perhaps the last time he thought about the profession as a career rather than a way to make his living.

It is nothing, and nothing, and nothing,
That I either think or see;—
The Phantom of dead illusions
Tonight are haunting me.

—W. D. HOWELLS, "Andenken," 1860

To his own and his parents' chagrin, the prodigal claimed homesickness, the one acceptable excuse for abandoning his job, and reappeared to take his post on the *Sentinel*. He did not intend to stay. In his words, he got up in a stew, boiled and simmered all day, and went to bed "sodden, and ferociously misanthropical."[59] "I am proud, vain, and poor," he told Vic. "I want to make money, and be rich and grand. But I don't know that I shall live an hour—a minute!"[60] Rheumatism kept him from sleeping, and the pain in his joints made it difficult to handle a knife and fork, "let alone a pen."[61] Because he had lived so long in isolation, he wrote one cousin, he supposed he "would rather be lonesome and miserable than not."[62] If nothing else, the Byronic posing reflected the failure in Cincinnati and the shame of coming home.

As the family world closed around him, Howells prepared himself for "a wider world and prouder pleasures" than the town's lectures on Mormonism or occasional minstrel show or circus performance.[63] His pocket diary for 1858 records:

Got up yesterday morning, per resolution, the instant I awoke. Made fires, read the papers, a chapter in Conde and a chapter of Aaron Burr's Life. . . .

After breakfast translated part of an article on "Vampires" from the Spanish; washed and went to the office, where I set up a job.

Afternoon—finished the translation mentioned; quite a lengthy affair—and read it to the women.

John and I went to the woods and brought home two raspberry bushes and planted them.

Last Monday, I cast my first vote.[64]

His record omits one ruling passion in these years, the poems of Heinrich Heine. After reading George Eliot's 1856 review of Heine's work, he made the German writer a model for his own poetry and fell in love with Heine's language. When he met an emigré bookbinder named Otto Limbeck, his German studies began in earnest. He had never read anything quite like Heine's witty, uncluttered verse or his self-questioning and unapologetic egotism. In an age that preferred lines like "Little fairy, smiling bright / In thine eyes a softened light," Heine struck him as revolutionary.[65] "Nothing is continual, but Change," he read, "nothing eternal but Death. Every beat of the heart gives us a wound, and Life were an endless bleeding, if it were not for Poetry."[66] Life carried with it a perpetual yearning for home or, in Heine's language, *Heimweh,* that "home pain" more like "world pain" brought on by the pangs of loneliness and separation.

But the young man with little formal schooling, large family obligations, and no visible mentors *was* at home and needed to make a living elsewhere. He fell back on what he knew. Before the legislature reconvened for the winter of 1858, he made arrangements to write letters for both the *Cincinnati Gazette* and the *Cleveland Herald;* together they brought him about twenty dollars a week, money the family could ill afford to turn down. In better health he set off for Columbus. Although a narrow Democratic majority had robbed William of the legislative clerkship he won in 1856, he left Joe to manage things in Jefferson and accompanied Will to the capital. If the father hoped his presence might avert his son's relapse, he was disappointed. The illness this time manifested itself as vertigo, which could be eased only by walking, rowing, or horseback riding. Almost before he began his new assignments, he had had enough, or *Genug,* the German word he used as pen name for the *Herald.* William assumed the larger part of his son's obligations, and in the coming winter Whitelaw Reid—not yet the nationally known journalist—took over from both of them.

Once again Howells went home to recover. He rose at six, usually heading for the woods to return with a new bush or tree for the front yard. He did a little print work in the office, came home for dinner, and went back to the office. In the evenings he read aloud to his sisters and mother. At a loose end, he decided to visit his Dean relatives in Pittsburgh before setting off on his Uncle Sam's steam packet—auspiciously named the *Cambridge*—for a twelve-hundred-mile trip to Saint Louis. Any river journey for Howells recaptured for him his boyhood days, when he watched the mile-long processions of river boats lining up to dock, each brightly decorated with the effigies of Indians for whom they were named. It seems almost a given that the boy who remembered his pilot uncles bringing home their wages in gold coins or who had listened to crewmen talk on the hurricane deck of a great riverboat would come to love Mark Twain like a brother—or that, with his own brother, he would repeat this 1858 journey a half century later.

In what had already become the pattern of his career, Howells made copy out of his riverboat experience for readers of the *Sentinel.* The voyage down "La Belle Rivière," as he called the Ohio in the first of nine letters, presented a world bordering on the "oriental."[67] He needed no reminder from *Uncle Tom's Cabin* that one side of the Ohio represented freedom, the other bondage. On the river, black cabin boys in starched white jackets served first-class passengers in the glow of crystal chandeliers. Finding himself in a whirl of revolving doors, uniformed bellhops, iced champagne, and illicit sex, he fell under its spell without overlooking the injustices making it possible. Signing his articles simply by the initial "W," he contrasted the lot of the penniless foreigners who cooked, ate, and slept together on deck without "the decencies of civilization" with that of cabin passengers who lounged before breakfast, then ambled, read, or dozed to their hearts' content.[68] As a guest of his uncle, he felt his own position to be somewhere between the groups he called the masses and the classes.[69] He published his last letter to the *Sentinel* on June 17, 1858, and returned to Jefferson to "rusticate" until offered an editorial position on the *Ohio State Journal,* a paper dedicated to the principles and policy of the state's Republican party. He could not explain his own inconsistency—taking at half salary essentially the same job he had turned down in Cincinnati—other than by saying that anything had to be better than his rut of inaction.

In November, he settled back into his old surroundings with surprising ease, boarding for $3.50 a week at the old Starling Medical College, a rooming house mocked by local sophisticates for its pretentious Tudor-Gothic façade. Howells loved it. Imagining himself and his fellow boarders as "Collegians," he decorated his mantel with casts of Goethe and Shakespeare and a medallion bearing the thorn-crowned head of Christ. He roomed with a young man named Artemas Thomas Fullerton, a lawyer and poet, who distinguished himself that year by publishing two poems in the *Atlantic Monthly*. Fullerton's presence, more than anything, kept the homesickness, the "intolerable gnawing and longing," at bay.[70] Fullerton also gave him a new incentive. To send more money home, Howells calculated that each month he might make eight to ten dollars above his salary from contributions to other papers. Learning that Fullerton earned twenty-five dollars a page for his *Atlantic* poems, he resolved to break into that market, too. He kept his sisters informed about each success, assuming that it meant as much to them as to himself, which in a practical sense it did. His monthly check made their circumstances a little more bearable—and reinforced the family belief in their collective genius. At times he could be insensitive when seeking encouragement: "O, how genially I come out in this ray of sunlight, after being frozen up so many years in Jefferson," he wrote Vic. "All my faculties expend, and the gloom leaves me, that haunted me forever. I have the assurance that I shall succeed, but, O God! sometimes, I tremble lest something should happen to destroy my hopes."[71] His enthusiasm let him forget for the moment that Vic was herself trapped in Jefferson, where she led a life of "monotonous drudgery."[72]

By the end of 1858, he had a job and some hope of literary success. Country editors had reprinted "Bobby," his most recent story, about a mischievous boy, albeit without permission. Welcoming the attention, he nevertheless deplored the piracy and the lack of payment, knowing that editors without legal responsibility to pay for already-published pieces cared for little beyond immediate deadlines. He enjoyed his work for the *Ohio State Journal* largely because Henry D. Cooke, a liberal Republican, had become one of the owners and the general editor. Cooke, who had prophetic ideas about the selling of newspapers, shifted the *Journal* from an evening to a morning paper and made it more readable with arresting formats and sprightlier articles. For a time the formula worked, thanks to Howells and another up-and-coming journalist, Samuel R. Reed. Cooke gave the young men joint responsibility for running the paper's news bureau. Howells looked up to Reed, a young man with an enviable and unflinching self-possession, who set his own style with a Rip van Winkle beard and, though he held nothing sacred, spouting from the Bible. Reed "always kept a countenance of bland calm, lit by pale-blue eyes which gave no hint of the feeling within, and if I had not loved him so much and known him so well, I might have thought the habitual smile of his clean-shaven lip sometimes a little cruel."[73] Later Howells decided that Reed's graciousness saved him from having a mean mind, but not from inflicting cruelty. Long after the Civil War, Reed wrote a scornful (some might say vicious) analysis of Ulysses S. Grant's leadership as commander in chief of the Union armies.

The two editors aspired to make the *Journal* more "metropolitan" in character, which meant urbane, with an Eastern flair, and above all not parochial.[74] The paper had something for everyone: crisp, satiric commentary on contemporary events, humorous glosses of stories poached (without apology) from other papers, literary reviews, and items of social, political, and human interest. Affecting a superiority toward the tabloids, writers of sentimental fiction, and Southerners of all types, the editors set themselves up as arbiters of taste. That did not stop them from printing off-color items like "Delightful Quarters," an anecdote about a man who took a free ride from Portland, Maine, to Newburyport, Massachusetts, under the voluminous hoops of a lady's skirt. Reed and Howells especially enjoyed "firing the Southern heart," as they called it, or deflating proslavery rhetoric. They reported national accounts of the torture, burning, and lynching of slaves and local stories like the murder of a tramp doused with kerosene and set on fire by local thugs. In the belief that the journalist and travel writer George William Curtis lost his job at Harper's for a lecture titled "The Present Aspect of the Slavery Question," they called his dismissal an example of "unspeakable flunkeyism."[75] The rumor cost Harper's in unwelcome publicity, but in fact Curtis had not been fired. He continued to write the Editor's Easy Chair column for *Harper's Monthly* until, at the turn of the century, William Dean Howells took his place.

The rehabilitation of the *Journal* coincided with the rise of Ohio's Republican party. In 1855 the state elected a Republican governor, Salmon P. Chase, soon to become President Lincoln's secretary of the treasury, then chief justice of the Supreme Court during the trial of Andrew Johnson. Originally a Democrat, Chase changed parties to defend escaped slaves and violators of the Fugitive Slave Act. Howells described him as "a large, handsome man of very Senatorial presence."[76] Chase's politics, like those of Giddings and Wade, reflected his New England background. He had been born in New Hampshire. Long before Ohio celebrated Thanksgiving, Chase did, and he opened his house to the *Journal*'s editors, inviting them to meet his daughter, Kate (a willful beauty who acted as his hostess), and share their holiday dinner.

That dinner marked Howells' entry into Columbus society. He soon bragged to Vic that only those of the "first-chop-est description" had been invited to another "extremely aristocratic" gathering, at the home of Judge Swan.[77] To use Edith Wharton's expression, Howells took to society as a duck takes to sewerage. "Wasn't this a different way of spending an evening from that of Jefferson," he asked Vic, "where the girls seem so stiff and constrained?"[78] However guilty he felt about boasting to his sisters or ignoring the humbler friends who first welcomed him to the city, he went to "almost any trouble" for the hostesses who made this Cinderella world possible.[79] During the day, he labored for the *Ohio State Journal;* at night he paid calls (sometimes four an evening) to mansions bursting with light and music before returning to his room at the College.

Not surprisingly, his new pleasures brought expenses and strife. Uncomfortable spending more money without justifying his purchases to the family, he could never convince them that he needed to dress better than Joe did at home. Because clothes cost more in the city than in the country, he wore his until they were threadbare but still could not send the money his mother expected.[80] "Now, mother, I had better have left off this explanation until I saw you," he wrote in May 1859; "but the suspicion that you tho't me perhaps neglectful of my duty, has been rankling ever since Sam told me this. I have never failed to send you money whenever you asked for it; and I have certainly wanted to do everything for you. But you know what a slender salary mine is; and I have to meet many expenses here that you don't know of."[81]

Howells lived in Columbus with a deep-rooted sense of his own difference and sometimes of his unworthiness. One day, for example, he watched a well-dressed young man close to his own age working on a chain gang. Seeing the prisoner as his counterpart and terrified by his own possible fate, he assumed that the man had been unjustly sentenced. He suffered with "that hapless wretch as cruelly" as if he had been in his place and even imagined himself the perpetrator of his crime. "Perhaps we are always meant to put ourselves in the place of those who are put, or who put themselves, to shame."[82] The word *shame* reverberates throughout Howells' memoirs. His youthful contempt for the world was, as he writes in *My Literary Passions,* "a refuge from the shame I felt for my own want of figure in it."[83] Judging himself against the social expectations of strangers, and identifying with his parents' ethical aspirations (and financial needs), he felt caught between extremes. Later he realized that some of his complaints had been rationalizations or shams, ways of hiding from himself the fact that his needs and those of his family could never be negotiated.

Howells' uneasy letter to his mother signaled yet another episode of bad health. This time he reached out to his brother Joe. He wanted to think that they had grown up rather than "apart," though his own emotional remove from family and home continued to distress him. For two months he fought the familiar hypochondria. Shutting his eyes, he imagined himself not in his room at the Starling Medical College but on the stoop of his house in Jefferson: "Aurelia is making a C of herself over a book," he wrote in his journal. "Mother has been sewing, but her hands and work have dropped into her lap and she looks up thinking,—as she often does. Henry plays all over the yard. Father is just come in sight . . . and John runs on before him, like an uncontrollable locomotive, announcing the arrival of the train, with piercing shrieks."[84] His friend and doctor Samuel Smith had age-old advice for what ailed him: giving the young man a clean bill of health, he told him to get on with his life. Dr. Smith's practicality helped, but the best remedy came in the form of good news. On August 14, 1859, he learned that the *Atlantic Monthly*, "that great periodical," had accepted his poem "Andenken" (1860).[85] He remembered taking the stage, which covered the ten miles between the nearest rail station and the house in Jefferson, and bursting in to announce the news. The *Atlantic* thought him a poet!

YEARS OF DECISION
1859–1861

I suppose you are all dreadfully stirred up about the Harper's Ferry
business. . . . In some respects, it is the most absurd and laughable event
of the age; but I'm sorry for poor crazy Brown.

—W. D. HOWELLS to William C. Howells, October 20, 1859

ON OCTOBER 16, 1859, the abolitionist John Brown raided the federal arsenal at Harpers Ferry, Virginia. His attempt to seize weapons
for arming slaves failed, and ten of Brown's men (including two of his sons)
died fighting. Brutal and useless as it turned out, the abortive raid stirred
passions across America. Not since Nat Turner's 1831 call to arms had the
Union seemed in such peril. Quick to take advantage of the incident, Democrats blamed Republican "fanatics" like Joshua Giddings and Salmon P.
Chase for inciting anarchy. Howells, caught up in the politics of his father's
possible appointment to the Senate clerkship, did not at first appreciate the
significance of what he called a "laughable event."[1] The more he thought
about the insurrection, however, the more it aroused his sympathies and
concern. In Columbus, an important stage in the main conduit to freedom
in Canada, he had seen men and women seized. He had been appalled by
the plight of Margaret Garner, who, having escaped to Cincinnati, killed
her own daughter rather than let her be sent back to enslavement in Ken-

tucky. Well over a century later, Garner's story prompted Toni Morrison to write her novel *Beloved.*

Ohio had more stations on the Underground Railroad than any other state, with lines converging at Ashtabula Harbor, Cleveland, Sandusky, and other ports on the shore of Lake Erie.[2] Columbus citizens who met to consider disobeying the Fugitive Slave Law turned a blind eye to black steamboat workers smuggling their human cargo. In an age when people violently disagreed on the issue of slavery, law-abiding men and women were judged criminals or accomplices by their silence. A Howells family friend like Justice Swan felt obliged to uphold the constitutionality of the Fugitive Slave Law even as he pronounced it immoral.

Although Howells and his colleague Samuel R. Reed, as editors of the *Ohio State Journal,* sought to separate Brown from the policies of the Republican party, they shared the common view of the raid as a terrifying but logical outgrowth of an immoral system by which free citizens of Ohio could be kidnapped with impunity and transported to slave-owning states. "Now Brown with twenty-one men has carried into the South the war he began [in Kansas]," an October 17 editorial ran: "We have little zeal to demand vengeance on Brown, while these monsters live and control the government." Another on November 4 protested "any backing down on the part of the democratic press." It argued that the Harpers Ferry raid, representing the highest principles, gave Brown standing among patriots such as Washington, Jefferson, Madison, and Patrick Henry. That left the Benedict Arnolds, Judases, and fratricides who denounced him. The irony that Brown saw his actions as steps toward the destruction of the federal government seems to have escaped his supporters, many of whom would fight not to end slavery but to preserve the Union.

The story of Brown had become fabulous enough, Howells wrote his father in early November, to promote war between the states.[3] Newspapers across the country carried accounts of the socially prominent Northerners called the "Secret Six," who by financing the raid risked prosecution for treason. They included social activists with transcendentalist leanings such as Theodore Parker and Thomas Wentworth Higginson, both Unitarian ministers, as well as Samuel Gridley Howe, the director of the Perkins School for the Blind and the husband of Julia Ward Howe, whose "Battle Hymn of the Republic" later emerged as the anthem of the North. Howells' identification with Brown aligned him with New England intellectuals and artists like Henry Wadsworth Longfellow, who saw Harpers Ferry as the whirlwind preceding the storm, before he met them personally. They would have appreciated the sentiment that led him to write to William, "If I were not your son, I would desire to be Old John Brown's—God bless him!" Disappointed not "to see something violent in the *Sentinel* on the subject of Harpers Ferry," he hoped that "Old Gid" would stand firm against the widespread revulsion.[4]

William, who had lost other jobs because of his political partisanship, showed surprising restraint. Nonetheless, in an October 27 *Sentinel* column that his son may have missed, he made clear the significance—some might say the righteousness—of Brown's actions. "No settled peace can exist between Liberty and Slavery. The weapons and the form of the warfare may be varied; but the battle goes on . . . and never can end till Slavery ceases;—for Liberty, being of Divine gift, cannot die. . . . The Harpers Ferry skirmish should serve as a beacon light of warning."[5] Weighing the connections between what amounted to his own ardent pacifism and the ethical and political benefits of Brown's violence, William felt troubled by the murders of innocent people and criticized Brown's tactics as impractical, if not insane.[6] His paper wrestled with issues of insurrection and justice until Brown's hanging in December 1859.

It proved a difficult time for all opponents of slavery. As Republican sentiment turned against Brown, the initial backers of the raid took cover. Gerrit Smith, one of the Secret Six, escaped trial for treason by pleading insanity and committing himself to a mental hospital. On December 1, the front page of the *Sentinel* featured Will Howells' lyric tribute "Gerrit Smith," an ode to Smith's principles that ignored his extraordinary backpedaling. The month before Brown's hanging on December 2, Howells could think of little else. "Old Lion! tangled in the net. . . . A captive but a lion yet," he wrote in "Old Brown." Thanks to this "hero of the noblest plan . . . men shall rise where slaves have trod."[7] How much Howells was drawn to Brown, Brown's sons, and other supporters of the raid can be seen in his admiration for the English-born poet Richard Realf—a protégé of Lady Byron—who was then lecturing in the United States. Realf seemed a dashing figure, a young man not much older than Howells himself, whose career combined the arts and politics. The son of an agricultural day laborer, he had won appointment as secretary of state designate in Brown's promised government.

The Howells family had profound sympathy for Brown, and they likely met him when Brown lectured in Jefferson, at Giddings' request, several months before the raid. After the raid, residents spotted Brown's accomplices on the streets of Jefferson. William, a self-described "life-long slavery abolitionist," supposedly gossiped with John Brown Jr.'s pursuers as the outlaw crouched in the *Sentinel's* loft.[8] When a new presidential campaign made Brown old news, William's outspokenness again increased. In the March 14, 1860, issue of the *Sentinel,* he asked people to attend a rally where John Brown Jr., Owen Brown, Barclay Coppoc, and James Redpath, every one an indicted fugitive, would mourn the hanging of their fellow conspirators Albert Hazlett and Aaron Stevens. He would like them "to feel safe to live in our country," William wrote, "because there was not a man mean enough to betray them." If decency failed, he said, stronger measures should be used to prevent treachery.[9] John Brown Jr. acknowledged his indebtedness to the Howells family. "Give our very kind regards to your Sister Annie," he wrote to Howells in 1874, "and say to her that we shall be more than glad to receive a visit from her next summer, and I will add from yourself, or from any of your Father's family."[10]

Brown's raid and Brown the man haunted Howells' imagination, no doubt because of the unresolvable issues they represented. He warned his sister Aurelia, swept up in the antislavery movement, that people can become "bigoted and narrow about even the salvation of souls."[11] The advice to Aurelia may explain why Howells refused to lend his autograph to a memorial volume called *Echoes of Harper's Ferry,* in which James Redpath reprinted his poem "The Pilot's Story," originally published in the *Atlantic Monthly,* with pieces by Emerson, Whittier, and Thoreau. "The Pilot's Story" dramatizes the suicide of a mulatto woman whose lover sells her to repay a gambling debt.

> Sold me? sold me? sold—And you promised to give me
> my freedom! . . . .
> What will you say to our God?[12]

Howells had mixed feelings not only about Redpath's reprinting his poem but equally about the raid and its consequences, which his signature would have seemed to condone. "My sentiments with regard to John Brown remain unchanged," he wrote his father; "but I am as yet a person of too little consequence to confer celebrity on a work by my connection with it; and, at any rate, I do not seek notoriety in any but a purely literary way."[13]

In his book of Ohio stories for schoolchildren, published in his sixtieth year, Howells summed up Brown for a younger generation: "Some think that Brown was mad, some that he was inspired, some that he was right, some that he was wrong; but whatever men think of him, there are none who doubt that he was a hero, ready to shed his blood for the cause he held just. His name can never die, so long as the name of America lives."[14] Brown also enters Howells' fiction. In *A Chance Acquaintance* (1873), he pitted the convictions of Boston against those of the West, to Boston's disadvantage, and invoked Brown, oddly enough, to compare the oppression of African Americans with that of women in Boston's hereditary aristocracy. He believed Brown's legacy to be one of conscience and creed, preferring it to a genteel, ineffectual alternative. When he wrote about Brown, he did not measure the horror or the triumph of the man's life but marveled at the conviction necessary to kill and die for a belief.

Given his fascination with Brown, it seems almost preordained that on his first trip to Boston Howells should have spied the conspirator Barclay Coppoc asleep in the coach. Making this encounter the centerpiece in one of his travel "letters," he was struck by Coppoc's vulnerability more than by his strength or determination. In a letter dated June 30, 1860, he quoted from Walt Whitman: "You are the same as I / You are no different from me."[15] Where, after all, *was* the line that one man crossed and another did not? Harpers Ferry taught Howells the significance of basic principles on the one hand and public harmony, along with due process, on the other. "No man or order of men," he would write in old age, "can pervert a whole people without their complicity."[16]

As Columbus grows old to me, it seems to contract, and I begin to feel here the gnawing discontent that I felt in Jefferson. Father need not be afraid that I should be seduced by Bohemianism in New York.

—W. D. HOWELLS to his family, April 21, 1860

For some months the *Ohio State Journal* had been on the verge of failing, and in the ensuing reorganization Howells lost both his ten-dollar-a-week salary and the prospect of collecting back wages of about two hundred dollars (which he received the following year). Casting around for a job in the spring of 1860, he found one as "professional reader" for the publishing house of Follett, Foster & Company, editing and sometimes entirely rewriting manuscripts. He worked with Joshua Giddings to promote his antislavery message and with William Coggeshall, the state librarian and booster of regional literature, on *The Poets and Poetry of the West* (1860), an edition that included poems by Howells.

Follett & Foster had published, with little success, Howells' first book of poetry, *Poems of Two Friends* (December 1859). Motivated by the *Atlantic's* acceptance of "Andenken," he had turned to John J. Piatt, a journalist he knew from his early years with the *Ohio State Journal*. In those days he had admired his friend's aim with wet sponges thrown whenever Piatt's uncle, Charles Scott, left the two apprentices unsupervised. Piatt had since won modest success as a poet, selling several pieces to the *Atlantic*. Howells would live to sigh about "poor Piatt," whose demands for preferential treatment from the magazine grew so persistent they seemed to exceed the debts of several lifetimes. In 1859 it was Howells who sought the favors. On September 19, he first approached Piatt about adding Piatt's poems to a Follett & Foster holiday book. Three days later he wrote: "When you are here, we can look your poems over together; and I constituting myself an awful judge of what you propose to print, could be a sort of pre-public to you. There, too, we might decide about publishing our verses together."[17] Within the space of two sentences, he moved from friendly editor to critic, and from literary agent to coauthor, as if in response to Piatt's invitation.

Howells' collaboration with Piatt added to his literary standing at a time when he may have lacked the confidence (or a sufficiently large body of work) to attempt a volume on his own. Overseeing the marketing of their book, he asked his more successful collaborator to approach Eastern publications such as the *New York Post* and *Boston Courier,* so that when their book came out editors would mention Piatt as a contributor and give them both free advertising.[18] Having learned from his father to push his own wares if he wanted them sold, he saw no conflict of interest in touting Piatt's genius when he wrote a long review of their book for the *Ohio State Journal* (in December 1859).

Howells' relationship with Follett & Foster proved to be one of those happy accidents that change the course of a life. Follett suggested that Howells write a campaign biography of Abraham Lincoln, then struggling against Northern opponents and Southern hostility in his bid for the presidency. Follett & Foster, who had published—in fact built their house upon—the Lincoln-Douglas *Debates,* hoped for another coup. Howells had little enthusiasm for an assignment he treated as hack work and that came with an early deadline: the book had to be finished within a month of Lincoln's nomination on May 18, 1860. Nor did he take Lincoln seriously as a candidate. Like most citizens of Columbus, he supported his mentor, Senator Chase, a scholarly man known for his good looks, social graces, and ardent antislavery positions, in comparison with whom Lincoln appeared awkward and uncommitted. Declining to interview or correspond with Lincoln or Lincoln's running mate, he wrote *The Lives and Speeches of Abraham Lincoln and Hannibal Hamlin* from published materials and from notes gathered by a law student named James Quay Howard.[19] Follett & Foster advertised that everything in the book came from either Lincoln's lips or those of his closest friends. Lincoln's backwoods-Quaker background and his self-deprecating tenacity hit home, however, and Howells soon came to admire his subject. He later regretted having missed a "great chance" of a meeting with Lincoln when too young to see its importance.[20]

With Eastern readers in mind, Howells remakes Lincoln, smoothing the rough edges, scorning the need to trace one's ancestors back to the *Mayflower,* and toning down accounts of the squalor of frontier living. He applauds Lincoln's efforts at self-improvement and rising above his station—qualities he would emphasize in his own autobiographies. A reviewer for the *Journal* observed that the Lincoln biography, with its abbreviated history of the Republican party and homey anecdotes, made for more interesting and entertaining reading than anyone could have imagined. The proud William Cooper Howells reprinted the review in the July 11 issue of the *Sentinel.*

From Howells' biography the Lincoln of legend emerges: the boy who could clear a field in a day, the golden-tongued orator who could swap tall tales with the best, the self-taught scholar who read Shakespeare by the flickering fire, and the man whose name became synonymous with moral courage. "In faith," ends Lincoln's Cooper Union address, "let us, to the end, dare to do our duty as we understand it." Moved by the "good-natured" man and his personal struggle, Howells played down the shrewd politician who saw the need to preserve the Union at any cost, including at times the suppression of civil rights, and highlighted instead the democratic process that made possible Lincoln's rise to power. "It is true," he writes, "that simply to have mauled rails, and commanded a flat-boat, is not to have performed splendid actions. But the fact that Lincoln has done these things, and has risen above them by his own force, confers a dignity upon them; and the rustic boy, who is to be President in 1900, may well be consoled and encouraged in his labors when he recalls these incidents in the history of one whose future once wore no brighter aspect than his own wears now." The less cluttered writing, the immediate connection to audience, and the portraits of American types—such as an emigrant at the head of a team of slow oxen dragging "his household goods toward the setting sun"—anticipated Howells' writing in years to come.[21]

He finished his biography in a little more than a week. "When one has written a hurried book," he explains in the preface, "one likes to dwell upon the fact, that if the time had not been wanting one could have made it a great deal better. This fact is of the greatest comfort to the author, and not of the slightest consequences to anybody else." However hastily written, his biography, the *ninth* to appear, proved an important resource for scholars because Lincoln himself borrowed and annotated the Library of Congress's copy on two separate occasions. Lincoln had the book in his possession shortly before his assassination, and historians have assumed, rightly or wrongly, that he found the unannotated sections accurate.

The biographer's task done, Howells left Lincoln's future to "Providence and to the people, who often make history without the slightest respect to the arrangements of sagacious writers."[22] He could not have guessed how much of his own future would be tied to Lincoln's presidency. The biography sold well enough for his publisher to suggest that he use $175 of his earnings to travel through Canada, New York, and New England to gather material for a book on the unlikely topic of "manufacturing industries of the northeast." With a $50 advance and a letter of credit addressed to Eastern publishers for $190 more, he set off, unaware that in an era of state banking, his Ohio dollar would buy only eighty-five or ninety cents in Boston. Even with less money, he would have left in high spirits for what promised to be a glamorous holiday.

Howells took a train to Erie, Buffalo, and Niagara, then traveled by steamer across Lake Ontario and down the Saint Lawrence to Montreal and Quebec. Stopping at Niagara Falls, ostensibly to study hydropower, he stayed for the views. He contributed fourteen travel letters to the *Cincinnati Daily Gazette* and the *Ohio State Journal* that trace his journey through July and August 1860. The early pieces from Niagara might be seen as the first installment of his developing argument against sentimentality. He advises readers to get over the first necessarily hackneyed look, which can never live up to expectations, then return to look again. Essentially he urges a new and independent angle of vision, something almost impossible at Niagara Falls given its popularity in magazines and paintings and its advertising images stamped on everything from picture postcards to ashtrays. Some of his aesthetic ideas Howells picked up from Godfrey and John Frankenstein, artists from Ohio whom he happened to meet at Niagara. By teaching him to see with a painter's eye and value the accuracy of his own observations, the Frankensteins kindled his lifelong interest in the visual arts. Together the three men walked to the usual tourist sites—the Falls, the Whirlpool, and Goat's Island—but the Frankensteins also took him to hidden nooks and thickets where, shielded by fragrant cedars, he could almost forget that Niagara had been made into a commercial center.

Visitors in the thousands crowded the town's hotels, boardwalks, and food stalls. The Prince of Wales returned for the second year in a row, and the Frenchman Charles Blondin, who had begun the year before to stage his death-defying feats on a tightrope, had, with increasing theatricality, crossed the falls pushing a wheelbarrow, walking backward, and with a man on his back, stopping midway to cook an omelet. Ordinary men and women climbed into wooden barrels and plunged over the falls or through the whirlpools. In after years, Howells associated the Whirlpool with Blondin, whom he saw "cross the river above the frantic Rapids not far from it" as if he were dancing on a dwindling thread for half a mile through space. Howells focused not on the man's face but on his feet, which seemed the most intelligent in the world, "pliable, sinuous, clinging, educated in every fibre, and full of spiritual sentience." Later he wondered why the government permitted a spectacle that courted death;[23] at the time he went back to his room and devoted a whole letter to Blondin's exploits.

Howells knew that his readers would also expect a description of one favorite tourist stop, the mist-covered, crumbling precipice called Table Rock. Weeks earlier a carriage full of people had dislodged a large piece of the formation, and the path that he himself trod would vanish within the next three months. On his visit to Table Rock, he came upon a long line of spectators taking turns to peer over the lip of the precipice. Suffering from vertigo, he crawled forward with difficulty and made out a corpse in blue overalls sprawled below. Imagining the dead man's green-and-yellow face swimming up toward his, he still managed to scribble a note before retreating to safety. The incident deeply disturbed him. He held the story back until 1893, when, with Mark Twain and Nathaniel S. Shaler, he published *The Niagara Book*.

Standing on the Canadian border, Howells thought about the Underground Railroad and the slaves who fled north. His guide, on the other hand, cared mainly about his livelihood. Apart from the fact that freed blacks in Canada got "uppity" and even married whites, he told Howells, they hurt the tourist trade. In protest and afraid of losing their human property, Southerners came to Niagara in smaller numbers. Not persuaded by the guide's arguments, Howells listened carefully and reported what he heard to his readers at home. And of course he had the last word: Intermarriage is the business of the individuals concerned, he wrote, whereas everyone shares the problem of slavery.

After crossing to Quebec, Howells took a more or less direct route to Boston, by way of Portland, Maine, the birthplace of his boyhood idol, Longfellow. Throughout the United States, England, and Europe, people from every walk of life read Longfellow's books. Howells himself began writing poetry based on the thumping rhythms of *Hiawatha*. With the audacity of an adopted son, he had signed some of his columns for the *Ohio State Journal* "Chispa," the Spanish for "spark" and the name of Longfellow's miscreant servant in his poetic drama *The Spanish Student*. Howells' passion for languages might also have been a conscious imitation of Longfellow, who was professor of foreign languages at Harvard. In any case, the young poet wanted to pay homage to Longfellow by visiting his house in Portland.

On the shore along Portland's Commercial Street, where fishermen unloaded flounder and haddock and ink-black heaps of mussels in the early morning light, Howells got his first glimpse of the Atlantic. Looking out at the islands dotting Casco Bay and the cobbled alleyways leading from the docks, he caught the competing odors of fish waste, drying seaweed, and engine oil. The landscape, with its slanted light, reminded him of the gentle valleys and uplands of southwestern Ohio. He came to think even the Western Reserve "a bit of New England flattened out along the lake shore," its villages "as scrupulously clean as any in Massachusetts," and the streets leafy tunnels of maples.[24] He had long imagined New England scenes. "I have never been able to see much difference between what seemed to me Literature and what seemed to me Life," he wrote some thirty years later. In 1860, it mattered little to him that Longfellow had never lived in the house he found.[25] Just as the poetry of the old seaport merged with the Portland of Longfellow's poetry, one venerable house served as well as another.

New England, which offered a strange mix of poets, changeable weather, codfish, and shoe-pegging machines, resisted easy reportage. So did New England traditions. Howells had never felt himself so surrounded by or so close to drowning in history as he did in Salem, Massachusetts, home to Nathaniel Hawthorne, the Custom House, and the witch trials. He began to learn—in the words of Henry James—that "it takes an endless amount of history to make even a little tradition, and an endless amount of tradition to make even a little taste."[26] His encounter with New England altered his scale of things. In the West people scurried to acquire histories by seeking out ancestors from the Eastern settlements. In New England he saw houses that for generations had belonged to the same families, to men and women who measured their inheritance by centuries. When people spoke their owners' names with awe, he understood the force of received privilege, a commodity (as *The Rise of Silas Lapham* suggests) that could be neither earned nor bought. When he walked the streets of Portland or Salem or Boston, he felt his own insignificance and, as perhaps never before, the sense of being at home.

He had taken a chance coming to Boston. Without friends in the area or letters of invitation, he checked into the Tremont House on August 1. Then—like Lemuel Barker, the countrified protagonist of *The Minister's Charge* (1886)—he took a horsecar to Cambridge. Howells did not wear Barker's outmoded pantaloons, but he had exchanged his Western broadcloth for a suit ordered from New York. Whatever confidence his new suit conferred soon evaporated. He intended to present himself to James Russell Lowell, the one man in Boston he knew through correspondence with the *Atlantic,* and had no idea where Lowell lived.

The rest of this story forms the Howells legend recounted in his own *Literary Friends and Acquaintance.* He eventually found the Apollo-browed Lowell, who quizzed him like a schoolmaster and admitted to delaying the publication of "Andenken" until he could be sure it was Howells' own work and not a translation of Heine. When Howells made the mistake of admitting that he had once wanted to believe himself a literary descendant of the well-known travel writer Sir James Howell, Lowell—who scorned pretenders of any sort—removed a volume of Howell's *Familiar Letters* to point out the different spellings of their last names. Nine years after their meeting, Lowell would respond to one of Howells' books by saying that its author deserved to have "James Howell on one side of him and Charles Lamb on the other—not to keep *him* warm, but for the pleasure *they* will take in rubbing shoulders with him."[27] Now Lowell may have felt trapped by his own kindness. As the wife of the minister in *The Minister's Charge* tells her husband: "You had no right to give the poor boy false hopes. You ought to have discouraged him—that would have been the most merciful way—if you knew the poetry was bad. . . . He will go on building all sorts of castles in the air on your praise, and sooner or later they will come tumbling about his ears."[28] At the end of their interview, Lowell walked his guest across a stretch of ground to a fence, which Howells bounded over. Lowell, who normally took the fence in stride, fell back twice, then succeeded on the third try. Before they parted he invited his visitor to lunch at the Parker House, the grand hotel on the corner of School and Tremont Streets in the heart of Boston.

When, on the appointed day, Howells arrived at two o'clock, he found the private room above the white marbled foyer and a table laid for four people. Lowell greeted him and turned to introduce a slight man of Napoleonic height. Like any literate American, Howells already knew about Oliver Wendell Holmes Sr.—the Parkman Professor of Anatomy and Physiology and the dean of Harvard's medical school—as "the Autocrat of the Breakfast Table," the pundit of fictionalized conversations set in a Boston boardinghouse. A contemporary described him as "the delight and ornament of every society he enters, buzzing about like a bee, or fluttering like a hummingbird, exceedingly difficult to catch unless he be really wanted for some kind act, and then you are sure of him."[29] Soon after, the bearish, affable owner of the *Atlantic,* James T. Fields, arrived. His pictures show a Byronic cast of face with full, pouting lips and long, curling hair swept up off a high brow. Howells had already met Fields at his office, where he had stopped to introduce himself and to collect, from Fields' partner Benjamin Ticknor, the five half-eagles of gold—each worth five dollars—owed to him for "The Pilot's Story."

Howells had never entered a building like the Parker House. The first Boston hotel to import a French chef, it had for several years provided the room where Emerson, Longfellow, Hawthorne, and John Greenleaf Whittier met on the last Saturday afternoon of each month for food and wine, readings and conversation. "Such feasts!" Holmes wrote over two decades later. "Such guests! What famous names its record boasts."[30] Howells flattered himself that he "breathed in that atmosphere as if in the return from life-long exile."[31] Not even at the governor's house in Columbus had dinner been served in separate courses. And the talk! When Holmes laughingly remarked to Lowell that "this is something like the apostolic succession . . . the laying on of hands," Howells felt that he had indeed been chosen.[32] The meal lasted four hours, ending as pleasantly as it had begun, with coffee and small glasses of cognac topped with flaming sugar. Howells left drunk with dreams, sure that he had made a triumphant start. After all, Lowell's hospitality might have had a practical purpose. With over a hundred unanswered letters on his desk, the *Atlantic* editor could have used an assistant, for which the dinner provided an informal interview. Tomorrow he was to breakfast with Fields and take tea with Holmes, who lived just a few doors away on Charles Street. Lowell promised that if Howells meant to go to Concord, he would write a letter of introduction to Nathaniel Hawthorne.

Howells presented himself at 37 Charles Street the following day. The Fieldses' house, packed with literary memorabilia, old portraits, editions, letters, and illustrations, appeared to have its very walls inscribed. Every surface held cherished objects gathered from their travels abroad. The room that Ole Bull had slept in one night might shelter Hawthorne or William Makepeace Thackeray the next. You found, as one friend wrote, "Christine Nillson or Celia Thaxter or Rebecca Harding or Mrs. Stowe . . . your vis-a-vis at breakfast or at dinner."[33] Known for her charm, Annie Fields showed Howells the library, which ran the whole length of the house with alcoves on either side. The moss-green carpet and draperies gave another writer, Harriet Prescott Spofford, the sensation of stepping into an "enchanted wood" owned by "a rarer race of beings."[34] Mrs. Fields pointed out books she thought Howells would find interesting, nearly all autographed by friends and contributors, including Longfellow. To be attended in that setting by the young and beautiful wife of the *Atlantic*'s owner flattered his dream of early success. Neither now nor later had he any clue to Annie Fields' impression that he lacked the "true poetic temperament" or sensibility she thought a writer and editor must have.[35] Her husband's editorial decisions helped to shape public taste, and she not only advised him, she also reigned over Boston's most famous literary salon (where "you heard the latest word from the world of books and book-men, and caught the first glimmer" of new talent).[36] She was, in Henry James' phrase, "the literary and social executor of a hundred ghosts."[37] Years passed before Howells recognized the provinciality of the Fields household, and of Boston and Cambridge, as a determined remoteness from the larger America.

Holmes' assurance, the day before, that literary Boston had room for newcomers, even for Westerners, highlights just how the *Atlantic*'s circle functioned. Taking "the autocrat" at face value, Howells saw the city as a mecca for anyone with artistic aspirations. He would learn to what extent it endured as a Yankee stronghold where family connections and educational background mattered most. When the idea for publishing *Who's Who in America* first arose, one Bostonian reportedly asked, "Wouldn't Harvard's catalog of graduates for the last five years answer every purpose?"[38] In Boston, and especially in the presence of Lowell, Howells felt "conscious of an older, closer and stricter civilization" than his own, a traditional and closed world that might be said to value the principle of democracy rather than its practical reality. A more sardonic Howells came to believe that Calvinism had shriveled the New England heart without affecting its outward hospitality. But not that morning at breakfast. Fields fed him his first blueberry cakes before sending him along to Holmes, who soon knew the story of Howells' troubled youth and uncertain health.

Howells left Boston with the introduction from Lowell in his pocket. After a brief stop in Lowell, Massachusetts, he boarded a stage to Concord, where he presented himself to Nathaniel Hawthorne. "I have no masonic claim upon you," Lowell had written, "except community of tobacco, and the young man who brings this does not smoke. But he wants to look at you, which will do you no harm, and him a great deal of good."[39] As might be expected, the two fumbled for conversation before Hawthorne sent him on to Emerson and Thoreau with his endorsement: "I find this young man worthy."[40] Thoreau made no effort to talk with him, and Emerson, whom he saw earlier the same day, humiliated him by searching back volumes of the *Atlantic Monthly* for his poems and then staring blankly at them and their author. When Howells took his leave, Emerson tried to dissuade him from future heartache. Poetry was worth "a pleasant hour . . . now and then." "A pleasant hour to poetry!" Howells protested. He meant to give it "all time and all eternity."[41] Much as they agreed about slavery, politics, the business of authors' royalties, and the unconscionable piracy of books, Emerson and Howells never took to one another. Howells dismissed Emerson's imperfect understanding of the West and Westerners and spoke of his "defective sense" of literature. Emerson managed consistently to forget Howells' name. Still, the meeting had not been the waste of time Howells thought. He went back to Boston with his tail between his legs, little knowing that Emerson's faint and secondhand praise of his poetry would help to secure him a coveted appointment abroad.

From Boston, he headed for New York to explore "the literary situation in the metropolis." In retrospect he thought that the August morning of his arrival must have been as sweltering as the day he was writing *Literary Friends and Acquaintance,* thirty years later. He could not remember. What he did remember was the "Niagara roar of the omnibuses" thundering night and day.[42] The city struck him as dirty, squalid, yet startlingly beautiful with its elegant and imposing buildings. His little knowledge of New York came from a woman who had stayed with the family for a month while painting his mother's portrait. She told him about transplanted Ohio writers, the literary Carey sisters and the journalist he came to befriend: George W. Curtis, author of *Lotus Eating* and *The Howadji in Syria.* Now and later, he looked for Ohio connections wherever he went, in fact for any connections that promised to help his career. He did not see Curtis but did seek out those he called the Bohemians, especially Henry Clapp, the editor of the *Saturday Press.* Clapp had accepted a few of his poems and called him a genius, though not of the highest order. Unlike the two paying magazines, the *Atlantic* in Boston and *Harper's Monthly* in New York, Clapp paid in promises. A born Yankee, in the words of a reporter for the New York *Leader,* he spoke French like a Frenchman, played poker like a Westerner, drank like a fish, smoked like a Dutchman, and conducted himself with the manners of a Russian. An open and avowed cynic, Clapp was the reigning spirit of Pfaff's beer cellar on Broadway, just north of Bleecker Street and not far from the New York Free Love League.[43]

It seemed to Howells that the staff of the *Saturday Press* spent their time drinking beer and holding the rest of the world, especially Boston's old guard, in contempt.[44] "How did he find Hawthorne?" Clapp asked. "Shy," Howells answered, like himself. "Oh, a couple of shysters!" Clapp retorted.[45] The experience at Pfaff's muddied Howells' response to Walt Whitman, a favorite with the *Saturday Press* set and with Clapp, who published poems from the forthcoming 1860 edition of *Leaves of Grass.* Clapp took credit for being Whitman's first supporter—beating the English, as Howells said, who claimed the honor.

Walt Whitman greeted him at Pfaff's by leaning back in his chair and extending his hand. Even sitting down, the man seemed gargantuan, with his "Jovian hair" and "branching beard and mustache, and gentle eyes that looked most kindly into mine."[46] By the time he met Whitman, Howells had already reviewed an early edition of *Leaves of Grass.* "Who is Walt Whitman?" he had asked, and responded with the poet's self-inventory:

Walt Whitman, an American, one of the rough, a kosmos.
Disorderly, fleshy, sensual, eating, drinking, breeding.
No sentimentalist—no stander above men and women, or apart from them.
No more modest than immodest.

"This," he had written, "is frank but not altogether satisfactory."[47] Realizing that he liked the "man-about-horses—slouch, insolent, 'cute,' coarse," he was at a loss for words.[48] Did he need to announce himself as a recent reviewer, and an unfavorable one at that? He decided not. But he had no interest in pursuing Whitman as he pursued Lowell or Emerson, or engaging with the group at Pfaff's. In 1885, he sent ten dollars for a subscription to buy Whitman a buggy, stipulating that his donation not be taken as an endorsement of the man's poetry or opinions.[49]

The "lawless, measureless, rhymeless, and inscrutable" Whitman confounded Howells as he did so many readers. If he were a poet, what could Howells himself be?[50] The answer to that seems obvious enough from a later perspective, but Howells still defined himself and his future by his writing of poetry. Without wanting to associate himself with the prudes or "Misses Nancy of criticism," he struggled with what he believed to be Whitman's repellent, egotistical genius.[51] How could he separate the man from the poet who celebrated catalogues and bodies electric and a broad, fleshy democratic vista? Whitman might have applauded Howells' summary of his work as "shaggy, coarse, sublime, disgusting, beautiful, tender, harsh, vile, elevated, foolish, wise, pure and nasty to the four hundred and fifty-sixth page, in a book most sumptuously printed and bound."[52] Howells himself struggled with a power he could not identify.

He would have disavowed Whitman's influence on his own writing, yet his call for an inclusive American literature written in natural language and his rejection of New England parochialism indicate that something may have rubbed off. Once he had met the man and liked him, he felt inclined to excuse what he saw as Whitman's horrendous breach of ethics: his publishing, without Emerson's consent, the famous letter extending a cordial greeting to the world of letters. He did not change his mind about the poetry. To his friend Edmund Stedman, who had himself enjoyed evenings at Pfaff's, he wrote: "The small but enthusiastic admirers of Walt Whitman could not make him a poet if they wrote all the newspapers and magazines in the world full about him. He is poetical as the other elements are, and just as satisfactory to read as earth, water, air and fire."[53] Instead of embracing Whitman as the pioneering writer he himself called for, Howells saw him a liberating force, an "anarch," whose prose he preferred to his verse and whose self he preferred to both.

New York's Bohemia, with its imported French theories and affected cynicism, depressed him. Years later he parodied Clapp's circle in *The Coast of Bohemia* (1893), the story of a village girl with a real but limited artistic gift who goes to New York to study painting. Coming from small towns himself, he liked the conceit that everyone in Cambridge knew Lowell or Holmes on sight, whereas New York bred a petty selfishness. "The Bohemians were the beginning of the story for me, and to tell the truth I did not like the story. I remember as I sat at that table under the pavement, in Pfaff's beer-cellar, and listened to the wit that did not seem very funny, I thought of the dinner with Lowell, the breakfast with Fields, the supper at the Autocrat's, and felt that I had fallen very far."[54] Intimidated by New York, he did not yet feel the lure of the metropolis that drew men like Stedman and Thomas Bailey Aldrich, or in times to come himself.

"Better fifty years of Boston than a cycle of New York," he wrote Fields from Ohio. "The truth is, there is no place quite so good as Boston—God bless it! and I look forward to living there some day—being possibly the linchpin in the hub. I wonder if I could not find enough writing there, on different journals, literary and otherwise, to employ me, and support me in comfortable poverty?"[55] Howells did his best to keep himself before his Boston acquaintances, corresponding with Holmes' son and namesake about art and religion (to the younger Holmes' discomfort), and mailing Lowell a copy of the recently published *Poets and Poetry of the West* in hopes of a review. Lowell declined to review the book but praised Howells' poems, the only poetry he found among the "rhyme-&-water," and urged him to stay in the West (to make himself "scarce") on the principle that native voices needed native soil.[56] Howells, who would change his views, protested that "the conditions in the west are rather against poetry, I think. It is hardly possible to assimilate and poetize the crude, harsh life we live."[57] Lowell had nothing to offer him beyond suggesting that the *Atlantic* might be interested in travel articles if Howells had the funds to do the research.

From a distance, New York seemed to have had fun at his expense. Boston, which appeared more generous, remained a citadel, the façades of townhouses along the Common forming a wall as impenetrable to the young man as the Great Wall of China. Not until he wrote *Suburban Sketches* (published in 1871) would he explore Boston's—or rather Cambridge's—neighborhoods of Irish, Italians, and freed blacks and come to appreciate that not all Bostonians were Brahmins (to use Oliver Wendell Holmes' word for Boston intellectuals) or that few outsiders had received the same welcome.

> He falters on the threshold,
> She lingers on the stair.
>
> —W. D. HOWELLS, "Convention," 1860

Howells arrived in "dear, little" Columbus glad to be home and among friends, and at the same time wanting to be free of both.[58] "Home," whether Columbus or Jefferson, had become the place he dreamed of but not the place he cared to live. Impatient with the "meanness and hollowness" of provincial life, he celebrated his homecoming by avoiding the people he had previously wooed, shunning invitations, and putting any free time left from the *Journal* into his writing.[59]

Much of his discontent went into a novel he called "Geoffrey: A Study of American Life," which begins with the titular character's return to "Dull-dale" after an absence of seven years. "It is hard to say with what feeling a young man goes back to the home of his boyhood after so long an absence," the narrator declares. "With his tenderest sentiment for the things of the past, is mingled a half contempt of them." However much Geoffrey despises Dulldale, he settles there, takes over the town newspaper, marries his widowed cousin, and lives unhappily ever after. After his wife's death, he is left responsible for a stepdaughter and the young woman who looks after her. In a typical romance, Geoffrey would have married the woman; instead he grows old in "apathetic seclusion," while she makes "her life an unthanked service" to him.[60] The book's subtitle—"a Study of American Life"—suggests that its author linked his own and his character's malaise with the state of the nation, and certainly a feeling of unease infected his countrymen in the years leading to the Civil War. Though fighting in Kansas had given way to drought, war seemed imminent in the new territories or along the Texas border with Mexico, and, worse, in established states divided on the issue of slavery. Americans already sensed the gathering violence that erupted with the secession of South Carolina and the bombardment of Fort Sumter.

The United States had become both more intimate and more diverse. The Pony Express raced in an unthinkable eleven days from Saint Louis to Sacramento and railroad workers labored to tie the Eastern seaboard with the far West. Emerging cities like Chicago, Cincinnati, and San Francisco reflected the country's changing demographics. San Francisco seemed to build itself in a matter of weeks; Cincinnati grew so wantonly that within a few blocks one could hear more languages than William Dean Howells could read. By 1860 America's center of population (then roughly 30,500,000) lay about a hundred miles east of Cincinnati and fifty miles south of Columbus, near Chillicothe, Ohio. Two million immigrants had arrived in the United States during the 1850s, nearly 70,000 of them from China—before the Chinese Exclusion Act of 1882. Across the land, dreams of gold mountains brought 100,000 fortune seekers to the Rockies in 1859 chanting "Pike's Peak or Bust." Silver drew con men and entrepreneurs to Nevada's Comstock Lode, where some emerged, like the father of William Randolph Hearst, millionaire. Others, like Mark Twain, left empty-handed and went on to rich careers.

Howells, too, hoped to better his life, as indicated by his trip to Boston and New York. Wishing to profit from the acquaintances he made, he had in a sense gone east under false colors and been made to feel the whimsy of others' power. He knew that when an opportunity came, as it did in 1861, he would have to make decisions. But deciding appeared to depend on something or someone beyond himself: a benefactor, a calamity, a new situation, or an unaccountable stroke of luck. He remained green when it came to closed social worlds and customs, overrating his ability to charm men like James Fields and powerful society women like Isabelle ("Belle") Carter, whose wrath he felt in Columbus. Irritated by his snubs, she and her friends kept him from meeting Abraham Lincoln, who had expected to see his biographer at entertainments in Columbus. Howells swallowed his pride, made the rounds again, and—thanks to the generosity of Senator Chase and Susan Smith, the wife of Howells' doctor—won forgiveness from Columbus society.

The return to favor coincided with new difficulties. Among James Russell Lowell's sundry pieces of advice, which included a warning not to "print too much & too soon," had been the recommendation, "Don't get married in a hurry."[61] A few months later, Howells' evident attraction to Elinor Mead, Laura Platt's cousin and guest for the winter, set Columbus tongues wagging. The two met sometime in December 1860, about a month after Elinor's arrival.[62] Coming from a "good" family in Brattleboro, Vermont, Elinor shone in Columbus drawing rooms as well as those of New England. Clever, amusing, and short in stature like himself, she would offer Howells almost everything he longed for, except, to be sure, a job.

Her hosts, the Platts, knew the Meads through the future president of the United States, Rutherford B. Hayes. Hayes' grandfather was Elinor's great-grandfather, a relationship that made her and Hayes, according to the byways of genealogy, first cousins twice removed. In his Ohio storybook for children, Howells would describe Hayes as "a great lawyer, a great soldier, a great statesman, a great philanthropist, a man without taint or stain."[63] Howells admired his friend so much he gladly wrote a campaign biography for Hayes before the 1876 election—as close and bitter as that of 2000. Hayes never lived down the taunt that "Tilden was elected, Hayes took his seat"—that he had in fact stolen the presidency. In 1858, not yet a politician or a major general in the Union army, Hayes paid a visit to the Meads' large and eccentric family and wrote a vivid account in his letters home. According to Hayes, Larkin Goldsmith Mead (1795–1869), Elinor's father, seldom stopped laughing or marveling at his good fortune in being alive. An older brother had saved him from drowning when they were boys, and Hayes heard the story of Mr. Mead's escape from death so many times that his shoulder ached from the older man's affectionate slapping. To Hayes, the children seemed a ragtag assortment, none of them alike. Particularly fond of Elinor, he called her "witty, chatty, and capital company." Some thought her "sarcastic," he wrote his niece, "but as she is not ill-natured in her satire, I like it. I did not expect them to enjoy me as much as I did them, but when I left was pleased to hear Eleanor say: 'Your visit has been perfectly splendid.'"[64]

The Platt-Hayes family probably considered Elinor, the fourth of nine children, a suitable guide through the social season for Laura, whose mother, Hayes' sister, had died. The visit served Elinor equally well. Though Brattleboro's numbers swelled in the summer with wealthy Boston and New York visitors seeking the country's most expensive water cure (at eleven dollars a day), the town could be stifling. In Columbus, "Squire Mead's daughter" became Laura Platt's cousin without any loss of status, and possibly the opposite. Laura's father presided over the Columbus Gas Company. In their Italianate mansion surrounded by three acres of park, the Platts lived on a grander scale than the Meads, whose modest colonial on Main Street overflowed with children.

If Elinor had been brought up to take the amenities of society in stride, the young man who now courted her had not. The Platt mansion must have seemed a long way from the house in Jefferson, let alone the dark, smoky cabin at Eureka Mills. Whether or not Howells saw Elinor as the embodiment of Boston or New York—and he probably did—she had the independence and artistic ambitions he associated with Eastern life.

The two heard about one another before they actually met. Surprised to find a copy of the *Atlantic Monthly* in her cousin's parlor, Elinor had been gently informed that at least one contributor to the magazine might be encountered among Columbus friends. By then Howells' résumé included five *Atlantic* poems. When they did meet, he saw a pert and pretty woman slightly shorter than himself; she saw a "tasty dresser" sporting long brown sideburns. Each looked into piercing blue eyes.

Beyond the physical attraction, Howells and Elinor shared similarities of taste and temperament as well as quirks of family history. Elinor had grown up in a family with the social, intellectual, and artistic pretensions of the Howellses, along with pride in living differently from their neighbors. Indeed they had once, like the family in Jefferson, skirted the edges of respectability. The year Elinor turned ten, the quiet, prosperous life of her family had been threatened by the arrest of her uncle, John Humphrey Noyes, for adultery. The spiritual leader of a utopian community in Putney, Vermont (and later in Oneida, New York), Noyes preached the doc-

trines of "perfectionism," a belief that individuals can free themselves of
sin through will and religious conversion, and of "complex marriages," by
which every man became the husband of every woman, and every woman
the wife of every man. Several months before her brother's arrest, Elinor's
mother, Mary Mead, made a public confession of salvation from sin and
accepted his interpretation of the Bible. The breaking scandal forced her
to defend her beleaguered brother and appease her husband, who did his
best to make light of the situation. "To all I hear of Putney affairs," Mead
wrote to one of his brother-in-law's followers, "I have only to say I am not
able yet to associate in my mind the names of my dear family friends there
with adultery."[65] He remained no less skeptical about Noyes, and Mary herself soon sided against her brother. Noyes blamed the defection on her husband, whereas other members of the community credited their escape from
imprisonment to Larkin Mead's intervention.

Having grown up in a household brushed by religious fanaticism and sexual scandal, Elinor knew the importance—and the absurdity—of social proprieties, in which regard she and Howells were well matched. He had felt
the shame of belonging to a family that remained, whatever its shifting status, eccentric and impecunious. Elinor's father, now solidly middle-class—
one son attended Amherst College—had, besides "lawyering," kept a guest
tavern in Chesterfield. Family parallels can be a source of mutual sympathy but also of secrets and awkwardness. Whatever they discussed privately
in the years to come, neither Howells nor Elinor willingly disclosed their
connection to Noyes and his experimental communities.

Elinor's appeal to Howells did not lie in her discretion. Describing himself as "always having a great deal to say without much disposition to say
it," he called Elinor someone who had nothing to "say with the greatest
possible desire to talk."[66] She was, he later joked, the one person he knew
who could chat while a dentist worked on her teeth. Mark Twain, in full
agreement, imitated for his wife's amusement the zany logic of Elinor's talk.
Elinor had just recovered from an ailment with the help of a hypnotist who
treated her with the so-called mind-cure, and Twain reported the conversation to Livy.

"People may *call* it what they like, but it is just *hypnotism* & that's *all* it is—
hypnotism pure and simple. MIND-CURE!—the *idea!* Why, this woman
that cured me hasn't *got* any mind. She's a good creature, but she's dull &
dumb and illiterate and—"

"Now *Elea*nor!" [Howells inevitably demurred] . . .

"*A-n-d*—when she tilts up her nose—well, it's—it's—well it's that kind of a nose that—"

"Now ELEANOR!—the woman is not *respon*sible for her nose—& it's not fair for you to—"

& so-on & so-on. Lord, it was just like the old days over again, & it didn't seem to me I had any right to be having this feast & you not there to have your share, sweetheart.[67]

Twain's mimicry of his friends matches Howells' fictional portraits of married couples, especially Basil and Isabel March, whom he loosely based on Elinor and himself. In *A Hazard of New Fortunes,* he wrote of the middle-aged Marches: "They often accused each other of being selfish and indifferent, but she knew that he would always sacrifice himself for her and the children; and he, with many gives and mockeries, wholly trusted in her."[68] This passage, published when the Howellses had been married for twenty-seven years, grew out of shared values but equally out of great and dividing personal anguish.

In 1860, they were merely two young people getting to know one another during one of the city's "brilliant" social seasons. Howells remembered pleasure seekers transforming the gymnasium at the Starling Medical College into a ballroom where, under the eye of a lone matron, couples danced in the glow of white candles to the music of Negro fiddlers. With the strains of the last song echoing in their ears, young men escorted Miss Julia or Sally or Elinor home, then gorged themselves on oysters at Ambos's, an eatery Howells described as an "uptown" restaurant.[69] Because of a relatively mild winter, with the snow clinging only to shadowed streets, Howells planned his days around walks with Elinor. Together they traversed the city, laughing in the delighted, secret way lovers do. "You are like two children," Laura told them. "What do we care?" Howells responded.[70] Their open affection and general flouting of conventions drew enough attention for Belle Carter to pass on the gossip to the family in Jefferson, who immediately doubted Elinor's character. Howells grew defensive. He sensed that the "proper people" they met on their walks looked at them askance— as well they might have if etiquette book warnings against private meetings and hasty courtships were taken seriously. Belle Carter, who had disliked Elinor or the idea of her from the outset, called the fun-loving New Englander a bluestocking.

As for Belle Carter's motives, they can only be guessed. Howells claimed in letters home that he preferred her to the younger women he met through her, and before Elinor arrived he had flirted with a number of his hostess's protégés. Seven years older than Howells, she paid him unusual attention and may well have been hurt by his sudden neglect. When Howells eulogized her in *Years of My Youth,* he wrote as if *she* had been the one he loved, and clearly he regretted his behavior toward her, no matter how innocent. The second wife of a wealthy man seventeen years her senior, Belle Carter seemed, as Howells remembered her, too young to be accepted by her stepdaughters as their mother. They preferred to call her "cousin." To Howells, she had "a social genius which would have made her in any great-worldlier capital the leader she was in ours. . . . [She was] herself a flower-like and bird-like presence."[71] Henry Adams' wife, Clover, who met Mrs. Carter at the Hayeses' White House twenty years later, saw a different woman. To her, Mrs. Hayes' guest "looked like a powder puff; fortunately, flour is cheap west of the Alleghenies."[72]

For all her impeccable reputation, Belle Carter had her own dreams, as she admitted to Aurelia: "It was always a fancy of mine if Will never married, that someday—when all my brood of girls were settled with husbands— to take him here with the Dr. and me—either here, or perhaps, somewhere in Europe."[73] Even if she was not a woman spurned, Mrs. Carter acted like one. Perhaps she had something to do with Howells' reluctance to propose to Elinor. While common wisdom said that no sensible couple should marry on short acquaintance, Howells' and Elinor's public show of affection, not to mention the apparent improprieties of the courtship, promised a quick resolution—and still nothing happened. On Elinor's leaving Ohio at the end of March, her relatives thought that "Nelly" Mead had enjoyed her stay. Howells may not have known what to think. He, who supposedly discussed everything with his family, including details about his laundry, remained silent about "the Angel" from Vermont, calling the rumors of a "violent flirtation" exaggerated, and falling back on evasive platitudes. "When I think of the good, unselfish life you live, devoting yourself to poor little Henry," he told Vic, "I am quite ashamed of myself, and want to do something better than achieve reputation, and be admired of young ladies who read the 'Atlantic.'"[74]

Vic and the others were understandably concerned. Howells virtually hid Elinor from his family and neglected to introduce her to his father when the two overlapped in Columbus. The mild-mannered William allowed himself anger at his son's behavior. Mary Howells—unless her letters from this period were destroyed—showed her disapproval with a telling silence.

Marriage to a woman with apparently low morals and high expectations spelled a catastrophic loss of income. In April 1861, worried that he would not be paid by the *Journal,* Howells wrote a desperate letter about providing. "Of course, dear mother, if I get this money, I will buy that carpet for you. . . . I am almost sick when I think of my labor being wasted, and of the disappointment you will feel in hearing of this."[75] Whether or not he regretted his conduct, he felt powerless to make Elinor or anyone else happy. On her part, neither Elinor nor her Columbus relatives wrote candidly about Howells to Larkin and Mary Mead. Elinor may have been embarrassed not to have received the expected proposal or worried about her family's acceptance of a man with few prospects. Or perhaps Howells' behavior—or Mrs. Carter's coolness—gave her pause.

Always alert to the importance of money and position in a world where a woman's status depended upon her husband's, Elinor believed in marrying but also insisted that a woman with a career could lead a happy life unmarried. She herself grew up nursing dreams of being an illustrator or a portraitist. Her parents kept paints and paper on the dining room table for the children to use at odd hours, and they often communicated by drawing pictures for one another. Her brother Larkin had dazzled the citizens of Brattleboro: they awakened one winter's morning to find an eight-foot-high angel sculpted in glazed snow, which led to the Vermont legislature's giving him his first commission.[76] He would win national renown for his sculpture in Springfield, Illinois, of Lincoln grasping the Emancipation Proclamation. Another brother, the architect William, went on, with his partners Charles McKim and Stanford White, to give late-nineteenth-century America many of its splendid private houses and public buildings. In 1902, King Victor Emmanuel honored him for designs that brought the Roman and Italian Renaissance to American civic institutions.

Elinor's knowledge of art was extensive, and Larkin, who treated her like an apprentice, had no doubt about her talent. "Yes I should think you might undertake to paint the head from Mother's portrait. . . . If you paint it I shall want it to hang in my room. But you of course know what it will be exposed to [the scrutiny of other artists], therefore work honestly and long, discover *all* of the beautiful modeling which there is in your mother's face."[77] Just two years her senior, Larkin sounded more like a father than a brother. The year he worked with the sculptor Henry Kirke Brown (1855), he wrote his mother that he expected Nell "to be very studious this winter. I hope so, for I am sure she is capable of doing great things and she must shake off the sleepy way of living."[78] "All artists make time, they catch at every spare moment."[79] And here he had a point. Elinor nurtured few illusions about being able to pursue a career if she married, though she would later provide some of the sketches for her husband's books and supervise the design, building, and renovation of various houses. She did not find the time or have the single-minded concentration her brother thought necessary for an artist.

All the Meads grew up talking about books. Larkin liked to recommend books his father should order for the town library, and, unlike his future brother-in-law, he idolized Walt Whitman. "Have you seen 'Leaves of Grass'?" he wrote Elinor. "I suppose that is one of the greatest books ever written in this country. . . . Walt is a printer here in Brooklyn and printed his own book. Mr. Brown has the book on the parlour table and any one coming in must have a few pages read. The first line is this—I celebrate myself,—the third line is this—I loafe and invite my soul."[80] Elinor shared both her brother's passion for reading and his critical faculty. She was, Howells said, an artist "in all but the profession of art." With her genius for knowing what did and did not succeed, she epitomized everything "aesthetically perfect."[81]

Marriages require readjustments, as Howells already knew. Many years later, possibly with Elinor in mind, he wrote in *The Story of a Play* (1898) about a woman who marries a journalist turned playwright:

> Though she never dreamed of giving him up again, she sometimes wished she had never seen him. . . . She believed that she understood his character better than any one else, and would know how to supplement it with her own. She had no ambition herself, but she could lend him a more telescopic vision in his, and keep his aims high, if his self-concentration ever made him short-sighted. He would write plays because he could not help it, but she would inspire him to write them with the lofty sense of duty she would have felt in writing them if she had his gifts.[82]

Fiercely protective of her husband, Elinor seems to have shared this view of her own role. She left no hint that she ever doubted her husband's talents.

———

As things are, marriage is very haphazard. . . . The belief that there is destiny in it—that there is only one person in the world you could truly love will not hold water.

—W. D. HOWELLS, interview, 1897

Howells' and Elinor's uncertain courtship took place in the months just prior to America's greatest calamity, though neither they nor anyone else anticipated its toll. "None of the rumors of war had distracted us from our pleasures or affairs," Howells remembered, "at least so far as the eyes of youth could see. With our faith in the good ending, as if our national story were a tale that must end well . . . we had put the day's anxieties by and hopefully waited for the morrow's consolations." A young man in Howells' position might have found the Civil War a temporary reprieve, perhaps even a way out of an awkward personal situation. Like many in the North and South, he believed the war would be over in sixty days. Reporting on troop maneuvers in Ohio for the New York *World,* he had a passing idea about entering the "adventure," chiefly because "business and especially literature" promised to be dull for the next year.[83] A friend of his had been in Columbus trying to get an infantry company he raised accepted for three years' service, and Howells informed his mother that he might sign on as a lieutenant. The friend failed to get the commission and had to earn his rank in battle. Long before this, however, Howells had decided against soldiering. His brothers Sam and Johnny, meanwhile, joined the Squirrel Hunters, a volunteer force armed mostly with shotguns, recruited to discourage Confederate guerrilla soldiers from penetrating the borders. In a deleted passage from *Years of My Youth,* Howells wrote: "I still thought of volunteering, and one night, as Price and I sat waiting for the latest dispatches, I was in question so extreme that I said to my fellow-editor, 'Price, if you will volunteer, *I* will.' 'Well,' he answered, 'I *won't*,' and that, for such reason as it had, seemed to close the question."[84]

As a man determined to be a writer of literature, he did not see the army as a logical stepping stone. "War," he told Vic, "is always stupid and foolish."[85] Yet his every comment on the war has to be seen as a reflection of his guilt, or at least ambivalence. *Not* fighting or sacrificing oneself for a noble cause carried its penalties. "Every loyal American who went abroad during the first years of our great war," he would write in *A Fearful Responsibility,* "felt bound to make himself some excuse for turning his back on his country in the hour of her trouble."[86] The fact that the Union cause, no less than the Confederate, soon depended on military conscription makes clear that vast numbers of citizens declined, like Howells, to fight.

For reasons of money as well as principle, Howells made a shrewd decision. Citing his Republican credentials, notably his campaign biography of Lincoln, he enlisted the help of friends and wrote to the German-born George (actually John George) Nicolay, one of President Lincoln's private secretaries, requesting the post of consul to Munich, Bavaria. Howells not only admired German authors, but he also knew the language. "I want to go [to] Munich," he wrote, "to pursue the study of German literature, and to have four years' opportunity. I do not conceive that I have any claims upon the president . . . but have thought that the rank I held in the 'noble army of' biographers might at least commend me to his notice."[87] Support for his application came from William Dennison, the governor of Ohio; Salmon P. Chase, now serving as secretary of the treasury; James A. Garfield, still a member of the Ohio Senate; and Charles Sumner, secretary of state. In other words, Howells and his father called in every outstanding Republican debt. Joshua Giddings testified to Howells' ability and integrity but emphasized William's service to the party. Those who signed a petition to Lincoln cited Howells' literary ambitions as evidence of his fitness; as Giddings remarked, "He is a regular poetic contributor to the 'Atlantic Monthly'—and holds a high place in the estimation of James Russell Lowell and O. W. Holmes."[88] Moncure Conway, the editor of the *Dial*, wrote that "Howells' friends—of whom I am one—love him very much; and covet for him a chance to pursue more freely the studies which they know may end in giving the West what she has not had—one real poet. Emerson told me last summer that he held Howells to be a high promise to us."[89] No one commented on the irony of his going to Europe to write about the American West. Howells himself must have spread a glowing story of his reception in Boston, which informs these exaggerated, though self-prophetic tributes. His supporters pressed his appointment—anointment may be the better word—expecting him to promote "the growth and influence of American literature."[90] It became his lifelong work.

The response to his application came from John Hay, at that time another of Lincoln's young assistant secretaries, later a novelist and biographer and secretary of state under two presidents. Hay told him that although no one else appeared to be so "well supported," it would be "easier to predict the destination of a thunderbolt than of an office."[91] He warned Howells to be ready for either an alternative post, maybe Vienna, or outright disappointment. Vienna or Munich? Did it matter? Any foreign consulate meant a job, almost a sinecure, and for a man of twenty-four who had seldom enjoyed a steady income and may have been thinking of marrying, the stipend seemed handsome. At the least it was a poor man's answer to the grand tour. He replied to Hay in a letter (of June 24, 1861) calculated to get whatever he could. "Vienna, I notice, is a consulate of $1,500 while Munich is only $1000. I would rather have had the latter at the lesser salary, for though I am certainly poor enough, money was not at all what I wanted. Indeed, I would rather go to almost any other German city than Vienna. Leipzig—is that spoken for? . . . I am acquainted with the Spanish language. Is Cadiz gone the way of Munich?"[92]

As the summer months dragged on, he heard nothing, until an envelope arrived without explanation for the "Consul at Rome, now at Columbus, Ohio." Since this position seemed to provide no salary except fees the consul himself collected, Howells had no idea how much he might earn. Reluctantly, he accepted the offer, "the inevitable," as he later wrote, adding that he had never been courageous about the appointment, only dogged.[93] In September, he set off for Washington to negotiate in person but won only George Nicolay's promise to inquire about the consulate at Venice.[94] Before returning home he stopped in Boston, where he met once again with Lowell and visited James Fields, hoping to find a place for the poems and travel accounts he could send from Europe, or, better yet, a last-minute opportunity for employment.

"After seeing Boston," he wrote to Dr. and Mrs. Smith, "I re-turned to N.Y. and so came home."[95] The "re-turned" implies a visit to Elinor, for a trip through New York allowed an easy stop in Brattleboro. He may or may not have gone to propose to Elinor; if that was his intent, he must have weighed his frustrated sexual attraction and reckless courtship against the consequences of a distant wedding day—to say nothing of the embarrassment and apprehensions of the visit. For the past several months he had made payments on insurance policies, presumably with a view toward marriage, though perhaps to provide for his family in Jefferson should he die abroad. *April Hopes,* his sardonic look at the obstacles to courtship—the clinging parents, disapproving siblings, and temperamental lovers—recalls his own waverings about the woman he came to see. Could he and should he commit himself? And did he or did he not come to an understanding with Elinor before leaving the Mead house? At the least, they agreed to write.

The uncertainties in Washington, DC, matched those in Brattleboro. At the time of Bull Run and widespread national crisis, State Department inefficiency made any planning difficult. As a condition of his consulship Howells had posted a bond, which somehow got lost and was found again when he arrived from Jefferson with a new one. The bond found, he lost Rome, again without explanation. The political lottery decided, Venice became his destination. "In that simple day of a united North," he wrote, patronage determined all such jobs, regardless of qualifications or expertise.[96] It was no "simple day"—in a far from "united North"—but it was a time when "office, like osculation" went "by favor," and when young men, avoiding the war and cashing in their political chips, seized the opportunity to serve themselves, the Republican party, and their country abroad.[97]

It has been said, not necessarily with malice, that Howells spent the Civil War in a Venetian gondola. Certainly he resided in Venice through those years, and he owned a gondola. But what others have seen as his happy escape, he regarded as daunting. He knew little of the Italian language and nothing of Venice, except that he would be posted to a city still straining under Austrian rule. Desperate for company on his voyage, the consul designate postponed his departure by a week to accommodate the plans of Harrison B. Brown, the new assistant consul at Civita Vecchia, the main port of Rome. With a stipend of $1,500 and a month's pay in advance, he spent ten days in New York with Quincy Ward, the friend he had met in Ohio, who was, like Larkin Mead, a student of Henry Kirke Brown. His Columbus walks with Elinor had frequently included a stop at Ward's studio. Now, giving a sympathetic ear to stories of interrupted courtship or lost opportunities, Ward tried to ease his friend's anxiety about the impending voyage and life in a country he had never seen. Howells' arrangement with Elinor to correspond gave him some consolation, though for how long or on what basis they would write remained in doubt. In one of his last requests before sailing, he asked that his mother tear his poems out of the *Atlantic* and have them bound into a chapbook. After years abroad, he wanted a past to return to.

CONSUL AT VENICE
1861–1865

Venice has been the university in which he fairly earned the degree of Master.

—JAMES RUSSELL LOWELL, review of *Venetian Life*, 1866

WILLIAM DEAN HOWELLS never felt more alone than on the morning of his first ocean crossing, November 9, 1861, a dark, drizzly day of the sort Herman Melville describes in *Moby Dick,* when the choice seems to be a gun to the head or a stint at sea. Damp and full of gloom, Howells had Quincy Ward to bid him safe passage, the only person he knew "in the sparse ten or a dozen well-wishers" who lingered on the dock.[1] As the ship built up steam and slipped from its mooring, Howells searched in vain for his traveling companion, Harrison Brown, who had failed to board with the other passengers. Looking back, he saw a small harbor craft chasing after them with painful slowness. He could just make out Brown, a "black-cloaked bulk" in the stern, "his boatman put[ting] forth a strength visibly frantic" in an effort to catch up. Determined to stop the ship, Howells shouted to members of the crew and pointed at the trailing boat. The men shrugged their shoulders, and the captain, a down-to-earth Scot whom Howells came to like, "turned with a Scotch ferocity" upon him and shrieked, "I wadn't stope ma ship for the Keeng!"[2] And that was the end of it.

He sailed on the *City of Glasgow,* hardly more than a tugboat compared to such renowned vessels as the *Great Eastern* and the sleek leviathans yet to come. Homesick from the moment he embarked, he was also seasick in a ship that labored through late-fall storms and high seas from the day it left harbor. "'She's built of rolling timber,' was the one joke of our one stewardess."[3] The voyage to Liverpool, via the Irish port of Cork, lasted two weeks. His arrival in Liverpool ended the seasickness but brought its own disappointments. At best England seemed a pale reflection of what he had read and dreamed, and, pleasant as he found the landscape and even London, his surroundings did nothing to ease his homesickness. Words like *loneliness, gloom,* and *sadness* mark his letters and diaries through the following year. "Exile is so sad," he was soon writing, "and my foolish heart yearns for America."[4] The phrase "my foolish heart" echoes Charles Dickens' autobiographical novel *David Copperfield,* which Howells relished as a young man, and which led him to lodge as uncomfortably as Copperfield at the Golden Cross Hotel. Copperfield, too, traveled to Italy, where for both him and the young man from Ohio, life changed forever.

As for Dickens' countrymen, Howells called them mean and wrongheaded. "I felt so bitter toward the English," he wrote Vic, "that I was glad to get out of England, where I was constantly insulted by the most brutal exultation at our national misfortunes."[5] What he heard may have sounded harsher than intended to a young man already sensitive about his absence from the war and on a mission to represent his government. From a British standpoint, the Confederacy's supply of cotton mattered more than the Union cause. Union embargoes, followed the next year by the Confederacy's withholding of cotton, interrupted trade and closed the mills. As Henry Adams and other American residents in England learned to their annoyance, Englishmen (and more discreetly the government itself) favored the rebel states. They would not have appreciated a young, jingoistic American setting them straight on domestic politics. Whether real or imaginary, the comments Howells heard confirmed a prejudice against the country. He would return to England and publish books in praise of its landscapes, customs, and history without ever dispelling that first impression of English political bigotry.

Rather than sail from London to Genoa then cross by train to Venice, Howells fixed on an overland route that allowed a stop in Paris. Mark Twain's account in *Innocents Abroad* makes fun of American pilgrim-tourists who take the guidebooks as gospel and Paris as the Holy City. The climax of a European tour—and for some Americans a civilized place to live—Paris offered Howells a brief rest on a long journey. Though he came to appreciate the city, he felt at odds with a strange society and intimidated by the scale of the place itself. Everything from the Louvre to the cathedral of Notre Dame to Haussmann's grand new boulevards left him cold. If a "cosmopolite" is someone who has seen too many countries and feels at home in none, Howells typified the opposite: a patriot who believed aggressively in his homeland and preferred the customs of fellow citizens.

From France, his itinerary took him across "the snowy breadth" of a Germany yet to be unified, almost every stop of the train bringing him to a different country.[6] He stayed in Munich, his first choice for a consulship, and in Vienna, his second choice, which had teased him. It seems a bit fantastic that a young man traveling toward an uncertain future would have to prove his identity, but that, in Howells' account, is what happened. At the end of a day sightseeing with his Viennese counterpart—a German American "and quite possibly a personal friend of Lincoln"—he entered his hotel to be told by the proprietor "that no gentleman resembling me had passed the night at his house."[7] The driver the night before had delivered him to the wrong hotel. After several hours of flustered explanations and the help of the police, he managed to find the place where he had slept. Duped, like many an innocent abroad, he set off on the night train for Trieste and Venice.

> The fact is, that in the course of time one becomes skeptical of one's whole youth, and Venice had been a great part, a vital part, of my youth.
>
> —W. D. HOWELLS, "Venice Revisited," 1907

Howells arrived in Venice before dawn on December 7, 1861, scarcely believing his luck and more anxious than he liked to admit. "It was five o'clock Saturday morning when I reached Venice," he wrote his father.

> There at the depot, I took a gondola, and glided up the Grand Canal, with its sad old palaces on either side, and through a hundred secret, winding streets of water to the door of the Hotel Danielli. You cannot imagine how weird and strange this little ride was. A perfect silence reigned, except for the starlit-silvered dip of the oars, and the groaning of the gondoliers. . . . I confess to you that I did not feel altogether comfortable. I had a little

money about me, and my gay gondolier might have dipped me into the water, and let me stay there.[8]

He came to a city that turned the mysteries of Paris into minor puzzles. Venice had no equivalent in Europe, and the reasons lay as much in its history as in its watery geography. Venice had been a republic for centuries. Its customs, its very character, had roots in the Roman civilization the city honored and devoutly maintained. Once a refuge on swampy, mosquito-infested islands with the Adriatic Sea protecting it from invasion from the east, Venice had flourished as a trading state, growing wealthy beyond measure while creating art and architecture perhaps unrivaled in Italy, which is to say unrivaled anywhere. In the 1850s John Ruskin had published his magisterial *Stones of Venice,* measuring what seemed to be every column and arch and nave in an area crammed with architectural splendor. In Ruskin's eyes, Venice epitomized Italian civilization at its height. Preferring the ancient city and mourning its decline since the High Middle Ages, he revered the Venice of his time as an incomparable relic of a greater past.

As Howells soon learned, there were other, more practical reasons why American and British visitors, and especially those residing in Italy, chose Rome or Florence over the city on the Adriatic. His appointment placed him among a people subject to Austrian domination in one of Europe's most baffling political situations. Since the Treaty of Vienna in 1815, Venice and the whole province of Venetia had been in Austrian hands. For a brief span during the revolutions of 1848, the city expelled the occupying army and, under the leadership of David Manin, restored the republic. Once Lombardy and Venetia failed to join forces, however, and France's Napoleon III declined to intervene, Venetians lacked the military force to keep their independence. The Austrians came back, and, as Howells put it, Venice reverted to its state of "mourning."[9] At the time of his consulship, every Italian province except Venetia and the Papal States had merged to form a united Italy. Venice and its province would join the new nation in 1866, the year after Howells went home.[10]

A good tourist and responsible consul, Howells read everything he could find about Venice, from the popular Baedeker's guide to scholarly histories and histories of art. He visited the ancient island town of Torcello (long given up, he wrote, to the frogs and mosquitoes), gazed at sunsets across the Grand Canal, and studied the Square and Cathedral (officially the Ducal Chapel) of Saint Mark's from the Caffé Florian, "the only common ground in the city on which the hostile forces consent to meet."[11] When not exploring the bizarre counterpane of islands and canals, he sought out the paintings that were the pride of Venice, the Bellinis, the Titians, above all the Tintorettos, and he discovered them—as Ruskin promised—tucked away in convents or the semidarkness of moldy, forgotten rooms.

"I love the place more and more every day," he wrote shortly after arriving.[12] Less than a month later he looked at the city "with a gloom that I cannot shake off."[13] Commenting later on Nathaniel Hawthorne's ambivalence about Italy, he drew from personal experience. "To the last," he wrote, "Hawthorne remained an alien in Italy, afflicted by the squalor, her shameless beggary, her climate, her grimy picture frames."[14] Protesting that no city could be more to his taste, he struggled to explain his feelings to his younger sister: "It is so quaint, so old, so beautiful, so sad. . . . Ah! Annie— Venice is everything that the poets and the painters have told us; but they have not always put the ruin and the melancholy desolation in their pictures." A poor imitation of former glory, it seemed at times a graveyard of "decay, rust, rot, damp, dirt."[15]

The plight of the city reminded him of the military struggle at home. Outside the ravaged convent associated with the Venetian hero Paolo Sarpi, Austrian troops practiced with bayonets. Elsewhere they paraded or manned the fortifications in readiness for battle. They had fought and lost and won again the year before, and they treated Venice as a hostile outpost. As a stranger in a place where the Venetians scorned the Austrians, and the Austrians despised the Venetians, Howells felt "planted between two hostile camps."[16] The hostility arose, he said, not between individuals but between fatally antagonistic groups. In this armed theater as at home, neutrality meant isolation, not safety, with the added difficulty that here his job prohibited taking sides. To dine or attend the theater with Austrians indicated political support, and since he spoke German but only scant Italian, "the simplest sentiments of the phrasebooks," he felt shunned by the Italians. "It comes hard," he wrote, "on a social nature like mine, that delights in talk and laughter."[17] When he grew fluent, he still pronounced the Venetians "eminently unsocial."[18]

Once more he confronted the symptoms of hypochondria, the "inscrutable feeling of shame and humiliation" that made him loathe himself. "I don't know from what it comes—I only know that I am very lonesome here."[19] He made only scattered acquaintances, including a few Russians and Austrians, and no real friends. One Sunday he planned with an American tourist to sail to the fishing port of Chioggia. The boat had already left, "so, we . . . went and spent the day at the Lido, or sea-shore. We began with a bath in the Adriatic—where the light surf breaks with a pensive cadence on the softest sand."[20] Such pleasant days were rare. During dog days and bad moods, friends seemed to disappear or not to matter. Indirectly he blamed his loneliness on the absence of women. Searching for lodgings one day, he felt tempted by a drab apartment because the landlord's young niece looked "extremely pretty indeed, with a fresh complexion and delicious eyes." He chided himself for such thoughts and apologized in his diary to Elinor, whom he addresses as "E.G.M."[21]

For three months, as he waited to begin his consulship, he remained the guest of his predecessor, J. J. Sprenger, "a good hearted man, but almost broken spirited from misfortune."[22] Hospitable as he seemed, Sprenger kept his office and continued to draw the consul's salary weeks after his scheduled departure. In Columbus, Howells had borrowed money from Dr. Smith to supplement his salary advance; he borrowed now from Sprenger. It cost him a dollar a day to live, eating one meal and drinking three or four cups of coffee, though he still pitied the Venetians. "No American would diet himself in the manner to which the beggarly bellies of Europe are accustomed. I don't speak of the poorer people—they live upon a kind of food for cattle,—coarse fish, mush, and a tough, filthy-looking decoction formed of old boots in slices, I should think. But even well-to-do people know nothing of abundance—a dish of soup, a plate of cauliflower, boiled beef, figs,—this is dinner. . . . The rest," he added with his own plight in mind, "is coffee and expectation."[23]

By the time he received his "exequatur" and began his formal duties on February 24, 1862, Howells knew his job to be at once ceremonial and lacking in ceremony. Neither the diplomatic corps nor the local administrators showed interest in the young American consul, whose duties, aside from running errands or securing ship passage for visiting compatriots, amounted to observing ship movement in the unused port and describing it once a year to the Department of State. Howells' accounts match those of consuls around the world, with one exception. Three years after his arrival, he wrote to William H. Seward, or Seward's underlings in the State Department, that he intended to waste no more time accounting for Venice's defunct commerce. Instead, he gave an overview of the city's history. "I think this will be more useful to those who look upon commerce as a means of civilization, and not merely a system of necessary transactions. . . . And I believe that the analogy which must always exist in the careers of republican nations struggling from small beginnings to great national prosperity cannot be without peculiar instruction to Americans."[24] From the first day, he studied the city for diplomatic purposes *and* for his future books. He published most of his 1864 report as the chapter titled "Commerce" in the second edition of *Venetian Life*. It typified Howells' writing in two ways: by recycling previous work and by addressing the larger issues of culture and civilization that underlie so much of his writing.

There must also have been a secret side to Howells' responsibilities. Any diplomat abroad serves as an acknowledged spy, the eyes and ears of the home government. In a passage cut from his memoir, *Years of My Youth*, he described a potentially damaging episode in 1862, when his Columbus friend Moncure Conway "offered on behalf of his anti-slavery friends in the North to bring our Civil War, then in a most hopeless hour, to a close if the friends of slavery in the South would consent to its abolition in the interest of Confederate independence." He presented this "amazing proposition" to a high Confederate official, who led him on before releasing the information through the London *Times*.[25] The blunder could have brought Conway to trial and prosecution, which he may have escaped by virtue of being a well-connected Unitarian minister. He did not escape embarrassment, however, and went to lick his wounds with his friends in Venice.

Conway's unsanctioned diplomacy suggests the intrigues to which Howells might have been privy. He lived in a crossroads of plotting. From Italy, overheard conversations, gossip, and reports of troop movements went to Washington by way of diplomatic pouches. Venetian rebels, along with the French, the Austrians, and even the British and Americans, schemed in and about the region. Howells' counterpart in Vienna went a step further than Conway, proposing to bring the charismatic Garibaldi to the United States in the capacity of general, and, when this plan failed, to give Garibaldi supreme command of Union forces—a job he might have handled with more success than any predecessor of Ulysses S. Grant. Howells described the farm boys of eighteen and twenty who first joined the Union army wearing "red shirts, as if the color of the Garibaldian war for Union in Italy had flashed itself across the sea to be the hue of our own war for Union."[26] In Venice spies or informers were assumed to be everywhere. They probably led to the firing of Howells' would-be traveling companion, Harrison Brown, who lost the job of vice consul at Civita Vecchia for what amounted to an act of treason: issuing false passports to Confederate Americans.[27] Although Howells left no hints about gathering or reporting information, his every contact with the State Department involved secret communiqués.

The irony, again, is that while he did his work creditably, there was precious little to do. He wrote in December 1861 about "loafing" "in the indolent desolation of Venice."[28] The smaller his responsibility, the less he could drive himself to write. "Lately I have been taking myself severely to task for idleness and neglect of opportunities," he confided to his diary, "but have not quite ascertained that I am wholly to blame, after all. There is something in my isolated situation . . . which accounts for my inaction as much as willful indolence."[29] If he pushed himself to keep his diary, write letters home, or toy with poems and stories, he "worked under great discouragement" in a state of "homesick despair."[30]

In time he began to widen his acquaintance and make connections with fellow diplomats. The distinguished historian John Lothrop Motley happened to be ambassador (still called "minister") to Austria, and as such Howells' superior. Tall, handsome, confident, and sporting a blond beard, Motley had studied in Germany after graduating from Harvard and had formed a lifelong friendship with a fellow student, Prince Otto von Bismarck, the framer of modern Germany. Motley had recently won renown for *The Rise of the Dutch Republic* (1856), a book committed to principles of American democracy rather than to Bismarck's "blood and iron" politics. He and Howells would share a common friend in Longfellow, a link with the *Atlantic Monthly,* and a failed ambition to write histories of Venice. They might have had a better relationship if Howells had not pushed for the rights of a naturalized American citizen whose fortune all but vanished in litigation. He did manage to persuade his chief to take up the cause, and he drew on the incident when writing *The Ragged Lady,* in which a Venetian vice consul fights for the inheritance of an American girl.[31]

He found a less threatening colleague in Richard Hildreth, the consul at Trieste, himself the author of a history of the United States and an acclaimed antislavery novel, *The Slave: or Memoirs of Archy Moore.* The diplomats Howells met were historians, painters, novelists, and poets. One reason for the appointments lay in a political system that rewarded party stalwarts, including writers; another in the strategy of young men like George Nicolay and John Hay, those private secretaries of Lincoln who picked men who shared their own artistic and intellectual agendas. Howells' friend William J. Stillman, the consul at Rome, for example, was a painter, critic, and journalist, and Harrison Brown a painter. Sprenger, a Pennsylvania brewer, proved the rule by exception.

Hildreth and his wife invited Howells to Trieste in April 1862. An older man who was ill much of the time (he died in 1865), the "dreamily incapable" consul once attended a public ceremony wearing his pajama bottoms below his formal coat. Deafness added to his eccentricity. Hildreth's wife welcomed the young man, not only laughing at his jokes but actually staying up after her husband had gone to bed to hear excerpts from his diary. On this first trip away from Venice, Howells found Trieste a happy contrast, a hilly place with "beautiful drives and footpaths," cheery and clean.[32] The beautiful "Triestians" he saw in the markets and the Exchange intrigued him, as did a woman he met at the Hildreths' house: Mrs. Hildreth's Italian tutor, a black-eyed, black-haired Jewish woman. Howells always appreciated black eyes and black hair. At one point in the conversation, he asked if Mrs. Hildreth knew a sculptor named Mead, or "M," as he called Larkin in his diary. She knew of him and, as it turned out, had met Elinor "(whereat my heart leaped to hear her praise your genius)."[33] Whether his heart leaped in love or alarm, the company of the women in Trieste intensified his loneliness and forced him to wonder if that other "lively person" still waited for him at home. It may have been around this time that he wrote his poem "Homesick," at the end of which he added "Venice."

Her hands they lie upon her knees.
And fold for comfort, each on each.
Yearning for other hands—that reach
To take them—over stormful seas.
Her lips that cannot part in speech,
Are shaken with sweet memories.
The loose hair faltering down her face.
Her breast leans to the far embrace.[34]

The Hildreths' friend appeared particularly engaging to Howells in months when his diary entries focus on attractive women and scarcely disguise his frustrations. He mentions one "pretty and pert" American woman, whose "presence is like wine to me."[35] Unlike many Americans, Howells did not welcome the idea of a less constrained life abroad. His future brothers-in-law, Larkin and William Mead, both married European women: Larkin a Venetian neighbor of Howells, Marietta da Benvenuti, and William a Hungarian, Olga Kilenyi. Howells felt the temptations even as he warned himself against such "mixed marriages."[36]

Given the enticements of Trieste, it seems predictable that his journey back turned into nightmare. As the single passenger on an unfamiliar ship, he may have feared being shanghaied or dropped off in some hostile port. "Put on board at midnight, and finding the ship so huge and deserted, I couldn't help a desolate sort of Manuscript-found-in-the-bottle feeling, which did not wear off with sleep, but made me dream all manner of fantastic things and only ceased in the morning, when I became seasick."[37]

Without colleagues or an American community in Venice, Howells relied for company on men he called his "young" and "old" Venetian friends. G. Antonio Tortorini, the "old" Venetian friend at fifty-six, had retired as an apothecary and won appointment as mayor of the small town of Monselice, near Padua. Despite signs of age in his gray moustache and thinning hair, Tortorini had kind blue eyes and a "friendly face of a comely fullness and a ripe bloom." Best of all, Howells says, "when we stood up to shake hands we were of that equal height which short men like other men to be of."[38] Tortorini lived in Venice much of the time, retreating in summer to his country estate. Having studied English with the former consul, he continued his lessons with Howells. Soon after their meeting, Howells suffered the most dangerous of his several illnesses in Venice. This one involved stupor and high fever lasting for ten days, throughout which Tortorini, distrustful of local doctors, nursed him as if he were his own child. To ward off the insects that blackened the night, he wrapped the young man's head and hands in a cap and mittens fashioned from mosquito netting. Tortorini must have thought Howells' illness life-threatening. When sure of the patient's recovery, he bent over and kissed him. It was Tortorini who helped him to find new and better lodgings on the Campo San Bartolomeo, not far from Saint Mark's Square, and who, in the early months, "acted like my social Mentor."[39] Tortorini also lent him money at an awkward time. Without hesitation—or interest or security—he presented Howells with twelve gold Austrian sovereigns from his strongbox, asking simply to be repaid with the same old-fashioned coins.

Howells commemorates Tortorini in a retrospective sketch, "An Old Italian Friend," describing him as a companion who "almost" became a comrade. The "almost" reflects in part his sense of a consul's necessary distance. He knew that no foreigner penetrated the byzantine politics of Venice and that the most innocent of statements might lead to dangerous consequences. In a "place so much given to gossip," he could talk freely only with intimate friends.[40] Since, for the moment, he had no intimate friends, he limited his confidences to letters home or to the best listener, his diary.

In later years Howells had an uneasy conscience about his "younger" Italian friend, Eugenio Brunetta, whom he described as tall, swarthy, and "full of alert intelligence."[41] In Brunetta's company, Howells roamed Venice, practiced his Italian, and met other Italians, so that doors began to open to him, however slightly. Brunetta introduced him in a highly "irregular" way to a young woman with whom Howells enjoyed "decorous" conversations, "she talking Italian poetry and Venetian patriotism, and the secretary, her chaperon, keeping her literary and revolutionary vivacity in bounds." For readers of *Venetian Life,* he wrote that "the Italian theory of morals does not admit the existence of opportunity without sin. It is by rare chance that a young girl makes acquaintance with young men in society; she seldom talks with them at parties to which she is sometimes taken by her mother, and they do not call upon her at her home." Later he protested that "I was already engaged in marriage beyond the sea," and the Venetian woman, too, "was promised," adding that "our association remained without romantic effect in real life."[42]

Long after the Venetian years, Brunetta sought help in immigrating to the United States. Howells told him flatly that he knew of no work for a teacher of Italian and had no place in his house for a long-term guest. "We had to say that we could not receive him into our family, and we explained why."[43] Plainly hurt even in Howells' account, Brunetta replied that he planned to live nearby, not with the family. As an older man telling the anecdote, Howells hints at his own responsibility for the misunderstandings and pays tribute to his Venetian guide. (He fails to mention that he won Longfellow's reluctant permission for Brunetta to translate "Evangeline," a project never realized.) Returning to Italy in the 1880s, Howells visited Brunetta, who by then lived in Verona, and Tortorini in Monselice. Just as important, he met with Padre Giacomo Issaverdenz, a brother in the Armenian monastery, whose acquaintance he made in the first year of his consulship. Set on the island of San Lazarro, the monastery attracted "every tourist" spending time in Venice. Aware that no book on Venice would be complete without a description of the monastery, Howells returned less for the sake of his writing than for the padre's stories, spoken in fluent and comforting English.[44]

If he had been different, she would not have asked him to be frank and open; if she had been different, he might have been frank and open.

—W. D. HOWELLS, *April Hopes,* 1888

Howells missed his family, to whom he wrote long and affectionate letters, but he missed Elinor Mead more. If he had not intended to marry her when he sailed for Venice, his first winter brought an awakening. Planning to turn his Italian diary and letters into articles, he wrote with Elinor as his audience and referred to her in coded ways, usually by her initials. The diary offered a way of sorting out responses to the enigmatic city on the one hand and riotous feelings about women, especially the woman in Brattleboro, on the other. "There is," he wrote, "nothing stranger in any romance than this affair."[45] The strangeness arose as much from the mechanics of correspondence as from the temperaments of the lovers. It took weeks or months to exchange letters. When news came, it was out of date, no longer pertinent to what either felt. Both grew prickly. Misunderstandings led to silences or evasions, even after Howells realized how much she meant to him. He had been a fool not to take his chance at home. The "dear absurdity of loving her!" he wrote in his diary, "and yet not saying it."[46] In early November, they had a serious falling-out. Howells told Richard Hildreth that he regretted "there should be no Mrs. Howells, nor any prospect of one to see you."[47] On January 7, 1862, everything changed. "Yesterday morning I got a letter from E.G.M. to my utter surprise; and it was such a letter as made all the past perfect again. To-day I answered it, in the only way I could, and now wait anxiously to hear again."[48]

In February, Elinor considered herself engaged "in a kind of half-way manner by letter. To be sure letters were the whole and only arrangement."[49] Neither she nor Howells had as yet written home about the news. Elinor, who was then teaching in Cincinnati, waited until she returned to Brattleboro before informing her family. Not until the end of May 1862 did Howells write about the engagement to his parents, and then mainly to defend his choice and past behavior.

Of course it wasn't because I didn't as perfectly confide in you, that I told Vic first about my engagement; but she and I were nearer the same size and age: and I knew you'd find it out directly. Your kind letter is a reproach to me, however, and I'm sorry if my seeming want of trust has given you the slightest pain. I don't expect any opposition from any of the family, after you have all seen E.G.M. and you particularly will like her.—She's not violently intellectual, by any means. She has artistic genius, and a great deal of taste, and she admires my poetry immensely. *I* think she's good looking, and rather suppose she was picked out for me from the beginning of the world.—The girls and mother have got their idea of her from Mrs Carter's descriptions, which were by no means just. She's as good as well as smart—

and in fine I love her very much, which may remotely account for my intending to marry her.[50]

Whatever their feelings about Elinor, Howells' marriage created problems for the family in Jefferson. William clung to the idea that his second son would return to Ohio and join the family business. Worried about Joe's conscription at a time when the *Sentinel* showed its first profit (they paid off the mortgage in December 1862), and with Sam no help, he expected Will to do his duty. Now he faced the possibility that this son's duty lay elsewhere. His future in the balance, Howells floated a compromise. Sam, he told his father, would benefit from enlisting; but should Joe be drafted into the Union army, he himself would provide for a substitute—a common and legal dodge for those with the means to pay. "It will cost me no effort to part with the money, though the loss of it will postpone my coming to see you, indefinitely, and will put off another event which I had hoped was to happen next summer."[51] When Joe escaped the draft, the sacrifice became unnecessary. Sam did serve in the Union army and was hospitalized twice.

Howells could not avoid thinking about home or worrying, even in his sleep. "The dream is pretty much always the same," he told his father: "I'm back in America, with a vague, regretful feeling for all the things left unseen in Europe, and an equally vague purpose of returning. Of late, I've got to arguing with myself in the dream, that though I've often dreamed before of being in America, this is at last reality—and then I wake up."[52] In this version he has returned to the United States, where people ask why he has given up his consulship. He realizes that, having exceeded his ten days' leave, he will be fired and publicly disgraced. Then suddenly the consul at Venice becomes the consul at Delhi, India, surrounded by "a splendid Oriental phantasmagory of elephants," a sign—in pre-Freudian days—that his dilemma would resolve itself in unexpected riches.[53]

Worn out by real and imagined arguments, Howells responded to his family's opposition by forestalling it. Having originally intended to make a trip home before his marriage, he now proposed an earlier wedding, with Elinor coming to Europe toward the end of 1862. His reasons ran the gamut from costs and complications with unpaid or disallowed leaves of absence to the unspoken truth that he did not want to lose or be tempted away from Elinor; just as important, a European wedding established a welcome distance from grudging parents. Whatever concerns she had about its impropriety, Elinor agreed to the plan, and, accompanied by her brother Larkin, she sailed for England. Howells' father responded to the news with unusual bitterness, angry at his son and distrustful of Elinor and her brother. "As to Will himself," he wrote a friend,

> I have little news to give you. On the tenth of this Month, a young lady sailed in the *Africa* for Liverpool where she is to meet him and marry him. I suppose you have some acquaintance with her—which I have not. It is Miss Mead, who visited at Platts' the winter before last. Her brother the sculptor, goes out to Rome, and she accompanies him. I suppose the arrangement will do—but not knowing her I cannot well judge. He was so secretive about it that winter, that I never got to see her, which I wish I had.[54]

As soon as Howells met Elinor and Larkin at the Liverpool docks, the three set off for London and the wedding. Howells' plan avoided awkward situations in Venice and gave Larkin, who (as William suggests) would not have been an appropriate chaperon, the briefest responsibility for his charge.[55] Larkin planned to stay on in Europe, where he joined his friend, the artist William Stillman, and met the woman who would become his wife. Having taken for granted a wedding in the American legation, the consul at Venice discovered that British law required a week's residence for proclaiming the marriage banns. Neither his diplomatic rank nor his diplomatic skills could alter the situation. He met his obstacle in the person of the ambassador's secretary, Benjamin Moran, who considered him a "sleek, insipid sort of fellow" and haughtily turned him away before he could talk to the minister or the minister's son, who happened to be Henry Adams.[56] A hard judge of everyone, himself included, Adams would later say that James' fiction showed he knew nothing of women "but the mere outside," never having had a wife, while Howells showed that he lacked the skill to deal with gentlemen and ladies.[57] On this occasion he learned of Howells' shortcomings secondhand.

His London plan having failed, Howells worried about trekking across Europe in search of an official or clergyman to perform the ceremony. He decided on Paris, and there, on December 24, 1862, William Dean Howells and Elinor Gertrude Mead became husband and wife.

———

> I made my first acquaintance with his writings when, as a very young man, in a rest-house on the edge of the Indian desert, I found a bro-

ken copy of some *Studies* of Venice in Austrian occupation. . . . I remember I spent most of a hot night reading it by the light of an unsteady oil lamp . . . and it awakened in me—as in who knows how many men since?—a deep desire to know this city of mixed nationalities and fantastic lives.

—RUDYARD KIPLING on *Venetian Life,* 1922

"Venice!" Elinor exclaimed in a letter to her cousin Lucy in Ohio. "I never imagined such a charming life in the way of luxurious ease and delight of the senses as one can live here. Everywhere you glance perfect beauty meets your eye."[58] Just as ecstatic, Howells for many years associated his love of Elinor with his love of Venice. The newlyweds glided in their own gondola or strolled along the shore. They read aloud, enchanted by the sound of each other's voices, and for a brief time kept a joint diary. Occasionally they invited Padre Giacomo for breakfast, and Elinor also took to the affable, storytelling monk. Although Elinor, an inveterate bookkeeper, listed the names Tortorini and Brunetta at the top of her thirty-three Italian acquaintances, Howells kept more distant from both. When he had first introduced her to Brunetta, the man could barely speak. "Your sister?" he asked. "No, my wife." "It was a long time before he could get the idea through his head," Elinor wrote her father-in-law, "and then he commenced laughing and scolding Mr. Howells all at once in the excited manner and voice of the Italians."[59] Howells had obviously kept his engagement secret from Brunetta, or at least given no hints that there might be impediments to his courting an Italian lady. Perhaps guessing more than she knew, Elinor took a dislike to Brunetta and said he bored her husband. But then she spoke of dodging Tortorini, "Bore No. 1," in the street.[60]

Encouraged by his bride, who gladly took dictation, Howells translated Adalbert Müller's *Venice: Her Art-Treasures and Historical Associations.* He added to Müller's work details about Italian words and desirable *caffés,* and he learned a great deal about the city while improving both his German and his Italian. He grew fluent enough in Italian to carry on sophisticated conversations and to read literary works as difficult as the *Divine Comedy.* In practical terms, the translation brought him seventy-five dollars. For that sum he considered buying either a gold watch from Geneva or—appropriately for a couple "reading up the history of art"—the much-prized *Kugler's Italian Art.*[61] He decided to buy both. In the evenings, he and Elinor attended the opera and the theater, where he discovered a passion for the plays of Carlo Goldoni and gathered material for his later essay "Recent Italian Comedies." The newlyweds had any number of visitors to keep them occupied, including Larkin Mead, who served for a time as his brother-in-law's assistant. They saw Larkin on a short trip to Florence in 1863 while sightseeing and visiting the studios of artist friends. Together with his brother-in-law, Howells contemplated a book on Florence, featuring Howells' text and Larkin's drawings. Instead he wrote a later book, *Tuscan Cities,* to be illustrated by the artist Joseph Pennell.

The Howellses began their marriage of almost fifty years in promising circumstances. Not having to go home protected them from family interference, or rather limited the claims on their lives. Except that neither went for long periods without some physical infirmity, they were at their happiest during this time: he writing and she sketching, or, as with the guidebook project, serving as his amanuensis. Both wanted children, and on December 17, 1863, almost exactly a year after the wedding, Howells wrote his father that he and Elinor had been "given a little daughter, who is just now trying to do all she can to keep her much-contented mother from falling asleep."[62] Elinor had gone into labor around ten o'clock, and, with Howells by her side, she gave birth three hours later. She delighted in the Saxon name Winifred (soon shortened to Winny, or Winnie), which she mistakenly chose with her husband's Welsh heritage in mind. When the baby was twenty-five days old, she described her as "very purple" and "hardly . . . pretty with so much dark hair hanging in her eyes."[63] The fond parents spent hours trying to decide whose eyes she had and what sounds and objects she recognized, and each kept records of her progress.

Howells enjoyed his role as head of a cozy household. Elinor's sister Mary had arrived for Winny's birth and would remain with them until May 1865, shortly before the Howellses' return to America. A lovely young woman who attracted attention everywhere she went, Mary seldom got through a week without a proposal of marriage. One day, staggered by her beauty, two women stopped on the street and "groaned out 'O bella! bella! bella!'"[64] Howells admired Mary's easy mastery of Italian and teased Elinor for having "the rare gift of learning to speak less and less Italian every day."[65] As Elinor recovered from the birth of their robust, eight-pound baby, he accompanied his sister-in-law to dinners and showed her the sights of Venice, which he now knew intimately. With his own uncertain wooing so recent, Howells might have sympathized with the men who laid their lives and fortunes at Mary's feet, had not irritation, and perhaps jealousy, won out. One man in particular annoyed him, a chief medical officer in the Austrian army, whom Mary had met on the train and who approached her afterward in

Saint Mark's Square. Mary showed her brother-in-law the officer's letter of proposal, asked his advice, and allowed him to reply for her, "declining not only correspondence, but further acquaintance. I did not think this officer in seeking her acquaintance except through me, was acting properly."[66]

Howells came either to regret his haughty manner or to revise his estimate of the man's behavior. Almost twenty years later he drew on the episode when writing *A Fearful Responsibility* (1881), a witty novella casting the protagonist in the role of chaperon fending off an Austrian suitor he both pities and admires for his ardor. In a stroke that seems less autobiographical, this smug, or possibly innocent, protagonist discovers his charge to be more ordinary than her looks have led him to believe. He intends to devote his life to writing a history of Venice, which, like Howells, he cannot finish. Except in the novel, Mary's wooing also remained unfinished. By choice or circumstance—and for all her charm and intelligence—she never married.

Howells and Elinor enjoyed Mary's company, as they did one another's. Their early letters from Venice spill over with cheerful gossip and news of acquaintances, as well as tales about "Pokey" when Elinor (affectionately called "Duck" or "Piggy") writes informally, and "Mr. Howells" otherwise. Howells kept the family in Jefferson supplied with "fotografs" of Winny, their "little girl, who grows so good and fair." He wanted them to "see how sunnily her hair is coming out of the darker color she was born with; and how sunnily her little life has issued from my gloomier nature."[67] Having a child made him think longingly about his mother, who had been ignoring him. He wrote letters designed to reconcile her to his absence and to the marriage she did not approve. "When I go home, I want to go home to live," he told her, and if she assumed that he meant Jefferson, Ohio, he did nothing to set her right.[68]

The Howellses made their Venetian home in two ancient houses, first the Ca' (Casa) Falier, on the Grand Canal, in which they took rooms. Once a family mansion, the Ca' Falier had been divided and subdivided over the years, and the Howellses' apartment made up part of a larger section leased by a British diplomat, Edward Valentine. Soon a close friend, Valentine shared the gondola and the evening entertainments. It was Valentine they asked to be Winny's godfather. "We live," Elinor wrote to Lucy Hayes, "in one corner of an old palace on the Grand Canal in little rooms fitted up in snug, English style by our landlord, the English vice-consul. We have carpets in every room—where the floors are made of marble or a kind of cement . . . , which looks like 'petrified-pudding'. . . . Our little parlor, or bower, has a balcony over the canal where we sit evenings and hear the Venetians sing as they go by in gondolas."[69] Above them lived a Dalmatian family; below a French family; elsewhere "a marquis in exile from Modena"; and on the same floor their landlord and friend, Valentine.[70]

Sitting on their balcony, the Howellses looked across at their counterparts on the far side of the canal and the boats plying the waters below. "*Anyone* must despair of putting Venice in June into words," Elinor wrote to Vic. "Even Dickens' description is vague and dream-like you know? It would be sacrilege for the practical Elinor to attempt it. I can only give you our indoor life. At last we have arrived at something like system—poetical system. After breakfast—a fairy-like repast of ham, baked potatoes and coffee—Mr. Howells retires into the cool, quiet office and, on the inspiration of beautiful intaglio table and a huge, bronze crab, writes most charming sketches of Venetian character and of things happening here."[71] "Such, then, was the house, and such the neighborhood," Howells writes in the yet unfinished *Venetian Life*. Here, "two little people, just married, came to live in Venice. They were by nature of the order of shorn lambs, and Providence, tempering the inclemency of the domestic situation, gave them Giovanna."[72]

A blend of inefficient maid and subtle tyrant, the matronly Giovanna took possession of them and, "acting upon the great truth that handsome is that handsome does, began at once to make herself a thing of beauty."[73] Within a few months she contrived to have the household support her entire family, several of whom appointed themselves supervisors of the gondola and purveyors of unwanted products. Giovanna's sister or son or husband made appearances in the kitchen, sometimes for extended stays, while she herself came ever later to work, so late toward the end that the "little people" ate their breakfast at lunchtime or in restaurants. As with wily and unrelenting tradesmen, so with Giovanna, who played them like instruments. Giovanna's sister visited one day; on the next, Elinor discovered that a carpet and a set of curtains had somehow vanished. Another time she woke to find a burglar—he seemed a shady relative of Giovanna—scaling the wall to her and Mary's bedroom window.

The Howellses solved the Giovanna problem as they solved, or tried to solve, most—by running away. They blamed Giovanna for this move; in times to come it would be the impossible Irish maids, or Elinor's or Winny's health, or the noise of traffic—or simply that it seemed time to go. Giovanna's antic disposition aside, they had perfectly valid reasons to move. They needed more room for the baby, for the office of the consul, and for long-term visitors like Mary Mead. To their surprise they found a better apartment in the more beautiful Palazzo Giustiniani, on the opposite bank of the Grand Canal. Here they lived for the remainder of their stay.

On either side of the canal, Howells and Elinor struggled with domestic affairs, for neither could manage a household. They disliked the routines of cooking, cleaning, and fixing the things that go awry in every house, and they usually found servants who made things worse. Soon after his arrival, Howells had suggested that Annie put aside her studies of French and begin Italian in order to come to Venice as his housekeeper. She declined. They also invited Aurelia, but that plan foundered on their reluctance to pay for her keep. (Lodging in the Palazzo Giustiniani cost a dollar a day; a dinner of five courses for three people, eight cents.) "Sometimes I think it is a pity that you cannot see the world, and learn what to esteem and to admire," Howells wrote to Aurelia, in lame consolation, "but perhaps your own instincts are better guides than experience."[74] Luckily they found Bettina, who attended to Winny and stayed with them until they left Venice. Of all the men and women they hired over the years, they remembered Bettina with the most affection.

Marriage brought Howells additional costs, some foreseen, like the birth of a child, others associated with his new sense of consular responsibility. Before Elinor's arrival, he had escaped all but a few social expenses; now costs piled up like the luggage of the American visitors he and his wife felt obliged to entertain. Why they felt obliged is another question, given his scorn for touring compatriots. "In truth," he wrote in his diary, "the average American traveler is a most dreary and uninteresting animal, and is altogether likely to go home I should think a duller beast even, than he came."[75] These transients nevertheless made up a large part of their guest lists. In addition to the guests on Saturday evenings invited for cake, coffee, and cards, the Howellses held occasional extravaganzas. On the Fourth of July in 1863 they took the gondola round to the hotels, leaving cards for any Americans. As Elinor described it, they "draped the parlor with our flags, put up the Washington [a copy of Frederic Church's painting], got a boquet of red white and blue," and made toasts to the country they missed.[76]

The month following their impromptu party, Harriet Beecher Stowe and her husband arrived. "We fell into pleasant conversation at once, and the ball kept moving for an hour without the least exertion."[77] A consul who aspired to be an author could scarcely refuse to honor the "little woman" Abraham Lincoln had supposedly credited with starting "the big war." Mrs. Stowe was one of many American dignitaries passing through Venice that year. "This has been an eventful week," Elinor informed her new sister-in-law, Aurelia, "and today a marked day, beginning with the postman's bringing us five letters while we were at breakfast. . . . Then one day this week we heard from Mr. [Moncure] Conway in London who said he was coming to Venice 'to see Howells' as he told Emerson—which Mr. Emerson remarked was 'a very anti-Ruskinian sentiment.' Yesterday we had the ex-vice-consul of Constantinople. . . . Shall I tell you what we had for dinner?"[78] And Elinor, who reveled in cataloging her pleasures, told at length.

Howells began a friendship, probably sometime in the spring of 1863, with Charles Hale, the brother of a later friend, the popular reformer Edward Everett Hale. Then on his way to Egypt as consul general, Hale not only knew the same people Howells knew in Boston but had also edited the *Boston Daily Advertiser,* his family's paper, which would publish parts of *Venetian Life* by their new "foreign correspondent," W. D. Howells.[79] Almost from the time of his arrival in Venice, Howells expected to sell individual sections of what became *Venetian Life* to the *Atlantic,* later to collect and edit them as a book. James Fields held the materials in "purgatory" for months before rejecting them. Apart from his narrative poem, "Louis Lebeau's Conversion," taken by the *Atlantic* in the spring of 1863, the young poet, touted by supporters for the consulship as a regular contributor to the *Atlantic,* felt neglected by the magazine.[80] Thanks to Charles Hale, his letters from Venice appeared in Boston at a munificent five dollars a column.

However much Elinor and Howells entertained, shared enthusiasms, or cooperated on projects like their diary, neither remained comfortable in their long exile. "I was so tired of the style of life we had been living for some time," Elinor wrote in her diary, "—trying to write & draw, but with no strength and spirit, hot mosquito nights without sleep, calls to be made, &c."[81] Howells' disquiet can be read in his hints of returning hypochondria and accounts of Elinor's bad health, a possible effect, as they thought, of the Venetian climate. Though he claimed himself to have been "scarcely ever" sick in Venice, and did enjoy better health, his old frustrations about work, his failure to find a publisher, and the artificial luxury—if not frivolity—of their life weighed on him.

The longer the war dragged on and the worse the reports became, the more he felt the unseemliness of living abroad. In a passage from *Years of My Youth,* he captures the bewildering cross-purposes common to untold Americans. "After the war actually began, we could not feel that it had begun; we had evidence of our senses, but not of our experiences; in most cases it was too like peace to be really war. Neither of the great sections believed in the other, but the South which was solidified by the slaveholding caste had the advantage of believing in itself, and the North did not believe in itself till the fighting began. Then it believed too much and despised the enemy at its throat."[82] Now, after years of miscalculations and lost hopes, the long-delayed Union victories depressed him, partly because they did not end the war as he and most people had expected, partly because he doubted they were genuine victories.

The former journalist thought that, intentionally or not, newspaper accounts lied. Beyond the unreliable news lay the larger questions about the nature of the war. Who, after all, did win at Antietam? Who won any of the hundreds of battles in which the victor seemed to be attrition itself? What could "victory" mean with friends killed in battle, the lives of those at home changed forever? Long before Wilfred Owen ridiculed the "old lie" about the glory of soldiers dying for their country during the First World War, Howells called war not "very glorious in any respect."[83] His "Battle in the Clouds," a song dedicated to the Army of the Cumberland, speaks of blood flowing

> like the water on the valleys down below.
> O green be the laurels that grow.
> O sweet be the wild buds that blow.
> In the dells of mountain where the brave are lying low.[84]

By his own estimate a confirmed pessimist, Howells could hardly have felt sanguine about the threat of Southern invasions, let alone the future of a divided nation. What he read from afar and after weeks of delay reinforced a sense of hopelessness. Even the well-informed Salmon Chase admitted to discouragement. "The War moves a little too slowly and costs a great deal too much to suit me. . . . It took our Head about a year to determine that negroes could be employed as military laborers, and nearly another year that they could be enlisted as soldiers. It took a year to find out that McClellan was unfit and unworthy. Meantime we have piled up a debt of twelve hundred millions of dollars and are adding to the pile about two millions a day."[85]

Through much of the war it remained unclear to what extent England or France would frustrate the North, or how the North would fare as it picked one incompetent general after another. "That army of the Potomac," Howells wrote to his brother Sam, "seems to paralyse every general set over it."[86] At this time (May 1864) he included among the paralyzed Ulysses S. Grant, who had assumed full command of the Union armies two months before. Despite the victories at Gettysburg and Vicksburg the previous summer, Howells came to think that the war would "cost more than the Union is worth, especially if we should get beaten, as seems likely." In this letter of 1862 to his mother, he added: "The Union will be of little value to the 20,000 killed at Richmond, or the mothers that sent them."[87] Only after hearing that Atlanta and Mobile had been taken did he speak about "encouraging" news.[88]

National disasters were one thing, Howells' own family another. Apart from Sam, who saw some heavy fighting, there were the girls to worry about. When Annie went foraging one day far from home, another girl warned her of rebel guerrillas nearby and said that a soldier had entered her house. True or not, the account would not have reassured a man with Howells' imagination. He had to live with both the guilt and the satisfaction of his absence.

In October 1863, his father won election to the state senate, where the next year he introduced the joint resolution by which Ohio ratified the thirteenth amendment to the Constitution. William called it the proudest moment of his life. His eldest son, Joe, would continue his work, serving on the board of Wilberforce, the country's oldest African American university. Of course William's new position gave him even less time for what he had never done well—earning an adequate living. He leaned, from a great distance, on his second son. At various times during Howells' stay in Italy, William—still full of inventions—proposed business ventures for his son's leisure. Howells never forgot his father's scheme for manufacturing paper from milkweed pods. He had a particularly difficult time explaining to his father the impracticality of bringing boat oars to Venice and selling them to the gondoliers. Apart from the laws against diplomats engaging in trade, he wrote, Venetian oars bore no resemblance to those William could manufacture in Ohio, and the local product happened to be cheaper.

Seeing the tragicomic quality of the situation did not solve the problems. Nor, for that matter, did writing letters. "And now, mother, in regard to my absence," he ended a letter in June 1863: "I know how it grieves you; and why you should feel it peculiarly, for I remember how hard it used to be for me to leave home, and you doubtless remember that, too, and contrast it with my present willingness to be away. But when you think, dear mother, you cannot believe that I love you less, but only that being now a man I judge more clearly of evils and bear them better. I wish we might always be together; but what comfort after the moment should we find in meeting, if with new cares and responsibilities before me, I left my place here to go to America?"[89]

The pull of home grew painfully acute in April 1863, when Howells' brother Johnny died from spotted fever at boarding school. Howells blamed himself for having insisted that Johnny get the formal education he himself had missed. "Let one Howells have the stamp of the schools," he had written.[90] Now Johnny was dead, and Howells wondered, as he looked at his own child, how he could keep her safe.

As Sam marched with Sherman to Atlanta and Howells wept thousands of miles away in Venice, the family buried their youngest son. "We have erected a beautiful monument to the memory of our Angel Johnny," Annie wrote in her diary. The consul at Venice could do nothing but offer a poem in his brother's memory.

> For this is the hardest of all to bear,
> That his life was so generous and fair.[91]

Although he mourned Johnny, rued his country's tragic course, and complained of life in Venice, he would always remember the city fondly. Nothing matched Venice in the early spring, when the Adriatic warmed up for bathing and the sun brought forth so many flowers that the ground and islands glowed in fresh colors. "Four weeks ago," he wrote in March 1863, "we gathered daisies on the Lido; and now the almond-trees are heavy with bloom and bees. Besides all this we live in the old Palazzo Faliero (where Marino Faliero according to all the gondoliers, was born,) and we have a piano, and a balcony on the Grand Canal, and the most delightful little breakfasts in Venice."[92] If William read this letter to his family at breakfast, with Mary hot from the kitchen, Vic trying to subdue Henry long enough to feed him (he grew worse after Johnny's death), and Annie looking out on a landscape still ravaged by winter, they must have realized that their son and brother could no longer be content in Jefferson, Ohio.

I've been reading Bayard Taylor's first book of travel—Views Afoot— very simple and natural. But *I* invented the modern travel [book], and can beat anybody else with one hand tied behind me.

—W. D. HOWELLS to his daughter Mildred, 1913

Years afterward, when he looked back over a prolific career, Howells found few faults with his first book. At most he wished that readers would refer to it by its correct title and stop calling it *Venetian Days*. *Venetian Life* appeared at a time when the market for travel literature had ballooned, with more and more Americans taking advantage of improved transportation, favorable rates of exchange, and group tours of the kind made famous by the English travel agent Thomas Cook. Twenty years after the publication of *Venetian Life*, *Scribner's Monthly* would announce that Americans had become "by nature 'Passionate Pilgrims.'"[93]

In an era when readers considered travel writing to be literature—if not with the status of poetry or fiction—a compelling travel book could make a reputation. Howells had long admired the work of Bayard Taylor, who joined Commodore Perry's squadron on the journey to Japan and wrote about Japan, China, Scandinavia, India, Egypt, Abyssinia, and Turkey. Even when donning an Arab burnoose and turban or other exotic costumes, Taylor wrote as a journalist with an eye to representative detail. A popular lecturer and a friend of Dr. and Mrs. Smith, he had met Howells at the Smith house in Columbus. Though Taylor forgot the meeting and inadvertently snubbed Howells on his 1860 trip east, the two corresponded between Venice and Saint Petersburg, Russia, where Taylor was secretary of legation. (Near the end of his life, Taylor crossed the Atlantic in the company of Mark Twain to become the U.S. minister to Germany.) Like Howells, Taylor began as a poet and built a career on travel letters that he turned into books. His popular *El Dorado*, written early in his career, recounts the Gold Rush, the beginnings of California statehood, and the birth of San Francisco at midcentury.

Aware of Taylor's example but preferring to "invent" his own kind of "travel book," Howells moves quickly in *Venetian Life*, as if opening windows to the city's history, art, politics, and customs. His metaphor, however, is the theater. He sets out for the reader the lesson he learned his first week in Venice: that any encounter with a foreign culture thrusts the traveler into make-believe, into a world of signs. Countries and their people remain finally unknowable because what we see are their external roles or trappings. If life abroad presents a kind of theater, what better beginning to his book than an anecdote about a play?

> One night at the little theatre in Padua, the ticket seller gave us the stage-box (of which he made a great merit), and so we saw the play and the by-play. The prompter, as noted from our point of view, bore a chief part in the drama (as indeed the prompter always does in the Italian theatre), and the scene-shifters appeared as prominent characters. We could not help seeing the virtuous wife, when hotly pursued by the villain of the piece,

pause calmly in the wings, before rushing, all tears and desperation, upon the stage; and we were dismayed to behold the injured husband and his abandoned foe playfully scuffling behind the scenes. All the shabbiness of the theatre was apparent to us; we saw the grossness of the painting and the unreality of the properties. And yet I cannot say that the play lost one whit of its charm. . . . The illusion which I had thought an essential in the dramatic spectacle, turned out to be a condition of small importance.[94]

The image of playgoing announces his perspective on the "grander spectacle" of Venice, which he watches—and allows his reader to watch—from the wings or box seats, and with a kind of intimate detachment.[95] As one of the first serious critics of the American theater, Howells would urge playwrights to approach social and psychological problems in the same ways regional writers approach and "deal with the humble life of New York and New England."[96] He might have added that he found his model in Carlo Goldoni, who did just that for the Venetian stage.

Having set off for Venice in the hope of becoming America's next great poet, Howells learned that he might be a better writer of prose. The letters that made up *Venetian Life* anticipate the dramatic scenes of his novels, in which the narrator and the characters primarily *talk*. He introduces a range of talk, from priests intoning at funerals to workmen shouting to one another to gondoliers marking their routes along the Grand Canal. Often the talk takes the shape of plays, miniature comedies like the one about two women arguing and near to blows:

ASSAILANT: *Beast!*

BESIEGED: *Thou!*

A: *Fool!*

B: *Thou!*

A: *Liar!*

B: *Thou!*

E via in seguito!

The comedy ends in happy anticlimax. "I returned half an hour later," he writes, to find "the assailant" laughing and playing with her baby.[97] Poking a little fun at the Venetians and at himself for neither fully understanding the exchange nor finding the words to convey the scene, he seems to surrender judgment in affectionate or compassionate laughter. Howells deflates anything approaching the operatic, anything at odds with the ways men, women, and children typically interact. The first of his "real" novels, *Their Wedding Journey* (still six years away), records the conversations of a married couple in transit, people so similar to Howells and Elinor that they follow the same routes—and rehearse some of the same conversations. Though travel narrative necessarily features the voice of a single observer, Howells' voice in *Venetian Life* suggests a running dialogue as he and Elinor cope with the challenges of the city. He uses dialogue to question the limits of language, whether in the mixed Italian of his mock translation or the absurd literalness of speech he renders from the Venetian alley.

The appeal of *Venetian Life* comes from one tourist talking to another. Howells intended his book, no less than his early accounts of the voyage to Saint Louis, to be read by eager, middle-class readers, "tourists" rather than travelers, amateurs rather than professional historians. He takes up the topics that tourists expect and others they may not, including the "Jewish Ghetto," "Venetian Dinners and Diners," "Churches and Pictures," and "Love-Making and Marrying," each giving glimpses into local lives and public rituals. The usual tourist complaints of dirt or inconvenience become in Howells' hands a way for readers to laugh at their own provincialism and open their eyes to a larger world.

When Henry James tried (again) to "do" Venice in his *Transatlantic Sketches*, he warned against "following the traveler through every phase of his initiation, at the risk of stamping poor Venice beyond repair as the supreme bugbear of literature."[98] Howells had learned that lesson and others besides. Few travel writers had worn knowledge so lightly or imparted it so engagingly. Within little more than two pages Howells moves from cookstoves and window sashes to wheelbarrows and the dredging of the canals, along with the cooking of poultry. "I do not offer the idea as a contribution to statistics," he writes, "but it seems to me the most active branch of industry in Venice is plucking fowl." Perhaps it is the worker's hard fate

> that the feathers shall grow again under his hand as fast as he plucks them away: at the restaurants, I know, the quantity of plumage one devours in consuming roast chicken is surprising—at first. . . . It may be that the Venetians do not like fat poultry. Their turkeys, especially, are of that emaciation which is attributed among ourselves only to the turkey of Job. . . . It is as if the long ages of incursion and oppression which have impoverished and devastated Italy had at last taken effect upon the poultry, and made it as poor as the population.[99]

Behind Howells' laughing account lies an understanding of Venetian history, economics, and domestic conditions.

Henry James knew that his friend's great talent lay in making strange places familiar. *Venetian Life* belonged "to literature and to the centre and core of it."[100] Howells had found a voice largely free from the self-conscious writing in his earlier poems, reviews, or general-interest essays. As James Lowell put it, he had "fairly earned the degree of Master." Yet he still needed a publisher for *Venetian Life*. After revising, he submitted the manuscript to the British house of Trübner. It would take this cautious but favorably inclined publisher and a piece of rare luck to get the manuscript into print. Trübner wanted an American publisher to share the costs, and Howells snagged the promise of one because he happened to befriend Melancthon M. Hurd, of Hurd & Houghton, on the voyage home. Though Hurd took some time to make a final decision, he liked Howells immediately and proved a reliable friend. On the ship he made a ready partner for shuffleboard and cards.

In 1863, Howells' sister Annie had started a new journal with the "life-giving words . . . *Richmond is ours*."[101] That report had been a hoax, but two years later Aurelia could confidently repeat her sister's words. The bitter news came soon after. On May 1, 1865, Howells wrote to William H. Seward: "Sir—I cannot refrain from uttering my share of the national sorrow which every American citizen feels with the poignancy of personal grief, in view of the untimely loss of the great and good man."[102] Lincoln's murder and the turmoil surrounding it increased Howells' longing to be home. He remained against his will consul at Venice with a job to do and without permission to leave his post. Evidently hearing nothing from Washington about his request for an early return, he approached his superior in Vienna, asking for support. Motley warned him that his "going home to *America* without permission would be deemed grave dereliction of duty."[103] Restless and sick of Europe but probably as intimidated as Motley wanted, he used the three-month delay to explore the Italian peninsula, a tour that resulted in *Italian Journeys* (1867). Like the tourists he mocked, he and Elinor went rapidly from place to place (as weather allowed), from Ferrara and Bologna across to Genoa, by sea to Naples, making an obligatory visit to the digs at Pompeii and Herculaneum, and returning by way of Rome before working their way to England and the voyage home. Some readers have preferred *Italian Journeys* for its range, others *Venetian Life* for its depth. Each represented a large step forward for its author.

When Howells and Elinor said good-bye to the places they had loved, "to islands and lagoons, to church and tower," to the Grand Canal that ebbed and flowed beneath their balcony, their future seemed as unbelievable as their past. "We had become part of Venice," he writes; "and how could such atoms of her fantastic personality" ever mingle with the now-alien world they returned to?[104] He confronted the obvious but no less tragic realization that time moved forward in damaging ways, and that—aside from death or the disasters of war—neither those he loved nor he himself had remained unscathed in the years they had spent apart.

5

ATLANTIC YEARS, 1

1865–1867

I find myself almost expatriated, and I have seen enough of uncountryed Americans in Europe to disgust me with voluntary exile, and its effects upon character. . . . But with what unspeakable regret shall I leave Italy! You see, that's the trouble—I am too fond of Italy already, and in a year or two more of lotus-eating, I shouldn't want to go home at all.

—W. D. HOWELLS to James Russell Lowell, August 21, 1864

THE STEAMSHIP *Asia* docked in Boston Harbor on August 3, 1865, four months after Robert E. Lee surrendered at the Appomattox Court House. The United States to which Howells returned was not the country he had left. Six hundred thousand soldiers had fallen in the war, and millions mourned. No matter how much they might wish to forget or undo the past, Americans now marked history by events before and after the War between the States. Years of conflict had altered a nation's perception both of its own fragility and of the bitter realities of life. Soldiers with missing limbs begged door to door. Women who had assisted at amputations, bathed dying soldiers, or worked the family farms returned to flat, devastated lives. In what remained of Richmond, Virginia, the former capital of the Confederacy, federal troops watched the flow of black-clad women trudging to the graves of men and boys who had found their share of peace in the Hollywood Cemetery. Watchers and watched alike belonged again to one nation, but that unity had come at a staggering cost.

The Civil War exacted sacrifices from almost every family, not excepting the Howellses. Vic had learned of the death of her fiancé, a surgeon with an Ohio regiment, when his corpse arrived on her doorstep; she buried him next to her brother Johnny. Her letter to Howells and Elinor, the saddest they ever read, amounted to "one wail of despair."[1] Sam, the only son to serve in the Union army, drifted after his discharge from job to job. A family friend, Harvey Green, cashiered for incurring the wrath of a senior officer, would, like Sam, drag out his life in one long "defeat."[2] Distant noncombatants, the intellectuals who supported the cause of black enfranchisement, also contended with its human toll. Unable to forget his three dead nephews, James Russell Lowell imagined ever afterward the autumn leaves of New England "stained with blood."[3] The James family turned out luckier than most: a friend searching for his own son rescued Henry's younger brother, Garth Wilkinson James, left wounded among the dead and dying.

From writers, the ordeal of war seemed to demand a more accurate representation of the ailing though formally reunited society. Walt Whitman understood this, as the war poems in *Drum-Taps* (1865) or the later memoir *Specimen Days* (1882) suggest. With its accounts of Whitman's informal nursing of soldiers in the military hospitals of Washington, DC, *Specimen Days* reflects the great changes in writing after the Civil War, above all the rise of literary realism. Unlike the American illustrators and photographers who went to the battlefields, novelists did not meaningfully confront the ironies of war before Steven Crane's *The Red Badge of Courage* (1895) and Ambrose Bierce's stories, written long after his service in the army. Howells found an early exception in John William De Forest's *Miss Ravenel's Conversion from Secession to Loyalty,* which depicted a soldier's psychology in battle and the general sordidness of war. "Our war has not only left us the burden of a tremendous national debt," Howells wrote in an 1867 review, "but has laid upon our literature a charge under which it has hitherto staggered very lamely. Every author who deals in fiction feels it to be his duty to contribute towards the payment of the accumulated interest in the events of the war, by relating his work to them."[4]

For Howells' generation, the Civil War made fiction, at least some fiction, more starkly historical. The native Virginian Ellen Glasgow saw her novel *The Battle-Ground* (1902) as an antidote to lingering Southern fantasies about a brighter past. "A war in which one had lost everything," she wrote, "was not precisely my idea of romance"; nor did it deserve the indignities of romantic fiction.[5] In the traditions of journalists like Whitelaw Reid, photographers like Matthew Brady, and artists like Larkin Mead (who followed McClellan's campaign for *Harper's Weekly*), novelists like Crane and Glasgow portrayed the war itself and its consequences, the broken lives of the men who fought and the women who were left behind.

As his review of *Miss Ravenel's Conversion* implies, even the consciously literary Howells felt the need to make the plainest events the subject of fiction or, as he thought, allow life to speak for itself. Unlike younger novelists such as Crane or Jack London, Howells did not write about battlefields or life on the streets or nature red in tooth and claw. Instead, he set a standard for honest, unsentimental fiction depicting the lives of average Americans, people we come to know, as contemporary reviewers tended to put it, better than our flesh-and-blood intimates.

Howells' way of living in a changed country might seem at odds with his literary principles. He chose not to go back to Ohio and the West, to Cincinnati or Chicago, a city burgeoning like none before it. However fitted by temperament and talent to the shaping of an unparochial *American* literature, he returned to his country through Boston, the city identified with social and intellectual elitism. But while he came to love Boston, he went back and forth between Boston and New York with trips to northern New England or New Jersey or rural Massachusetts or Hartford, Connecticut, itself a busy corner of Eastern literary life. Much later, he would find in Chicago's Columbian Exposition (1893) the signs of a new America. The Westerner became less a Boston man than a man of the nation, his restless ways confirming an unavoidable, often painful rootlessness. Howells' theories of realistic fiction may have owed less to the state of his country than to the fact that he never felt completely at home wherever he found himself.

Since his first journey east, he had dreamed of a triumphal entry into Boston, accepting the keys to the great city and the mantle of its literary heritage. He dreaded a return to Jefferson and working again for a provincial paper—or even for his brother Joe, who wanted him for the *Sentinel.* "I'm sure I can't lose much in doing my duty as a son," he had written his father from Italy. "At the same time, I do not conceal from you that I have not yet in three years shaken off my old morbid horror of going back to live in a place where I have been so wretched. If you did not live in J. and my dear Johnny did not lie buried there, I never should enter the town again. It cannot change so much but I shall always hate it."[6] Apart from undoing the benefits of a four-year absence, it would also test his marriage. In *A*

Chance Acquaintance (1873), he describes Elinor's likely plight in the person of Kitty Ellison's aunt, whose in-laws never come to terms with her husband's choice of wife, "except as a joke, and [they] sometimes questioned if he had not perhaps carried the joke too far."[7]

His reluctance to live in Jefferson left open the questions of home and career. Once more he felt stymied, "a mere supernumerary," with his prospects as uncertain as ever.[8] Where *did* one begin a great future? And how? If Venice, as Lowell quipped, provided Howells his university, it remained to be seen whether the degree would pay. "My notion," Howells wrote, "was that which afterwards became Bartley Hubbard's [in *A Modern Instance*]. 'Get a basis,'" which meant at this moment any tolerable, salaried place.[9] How that notion struck him in retrospect might be guessed from Squire Gaylord's remark to Hubbard, his daughter's suitor: "Editing a newspaper aint any work for a *man*. It's all well enough as long as he's single, but when he's got a wife to look after, he'd better get down to *work*."[10] Accepting that he could not yet earn a living as a freelance writer, Howells may have remembered his own father's advice, that "we are to seek the best opportunities, and failing to find the best, to improve the second best."[11] He decided that a good second-best might be joining the staff of an Eastern paper, and he tried the *Boston Daily Advertiser*. When that failed, he called on James Russell Lowell.

The years had brought changes in Lowell's life as great as in Howells' own. Beyond the heartache of his nephews' deaths—in all he lost eight relatives to the war—Lowell counted the names of Harvard students who died in battle, the men honored in his "Ode Recited at the Harvard Commemoration." After a disagreement with James T. Fields about the direction of the *Atlantic,* he had resigned from the magazine in 1861. Two years later he joined Charles Eliot Norton as coeditor of the *North American Review.* He still spoke out on political issues, as in the second series of his *Biglow Papers* (1867), with its criticism of England's wait-and-see policy during the Civil War. In time, the British overlooked what they saw as a lapse of etiquette and welcomed him as ambassador to the Court of Saint James.

Howells' visit marked the real beginning of his friendship with Lowell, to whom he brought a bronze lobster containing a hidden inkpot and a sandbox. Lowell placed the lobster in the middle of his writing table, where it remained for the rest of his life. Howells arrived in the afternoon, stayed for dinner, and then joined Lowell in his study, where they spoke Italian together and sipped wine until dawn.[12] In the meantime, Lowell had gone from addressing Howells as "dear sir" to embracing him as "dear boy." Lowell still thought Howells should return to the West, which would allow him to keep an independent voice and stay clear of seductive Eastern legacies. His opinion given and rejected, he offered advice about finding editorial positions (not with the struggling *North American*) and agreed to speak with James Fields about an American edition of the still-unplaced *Venetian Life.*

In what was almost a reprise of his 1860 visit, Howells made a round of calls. He called the next morning on Oliver Wendell Holmes, who, as an old friend of James Fields, had influence with the *Atlantic,* and for good measure sent Lowell a note to prod his memory: "Now, if you think it doubtful that Mr. Fields will act even the step-fatherly part toward my book . . . I am sure that Dr Holmes would unite in pulling the wires of that sensitive organization."[13] Despite his unabashed plea for Holmes' assistance, he felt genuinely drawn to the man, who remained a friendly supporter. Oddly, when Howells came to write his intimate portraits of men like Lowell and Fields and Longfellow in *Literary Friends and Acquaintance,* he failed to catch Holmes' spontaneous affection, his impish appeal to almost everyone he met. Besides being a doctor of medicine (he coined the word *anaesthesia*), Holmes had played a part in creating the *Atlantic* (which he also named) and could be counted on like a Boston poet laureate to write verses for any occasion. On this visit, Howells received another warm welcome from the "Autocrat" but no immediate help with employment.

From Holmes he went to James and Annie Fields. As the influential editor of the *Atlantic* and a partner in the publishing house, Fields often needed new talent. At this time, however, he had his hands full overseeing Nathaniel Hawthorne's posthumous publications—and coping with the demands of Hawthorne's widow—without taking on a man whose talents his wife still questioned. In everything except title her husband's assistant, Annie Fields read submissions to the magazine and corresponded with contributors. She may still have seen in Howells a threat to her own influence.[14]

Much as Howells wanted Boston, the city at this moment seemed not to want him. With a wife and child in need of support and visits to pay in Vermont and Ohio, he decided to look elsewhere. The family traveled first to Brattleboro, then to Jefferson; the talk in both houses focused on employment, as that would determine where he and Elinor settled. Elinor's father proposed founding a newspaper in Cincinnati underwritten by himself and other investors. The Jefferson family spoke about Columbus, where Howells might join his friend Jim Comly, a son-in-law of Dr. Smith, who had recently become proprietor and publisher of the *Ohio State Journal.* Opposed to taking any job in Ohio, Howells flirted with the idea that he might, as Lowell once suggested, fall back on a professorship in modern languages—hardly the position he wanted, though a better last resort than newspaper life back home.

In Jefferson, Elinor and Winny met their in-laws for the first time. Letters between Howells and his sisters play down the delicate negotiations and the sensitivity of each person to hints of ill will. Mary's and the sisters' resentment, to say nothing of Henry's interruptions and Winny's coming down with whooping cough, almost certainly dampened Joe's easy humor and William's stoical decency. Winny quickly recovered to take her first steps and, a day later, carried to her mother and everyone in the room a purple verbena. With the baby as a common focus, both sides considered the meeting a success.

After the visit Elinor returned to her parents' house in Brattleboro, by which time Howells had gone on to test the waters in New York. The city now appealed to him as a noisy, exciting alternative to Boston. "Dearest Sweety," he wrote Elinor, missing her and weary after days spent knocking on editors' doors. He spoke of going on to Washington, or even, as his early job possibilities vanished, returning to Ohio. Soon, however, his letters began to list the fees received for freelance articles (seventy dollars within a week or ten days), and his unexpected success. He managed to persuade the house of Hurd & Houghton to consider a collection of his ballads, and, even better, he won a definite and enthusiastic commitment from Melancthon Hurd to bring out the American edition of *Venetian Life.*

Reassured about his progress, he felt optimistic enough about New York not to seek a job in Washington. Like others, he considered the capital unsafe. One contemporary wrote about the impossibility of later generations comprehending "the uneasiness that pervaded Washington," the morbid sensationalism and fear of secret plots following the war and Lincoln's assassination.[15] With the possibility of an opening at the *New York Times* paying thirty dollars a week, he wrote hopefully to Elinor. "If I *could* get such a place! I hardly dare think of it. Why I could average $50 a week the year round. I tell you I don't leave a stone unturned, nor a wire unpulled."[16]

It took Howells a month to land a job, but with the *Nation* instead of the *Times,* at a salary of *forty* dollars a week. Founded during the post–Civil War confusions, the weekly *Nation* had already set its political course. More conservative then than in later years, it stood for principled journalism and presented itself as a broker for "the topics of the day."[17] To quote one of its recent publishers, the *Nation* has always called "attention to the symptoms of some of our age-old illnesses as they appear today—anti-intellectualism, intolerance, jingoism, imperialism, for starters."[18] Howells found a near-perfect match for his own interests. "Are you happy?" he asked Elinor in November 1865.[19] He needed no answer. "There were two months of struggle and distraction," Elinor wrote to a friend, "and, now, we have come out of it all into calm weather and clear sailing. Mr. Howells has got an engagement on one of the best literary papers in the country—*The Nation,* just started in New York."[20]

When asked his opinion about work in journalism, Lowell had offered a sibyl's reply. Addressing some of Howells' own doubts, he called journalistic lives "unhappy," then, flinging a token "old shoe . . . for luck," he laid out his cautions. "Keep your ideal alive in your soul, a thing sacred & apart from all your drudgery & yet ennobling even that. Do not write in a hurry, for one thing *well* done is worth more in 'the end to a man's reputation' & therefore also to his pocket, than a thousand pretty-wells or even very-wells." Except for the warning about writing "in a hurry," this may have sounded to Howells like Shakespeare's hypocritical Polonius setting straight the wayward Laertes. But Lowell's last comment drove home. "Never write anything personal," he said. "People are small, but principles . . . great."[21] Taking "personal" to mean "confidential," Howells lived by this precept throughout his career.

By an ironic twist, he got his job thanks to Lowell, or rather to Lowell's friend and coeditor, Charles Eliot Norton, who had published Howells' essay on Italian comedies in the *North American* and recognized his talents in the Venetian pieces that had appeared in the *Boston Advertiser.* One of four cofounders of the *Nation,* Norton recommended Howells to Edwin Lawrence Godkin, another of the founders and the magazine's first editor. On November 17, 1865, Howells started work for Godkin, an Irish-born immigrant of English parents who had served as a war correspondent in the Crimea before immigrating to the United States. Godkin, who had a reputation for blunt prose and an irascible personality, intended the *Nation* to be a leading voice on public issues and—especially appealing for Howells—to publish better book reviews than any competitor. Howells, who called Godkin a "substantial and solid man—a bit of meat in a world of thin soup," had every reason to like his editor.[22] Godkin liked him and agreed to his writing for other magazines in addition to delivering the contractual book reviews and a Minor Topics column for the *Nation,* which ranged from political shenanigans to the scandals of divorce trials. The job turned out to be more to his taste and far less onerous than he or Lowell could have imagined.

Once Elinor and Winny arrived in December, the family rented a house on Ninth Avenue they named "Berickity-Barackity." On Sundays Howells wrote his *Cincinnati Gazette* column Letters from New York, an omnibus commentary like the Minor Topics. The freelance work boosted his weekly income to a handsome fifty-five dollars. At the same time, thanks to the success of Joe's scheme for selling Civil War songbooks, the family in Jefferson relaxed their demands for a share of his earnings.

Content with his new prosperity and a job he enjoyed, Howells quickly established a circle of friends. He formed a lifelong if uneasy relationship with the laconic poet Richard Henry Stoddard and Stoddard's wife, Elizabeth. Self-educated like himself, Stoddard had begun his working life as an iron molder in New York. Nathaniel Hawthorne read his first volume of poems and helped him land a job as inspector of customs. Stoddard went on to be an influential book reviewer as literary editor of the *New York Mail and Express*. His wife, a poet and novelist, made her reputation with a loose, baggy monster of a novel, *The Morgesons,* published in 1862. Part gothic, part sensation fiction, its evocation of place and its unsentimental portrayal of female psychology led Howells to call *The Morgesons* a "foretaste of realism."[23] He admired the Stoddards' snug literary life, the raciness of their talk, and the friends—among them the unsung Herman Melville—who gathered in their "salon." At the Stoddards' he renewed acquaintance with Bayard Taylor, the fellow travel writer and diplomat with whom he had corresponded in Venice. Toward the end of Taylor's short and money-troubled life, Howells helped him by accepting extra pieces for the *Atlantic* and paying above scale. Now Taylor invited him to a New Year's party, where Howells again, and this time more auspiciously, met James Fields. "Don't despise Boston!" Fields told him in parting.[24]

Ten days later, Fields offered him the position of assistant editor of the *Atlantic Monthly.* Lowell and other Cantabrigians, impressed by Howells' work for the *Nation,* endorsed this decision. But with the long-hoped-for offer in hand, Howells himself held back, as did Fields, whose hesitant letter may have reflected his or his wife's misgivings. "Perhaps you are permanently engaged at 'The Nation' bureau, and dont wish a Boston or Cambridge life," he wrote; "and it may be your present emolument is larger than I could offer you for the place to be filled in our establishment. . . . If you care to come East let me know, and tell me what salary will content you."[25] Already holding a good job, Howells felt he was in a position to bargain with Fields, which he did, raising the proposed salary by five dollars a week. At the same time, he had reservations about the *Atlantic* position and good reasons for staying in New York, where he and Elinor had only just settled in. It did not escape him that Fields seemed too interested in his practical background as printer and proofreader, which suggested limited and mechanical duties he avoided at the *Nation*. Besides, Fields had shown himself tentative, if not reluctant, whereas Godkin wanted him as a writer.

The lures of Boston and the panache of the *Atlantic* eventually won the day. Reassured by Fields that he would have time for his own writing and might inherit, if he chose, the editorship of the magazine, Howells accepted what had long been his ideal "basis." Almost immediately he had doubts, reminding his father—and perhaps himself—that the object of his life was "to write books, not to edit magazines."[26] Sharing the misgivings, Elinor apparently questioned his decision. "It does seem retrograding," she wrote her father-in-law, "to go from New York to Boston."[27]

You young fellows are dreadfully irreverent—but don't you laugh—
I take a kind of credit to myself in being the first to find you out.
— JAMES RUSSELL LOWELL to W. D. Howells, June 16, 1869

Howells and Elinor arrived in Cambridge on February 19, 1866. Unable to rent a convenient house, they boarded temporarily with friends they had met in Venice, then lived in two separate houses on Bullfinch Street, Boston, the second a comfortable flat where they had an upper floor to themselves. A few weeks later, they canvassed the market for a house to purchase. The "carpenter's box" they found on Sacramento Street, a few blocks north of Harvard Yard, resembled something in a Dickens novel, with rooms so small that friends praised its snug compactness. Elinor's father lent them the down payment. E. L. Godkin and Charles Eliot Norton arranged and cosigned the mortgage—despite Godkin's wishing Howells to stay in New York and Norton's scarcely knowing him.[28] Discovering that Howells had agreed to an inflated price for the house, Norton confronted the seller and renegotiated the contract. He had experience with such transactions: among his social projects, Norton helped the needy poor find housing and shamed slum landlords on their behalf. A successful businessman, he had spent money on national causes, including the campaigns of John Brown and the abolitionist movement in virtually every form.

Unlike Lowell, who, as Emerson put it, improvised "conversational fancies as a child builds his castle out of cards," Norton spoke deliberately.[29] Against a background of books in his library, his "frail presence, the low voice, the ascetic features so full of scholarly distinction, acquired their full meaning, and his talk was at its richest and happiest." When Norton conversed, Edith Wharton remembered, each word, each question worked "like a signal pointing to the next height, and his silences were of the kind which serve to carry on the talk."[30] Cantankerous when roused, he was known to berate his Ashfield, Massachusetts, neighbors for erecting ugly buildings or neglecting to cut their grass. A self-appointed but well-received feudal prince, Norton thought his fellow citizens would benefit from contact with the country's leading artists and intellectuals, and vice versa. Beginning in 1879, he accommodated both groups as toastmaster at a dinner held in the village hall to raise money for the local academy. (In 1886, he and Howells planned an unrealized series of "Ashfield Readers" or a "Library of School Reading.") The fact that Norton's houseguests continued their discussions savoring creamed oysters and old brandy did not make his type of liberalism less attractive to Howells, who soon considered Norton a friend, a man he turned to for advice or solace and whose often contrary views he found hard to ignore.

With Norton he debated two topics that each man held dear: democracy and culture, or rather the meaning of and obstacles to culture in a postwar republic.[31] The paradoxes here were many. Norton both supported and struggled with American democratic ideals while envisioning a self-appointed group as educators of a rising and increasingly literate citizenry. Fittingly, he had accepted Harvard's offer to serve as its first professor of fine arts. Howells himself, when recalling the intellectual life he had found in Cambridge, credited Norton as its guiding, democratic force. *Oligarchic* might have been the better word. With portraits of John Brown and Abraham Lincoln prominent in his Cambridge house, Shady Hill, Norton in at least one respect rivaled Howells' egalitarianism. He welcomed the democratic vistas of Whitman, whose poems he imitated and loved as his younger friend did not. At the same time, when Norton and other friends born to Cambridge entitlement spoke against the damaging effects of class, or accepted outsiders like Howells, they did so with no diminished sense of their own social importance.

Norton was an anglophile with connections to England, among them John Ruskin. Ruskin himself admired Norton as a scholar free of envy and ambition and not merely "a *man* of the world, but a *gentleman* of the world," in whom people of any class might recognize a fellow citizen.[32] Though serving as an unofficial mediator between England and the United States, Norton, like his *Atlantic* friends, cared first about the cultural state of his own nation. "Whether you like it or not," Howells told Norton in 1880, "you are always one of the half score readers I have in mind. . . . I don't write *at* you but *for* you; and no doubt you sometimes save me from myself."[33] He might have added that he also wrote *of* Norton, or of Norton's particular class of Bostonians in, for example, *A Chance Acquaintance*. His criticism of that class lies behind the observation of another privileged friend, Lowell, who joked that Howells wrote "as if some swell had failed to bow to him on Beacon Street."[34]

In the spring of 1866, Norton materialized as the benefactor helping the Howells family to "the long-deferred process of feeling at home."[35] "What is fame when you have a *house* of your own?" Elinor asked, delighting in their good fortune and proud of her husband's breadwinning.[36] Content at first to camp on the floor or borrow knives and forks from neighbors, they described themselves as "perfectly happy." "Everything is beyond our expectations," Elinor wrote gleefully. "The library is sunny and inviting. The dining-room is a *great* favorite with us. We sit here & write evenings. I am writing here now on our chestnut extension table. Our room is gorgeous." She agreed with those who called the kitchen "the pleasantest room in the house," and she judged the hall—soon to sport an elk-horn hat rack from Howells' father—*"not so bad."*[37]

The couple did what couples usually do when buying their first house. With eight hundred dollars set aside for purchases, they picked out furniture: green for the parlor, a chestnut set trimmed with black walnut for the guest room—perhaps an unwitting imitation of Fields' house and his parlor in the *Atlantic* building. They hung curtains, debated the merits of different cooking stoves, planted flowers and fruit trees, and looked forward to picking their own grapes and blackberries in summer. In 1866 much of Cambridge still opened to the countryside. Howells laughed about "the agitation of a cow in the pasture across the street" being "very stimulating." He felt less content when a large dog materialized at the corner of their fence. Otherwise he found the neighborhood peaceful and "free from tumult."[38] Here, rather than in the *Atlantic* office, he preferred to work.

Both parents doted on Winny, who had been staying with her grandparents in Brattleboro. Howells mimicked her quaint attempts to talk; Elinor sewed her a scarlet dress to be worn with matching stockings, for livening up Boston. "How do you like that?" she asked her mother-in-law, thinking she probably would.[39] The Howellses were so infatuated with their daughter that they considered writing a book about her first year in Venice, based on their letters and diaries, which Elinor would illustrate. Putting that idea aside, they later collaborated on a poem set in Venice, *No Love Lost: a Romance of Travel* (1869). Lowell, who had been married to his daughter's governess for the last thirteen years, wrote that "the plot of your little poem is so charming that it will take all the lovers & loved, & who else is worth caring for? I tried it on Mrs Lowell (You know we have a bit of Darby & Joan left in us still) & she *purred* at once."[40] Around sunset, neighbors got used to the sight of the "literary people" walking Baby, Winny's pet name for several years. Their evenings ended with the parents retiring to the dining room to write or read aloud.

James and Annie Fields, who knew practically everyone, did their best to make the Howells family welcome, introducing them to useful acquaintances and making sure they met the local contributors to the *Atlantic*. At the end of August 1866, the Fieldses persuaded them to visit their cottage in the resort town of Manchester by the Sea, some twenty-five miles from Boston. Elinor, who had very reluctantly left the baby behind with Katy, the new maid, found Manchester the dampest, muddiest, saltiest, most disagreeable spot on earth and, in an age before suntans became desirable, sneered at her hostess for being "brown as a bun." In turn, Annie Fields thought that Elinor just missed looking spiritual by the quaint childishness of her enjoyments. For many years Annie tried to keep an open mind about Howells, whose Italian vocabulary and allusions to Venice struck her as pretentious. Intending no compliment, she thought he had the makings of an academic historian. The end of the visit brought relief to both couples. "I feared they would be actually ill, if they stayed longer," Annie Fields wrote in her diary. "Their five years sojourn in Venice has helped to enervate constitutions by no means very strong in themselves and their pallid faces were in strange contrast with our healthy sunburnt countenances. Besides they have no rapturous love of country sights and sounds—they love the sea because it reminds them of Venice and their days of early married life specially when it laps up softly on the sands but they did not seem to hear this lonely voice in the nighttime when it brings us news from the far misty deep."[41]

Despite her own pretensions, Annie Fields saw in the Howellses something they themselves did not. Although they prided themselves on loving "nature," they often preferred it tamed or peopled. Howells confessed to feeling an "intolerable despondency of spirit" in the presence of great beauty, and if he meant by this the sunsets of Venice, he could have made the remark about any natural prospect.[42] Whether at Cape Ann in Massachusetts, the shore in southern Maine, or Niagara Falls, he and Elinor relished the outdoors, and both had the acuity of landscape painters when describing scenes that moved them. For entertainment or escape, however, they enjoyed the "summer people" almost as much as the vistas. Pitying those who filled their lives with a "continual round of dressing, dancing and gobbling costly liquids and solids," Howells himself spent a part of each year seeking their company.[43] He and Elinor also enjoyed the social life of Cambridge. With the unsuccessful summer visit behind them, Annie and James Fields continued their hospitality, and extended an invitation to spend Christmas Day at their house. This began a long tradition, which took the Howells family first to the Fieldses'—where Howells played Santa Claus— then on to the Longfellows'. Longfellow's kindness to children was legendary. Given a copy of *Jack and the Bean Stalk* by a little boy, the poet asked for a dedication before finding it a place of honor in his library.[44] In years to come, he became a surrogate uncle to Winny.

When the Howells family arrived in Cambridge, according to Elinor, Longfellow had inquired *"particularly"* where they lived.[45] Lowell seemed to keep aloof during the first month, and Howells worried that he would pronounce his protégé a fraud. Soon, however, the two were striding the length and breadth of the town deep in conversation.[46] New acquaintances came with the old. Quincy Street alone was home to the eminent scientist Louis Agassiz, the author Richard Henry Dana, and the brood of Henry James Sr. From Quincy Street it was a short walk to Longfellow's house on Brattle Street or later to Higginson's on Buckingham.[47] Old Cambridge, as the area around Harvard College came to be called, exuded history, making Ohio seem as young as Venice made Boston. Parents took their children to the graveyard to show them holes in tombstones that had once borne the leaden escutcheons melted into balls for the muskets of the Revolutionary army; or to the old First Church, where John Hancock had presided over the First Provincial Congress. George Washington really did sleep in the Craigie House, which Longfellow had boarded in and now owned. The city's past, its lofty elms and stately architecture, inspired poets like Longfellow and Holmes, both of whom revered the historic Old Burying Ground.

Much of Cambridge's cultural life centered on Harvard College, where Longfellow, Lowell, Norton, and Henry Adams had studied and taught, and which, across the years, spawned such literary dynasties as the Danas. In biblical idiom, Richard Dana (who died in 1772) begat the jurist and diplomat Francis Dana, who begat Richard Henry Dana, a lawyer and founder of the *North American Review*, who begat yet another Richard

Henry Dana, himself a lawyer but better remembered for his popular *Two Years before the Mast* (1840), which, according to Howells, "probably carried the American name farther and wider than any American books except those of Irving and Cooper."[48] Howells met this Dana (whose son married Longfellow's daughter) shortly after moving to Cambridge.

Like the rest of the United States, Boston and Cambridge had changed through the years of war, and in the eyes of some critics not for the better. By the time Howells joined the *Atlantic* in 1866, New England had entered upon what Van Wyck Brooks called its "Indian Summer."[49] The phrase captures the self-consciousness of Boston and Cambridge in transition—a period marked by the deaths of Hawthorne and Thoreau and the aging of Holmes and Emerson—and, like any such labels, including Twain and Warner's "Gilded Age," "Indian Summer" offers at best the sense of a passing world. Boston, with its educational and cultural institutions, had long competed with New York and did not suddenly lose its publishing or its literary clout, let alone its strategic importance, to the larger city. The changes came surely enough, but to newcomers like Howells they came piecemeal, with overlaps, complications, and paradox. In 1866, when Howells arrived, Norton was in his thirties, Lowell and Fields in their mid- to late forties—distinctly not in the autumn of their lives. Boston had outstanding young artists like John La Farge, scientists like Louis Agassiz, and writers like Howells, whose friends would include Henry and William James, Thomas Sergeant Perry, Henry Adams, and other men more or less beginning their careers in that springlike Indian Summer.

What would "Indian Summer" mean for these and others of Howells' generation, whose meetings and clubs kept Boston and Cambridge energized for decades to come? And how does the phrase fit older figures like Longfellow, saddened and still reclusive after the death of his wife in 1861? With other close friends, Holmes and Henry James Sr. persuaded Longfellow to translate Dante, and on Wednesday evenings the Dante Club convened at the poet's house to discuss the *Inferno* and the work of its translator. Enter Howells, who brought fresh and self-taught knowledge of Italian literature to these discussions, as well as an appetite for the suppers of cold turkey or venison. "It is not so much what an old man says to a young man that encourages him," Richard Stoddard wrote of Longfellow, "as what the old man himself is to the young man. Words are one thing, manner another, and the manner of Longfellow was the perfection of courtesy, kindness, and sincerity."[50] Older and younger generations came together in those years, to the benefit of both. If it was not New York, Boston was still Boston—

or Cambridge. It would be another quarter century before Henry Blake Fuller described the United States as a sailing ship with Boston its mizzenmast, New York, the mainmast, and Chicago, home of hogs and the Columbian Exposition, the foremast. Most Bostonians still considered their town the whole ship.

Soon intimate with Longfellow and a string of luminaries, Howells felt that he had gone to sleep and awakened in the Elysian Fields. Cambridge's elite allowed him to feel that he was, almost, one of their own. "At every moment," he remembered, "I was as sensible of my good fortune as of my ill desert. They were the men whom of all men living I most honored, and it seemed to be impossible that I at my age should be so perfectly fulfilling the dream of my life in their company. Often the nights were very cold, and as I returned home from Craigie House to the carpenter's box on Sacramento Street, a mile or two away, I was as if soul-borne through the air by my pride and joy."[51] It flattered him to be part of the *Atlantic* circle, even when he came to think its senior occupants naive or old-fashioned, or, like Fields, overbearing. By then he enjoyed relationships with men and women his own age, many of them from around the country or abroad.

Socially as well as professionally, the Howellses made their way. Howells found a particular favorite in the historian John Fiske, his neighbor and soon his friend, with whom he dined and talked philosophy and history. They determined that, when the first of them died, the survivor might attend to the other's affairs. Fiske's spirited support of Charles Darwin's theories may have led Howells to believe that literary study needed a more scientific— and evolutionary—basis, or to nurse ambitions about his own history of Venice. Given the evenings with Fiske, the Wednesday night meetings of the Dante Club, dinner once a week at Lowell's, an occasional Saturday at the Parker House, and the usual round of teas and dinners to give and attend, Howells struggled for time to do his job.

December 1866 brought Howells together with Henry James Jr., a new contributor to the *Atlantic* in whom he found a kindred spirit. Soon James visited regularly at the Sacramento Street house, where he amused his hosts by eating nothing "except a biscuit he crumbled in his pocket and fed himself after the prescription of a famous doctor then prevalent among people of indigestion." Recognizing in James a capital talker as well as "a constant sufferer, tacit and explicit," Howells believed James' conversation to be an escape from physical ills and the strain of writing.[52] He never wearied of his friend's verbal acrobatics or the pregnant silences. Nor did another of James' friends, Edith Wharton, who said that James' slow speech, "sometimes mistaken for affectation—or, more quaintly, for an artless form of Anglomania!—was really the partial victory over a stammer which in his boyhood had been thought incurable. The elaborate politeness and convoluted phrasing that made off-hand conversation with him so difficult to casual acquaintances probably sprang from the same defect." Intimates enjoyed his "silver-footed ironies, veiled jokes," and what Wharton called his "tiptoe malices."[53]

To Howells, James appeared "earnest" and "extremely gifted—gifted enough," he told Stedman, "to do better than any one has yet done toward making us a real American novel."[54] Disagreeing with Fields, who had already published James but balked at a piece he thought too bleak from "an author with his mother's milk scarce yet dry on his lips," Howells overrode his senior's objections and solidified a friendship that lasted until James' death.[55] It is true that James later and secretly agreed with friends in thinking Howells' fiction too "social," by which he meant "superficial," and that Howells occasionally wondered about James' self-indulgence or the ill effects of his French upbringing. Still they shared, as Howells thought, a "Celtic" heritage with a commitment to "an American present," and each valued the other's support.[56] "There seems at last to be a general waking-up to your merits," Howells wrote James in 1869; "but when you've a fame as great as Hawthorne's, you wont forget who was the first, warmest and truest of your admirers, will you?"[57] Several years into their friendship, James wrote from Switzerland to "thank you for everything, for liking my writing and for being glad I like yours."[58] "We seem to have been presently always together," Howells recalled, talking "of methods of fiction, whether we walked the streets by day or night, or we sat together reading our stuff to each other."[59] As they grew into rivals and competed for magazine space, they continued to write and talk as a way of defining their respective ambitions and values. "I was seven years older than James," Howells would say, "but I was much his junior in the art we both adored. Perhaps I did not yet feel my fiction definitely in me."[60] He would "feel" his fiction well before he wrote it, thanks in part to James and the scores of novelists he read and reviewed for the *Atlantic*.

A few months after the Howellses moved to Sacramento Street, the English edition of *Venetian Life* appeared and won glowing notices in the *Examiner, Athenaeum,* and other London papers. Howells carried these reviews around for months and read them long after he knew them by heart. A love letter could not have been sweeter than people likening his talents to Hawthorne's. Closer to home, Longfellow wrote that "It is curious that the two most poetical books about Venice should have been written by persons bearing the same name; I mean yours and the 'Signorie of Venice' by another Howells! some two centuries ago."[61] *Venetian Life,* wrote Bayard Taylor, had an immediacy and ease of style in which "the refining processes" remained invisible.[62] From a distinguished writer of travel literature this was heady praise, though apparently not enough. Eager to get as many reviews as possible, Howells asked Lowell and Norton to divide their forces. They complied, Norton reviewing the book in September for the *Nation,* and Lowell, who pronounced it the best book ever written about Italy, for the October *North American.* Howells wrote James Comly at the *Ohio State Journal* to make a similar request. "Don't think I sent you the London Review's notice of my book in order to 'bone' a notice out of you. I merely hoped that you would like to read an English criticism of me. . . . I have seen the flattering allusions the Journal has made to me, and I may confess that they have given me great pleasure, because I valued both your friendship and your judgment."[63] When the *Ashtabula Sentinel* put forth Comly's name as a possible candidate for governor in April 1867, Howells offered whatever help he could extend through the *Atlantic,* and his father obligingly wrote his own endorsement.

Pleased as he was with *Venetian Life,* Howells regretted his lack of opportunity to correct the proofs. Finding the English edition riddled with repetitions and errors, he offered to relinquish any claim for royalties if Trübner would reprint a revised text. "By dint of cancelling and reprinting *eighty* of the worst pages," he told Norton, "it will be brought out here almost free of errors—but the correction absorbs all the profit I should have received from it. . . . I'm disposed to think your friendship a compensation for all I have suffered in the cause of letters—if it *is* a cause, and if I *have* suffered."[64] After publication of the American edition (in August 1866), Howells lobbied Melancthon Hurd about a second edition, flattering him that in spite of widespread praise, none mattered so much as his publisher's. And since Fields, that wizard at predicting popular taste, had a good opinion of the book, it would surely find success with a broader public.[65] Howells won his point, launching *Venetian Life* as a new, expanded edition in 1867.

Beyond its sales and favorable reviews, *Venetian Life* brought status in Cambridge. Men Howells respected, like Francis James Child, the scholar still credited for his work on English and Scottish ballads, read *Venetian Life* and hurried to make the author's acquaintance. Decades after its publication, Mark Twain explained what he and so many others found unusual in *Venetian Life.* "For forty years," Twain wrote, "[Howells'] English has been to me a continual delight and astonishment. In the sustained exhibition of certain great qualities—clearness, compression, verbal exactness, and unforced and seemingly unconscious felicity of phrasing—he is, in my belief, without his peer in the English-writing world."[66] If some critics found it amusing that Howells sprinkled his letters and conversation with bits of Italian, he had nevertheless come to be seen in Cambridge not just as an editor but as "a wholly literary spirit."[67] Norton's daughter Sally spoke for the majority when she described the effect of Howells' Italian writings. "I am not quite sure whether Cambridge is in Italy," she said, "—though now I think of it, I know Italy is sometimes in Cambridge!"[68] No wonder Howells felt more comfortable in this city than anywhere else. For the first time in his life, people saw him as he saw himself or as he aspired to be.

Even in Cambridge, however, he could not shake off the chronic sense of being apart: at ease in Zion but at heart a tourist. Having lived long in Cambridge, James offered a corrective to Howells' "prodigious satisfaction" with the place as less intellectually vulgar than the rest of America. James shared Henry Adams' view that the country's best-educated people "united in Cambridge to make a social desert that would have starved a polar bear."[69] He felt oppressed by the "bondage" of the town and eager to distance himself from the self-congratulatory kindness of Longfellow and especially Norton, whom James thought "deluded" in thinking himself James' "guide, philosopher, and bosom friend."[70] Though he came to share James' double vision, Howells stuck by his older friends and lived and worked in Cambridge for years to come.[71]

He explored his relationship with the town in "First Sketches of American Life," the subtitle of *Suburban Sketches*. A collection of *Atlantic* articles from 1868 to 1870 based on his early years on Sacramento Street, it might well have been titled "Cambridge Life." In the vernacular of travel literature, Howells—or his narrator—draws the town with an affectionate irony similar to the tone of *Venetian Life*. He appreciated that while little more than a village in size, "Charlesbridge" extended beyond the affluent neighborhoods around Harvard Square. Envisioning the outlying districts as a series of city-states (and cityscapes) peopled by immigrants, he casts himself as an open-minded observer of ethnic and national groups arriving both in the town and on his doorstep. His portraits include an Italian organ grinder as well as an old sailor, "Jonathan Tinker," whose lies rise to the truth of storytelling. Howells describes Irish families living in makeshift shanties around the brickyards of North Cambridge, the "Dublin" slum of old New England. Railing against the Irish propensity for large families, with their damaging effect on real estate values, he writes that "none but the Irish will build near the Irish. Values tremble throughout that neighborhood, to which the new-comers communicate a species of moral dry-rot."[72]

A kind of counterawareness underlies Howells' comments about the Irish as he looks around their graveyard and sees an old woman wailing and boys singing ribald songs. He acknowledges that the same scene would strike him differently in Italy, "as an aesthetical observer; whereas I was now merely touched as a human being, and had little desire to turn the scene to literary account."[73] He did, however, turn it to literary account, and his unsentimental scrutiny would provide a model for the *Atlantic*'s new wave of local color writers. Howells confessed and fought his prejudices without overcoming them; he admired Lowell for his freedom from any enmity toward the Irish. He may have recalled the New York draft riots during the Civil War, when for three days an Irish mob of fifty thousand looted, lynched, and burned a black church and orphanage. Perhaps the Irish slums reminded Howells of his own extraordinary luck and the family's desperate "year in a log cabin." Whatever the reasons, his prejudice touched the larger fears of his countrymen in an era when signs proclaimed that "No Irish need apply."

In addition to taking walks through Cambridge, rides on the horsecar to Boston, and trips to the seashore, the narrator of *Suburban Sketches* finds his grotesque and sympathetic characters in his own household. The first two "sketches" describe a pretty servant, based on Katy McGuire, the maid Howells and Elinor hired early in Cambridge and feared losing to a young man (as they did), and an African American cook called Mrs. Johnson. Howells draws these representative "domestics" from his household experience, in the tradition of the Venetian Giovanna. As in Venice he and Elinor had eaten meals in restaurants to avoid Giovanna, so now they could have their breakfasts and dinners sent from a tavern above Porter's Station. "We have a series of tin covers fitting one into another and united by a common handle in which the meals come," Howells explained to his father in 1869, "and we get them nice, warm, and abundant for $5.00 a week less than the raw material cost us."[74] When he speaks about the difficulties created by Katy's leaving or the saga of replacing her, he pokes fun at their own incompetence, a self-conscious legacy from the Venetian days.

From *Venetian Life* Howells takes another legacy, writing sections of *Suburban Sketches* in the form of dialogue. Sometimes the narrator overhears; sometimes he engages people in conversation. He also seems to chat with his reader about topics as random as his wanderings, including the follies of bad travel books or the effect of romantic stories in "this fiction-ridden age, when we must relate everything we see to something we have read."[75] Here, as in the later books, he plays with the boundaries between facts and fiction, the ways by which fiction can grow from observed life, however distasteful, into a new reality that corresponds to an actual world. In dialogue and unembellished language, Howells finds his best expression of *truth* or *honesty*, which is to say verisimilitude. If some contemporaries found the descriptions of *Suburban Sketches* low-key or undramatic, most—at least most reviewers—considered the book a worthy successor to *Venetian Life*. In the words of a writer for the San Francisco *Overland Monthly*, "More than any other living American writer, Howells has both the gift of insight into common things, and the genius to describe them."[76] The reviewer, perhaps Bret Harte, who had just resigned his editorship of the *Overland*, saw in the book what Howells himself announced as the principles of literary realism.

Suburban Sketches draws, too, on the less humorous practicalities of Howells' domestic life. How does one find good and reliable servants? Why can't the immigrant Irish be more reliable and the blacks less inscrutable? How can people in need of money dare to set limits or show displeasure? After losing Katy McGuire, he goes to the employment office, where he finds that applicants from the nether world of "Charlesbridge" refuse to work far from their families. Whether in his shamefaced handouts to the "cons" who knock at his door or describing the dignity of his cook's self-possession, an old soldier's maimed body, or a mentally ill servant who threatened to kill Winny (and for whom he got help), he admits to using needy people for his own domestic and literary purposes, paying them as a painter might pay his models. In a private letter, he describes an unnamed boy— a "Negro page"—hired through the Freedman's Bureau. "He's ten years old, and about a yard square," Howells wrote to his family, "but bright and very helpful. Winny adores him—tucks her chair close to his, and manifests none of our 'natural antipathy' to the black race."[77] As the quotation marks suggest, neither he nor his family believed in any natural antipathy, and he wants to suggest that the boy has become a part of their family; yet Howells' accounts—in print or in letters—raise discomfiting questions. What about the boy's mother or father? Did Howells think it appropriate for a child so young to be working, even in a house of caring people? He, or his narrator, remains as far from the lowly neighbors he meets as from the plutocrats like Andrew Carnegie. Indeed, the description of the "page" is a rare mention in Howells' letters about any individual servant; domestic help came and went as the family itself came and went from house to house.

In the 1880s, when he had read Leo Tolstoy's Christian-socialist writings,

Howells' thinking about social justice underwent a drastic change. He began to hope—or at least speak—for a society without servants and underclasses used by those who happened to have more money, and he no longer glossed over the implications of class difference to himself or to American society. Never a Marxist, he tended to look at issues of social justice from a personal or moral perspective but with an increasing awareness of larger, historic forces.

With little choice, as middle-class Americans, the Howellses continued to rely on servants and never quite got the help they wanted—or, as they aged, the help they needed. In the late 1860s and early seventies, however, they were happy enough joking or fretting about their servants and making the most of their lives. They liked and admired their neighbors, and, for all its challenges, they enjoyed their comfortable house in the "suburb." When Cambridge or Howells' job occasionally palled, they told themselves that they lived in a town more intellectual and no less rural than Brooklyn, where Larkin Mead's mentor, Henry Kirke Brown, kept a tame bear. In search of their own Bohemian elegance, they settled for raising chickens.

Boston is my destiny, so far as I can shape it.

—W. D. HOWELLS to Annie Fields, February 8, 1866

Howells' life in these years cannot be separated from the *Atlantic Monthly,* through which he established himself as America's foremost writer. Twenty-nine years old, he had assumed his duties as assistant editor on his birthday, March 1, 1866, at an annual salary of $2,500, or slightly more than $48 a week. His term lasted five years, and he continued for another ten years beyond that as editor, succeeding James Fields. The position meant, as he knew, relinquishing the independence he admired in Henry James and accepting a slower start to the writing of his own fiction. It amused him when his mother thought him slighted because the magazine carried too few of his stories and poems. His duties went beyond reviewing and writing at least five pages for each issue to reading proof, checking facts, soliciting and often revamping articles, and composing delicate letters of rejection. Though he managed to finish several books after *Suburban Sketches,* and at an accelerating rate, his main energies during the next few years went into the magazine. It would prove an exacting and frustrating master.

As late as 1853, Henry David Thoreau had complained that no literary magazine could survive in Boston. Thoreau overlooked the efforts of the second Richard Henry Dana who, emboldened by the success of Scottish quarterlies of his day, founded the *North American Review* in 1815. Never achieving a large readership or financial return, the *North American* managed to set a high intellectual standard and a record for longevity. Boston still lacked a magazine with the popular appeal of New York's *Harper's* or Philadelphia's *Putnam's*. Four years after Thoreau's prediction, the editor Francis Henry Underwood, in company with Boston poets, historians, and fiction writers, decided to prove him wrong.

The *Atlantic* came into being on May 5, 1857, over an elaborate five-hour dinner at the Parker House. Among the sponsors were the historian John Lothrop Motley, Howells' chief in Venice; James Russell Lowell, the magazine's second editor; James Elliot Cabot, known later for a biography of Emerson; and of course Emerson himself, Longfellow, and Holmes. The guest list that evening highlights the theologically liberal bent of the *Atlantic* as well as its Brahmin cast. Harriet Beecher Stowe may have missed the Parker House dinner because of her objection to alcohol, but in any case women were rarely invited to these events. Stowe did support the project and soon became a highly paid contributor to the *Atlantic,* which drew as many female as male readers. The magazine's founders proposed to speak for a meritocracy of independent individuals in the spirit of Emerson's "American scholar."[78] They attended to European, mainly English, voices, in hopes of promoting a broad American readership, however much it might be split by class, politics, taste, or regional parochialism.

Howells thought that if any one person characterized the *Atlantic* it was Lowell, who gave the magazine a literary conscience that his successors tried to maintain. Not that the *Atlantic's* editors and contributors always agreed. They were torn, for instance, between Asa Gray's defense and Louis Agassiz's rebuttal of Charles Darwin's theories of evolution, a topic to be argued in the pages of the magazine. They agreed to disagree on a range of issues from Reconstruction to education and suffrage. Yet none would have disagreed with the notion that culture, like a river, "spreads its fertilizing waters over a continent, and the whole nation drinks of its refreshing stream," or that the *Atlantic* represented American culture at its best.[79] Committed to his principles, Lowell offered reduced-price subscriptions of the magazine to priests, postmasters, and teachers—men and women he saw "fertilizing" their own communities across an uncultivated nation. Charles Eliot Norton—a man close to the magazine though editor of the *North American*—maintained that both Howells and Henry James would have been better writers for just a small acquaintance with Homer and Virgil.

The early *Atlantic* voiced the political stands of those radicalized against slavery, among them Emerson, Whittier, and Thomas Wentworth Higginson, the Civil War hero who became the friend and first editor of Emily Dickinson. Howells shared with Higginson an almost righteous passion against slavery and about the "Promethean" role to be played by the magazine. In fact, he shared Higginson's (and Lowell's) commitment to the *Atlantic*'s enterprise both as a distinguished literary magazine and a monthly messenger shaping American thought. He still needed every scrap of diplomacy. Higginson quarreled with him about principles, policies, and literary opinions, sparing neither personal feelings nor perceived errors of grammar. With studied courtesy, the two dueled in and out of print for years to come. Higginson, who thrived on conflict, took Julia Ward Howe to task publicly in 1882 for entertaining Oscar Wilde. Refusing to be bullied, Howe declared that contact with the women of Boston might well improve the bad young man.

Unlike Higginson and Lowell—pedigreed and cultured men from old Massachusetts families—James T. Fields worked his way up from poverty. The son of an indigent widow from Portsmouth, New Hampshire, he had started as a clerk in the firm he now owned, and appointed himself to succeed Lowell as editor of the *Atlantic*. Fields congratulated himself on how well his new assistant fit. He may have seen his younger self in Howells, who also lacked formal education and impressed his seniors by hard work, charm, and an uncanny grasp of popular taste. Both had grown up among rural and small-town readers who ignored trade publishing houses to buy their books—the bigger and gaudier the better—by "subscription," and both read as widely as the privileged men they came to associate with. Fields had the reputation of being able to tell within minutes after customers entered the Old Corner Bookstore what books they would buy. Through Annie Fields, a descendant of John Adams, he had ties to Boston's oldest families and literary lights, who gathered at their Charles Street house to hear Longfellow read his poems or meet a visiting celebrity like Charles Dickens, who stayed with them on his American tours.

Fields had edited the *Atlantic* during the war years and would continue until Howells replaced him in 1871. Whereas Lowell refused to appeal to any "mob," however well-dressed, Fields wanted the magazine to make money.[80] Some thought his methods undercut what the founders and previous editors of the magazine, Underwood and Lowell, had stood for: they suspected that he put profits over principles, favored light over serious contributions, and would reduce the *Atlantic* to a level as banal as, well, a New York magazine. Emerson, on the other hand, praised him as the great "guardian," and highly paid *Atlantic* writers testified to his generosity. More practical than Lowell, Fields sought a larger audience with the fewest possible compromises—a description that would apply equally to Howells.[81] Fields paid more attention to details than the absentminded Lowell, who, on his way to work one day, stumbled into the Charles River, saving himself but drowning a bundle of *Atlantic* manuscripts.

At once relishing his job and objecting to the weight of work, Howells developed a love-hate relationship with the *Atlantic.* Almost as soon as he began, he longed to decrease the drudgery and focus his energies on the substance of the magazine and his own writing. He chafed at Fields' constant if benign supervision. Lowell had in fact warned Howells about his boss. "I would find Fields easy to work with," Lowell had said, "though he advised me to work in entire subordination, even (I remember his word), to *écraser* myself if necessary."[82] Without Fields' consent, Howells could not make plans for a vacation or complete the makeup of a future issue. To be sure, he had influence. After only a few months, for example, he asked Fields to recommend Larkin Mead's design for the Boston Soldier's Home, and he often stood up to Fields when they disagreed about submissions.

On parts of the magazine Howells worked independently, especially the *Atlantic's* reviewing, which Fields left entirely in his hands. Both men appreciated that what gets reviewed may be more important than how it gets reviewed, but, for his part, Howells intended to focus on books that would supply "the great want" of original voices in American letters.[83] In essay-length book reviews, themselves a major innovation, he honed his literary ideals and made them felt. He never ceased asking, "What is literature in America? Almost any one can tell us what it will be, but it wants a prophet to tell us what it is and has been."[84] Howells became that prophet, slogging through desert stretches of literary drought or personal discouragement to find astonishing oases. In 1869 he put his stamp on W. E. H. Lecky's monumental *History of European Morals,* Mark Twain's *Innocents Abroad,* John Greenleaf Whittier's *New England Ballads,* memoirs by a Civil War soldier, and works by George Eliot, Francis Parkman, and Horace Greeley, among dozens of others. From history to fiction to poetry to memoirs to civil-service commission reports to the Italian press, he scoured the publishers and magazines across Europe and America in search of the best in contemporary literature. All this as he edited the magazine, gave public lectures, and wrote poetry, parts of *Suburban Sketches,* and theater reviews. An omnivorous reader and reviewer, he mixed the orthodox and the unexpected, his Western past with his Eastern present. He would joke that the elder Henry James had written and kept *The Secret of Swedenborg* (which he himself reviewed) yet would still take the time to tell his father that a notice in the *Sentinel* would gratify James "immensely, even if you shouldn't agree with him, for all he wants is thoughtful consideration."[85]

Besides training Howells' instinct for good writing, the reviews brought fresh talent to the magazine. Howells became friends with Thomas Bailey Aldrich, Bret Harte, and Mark Twain after praising their books. Following Godkin's example at the *Nation,* he dramatically increased the number and quality of reviews. During his first year, when he wrote eighteen full-scale reviews, he essentially invented the art of reviewing for American readers; and he outlined his practices for his sister Annie as she began her own career. "Set the author honestly before the reader," he advised her. "If you don't like an author, say *why* and let him *show* why. Never try to be funny at his expense; that's poor, cheap, cruel business. Read a book, or else don't write about it."[86] Reviewing began with the acceptance or rejection of manuscripts, and Howells' rejection letters became miniature correspondence courses in which he urged would-be authors to speak distinctly, simply, and directly, and to make everything vital to the topic.[87]

His work for the *Atlantic* had not gone unnoticed. Harvard University granted him an honorary Master of Arts degree in 1867 for achievements that "endeared him personally to so many scholars."[88] Two years later, Charles W. Eliot, Harvard's new president, asked him to share with Francis Child and other eminent academics a new kind of seminar "on modern literature." Eliot saw the course as part of the reform he planned for Harvard's curriculum. Himself a contributor to the *Atlantic,* he valued Howells for the range of his interests. Howells at first declined the offer, then changed his mind when Eliot showed up at his house to plead. Throughout his career, Howells negotiated the competing worlds of newspapers, magazines, publishing houses, and academies. He would be offered professorships at Harvard, Yale, Johns Hopkins, Union College at Schenectady, and Washington University at Saint Louis. He realized early, however, that he belonged in a wider world than the university. The Harvard seminars turned out to be his first and last academic appointment, though only the start of his teaching.

6

ATLANTIC YEARS, 2
1867–1871

Dear Mother: The peacock came yesterday just as the last course was put on the table; and we all ran down with our mouths full of hot pudding, and welcomed him. . . . We are very grateful to you for sending him, but I don't conceal that he is as yet a blessing in disguise which might easily be taken for a calamity. If you have any thoughts of giving us Charles, the horse, please consider our unprepared state.

—W. D. HOWELLS to Mary D. Howells, June 30, 1867

COMICAL AS HE FOUND IT, the peacock's arrival illustrated for Howells the misunderstandings between Jefferson and Cambridge and the need for diplomacy in family dealings that made his *Atlantic* negotiations pale by comparison. Elinor told Mary Howells that they had been thinking of a pet and, when asked, said they would be pleased with the gift of a peacock. Neither she nor Mary reflected that even with cows grazing in the pasture across the street, a noisy bird might be no more suitable for their backyard than a pet bear. The episode went beyond the matter of domestic animals or a large bird in the hand. Even honey sent and inadequately appreciated could bring unexpected ill will, packed in with the letters and goods. Fruit trees and photographs, hand-me-down clothing, unwanted advice, even Elinor's drawings went back and forth with doubtful success. The principals themselves visited with similar effect.

Howells and Elinor entertained the relatives from Brattleboro and made an effort to entertain those from Jefferson. William visited several times, as did Mary, Aurelia, Joe, and Vic. Although more acceptable than the peacock, they could be troublesome in a household about to have two, then three children, and struggling with "unreliable" servants, the demands of Howells' writing, and, far too often, Elinor's poor health. There were, happily, good times and successful family exchanges. In the early months of 1867, Annie Howells came for an extended and what turned out to be ideal visit. Just twenty-three, she was in her own eyes a provincial young woman from a small village in Ohio. Joe accompanied her on the train, which stalled after plowing through deep drifts of snow. They watched as a small army of shovelers worked through the night to dig them out. "I don't remember being either sleepy or tired," Annie wrote more than fifty years later,

> for my busy mind went skimming through space to the wonderful city which stood for so much in all that was then building our national life. To me Boston meant great writers, great reformers, great orators and learned men. It was the place which was most talked about by intelligent, intellectual or serious minded fathers and mothers. And their talk was listened to by eager children until it came to mean to them Theodore Parker, Wendell Phillips, Longfellow, Holmes, Lowell, Julia Ward Howe and a dozen other men and women whose names belonged to the west as well as to the east.[1]

Charles Eliot Norton made a point of adding William Dean Howells' name to that list. "Remember," he told her, "we dont merely regard him with admiration but also with affection." Annie wrote home that "Will was to fill the very place in American literature which had always been vacant—he [Norton] thinks that when Will exhausts his Italian stock—he will settle into an essayist and refined art and social critic. I never heard such unbounded admiration as he confessed for him."[2]

In part because she was pretty and good-natured, the Howellses' friends did their best to make Annie welcome. Feeling immediately at home, she helped her brother by filling out blank forms for rejecting manuscripts, and she received callers when he and Elinor went out. At the Fieldses', she met and charmed Longfellow, who later sent her a volume of *Miles Standish.* (When she returned home, her brother told her to write "a nice letter of thank you *at once,* and have father see that the capitals and punctuations are right.")[3] Elinor informed her mother-in-law—worried about her daughter alone and vulnerable in the wicked city—that Annie had "several *ad-*

miring gentlemen friends." She added less helpfully: "I hope they wont prove themselves *savages!*"[4]

Annie had no such fears. In the house of Henry James Sr., surrounded by old paintings and soft-colored walls, she mingled with exciting guests: "Henry James, who is going to be a great author—Will Howells, with a literary reputation already established, Arthur Sedgwick a writer for the N A Review, Leon Richard, H. Dana, Ex.-Gov. Washburn, Professor Child and Wright, and our host himself." Of that "distinguished" company, Annie particularly liked William James, whom she portrayed as "handsome but not tall with very beautiful hair parted almost in the middle."[5] He asked her if she had attended the "Cretan concert," a charity affair. She in turn "asked him if he thought they would succeed in establishing their independence. He looked very wise for a moment and then we both began to laugh and he said that if I would confess just how much I knew about their cause, he would do the same. I told him I always looked solemn when their wrongs were spoken of, because it seemed the proper thing to do, and I supposed I was on their side, but was not quite certain. He was delighted with my truthfulness, and said his ideas were equally definite."[6] She did not record whether they went on to discuss philosophy or psychology.

Annie's memories of Cambridge would have made a good children's story, along the lines of her brother's wanderings in *Suburban Sketches*. One day she went walking down Charles Street quoting poetry when her veil blew off and snagged in a tree. A sweeper retrieved it with his broom as Longfellow looked on. Another time, on her way home from the opera, she lolled against an iron grating and toppled over; Joe told her she was lucky not to be fined for creating a public disturbance. Henry James Sr. took her to the Natural History Museum to see a collection of South American birds he and Louis Agassiz had collected along the Amazon. Professor Francis Child invited her to a Scottish concert at the Music Hall, which ended with the audience singing "Auld Lang Syne." "I suspect they miss you [at home]," one elderly gentleman told Annie. "Well I can imagine it, I can imagine it," and, she repeated, he seemed to think the Howellses in Jefferson "a bereaved family."[7] In 1870, while staying with the Garfields in Washington, her sister Vic wrote home with mixed pride and exasperation, "I am *always* my brother's sister!"[8] Annie met with such success in Cambridge that Howells might have wondered if he had become this sister's brother.

The round of tea parties, parlor concerts, and large gatherings took their toll on Elinor, who miscarried in February. Reconciled by the sad news to Annie's absence, Mary Howells advised her daughter to treat Elinor with fancy food, port wine, and French brandy. Still recuperating in April, Elinor went for three weeks to Brattleboro, leaving Annie to care for her brother and Winny. In March, Annie had a story accepted by Ticknor and Fields for the magazine *Our Young Folk*. "Oh how I hope I can make a name for myself," she wrote. "Dear Will seemed almost as much pleased as I was."[9] Like him, she had wanted to go to school and, like him, she had not been allowed. After long debate the family decided they could not afford to send her to a commercial college. Annie returned to Jefferson in May, dreaming of another trip to Boston and of supporting herself as Will had done: if not working for a magazine, then teaching in a kindergarten. She developed a much closer relationship with Howells than her other sisters did, including Vic, with whom he had once been so intimate. When they were apart in later years, he awaited Annie's letters about her life and work as if each brought a new installment of a Dickens novel; those letters may be her best writing. In his return letters, he recommended she try regional and realistic fiction of a sort he never quite chose for himself. "You may be sure that the imagination can deal best with what is of most familiar experience. I want you to celebrate incidents of our western life, no matter how rude or how thinly disguised, and then you cannot fail. Have patience and courage, for a great prize is within your reach."[10]

Howells himself received something of a prize on his thirtieth birthday in March 1867: a thousand-dollar increase in his *Atlantic* salary, along with the assurance (false, as it turned out) that he would be spared tedious duties like reading proof. For a yearly salary of $3,500, he was to continue as assistant editor and "contribute as much to the body of articles of the magazine" as time permitted.[11] "You can get along with discomfort or unhappiness because you're sure of it," he quoted Elinor, "while bliss is appalling from its insecurity."[12] He managed now, perhaps for the first time, to recall the awful summer of 1854 and believe that he had seen the last of his old hypochondria.

Elinor's pregnancy through the spring of 1868 delighted them. She gave birth on August 14, 1868, to a son, referred to as Brother until they named him John Mead Howells, after deceased brothers of both parents. Howells wrote gleefully to Norton, "I am wracked by too great good fortune—I am dashed to pieces on the Happy Isles. . . . You must know before this—one continent could not contain the news—that we have a boy . . . who came into this republic with as little disturbance as ever attended a citizen's advent."[13] Because she had an easy birth and recovered with not so much as a headache, Howells believed that Elinor's health might at last be reestablished.

John's birth marked both beginnings and endings. Howells' mother had been frail throughout the summer. When the Howells family learned she was gravely ill, Winny, with a child's untouchable sadness, told her parents that her grandmother could not possibly die before the election. But on October 8 Mary suffered a stroke and after two more days slipped away without regaining consciousness. Arriving in Ohio five hours too late, Howells found some comfort in recollecting that his mother had stayed with them the year before and that he and Elinor had done everything possible to make her happy. Incapable as he felt of writing intelligibly about his mother's death, he tried to explain his feelings to an old friend. "Partly, perhaps, because my grief was too violent to be opposed, the first sorrow exhausted itself, and left me more calm and cheerful than I could have dared to hope. I don't think any of us wholly realize the fact of mother's loss." Yet, as he reflected, "Every one has lost a mother or has one to lose."[14] Mary's death, which loosed a host of self-recriminations or "might haves," brought back anxieties about the passing of time and its inevitable end. He had loved his mother with a "child's heart," he told Aurelia. Now he had a man's grief.[15]

Despite the higher salary, Howells' money worries increased, perhaps as a symptom of his overall unease. He compared himself to a mill, ceaselessly grinding, halting, or "elevating something for market."[16] Bad health coupled with servant problems (what he called the flight of the Biddies) drove them to a boardinghouse for three months. When Elinor visited her family before Christmas in 1868, he could not concentrate on the tasks at hand. He felt it increasingly hard to tie his mother's death to any larger purpose and dreamed of her each night in "characteristic ways," by which he meant jumbled together with his fears and hopes. "There was some person of distinction whose attention she wished to draw to me," he wrote his father in January 1869, and when the person "simply bowed, and went on talking with another, she wore such a grieved and hurt expression" that he woke up. He could not escape the image of "the awful beauty" of her dead face.[17] In May, seven months after she died, Mary appeared to him three times in one dream, the first time to reassure her family about immortality, the second to show her happiness, and the third to say good-bye.[18]

On Sundays Howells began writing to his father about the morning's sermon, often in a different church each week. His accounts stress the impossibility of finding faith through intellect or ethical behavior, the only means open to him. He liked talking with Henry James Sr., less for his piety and severity than because he admired the man's stoicism: he bore without complaint the loss of a leg. Impressed by James' courage, he was moved to consider his father's beliefs and what as a child he had absorbed from Swedenborg's writings. He asked his father where he could find the doctrine of *vastation,* that sense of loss and perplexity central to Swedenborg's thinking—and to the senior James' sense of his life. He found himself musing on his own and his family's past and began urging William to write what would be published, after his father's death, as *Recollections of Life in Ohio from 1813 to 1840.*

Perhaps because of his intimacy with his father, he had sought out older men like James—as well as Holmes, Longfellow, and Lowell—whose wit or wisdom he enjoyed. Without growing close to Larkin Mead Sr., that "kind old man," he respected his father-in-law's integrity and had adopted Elinor's entire family as his own.[19] In the summer of 1869, Elinor left the children with Howells in Cambridge and made a sad return to Brattleboro to nurse her dying father. Worried about possible infection, Howells advised against inhaling her father's breath. "I had an awful pang of wife-sickness," he wrote when a satchel of her clothing arrived. "I took out your old dear drab dress. I've got such ideas of your thinness lately that perhaps I half expected to find you in it and was disappointed."[20] Except for a few hopeful rallies, Larkin Mead gradually weakened and died in August after a stroke. Howells blamed the "treacherous and cruel treatment" his father-in-law had received from the Windham Provident Institution for Savings, a bank Mead had started in Brattleboro that apparently forced him from his post as treasurer.[21]

The deaths of his mother and Elinor's father caused Howells to draw his own family closer. Johnny slept in a crib beside his parents' bed, and in the morning they awoke to his little blue-flanneled figure silently peering at them. At this Christmas as at most, Howells admitted to finding anniversaries painful, "hollowdays," as his youngest daughter would pronounce them. Christmas recalled the meager feasts and presents that used to make him happy as a boy. Now, looking at the abundance of Winny's Christmas, he felt the perversity of life. Even praise lost its charm, and blame cut deep as ever. What did it matter? In thirty years, he told himself, he would not care what happened to the world as long as the children flourished and John wrote to him with the love he himself felt for William.[22]

I've read Shirley Dare's article with the greatest delight, but of course it wont do for us. With what a kind of bad-girl cleverness it's done, and at what wicked Parisian possibilities does it not hint! . . . I'll send

back the Ms. to-morrow. Tell her it's too sensational for us . . . after
the Byron business.

—w. d. howells to James R. Osgood, November 7, 1869

In April 1869, James and Annie Fields sailed for Europe, leaving Howells—
under the benign thumbs of Lowell and Holmes—in charge of the *Atlantic*.
Fields approved the contents of the magazine through June, giving Howells
free rein to plan the issues from July through December. The summer passed
without major surprises, but in late August, when the September issue appeared, Howells had to report new developments to Fields: "Mrs. Stowe's
sensation of course benumbs the public to everything else in it. So far her
story has been received with howls of rejection from almost every side where
a critical dog is kept." He reassured Fields that the tide would turn and he
chatted on about "editorial business" before launching an abrupt defense:
"I believe I haven't got into difficulty with any one, made you enemies or
changed the general policy of the magazine."[23] This turned out to be wish-
ful thinking. The storm that broke over Harriet Beecher Stowe's "The True
Story of Lady's Byron's Life" brought trouble for both Howells and Fields,
made more than enough enemies, and, without actually changing policy, reduced the magazine's readership to a level from which it never recovered.

Ever since *Uncle Tom's Cabin* had given a face to slavery, Stowe had
remained an international celebrity, honored by Queen Victoria, no less,
as the conscience of America. Believing herself an instrument of the Divine Spirit, she had pushed for women's rights on the premise of women's
"higher" nature and the sanctity of the home, notably in her *House and
Home Papers* (1864) for the *Atlantic*.[24] After half a century, Byron no longer
made headline news, though scandal about his life and habits titillated readers on both sides of the Atlantic, and young people still cultivated his mannerisms, dress, and literary affectations. Stowe wrote her startling account
of the affair with his half-sister, Augusta Leigh, in response to a book by
Byron's last mistress, the Countess Guiccioli. Incensed that Guiccioli had
painted her friend as a frigid stifler of genius, Stowe transformed Lady Byron into a Christian symbol of every wronged wife.

No one, least of all her editors, anticipated the outrage over Stowe's rev-
elations or the storm she brought upon the magazine and herself. The
executors of Lady Byron's estate faulted her for unauthorized use of their
client's papers, not to say a flagrant breach of trust. The British press took
her remarks as a national affront, whereas American critics called her a man-
hater, a royal-chaser, and—what must have been especially galling—a blas-

phemer. The angry exchanges spawned a volume entitled *The Stowe-Byron Controversy: A Complete Résumé of Public Opinion, with an Impartial Review of the Merits of the Case.* Declining to contribute, Charles Dickens allowed himself a private jab to Fields. "Wish Mrs. Stowe was in the pillory."[25]

How could Howells, who hated gossip, have agreed to print the article? Holmes speculated that he feared losing Stowe as a contributor, and it is true that with Longfellow Stowe had established herself as the *Atlantic's* most popular writer. But Stowe's avowed purpose—to rescue young people from the influence of Byron's "seductive genius"—may also have clouded Howells' judgment.[26] As a young man, he first loved and later repudiated Byron. It made him sick, he had written his brother Johnny, to remember how much he had admired Byron's worst poems. "If such things don't spoil you, they'll make you ashamed and remorseful, some day."[27] The issues went beyond sexual proprieties, personal squeamishness, or shame. Howells proudly called himself Victorian in his preference for decency; while shame could be harmful, it also kept people honest. "The style is the man," he wrote, "and he cannot hide himself in any garb of words so that we shall not know somehow what manner of man he is within it."[28] Much as he loved the ribaldry of Chaucer and Shakespeare and laughed at human folly, Howells could appear prudish when it suited his purposes. He knew from experience that books *do* change people's lives, and he never backed away from considering a poet or novelist a member of society with critical, if never quite definable, responsibilities. That said, he praised any poem, novel, or painting he thought outstanding, without concern for the public's squeamishness or the charge of immoral subject matter, and he wrote books that others believed trespassed on forbidden ground.

The Stowe blunder may in the long run have opened his eyes to mistakes in judgment. At the time, he was intent on justifying his decision. "I don't at all agree with those who condemn her," he wrote to his father. "Always supposing that she has producible evidence in support of her story, I don't see why it shouldn't have been told. The world needed to know just how base, filthy and mean Byron was, in order that all glamour should be forever removed from his literature, and the taint of it should be communicated only to those who love sensual things."[29] Apart from having no "producible evidence" himself, Howells blurs his argument. For "The True Story" exemplified what he later called chromo- or sensational journalism—it was packed with melodrama, error, and its own "sensual things"—and he bore the main responsibility for its publication. In an effort to deflect criticism, he reminded Fields that Holmes and Lowell accepted the truth of Stowe's report. The two had, however, disagreed about its publication, and in siding with Holmes Howells went against the better judgment of his mentor. Fields himself had approved the decision from afar and arranged for the article's simultaneous printing in Britain's *Macmillan's Magazine.* As well as wanting to support a contributor—and one of his wife's best friends—he probably smelled profit in a bit of scandal.

The Stowe incident marked a turning point in the history of the *Atlantic,* costing the magazine fifteen thousand subscribers and at least part of the moral high ground it had earned and enjoyed since the founding days. Annie Fields, who admitted the Byron article to be misguided, later edited the *Life and Letters of Harriet Beecher Stowe* (1897) in vindication of the friend who braved the world for her principles.

The fateful year 1870 . . . was to mark the close of the literary epoch, when quarterlies gave way to monthlies; letter-press to illustration; volumes to pages. The outburst was brilliant. Bret Harte led, and Robert Louis Stevenson followed. Guy de Maupassant and Rudyard Kipling brought up the rear and dazzled the world.

—HENRY ADAMS, *The Education of Henry Adams*

Howells' job brought him into contact with some of the best and brightest of his generation, including the young, "long-headed" intellectuals (to borrow Henry James' phrase) who called themselves the Club.[30] Formed in the late 1860s, the Club—a loose connection of friends and guests modeled after Boston's Saturday Club—met on the second Tuesday of every month for dinner and counted among its members a future Supreme Court justice, Oliver Wendell Holmes Jr.; the Harvard philosopher William James; Howells' Cambridge neighbor, the historian John Fiske; the Adams brothers, Henry and Brooks, both historians; and literary men like Henry James and Thomas Sergeant Perry. As legend has it, no food could rival these men's talk. James spoke in stammering paragraphs that seemed to rise like the sections of a pagoda. Fiske, who never did anything in moderation—whether eating, working, singing, smoking, or talking—had a prodigious memory for dates and facts and a photographic memory for print, and if asked a question could deliver a perfectly constructed lecture on the topic. Howells, now a widely read raconteur and thinker, more than held his own.

Because of his position with the *Atlantic,* Howells had business dealings with most of the Club's members—publishing, for example, Fiske's *Myth and Myth-Makers* (1872), a corrective to the "monument history" of William Prescott or Francis Parkman. Fiske dedicated the book to Howells "in remembrance of pleasant autumn evenings spent among were-wolves and trolls and nixies." The two might have stepped out of the pages of the Grimm brothers: Fiske, a tall, burly man with a large head and a full, rather carelessly kept brown beard, dwarfed the broad-shouldered, full-chested, but short-legged Howells. Fiske grew so heavy in later years that Howells described him as the fattest man he ever met. "He must have weighed 300 pounds," he told Aurelia, measuring at his middle "nearly a yard through."[31] Howells associated with these men in the years when he formulated his creed of literary realism, taking into account Fiske's anthropological approach to history and William James' conviction that history, whatever the larger social forces at work, could be changed by the intervention of individual men and women. Like many of the Club's pioneering thinkers, Howells distrusted received ideas or absolute standards and accepted the role of chance forces at work in human lives.

Although most of the members came from the New World aristocracy, they believed in practical social engineering to bring about a more inclusive society. So, surprisingly, did Charles Eliot Norton, who trod common ground with the slightly younger prodigies of the Club. He too sought "pragmatic" solutions to contemporary problems, whether Negro education or tariff reform or industrial relations. When Howells characterized what Hawthorne or Lowell, Fiske or Norton stood for, he spoke of faith in humanity. Readers today might still think of most American nineteenth-century writers as Bohemian outsiders plying their trade in isolation. Howells' association with so many different groups in his life, from the Club to the Academy of Arts and Letters, betrays no lack of "genius" on his part, or theirs. Melville, who would probably have liked to join, proved the exception, Howells the norm. Most writers conceived of their clubs—and there were many—as intellectual communities, perhaps the urban counterparts of utopian associations like Brook Farm.

Howells' satisfaction with Cambridge life might be inferred from his decision, in August 1870, to move from its outskirts to its center, which is to say from Sacramento Street to 3 Berkeley Street. Apart from the difficulties he claimed to have concentrating after an Irishman with a large family built a double house across the street, he and Elinor felt obliged to find space for Elinor's mother and her sister, Mary, who planned to spend part of each year with them.[32] Then, too, Elinor's usually precarious health had improved, so much so, according to Howells, that her social aspirations required something larger than the "carpenter's box."

It was at the Berkeley Street house, with its study looking out on a small garden, that the Norwegian translator, poet, critic, and novelist Hjalmar Boyesen became a frequent guest. Boyesen, who stayed with the Howellses for several weeks in 1871, remembered descending to Howells' cellar in the middle of the night for champagne to complement cheese, crackers, and watermelon. He first met Howells through Professor Child, who had discovered the lonely foreigner in the Harvard library and taken him in hand with the same generous spirit in which he responded to *Venetian Life*. With Boyesen, Howells spoke Italian and discussed Scandinavian literature. A Swedenborgian, Boyesen found himself at home with the Howellses, including those in Ohio, where he met the "lonesome girls" and "our poor crazed Henry."[33] He went on to publish his first novel, *Gunnar*, in the *Atlantic*, win faculty appointments at Cornell and Columbia, and marry a woman whom Elinor could claim as distant kin. If, as Elinor complained, Boyesen sometimes took advantage of their hospitality or—as her husband complained—talked too much about himself, he never hesitated to praise Howells or couple his name with prominent novelists like Ivan Turgenev.

Professor Child played benefactor to Howells as well, arranging for him to lecture on "New Italian Literature" at the Lowell Institute in the fall of 1870. Though Elinor thought his subject "scarcely of the kind to interest" a general audience, two hundred and fifty people ventured through the slush in full evening dress.[34] Word of mouth may have swelled the audience. Henry James had heard Howells lecture the previous May at Harvard, and as his friend spoke, James said, he had closed his eyes and imagined a window opening out to Florence. Awakening in Cambridge, he had been consoled by the thought that his Florence remained within.[35]

The lectures over, Howells focused again on the magazine and began to correspond with the rising star Bret Harte about Harte's literary plans and contributions to the *Atlantic*. Learning of Harte's intention to come east in March 1871, Howells invited him to stay with the family. Harte agreed, casually adding wife and children, and Howells obliged—to Elinor's indignation. How could Mrs. Harte accept their hospitality without a personal invitation from her? On the day of the guests' arrival, Howells, who was told that Harte demanded such attentions, rented the "handsomest hack" that "the livery of Cambridge afforded." The "fairy prince" proved to be human after all.[36] He had what Howells called a "golden nature," the ability to take the bad as lightly as the good. As it turned out, Harte could be as exasperating as he was charming. Perennially and unapologetically late, he also had no qualms about showing up at a friend's house because he found his hotel room dreary. Lilian Aldrich remembered that Harte expected night-clothes and toothbrushes to appear magically, and in return did her husband the favor of smoking his choicest cigars.

On the Hartes' arrival, Elinor took them to the drawing-room, where she had placed—on Harte's order—the flower stand sent in advance. She found their guests' two boys well-behaved, their parents surprisingly dignified and sensible. "Of course they are not quite au fait in every thing," she told her sisters-in-law, perhaps referring to Harte's stylish dress or the fact that he reminded some people of a French marquis, "but they give you the idea of polished, cultivated people."[37] Cambridge embraced Harte, and so finally did his hostess, who enjoyed the recognition, indeed the coup of introducing their new friends. *"The party!"* she said of their first big entertainment: "How shall I do justice to it?"[38] Howells had no such difficulty. It had, he said, brought together "the genius and 'beauty' of Cambridge," with genius predominating.[39] Elinor had hired a caterer who provided linen, silver, dishes, coffee, chocolate ice cream, salad, bread, and cake for a dollar and a half a head—"as cheap," she told the folks at home, "as we could have got it up any other way."[40] Harte joked about the disparity between the caterer's china and that of his hosts, who lived, as Howells liked to think, in semivirtuous poverty. John Fiske reported that "everyone wore his best bib and tucker . . . the supper was delicious . . . [and] Mrs. Howells . . . very pretty and charming, vivacious and amusing as always."[41]

The Hartes' visit brought uneasy questions from Jefferson. Aware of Fields' planned retirement, William warned that Harte might prove a dark-horse candidate for the editorship. His son reassured him that Harte had no further editorial ambitions nor, as a salaried contributor, any need of them. Fields paid Harte ten thousand dollars a year, more than his own salary as publisher and editor. From Howells' vantage point, securing one of the country's most popular writers seemed money well spent, a way for the *Atlantic* to attract new readers and convince a growing number of lapsed subscribers to return. He began touting Harte in print and arranged with *Every Saturday,* the weekly owned by Fields and James Osgood, to have Harte's portrait on the magazine's front page.[42] Over time, Harte's relationship with the *Atlantic* grew strained because he rarely met his obligations as a contributor, submitting older work or none at all. He resented Howells' meddling with his manuscripts, which he thought untouchable, and challenged the firm's policy of reimbursement. Perhaps the editors thought it worth only $300 to him to appear in the *Atlantic,* he wrote in 1874. "The *Times* paid me $600 for 'The Roses of Tuolumne,' $500 for 'John Oakhurst.' Scribner paid me $1000 for 'Fiddletown'—16 pp. long and 4500 for 'Monte Flat Pastoral'; 7 pp."[43] Harte claimed to have had every previous story accepted and the fee fixed before putting pen to paper.

At the time of Harte's leaving Cambridge, when Howells looked "forward to the fatness of the future with lively alarm," he had a moment of genuine alarm.[44] Seeing his guest off at the train, he slipped on the platform and barely escaped being crushed against the station wall. (In a novella he called *The Shadow of a Dream,* he made use of this experience to dispose of a character.) Glad to be alive and satisfied with the *Atlantic's* fortunes, he felt that even if the magazine failed him, he had options. The previous fall, after scouting job possibilities, he had found himself marketable. More important, he vowed to put the magazine second to his own work. "I am a writer, and nothing else," he had told his father several months before the Hartes' visit, and should "be wiser and happier if hereafter I attempt nothing outside my proper sphere."[45] Brave words from a man about to accept the responsibility for America's premier magazine.

As he looked ahead, Howells as usual looked back. He would not write an autobiography for years to come, but on the eve of his appointment to the *Atlantic* editorship, he offered a thumbnail sketch of his life to a Princeton professor seeking information.

Dear Sir:

I have your obliging note of the 27th [June 1871], and I will now try to give you the information you ask.

I was born at Martin's Ferry, Belmont co., Ohio, on the 1st of March 1837, of Welsh parentage on my father's side and Pennsylvania-German on my mother's. I learned the printing-business in my father's offices at Hamilton and Dayton, Ohio, and worked pretty steadily "at case," from my twelfth to my nineteenth year. Then I became legislative correspondent of the Cincinnati Gazette from Columbus, and two years later, news-editor of the Ohio State Journal. In 1861 I was appointed Consul at Venice, where I remained till July 1865, when I returned to America, resigning my office in October of the same year. I was engaged for a few months on The Nation, at New York, and on March 1st, 1866 came at Mr. Fields's invitation to be his assistant editor on the Atlantic. I succeeded him yesterday as chief-editor. I live in Cambridge.

You will have noticed that I have to lament an almost entire want of schooling. However, my father had ardent literary tastes, and an excellent library, and I studied and read as I could, and repaired to some extent a loss which can never be wholly repaired. I learned with little or no help Spanish and German, a trifle of Latin and a soupçon of Greek. Italian was a necessity and a pleasure at Venice, and a little French one knows naturally.

Perhaps I have troubled you with more facts than you care for. You can suppress them at pleasure. I enclose a list of my books.[46]

His modest overview suggests the skeletal lives recorded in dictionaries of biography—or the annals of time. Maybe he felt the catalog of books spoke for itself, or he feared jinxing the future. The Harriet Beecher Stowe fiasco had shown him how the best of intentions could and commonly did go awry.

Americans I remember fifty years ago had a consciousness of standing firmer on their own feet and in their own shoes than those of the newer generation.

—CHARLES ELIOT NORTON to James Russell Lowell, June 12, 1879

Regarded by many as the country's most successful publisher, James T. Fields had announced his retirement on New Year's Day 1871: the place was his elegant, *Atlantic* office in the Tremont Street building, the fare peanuts. His reasons for stepping down went beyond the burden of deadlines or the tedium of reading manuscripts. According to Howells, Fields "wanted time and a free mind to do some literary work of his own. 'Besides,' he added, 'I am past fifty and do not expect to live long.'" Whether or not the robust-looking Fields actually "felt himself a stricken man," he had misgivings about the ailing firm.[47] Going over its finances, he reckoned that the previous twelve months had cost almost sixty thousand dollars in general expenses and over fifty-one thousand in advertising.[48] When James Osgood, with two silent partners, agreed to buy him out, the firm once known as "Ticknor & Fields" and then as "Fields, Osgood & Company" reemerged as "James R. Osgood & Company," so that the entire publishing enterprise, the *Atlantic* included, fell into Osgood's hands.

Fields had hired the diminutive nineteen-year-old from Fryeburg, Maine (Howells' model for "Equity" in *A Modern Instance*), to learn the publishing business, and in 1864 he made Osgood a partner.[49] Osgood was by all accounts a tireless worker—not just an enfant terrible but the "Boston

Bantam"—despite the severe rheumatism that kept him in bed for days and caused him to limp. An extrovert, he once crashed a meeting of the Kinsman Club and so charmed its members that Mark Twain, the president, proposed a change of name to The Osgood Club.[50] A man who seems to have lived for work, Osgood played a major part in Howells' life, evolving from his early adviser on the *Atlantic* into his employer, literary agent, and friend.

Between Fields' resignation at the beginning of the year and his own formal acceptance of his editorship in July, Howells bore the magazine's responsibilities without the title. In June, he made his memorable trip to Ohio, visiting with James Garfield and accompanying his father to the old homestead. On July 1, more than a decade after Holmes prophesied his succession, he gained the right to put his own pen, and perhaps his feet, on Fields' desk. The event passed with little fanfare. He had in a sense been anointed in January through tributes paid by Longfellow, Whittier, Holmes, and Emerson at Fields' retirement party, so that the official transfer seemed a technicality. Of his joy or anger about past grievances, lost hours, or salary, Howells left no record. He described "a sort of incredulous gasping" at finding himself in charge and accountable only to himself and his publisher.[51]

From Fields he inherited a mixed bag of responsibilities. Tallying benefits against deficits, he could list the new employer he both liked and trusted along with the man's largesse.[52] Osgood increased his salary to $5,000 a year, the equivalent of about $100,000 today.[53] Fields—who had paid himself $5,000 for work on the press and $2,000 for editing the *Atlantic*—also allowed himself a house and $1,000 a year toward entertaining. Howells, without the bonuses, did have the public recognition of being editor in chief. At the same time, his old job had been rolled into the new one, so that he paid for his title with double the work. Elinor described his situation in November 1871: "Will's place is as secure and good as ever," she wrote to Annie Howells; "but he has to work tremendously now. By & by he is to have more help—but just at present he must do it all himself, to be sure it is well done."[54]

Answerable for a magazine with a shrinking circulation, Howells faced a host of issues, not least the egos of contributors. The *Atlantic* had managed to retain its reputation for high culture because of its stable of writers, a mix of old favorites who—however much Stowe taxed the patience of her editors or Lowell's elitism irked some readers—had a popular appeal.[55] After five years as assistant editor, Howells was a known entity and enjoyed little of the cachet or indisputable authority a new editor in chief might have expected. Long-standing contributors, some of them national heroes like Higginson, condescended to the Westerner they saw as asserting himself unduly or patronizing his betters. When Howells hesitated about one of his submissions, Higginson fired off an indignant letter. "I would not on any account have you print anything of mine which you only thought 'well enough,' so I have arranged for it elsewhere—with a regret which you can hardly understand, as you have not, like me, written for but one literary magazine for thirteen years & felt identified with it." From now on, he would allow himself "a merely business relation with the Atlantic."[56]

The editor's job had never been easy, as Howells knew, but the magazine's history of inbreeding complicated his work even more. His intimacy with his contributors, many of them old friends or enemies, made it all the harder to appear impartial or to sustain the magazine's commitment to shared cultural ideals. As with Higginson, squabbles over submissions quickly became personal. Years before, Thoreau had refused to contribute to the magazine after Lowell deleted lines from a poem. Annie Fields thought the mercurial Lowell incapable of a joke. Etiquette forbade direct criticism of Mrs. Fields, so Henry James Sr. applauded her work for local charities one day and on another spoke about women forsaking the sanctity of their homes "to battle and unsex" themselves in the world.[57] James Fields blamed Holmes' irreligious sense of humor for a loss of readers. Henry James Jr. considered Fields a Philistine, his taste in literature a joke. Howells, who laughed with James about Fields, would have been surprised to learn that James had complained about the magazine's low standards since Howells became "absolute monarch."[58] (In 1871 Howells pushed Fields to accept James' first novel, *Watch and Ward,* for serialization, which its author touted as "one of the greatest works of 'this or any age.'")[59] The poet Paul Hamilton Hayne thought Howells cantankerous and said so to anyone who would listen. And on it went. The new editor began to imagine an *Atlantic* supplement consisting of irate letters like Higginson's and threats to his person—"war to the knife," in the words of one rebuffed poet from Kentucky.[60]

The job brought less histrionic and far more hurtful misunderstandings. It became apparent to Annie Howells that her brother's position with the *Atlantic* hampered her own career. On the one hand, she did not want to compromise him with her submissions; on the other, she knew the importance of the magazine to literary success. "I do not intend ever to embarrass you by offering anything to the Atlantic," she told him. "I know it will be next to impossible to make a reputation except as a contributor to it, still I know your reasons for keeping me out, are convincing to you."[61] Howells must have read "to you" and winced, for Annie had a point: he too depended on the *Atlantic* for his career. Besides his unhappy sister, he had to face his old friends. Long ago he had sought favors from John Piatt, the coauthor of *Poems of Two Friends,* who now expected to see his submissions automatically accepted and his work reviewed in the *Atlantic.* Like Fields, he understood that reviews provided free advertisement. Fields' phrase, "Pills thus puffed will sell," highlights Howells' unending quandary (later a topic in his fiction) about what to publish and what to decline.[62] Every decision mattered because the magazine mattered to every contributor. An indication of its influence can be seen in President Lincoln's remark during the Civil War that a favorable piece in the *Atlantic* might save him a dozen battles.[63]

Howells faced daily reminders of how much his editorship and later his fame affected his relationships. Since so few authors earned a living by writing, his editorial decisions could protect a contributor, even one as established as Bayard Taylor, from bankruptcy. Taylor, who acknowledged Howells' generosity, still taxed him with almost everything he wrote, including letters of complaint about rejections. Lowell praised Howells' treatment of veteran authors without apparent awareness of the special advantages he received. Over the years their roles had gradually changed: when Lowell worried about providing for his daughter after his death, Howells, then at Harper's, would spare him from drawing on his principal by paying extra well for his poems. "The money will be a godsend to me," Lowell confessed, "—but is it [his new poem] worth so much? I suppose it isn't for me to decide—if they think so. I will send it to you tomorrow."[64] "They," as both understood, meant Howells himself.

Any editor walks a moral tightrope, and Howells, who balanced profits and his own integrity, occasionally stumbled. In a world tacitly endorsing a system of quid pro quo, the editor of the *Atlantic* received as many advantages as he bestowed. Delicacy might have precluded "any mention of himself, whether for praise or blame within his own pages," but serialization in the magazine of *Suburban Sketches* or his novels enhanced his reputation and his income by keeping his work before the public.[65] To this extent he did puff his own books. And, as Higginson pointed out, so did his friends, from whom Howells expected, and usually received, positive reviews. He may not, however, have benefited from rigorous criticism, since he soon dismissed all negative reviews as wrongheaded. In the years to come, he would get his share.

Intricacies of family, friendships, and ethical complexities aside, Howells had other challenges. The magazine business had changed dramatically since the early *Atlantic* days. Competition for advertising and sales grew in intensity; readers demanded expensive, eye-catching formats; new publications appealed to and encouraged less highbrow tastes. Rather than tamper with the *Atlantic* itself, the firm had invested in the spin-off *Every Saturday*, a magazine edited by Howells' friend Thomas Bailey Aldrich that paid contributors too much and sank money into unused illustrations. When the magazine folded in the aftermath of the 1871 Chicago fire, Osgood and his partners turned away from illustrated magazines. The failure meant a personal loss for Howells, who had negotiated a position for Annie as *Every Saturday*'s Washington correspondent and saw her job disappear with the magazine.

Howells' major competitive challenge lay in broadening the *Atlantic*'s appeal. To hold ground against the illustrated magazines, he gradually added sections on art and music, another on politics, and then, in 1877, a spirited, anonymous forum called the Contributor's Club, designed to introduce young writers and offer new venues for the old. (His father submitted an article on Canadian Indians.) "If you know any bright women who are disposed to write in the Club," Howells wrote Edmund Stedman, "invite them for me. I much desire the discussion of social matters."[66] "Spit your spite at somebody or something," he told Mark Twain, who wanted no prompting.[67] Half the fun for readers and contributors alike came from guessing who wrote what.

Clever ideas alone could not restore the *Atlantic*'s lost glory. Whereas *Harper's* targeted "the average American," the *Atlantic* did not, or could not, since lowering its intellectual level risked alienating core subscribers.[68] In terms of sales, the *Atlantic* never competed with *Harper's* or, later, *Scribner's*, which printed 100,000 copies of its first issue in 1887. The *Atlantic*'s circulation peaked under Fields at 50,000, dropped to 35,000 in 1870 (after Stowe's attack on Byron), and sank to 20,000 four years later. For all Howells' efforts, it hovered around 12,000 by the end of his tenure.[69] The "illustrateds" had come to stay, and he could do nothing to boost the *Atlantic* unless or until he joined them. To some extent *Atlantic* standards depended on the quality of submissions and readers' tastes. Howells occasionally resorted to sentimental fiction that he despised. In the March 1870 issue—when he still served as assistant editor—the magazine carried an improbable story of mistaken identity, "The Blue River Bank Robbery," as well as "Time Works Wonders," in which a character exclaims: "Keep pretty women out of my sight, and the thunder-stroke shall not make me swerve. But with their eyes looking into mine, I am like wax over the flame of a taper."[70] A further problem for the new editor lay in maintaining the *Atlantic's* intense focus on literature when established writers found it more advantageous to publish with *Harper's* or *Scribner's Magazine* (soon to be *Scribner's Monthly,* later the *Century*) than with the *Atlantic,* if only to reach more readers.

One irony about Howells' tenure is that, more than any editor in his day, and in spite of his own impatience with reviewers, he devoted space in his magazine to commentary on literature rather than literature itself. "We all read in such a literary way, now," his protagonist of *The Lady of the Aroostook* explains; "we don't read simply for the joy or profit of it; we expect to talk about it, and say how it is this and that; and I've no doubt that we're sub-consciously harassed, all the time, with an automatic process of criticism."[71] If right about this, Howells might have blamed himself. At its best, he saw reviewing or criticism not as personal vendetta, disguised envy, or "mere trade-puff," "the financial comments of the advertiser, or the bought-and-sold eulogism of an ignorant, careless, or mercenary journalist," but as a collaboration between the author and reviewer on the one hand, and the reader and reviewer on the other.[72] On this basis, he did not hesitate to call some books bad. In April 1870 the magazine carried a review of "'Red as a Rose is She' by the author of 'Cometh up as a Flower' and 'Not Wisely, but too Well, etc.'" Almost certainly Howells', the unsigned review faulted the author's "loathing of all persons in sickness, poverty, old age, or calamity of any kind, except unhappy love."[73] Three months later, the same reviewer summed up Mrs. Steele's "So Runs the World Away": "A novel of the 'Red as a Rose is She' sort; but entirely stupid, and without any of the redeeming originality of that book,—if original sin may be considered a redeeming quality."[74] The best criticism, Howells explained in 1901, "gives the critic, as well as the author, to the reader's knowledge," and *perhaps* helps a writer to make the next book better.[75] Knowing most standards to be personal prejudices, he objected to templates for "good" literature and critical assumptions based on intrinsic merit, or what he called "a supposed law of aesthetics applicable to every exigency of literary development." There is no law for criticism, he had written in 1867, "which has not been overthrown as often as the French government."[76] Of course he had his prejudices: his taste leaned toward character over elaborate plotting, dialogue over authorial intrusion. If he envisioned American criticism and American literature evolving like fraternal twins, his early essays on literary criticism might be taken as a manifesto: a challenge to both writers and reviewers for a just, true handling of subject.

As with the twentieth-century editor T. S. Eliot, Howells' importance as a writer and critic is as hard to define as it is to overstate. Like Eliot, he had a broad, eclectic (if less classical) knowledge of literary culture, and Howells too weighed the merits of tradition and the "individual talent." More than Eliot, he wrote journalistic or what might be called opportunistic criticism, running commentaries, liberal and without snobbery, on the state of the arts, which he collected in books like *My Literary Passions* and *Literature and Life.* In part because of his openness to European writers, he appreciated developments that others ignored or belittled in American fiction. Imagining American literature as both a new entity and of a piece with European writing, he believed his countrymen to have a natural affinity for Continental literature because they shared common cultural values with European authors. The year before becoming editor, he had written James to praise the English writers George Eliot and William Morris as the best available.[77]

His convictions are typified in a review of the Norwegian author Bjørnstjerne Bjørnson's *The Happy Boy; A Tale of Norwegian Peasant Life.* The bleak world of Bjørnson's fiction appealed because of its "simplicity and self-control" and the author's "confidence in the reader's intelligence."[78] Without addressing issues of translation (he read Bjørnson in either German or French translations), or how a Norwegian writer might speak directly to American readers, Howells assumed that authentic literature grew from a writer's singular imagination and sensibility; that a national literature developed from national characteristics and conditions, and that, if honestly studied, any life, no matter how alien, could be compelling. During the winter of 1880–81 he met Bjørnson, who stayed a few months in Cambridge with the widow of the great Norwegian violinist Ole Bull. "I like him extremely," Howells told his father. "He is a hot Republican, and just now is in disgrace at home for having spoken disrespectfully of the king; I think he called him a donkey." Howells was one of the few people with enough patience to carry on a conversation with Bjørnson, "a great genius" but a beginning speaker of English.[79] They would remain friends.

Probably no writers inspired Howells as much as the Russians. It was Thomas Perry who first introduced him to Russian novelists, including Ivan Turgenev, whom Perry—the editor of an *Atlantic* section called "Recent Literature"—knew personally and whose works he translated. Howells wrote the bulk of the *Atlantic* reviews until Perry, among others, slowly replaced him, Perry contributing over four hundred reviews of his own, in tone and substance like those of the senior editor.[80] To Howells, the uncompromising craftsmanship of Turgenev or Bjørnson (later the scope and power of Dostoyevsky or Tolstoy) set standards for an American fiction based on a profounder psychology, a broader sense of the political and economic weave of society, and, above all, the way people live. He called Turgenev's novel *Liza,* which he reviewed in February 1873, "life, nothing more, nothing less; and though life altogether foreign to our own, yet unmistakably real. Everything is unaffected and unstrained." Neither in style nor substance is Turgenev false. "This author never calls on you to admire how well he does a thing; he only makes you wonder at the truth and value of the thing when it is done. . . . One feels the presence, not only of a great genius, but a clear conscience in his work."[81] Despite his debunking of the word *genius,* Howells uses it here to suggest Turgenev's rare talent and to illustrate his own evolving principles. Seven months later he wrote of Turgenev's *Dimitri Roudine:* "We are not quite sure whether we like or dislike the carefulness with which Roudine's whole character is kept from us, so that we pass from admiration to despite before we come finally to half-respectful compassion; and yet is this not the way it would be in life?" He would praise in James what he saw in Turgenev—and had suggested in his own *Venetian Life*— the understanding that no person, no character or narrator, can wholly know another person, let alone himself.[82] When Turgenev read *Their Wedding Journey,* a gift from his friend Boyesen, he returned Howells' compliments: "Your literary physiognomy is a most sympathetic one . . . it is natural, simple, and clear . . . full of unobtrusive poetry and fine humor . . . [with] the peculiar american stamp."[83]

Like Lowell and Fields before him, Howells saw American literature—its authors, readers, and place in the general culture—as a personal responsibility. Unlike his mentors, he had arrived at new valuations of literary types and regional literatures. The man who railed at "plantation romances" and other less auspicious fiction believed that postwar Southern writing achieved a realism akin to Turgenev's depiction of rural Russia. Howells anticipated a range of issues that would be addressed by twentieth-century Southern Agrarians such as John Crowe Ransom and Allen Tate, whose social views came from a consciousness of history, and whose fiction presented—in often lyrical language—a cross section of the South's races and classes. The politics of the Southern Agrarians pitted them against industrialists and developers in the years after the First World War.

Henry Adams, singling out 1870 as a pivotal year for American fiction, might have exchanged temperaments with Howells: the pessimist turning optimist, the optimist seeing only the worst. With a few rare exceptions, Howells felt that the American novel hovered in the country's mental atmosphere like a "pathetic ante-natal phantom, pleading to be born into the world."[84] A promising star like Bret Harte had already begun to repeat himself, taking good *Atlantic* money for second-rate work. Meanwhile, the magazine's stable of writers, the old standbys from a previous generation, could not build a future for literature. Howells' low spirits seem to have been both real and temporary. "Perhaps I am painting the case in rather blacker colors than the fact would justify," he wrote of this time.[85] He had exaggerated the "pathetic" and ignored the positive, and what he first found overwhelming, he learned to face and to some extent change. Committing himself to the mentoring of contributors and would-be contributors, he meant to praise and coax—and winnow out the chaff.

In a sense, Howells became a critic in spite of himself, a critic impatient of others and of the critical enterprise itself, writing shrewd personal essays rather than intense scrutiny of texts or systematic commentary. Always informed, he was not always careful or thorough—nor did he try to be. His reviews are genial introductions to or defenses of books, pleas to read them, and endorsements for the kind of literature he advocated. A reviewer of his *Modern Italian Poets* wondered how any such study could be so casual if the critic took his work seriously. Had he read it, Howells might have taken the criticism for praise. He worked hard to rid himself of what he called *literosity* and to engage the common reader through the simplicity of spoken language.[86] He produced enormous amounts of literary commentary, taking on British critics, American critics, indeed any critics who disagreed with his ideas or his values. He would have agreed with a later critic, Carl Van Vechten, who said that "good critics should grope and, if they must define, they should constantly contradict their own definitions."[87] By anyone's definition, Howells wrote a body of commentary impressive enough to make another writer's reputation, quite apart from his plays, poems, travel and children's literature, and more than forty novels.

The young Howells thought of himself as a poet and of poetry as the highest art, and the magazine certainly published poetry (and plays), but poetry had imperceptibly given way to fiction as both his literary passion and literary measure. The shift is understandable in someone whose poems had met with little success and who had been rewarded for his prose. Over the past century, Howells' name has been synonymous with literary realism, and rightly so—with qualifications. In his time, as now, "realism" meant many things and took many forms. How can the term meaningfully embrace Rebecca Harding Davis' *Life in the Iron Mills* (1861), Herman Melville's then-neglected *Moby-Dick* (1851), Twain's *Tom Sawyer* (1876), and Henry James' *The American* (1877)? Howells himself used the word loosely and managed to speak about "realism" in books he labeled romance. Although he disliked Elizabeth Stuart Phelps' "shuddering, gasping style," he later voted for her inclusion in the American Academy of Arts and Letters. He knew that his *truth* (or applied truth, *realism*) could not be transposed into a simple aesthetic formula; nor, on the other hand, could *sublimity, sincerity,* and *genius,* the dross of an outdated aesthetics. *Real, realistic,* and *realism* simply offered his best markers for the writing he admired. Howells' flexible terms raise a number of issues about his editorship and the shape of his career. His efforts would leave the *Atlantic* the major voice for literary realism and a weaker competitor of *Scribner's* and *Harper's,* which had drawn away both readers and contributors. Aware of the irony, Howells himself served the firm of Harper & Brothers for the last three and a half decades of his life and worked in various editorial capacities.

In 1871, after he had spent five years with the *Atlantic,* Howells' goals remained the same: to make his name in literature, establish his own critical principles, and finish the first of his novels. Between July and December of that year he serialized *Their Wedding Journey* in the *Atlantic.* In this and the novels to follow he attempted to reproduce the world as he knew it, and in one respect at least his aims overlapped with those of Whitman.[88] "The trouble has always been," Howells told his journalist-friend Ralph Keeler, "that we have looked . . . through somebody else's confounded literary telescope. I find it hard work myself to trust my eyes, and I catch myself feeling for the telescope, but I hope to do without it, altogether, by and by."[89]

HIS MARK TWAIN

FROM 1869

Not to lose time in banalities I began at once from the thread of thought in my mind. "I wonder why we hate the past so," and he responded from the depths of his consciousness, "It's so damned humiliating," which is what any honest man would say of his past if he were honest, but honest men are few when it comes to themselves.

—W. D. HOWELLS, *My Mark Twain*, 1910

HOWELLS FIRST SAW MARK TWAIN in late 1869, when a tall man with drooping red moustaches strode into the *Atlantic* office on Tremont Street, eager to thank the anonymous reviewer of *Innocents Abroad*. Twain had declined a letter of introduction to Howells, professing a "delicacy" some might say he lacked, and on this occasion introduced himself unannounced to Fields, who introduced him to Howells. Already aware of Howells as an influential editor, he could now put the reputation with the reviewer and, just as important, ally himself with the *Atlantic Monthly*. It was an auspicious moment for both men, whose careers and private lives intertwined for the next forty years.

They met as kindred spirits with contrary temperaments, which may suggest why Howells remained Twain's close friend when Bret Harte and so many others did not. Howells, then thirty-two, had married seven years earlier, fathered two children, and grown gradually more respectable, or what he called in the aftermath of the Stowe fiasco more "prudish." Sometimes he seemed to blur the distinction between his personal life and his stewardship of the *Atlantic Monthly*. His new acquaintance, thirty-four and about to marry, could not let even Olivia Langdon reform him beyond promises to stop drinking or become religious—and she may not have tried very hard. Twain's appeal lay in his flamboyant disregard for convention. Howells remembered that on the day of their first meeting, Twain wore a sealskin coat turned fur side out (as it would now be worn), while he, with "cold chills," escorted the coat down Boston's Broadway past gawking pedestrians.[1]

Whereas Howells already felt settled in his job and established in Cambridge, Twain remained in transit. Over the last few years he had traveled to Hawaii—still the Sandwich Islands—to Europe, South Africa, Central America, the Holy Land, Spain, and Russia. He had lectured in towns like You Bet and Red Dog, California, and crisscrossed dozens of states. In addition to writing for New York and California papers, he had chased jobs in Cleveland and Hartford and visited Elmira, New York, with his friend Charles Langdon. There, already smitten by Livy Langdon's photograph, he fell in love with the woman herself.

Howells' public credentials as a writer and editor notwithstanding, he and Twain met at comparable stages in their careers. Howells had been footloose and unsure not very long before, and, like Twain, he had published his first two books and miscellaneous articles without producing the work he dreamed of. Though his editorship and alliances with elite publishing houses gave him better connections than Twain's, Howells knew that these amounted to little. Twain's iconoclastic thinking, his ways of looking at the world, and his bold conversation teased Howells out of complaisance and reminded him of a calling beyond the assistant editorship or his duties as James Fields' clerk. His review of *Innocents Abroad* (1869) announces "the bounty and abundance," "the good-humored humor . . . that [Twain] lavishes on the reader," and he guessed right about the man. "As Mr. Clements writes of his experiences, we imagine he would talk of them; and very amusing talk it would be; often not at all fine in manner or matter."[2] Whether or not this early review changed Twain's career, as Twain insisted, Howells drew his new friend into Cambridge life while opening doors to the publishing world that Twain quickly mastered. With a similar guile, he too sought out useful people, including Ulysses S. Grant and Oliver Wendell Holmes, whom he visited before calling on Fields and Howells.

Given their mutual affection and admiration, it seems odd that the initial friendship lapsed as quickly as it began. After finishing his Massachusetts lectures, Twain left for Elmira to marry Livy and, as he thought, settle down to run a newspaper in Buffalo, New York. At least a year and a half passed before he returned to Boston on the lecture circuit, and afterward he and Howells lost no opportunity. When Twain went back to sell his business in Buffalo and plan his new home in Hartford, letters shuttled back and forth, soon followed by the men themselves. Livy and Elinor met and liked each other, and the two couples duly exchanged photo portraits, the mark of friendship in that emerging age of professional photography.

Each man must have felt that he had found a missing brother, someone without Orion Clemens' or Sam and Henry Howells' insatiable needs or penchant for failure. Physically unlike, especially in later life—Howells balding, short, and stocky; Twain tall, wild-eyed, and feathery-browed—they shared professional, social, and financial aspirations that made them almost Janus-like halves of the same person. They came from what they saw as comparable places, and, though both flourished in the New England establishment, they clung to their roles as "Westerners" in Eastern society. Hamilton, Ohio, scarcely resembled Hannibal, Missouri, "a loafing, out-at-elbows, down-at-heels, slave-holding" town, yet for Howells a boyhood in either Hamilton or Hannibal meant knowledge of a greater America than the eastern seaboard.[3] Besides, Twain "was the most desouthernized Southerner" he ever knew.[4] In the small frontier towns where they grew up, both had, like Benjamin Franklin before them, apprenticed as typesetters and journalists. Twain moved westward as a young man, the journey in *Roughing It*, and Howells east, to Venice and old-world Europe, with neither losing his pride in his place of birth. About *Innocents Abroad* and *Roughing It* Howells wrote in 1887: "Let fiction cease to lie about life; let it portray men and women as they are . . . ; let it speak the dialect, the language, that most Americans know—the language of unaffected people everywhere—and we believe that even its masterpieces will find a response in all readers."[5] From the early 1870s, Twain's language found an eager welcome from his reviewer, who through a long career defended everything he felt Mark Twain embodied, everything *natural* as well as *national,* however broad the definitions.

No wonder the two planned a never-realized trip down the Mississippi, which was to be a return home for Twain and a surrogate return for Howells, who had heard as a boy the call of the river and traveled on his uncles' paddle wheelers down the Ohio. Once, interviewed about his work habits, Howells drew on childhood images to describe his writing. "I work like a pilot on a Mississippi river steamboat," he said, "with certain landmarks to shape my course by; I keep a phrase, an attitude, a situation in mind, from the beginning, and steer by those successive points to the end."[6] Along with himself, Howells saw Mark Twain and Henry James writing unmistakably American books. He spoke of both friends as realists and masters of language. Howells could and did compete with James, the craftsman whose social and novelistic worlds in certain ways mirrored his own. But the metaphor of the riverboat addresses the common past, the intimacy he felt with the apparently "unliterary" Twain, and the power he saw in Twain's writing.[7] Twain remained so different, so immeasurable, that his work belonged to another order. Perhaps echoing Howells, Ernest Hemingway declared that "all modern American literature comes from one book by Mark Twain called *Huckleberry Finn.*"[8] Howells had gone further, calling Twain "the Lincoln of our literature."[9]

Howells liked to speak about his *two* new friends, Samuel L. Clemens (1835–1910) and Mark Twain—a distinction that has shaped later biographies and commentary on Twain. At the beginning of *My Mark Twain* (published after Twain's death in 1910), he wrote that he would call his subject Clemens "instead of Mark Twain, which seemed always somehow to mask him from my personal sense."[10] The tribute of course bears the title *My Mark Twain,* as though claiming for Howells alone the private man in his public role. To stretch another of his own metaphors, Howells offers a double exposure, two superimposed photographs of a complicated and sometimes baffling man.[11] If Twain is a separate entity, the creation and alter ego of Samuel Clemens, Clemens himself often forgot or elected to blur the distinction, and so did Howells.

Howells' Mark Twain combined the man to whom he became personally, socially, and professionally attached with the character Clemens loved to present: the extrovert who, on their first encounter, appeared so compelling, so much larger than life that Howells scarcely knew whether to hide in embarrassment or join in the antics. In retrospect, it may not have mattered to him that throughout his letters he addressed Twain as *Clemens* (and first reviewed him as *Clements*), or that, except in early letters, his correspondent signed himself "Mark Twain" and soon, simply "Mark." Even with Twain, Howells never put aside the formal signatures "W. D. Howells" or "W.D.H."

The pleasure they took in each other's company led to the sharing of friends. Howells introduced Twain to his wide acquaintance; Twain had already met John Hay as well as Holmes, whose *Autocrat of the Breakfast Table* he and Livy made their "courting book."[12] In Hartford, Howells made friends with the Reverend Joseph H. Twichell, a Congregational minister and Twain's confidante. Persuaded by Twichell and Charles Dudley Warner, along with Harriet Beecher Stowe, Twain settled in Hartford, seeing it as a good place for writing and raising a family. Warner, himself a journalist and part owner of the Hartford *Courant,* had connections with Howells through the *Atlantic* and collaborated with Twain on *The Gilded Age.* Both Warner and his wife Susan, who welcomed Elinor and Howells, remained as close as time and distance allowed.

Twain began to stay over with the Howells family whenever he came to town, and he came often. "I am delighted that you entered so thoroughly into the spirit of our family group," Howells wrote playfully in February of 1875. "[The photograph] shows Mrs. Howells and me in our true relations of domination and subjection. But don't you think I've made a very successful stagger at looking knowing, and as if I just gave way to humor her?"[13] Sometimes with Elinor, more often alone, Howells escaped the magazine to board a train to Hartford, an easy half-day trip. In May 1875, Twain had moved into the mansion he built for his family in Nook Farm, then a rural development on the outskirts of the city. Big and extravagant, the house mightily impressed Howells—always an honored guest—and suited its owner like his sealskin coat.

Howells felt as much at home in Hartford as Twain in Cambridge. Clara Clemens (the one child to survive her father) remembered Howells bringing "cheer into their house as no one else could. Everyone loved him and wanted him to stay a long time. His sense of humor and capacity to show it refreshed the hearts of all. To see him and father enjoy a funny story or joke together was a complete show in itself. . . . I am sure no children ever laughed with more abandon."[14] The reminiscence captures two great humorists together, which is how Twain and Howells saw each other. "I do not know," Twain wrote, "any one else [who] can play with humorous fancies so gracefully and delicately and deliciously as he does. . . . His is a humor which flows softly all around about and over and through the mesh of the page, pervasive, refreshing, health-giving, and makes no more show and no more noise than does the circulation of the blood."[15]

On those visits to Hartford, Howells savored the times when other guests had left and the children had gone to bed. The two men sat up late in Twain's study—not the planned study, but a room above his stable—"smoking the last of his innumerable cigars, and soothing his tense nerves with a mild hot Scotch, while we both talked and talked and talked, of everything in the heavens and on the earth, and the waters under the earth."[16] When Howells retired to his majestic chamber on the ground floor, there would come a predictable knock at the door. Twain's excuse was that he wanted to see him settled before turning off the burglar alarm and did not want his family disturbed if an intruder entered through Howells' window.

Among their mutual friends in Boston, Twain and Howells shared a fondness for Ralph Keeler, like Bret Harte a refugee from California and a popular freelance journalist who worked on *Every Saturday* under Thomas Bailey Aldrich. Years later, after an elaborate lunch with Twain in New York, Howells reminisced in a letter to Aldrich. "And do you remember a lunch that Keeler gave us all at Ober's, where Clemens first appeared among us, and after Fields told a deliriously blasphemous story about a can of peaches, Harte fleered out that this was 'the dream of Mark's life'? Those were gay years, and bless God, we *knew* they were at the time!"[17] Howells admired Keeler's scapegrace daring and quipped that he "wrote the *Vagabond Adventures* which he had lived." Orphaned as a child, Keeler had worked as a cabin boy, bootblack, and dancer. A man of misadventures who could always laugh, he lived by his simple philosophy. He told Howells to put his finger "on the present moment and enjoy it. It's the only one you've got." "I loved him," Howells wrote, remembering that he had published Keeler's book in the magazine and that the man died "during the Cuban insurrection of the early seventies."[18] Keeler did not die in battle; like Hart Crane after him, he disappeared mysteriously from a ship at sea.

Keeler, Twain, and Aldrich and the rest of this circle appealed to Howells because of their boisterous pleasures, which differed from the "long-headed" intellectuality of the Club. They came and went as iconoclasts, neither Boston Brahmin nor New York Bohemian. Unlike the bachelors Howells met at Pfaff's on lower Broadway, the Keeler group—with Keeler himself excepted—were mainly middle-class family men. They might have seen themselves positioned somewhere between the diners at Norton's house and the drinkers at Pfaff's, transients, in Howells' phrase, on "the coast of Bohemia."

In Twain, who sympathized with his ambitions and admired his writing, who was a doting father, supported his extended family, and rescued a feckless brother, Howells found a validation of his choices. Both men married Eastern women higher on the social scale than they themselves. Livy, from upstate New York, grew up with more-than-ample means, a long family tree, and extensive connections, which Twain used and burlesqued. Elinor, from Brattleboro, had family ties beyond rural New England, indeed back to old England, not to mention present-day Washington, DC, where for a term her cousin Rutherford B. Hayes occupied the White House. Twain, while laughing at Elinor's unbridled talk, appreciated her wit, which had an edge lacking in her husband's, and thought of her as a free spirit in tethers. He gave her a blank notebook affectionately inscribed: "I beg to place this copy of my last & least objectionable work before Mrs. Howells with my kindest regards."[19] Howells in turn considered Livy "a delicate little beauty, the very flower and perfume of *ladylikeness*," yet as remarkable in her way as Twain in his.[20] All four were close enough to enjoy friends like Charles Warner and disagree about others, like Henry James or, after Twain broke with him, Bret Harte.

Claiming not to be able to think about Twain separately from Livy, Howells liked him all the more for the quality of their marriage. "Marriages are," as he said, "what the parties to them alone really know them to be, but from the outside I should say that this marriage was one of the most perfect."[21] He thought that their love defined much of Mark Twain. "It was a greater part of him than the love of most men for their wives, and she merited all the worship he could give her, all the devotion, all the implicit obedience, by her surpassing force and beauty of character. . . . I suppose she had her ladyhood limitations, her female fears of etiquette and convention, but she did not let them hamper the wild and splendid generosity with which Clemens rebelled against the social stupidities and cruelties."[22] From the outside, his own marriage after the early years appears at times to have grown if not more testy, then companionable rather than passionate, and more studiously courteous. Henry James teased Elinor about referring to her husband as "Mr. Howells" when speaking to an old friend, and Howells found some truth in a generalization that marriages pass from passionate love to hate and quarrels and then back to love of a more spiritual kind—assuming the man and woman remain true to their bonds.[23] He could not, however, imagine life without the woman he described as half himself and whose loyalty he never doubted.

Howells had a keen sense of privacy and propriety in an age that had not entirely disowned the rule that a lady's name should appear in print only upon birth, marriage, or death. Deep feelings remained for him "inexpressible." The remarks he made as an older man and those of his narrators scarcely convey his affection for Elinor but they do seem consistent with what he wrote as a young man, excepting the urgent appeals in the "Venetian diary" before they married, or the letters from New York before he joined the *Nation*. In *Their Wedding Journey* he says that, no matter how welcome, duty robs life "of the sweetness of even a neglected pleasure."[24]

Neither he nor Elinor left any record that their own relationship remained anything save close and cordial, and, in the years following her death, he would pay her heartfelt tributes when corresponding with friends and family.

Having grown up in poverty, Howells and Twain liked to joke about their wives dragging them kicking and screaming into a mannered and moneyed world. Sallies about henpecking and proprieties grew into routine patter. "Mrs. Clemens received the mail this mor[n]ing, & the next minute she lit into the study with danger in her eye & this demand on her tongue: Where is the profanity [in *Tom Sawyer* that] Mr. Howells speaks of? Then I had to miserably confess that I had left it out when reading the mss. to her. Nothing but almost inspired lying got me out of this scrape with my scalp. Does your wife give you rats, like this, when you go a little one-sided?"[25] She did, and Twain heard about it. When Howells and Twain planned their voyage down the Mississippi, Howells wrote: "About New Orleans, I can't tell. Mrs. Howells is behaving very handsomely about it, and so am I; but the probabilities are that as she would not like to go to N. O. under the circumstances, I shall go to Bethlehem, though she *says* in the noblest way, 'Well, *go* to New Orleans, if you want to so *much*.' (You know the tone)."[26] At another time: "And speaking of Mrs. Howells brings me to New Orleans,— or rather it doesn't."[27] (The *Atlantic* had inaugurated the new year with Twain's series of articles about the Mississippi, "Old Time on the Mississippi," January 1875, written at Howells' urging.) Much like Twain, Howells deferred to his wife on topics from personal whim to social etiquette, and perhaps on matters of business. When he and Twain lost money on a collaboration, he wanted his part of the loss kept secret from Elinor. Twain insisted he had to be careful about showing his writing to Livy, particularly if it contained a "cuss," yet he relied on his wife's judgments about early drafts. Howells relied on Elinor, who listened patiently to his reading, minced no words, and checked his proofs. He also read to Twain, and Twain to him. On this matter Twain allowed that he himself read brilliantly, Howells adequately at best.

The deference to their wives seems tied to the matter of health, or rather, as their husbands said, the lack of it: Howells called Livy and Elinor "tearing invalids."[28] Injured by a fall on ice at age sixteen, Livy suffered for two years before a faith healer gave her the strength to rise from her bed and walk again. Because of her frailty, Livy's father had doubts about trusting her with any man, let alone a rough Westerner. Twain delighted in the story of Jervis Langdon's seeking testimonials about him from California and, receiving no word of support, accepting the brash suitor on his own hunch.

The correspondence between Howells and Twain recounts their wives' constantly changing and often doubtful state of health. Only to Twain, perhaps, could Howells write, "Mrs. Howells salutes Mrs. Clemens from the habitual sick-bed."[29] Medicine had cures for few illnesses, and families often faced chronic bad health. Twain and Howells contended with their own as well as their wives' and children's indispositions. Throughout his letters, Howells reports his recurrent hypochondria, dyspepsia, and sundry ailments and responds to similar complaints from Twain. "I'm ever so sorry to hear of your sickness," he wrote in 1876, "which seems a thing altogether out of character with you, and hardly fair on a man who has made so many other people feel well. How do you pretend to justify it?"[30] Elinor and Livy suffered through long periods of ill health, as baffling in their kinds as in their cures, which made travel, visits, and children into overwhelming burdens.

Twain never lost his awe at having won Livy for his wife. His merriment with Livy's genteel sensibilities suggests that they laughed together and that she set few restraints within the privacy of their home. Twain's role as a repentant if incorrigible curser and hothead remained a long-standing family joke and to some extent a source of pride. "He *has* got a temper," his daughter Susy wrote, "but we all of us have in this family."[31] The mock-censorious role Twain assigned to Livy pokes fun at contemporary prudery like that of Richard Watson Gilder, the *Century* editor (and a friend of both Howells and Twain), who frowned even on the mention of offensive smells or the blowing of noses. Twain admitted to abusing his own innocent editor with language designed to delight his children before Livy censored what he all along intended to cut. "I often joined my supplications to the children's for mercy and strung the argument out, and pretended to be in earnest. . . . But it was delightful and I could not resist the temptation. . . . Then I privately struck the passage out myself."[32] It had not always been this way. Before their marriage he had wanted to bowdlerize one of his favorite books, Swift's *Gulliver's Travels,* to "mark it & tear it until it" was fit for Livy's eyes. "You are as pure as snow, & I would have you always so—untainted, untouched, even by the impure thoughts of others."[33]

In his *Ordeal of Mark Twain,* Van Wyck Brooks faulted Livy and Howells for trying to tame Twain's native genius. Thomas Perry, well acquainted with both Twain and Howells, set him right. "I don't agree . . . that Howells and Mrs. Clemens were of too great influence. . . . I knew Howells very well and know that he was far from being an authoritative person who moved people by force of will. He could gently suggest or amiably persuade in minor matters, and often did, but he was never masterful. Nor was M.T. an easy victim of the authority of others. No, the trimming, the modifications, sprang from his immense love of popularity which was in him from the beginning."[34] In the expectations of readers, or editors like Gilder who had say over book serializations, or the clamor of religious and political groups, censorship touched every kind of writing. When Howells took up scandalous topics or taboo issues such as failed marriage, divorce, and sexual strife, he paid the price with angry reviews. Twain, who goaded readers even as he pleased them, appears—as Perry insisted—to have censored his own writings in response to economic pressures. Like Howells, he made his living by guessing just how far the public could be nudged.

In financial matters, the two might be seen as the hare and tortoise. Twain had trouble walking away from a good deal, especially one that was manifestly too good to be true. He invested in a patent steam generator, a cash register, a mechanical organ, a carpet-pattern machine, and a synthetic food for invalids called "plasmon." Howells introduced him to one of William Cooper Howells' devices, grape shears, though Twain, who lost money on almost all inventions, would have done as well trying to find buyers for the Brooklyn Bridge. The story of his vast losses with the Paige typesetter, which drove him to bankruptcy in the panic of 1893, and the lecture tour that helped recoup his losses have only added to the man's legend. Less of a gambler, Howells steadily made a modest fortune from both his writing and his investments in stocks and real estate.

Twain's material extravagances exceeded Howells' in proportion to his income. The nineteen-room manor he and Livy unblushingly built for themselves in Hartford—partly on profits from *The Gilded Age*—cost nearly two hundred thousand dollars and required six servants and, if Twain did not as usual exaggerate, a hundred thousand a year to maintain. Was this for love of Livy? Were Howells' successively grander houses bought or built for Elinor and the children? Twain and Howells understood one another for their common failings no less than their virtues. Each had something to prove, and neither was above excusing his own indulgences in the name of family responsibilities.

And that reminds me—ungrateful dog that I am—that I owe as much to your training as the rude country job printer owes to the city boss who takes him in hand & teaches him the right way to handle his art.

HIS MARK TWAIN, FROM 1869

I was talking to Mrs. Clemens about this the other day & grieving because I had never mentioned it.

—MARK TWAIN to W. D. Howells, March 23, 1878

In both small and large ways Twain and Howells made their friendship collaborative. Whether struggling to write plays together, planning new books, or editing a manuscript, they depended upon and—with a few exceptions—trusted one another unconditionally. Apart from the friendship itself, the most important of their collaborations may have been the more than seven hundred letters they exchanged during four decades of friendship. The letters reveal the writers as well as such documents can, which is to say that they necessarily leave piecemeal and implicit the nuances, the gestures, the expressions, and the moods of writers long since dead. Words remain as elusive as the individuals themselves, and "evidence" or "documentation" raises as many questions as it answers. What drew and held the two men together? Why did their friendship matter so much to both? How did it survive their long absences and busy careers? And what was it about each that prompted the honest and engaged responses from the other? There are no defining answers to these or any other questions we may want letters (or biographies) to yield. We can appreciate that the openness and intensity of the Twain-Howells correspondence testify to an extraordinary friendship. What Howells wrote of Twain applies also to himself: "Clemens had then and for many years the habit of writing to me about what he was doing, and still more of what he was experiencing. Nothing struck his imagination . . . but he wished to write me of it, and he wrote with the greatest fulness."[35]

Howells, who valued directness, admired it in Twain and responded in kind. His letters to Twain, spontaneous and confidential, have the quality of easy conversation that Twain so valued in his friend's fiction. Whether commentaries on political events, reports of family life and professional work, uninhibited, laughing gossip, or political rants, they read like an epistolary novel, a form he chose for the underrated *Letters Home* (1903). As in any good letters, Howells' thinking unfolds as he writes, a simple complaint or idea growing by association into a larger commentary. He says, to give an example, that he does not feel "natural" writing with pen and ink, then admits that typing letters plagues him more. Henry James, he relates, has begun to dictate his novels, claiming that Howells suggested it. Howells insists he said no such thing and never tried dictation; he would find talking to a human "machine," as James does, pure agony.[36] With its jokes about

James and himself and the final impossibility of any comfortable writing, this one passage raises questions about the new technologies, the differences in writers' approaches, and the whole eccentric process of composition. Howells' correspondence with James ranged widely over family and Cambridge life, books and friends and travel. But he focused largely on their fiction—apart from reassuring or trying to cheer James in later years—and on their shared vision of a greater American literature. In both subject and style, these letters tend to be more "literary" than those to Twain, in the sense of being more composed.

With Twain, Howells could be bluntly direct. Occasionally he complains that without Twain near and able to reply, he finds it burdensome to carry on the written conversation, which represents time and effort borrowed from other projects. He gets irritated or impatient, and he drops his gloves. "Dear Clemens," he writes in November 1875:

> Here is the Literary Nightmare [proofs of an article for the *Atlantic*], which I am going to put in the January, and want back by the return mail. I couldn't give it up.
>
> —I finished reading Tom Sawyer a week ago, sitting up till one A.M., to get to the end, simply because it was impossible to leave off. It's altogether the best boy's story I ever read. It will be an immense success. But I think you ought to treat it explicitly *as* a boy's story. Grown-ups will enjoy it just as much if you do; and if you should put it forth as a study of boy character from the grown-up point of view, you'd give the wrong key to it. I have made some corrections and suggestions in faltering pencil, which you'll have to look for. They're almost all in the first third. When you fairly swing off, you had better be let alone. . . . I shouldn't think of publishing this story serially. Give me a hint when it's to be out, and I'll start the sheep to jumping in the right places.
>
> —I don't seem to like the last chapter. I believe I would cut that.
>
> —Mrs. H. has Mrs. C.'s letter to answer. In the meantime she sends love, and I will send the Ms. of my notice some time this week—it's at the printer's. How shall I return the book MS?
>
> *Yours ever*
>
> *W. D. Howells*

Took down Roughing It, last night, and made a fool of myself over it, as usual.[37]

This letter stems from Twain's appeal to Howells to help dramatize *Tom Sawyer,* a book Twain withheld from the *Atlantic* for financial reasons.

Howells accepts the decision to publish elsewhere, offers his usual supportive critique, and advises like a literary agent.

Putting *Tom Sawyer* or another novel or a new play or spin-off onstage made sense to Howells as to Twain. From his boyhood days in Dayton and again in Columbus and Venice, Howells attended any theater productions he could and continued the habit until, in later years, the effort wore him down. By then he preferred reading plays to seeing them and said he would attend another play only on condition that the actors performed it in his living room. During his years as assistant editor, his writings inclined almost as much toward the theater as to fiction. With Twain's example and prodding, he had agreed to translate *Sansone,* a French play about the biblical hero, for the actor Charles Pope. "As it is owing to your kindness that I'm thus placed in relations with the stage,—a long-coveted opportunity— I may tell you the terms on which I make the version": they included four hundred dollars outright on acceptance, an additional hundred after the play ran for fifty nights, and one dollar a night thereafter for the reminder of its run.[38] The next year, in 1875, one of the country's theatrical impresarios, Lawrence Barrett, approached him about writing what had been too long missing in the theater, an "American hero," or what Barrett imagined as a representative character in search of an author.[39] Howells could be that author; might he be persuaded? Howells scarcely needed persuasion. In the first place, he agreed with much that Barrett said about the wasteland of American drama. He had recently published a scathing review of the theater season in Boston, condemning everything from shoddy writing to exaggerated acting to the displays of female flesh that turned theater into burlesque—though he enjoyed burlesque. Offering to produce the first "genuine American comedy," Barrett more importantly promised heaps of cash.[40]

From afar, Twain guided Howells through his negotiations with Barrett as he had guided the dealings with Pope about *Sansone.* At a time when writers could earn more money from plays than from novels, the author of a popular play stood to make a small fortune. Bret Harte, for example, took an advance of three thousand dollars for the play *Two Men of Sandy Bar,* with the promise of another three thousand in earnings.[41] John T. Raymond's version of *The Gilded Age* netted Twain, on average, a thousand dollars a week. James Fields had challenged Howells to compete with the likes of Harte and Twain. "If *you* can't write a play you aren't the man I take you to be."[42] His collaboration with Barrett resulted in Barrett's performing *A Coun-*

terfeit Presentment about thirty times, beginning with a much-heralded opening at the Grand Opera House in Cincinnati on October 11, 1877. Barrett added to his repertoire Howells' adaptation of Manuel Tamayo y Baus' *Un drama nuevo,* a melodrama titled both *A New Play* and *Yorick's Love.*[43]

Their collaboration proved lucrative but left Howells feeling overworked and hounded by Barrett's demands, to which he surprisingly deferred. He found himself in the role of reluctant apprentice lured on by the promise of riches and wider fame. According to Barrett, Howells' work charmed cultivated theatergoers who found "fine writing and pretty dialogue" as pleasing as complicated plots.[44] When Barrett played at the Boston Museum, for instance, the audience, filled with friends of Howells, positively *"roared"* their appreciation.[45] *Yorick's Love* ran for three weeks at the Museum. From Barrett, Howells learned two main lessons: how the theater worked as a commercial and artistic enterprise and how to write directly for the stage. He later borrowed Barrett's tics and mannerisms for a character in a novel about the theater, *The Story of a Play* (1898).

Although his plays would be staged by professional companies in England and the United States, they lent themselves better to amateur theatricals than to commercial productions. The novelist Booth Tarkington remembered that when he came home from college at Christmas, everyone seemed to be either reading or performing in Howells' most recent play.[46] After the collaboration with Barrett, Howells went on to write the lyrics for a comic operetta, *The Sea Change, or Love's Stowaway* (music by George Henschel), and dramatized his own novels *The Rise of Silas Lapham* and *A Foregone Conclusion;* none of these projects matched the success of *Yorick's Love.*

Playwriting may seem for Howells a kind of busman's holiday, yet he once told Twain that he would "ten times rather write plays than anything else."[47] Twain offered up his own brother as material for a stage comedy: "Orion is a field which grows richer and richer the more he manures it with each new top-dressing of religion or other guano."[48] Howells actually began writing the play before convincing Twain that Orion might find the publicity unwelcome.[49] While he held back from some of Twain's more outrageous suggestions, he had trouble resisting any appeal to collaborate. Twain once sent an actor with what would now be called a concept, asking that Howells turn it into a play. Howells' awareness of Twain's collaboration with Bret Harte and the rancor that followed must have given him pause, however. During the fall and winter of 1876, Twain and Harte had worked on the play *Ah Sin*. By March their friendship was beyond repair. Harte accused Twain, who had lent him money, of being responsible for a number of his financial problems. When Twain offered to pay him twenty-five dollars a week, with board, during his work on another play, Harte fired off a letter of refusal with this final thrust: "I have kept a copy of this letter."[50]

Howells sided with Twain without wholly deserting Harte. The year following the *Ah Sin* episode, he passed on damning letters from Twain about Harte to Rutherford B. Hayes when Harte sought a consular appointment. Having this on his conscience, he recommended Harte the next year for a consulship to Germany.[51] Howells asked Hayes to return his letter, perhaps because he did not want Twain to know about it but more likely because of its candid appraisal of Harte:

> He is notorious for borrowing and *was* notorious for drinking. This is *report*. He never borrowed of *me,* nor drank more than I, (in my presence) and yesterday I saw his doctor who says his habits are good, now. . . . From what I hear he is really making an effort to reform. It would be a godsend to him, if he could get such a place; for he is poor, and he writes with difficulty and very little. . . . *Personally,* I should be glad of his appointment, and I should have great hopes of him—and fears.[52]

Harte soon left the United States for a consulship in Krefeld, Germany, with Twain complaining that he could have stood it had Harte—"a liar, a thief, a swindler, a snob, a sot, a sponge, a coward, a Jeremy Diddler"—been made only "a home official . . . but to send this nasty creature to puke upon the American name in a foreign land is too much."[53] Howells kept discreetly silent.

He succumbed to Twain's offer of a joint venture in 1882. "He seemed always to have the notion of making something more of *Colonel Sellers,*" the character he had already used in a profitable adaptation from *The Gilded Age.* Twain told Howells that his "refined people & purity of speech would make the best possible back ground for this coarse old ass. And when you were done, I could take your MS & rewrite Colonel's speeches & make him properly vulgar & extravagant. For this service I would require only 3/4's of the pecuniary result. (How liberal, how lavish I seem to grow, these days!)"[54] They embarked on *Colonel Sellers as a Scientist,* but, as with *Ah Sin,* what started off well eventually soured. The playwrights' exuberance drove them to devise scientific skits and spoofs that amused them and convinced Twain, sporadically at least, that they had written a good play. John T.

Raymond, the actor who had played the original Sellers with great sympathy, protested the character's transformation into a maniacal scientist who believes himself a British earl. Like those of his authors, Sellers' inventions backfire, literally blowing up and poisoning or crippling bystanders. In the end, the project that was to have brought "big money" cost money and time.[55] When Twain arranged to have it read by the professional elocutionist and ventriloquist Alfred P. Burbank, Howells withdrew, though Burbank convinced Thomas Edison to furnish, at his own expense, a museum of inventions that would "be memorable in the history of the stage."[56] "Here is a play," Howells recalled telling Twain, "which every manager has put out-of-doors and which every actor known to us has refused, and now we go to an elocutioner. We are fools."[57]

The collaboration had as many farcical moments as the play itself. Twain hired the Lyceum Theater unaware that a letter from Howells awaited him. "Withdraw the play *absolutely* . . . on the ground that it needs revision which we can't now give it; making what terms you can *with the manager*."[58] Howells insisted on paying his share of their contracted expenses, and after some wrangling Twain consented, clearly impatient with what he saw as Howells' waffling. Neither man could bear to waste anything he put down on paper or give up the chance of profit. Parodying this practice in *The Undiscovered Country*, Howells has a character explain: "I've taken my letter for a text, and I'm working it over into an article for a magazine. If I were a real literary man I should turn it into a lecture afterwards, and then expand it into a little book."[59] As late as 1899 Howells offered a revised version of their *Colonel Sellers* to the playwright and actor James Herne, whom he met through Hamlin Garland. Celebrated for his "realistic" or understated style of acting, Herne did not object to the play's slapstick qualities as Howells outlined them—"fire extinguisher, phonograph, telephone scene, drunken scene." He did urge Howells and Twain to keep Sellers "sane, and broadened, deepened, softened."[60] Herne refused the play, but parts of *Colonel Sellers as a Scientist*, reluctant to die, eventually found their way into Twain's *The American Claimant*.

According to Howells, "No dramatists ever got greater joy out of their creations, and when I reflect that the public never had the chance of sharing our joy, I pity the public from a full heart."[61] By the time he wrote *My Mark Twain*, he had transformed the wasted effort and the ill will into a tribute to the friendship. The plays he would write with greater social and psychological realism than *Colonel Sellers as a Scientist* never had the depth he achieved in his novels.

I think we may hope for the best he [Twain] can do to help us deserve our self-respect, without forming Mark Twain societies to read philanthropic meanings into his jokes, or studying the Jumping Frog as the allegory of an imperializing republic.

—w. d. HOWELLS, "Mark Twain: An Inquiry," 1901

In the year he worked with Twain on the abortive comedy, Howells wrote to their friend John Hay: "I have lately been at Hartford, and have seen a great deal of Mark Twain. We confessed to each other that the years had tamed us, and we no longer had any literary ambition: before we went to bed we had planned a play, a lecturing tour, a book of travel and a library of humor. In fact he has life enough in him for ten generations, but his moods are now all colossal, and they seem to be mostly in the direction of co-operative literature."[62] Although in the long run Howells and Twain collaborated little in a formal way, they prompted one another to try different kinds of writing or to stick with difficult projects, whether flops like *Colonel Sellers* or international triumphs like *Tom Sawyer*.

Because of Twain—and writing to Twain—Howells broadened his thinking about the ways in which humor worked from the inside out, through character or deeply ingrained traditions or prejudices, rather than through chance situations (the method of their play and some of his early fiction). In a letter of 1880 he would say of *The Prince and the Pauper*, "I think the book will be a great success unless some marauding ass, who does not snuff his wonted pasturage there should prevail on all the other asses to turn up their noses in pure ignorance. It is a book such as *I* would expect from you, knowing what a bottom of fury there is to your fun."[63] When aroused, Twain resembled a dog with a bone, which meant at times a very angry dog. "I warn the reader," Howells wrote, "that if he leaves out of the account an indignant sense of right and wrong, a scorn of all affectation and pretense, an ardent hate of meanness and injustice, he will come indefinitely short of knowing Mark Twain."[64] It was of course Twain who said that "there is more real pleasure to be gotten out of a malicious act, where your heart is in it, than out of thirty acts of a nobler sort."[65] Irreverent, indignant, disruptive, Twain's "fun" had for Howells the moral force of tragedy. It was, like Balzac's, a comment on "the human comedy," if not a plea for equality and social justice.

Whether or not the friends' books continued the dialogue of their letters, they highlight the similarities and quirks of overlapping imaginations. Both men published travel books—Howells' *Venetian Life* and Twain's *Innocents Abroad*—before attempting novels in the early 1870s. Twain, who claimed to detest novels, poetry, and theology, admired Howells' travel writings as much as Howells admired his. Like Howells, he brought the elements of travel writing—following characters from place to place—to novel writing, and Twain too has been criticized for weak plotting. Rafts carry the story line of *Adventures of Huckleberry Finn,* a brilliant pastiche of boy's book, tall tales, and digressions that finally lacks a coherent structure. Howells might have argued that the anarchy of Twain's novel made it most "realistic." Given Twain's glowing memory of *Venetian Life*—"the spirit of Venice is there"—it seems fitting that Howells thought Twain a better writer of autobiographical travel books than of fiction, with the exception of his bitter and visionary social novel *A Connecticut Yankee in King Arthur's Court.* Under "cover of his pseudonym," he writes, "we come directly into the presence of the author, which is what the reader is always longing and seeking to do."[66] Dissimilar as the madcap narrator of *Innocents Abroad* and the sophisticated speaker of *Venetian Life* may be, they have in common their authors' humor, empathy, and never-failing irony.

In their own remarkable ways, Twain and Howells turned the absurdities or wrongs they saw into the subject of their fictions. *A Chance Acquaintance* and *The Gilded Age,* which both came out in 1873, address changes in American society after the Civil War. In 1885 Twain published the American edition of *Adventures of Huckleberry Finn* and Howells *The Rise of Silas Lapham,* books that for many people represent the authors' finest work and that deal directly with the difficult, divisive, and inseparable issues of race and class. *A Connecticut Yankee in King Arthur's Court* (1889), a sequel in its own way to *The Gilded Age,* predates by one year *A Hazard of New Fortunes* (1890), Howells' condemnation of the economic basis of most human exchanges. Twain fired his guns at the aristocracy with *The Prince and the Pauper* (1882), a tale of trading places that anticipates the switching of babies, one white, one black, in *Pudd'nhead Wilson* (1894). Two years before, Howells had brought out *An Imperative Duty,* the story of a woman ignorant of her African American lineage. The year *Pudd'nhead Wilson* appeared, Howells published the first of his utopian romances, *A Traveler from Altruria.*

Twain and Howells were political writers in the sense that they took stands, sometimes unpopular stands. It might be said that their fun fed their fury until life interceded—Howells growing more pointedly political from the 1880s and Twain more misanthropic. Howells thought Twain "romantic" as only disillusioned idealists can be. He recognized in Twain his own compulsion to make the world righter and the same ruthless honesty, which held him accountable and found him wanting.

Howells recalled one evening when he helped Twain through a bout of self-questioning. "I went with him to the horse-car station in Harvard Square, as my frequent wont was, and put him aboard a car with his MS [of *Tom Sawyer*] in his hand, stayed and reassured, so far as I counted, concerning it. I do not know what his misgivings were; perhaps they were his wife's misgivings, for she wished him to be known not only for the wild and boundless humor that was in him, but for the beauty and tenderness and 'natural piety.'"[67] Livy's wish led to Twain's anonymously publishing a serious book about a controversial saint, *Personal Recollections of Joan of Arc*.

For Twain, Howells proved not just an editor or a literary broker but the ideal reader and reviewer. From at least late 1871 or early 1872, when Twain returned to Cambridge, he sent Howells most of his writings. Once Livy passed judgment, the work went to Howells. "Give me your plain, square advice," Twain wrote, "for I propose to follow it."[68] Howells gave advice, which Twain took, and followed the advice with glowing reviews in the *Atlantic*. "The newspaper praises bestowed upon The Innocents Abroad were large & generous," Twain told him in 1875, "but I hadn't *confidence* in the critical judgment. . . . *You* know how that is, yourself. . . . Yours is the recognized critical court of Last Resort in this country; from its decision there is no appeal; & so, to have gained this decree of yours before I am forty years old, I regard as a thing to be right down proud of."[69] Neither Twain nor Howells saw anything unethical in their mutual partisanship; not so Whitelaw Reid, who wrote his acting editor, John Hay, that "It isn't good journalism to let a warm personal friend, and in some matters literary partner, write a critical review of him in a paper wh. has good reason to think little of his [Twain's] delicacy and highly of his greed."[70] His objection to Howells' reviewing *The Prince and the Pauper* would seem reasonable enough, except that Reid's own principles coincided with his dislike of Twain—who had twisted his arm to let a friend, Edward House, review *The Gilded Age*— and that Reid himself had been known to swallow his scruples. "What a splendid success you are making!" Reid assured Howells shortly after he assumed editorship of the *Atlantic*. "I have allowed [as the new *Tribune* editor] more space to notices of *The Atlantic* in advance than my own theories of good journalism would warrant, mainly because it seems to me of all things desirable that so excellent and splendid an attempt at making the best magazine in the world, should be heartily sustained. I do hope that the cash corresponds with the excellence."[71] In the end, Hay chose friendship over his boss and his own scruples, allowing Howells three full columns of Twain puffery.

More than anyone, Twain appreciated Howells' grasp of audience and market, along with his unerring instinct for stylistic problems. As he says in a letter of 1876: "There [never] was a man in the world so grateful to another as I was to you day before yesterday, when I sat down . . . to set myself to the dreary & hateful task of making final revision of Tom Sawyer, & discovered . . . that your pencil marks were scattered all along. . . . Instead of *reading* the MS, I simply hunted out the pencil marks & made the emendations which they suggested."[72] He gave Howells carte blanche to make corrections on the proofs of *Huck Finn*.[73] Howells, whom Twain laughingly called "Pap Finn," asked only that posterity value him as the friend who valued Twain "aright" in their own day.[74]

Twain, who otherwise hated critics, had the sense to recognize—quite apart from Howells' practical help—that his approach to books represented a new and overdue relationship between writer and critic. "As a rule," Twain told him, "a critic's dissent merely enrages, & so does no good; but by the new art which you use, your dissent must be as welcome as your approval, & as valuable. I do not know what the secret of it is, unless it is your attitude—man courteously reasoning with man & brother, in place of the worn & wearisome critical attitude of all this long time—superior being lecturing a boy."[75] What Twain appreciated, writers as dissimilar as Bayard Taylor and James Lowell, Sarah Orne Jewett and Stephen Crane, Henry James and Paul Laurence Dunbar also came to appreciate: that Howells put into words an author's known and sometimes unknown intentions. His reviews deliver not so much judgments as understanding.

To call Twain the genius and Howells the skilled critic or literary broker misses the point. Certainly, his friend saw Howells as an equal: a humorist, critic, and novelist unmatched among American writers. "I have just finished reading the Foregone Conclusion to Mrs. Clemens," Twain wrote in 1874, "& we think you have even outdone yourself. I should think that this must be the daintiest, truest, most admirable workmanship that was ever put on a story."[76] And from Heidelberg four years later: "Look here, Howells, when I choose to gratify my passions by writing great long letters to you, you are not to consider anything but the briefest answers necessary—& not even those when you have got things to do. Don't forget that. A lengthy letter from you is a great prize & a welcome, but it gives me reproach, because I seem to have robbed a busy man of time which he ought not to have spared."[77] In these years, when Twain lived in self-imposed exile, Howells would offer a mild complaint that his friend did not read his books "as much as you ought," which Twain conceded, adding that his travels made reading difficult, in part because of Howells himself. Was it his fault that sneaky "admirers" of Howells hid in hotel lobbies waiting to purloin unattended books?[78]

Despite Howells' peevishness and Twain's facetious reply, both consistently honored the other's work. "You are really my only author," Twain told Howells in 1885. "I am restricted to you; I wouldn't give a damn for the rest," adding by way of contrast that he had "bored through Middlemarch during the past week."[79] He put George Eliot in the same class as Henry James. "I would rather be damned to John Bunyan's heaven," he said, than finish reading *The Bostonians*.[80] Twain saw Howells as an unmatched craftsman. "In the matter of verbal exactness, Mr. Howells has no superior.... He seems to be almost always able to find that elusive and shifty grain of gold, the *right word*." He wrote this late, in a *Harper's* essay of 1906, where he insisted that from the time of *Venetian Life* to a recent essay on Machiavelli, Howells had proved himself the best and most consistent American writer.[81]

If, like Hemingway, John Updike, and Norman Mailer after them, they fostered public personalities (Howells becoming the respected dean of American letters, Twain the gleeful, immensely popular curmudgeon), Howells and Twain were not above calling one another's bluff. Each of us has to face the "black heart's-truth," Howells told Twain after reading his autobiography. "I fancy you may tell the truth about yourself. But *all* of it? The black truth, which we all know of ourselves in our hearts, or only the whity-brown truth of the pericardium, or the nice, whitened truth of the shirtfront? Even you wont tell the black-heart's truth."[82] Here he turned the tables on his friend, a man otherwise "so promptly, so absolutely, so positively, so almost aggressively truthful." Howells spoke personally. He did not consider himself more courageously honest than Twain; if anything, the contrary. He knew that Twain could, "of course," lie, "and did to save others from grief or harm."[83] Acquaintances might associate him with ribaldry and profanity. Howells called him "the most serious, the most humane, the most conscientious of men."[84]

I encountered Sam coming up as I turned the lower corner of the house, & he said . . . a stranger . . . insisted on seeing me—"a stumpy little gray man with furtive ways & an evil face. . . . [who] called me a quadrilateral astronomical incandescent son of a bitch." "Oh that was Howells."

—MARK TWAIN to W. D. Howells, February 13, 1903

As in any long friendship, Howells and Twain created their private myths with self-consciously jesting roles, Howells playing the honest laborer to his friend's impulsive genius, or Twain the slothful or inept or surprised innocent to Howells' sly hypocrite. Howells particularly liked the myth about their shared failures, which began on the day of the country's centennial in July 1876. The two men intended to go from Cambridge to Concord to take a formal part in the festivities. Setting off to catch the reserved train in Boston, they decided instead to take a train directly from Cambridge, where they discovered to their chagrin that trains and all other means of transportation were full. In his affectionate and self-mocking account, Howells reports the consequences:

A swift procession of coaches, carriages, and buggies, all going to Concord, passed us, inert and helpless, on the sidewalk in the peculiarly cold mud of North Cambridge. We began to wonder if we might not stop one of them and bribe it to take us, but we had not the courage to try, and Clemens seized the opportunity to begin suffering with an acute indigestion, which gave his humor a very dismal cast. I felt keenly the shame of defeat, and the guilt of responsibility for our failure, and when a gay party of students came toward us on the top of a tally-ho, luxuriously empty inside, we felt that our chance had come, and our last chance. He said that if I would stop them and tell them who I was they would gladly, perhaps proudly, give us passage; I contended that if with his far vaster renown he would approach them, our success would be assured. While we stood, lost in this "contest of civilities," the coach passed us, . . . and then Clemens started in pursuit, encouraged with shouts from the merry party who could not imagine who was trying to run them down, to a rivalry in speed. The unequal match could end only in one way, and I am glad I cannot recall what he said when he came back to me. Since then I have often wondered at the grief which would have wrung those blithe young hearts if they could have known that they might have had the company of Mark Twain to Concord that day and did not.

We hung about, unavailingly, in the bitter wind a while longer, and then slowly, very slowly, made our way home. We wished to pass as much time as possible, in order to give probability to the deceit we intended to practice, for we could not bear to own ourselves baffled in our boasted wisdom of taking the train at Porter's Station, and had agreed to say that we had been to Concord and got back.

After creeping "quietly into my library" and building a "roaring fire," they regained their courage—temporarily. "With all these precautions we failed, for when our statement was imparted to the proposed victim [Elinor], she instantly pronounced it unreliable, and we were left with it on our hands intact."[85]

The pretended joy in failure, which both men relished, extended from the collapse of *Colonel Sellers as a Scientist* to the never-realized voyage down the Mississippi to a lecture tour with Thomas Bailey Aldrich and George Washington Cable. In the original plan for the tour, they were to meet with other friends and impromptu speakers along the way and to enjoy a private railroad car, "a cook of our own, and every facility for living on the fat of the land." Twain, as "the impresario . . . would guarantee us others at least seventy-five dollars a day."[86] After Howells and Aldrich begged off, that left Cable and Twain, both sensational performers, touring as a pair. Profitable as it was, the tour lost Twain his unbounded affection for Cable, whom he accused of being cheap and hypocritical, the kind of man who stuffs himself at others' expense and starves himself when it comes his turn to pay.[87]

In this, as in every magnificent scheme, Twain had expected Howells to participate with enthusiasm, and his refusal to join the tour and save the Cable friendship, as he might have done, left them with yet another failure— and a real one—to laugh about. Howells himself laughed at Twain's unending efforts to enlist him. At one point, Twain wanted the two of them to edit a kind of collective novel, written by themselves and friends, contributing chapters in turn. Once again Howells turned him down. Later, when he asked for Twain's help with essentially the same project, Twain forgot or chose not to remember his own scheme, telling Howells he had absolutely no interest in such things. The stories of their failures became a way of celebrating their friendship and also a kind of knocking on wood.

Among their failures they could count a partial success, Congress's extension of the copyright law in 1909. No fight engaged them longer. "There is one book better than a cheap book," James Lowell quipped, "and that is one honestly come by:

In vain we call old notions fudge
    And bend our conscience to our dealing;

The Ten Commandments will not budge
  And stealing will continue stealing."[88]

To protect his Canadian royalties, Twain spent two weeks across the border conspicuously fulfilling the country's residency policy. He also registered his pen name as a trademark and formed the Mark Twain Company. Learning from his friend, Howells told Augustin Daly, owner and manager of Daly's Theater on Broadway and the Fifth Street Theater, that he would rewrite a play for two thousand dollars, unless Daly wanted to use his name; then it would cost him more.[89] As a guest of Rutherford B. Hayes at the White House, he persuaded the president to act on copyright legislation—if authors and publishers agreed first among themselves. "Now," he wrote Twain in 1880, "could they not agree on this basis: Englishmen to have copyright if they have an American publisher, and Americans, vice versa . . . ? If some such house as Harpers would send this proposition to all the authors and decent publishers for signature, I believe that it would be universally signed, and that if presented as a memorial to the State Department, it would before this administration goes out, become a treaty."[90] In 1906 the friends—still working to guarantee an author's rights over his or her own work—appeared before the House Copyright Committee (Twain in his signature white suit) to make an argument for extending an author's rights from forty-two years (twenty-eight for the original copyright, fourteen for renewal) to at least fifty. Twain would have preferred to be able to will the rights, like real estate, down through the generations. In that, they failed.

Circling back near the end of *My Mark Twain* to his and Twain's "failures," Howells writes: "From our joint experience in failing I argue that Clemens's affection for me must have been great to enable him to condone in me the final defection which was apt to be the end of our enterprises. I have fancied that I presented to him a surface of such entire trustworthiness that he could not imagine the depths of unreliability beneath it; and that never realizing it, he always broke through with fresh surprise but unimpaired faith."[91] This recognition, expressed by an older man who tended to be self-effacing, captures Howells' notion of Twain as larger than life, someone who, by reason of his own fine nature, in a sense loved mistakenly. The irony also suggests that each knew the other's weaknesses and that the affection—tested at times and strained by distance—overcame any failure because, as both liked to say, they could do anything together.

Howells sensed that his relationship with Twain remained to some extent one-sided. "He glimmered at you," he writes, "from the narrow slits of fine blue-greenish eyes, under branching brows, . . . and he was apt to smile into your face with a subtle but amiable perception, and yet with a sort of remote absence; you were all there for him, but he was not all there for you."[92] The statement may reflect a sense of lost opportunities more than of Twain's absence as a friend; still it speaks to strains in the relationship. It has been argued, for example, that the two men remained friends partly because they saw relatively little of one another.[93] In New York, when they actually lived nearby, they would visit frequently and then for long stretches not at all. Howells bemoaned the missed meetings, though they may have been unavoidable. By then they were older men, not so likely to leave ailing families or test their constitutions with travel.

Yet it may be true that they were at once intimate and distant—distant in the way Howells suggests, which has little to do with physical separation. Twain the storyteller silenced others and indulged himself, making him harder to know and a less consistent friend. Intense and touchy, he could talk through the night or keep himself at a remove, which Howells accepted without liking. "I wrote you a long and affectionate letter just before you left Hartford, and you replied with a postal card; on which instantly forgiving all the past kindnesses between us, I dropped you. You may not have known it but I did. Now I find I can't very well get on without hearing from you, and I wish you would give me your news—what you are doing, thinking, saying."[94] Twain responded in the only way he could: "I was just about to write you, when your letter came—& not on one of those obscene postal cards, either, but reverently, upon paper."[95]

Perhaps Howells felt for Twain more than Twain felt for him. In his *Autobiography,* Twain mentions him only eight or ten times in a book packed full of names. By contrast, Howells rewrote *Literary Friends and Acquaintance* to include Twain (and more oddly, Bret Harte, a man he had reservations about—"you could never be sure of Harte").[96] He was also the first critic to publish a full-length appraisal of Twain's work, *My Mark Twain,* the second half of which reprints his reviews and essays of Twain's writings. On the other hand, Twain's 1906 tribute to Howells matches the enthusiasm of *My Mark Twain* and ends with something like a toast to friendship: "I know by the number of those years that he is old now; but his heart isn't, nor his pen; and years do not count. Let him have plenty of them; there is profit in them for us."[97] The most telling tribute that Twain paid to Howells may be one his friend never read. Near the end of his life, when Twain discovered that his assistant, Ralph Ashcroft, had gained control of his estate with the help of Isabel Lyon—the secretary who, before her marriage to Ashcroft, had hoped to become Mrs. Clemens—he poured out his venom and hurt in unsent letters, all addressed to Howells, the man he trusted most.[98]

Before these tributes, there came from Yale University another, or two others, in the form of honorary degrees. Remembering the Concord Centennial of 1876, Howells asked Twain about his plans for skipping the celebration. "I suppose you are to come up for your degree of Doctor of Divinity when I am to get mine of Doctor of Letters. Now, how can we best avoid being present? We ought, if we try it together, to be able to do something handsome."[99] Neither missed the ceremony, though Howells complained that in the program Twain's name came *first,* and his followed with "and others."[100] Afterward it was, as Mildred Howells remembered, "Doc Clemens" this and "Doc Howells" that, as if they belonged in *Roughing It.*[101] Twain himself would remember the Centennial episode in 1910, just a few weeks before his death. He was in Bermuda, visiting with Joe Howells, and according to Joe he "exulted" in a day that, having gone all wrong, signified everything that was right.

Much of this chapter, like Howells' *My Mark Twain,* has leapt across years and topics well beyond the time when Twain came knocking at the door of the *Atlantic,* and the two unlike men, already delighting in each other's company, strode together through Boston's streets. In the 1870s, successes and joyous failures lay still ahead.

8

FICTIONAL LIVES

1871–1878

We hold the unhappy author to a logical consistency which we find
so rarely in the original; but ought not we rather to praise him where
his work confesses itself, as life confesses itself, without a plan?

—W. D. HOWELLS, "Mr. Henry James's Later Works," 1903

HOWELLS' FIRST NOVEL, *Their Wedding Journey,* appeared in December 1871 (with the 1872 imprint), just in time for Christmas sales.
By December 20 it had essentially sold out. Another thousand copies would
not be available until December 27, and the author, who received royalties
of 10 percent, complained that he might have sold five thousand copies had
his publisher, James Osgood, shown more foresight. "I put the last touches
to Their Wedding Journey a few days ago," he had written James Comly,
in October. "I found a pleasure in writing the thing, though I groaned over
it, too. . . . There's nothing like having railroads and steamboats transact
your plot for you."[1]

Howells had been a traveler, as he said, before he turned "noveller." As the
author of two books on Italy, he knew that the advantage of a fictionalized
travelogue lay in the credible familiarity of a train, boat, or happenstance
pushing his people through time and space. *Their Wedding Journey* reflects
the touristic and autobiographical ease of *Venetian Life,* except that, like

Suburban Sketches, it offers an American scene. Playing with the notion of parallel lives, fictional and personal, Howells takes Basil and Isabel March over ground he and Elinor had covered the previous summer when, after visiting Boston, New York, and Buffalo, they followed the itinerary of his 1860 trip east. He aimed for an almost plotless book, the success of which depended on the realizing of vivid personalities and what he always did well, the creating—or re-creating—of places.[2] For Osgood he sketched a summary of the book. "Hereafter follow descriptions of New York, especially the hottest day of last summer there, the Night Boat on the Hudson; the RR. from Albany to Niagara with a night's pause at Rochester; Niagara— very full; the steamboat ride down the St. Lawrence; Montreal, Quebec, etc., etc. Of course fresh characters and incidents are introduced throughout."[3] Even when Howells came to write radically different kinds of novels and developed more complex approaches to character, he never quite abandoned either tourists' wanderings or understated plots.

Commenting ironically on the ways that Basil March mirrors Howells and Isabel mirrors Elinor, Howells allows the narrator of *Their Wedding Journey* a burlesque version of his own approach to character.

> As in literature the true artist will shun the use even of real events if they are of an improbable character, so the sincere observer of man will not desire to look upon his heroic or occasional phases, but will seek him in his habitual moods of vacancy and tiresomeness. To me, at any rate, he is at such times very precious; and I never perceive him to be so much a man and a brother as when I feel the pressure of his vast, natural, unaffected dulness. Then I am able to enter confidently into his life and inhabit there, to think his shallow and feeble thoughts, to be moved by his dumb, stupid desires.[4]

Instead of "unaffected dulness," contemporary readers of *Their Wedding Journey* found only wit and charm in the portraits of its mature newlyweds. They bicker in the friendly way of married people, with Basil foiled at every turn by Isabel's zany illogicality and her biased knowledge of geography, which places Boston at the center of the universe. (A more impatient William Cooper Howells, wanting more plot, complained that the novel took too long to get the Marches out of Boston.) Just as Howells depicts Isabel as another Elinor—a woman hating to appear foolish or provincial while loving "any cheap defiance of custom"—he gives the Ohio-born protagonist his own affectionate resignation.[5] Variations of Isabel March appear in later novels, in which Howells has fun with combinations of the perfect lady and perfect fool who is often less a fool than the man she loves.

His novels survey the roles life assigns to men and women, as did literature by women of the time, wherein wives dutifully put aside writing tablets and sketch pads to serve their families. "I'm 'Wife'!" Emily Dickinson wrote. "Stop there!" Howells sympathized with the plight of trapped women while seeing social advantages in their position. His narrator in *The Lady of the Aroostook* (1879) explains that women "are seldom forced to commit themselves. They can, if they choose, remain perfectly passive . . . ; they need not account for what they do not do. From time to time a man must show his hand, but save for one supreme exigency a woman need never show hers."[6] Howells often introduces men who condescend lovingly to their wives, and wives whose husbands determine their labor and position. They include couples struggling with the realities of their union as they honor the romance of their youth.

Howells' less satiric side coincided with an eye to sales, for he recommended to his publisher a white, beribboned edition of *Their Wedding Journey* as a suitable gift for new brides. Evidently responding to its amiability more than to its irony, Henry Adams gave a copy of the book to Clover Hooper, his future wife. In a review , he called it "a lover's book [a *virgin*, to borrow his own contraries, rather than a *dynamo*]. It deserves to be among the first of the gifts which follow or precede the marriage offer. If it can throw over the average bridal couple some reflection of its own refinement and taste, it will prove itself a valuable asset to American civilization."[7] Forty-five years later, a man Howells' age said that before and after their wedding, Howells' early novels helped him and his wife to hold hands or swing in the hammock and create the atmosphere of their marriage.[8]

When, in later novels such as *April Hopes* or *The Landlord at Lion's Head*—even to some extent in his next novel, *A Chance Acquaintance*—he depicted love or marriage in terms of social and sexual strife, Howells still touched lightly on the subjugation of middle-class husbands like himself, who see no alternative to getting and spending, and submitting to the mothers of their children. The terrifying *impedimenta,* as Henry James called Howells' children, must be housed and fed, educated and "finished." Notwithstanding that the hard lessons of marriage have little to do with the romance of youth and much to do with *impedimenta,* many of his couples jog along contentedly. As in his fiction, so in his own life: "Love at its best means marriage," he would write at eighty-two, "and is altogether the most beautiful thing in life. It is never self-consciously ridiculous, though often ridiculous enough to the witness. Its perversion is the ugliest thing in life and the shamefullest, but for a day, for an hour of its bliss, one would give all one's other years; yet it does not escape the imperfection which mars everything."[9] His first novel admits the imperfections of marriage in a genial if imperfect world. But at least one male reader of his next, *A Chance Acquaintance* (1873), thought he went too far. Was the husband "good natured and blind" to his wife's deficiencies or did he philosophically shut one eye? The men at his club could not agree. The husband had a perfect understanding of his wife's character, the author explained, loving her "unreason" as much as anything else.[10]

Howells wrote *A Chance Acquaintance* shortly after the publication of *Their Wedding Journey*. "I know that there's good material in the plot," he had told his father in April 1872, as he struggled to avoid caricature at one extreme, high seriousness at the other.[11] Convinced that any successful story needed flesh-and-blood characters, he goes beyond the previous novel in his skepticism and in the barriers he sets up between people. He may allow secondary characters to be united by love and "unreason," but not his central couple, the orphaned daughter of an assassinated Free Soiler and a priggish Bostonian, who struggle through an unsuccessful courtship. In this novel Howells saw himself making a leap forward, expressing through a limited cast of characters what he called "the true spirit of Democracy." The novel announced his coming of age by setting him "forever outside of the rank of mere *culturists,* followers of an elegant literature."[12]

Put another way, *A Chance Acquaintance* allowed him to separate himself from the aristocratic Boston values embodied in his flawed protagonist, Miles Arbuton. Howells presents Arbuton—whom Thomas Perry believed to be modeled on himself—as the kind of snob who can appreciate a landscape only secondhand, through the lens of a critic like John Ruskin. In contrast, the pert and unschooled Kitty responds with her eyes and heart. As Arbuton beholds picturesque waterfalls, she sees both the beauty of the falls and the plight of the local poor. She recognizes the injustice that denies the basic needs of others to promote her own leisure. In the tradition of *Their Wedding Journey,* Kitty remains a traveler, though a socially conscious traveler.

From the beginning of his career, Howells argued that aesthetics must be moored in social and political realities. One of the last ironies of *A Chance Acquaintance* occurs when Kitty mistakes a shopkeeper dressed in Arbuton's damaged overcoat for Arbuton himself. The image reinforces her earlier observation that Arbuton dons his opinions like his wardrobe. He mystifies

Kitty because "he talks of the lower classes, and tradesmen, and the best people, and good families, as I supposed nobody in *this* country *ever* did,— in earnest. To be sure, I have always been reading of characters who had such opinions, but I thought they were just put into novels to eke out somebody's unhappiness. . . . Such things sound so differently in real life."[13]

The larger irony of *A Chance Acquaintance* is that a novel dedicated to "real life" bore the title "Romance of a Summer Month" until Howells realized that potential buyers might confuse it with another author's recently published *Summer Romance*. Poorly as the original title fitted his intent, he meant it to poke fun at sentimental fiction. In Arbuton he drew an unmistakable narcissist, who after thrusting himself between Kitty and an attacking dog, sees the heroine "in the enrapturing light of his daring for her sake."[14] Arbuton's lack of courage keeps the novel from ending as a typical "summer romance," in reconciliation and marriage. When he fails to introduce the shabbily dressed Kitty to his Boston acquaintances, she breaks the engagement. Deciding that the man is "Boston," and that Boston would cut her off from her friends, her past, and herself, she will not let even the acknowledgment of his heroism change her mind.

Howells drew Kitty Ellison from a woman he admired, his sister Annie. An accurate portrayal of Annie's character would, he felt sure, "be the fortune" of his story, and so it turned out.[15] Annie felt flattered, and she probably welcomed a little publicity on the off chance that it might boost her career. But when she wrote an article identifying herself as the model for Kitty, Howells asked her not to publish it, claiming that because he had "fully treated" the subject, she could do no more than repeat him. Adding insult to injury, he offered to compensate her for the loss.[16]

Reviewers, like the *Nation*'s, agreed that the spirited heroine made *A Chance Acquaintance* good enough to promise the great American novel. Those in Cambridge who had met Annie congratulated Howells on catching her spirit. His other sisters, in agreement about the likeness, took the portrait as an insult. Appalled by what they saw as unflattering comparisons between the sprightly Kitty, or Annie, and themselves, they appealed to their father to demand an explanation. Put on the defensive, Howells denied what he had already acknowledged. "Now in regard to my story, and the resemblances you fancy," he wrote his father,

There are some faint outlines of Annie in "Kitty," and I have used her little adventure of coming on without preparation to Quebec. There all resemblance, except of the most casual kind, ceases. The "girls" at Erie are Kitty's *aunts*, represented as 15 or 20 years older; she as born in Illinois. . . . It isn't a question of our girls at all, or of my opinion of them. . . . I beseech you to dismiss forever from your mind the notion that I regard either Vic or Aurelia as inferior to Annie, or had any intention to exhibit them in the Ellisons.[17]

As Howells should perhaps have expected, *A Chance Acquaintance* trod on real and imagined family corns.[18] When Virginia Woolf speculated about the fate of Shakespeare's sister, she had in mind women like Vic and Aurelia Howells (both of whom lost their fiancés and remained in family servitude). Annie benefited from being the youngest of Howells' sisters. She avoided conscription into nursing the troubled Henry and, following her brothers, entered a career in journalism—not without Howells' stringent advice. More doubtful than pleased about her editorship at Chicago's *Inter-Ocean* in 1872, he warned her that working alone in an office of men smacked of immodesty. Understandably irate, Annie complained to Aurelia that his letter brought on a headache. "I told Will that if I gave up my room at the office I would give up my place too, for I *could not* write at my boarding place."[19] His lack of trust struck her as cruel and unfair. "I think no *lady* can be cheapened," she let him know, "except by some act of her own."[20]

Vic, possibly the most talented of the sisters, lived with a passion to write and frustrated ambitions. She never found the opportunities nor, as she made clear, the help to pursue a career, yet she held to her dreams of writing, especially playwriting, through the 1870s. "So at last," she wrote at age thirty-three,

I have launched my frail bark [a play she had written], out on the Sea of literature, with what result, only time can tell. . . . And Oh how much depends on its success. I shall cease to be a household grub and suddenly expand into a brilliant career, floating on the gauzy wings of, well! what? I cannot tell. Only I should be proud to suddenly announce to Father, that I had dramatized a book and it was to be played on the stage, then too how Will would gasp with astonishment. . . . I have been helped so constantly by our dear friend Col. Hinton [a newspaperman and supporter of John Brown]. Ah, that he had been my brother![21]

In 1871, Vic corresponded with the well-known actor Frederic Hugo Robinson, who, after showing initial enthusiasm for her play, rejected it as undramatic. A few years later, she sent Howells a script—possibly a revision of the one she had sent Robinson—asking him to get copyright if he and Elinor liked it. When he expressed reservations, she still pushed for the copyright. "You know I have the greatest confidence in you, as authority on the literary merit of any work, but perhaps an actor might see it in a different light, knowing better than you, or I, what most pleases the popular taste. And Will, above all do take care of my own little ewe-lamb. Those actors are such devouring wolves."[22]

Vic's brilliant career never materialized; not one of her plays found a producer or director. Whether Howells—who promised that if she dramatized a book he would get Mark Twain to promote it—did enough to help, or whether the help would have satisfied Vic, can only be surmised. But the depth of her disaffection can be read in a dream she recounted later in life about keeping her own house in suburban Philadelphia. She pictured Annie writing for a newspaper, Aurelia a commissioned buyer for ladies in the country, and she herself earning money from copying manuscripts. The three would have plenty of help and a garden just big enough for their needs. Will and his little children could board.[23] Not only does Vic relegate her brother to the status of paying guest; she omits Elinor, along with her father and Henry, altogether. Though Howells wondered why he seldom heard from Vic, her silences came as reprieves.

If it's a girl—poor thing—I incline strongly to another family name— Eve. She was a relative—"true, a distant one," as Mark Twain said at the tomb of Adam, but indisputable, all the same, and the name is very soft and beautiful, to my thinking.

—W. D. HOWELLS to William C. Howells, September 22, 1872

As 1872 began, the Howellses might have breathed a self-congratulatory sigh, except for fear of angering the gods. God, as it happened, made up a part of their reading in January—Swedenborg's God, that is, who set conditions as strenuous for life on earth as for entry into heaven. "Swedenborg tells me I shall pass my eternal life in an insane asylum," Howells wrote his father. "This is hard."[24] Theological conundrums aside, he and the rest of the family felt comfortable and well. "Howells *grows* steadily," E. L. Godkin wrote to Norton, "in all ways, for he has become very stout."[25] Elinor, sickly after having had a tooth pulled in April, benefited from a twice-daily concoction of whiskey, beef tea, and milk, and "enough iron to run a machine-shop."[26] She regained her normal weight of ninety pounds.

With Elinor's health improved they thought again of buying their Berkeley Street house, which they had rented for the past two years. Unable to persuade the landlord to sell, they saw an opportunity for something larger and better. In August 1872 Howells wrote his brother-in-law Larkin that he had bought a lot on nearby Concord Avenue, with lovely pines and maples, for thirty-three cents a square foot. By late September the carpenters and bricklayers had everything looking "very large, and very compact, and altogether satisfactory," although the family would not move in until the following summer.[27]

Elinor gave birth on September 26 to their third and last child. The anticipated boy would have taken the name Owain Rhys Howells (Howells laughed with his brother about naming the child "Gwyneth Howells ap William ap William ap Joseph ap Thomas"), so the arrival of a girl presented something of a problem.[28] At odds over Howells' bid for Eve, they settled on Mildred and called her Milly, or Peelah, soon spelled Pilla, a name that stuck. Elinor, despite her small frame and the bearing of an eight-pound baby, had another easy delivery.

The couple greeted each new child with delight. Howells bragged to Mark Twain that Mildred would turn out the prettiest of the lot. Winny remained the smartest, and John, still finding his way, was as good as could be. Elinor kept a scrapbook of her children's sayings and doings, taking pleasure in their self-assurance: "They call me 'The Ogress' in the most innocent way to my face," she wrote.[29] The parents sought to teach their children to find poetry in everyday things. It kept life fresh, as Howells says in *Their Wedding Journey,* for the grown-ups and the children.[30] Winny's autograph book, which she began at age fourteen, bears witness to the kind of household in which the children grew up. Among its signers are Sarah Orne Jewett, Louisa May Alcott, "Members of the Association of Writers and Artists of Spain," and Samuel L. Clemens, who offered the girl these maxims:

1. To be as others are, speak the truth occasionally.

2. To attract attention, speak it frequently.

3. To astonish, speak it all the time.

   This plan works. It has been tried by your friend
   & well-wisher.

Longfellow composed a verse-riddle playing on her name:

> Two sweet words together wed
> Form the name of Winifred,
> Breathing soul into the sound;
> Joy, the winsome first; the Peace
> Following with its soft increase,
> Till the two in one are bound.[31]

The children occupied a world rich in imagination and people. They felt as comfortable in Annie Fields' drawing room as with Tekahionwake, the son of Chief Johnson of the Six Nations, who married a remote Howells cousin—the "demi-semi-squaw," as Howells called her.[32] They knew artists and politicians. As a little girl, Winny had been held in the arms of "Presentdent" Grant, who kissed her. She swore to keep the cheek he kissed "sacred," and did so for half a day.[33]

By tradition the family defined themselves as readers, if not artists, and set apart. "It is a regular Howells gift," Elinor flattered Vic, "—that faculty of seeing more than other people."[34] Howells at once fostered and laughed at the myth of family superiority. Describing the children to his father, he said that "Bua [his pet name for John] has been in doubt lately whether he should be a soldier, a sailor, or an artist; but this morning he came swaggering into the library and said he was not going to be either of those: 'I'm to be *just a common man,*—like you, papa!'"[35] Winny, as the oldest child, perhaps had little choice but to gravitate toward poetry—she especially loved Tennyson—and scholarly pursuits. First following her mother, Mildred chose art, then poetry. John—allowed the most independence of the three—decided early on architecture, and, though he and his oldest child became authors, he went on to design buildings as different as Gothic-capped New York skyscrapers and Mark Twain's Stormfield.[36] (Wanting to call Stormfield "Innocence at Home," Twain finally submitted to his daughter Clara's appeal for an apter name.)

When not attending to the children, Elinor busied herself with house plans and social engagements and tried to keep up with her drawing. Howells set mornings aside for writing and worked at home so that the children had the almost constant attention of both parents. He involved them in his own writing, and wrote with Winny a poem called "A Day in the Life of a Certain Little Girl":

Now—This is the life of
A queer little Girl
Whom Nobody Knows.

The stories he wrote specifically for children (published first in *Harper's
Young People* and partly collected in *Christmas Every Day and Other Stories
Told for Children*, 1893) tell much about his own children as well as their
parents. He begins "Christmas Every Day" with a girl coming into her
"papa's" study and demanding a story. When the father acquiesces, she inter-
rupts. He finally tells her about a greedy little girl who wants Christmas—
not to mention her father's attention—every day. The story ends with the
ogreish mother calling them to breakfast. "What have you been telling that
child?" the mother asks. "Oh, just a moral tale."[37] Mostly humorous, these
"moral tales" move toward rollicking endings with the hapless father laughing and laughed at by his children for his finger-wagging or unoriginal storytelling. "The papa had told the story so often that the children knew exactly what to expect the moment he began. They all knew it as well as he
knew it himself, and they could keep him from making mistakes, or forgetting. Sometimes he would go wrong on purpose, or would pretend to
forget, and then they had a perfect right to pound him till he quit it. He
usually quit pretty soon."[38] Assuming the stories reflect his own household,
Howells must have taken a lot of pounding, and the children, "awfully severe with him[,] . . . made him do exactly what they told him; it was the
way they had brought him up."[39]

At the same time, the Howells children had a sense of their father's importance, reinforced by his habit of reading aloud from his latest book; all
had to make their peace with being the child of a public man and chronic
worker. From habit and need, Howells wrote or prepared to write for several hours each day. One summer, when his hand hurt too much to hold a
pen, Elinor acted as his amanuensis. It could be a strain to write at home,
or to have a husband or father who did not leave each morning for work.
One day, spying her father in the nursery, Mildred remarked: "I didn't *know*
this was your *library!*"[40]

Howells talked with his children as few other fathers did, even sharing
details about the family's finances. The older they grew, the more he told
them about matters such as real estate holdings or negotiations with publishers. He had much to talk about in November 1872, after a great fire swept
through Boston's business quarter, burning for thirty hours and destroying

seven hundred buildings over sixty acres—at a cost of nearly $70,000,000 or well over a billion in today's dollars. Admitting he found a savage beauty in the devastation, he also knew what to expect. The fire and its physical and economic aftermath ruined many businesses in what another witness, George Santayana, recalled as a "financial deluge."[41] Osgood lost $30,000 (now about $500,000) in presses, paper, stock, and plates stored in various printing offices, binderies, and warehouses.[42] Little as Osgood's situation touched Howells, he felt immediately poorer and began to cut expenses.

When he wrote home to Jefferson to say he would not be able to give Sam the $300 to $400 a year he had been sending for emergencies, the family reacted with hurt surprise. Vic seemed the most upset—or most vocal—about the contrasting lives in Jefferson and Cambridge. For years she had longed for a black silk dress, indeed for anything beautiful, and had settled for cutting and resewing her mother's old garments. In her more generous moods, she conceded that whatever either brother sent to them robbed his immediate family, but that did not make up for her own humiliating poverty or the one brother's evident wealth. He appeared to those in Jefferson more prosperous than ever. He had built and would soon move into his own house on Concord Avenue, which, from their perspective, seemed a mansion. Besides, who but the affluent dined at places like the Union League Club, the Parker House, or Delmonico's? In the eyes of people whose biggest annual event might be the honor of driving spikes into the new railroad bed, Elinor and Howells were stepping in very high cotton.

Apart from financial strains and misunderstandings in Jefferson, the Howells family suffered through the winter of 1872–73. John came down with measles, Elinor was sick and housebound for eight months, and Howells himself fell ill with nervous prostration and stomach palpitations. John's illness had worried them, especially when the doctor said that talking in his sleep could be symptomatic of blood on the brain. Howells recalled that his brother Henry's trouble "began in much the same way." Henry's "tonsils remained swollen for years," he wrote his father. "Doesn't it almost seem as if he might have been relieved and restored to sanity, by an operation on the tonsils, which is very common? You know he always seemed to suffer pain in his head."[43] Unlike Henry, John recovered fully, and so did his anxious father, who could now take pleasure in the success of his novel and the completion of his new house.

On July 7, 1873, he moved the family to Concord Avenue. Elinor designed the elegant library, which boasted a frescoed ceiling with walls painted dark red below and papered a dull pale yellow above the chair rail. She had selected heavy chestnut for the bookshelves, drawers, and closets and tile for the fireplace, the mantel of which rose in three broad shelves almost to the cornice. The design of the whole reflected the precepts of the English-man Charles L. Eastlake (the nephew of Sir Charles Eastlake, president of the Royal Academy), the acme of conservative good taste in the 1870s. For weeks whenever Howells entered the library, he looked first at the carved monogram on either jamb of the mantel, which Elinor had painted as a surprise. "I try not to be proud," he wrote Henry James, warning himself not to exult in a house with such tangible signs of success as six bedrooms, servants' quarters, a nursery, a state-of-the-art furnace, hardwood floors, and William Morris wallpaper (which he liked better than Morris' poems).[44]

Three months after the Howellses took possession of their new house, Annie and Aurelia came to stay in Boston. Howells had urged Annie to give up her position on the *Inter-Ocean* to avoid angering the editor of the *Boston Literary World,* who needed her work himself. "I'm quite in earnest on this point," he told her, "and I hope you will yield it to me even if you do not see it in the same light."[45] Annie's correspondence for various Ohio magazines, as well as the New York *Hearth and Home,* earned her eighty dollars a month with which to finance the winter in Boston. Howells wor-ried that the freelancing would barely cover food and other expenses while robbing time from her writing of fiction. Elinor felt that Annie's recent story "Fireworks"—itself turning on a "chance acquaintance"—showed a dra-matic improvement. Soon, she predicted, reviewers would be praising "*Miss Howells* as well as *Mr. Howells* in the magazines."[46] Annie did manage to support both herself and Aurelia in Boston, beating out other reporters in February by interviewing the popular British novelist and Christian socialist Charles Kingsley. After congratulating her on the coup, Howells advised her against further interviewing on the grounds that it appeared undignified.

Perhaps tired of her brother's meddling, Annie returned to Jefferson on May 1, and when President Grant appointed William C. Howells consul at Quebec City in 1874, she joined her father there. She contracted to write letters on Canada for the *New York Tribune,* edited by Howells' friend Whitelaw Reid. Life in Canada proved, for the most part, a happy choice. She and her sisters, recognized as charming hostesses, enjoyed the city's cul-tural life, especially the meetings of a club called Tête-à-Tête. Her family befriended the Spanish diplomat Count Premio Real, who soon collabo-rated with Annie on a collection called *Popular Sayings from Old Iberia,* which her brother puffed in the *Atlantic.* Annie would name her son Louis de Premio-Real William Cooper Howells Fréchette in honor of her father and the count, a man who later baffled friends by committing suicide after a hearty breakfast of fried oysters, eggs, bacon, steak, and potatoes.

Howells hoped that William and the family, once settled on Hamel Street near the ramparts of the walled city, might be self-supporting. The equivalent of less than $30,000 today, his father's stipend of $1,500 a year—the same as his son's in Venice—had to cover the costs of consular entertaining and travel as well as his family's heightened expectations. For immediate expenses, Howells advanced his father all the money he had in the bank. Less generously, he urged Joe to curb William's liberties with the French language and "counseled" William about the respect due his position and himself.[47] "*It is below your office to run about after people,* and it will tire you out, very soon. Remember that the whole U.S. reside with you at Quebec."[48] Squabbles arose between Joe and his sisters, who resented Joe's living, as they put it, rent-free in Jefferson. Always frustrated when drawn into family affairs and anxious when he was not, Howells tried to mediate between his warring siblings. Vic now enlisted his aid.

> We girls have a load of care on our shoulders all the time. What no one but ourselves can feel, because we hide it from all eyes but our own. Poor Henry, is an incessant care but he is so much the greater sufferer and loser that it seems wicked to name him, as a care. But besides this for almost a year Joe has harassed our lives. . . . What has he done? simply cheated us. It's an ugly way of putting it, but it['s] the only way to say it. . . . I can send you the different bills and prove it. But I don't want any body's money but our own. I don't want yours, no matter how much you may have. If we only have *twenty-five* dollars in Jefferson, I don't want *thirty.* But I insist that we ought to have what is our own.

Vic's letter details Joe's salary from the post office and her estimate of his legitimate and frivolous expenses, including dainties for his ailing wife, Eliza. She felt that the family in Quebec were owed at least a hundred dollars, whereas Joe had sent only a box of apples from their own orchard—with freight costs due on delivery.[49] The rift between Joe and his sisters would be repaired by a "memorandum" signed in 1880, which gave him a half interest in the Sentinel building, printing business, and bookstore for the sum of $5,000. He agreed to assume all outstanding debts. No one else would pay as much or sooner, he argued; the mansard roof alone would cost him another $1,000.[50] Being Joe, he could not resist making a joke. If Annie designed a guide to letter writing with sample forms for invitations and business correspondence, or, better, if Will bought the *Atlantic*, paid $20,000 a year for literary talent, a certain amount for paper, printing, and binding, and paid his older brother $10,000 to act as business manager, they would all be in clover.[51]

Joe may have been referring to the sale of the *Atlantic* in the fall of 1873, when Henry Houghton bought the magazine from James Osgood.[52] A fiscal conservative, Houghton did not raise Howells' salary or treat him with great generosity, though he supported his editorial policies and kept the magazine afloat through the rest of the century. "I'm glad to say that the change in ownership makes no difference whatever in my relation to the magazine," Howells wrote James Comly. "I am still 'sole master of the situation.'"[53]

At forty, one has still a great part of youth before him—perhaps the richest and sweetest part. . . . We have learned to smile at many things besides the fear of death. We ought also to have learned pity and patience.

—W. D. HOWELLS, *Indian Summer*, 1886

A few days before the appearance of his new novel, *A Foregone Conclusion*, in late November 1874, Howells became a member of the Saturday Club— a more exclusive but in its way no less intellectual group than the Club.[54] Despite the good relations with men like Norton and Henry James Sr. and his business connections with club members, his election had been doubtful; he had been blackballed twice before. This time, Henry James Sr. brought his name forward, Ralph Waldo Emerson graciously seconded it, and Howells received no blackballs. With this mark of respect, his wife and children healthy and settled, and three thousand copies of his new novel selling in three weeks, he probably enjoyed a happier Thanksgiving than usual.

A Foregone Conclusion speaks to a different world from that of Boston-Cambridge clubs, snobberies, or Mayflower ancestors.[55] An international comedy of manners, it presents Howells' version of the American girl abroad, four years before James' *Daisy Miller*. Howells obviously draws the elements of the story from his own experience. Florida Vervain has come to Venice in search of a better climate for her ailing mother. There she meets the American consul and professional painter Henry Ferris. After Ferris arranges for her to take Italian lessons from a priest named Don Ippolito, she cannot decide what appalls her most: that an agnostic priest (also an inventor of weapons) hears confession, that he feels comfortable in street clothes smoking a cigar, or that he has fallen in love with her.

To this point, the plot seems predictable enough: a woman and two suitors, with one foregone conclusion. Like James' Winterbourne in *Daisy Miller,* Ferris loses the heroine after misinterpreting her kindness toward Don Ippolito; unlike Winterbourne, he reunites with her two years later in a New York gallery where he exhibits his portrait of the now-dead priest. Crippled and chastened by the Civil War, Ferris gets his heiress, and she gets the dubious privilege of reconciling him to the loss of his art.

The setting of Howells' story makes it more than another ironic look at romantic love. In occupied Venice, priests spied for the Austrians, and soldiers of fortune offered the American government their services in the Civil War. The political backdrop of the novel, which invites comparison between the destinies of two republics, Venice and the United States, also connects private lives to official history. The narrator's references to the suppression of the Seminoles in the state of Florida and his skepticism about democratic processes—whether in nations or marriages—qualify the novel's "happy" ending. Had he been true to his purpose, Howells told Charles Norton, he would have ended his story with Florida's rejection of Don Ippolito's grotesque but touching offer of marriage.[56] Instead he resorted to an improbable conclusion resembling Charlotte Brontë's in *Jane Eyre.*

The contrived ending did not, however, hurt the novel's reception. Edmund Stedman summed up the critical acclaim when he congratulated Howells on gradually (he underscored *gradually*) moving toward traditional plotting. "Each of your books has had a little more *story* to it," wrote Stedman, "and this is a story throughout and therefore the best of all."[57] Howells welcomed Stedman's insight, telling him that no man had "ever felt his way more anxiously, doubtfully, self-distrustfully" than he.[58] But it was Twain who best understood his aim. "If your genuine stories can die," he wrote, "I wonder by what right old Walter Scott's artificialities shall continue to live."[59] Not long, perhaps—except in Twain's own elaborately bound set of Scott's works.

James endorsed *A Foregone Conclusion* in both the *Nation* and the *North American Review.* Although no novel could be more different from his own *Golden Bowl,* James might have been describing the style of his late fiction when he praised Howells' "suggestiveness," the ability to present a complete drama about four persons on a narrow stage, "with all glowing Venice for a back scene." James and Howells did not borrow directly from one another; they did use their mutually respectful and reciprocal reviews to sharpen their own writing. James picked up on Howells' "free-stepping" heroines, his concentrated canvas, and "balanced composition."[60] Howells wrote about James' unique voice, the stateliness of his style, and respect for his material. The distinctions characterize their differently weighted novels yet to come.

Somehow the young "novellers" had reached middle age. Howells, overwhelmed by the passing of time, learned in November 1874 of the death of Samuel Smith, the Columbus doctor who had been a second father to him. When writing to his friend and Smith's son-in-law, James Comly, he took the risk of enclosing a check for fifty dollars, money Smith had refused to take years ago when treating his diphtheria. His widow Susan accepted the money with gratitude, all the more, she told him, because it was the first and most likely the last she would receive in acknowledgment of her husband's generosity. Howells' reconnection with the Smiths brought memories of the Columbus years: the night sweats of hypochondria on the one hand, the first meeting with Elinor and the glorious winter they had enjoyed together on the other. The future seemed all promise then. Success had brought its dissatisfactions, the effect of lost time and jaded pleasures. "Cambridge is as sanely and morally organized as it can be," he wrote his father after dining with Longfellow, Holmes, and Norton one night and attending private theatricals at Longfellow's the next; "people are amiable and benevolent, and yet it always leaves a bad taste in the mouth."[61]

He may have had in mind something as innocent as the annual *Atlantic* dinner in December 1874, when the editor in chief played his required role as master of ceremonies. Among the thirty or so magazine contributors various people spoke, and Mark Twain spoke twice. When it came to Howells' turn, he made a joke about the magazine's rejecting his own early contributions. Everyone there knew the story of his progress from the Parker House dinner fourteen years ago to the dinner that evening. And no doubt everyone laughed at his characteristic diffidence—at the idea of the *Atlantic*'s editor turned down by what was now in a sense "his" magazine. Reading about the event in the *Evening Transcript,* Howells felt compelled to correct their account, which implied that he held James Fields responsible for rejecting his early submissions. Aware that Fields would probably have enjoyed the publicity, Howells still needed to set the record straight. "When I mentioned Mr. Fields," he wrote the paper's editor, "I ought to have added that in the vastly greater number of cases, he was quite right in sending back my contributions."[62] Either the strain of the job was telling, or he had lost perspective after years as editor-agent of the *Atlantic*. He saw the problem as the need for privacy. "A great amount of quietness is necessary to the possession of one's soul," as he wrote his father in January 1875, "and to the protection of one's self against one's self."[63]

A more damaging incident occurred in December 1877, when Howells again hosted the *Atlantic* dinner and again overreacted. At this celebration of the magazine's twentieth anniversary—and the seventieth birthday of John Greenleaf Whittier—guests gathered in the new wing of the Hotel Brunswick to work their way through almost as many courses as speeches. The menu, printed the following day in the *Boston Daily Globe*, makes clear the reasons for Howells' expanding waistline and why he considered writing a novel organized around a series of dinners:

Oysters on Shell. Sauterne.

SOUPS
Puree of Tomatoes au Croutons.
Consomme Printanier Royal. Sherry

FISH
Boiled Chicken, Halibut a la Navarre.
Potatoes a La Hollandaise.
Smelts Panne, Sauce Tartar. Chablis

REMOVES
Capon a L'Anglaise.
Rice. Cauliflower.
Saddle of English Mutton a la Pontoise.
String Beans. Turnips.

CHAMPAGNES
Mumm's Dry Verzency.
Roderer Imperial.

ENTREES
Filet of Beef, larded, Sauce Financiere.
Epinards Veloutes.
Vol au Vent of Oyster a l'American.
Squabs en Compote a la Francaise, Tomatoes.
Sautees
Terrapin Stewed, Maryland Style.
Sorbet au Kirsh. Claret.

Broiled Partridges on Toast. Canvasback Ducks.
Water Cresses, Sweet Potatoes, Dressed Lettuce.
  Burgundy.

Charlotte Russe. Gelee au Champagne.
Gateaux Varies.
Confectionery.
Fruit. Dessert.
Coffee.

The after-dinner speeches completed an orgy of self-congratulation, and Howells, the toastmaster, put aside any private criticisms and summed up the jubilant mood of the celebrants: "It was not given to all of us to be born in Boston, but when we find ourselves in the *Atlantic* we all seem to suffer a sea-change, and aesthetic renaissance; a livelier literary conscience stirs in us; we have its fame at heart; we must do our best for Maga's name as well as for our own hope; we are naturalized Bostonians in the finest and highest sense."[64] Charles Eliot Norton, representing the magazine's founding generation, spoke next, followed by Twain, representing the new. And here the problems began.

Twain's talk turned on an opportunistic trio of tramps, called Emerson, Longfellow, and Holmes, who con an old miner. According to Howells, Twain fired one joke after another into a thundering silence. Other witnesses recall it in different ways. Emerson said he had neither heard nor understood Twain's jest, while Francis Child called the speech the richest piece of humor in the world. Howells believed (and several papers reported) Twain to have slighted the guest of honor, insulted the magazine's sponsors, and ruined the evening, and he told Twain what he thought. In fact, he told him more than once and almost browbeat his friend into abject shame. When Twain capitulated and wrote formal apologies, Longfellow replied that he was disturbed only by Twain's personal distress. Holmes brushed over the matter and later wrote a glowing tribute to Twain on the occasion of his fiftieth birthday.

I know whence all your magic came,—
    Your secret I've discovered,—
The source that fed your inward flame—
    The dreams that round you hovered.

Before you learned to bite or munch
　　Still kicking in your cradle,
The Muses mixed a bowl of punch
　　And Hebe seized the ladle.[65]

Why Twain's joking offended Howells—what made him so unforgiving—
is hard to pin down. He had introduced Twain as a humorist "who never
makes you blush to have enjoyed his joke; whose generous wit has no meanness in it, whose fun is never at the cost of anything honestly high and
good."[66] As Howells' labored accounts of the dinner suggest, the problem
ran deeper than simple bad manners or embarrassment. Of the various rules
of etiquette Twain had ignored, Howells wrote, "One was the species of religious veneration in which these men were held by those nearest them,"
another that the men themselves were present.[67] It is of course possible that
Twain intended a little deflation of the men whom Howells praised as gods
and of the praiser himself. Whether Howells feared that he acted no better than Twain on the ill-fated evening, or that Twain somehow exposed
his own hypocrisies about the magazine and its patrons, Twain's performance
depressed him more than he acknowledged.

Whatever his motives, it took Howells years to realize how oversensitive
he had been for his *Atlantic* acquaintances and, worse, how foolishly he had
acted toward his closest friend. In September 1878 he asked Twain: "Have
I offended you in some way? The Lord knows it is my disposition, my
infirmity, to do such things; but if I have done it in your case, I can truth-
fully say that if I had known it at the time, I would not have done it, & if
it were to do again I would not do it—& in any case I am sorry."[68] When,
near the end of his life, Twain asked Howells if he might try his lampoon
on a meeting of newspapermen, Howells dissuaded him. "I do not know
whether he ever printed it or not," he writes in *My Mark Twain,* still trying to sort out his feelings: "but since the thing happened I have often wondered how much offense there really was in it. I am not sure but the horror of the spectators read more indignation into the subject of the hapless
drolling than they felt. . . . To be sure, they were not themselves mocked;
the joke was, of course, beside them; nevertheless, their personality was
trifled with, and I could only end by reflecting that if I had been in their
place I should not have liked it myself."[69]

The time had come for Howells to recover his sense of humor. Apparently aware of his state of mind, he wrote to his father that "There should
be no anniversaries for a man past thirty. . . . Joe sent me a scrap from some

old diary of mine the other day, written on New Years eve of 1853. It was like my dead self speaking to me. Do you remember how you and I used to walk to and from that first house out of Jefferson, and I used to talk of writing a life of Cervantes? It's all immensely melancholy to think about, but no doubt there is a meaning in all this business, which we shall yet find out."[70]

If admission to the Saturday Club had crowned Howells' acceptance by Cambridge literary society, it coincided with growing doubts about his competing roles as editor and novelist. Higginson spoke for many when he complained about Howells' tenure as editor, his changing the course or lowering the standards of the magazine; and while Higginson's reasons may have been personal, the magazine did not flourish economically under Howells' stewardship. Moreover, he *had* been blackballed twice by the Saturday Club. Perhaps he guessed about the gossip Norton, Higginson, and even his friend James engaged in at his expense. "Howells came in to dine," Norton told Lowell in 1874, "plump and with ease shining out of his eyes. He has passed the poetic stage, and bids fair to be a popular American author. As for art in American letters,—recent numbers of the 'Atlantic Monthly' forbid one to think of it."[71] It would have hurt him more to learn that in a particularly unkind mood James had called him a "tertiary talent . . . destined to fade slowly and softly away in self-repetition and reconcilement to the commonplace."[72] By this time Howells had as many reservations about the parochialism of the Cambridge world, about the rivalries of former idols and present friends, as about his own behavior.

When he finally hired an assistant editor, in the late 1870s, he proved, like Fields before him, an exacting boss, even more reluctant than Fields to delegate responsibility. George Lathrop—a man well connected socially, having married Nathaniel Hawthorne's daughter Rose—considered his abilities wasted as assistant editor and, no less than Howells before him, resented being patronized by his editor. Feeling underused and underrated ("a merely mechanical clerk," as he phrased it), Lathrop no doubt imagined himself the next editor of the magazine.[73] His resignation in 1877 surprised Howells. It certainly left him drowning in manuscripts and questioning his own conduct. Whether he or Lathrop bore the blame—most likely both—Howells had lost needed help in less than amicable circumstances. The previous year he had missed his chance of hiring a more compatible assistant. George Gissing, the English novelist, who stayed in Boston in 1876, had been looking for work. He wrote home that the editor and abolitionist William Garrison could get him a job on "one of our best periodicals," by which he meant the *Atlantic Monthly*.[74] As it turned out, the two realists never met, and Gissing came to disparage Howells' writing as too tame by the standards of his own *New Grub Street* and *The Odd Women.*

For all his discontents, Howells had at least one cause to rejoice. Annie Howells, whose move to Canada spelled a new beginning, published installments of her novella "Reuben Dale" (1875–76) in the *Galaxy.* Better yet, she wrote to Elinor in early March, asking her blessing and begging secrecy, even from her brother, about a proposal of marriage from the Canadian poet and journalist Achille Fréchette, who served as translator for the House of Commons in Ottawa. Though she rarely kept secrets from her husband, Elinor did for once wait to tell him. In the meantime she wrote back to offer practical advice. She had a list of concerns: Would Achille encourage Annie's literary aspirations? Did she have a choice as to where they would live? "You *must* tell just as soon as possible. I dont promise to keep another letter from Will. And things must come to a point soon. . . . Would it be thought a good match in Quebec? . . . Is he rich enough to take you to Europe? I'd make that a condition."[75]

Annie told Elinor that she most valued Achille's "exquisite refinement"— a quality lacking in every man who had "pretended" to love her. (Her sister Aurelia once said that she never tired of "refined" people, while coarse people made her physically ill.)[76] Unlike her democratic twin in *A Chance Acquaintance,* Annie valued social distinctions and described Achille as a gentleman in a society where "the lower classes yield to the higher." His Catholicism would not interfere with her religious position since he did not go to confession and had no affection for the Church; they would also be well off with his salary of $1,600 a year and the promise of future promotions.[77] Annie's marriage had several consequences. The responsibility of Henry would be left wholly to her sisters, an issue that troubled her and made Vic more resentful, and the marriage also required giving up her country and bearing children who would be Canadian.

Much as Howells and Elinor worried about losing Annie, they found Achille (whose full name was Antoine Leonard Achille Fréchette) "quiet, cultivated and perfectly natural in his manners."[78] Both approved of her choice. On the day of Annie's wedding (June 20, 1877), Elinor and the children walked down to the shore on the Island of Conanicut, near Newport, and threw three stones into Narrangansett Bay: a red one for health, a yellow for wealth, and a white for domestic peace. Howells, who attended the wedding, sat down with all his siblings for the first time in years.

Very few things are worth as much as they cost.

    —W. D. HOWELLS to Charles Eliot Norton, June 14, 1866

In the aftermath of the 1876 election, Howells had written his father in near despair.

> What an awful week this has been to me. I hardly dare hope yet that we [Rutherford B. Hayes and the Republicans] have carried the election, but unless we are cheated in Florida or Louisiana, it seems probably we have. Grant's having sent troops to both States is applauded by all, and will ensure a fair count. We may not know what the result is till the end of the week. . . . There is no use trying to write about it—I get perfectly frantic. Last night when I went to bed I felt sore from head to foot.[79]

Howells remained through the 1870s a committed Republican; this was perhaps his first qualification for the editorship of the *Atlantic*, which carried the unspoken charge of keeping the magazine a Republican and a national political force. Lincoln's comment about the *Atlantic*'s saving him battles suggests the magazine's sway in the national consciousness and its role in supporting the idealized antislavery, pro-Freedman aims of the party. The *Atlantic*'s editorial policy squared with Howells' aims.

While he sometimes argued with Norton, differed with Lowell and Fields, and, more often, clashed with Higginson about aesthetic issues, Howells shared the founders' broader social values and supported their positions. The *Atlantic*'s political underpinnings might be read in the guest list of an 1874 dinner in Howells' honor. The company included an associate justice of the Supreme Court, Benjamin R. Curtis, who had objected to the court's decision in the Dred Scott case; Thomas C. Amory, a Boston politician; and Horace Gary, chief justice of the Massachusetts Supreme Court. Throughout his tenure with the magazine, Howells remained a "capable Republican partisan," working on a national scale in the spirit of his father, the small-town editor who helped to make presidents. In 1875, he wrote to General Garfield offering him the *Atlantic* platform in the debate over paper money and the gold standard. His friendships with presidents reflected their appreciation of his political writings and his campaign support.[80]

His relationship with Grant—whose presidency Henry Adams and so many others dismissed with contempt—came through his friendship with Twain and from his own *Atlantic* piece "The Next President" (1868). Of course he knew Garfield from boyhood, and Garfield's favors to the family partly repaid those he had received from William. When Hayes won the Republican presidential nomination in 1876, Howells wrote, "We are most glad and happy in it," and Hayes responded, "You don't know how fond we are of managing to let friends know in a casual way that the editor of the Atlantic, the author of &c &c is our Cousin."[81] Fully aware of the scandals that plagued Garfield and Hayes, Howells publicly expressed no doubts about their ethical character. Even faced with Grant's reputation for corruption, he offered his support.

The peak of Howells' Republican partisanship came with the Hayes biography, about which he seems to have been both eager and doubtful. "Dear General, I have just received this letter from my 'owner' [Henry Houghton, the *Atlantic* publisher], proposing something that I confess I felt tempted to propose to him the instant you were nominated. The objection is 'nepotism,' not to say 'Caesarism.' I desire your election far more than any profit the book would bring me; but if you think a biography from my pen would help, and not hurt the good cause, I will gladly go on and write it."[82] Undeterred by the competition of another biography (at least three would be published), Howells took the materials gathered from Hayes, Hayes' family, and Elinor's genealogizing, and finished his "horribly crude" work "in twenty-eight days."[83]

The *Sketch of the Life and Character of Rutherford B. Hayes* appeared with the Riverside Press, otherwise Hurd & Houghton, in mid-September. Its low sales notwithstanding, Hayes appreciated the overstated, underwritten book, and Charles Norton, a staunch Republican (if tentative republican) called it "something more than the best of campaign documents . . . [which] will be read as an excellent story of the life of one of those Americans who in this generation justify our faith in American politics & society."[84] Howells replied that Hayes—who campaigned on the issues of minority representation, better schools, and a reformed judiciary, civil service, and tax system—deserved better than his four weeks' labor. His description of the candidate as "a very brave, single-hearted, firm-willed, humorous, unpretentiously self-reliant man" certainly fits the commanding officer who wrote home after battle pleading with his family to honor the Confederate soldiers, brave if mistaken men who would be citizens once more. At the same time, and fully aware that a book written for a crassly political cause risks hagiography, Howells overlooks any detail harmful to the saintly candidate.

The cottage where William Dean Howells was born, March 1, 1837. Reproduced by permission of William White Howells.

Howells' mother, Mary Dean Howells, whom he described as a handsome woman, with irregular features. Courtesy Herrick Memorial Library, Alfred University.

Howells' father, William Cooper Howells, in 1863, the year before he served in the Ohio Senate. Courtesy Herrick Memorial Library, Alfred University.

Howells the dandy, 1864–65. Courtesy Herrick Memorial Library, Alfred University.

Howells' older brother, Joseph (Joe), printer, editor, and supporter of civil rights. Courtesy Herrick Memorial Library, Alfred University.

Howells and his younger brother Johnny, who died at school while Howells was in Venice. Courtesy Houghton Library, Harvard University.

Victoria (Vic) M. Howells, Howells' closest sister during his teenage years.

Henry, Howells' long-suffering brother, who was cared for by his older sisters. Courtesy Herrick Memorial Library, Alfred University.

Aurelia Howells, 1869, drawing by Elinor Mead Howells: "The most beautiful and most terrible example of self-sacrifice." Courtesy Herrick Memorial Library, Alfred University.

Annie Howells (Fréchette), the model for Kitty Ellison in Howells' *A Chance Acquaintance*.

Elinor Mead shortly before her marriage to Howells. Courtesy Herrick
Memorial Library, Alfred University.

The newlyweds in Paris, 1862. Courtesy Herrick Memorial Library, Alfred University.

Ca' Falier, the Howellses' first residence on the Grand Canal.
Courtesy Houghton Library, Harvard University.

Palazzo Giustiniani, on the other side of the Grand Canal, where the Howellses escaped
their maid Giovanna. Courtesy Houghton Library, Harvard University.

The writer at work in
Venice, a sketch of Howells
by Elinor, 1863. Courtesy
Houghton Library,
Harvard University.

Title page from
Howells' *No Love Lost,
A Romance of Travel,*
with Elinor's illustrations.

Howells in Venice, May 1865, shortly before his return to the United States. Courtesy Houghton Library, Harvard University.

Howells and his family. From left to right: Elinor, Mildred, John, and Winny. Courtesy Herrick Memorial Library, Alfred University.

James Russell Lowell
in 1859, aged forty.
Courtesy Rutherford B.
Hayes Presidential
Center.

Henry Wadsworth
Longfellow. Courtesy
Lilly Library, Indiana
University,
Bloomington, Indiana.

Oliver Wendell Holmes, the "Autocrat of the Breakfast Table." Courtesy Lilly Library,
Indiana University, Bloomington, Indiana.

Annie and James T.
Fields, from contem-
porary daguerrotypes,
1861. Courtesy
the Metropolitan
Museum of Art.

Mark Twain in his
sealskin coat, circa
1869. Courtesy
Houghton Library,
Harvard University.

Mark Twain striking a
pose. Courtesy the
Mark Twain Project,
The Bancroft Library.

Bret Harte, circa 1871, from T. Edgar Pemberton, *Life of Bret Harte,* 1902.

An 1871 portrait of John Hay, secretary of state under McKinley and Roosevelt. Courtesy the Mark Twain Project, The Bancroft Library.

His account reads like a promissory defense of the president whom many suspected of stealing his office. It ends with one defiant word—"a word which has always been the instinct and the principle of the man whose life we have so imperfectly portrayed—'Recte!'"[85]

The biography marked the beginning of the end of Howells' party politics, though not before he had reported to Hayes on the political views and character of various Bostonians and defended Hayes through the charges and countercharges following his one-vote Electoral College victory. In later years Howells came to dismiss the Republicans as a failed party, morally bankrupt like the Democrats. He would take a metapolitical view, writing defiantly about the status of the "masses" (his own word) and about fundamental change in the capitalist system and the conduct of American life. His new politics developed after he left the *Atlantic* and when, like the radicals Laurence Gronlund and Edward Bellamy, he began a personal campaign for social reform. Now, in the late 1870s, he continued to serve the Republican cause and to benefit from it.

With Hayes in office, Howells was approached by the outgoing minister to Switzerland about assuming the post. Howells' mention of the idea brought an impassioned rebuke from Vic. The family would be lucky to get one position, she said. How could he put himself in direct competition with his father, who might lose his consular job in Quebec and hoped, in any case, for a more lucrative post in Toronto? "Every thing we have is wearing out," she told him. "The office to us would be to relieve our actual needs[;] with you, it would be nothing more than a pleasant holiday."[86] She made her point. "I am not going *to ask* nor *to be asked for*," Howells told one of his advocates.[87] After much family hand-wringing and bureaucratic politicking and delays, William's new appointment finally materialized, and he moved to Toronto in 1878 as the United States consul.

William had thought about bringing Sam and his family with him, but in the end saw the wisdom of Howells' argument: "[Sam] has no education to make him useful, and he would load you up with his family and be no end of trouble and expense. Besides, it would be contrary to the spirit of the service for you to employ him. If you wish to help him, it would be far better to pay him $500 or $600 a year outright, and let him stay at home. . . . I earnestly trust that you wont let yourself be governed by a mistaken sense of kindness in the matter."[88] Henry would be liability enough in their new life without including Sam. In Toronto, Vic and Aurelia planned to open their house to the international community, staging musical evenings or literary discussions, and if the teasing letters of Elinor—who would sketch Aurelia in poses affectionately titled "Aurelia fat & saucy," "under a cloud," and "fashionable at forty"—can be taken as a guide, they expected a little courting.

Howells himself, at a difficult crossroads, had begun to look at his life more critically. Henry James chose European exile, and Mark Twain continued to travel, either to escape the costs of living at home or because he remained a chronic wanderer. James' ironic assessments of Cambridge society coupled with Twain's fiery independence worked to increase Howells' disaffection. He did not have a free hand to write his books or express himself without some sort of censorship, his own worst of all. In a few years he would follow James for long stays abroad, visiting England and returning to Italy; and while his stated reasons included escape, boredom, bad health, or search for new materials, the wanderlust he saw in James and Twain was something he also acknowledged in himself. For the moment, however, his escape required him to live within commuting distance to Boston and his office at the *Atlantic*.

9

"FROM VENICE AS FAR AS BELMONT"

1878–1882

> We like Belmont extremely, and I feel an ease and independence here
> that I never did in Cambridge. I am very impressionable, and try to
> live up to people's supposed expectation: that made C. a burden. Here
> there is no literary opinion but my own.
>
> —W. D. HOWELLS to Victoria M. Howells, October 20, 1878

IN 1877 ELINOR HOWELLS began working with her brother Will, an architect with the New York firm of McKim, Mead, and Bigelow, on plans for a new house. The land, a knoll on Holiday Farm in Belmont with a view east toward Boston, belonged to a friend, Charles Fairchild. A wealthy partner in a paper-manufacturing firm, Fairchild had in 1874 provided the twenty thousand dollars that allowed Hurd & Houghton to purchase the *Atlantic Monthly* from James Osgood. This good friend and drinking companion of Osgood and Twain could think of nothing better than having the Howellses as neighbors. At first Howells and Elinor envisioned a modest summer retreat, but, thanks in part to Fairchild's generosity, their plans quickly changed. He agreed to finance the building of the house, which they would then rent for 10 percent of his costs. If and when they sold their Concord Avenue house, they would buy the Belmont property outright.

For several years, Howells had thought about alternatives to Cambridge. Their foray into society had been if anything too successful, so much so that he spoke of being distracted by the waste of "time and substance . . . upon people and things" for which he cared nothing.[1] What with fancy balls, theatricals, fairs, suppers, and informal luncheons, they had so many invitations that Elinor felt overwhelmed, without time or energy to pay the next day's courtesy calls. Try as she did to take drawing lessons with an eye once more to illustrating books, she could never heed Larkin's counsel to commit herself fully to her art. By the beginning of 1876, her ambitions had shrunk to painting a white bureau with flowers, and those "conventional, furniture flowers, and *copied at that!*"[2] There were weeks when the couple spent more evenings out than in, to the chagrin of their children, who complained from the moment they saw their parents dressing to the moment they left. John learned to dread the sound of the closing door.

Howells' profession compounded the busyness of his life. Not only did he work mostly at home; he worked for an organization with a commitment to hospitality. In Elinor's view, which alternated between pride and irritation, her husband's growing fame added nothing to their *Atlantic* income and mightily increased the troops of petitioners and callers. Apart from business connections, there were people they felt obliged to entertain, including a second cousin who (to Howells' annoyance) fled to them from Wellesley College during a scarlet fever epidemic. Less dangerous but still irritating, old and new friends like John Piatt and Hjalmar Boyesen dropped by often enough for Elinor to characterize them as sponges. Other friends, such as John Hay, they genuinely wanted to entertain, and in his case did so with a luncheon for fifty. If they never repeated the extravaganza thrown for Bret Harte, their hospitality grew more elaborate—with one notable exception. When Hay sent the millionaire artist William Waldorf Astor to be fed, Howells consulted with his caterer about pleasing a young man who had everything. On his recommendation they served the simplest possible meal, with great success. Some friends they slighted. They had too few opportunities to see favorites like the Twains and the Charles Dudley Warners— he an extraordinary listener and conversationalist, she a favorite of Elinor's— whose company they missed.

Summers offered a respite when work at the magazine slowed down and lucky acquaintances scattered to lakes and mountains. The Howellses had long flirted with the idea of a place they could live in year-round, a convenient distance from city heat and humidity. The family worried about Howells' health during these months. On a trip to New York City in 1871, he had collapsed and needed to be driven back to his lodgings. It took him weeks after such incidents to regain his health and his confidence to write. Even when healthy, he still had summer deadlines, which meant that he commuted like any executive between his shifting residences and town. Commuting forced him to leave Elinor and the children, sometimes in unpleasant circumstances. During the summer of 1875 they had boarded with an old abolitionist and temperancer Christopher Robinson and his unruly family. Returning the next summer to another lodging, the Howellses found their food rancid, their hostess a "slut," and the landlord a "ruffian." With Howells suffering from heatstroke, the family fled to better accommodations.

Always anxious about time and how he used it, Howells feared his children's growing up too fast. Before Annie's marriage to Achille Fréchette, he and Elinor sent Winny to stay with her grandfather and aunts in Quebec. They wanted her to be fluent in French. Winny came home six months later strangely mature and quiet. The change in his daughter disturbed Howells without raising suspicions about her health or situation. He had evidently felt unconcerned about her living in the same household as Henry, although because of Henry he insisted that his father not take boarders. "I should be to blame if with my knowledge of the matter I didn't press the fact."[3] Knowing that Winny would have to witness Henry's unpredictable behavior, he might have applied the advice to himself.

Some changes came naturally in a girl her age, as William pointed out, telling his granddaughter that she would be a taller, older, wiser, better girl when next they met. Possibly hinting at other problems when she spoke of Winny's unhappiness at school, Annie had recommended that the girl return home. Howells, agreeing to fetch her if Annie believed it necessary, had fretted more about the girl's schooling in French. It seems peculiar that parents who monitored so many aspects of Winny's life hesitated in this situation. From a distance Howells had tried to protect her from dangerous reading, telling Annie, for example, that he considered *Jane Eyre* too "excruciating" and that she should not read such books.[4]

Like most parents, he and Elinor struggled between giving their children freedom to grow and trying to keep them from harm. In the year Winny went to Quebec, they allowed her to submit her poems to various editors, and to their delight she had a sonnet accepted by the children's magazine *St. Nicholas.* The *Tribune* drew attention to the fact that she was *Howells'* daughter. Howells was distraught. "Did you see that disgusting paragraph in the Tribune in which poor Winny and her sonnet were dragged out before the public?" he asked his father. "I don't know when any-thing has vexed me more. We were especially trying not to have any publicity about it, and we shall not let her see the silly notice."[5] No doubt Winny did learn about the paragraph, and Howells, who wanted his daughter's talent recognized—and promoted her work as he would Mildred's—did not anticipate the supposed indignity.

Prompted by Winny's condition, whatever its cause, Howells wanted to make sure his children grew up surrounded by fresh air and natural beauty. Belmont offered the ideal location. Since the extension of the Fitchburg rail line in 1843, Belmont had become a popular destination for day excursions from Boston and Cambridge. Summer estates that might have graced a Tuscan hillside sprang up in the 1850s and 1860s. Accessible by trolley in the 1870s, Belmont, with a population of slightly more than two thousand, attracted such well-heeled vacationers as Elisha Atkins, director of the Union Pacific Railroad; George Fuller, who painted portraits of Elinor's parents and became the subject of a Howells biography; and the family of the painter Winslow Homer. A summer tourist might have seen the sculptor Anne Whitney visiting her family or the actors Edwin Booth and Lawrence Barrett (the producer of Howells' *Counterfeit Presentment*) strolling the streets.

Elinor and Howells met with the architects William B. Bigelow and Charles McKim in July 1877, when the family summered on Conanicut Island near Newport. William Rutherford Mead (Elinor's brother Will) had already sketched preliminary plans. Mead served as man of business and go-between for the project. The main work fell to his partner, McKim, who staked out the land, adapted the original plans, and supervised most of the site preparation. (Howells drew the architect in *The Rise of Silas Lapham* with McKim in mind.)

McKim and Mead are remembered for their collaboration with another partner, Stanford White, who replaced Bigelow in 1879 but had no hand in the building of the Howellses' house. From that year until around 1910, McKim, Mead, and White became the dominant architectural firm in the nation, and the largest. They built monumental edifices such as Pennsylvania Station, Madison Square Garden, and major structures in the World's Columbia Exposition. They also took part in the renovation of the White House and designed sections of the Washington Mall. Each of the partners had distinct gifts. Stanford White (who would be murdered by a jealous husband) specialized in decorative details and interiors. Mead was a shrewd and practical engineeer who, in his own words, kept his partners "from making damn fools of themselves."[6] McKim, known for his innovative layouts, created in the Belmont house a forerunner of hundreds of striking houses in rural settings.

McKim, Mead, and White's early designs, mixing the popular Queen Anne style with American colonial and Japanese features, stressed broad and sometimes gabled roofs.[7] The Howellses' house typified the firm's emphasis on color and bold contrasts, the signature of their so-called Shingle House. Inside they created a dramatic, horizontal space complemented by wide staircases, entryways, pocket and oversized doors, and great stone fireplaces. Howells may have had mixed feelings about the scale of the design. In *Annie Kilburn* (1888) the heroine returns to her native village and finds "herself in a strange world—a world of colonial and Queen Anne architecture, where conscious lines and insistent colours contributed to an effect of posing which she had never seen off the stage. . . . In detail it was not so bad now, but the whole was a violent effect of porches, gables, chimneys, galleries, loggias, balconies, and jalousies, which nature had not yet had time to palliate."[8] Written years later, the novel recalls the design of his own house and the effect it had on him. He could not know that the house would endure. Most of McKim, Mead, and White's early buildings have been lost, but the one built for the Howells family was declared a National Historic Landmark by the Department of the Interior in 1971.

Elinor involved herself with every phase of the construction. She worked with the architects, and her careful attention to the project rivaled that of a contractor. "You'll have to come soon," she wrote her brother, "we must build now or never." She had no hesitation telling him that his "plan was wrong because [he] did not know the lay of the land. House faces east. . . . The magnificent view is towards Boston—directly east."[9] Elinor, "the driving force" behind the project, got what she wanted.[10] With Elinor calling for extra windows or wider rooms or additional exterior space, the house expanded—before and during the actual building. A supplemental bill from Myers, the builder, reads:

Extra 4 inches of thickness of foundation wall $75.00

Addition for Pantry 85.00

Addition to Reception Room 75.00

Extra one foot 8 inches to height of kitchen 10.00

Window in Pantry 9.50[11]

A house that was originally to have neither furnace nor frills got both as the Howellses rethought the purpose of their new residence. In the process they discarded names such as Sub-Hub, Monte Rose, the Parlor Car, and the Spindles, settling on Redtop for a house whose lower story was brick, the second and third sheathed in redwood shingles beneath a red-painted roof. "The shingling is all red," Elinor wrote. "It is red and on top of a hill."[12] Her husband, who according to Elinor talked of nothing but the Belmont house, watched the building almost as carefully as his wife and sounded equally excited. "Back of our house are lovely hill-tops, and gardened slopes," he wrote, "and our road frays off into the most delightful country lane to be found anywhere within a hundred miles of Boston." Then, laughing at his own hyperbole: "You can see Europe from our hill-top."[13] At last the imposing "cottage" loomed on the hillside, a distinctive structure with sweeping rooflines and solid, uncluttered walls.

Though the painter would not leave for another two weeks, the Howells family moved to Redtop on July 8, 1878. The children, proud of their own large rooms, lived in a state of wild delight. They could celebrate birthdays with fireworks, hide in the woods, and explore with newfound abandon. Elinor wrote her brother Will: "This life is going to be a benefit to our children," and the family did appear to come together in the new house. The children made a new passion of baseball and taught their father the vocabulary of "hot balls," "grounders," and "licks"—until another craze called for bows and arrows and straw targets. On most evenings the family gathered in the library to read and talk before father and children tumbled into bed to tell one another stories.

The rent from the Cambridge house paid for expenses and a horse besides. It should come as no surprise that Howells used the story of Winny's new pony for a sketch in the *Atlantic* titled "Buying a Horse," or that Winny's pony turned out to be two. Skilled as a storyteller, Howells faltered as a trader of horses. The first of his purchases, an unmanageable and ill-tempered beast, smashed its buggy against a stone wall and had to be replaced.[14] Winny got her pony; Mildred longed for and got a playhouse, which she named Buttercup Cottage in honor of the character in *H.M.S. Pinafore*. John, who looked likely to become a naturalist, had a range of hobbies, among them the "deadly" passion for collecting butterflies and moths, and he begged for his uncle Will's egg collection.[15] He loved gardening, like his father, who specialized in growing hyacinths under glass.

At Belmont, Howells and his son grew closer, as Howells and his father had grown closer in Columbus. He began to appreciate the boy's temperament and interests, even those he could not share. His kindness as a father can be seen in a piece he wrote entitled "A Perfect Success," in which—

anticipating the storyteller in *A Boy's Town*—he refers to both himself and John as "the Boy." Against his better judgment, Howells let John have an air gun and showed him how to trap squirrels. John grieved over his success, and Howells hid his own guilt by telling him how the poet Wordsworth "had bidden us,—

> Never to blend our pleasure or our pride
>   With sorrow of the meanest thing that feels."

"In this way," Howells writes, the father "put it all on the Boy."[16] His "all" captures the importance he placed on personal responsibility, and he vowed to live more for family and friends. Within two months of moving in, he complained about the number of uninvited friends and other visitors showing up to see the house.

Howells found Redtop good for writing. As in the Concord Avenue house, he worked in an elegant study, this one white-paneled with a carved inglenook and built-in settee for napping. He could read the tags or titles Elinor had painted from favorite authors, such as "Home-Keeping Hearts Are Happiest" or "Far from the Madding Crowd," and if he got restless he gazed out the windows on the south wall across lawns and meadows to the Fairchild house.[17] They had inscribed Shakespeare's line from *The Merchant of Venice* above the library door: "From Venice as Far as Belmont." So far had they come, in miles, in years, in circumstance. In this room, he worked on and put aside *A Woman's Reason* (1883) and took up *The Lady of the Aroostook* (1879) and *The Undiscovered Country* (1880).

These very different books, which range from a comedy of manners to a book William James might have written about "religious experience," have one element in common: they deal with characters struggling to come to terms with themselves and others in indeterminate social spaces or, to twist the Japanese phrase, in their own "floating worlds." *A Woman's Reason,* for example, depends on a fantastic leap of imagination when Howells shipwrecks his hero on an uninhabited South Pacific island. In *The Lady of the Aroostook,* he suspends his characters between continents on a ship sailing from Boston to Europe, which provides a morally nebulous theater at sea. And in *The Undiscovered Country,* begun in 1877, he capitalizes on the public's obsession with spiritualists like the famous table-rapping Fox sisters, setting part of the novel in Boston, part in a rural and to most readers unfamiliar Shaker community.

Howells' fiction shifted in its portrayal of characters as in its investigations of place. The success of Henry James' *Daisy Miller* may have sharpened his analysis of female psychology in *A Woman's Reason* and *The Lady of the Aroostook*. The ironic first title implies (as in Jane Austen's novel) the conflict between good sense and sensibility; the second refers to the heroine's questionable status and to the name of the ship carrying her to her destiny. In these books Howells bent his own rule about writing from knowledge. He did limited research for each book, borrowing one friend's travel journal for *The Lady of the Aroostook* and relying on another's expertise in naval procedure for *A Woman's Reason*. But even if he had been nowhere near Hong Kong or the Pacific islands, he knew enough about social intricacies—on board ship or elsewhere—to write unsettling analyses of men and women in transition.

The lady of the *Aroostook,* Lydia Blood, travels "under the chaperonage of her own innocence" from South Bradfield to Venice—or as her aunt calls it, "Venus"—the journey Howells had taken from his provincial town.[18] The lone woman on board, Lydia of course meets the man she will marry, a Bostonian named Staniford who belongs to the same class as Miles Arbuton in *A Chance Acquaintance*. Lydia comes from a rural village where "there's a decay of the religious sentiment, and the church is no longer a social centre."[19] The last dance had taken place in the town's tavern half a century before, and only one "octogenarian remembers seeing something famous in the way of theatricals on examination-day; but neither his children nor his grandchildren have seen the like."[20] Howells evokes a world passing from history—if not from the fiction of regional writers such as Mary Wilkins and Sarah Orne Jewett—and he suggests that from the loss of local traditions and institutions comes a consequent loss of personal identity. At the close of the novel, Lydia's husband plans to take her to California, a move that will either remake her or place her once again in a condition of *un*belonging. *The Lady of the Aroostook* was during Howells' lifetime one of his most popular novels, selling five thousand copies before publication. James recognized *The Lady of the Aroostook* as Howells' "American-est" novel to date. "Continue to Americanize & to *realize,*" he wrote: "that is your mission;—& if you stick to it you will become the Zola of the U.S.A."[21] With Balzac substituted for Zola, James repeated his "write American" advice to various friends, including Edith Wharton (who set her first novel in eighteenth-century Italy). Europe he claimed for himself.

Howells had moved to Belmont for a simpler, less cluttered life—without giving up the city. Boston continued to be his place of employment and, contrary to the family's expectations, the center of the children's schooling and friendships.[22] Perhaps speaking for himself through his character Kitty Ellison, in *A Chance Acquaintance,* Howells describes Boston as a city "of mysterious prejudices and lofty reservations; . . . of high and difficult tastes, that found its social ideal in the Old World, and that shrank from contact with the reality of this; . . . proud only of the things that were unlike other American things; a Boston that would rather perish by fire and sword than be suspected of vulgarity; a critical, fastidious, and reluctant Boston, dissatisfied with the rest of the hemisphere."[23] A Boston, in other words, that differed as much from Howells' boyhood dream of a sacred, principled city inhabited by slavery-hating republicans as it did from countrified Belmont. Howells looked back at the city from the bucolic perspective of the suburb, resolute in his escape but, as always, ambivalent.

If he expected to be "humanly speaking content," he also begged James Lowell's forgiveness for "leaving Cambridge. Do you know that at the bottom of my guilty heart, I had all along felt that my going was a sort of disloyalty to you? This grieved me, and secretly embittered Belmont. But now that you don't reproach me, I shall like the new home without a pang."[24] The pang, however, went along with the guilt, so much so that he eventually liked his new home less than the old.

Howells would come to see the fulfillment of his dreams as a kind of economic and moral entrapment, a self-imposed exile from the city and a place with its own tragedies. The building of their cottage-castle brought the predictable strained relations and unforeseen problems, not to mention escalating costs. (Redtop cost double its first estimate.) As so often with people who build houses, they got what they wanted and found that it was not what they wanted after all. In what might be viewed as a portent of the Howellses' change of heart, one of John's young friends sledded into an oncoming train. Maimed and in shock, the boy died. Howells, deeply saddened by the accident and feeling helpless, blamed the railroad and lobbied for the construction of a strong wicket gate. "Et in Arcadia ego:" "I, too, am in Arcadia," as Death says in the iconography of pastoral paintings.

The Belmont house, which represented to Howells an imaginary, moneyed equivalent of his father's Eureka Mills, was, though not the last, perhaps the most important of the houses they intended to live in forever. Choosing to belong to a semirural, affluent community "brought home" to him the dilemmas he had struggled with since the years in Ohio. In *The Undiscovered Country,* a novel he would soon write, a character addresses the problem directly: "No man of simple social traditions like mine fits into a complex society without a loss of self respect. He must hold aloof, or commit insincerities,—be a snob."[25] Deeper soul-searching about place and class would come later, with far worse pain.

However fed up Howells might have been with Boston, his identity lay there, in the city he considered snobbish, provincial, and occasionally hostile to himself and his values. Even when he participated in fund-raising for charitable organizations run by the wealthy and socially prominent, he saw the ironies of his position. After congratulating the Boston Ladies' Association for their efforts to educate the discarded children of Rome, he said his good-byes to the president, Mrs. Richard H. Dana, and the secretary, Mrs. Horace Scudder, the wife of a later *Atlantic* editor. Yet Oliver Wendell Holmes spoke shrewdly when he said: "You have brought us an outside element which Boston needed, and have assimilated all that Boston could do for you (If you can be said to have needed anything) so completely that it seems as if you had cheated some native Esau out of his birthright."[26] Consciously or not, Howells had become wedded to Boston even as he exiled himself to Belmont.

The events . . . have the quality of things dreamt, not lived.

—W. D. HOWELLS, *Years of My Youth*, 1916

No matter how dull or monotonous he found the *Atlantic* editorship, Howells could not easily give up the income or find an attractive alternative. At forty-two he was entrenched, respected, and well-off. He might have seen himself as the maker of authors and ambassadors, having secured Lowell's appointment to Spain through his friendship with President Hayes; and acknowledged himself the public man, hosting a testimonial breakfast for his old friend, the Autocrat of the Breakfast Table. As the private man, he had the pleasure in early December of Twain's forgiving company at Belmont.

The public man found himself criticized in 1879 for the "immoral" theme of a Spanish play he had translated. The criticism marked the beginning of complaints that built to a climax a few years later, when his support of Tolstoy and other socialists brought angry derision. The play itself remained a minor item in a list of projects for that year. Howells continued to edit an unsuccessful series for Osgood called *Choice Autobiographies* and worked to finish his new novel, *The Undiscovered Country*. He got nowhere trying to stop the Canadian pirating of his books, most recently *The Lady of the*

Aroostook, which tourists could buy there for half the American price. "It is robbery, pure and simple," he wrote, "a shame and an outrage that the only property which is absolutely created by man should not be protected by law."[27] No American writer solved that problem before the international copyright agreement, still a decade away.

As the old year tolled out, Howells hoped that *The Undiscovered Country,* beginning its run in the *Atlantic,* would make his future. Elinor thought the novel his best yet, and it remained her favorite. An ambitious book, it tries to come to terms with large questions of faith by touching on the topic of mesmerism. Howells may have remembered the sinister mesmerist in Nathaniel Hawthorne's *Blithedale Romance* (1852). Aberrant states of mind continued to fascinate readers. Fourteen years after *The Undiscovered Country,* George du Maurier's spectacularly popular *Trilby* (1894) spawned a craze for anything "Trilby"—from Trilby dolls to Trilby hats and shoes. *The Undiscovered Country* has little of the obvious sexuality that made du Maurier's book a best seller, though Boynton, the heroine's father, is a lesser Svengali whose interest in spiritualism loses him his medical practice, his good name and home, and finally his daughter Egeria. (Her name means a female adviser.) The plot centers on Boynton's hypnotic power over Egeria, whom he has raised to be a medium, and his efforts to engage the Shakers in his extrasensory experiments.

Howells had been fascinated by the Shaker sect since reading F. W. Evans' "Autobiography of a Shaker," which Fields had commissioned for the *Atlantic* in April and May 1869. Like most readers, he knew the Shakers for the style of their feverish praying and their practices of segregating the sexes and adopting orphaned children, as well as for the quality of their produce and brooms. After his six-week summer stay near Shirley, Massachusetts, where he and Elinor attended Shaker meeting each week, he published an article, "A Shaker Village," in the June 1876 issue of the magazine. His article outlines the history, organization, and living arrangements of the community, including the material aspects of Shaker culture: the foods they ate and the books they read. Some read Bret Harte and Mark Twain. Worried that his novel might seem to violate the rules of hospitality, Howells had added a footnote at the beginning of chapter 12 stating that *his* Shakers "are imaginary in everything but their truth, charity, and purity of life, and that scarcely less lovable quaintness to which no realism could do perfect justice."[28] This note did not of course forestall criticism: his novel offended both spiritualists and Shakers.

Taking his title from Hamlet's soliloquy about death and afterlife—"the undiscovered country from whose bourn / No traveler returns"—Howells uses it to incorporate mesmerism, faith, states of grace, religious communities, and the sort of restless and tyrannized souls William James studied for *Varieties of Religious Experience.* In the general exploration of spiritual struggles, the novel focuses on Egeria's efforts to free herself of her father's unnatural control. "If I willed her to put her hand in the flame of that lamp," her father brags, "she could not refuse; neither would she feel any pain, if I forbade her to feel pain. She sees, hears, tastes, feels, whatever I will. She has no being except in my volition, and I have not a doubt that, terrible as it may seem, if I were to will her death, she would cease to breathe."[29] Egeria almost does die, falling into a coma that destroys her extrasensory powers. The loss, coupled with the knowledge of her impending marriage, brings about her father's death. In his melodramatic climax, Howells fulfills the fated struggles and burden of parent-child love, with its mix of devotion and power and certain loss.

Henry James found *The Undiscovered Country* the least entertaining of Howells' novels because of its tone. "You strike me, once you have brought in Shakerism, as not having made quite enough of it—not made it grotesque, or pictorial, or whatever-it-may-be, enough; as having described it too un-ironically & as if you were a Shaker yourself. (Perhaps you are—unbeknown to your correspondents & contributors!!—& that this is the secret of the book!)"[30] If James accurately described Howells' fascination with the Shakers, or even his larger focus on questions about matters of faith, he may not have understood the difficulties of parents and children—James' *impedimenta*—which Howells came to know too well.

On December 28, 1879, another fire struck the Boston office of Houghton, Osgood & Co., with a loss amounting to $1,500,000. Fire hoses did so much damage that axes had to be used to free sodden paper, which had swelled in the bins. Before the debris had a chance to cool, a secretary began notifying customers that all orders would be filled.[31] Howells did his best to assure contributors and readers alike that nothing would stop publication of the magazine. The fire and its devastation might have seemed in hindsight an omen.

In 1880, Winny was sixteen and showing the first obvious signs of decline. That June, Howells left her with friends for a fortnight's stay in Magnolia, Massachusetts, to recover from fatigue. In November, she had a poem, "Magnolia," published in *Youth Companion.* Longfellow sent his congratulations. "Give a kiss to Winny, for me, and tell her that I have read her beautiful poem . . . with uncommon pleasure." Howells reported to his father that the praise had no ill effects: Winny remained "the same simple, good child; only very happy."[32] Her poem, a paean to the recuperative powers of nature, would suggest the opposite, that this was an unhappy child, or at least someone with a young poet's melancholic disposition.

My heart of late had been full sore oppressed
    Vext with some trifling trouble hard to bear;
    But now at length there was an end to care,
And all things seemed to join with me in rest. . . .
Then to my glad heart, lightened of its pain,
    There came this happy thought which here I write;
    And though to others it seem old and trite,
To me it spoke return of hope again;
The breaking waves seem like our troubles sore,
    Which darken ever with their gathered weight,
    Till as we cease to strive against our fate,
Behold they break in foam and are no more!

Winny earned five dollars for her poem. Howells cashed the check for her and—maybe recalling his first visit to the *Atlantic* office—gave her a gold piece, with the advice to spend it frivolously on herself. After much deliberation, she asked him to give it to the destitute ex-slaves flocking into Kansas. Howells did as she asked. By an odd twist of fate he met a man a few years later who knew the story and owned Winny's coin. He had kept it as a lucky piece and, to honor her contribution, sent along his own money instead.

From both parents' accounts, it seems clear that Winny inherited her father's dogged ambition and insistent need for self-improvement. According to Elinor, she drew abundantly and well, a talent she shared with John and Mildred, who became the designated family artist. Until she fell ill, she had none of her younger sister's "bob-tailed" temper, which probably saved Mildred from Winny's self-recriminations. When reprimanded for striking John, Mildred had retorted, "Well, he put me in a *terrible* rage."[33] She also resented Winny's demands, telling her: "You're always asking me to do things for you."[34] Winny was fifteen at the time, and Mildred six, a girl, in her mother's eyes, who managed to do "*everything* well." Elinor announced that "We are beginning to respect Pill a great deal. She is both clever and good, and seems to have a great deal of character."[35]

Maybe sensing that her parents thought her sister the brightest of the children, Winny pushed herself to excel. Even Howells had trouble appreciating that she took more pleasure discussing the theories of John Stuart

Mill than in dancing, and felt comfortable accompanying him to Ashfield, Charles Norton's woodland "cottage," where Norton once a year gathered together those he considered the best and the brightest. "What is she coming to!" Elinor wrote Annie about Winny's reading of Froude's *Caesar* and Bacon's essays.[36] However proud of their daughter's achievements, Elinor and Howells were taken aback by her earnestness. Howells must have forgotten his own obsessive study of foreign languages and literature at a time when books had seemed his life. Probably sensing her parents' contradictory signals to excel and to enjoy herself more, Winny begged her parents not to expect too much of her. Without better answers, Howells would later ascribe his eldest daughter's illness to a kind of family curse or "the cruel inheritance of insufficient nervous force."[37]

In *The Undiscovered Country,* Egeria asks Ford, Howells' fictional surrogate and Egeria's future husband, whether he enjoys the influence a writer has. "It must be a pleasure to feel your power over people." Ford objects that it shocks him to "think of people turned this way or that by . . . [his] stuff." "Then you believe," she insists, "'that we can have power over others without knowing it, and even without wishing it?' 'Oh,' he answered carelessly, 'we all control one another in the absurdest way.'"[38] Egeria fears this truth, as well she should from Howells' point of view. His first letter to his father from Belmont had carried what seems a startling admission. "My own life has been too much given to the merely artistic and to worldly ambition," he wrote. "My morality has been a hand to mouth affair."[39] It was undoubtedly a topic on his mind as he struggled with ethical issues at work, issues of privacy in the gray areas between work and private life, and above all worries about his sick daughter and his own behavior toward her.

He [Osgood] gives me for the story alone as much as I got for a story and all my editorial work, and he leaves me free to live anywhere, and to do any other work I like after the story is finished.

—W. D. HOWELLS to William C. Howells, February 13, 1881

Howells officially resigned his editorship of the *Atlantic* on his birthday, March 1, 1881. He had contracted with James R. Osgood & Co. for a fixed salary of $7,500, in exchange for which he would forgo royalties from the first ten thousand copies of each of his books. With royalties and other investments, he earned about $10,000 a year. The "fifteen years' fret and sub-

stantial unsuccess" had come to an end. "To see a good thing go unwel-
comed, or sniffed at!—The chance came to *light soft,* and I jumped out."[40]
Leaving his job as quietly as he would leave Belmont at the end of the year,
he turned the magazine over to his friend Thomas Bailey Aldrich, who,
over the next eight years, moved it politically to the right while slowly but
noticeably making it more consciously "arty" and certainly less "Howells-
ian." As Houghton had not increased his $5,000 salary in the last eight
years—one reason he was pushed to write novels at the pace he did—and
the editing had long been wearisome to him, it seems remarkable that no
one had lured Howells away before. The new arrangement allowed him to
live anywhere at the same pay he had received for his editing and other
projects together. Osgood had the rights to one book a year in serial form;
Howells kept the copyright, which guaranteed royalties from all subsequent
editions of his books. Any income beyond the terms of the contract he put
directly into his own pocket.[41]

Glorying in his new leisure, he first paid a long-overdue visit to the president of the United States. He had sent numerous letters of regret to Rutherford B. Hayes, who this time offered an inducement Howells did not refuse. Hayes sent Elinor "a magnificently bound set" of her husband's books
issued by the Riverside Press. Now, Howells told his father, he had volumes
of his own books he could not give away.[42] The Howellses visited Washington in May 1880, and in Elinor's words they saw everybody—General
Sherman, the wife of the Marquis de Chambrun, and Lafayette's granddaughter and niece, not to mention (all in one breath) Indians, the John
Hay family, and James Garfield, who complimented Howells on growing
very much like his father.

In letters of the time Howells does not comment on the White House
itself, nor on what might be called the shadow White House behind the
presidential mansion on Lafayette Street, the home of Henry and Clover
Adams. The Adamses had various presidents, including Hayes and the soon-
to-be-elected James Garfield, as neighbors. Henry Adams held Western
politicians, including presidents, to be generally of "mixed ability, cant, vulgarity, and shrewdness."[43] Clover Adams liked Mrs. Hayes' kind, school-
mistressy ways, in spite of the smile that reminded her of "a basket of chips."
She had, Clover said, not a bit of nonsense or vulgarity, and it was touching that she so liked being first lady. The presidential mansion itself, still
unrefurbished, offered no amenities. Clover told of the president and first
lady awakening one night to find their bed overrun with rats, one of which
nibbled at Hayes' toe. Worse, for guests, the Hayeses did not—in deference

to the Prohibitionists—serve wine. Dining at the White House did not improve with the Garfield administration. "To eat one's soup calmly with a coyote springing at you from a pine tree is intimidating," Clover wrote her father, "and ice cream plates disguised as Indian snowshoes would be aesthetic, but make one yearn for Mongolian simplicity."[44] Ohio people like the Hayeses and Garfields tended, as she put it, to be "sensitive about 'stuck up Boston folks.' They sniff at Beacon Street, but I believe even Howells underestimates the [Irish] 'South End.'"[45]

Howells and Elinor stayed a week in Washington. Years afterward he would write an article about their visit that neither Hayes' son, Webb C. Hayes, nor his nephew, Rutherford Platt, found tolerable. Howells destroyed it. Invited by President Hayes in the fall of 1880 to join his family on a two-month tour of the West, he again declined. He could not spare the time. The trip turned out to be Hayes' swan song. He and his wife left Washington at the end of August. The first president to visit California, he journeyed to Yosemite and went as far as Walla Walla, Washington, speaking to well-wishers at each stop. In Sacramento, he deplored the hostility directed at Asian workers. "Whatever difficulties you have here will all work out right if the Anglo-Saxon race will stand on that great principle of equal right of all men. . . . now it is for you . . . to see that . . . American institutions and the American name shall lose nothing at your hands."[46] Perhaps nothing fed Howells' respect for Hayes more than his veto of the Chinese Exclusion Act. Hayes returned to Fremont, Ohio, to cast a vote in the 1880 election for his friend and colleague, James Garfield.

In July the following year, Hayes and Howells, like all Americans, heard of the attempted assassination of the new president. For eighty days, he lay dying from a bullet no one could find to remove. The nation hung on the daily reports and put its faith in Thomas Edison's recently invented metal detector. By a grim coincidence, the president's bed contained another recent invention, coiled-steel springs, which rendered the detector useless. When Garfield died on September 19, Howells worried about the strain on his father, who had supported Garfield for so long and followed the minutest details of his progress.

Worry about his father's response to Garfield's death might have been offset by Howells' honorary M.A. degree from Yale in 1881, and his growing list of honors and accomplishments, had not Winny's worsening health overshadowed everything else. She grew worse at a time when Elinor suffered from an obscure and debilitating back pain as well as bad nerves. Mother and daughter checked themselves into a clinic in Arlington Heights. Elinor responded to treatment, but Winny did not. "So far, nothing really seems to do the child any good," Howells wrote his father in July, "and she is a burden on my heart. I see these days of her beautiful youth slipping away, in this sort of dull painful dream, and I grieve over her. 'Oh, papa, what a strange youth I'm having!' she said once with a burst of tears that wrung my soul. Well, to every one his own care."[47]

In August, despite the attention, the bathing and massages, Winny showed few signs of improvement from the rest cure and its regimen of eight meals a day. Unable to concentrate on anything else, Howells plugged away at his six-hundred-page manuscript of *A Modern Instance*. September found Winny still in bed, and Howells, who employed a nurse to spare Elinor's health, losing patience. "You can't think how tedious this sickness, or no-sickness has been," he told his father.[48] Wanting her up and about, he decided to put her case in the hands of one of her old doctors who would soon be returning from Europe. If she recovered, he proposed to take the family abroad by January 1. At the end of October, he could write his father that Winny had finally made headway. "She is not strong yet; but she is down stairs, she walks out, is cheerful, and seems to be getting rid of her vertigo. Of course she has her ups and downs, and at times is very morbid; but still she is gaining, and gaining fast."[49]

With the unfailing logic of bad health, Winny's remission came just before her father fell desperately ill. Bedridden for seven weeks, he lost twenty-six pounds, his heart beat arrhythmically, and he felt so weak that he dreaded climbing the hill to Redtop. As with his boyhood illness in 1854, Howells himself and others after him have described this episode as a "breakdown," for which his old terms *hypochondria* or *neurasthenia* serve equally well. He also suffered from cystitis, a painful bladder infection, but that and sundry other ailments may have been symptoms of a more general condition. He was a man worn down from the strain of his wife's and daughter's misery and from his writing. Through the previous months, he had worked superhumanly hard, publishing in 1881 both *A Fearful Responsibility, and Other Stories* (based on Mary Mead's stay in Venice) and *Dr. Breen's Practice,* the story of a woman doctor who finds her true vocation in marriage. He had also begun a longer-than-usual novel in *A Modern Instance* (which he temporarily set aside at the point when the protagonist deserts his family), at the same time collaborating with Twain on the frustrating *Colonel Sellers as a Scientist.* He still had unfinished business with the *Atlantic* and took on miscellaneous additional writing to finance the trip to Europe. When he recovered his health to finish *A Woman's Reason* (1883), *Tuscan Cities,* and

The Rise of Silas Lapham (these last two in 1885), the pace of his writing would once more become frenetic.

The changes in Howells' life had their usual effect on the family's housing. Before setting off for Europe they moved back to Cambridge. Howells spoke of saving money and being closer to the doctors treating him and Winny. Their leaving Belmont reads in his letters like an unfinished story, as if they simply lost interest—and the house its magic. Howells would later say that it had been a mistake to take the children so far from Boston. Charles Fairchild reluctantly reclaimed his property as the Howellses turned nomads. At first he boarded alone, until Elinor finished shutting up Redtop. The family joined him in Cambridge at 7 Garden Street before moving to Boston at 16 Louisburg Square. Now it was the cost of the rented house, an old-fashioned Greek Revival building, that made him shudder.

Perhaps nothing made him more aware of fragile health and middle age that winter than the passing of Longfellow. "It is awful," he wrote his father, "to think of his lying in the beautiful old house, which he seemed to fill with his goodness. I can't reconcile myself to his death. I had the sad and curious fortune to ring at the door and ask how he was at almost the moment he died."[50] Howells remembered the times he had let himself into the Brattle Street house with lines of Dante chasing each other in his mind, and now Longfellow was dead. He wondered if "poor old" Emerson even remembered the name of his friend.[51]

From a distance, Howells followed the fortunes of the *Atlantic* under Aldrich (*he* insisted on spending six days a week in the office), and as part of his recovery read as many books as he could by his friend George Washington Cable. He and Elinor were so taken with *The Grandissimes* that they chattered at one another in Creole. Life had settled into manageable routines when Vic and Aurelia began to panic about William's losing his Toronto consulate under Garfield's successor, President Chester Arthur. John J. Piatt, then stationed in Washington for the *Cincinnati Commercial*, confirmed the rumor that Senator John Sherman aimed to get the political sinecure for a friend. Thinking immediately of Mark Twain's friendship with Ulysses S. Grant, Howells begged for help, and he and Twain traveled together from Hartford to New York to meet with the general. When Grant used his influence with the president, Howells could leave the country knowing that his father and siblings had for the moment a secure income.

By the end of January 1882, he could face the practicalities of travel sufficiently to get vaccinated against smallpox. He had endured "great suffering," as he managed to joke, "to which variety of pain gave no charm, or even relief. I got well because there were no more things to have."[52] In February he came down with influenza; then, as he mended, Elinor had her annual spring breakdown. Neither's illness seriously interrupted their preparations for travel.

After years of daily routines and the labor of finishing *A Modern Instance*, Howells needed a break. No doubt with Winny in mind, he longed for Italy as the place of better times, where he and Elinor kept house as newly-weds and where their first child had been born. Beyond the hopes and nostalgia, Italy would of course provide material for future books. In his habitual way, Howells spoke of growing old—at forty-five—and, for this and a string of competing reasons, he questioned the decision to travel almost before he made it: "How I hate to go!" he wrote to Charles Warner and through him to Livy and Mark Twain. "I would almost as soon spend a year in the Western Reserve. I loathe the idea of the voyage, and I despise the pictures and the scenery and the sunsets and the antiquity. But we are going."[53] By this time he and Elinor had recovered, and Winny appeared to be convalescent. As an added incentive, John Hay and his family intended to spend the summer in England and to winter in Florence, where they could meet for a long-postponed reunion.

As I write this I look out on Louisburg Square, where Howells pitched his tent, & I reflect, with envy, that he has the advantage of not wanting to go abroad, finding his native land more than sufficient for literary purposes. He is right in being shy of the dismal fate of trying to live in two countries—in two worlds—at once. There is a woeful intellectual straddle in the attempt, & my poor legs ache with it.

—HENRY JAMES to John Hay, April 5, 1882

At the time of this letter, shortly after his mother's death, Henry James felt the tug of conflicting allegiances. Coming home meant leaving his adopted home, while his mother's funeral added to a reluctance bordering on despair. In 1884 he would return to bury his father; after that he would not cross the Atlantic again for twenty more years. James' letter includes a mild jab at Howells. He knew perfectly well that by giving up his editorship of the *Atlantic,* his friend had jumped bravely from security into the ranks of the unemployed—though of course not the destitute. He also knew that

Howells planned an extended sojourn in Europe, an overdue return for a man who had spent four apprentice years in Venice. Howells never permanently "pitched his tent," in either his places of residence or the settings for his novels, and he had come to share James' reservations about Cambridge, though not yet about American society. He had found his place in Cambridge but changed his "tents" almost as regularly as some people change their clothes. Belonging fed rather than curbed his restlessness, and he had the example of friends like James and Mark Twain to prod him.

One of Howells' consolations through bad health and unsettled times had been the company of James. The two resumed their old walks and talks. People who had seen them ten years before, strolling deep in conversation, might not have recognized either—Howells suddenly thin and sporting a gray beard grown during his illness; James rounded and balding, but with dark brown hair and a darkish brown beard that made him appear "shadowy."[54] They were, in Howells' words, a pair of "badly assorted Siamese twins."[55] For James, Howells represented the reader he wanted to win over—astute, informed, and ready to appreciate narrative innovations. For Howells, James set high standards, giving shape to the majesty and longings he himself had always found in literature.

In 1882 James and Howells might have anticipated their brilliant futures. James had published *The Portrait of a Lady* the previous year, and Howells brought to conclusion his most ambitious novel so far, *A Modern Instance*. Both novels represented what critics hailed as a new school of fiction. Although John Hay assured Howells that authors who had chosen such different scenes (James the European, Howells, in *A Modern Instance,* New England) need not be considered rivals, no one, least of all the principals, believed that. Reviewers at home and abroad frequently coupled their names, prompting Howells' description of himself and James as the mismatched but somehow united twins. The differences that they saw in their own approaches to narrative or character meant little to an observer like Henry Adams, who regarded them as cut from the same mutually complimentary cloth. While subsequent critics have dismissed Howells' realism as too tepid and seen James as a forefather of every literary movement from realism to postmodernism, contemporaries reading their books, at times in the same magazine, noticed striking similarities—not always to James' advantage. In *A Foregone Conclusion* (1875), set in Venice, the reader views Howells' heroine, the American-born Florida Vervain, through the eyes of the dilettante artist and consul Ferris:

She was a girl of about seventeen years, who looked older; she was tall
rather than short, and rather full. . . . In the attitudes of shy hauteur into
which she constantly fell, there was a touch of defiant awkwardness which
had a certain fascination. . . . Miss Vervain seemed sometimes a little bur-
dened by the passionate nature which he [her father] had left her together
with the tropical name he had bestowed in honor of the State where he
had fought the Seminoles in his youth, and where he chanced still to be
stationed when she was born; she had the air of being embarrassed in
presence of herself, and of having an anxious watch upon her impulses.[56]

Daisy Miller (1879) presents the heroine, a cousin to Florida Vervain, from
a similar perspective:

The young lady inspected her flounces and smoothed her ribbons again;
and Winterbourne [another expatriated American with artistic pretensions]
presently risked an observation upon the beauty of the view. . . . There
had not been the slightest alteration in her charming complexion; she was
evidently neither offended nor fluttered. If she looked another way when
he spoke to her, and seemed not particularly to hear him, this was simply
her habit, her manner. . . . [Her face] was not at all insipid, but it was not
exactly expressive; and though it was eminently delicate, Winterbourne
mentally accused it—very forgivingly—of a want of finish.[57]

Individual styles aside, the friends improvised upon each other's themes
and provided a legacy for future writers. In *The Lady of the Aroostook,* the
heroine says, "Sometimes I wondered if I had any real self. I seem to be just
what people made me, and a different person to each."[58] In James' *Portrait
of a Lady,* Madame Merle explains to Isabel: "There is no such thing as an
isolated man or woman; we are each of us made up of a cluster of appurte-
nances. What do you call one's self? Where does it begin? where does it
end?"[59] Other examples suggest the range of their often overlapping topics,
including spiritualism in Howells' *The Undiscovered Country* (1880) and
James' *The Bostonians* (1886); controlling fathers or surrogate fathers in Howells' *A Fearful Responsibility* (1881) and James' *Washington Square* (1881); divorce in *A Modern Instance* (1882) and *What Maisie Knew* (1897); and anarchy in *The Princess Casamassima* (1886) and *A Hazard of New Fortunes* (1890).

As to the question of style, who can make qualitative distinctions between
different but perhaps equally gifted craftsmen, who in a sense played novelistic leapfrog through long careers? Each pushed the other to new heights,

and each looked critically at his own and the other's work. Early sections of *The Portrait of a Lady* set the table, so to speak, for a fortune hunter gobbling up Isabel. "Under certain circumstances there are few hours in life more agreeable than the hour dedicated to the ceremony known as afternoon tea."[60] *The Bostonians* begins in the middle of things: "Olive will come down in about ten minutes; she told me to tell you that."[61] Howells, opening *A Foregone Conclusion* as though it were a cloak-and-dagger melodrama, creates a stage for the seemingly benign yet nefarious events that follow the courtship of Florida Vervain:

> As Don Ippolito passed down the long narrow *calle* or footway leading from the Camp San Stefano to the Grand Canal in Venice, he peered anxiously about him: now turning for a backward look up the calle where there was no living thing in sight but a cat on a garden gate, now running a quick eye along the palace walls that rose vast on either hand, and notched the slender strip of blue sky visible overhead with the lines of their jutting balconies, chimneys and cornice, and now glancing towards the canal where he could see the noiseless black boats meeting and passing.[62]

One word in the first sentence of *Silas Lapham*, "solid," expresses the character and contradictions of Howells' materially driven, steadfast protagonist: "When Bartley Hubbard went to interview Silas Lapham for the 'Solid Men of Boston' series, which he undertook to finish up in 'The Events,' after he replaced their original projector on that newspaper, Lapham received him in his private office by previous appointment."[63] Almost any line in a given Howells or James novel can be used to belie stereotypes about James' long-windedness or scope and Howells' transparent immediacy. In the end, what mattered most to each seems to have been the shared knowledge that another understood the struggle not simply to get words on paper, but to push one's natural talents to the limit.

In their correspondence James tended to be the more pointed critic. "I sometimes wish in this manner [of *The Lady of the Aroostook*] for something larger—for a little more *ventilation*, as it were; but in this case the merit & the charm quite run away with the defect. . . . You are sure of your manner now . . . & you have only to apply it. . . . Don't be afraid, & you will do even better things than this."[64] Howells, who spoke more about his difficulties, especially in bringing a story to conclusion, seldom criticized James' prose, maybe because he did not want to interfere with a writer who had such a distinctive style. As he wrote in an 1875 review of James' *A Pas-*

sionate Pilgrim and Other Tales, "few have the abundance and felicity of his vocabulary" or the exquisite "precision with which he fits the word to the thought."[65] Then again, maybe he knew that, aside from the practical, the best help he could offer was praise. After reading *The Bostonians,* and with *Princess Casamassima* still to be enjoyed, he conceded that the international scene (the setting also of his early novels) "is pre-eminently and indefeasibly your ground; you made it, as if it were a bit of the Back Bay."[66] Not only they themselves but their contemporaries appreciated what they had in common and how they differed in their parallel careers.

To picture Howells' and James' late years, when readers no longer clamored for their novels, when politics and economics and war pushed discussions of literature to the national margin, is to appreciate the poignancy of their meeting in Boston. James would unsuccessfully concentrate on the stage and be hooted at the premiere of *Guy Domville* in 1895; Howells followed the controversial *A Modern Instance* with *Silas Lapham,* and he too would find himself hooted, in his case for political radicalism on the floor of the United States Senate. During that spring of 1882, each man felt himself at last hitting his stride. They would soon spend time together in England, where Howells' defense of James in the *Century* began a testy transatlantic feud about what was and was not American literature, complicating his relations with the English for decades to come. Now, released from editorial responsibilities and with his health renewed, he was ready to devote himself to the writing of novels—and to pass the next year in European travel.

10

IN ENGLAND AND ITALY

1882–1883

> We live in a true fairy-land after all, where the hoarded treasure turns
> to a heap of dry leaves. The almighty dollar defeats itself, and finally
> buys nothing that a man cares to have. The very highest pleasure that
> such an American's money can purchase is exile, and to this rich man
> doubtless Europe is a twice-told tale.
>
> —W. D. HOWELLS, *Their Wedding Journey*, 1872

THE HOWELLSES BEGAN THEIR YEAR ABROAD in late June with a visit
to William Howells and the family in Canada. As the American consul
in Toronto, William held a position that Quebec society honored and that
gave him and his son satisfaction. "Father never seemed to me so dear and
good [as on this visit]," Howells wrote, overlooking past frustrations and
perhaps seeing in his father's good fortune a promise for his own.[1] Leaving
Toronto for Montreal, they picked up the Fréchettes' little daughter, Vevie,
and took the mail boat down the Saint Lawrence to Quebec City. Annie
met them at the dock. "We are here in Quebec at last," Howells reported to
Vic, "—what is left undevoured by the hospitalities of the Count." Count
Premio Real, Annie's wealthy Spanish collaborator, appointed himself their
host, guided them around the old city, and entertained them lavishly, partly
as a courtesy to Annie and Howells, partly because he admired their father.[2]

On July 22, 1882, happy with their Canadian visits and replete with Quebecois cuisine, the Howells family passed through the dockside bustle and boarded their ship for England. Howells could not help recalling his last European departure, when, on that bleak November day in 1861, Quincy Ward had come to see him off. Now, in warm summer weather, family and friends waved from the docks. Achille Fréchette accompanied them a few miles downriver, and Will Mead joined them for the voyage out.

With Annie and the full entourage looking on, the S.S. *Parisian,* horns blaring, smoke belching from its stacks, edged into the Saint Lawrence. Unlike the clumsy *City of Glasgow,* the sleek *Parisian* epitomized speed and luxury and made record time between Quebec and Cork, Ireland, before docking in Liverpool. Except that the children came down with mumps, the family enjoyed an easy journey. Twenty-one years earlier, Howells had arrived in the same port to set off, curious but apprehensive, for London. This time he brought a wife and three children and the wherewithal to travel in comfort. Pleased as he looked back, he told his father that "great improvements have taken place in R. R. travel since I was here, and on applying for it, I got without extra charge, what they call a lavatory compartment. . . . The place was marked with a placard 'Engaged for Mr. Howells' family.'"[3]

They were met in London by the international straddler himself. Henry James took them to their lodgings, which he had described as "dearer than some & cheaper than others . . . in a quiet, salubrious, genteel, but unfashionable situation."[4] A hospitable and a cost-conscious host, James had chosen well. They liked the house on Pelham Crescent in South Kensington, "where our five rooms with private dining-room and exquisite feed cost us only $50 a week." An elegant Georgian terrace house with stucco façade and fronting on a tree-lined park, Howells called it "the prettiest and comfortablest kind of lodging."[5] They found it attractive enough to extend their stay in England until late September.

The British aristocracy, which reads the British novel so little, and the British novel, which derides the British aristocracy so much, are twin monuments whose perfection no foreigner may doubt, under pain of British criticism's high displeasure.

—w. d. howells, *Harper's Monthly,* June 1887

Howells once wrote that "no American complexly speaking, finds himself in England for the first time."[6] If he meant that Americans shared the language or culture of England, he could also have included, for this visit, the friends in London who made the foreign city familiar. A transatlantic community of artists and intellectuals, many of them from Boston, welcomed the Howells family. The *Athenaeum* listed a sampling of Howells' compatriots at a party thrown by his agent and publisher. "A LARGE number of American literary men are just now in London, and were recently entertained by Mr. J. R. Osgood, of Boston. Among the guests were Messrs. W. D. Howells, Henry James, T. B. Aldrich, Bret Harte, John Hay, Moncure Conway, Charles Dudley Warner, Clarence King, and Edwin Booth."[7]

Osgood's hospitality gave Howells a chance to renew his acquaintance with Clarence King, a close friend of the Hays and Adamses who charmed friends and strangers alike. Best remembered as a man of action, the leader of the U.S. Geological Survey and surveyor of the Fortieth Parallel, King had ridden across the continent on horseback to work in the mines of the Comstock Lode. He won Howells' heart the day he arrived in the *Atlantic* office wearing a pith helmet to proofread his *Mountaineering in the Sierra Nevada*. Sharing Howells' love for Cervantes, King collected Spanish art and artifacts, from spangled matador costumes to ecclesiastical ornaments, and when Howells praised his paintings by the contemporary artist Mariano Fortuny, King insisted on giving him one.[8] Living a double life, he was also known as "James Todd," the common-law husband of a black woman named Ada Copeland, whom he installed in a house in Brooklyn; he himself resided at one of his clubs or with friends abroad.

For the past two years James Russell Lowell had served as ambassador to the Court of Saint James, another appointment Howells had helped to engineer through President Hayes. The British admired Lowell so much that when Nathaniel Hawthorne's son, Julian, published a private conversation in which Lowell made apparently anti-British remarks, it was Hawthorne rather than Lowell they denounced.[9] After Lowell's death in 1891, the British press compared him to Chaucer, Shakespeare, Spenser, and Milton, and two years later friends held a memorial service in the Poets' Corner of Westminster Abbey. Leslie Stephen, the father of both Virginia Woolf *and* the *Dictionary of National Biography,* unveiled a bust of Lowell beneath a window featuring his role in the emancipation of slaves. More personally, he paid homage to the man he had asked to be Virginia's godfather.

Very much alive in 1882, Lowell entertained his visiting friends. "Lowell took me to [Prime Minister] Gladstone's reception," Howells told his father, "and next week he dines me to meet swells, who it seems wish to see me."[10] Elinor triumphed, winning Lowell's admission that Annie's Count Premio Real was as real as his name. "Lowell, who is awfully schoolmasterish [people couldn't believe anyone dared call him 'Jim'], would have it that Premio Real must be a Count of a very new creation—because he was stationed in Canada as Consul. . . . But afterwards finding his credentials in some Spanish official guide he wrote a charming note in which he said he would eat any amount of humble pie I would prescribe."[11]

As the *Athenaeum* notice suggests, Elinor and Howells crossed paths with people like Moncure Conway, the man who supported Howells for his consulship and fled to Venice after negotiating with Confederates during the Civil War. Conway pursued an active career as editor, novelist, and reviewer. Other countrymen they met for the first time. On a visit to Cambridge, Howells got to know the New York–born Charles Waldstein, a respected classicist at Cambridge University with a passion for ancient Greek plays, which he staged, and for modern fiction, particularly Howells' *A Modern Instance*.

Soon English connections outnumbered American. Elinor's letters from Europe show how much they crammed into their stay: "Charles D. Warner lunched with us," she wrote her father-in-law. "Monday we go to Mrs Anna Lea Merritt's to meet [the painter] Holman Hunt . . . and this Saturday we all lunch with Green the historian. He is far gone in consumption. [John Richard Green had written a history of Venice that Howells probably read for *Venetian Life*.] I have just refused an invitation to the [publisher] Kegan-Paul's as our time is so taken up that we cant go to see sights. . . . Mrs Conway has invited us for the 12th to meet Mrs William Morris at dinner—a thing I greatly desire."[12] The climate agreed with everyone, and the Howellses "lived faster" than they "could have possibly done at home."[13] Between Lady Rosebery's reception and the Lord Chancellor's daughter asking him for a Friday evening, Howells soon felt "consumed by engagements."[14] Altogether Elinor counted two hundred callers during the three-month visit.

Charles Eliot Norton had provided introductions for Howells—who jokingly drew the line at "a letter to any such fairy as a real nobleman"—and thanks to Norton or Lowell he met one of the Darwins, perhaps Francis, the son of the author of *Origin of Species,* published twenty-three years before. Howells wrote to Norton that they came to know "all kinds of desirable people," and he, too, meant the English. "I must name Burne-Jones [another of Norton's English friends] first among these. . . . I had enough talk with him to feel his gentle and exquisite spirit, which had already delighted me in his pictures at the Grosvenor and the Royal Academy."[15] Edward Burne-Jones carried on the traditions of the Pre-Raphaelites in the generation after Dante Gabriel Rossetti, who died that year. The "brotherhood" he and William Michael Rossetti founded in 1848—without including their gifted sister, Christina—had long ago disbanded, damned by Dickens and others for immorality. Neither Howells nor Elinor found anything untoward in the Pre-Raphaelites' eroticizing of religious scenes or in their voluptuous female models with thick auburn hair, prominent among them Jane (Mrs. William) Morris. Much as he fussed about his sister's working in an office full of men, Howells had no hesitations about his wife's lunching with Rossetti's former mistress or buying his own Rossetti painting.

Howells, who liked to profess his ignorance of painting, had of course educated himself in the visual arts. Venice had seen to that, along with the Frankenstein brothers at Niagara and Elinor and Larkin Mead. Despite the dreamlike quality of the work of so many Pre-Raphaelite painters, he probably admired their bid to restore and renew British art, an ideal exemplified by Morris & Co., founded in 1861 and known as "The Firm." The consummate craftsman—poet, public designer, and maker of books and wallpaper, as well as political reformer—William Morris worked to bring beauty into English houses and justice into English society. His stand against the ugly commercializing of the arts (the Firm itself sold for a profit) matched Howells' ambivalence about "letters" and "business." Morris imagined a socialist future in his own utopian novels, and, like Howells in the United States, would lead English protests against the Haymarket trials.

Howells' taste in art might predictably have rested with American genre and landscape painters—such as Winslow Homer, Frederic Church, and Thomas Eakins—or with the Italian painters he encountered in Venice. Instead his interests stretched from quattrocento Italian to Pre-Raphaelite British, from Ohio realists like Frank Duveneck (a model for his artist in *Indian Summer*) to the American Impressionists, whose exhibitions he reviewed with enthusiasm. Childe Hassam shared a friendship with the poet Celia Thaxter and became Howells' neighbor in a New York artists' cooperative. Howells remained as open to different artists as to the diverse writers he berated for bad methods but commended for individual books.[16] During the summer of 1883 he attended the Royal Academy exhibitions, where he encountered the work of William Powell Frith, known for his panoramic, if staged, depictions of Victorian life. He also met two other painters, the German-born Hubert von Herkomer and the Dutch-born Lawrence Alma-Tadema.

Herkomer—who spent part of his boyhood in Ohio's Western Reserve—

made his reputation with sympathetic paintings of the poor and outcast, including his famous "Hard Times" (1885). When Vincent van Gogh visited England as a young man in the 1870s, even he associated Herkomer with "the highest and noblest expressions of art." In the next decade, Herkomer exchanged "social realism" for portraiture, made enough money to build a castle in Bavaria, became Sir Hubert, and painted the likes of Kaiser Wilhelm II and the family Krupp.[17] The Pre-Raphaelites' champion, John Ruskin, dismissed Alma-Tadema as the worst painter of the nineteenth century. Howells, who obviously disagreed, owned a Tadema painting along with his Fortuny and Rossetti. At the time of his visit, Tadema had been elected to the Royal Academy and was one of England's wealthiest painters. Buyers were eager for his large canvases of ancient Greece and Rome, peopled with latter-day Britons in classical costume, and for his languorous harem scenes. In an age when writers faced censorship for any hint of nudity, let alone sexuality, one of Alma-Tadema's nudes might fetch ten thousand pounds, a fortune to a middle-class family.

Howells met Alma-Tadema through a new connection. Waiting for him in London he found a note from a young Englishman, a writer of poems and literary reviews who held the position of translator for the Board of Trade. Twelve years Howells' junior, Edmund Gosse had a talent for gathering and using people. Admiring Henry James because he had seen people reading James' novels across Europe in French and German translations, Gosse had been "dazzled" by the connections that James enjoyed, and he himself coveted, in London and Paris. "Benign, indulgent, but grave, and not often unbending beyond a genial chuckle," as Gosse described him, James would make a valuable friend.[18] James, with his nose for weakness, called Gosse "very intelligent, but *manqué de fonds.*"[19]

Introducing himself to Howells as "the English representative of the *Century*" (formerly *Scribner's*), which appealed to English and American readers abroad, Gosse, who worked for the *Century* as Richard Watson Gilder's agent, had an interest in things American; years later he discovered that his mother had been born in Massachusetts. He already claimed Edmund Stedman and John Hay, along with Gilder and James, among his transatlantic friends. When he invited Howells and Elinor to dinner, he spoke of including "the much-engaged" James (who declined) and Alma-Tadema, who happened to be his brother-in-law. "I found your very kind note at the American Exchange to-day," Howells replied, "and I have to thank you for the acquaintance you give me. I shall be only too glad to meet you and make it personal."[20]

Howells and Gosse leapt into friendship. Within a few weeks Gosse wrote to Edmund Stedman: "W. D. Howells is over here, and we have seen a great deal of him. To know him is to love him: I think he is one of the most winning personalities I have ever met . . . with such a fund of genius and strength. He is your best novelist, I think."[21] Nothing if not politic, Gosse knew that any praise to joint American friends would get back to Howells himself. In a letter to Howells that teetered between shrewd judgment and lavish compliments, Gosse called *A Modern Instance* "altogether the greatest work of fiction that America has given us since the death of Hawthorne. I am quite sure of that."[22]

Different as they may have seemed, both Howells and Gosse had joined the "establishment" as young men and perhaps, as Gosse believed of himself, succeeded too easily. Both had grown up in religious families that set rigorous moral and spiritual standards. Gosse's father, Philip, a renowned biologist and, like his wife, a religious fundamentalist, argued in his book *The Omphalos* that God had planted fossils as a test of faith, a proposition laughable to scientists and unacceptable to religious believers. Gosse rejected the tenets of his parents' Plymouth Brethren and broke with his father. Howells, if never wholly embracing his father's Swedenborgianism or any formal religion, remained fascinated by matters of faith and conscience. He once contemplated making Swedenborg a character in a novel. Gosse published a biography and a poignant memoir, *Father and Son,* and Howells persuaded William Howells to write his recollections of Ohio, which he himself edited. Above all, Howells and Gosse were writers and readers of books, men of letters in the broadest, most paradoxical sense of that phrase, who would later cling "by their eyelids," as Gosse joked, "to the outer cliff of fame."[23]

Gosse set the pattern of their correspondence with flattery followed by extravagant protestations of affection. Howells, as he had with Twain, responded in kind. "I had such a lovely time last night," he wrote after a visit in late August, "that I would now like to cut the ties of a husband and father, and come to live with you. Is there not some law or privilege by which you could adopt an elderly foreigner of fading intellect?"[24] Even discounting the humor, this was an unusual letter to a man he scarcely knew. Gosse, on holiday at the seaside, went farther: "You shall be welcomed, oh! how gladly. . . . If it were not selfish I should wish you here. What endless talks by the sea, what rambles over the brown sweet-scented moors that would mean. And we would take a boat over to the Fern Islands, and start a monarchy. You should be King, because you are so very democratic, and I would be your Fool."[25]

Gosse normally reserved such language for friends, notably his lover, the sculptor Hamo Thornycroft. Like Oscar Wilde before the notorious trials, Gosse managed—without upsetting social proprieties—to be openly affectionate with Thornycroft while remaining happily married to his wife, Nellie, and devoted to his children. When someone asked Lytton Strachey, Bloomsbury's debunker of things Victorian, whether Gosse might be a "homo-sexual," he quipped: "No, but he's Hamo-sexual."[26] Howells, who met Thornycroft, may not have suspected his friend's bisexual leanings.[27] Yet he must have been aware that his own terms of endearment went beyond the ordinary. His friendship with Gosse lasted several decades, but not at the pitch of those first months. Though Howells arranged an 1884 American lecture tour for Gosse, and Gosse returned the favor with reviews and support, their summer exuberance gave way to a more careful or diplomatic friendship. In retrospect, the friendship may have mattered little to either man: Gosse at least would write a tepid eulogy of his old friend.

In 1905 Howells acknowledged that "he had always been more or less busy bothering about England," and from the time of his fascination with Dickens' novels, or with Richard Realf, John Brown's "secretary of state," his observation is apt, for he had what might be called his "English problem."[28] Until at least the turn of the century—and fitfully after that—he looked askance at English politics and had serious reservations about the English themselves. His social successes and new friendships notwithstanding, the ill will he had felt on his first visit rebounded now. Howells believed the English to be caste-ridden, narrow-minded, ambivalent about democratic principles, and of course colonialist, and he must have deplored such events as the British occupation of Egypt, which took place during his 1882 stay.

The reasons for Howells' almost blanket dislike of the English lay in a combination of old prejudice and new misunderstandings. Since the publication of *Venetian Life* in Trübner's English edition, he had been politely, at times generously, reviewed in England, and critics welcomed him in London with evident goodwill. "English novel-readers," wrote a reviewer for the *Athenaeum*, "will probably be disposed to congratulate themselves on the fact that the late editor of the *Atlantic Monthly* has by his retirement given himself leisure to superintend the production of his works in this country."[29] Readers in England admired his "careful picture" of American life and compared him favorably with James, a writer some accepted as one of their own. None of this regard prevented his attack on British critics and novelists.

About a month after his "Mark Twain" appeared—and after his family had left for Switzerland—Howells published "Henry James, Jr." in the *Century*. Previously he had restrained his digs at the English or limited himself to passing barbs, as in *Their Wedding Journey,* where he mentions England's hereditary aristocracy inspiring "no great culture, no political influence, no civic aspiration."[30] With the *Century* essay he made a direct assault, defending James against imaginary enemies who became real soon enough. Even granting a complicated relationship with the English, he had no immediate grounds for attack. A cynic might call his essay a response to less-than-gushing English reviews which agreed that, for all his talent, Howells' novels clearly lacked plot. To a writer emphasizing other aspects of fiction, this might have seemed either an unwitting compliment or a call to arms. The year before he had told his father: "I think that I know rather more about the business of writing novels than any critic living, and where I don't feel obliged by my consciousness to side with a man against my work, his censure doesn't worry me."[31] The James essay expressed his contempt for critics in a general debunking of English literary pretensions, yet in a sense it went further. It can be read as Howells' ultimatum: that the English had no standing in the world's literary court and no business treating superior American writers as fledgling colonists.

After easing into his essay with a sketch of James' Irish and Scottish background, his ties to Cambridge, Massachusetts, and his "universal" popularity following publication of *The Portrait of a Lady* (1881), Howells fires his main guns. James has set a standard the English cannot or have yet to meet, he says, and implies that the present writer, James' friend and discoverer, stands on the same pedestal. It is James' "reserve" and "artistic impartiality" that stamp him as a modern author, an American author, at a time when the English muddle along with nostalgic and outdated models.

> The art of fiction has . . . become a finer art in our day than it was with Dickens and Thackeray. We could not suffer the confidential attitude of the latter now, nor the mannerism of the former, any more than we could endure the prolixity of Richardson or the coarseness of Fielding. These great men are of the past. . . . The new school derives from Hawthorne and George Eliot rather than any others. . . . The moving accident is certainly not its trade; and it prefers to avoid all manner of dire catastrophes. It is largely influenced by French fiction in form; but it is the realism of Daudet rather than the realism of Zola that prevails with it. . . . This school, which

is so largely of the future as well as the present, finds its chief exemplar in Mr. James; it is he who is shaping and directing American fiction.[32]

The British press might have excused this patriotic defense of James as an *American* writer—who to be sure lived in England—or even a little boasting by Howells, his prophet. They could not, however, swallow three related pieces in the same November *Century*, which ran an essay by James himself (on Venice) and a diatribe by Charles Dudley Warner, berating the ignorant "snobbishness of English critics."[33] Taking the *Century* issue as an affront to their country, they retaliated. A writer for the London *World* spoke of the "intellectual trinity [Howells, James, Warner], which it is the proper thing for all would-be 'cultured' Americans to bow down and worship. . . . Mr. Henry James jun. writes of 'Venice' in his usual tepid, invertebrate, captain's-biscuit style; and Mr. W. D. Howells writes of 'Henry James Jr.,' and places him at the head of the 'new school' of fiction, which is, it seems, a very fine thing."[34] The Anglo-Irish novelist George Moore had little patience for any competitor and none for Howells. "James went to France and read Tourgenieff," he wrote. "W. D. Howells stayed at home and read Henry James. . . . Henry James said, I will write the moral history of America, as Tourgenieff wrote the moral history of Russia—he borrowed at first-hand, understanding what he was borrowing. W. D. Howells borrowed at second-hand, and without knowing what he was borrowing."[35] Moore was as fair about Howells' provincialism as Howells about British fiction of the time, which included writers such as Moore himself, George Gissing, and Thomas Hardy, each a "modern" in his way. He could not have anticipated Olive Schreiner's *Story of an African Farm*, which appeared the following year, but he could (and later did) acknowledge powerful new voices in British fiction.

Margaret Oliphant, herself a novelist, wrote a damning critique of his essay in an anonymous review for *Blackwood's Magazine*. (She would soon write a book on Venice, for which she probably read and learned from *Venetian Life*.) Oliphant preferred James to Howells because Howells himself seemed the more American and therefore the *weaker* writer. In a critique to make anyone cringe, she wrote that great writers rise above provincial crankiness. Not Mr. Howells. "When a writer of fiction alleges . . . that the art of which he is a professor is finer than the art of Thackeray, the punishment which he prepares for himself is so prodigious that it becomes ridiculous. But no one we believe will be cruel enough to make the suggested comparison."[36] And no one remarked that Howells himself owed a debt to Thackeray—for creating, as he put it, a "world of flesh and blood"—or that his arguments undercut both his principles and practice. If he called Thackeray inartistic, chattily confidential, or outmoded, he later placed him in the company of Tolstoy, James, and Hawthorne. Rarely is Howells the narrow-minded reader or patriot he appears in his essay on James; he either misjudged his audience or, more likely, deliberately provoked it.

From his refuge in Switzerland, he professed surprise at the British reactions. "I always thought myself quite unapproached in my appreciation of the great qualities of Dickens and Thackeray," he told Gosse, "and I can hardly believe that I have 'arraigned' them."[37] This sounds, and was, disingenuous. It had incensed him, for example, that Thackeray presented "the American girl" as a predatory coquette incapable of speaking correctly.[38] In a vexed literary and economic climate, he understood as well as anyone the depths of English and American literary rivalry: the American assertion of literary independence and its counterpart, the British contempt for America's lack of culture. Literary piracy (ended in 1891 by overdue copyright legislation) added to the tensions. American publishers printed unprotected English books without paying royalties to their authors or to those American authors who could earn no royalties from their unpublished books. These were among the battle cries in the magazines and another underlying basis for Howells' attack. He does not mention that the British often welcomed American writers, Whitman among them, before Americans did, and that they welcomed William Dean Howells.

The *Century* debacle did not ruin either James' or Howells' book sales in England. Both writers had received and would continue to receive complimentary British notices, though none of their books approached the popularity of James' *Daisy Miller*. Despite the success of that book and the critical acclaim for *The Portrait of a Lady*—or their relative reputations today—Howells actually outsold James in the early 1880s. By 1885, he had sold a total of 131,000 copies to James' 33,000, and he managed limited but steady sales for decades to come.[39] That his British publisher issued few of the later novels does not mean they were unpopular with British readers, who bought his books, or British critics, who often gave him better press than he received at home. In the years after publication of *The Rise of Silas Lapham,* when Howells began to be reviewed as a "realist," American critics bristled at what they thought the luridness of, say, *A Hazard of New Fortunes,* while British reviewers responded with enthusiasm to the novels and pronounced their author worthy "to be ranked among men of genius."[40]

James had been away in France and "missed the little breeze produced, as I am told, by the *November* Century." Back in London he sent his reassurance that Howells had done the right thing, urging him not to take the attacks to heart. Well aware that he might have been the one more damaged, James dismissed the commotion as "rubbish." Warner's essay he called "crude, boyish & not well written."[41] Like James, Edmund Gosse reacted to the situation—with Howells at least—by making light of it: "So you have demolished poor old Dickens and Thackeray, have you? Well, I am glad I was born in the good old times when they were thought good enough for week-day reading." Setting the banter aside, he wrote a more pointed postscript.

"Motto for the American Critic"
Ho! the old school Thackeray, Dickens!
Throw them out to feed the chickens.—
Ho! the new school! James and———
Lay the flattery on with trowels.

   (Doggerel by a candid friend.)[42]

A few days later Gosse, evidently wondering whether *he* had overstepped the bounds of friendship, wrote to Howells with a delicate justification of his "flippant" verses that addressed the bias on both sides.[43] For home consumption, he sent a lame defense of Howells to the *Athenaeum,* claiming that Howells, at work on a novel in Switzerland, had not seen the magazine and could not remember what he had said. "But he is sure that he has been misprinted or misunderstood if he seems to be disrespectful to those great writers."[44] In a sense, the James article became for Howells the equivalent of Twain's speech at the Whittier dinner. It was ill-considered and ill-mannered but probably had few lasting consequences.

Howells' recurrent clashes with the English stand at ironic odds with his attraction to the country, his delight in its landscape, his association with people such as the novelist Anthony Trollope and Thackeray's daughter Ann, his pride in an Oxford degree, and, when it suited his purpose, his acknowledgment of England's cultural achievements. He welcomed a range of British novelists and wrote sympathetically about Britain itself in novels like *A Woman's Reason,* published soon after his 1882–83 visit. Much later, in an 1896 essay for *Harper's Weekly,* he berated his countrymen and President Grover Cleveland for using England as a political whipping boy. "There is in the American heart a hatred of England which, if not dying, is certainly not dead yet."[45] He might have been making a personal confession.

> My wife did me the honour to divorce her husband in order to marry
> me. This, neither more nor less, it is at once my duty and my plea-
> sure to communicate. . . . It will be a sincere disappointment to find
> that you cannot be my guest. I shall bear up however; for I assure you
> I desire to know no one who considers himself holier than my wife.
>
> —ROBERT LOUIS STEVENSON to W. D. Howells, December 4, 1882

Howells and his family had escaped to Villeneuve, on the shore of Lake
Geneva and near the Castle of Chillon, the setting of Henry James' opening scene in *Daisy Miller*. The extended stay in London had made Howells
anxious about delays in his work, and he wanted a retreat in an area where
the family could entertain themselves. After weeks of rain, he joked about
his "imprisonment," which also meant displacement. "I consider myself,
especially fictionable," he wrote to James, "and I am sorry you are not here
to study me in the character of a thoroughly bourgeois American: a man
who had once some poetical possibilities, but who finds himself more and
more commonplace in surroundings that twenty years ago appealed not in
vain to something fine in him. I daily put on more *sitzfleisch* [extra weight
from sitting]." The sight of pretty girls gathering the crimson leaves of Virginia creeper made him feel "hopelessly middle-aged. . . . Somewhere, deep
within my awkward bulk, I know that I am as young and stylish and slim
as any of them, but I know also that I don't look it."[46] He would draw on
such feelings for *Indian Summer,* his novel about middle-age love. To Twain
he spoke of being lonely and "a little downhearted" and wishing that his
friends might share his Spartan life. Meanwhile, he settled down to write.

He had gone to Europe planning to begin several books and to finish *A
Woman's Reason.* With Osgood he broached a topic very much on his mind,
the disappointing sales of *A Modern Instance.* Osgood speculated that, contrary to the rule of thumb, publicity about its unpleasant subject had hurt
sales. The most psychological of his novels, *A Modern Instance* chronicles
the courtship, marriage, and divorce of Marcia Gaylord and Bartley Hubbard. Having originally cast Bartley as a schoolteacher, Howells had the inspired idea of making him a newspaperman. "Why has no one struck journalism before?" he asked a friend.[47] As Bartley's profession implies, the novel
allowed Howells a kind of meditation on career and marriage, which may
have contributed to his low spirits and bad health through the winter of
1881. Despite thinking the final episodes of chapters 7 and 8 the strongest

he had written, he could not approach them without a tremor of nerves. He wondered that other people could bear to read about Hubbard seducing one coworker and nearly killing another, or to see the overtly sexual Marcia groveling at his feet.[48]

Thirty years after the novel appeared, Howells told a friend that he had "drawn Bartley Hubbard, the false scoundrel, from himself."[49] He obviously touched a responsive chord in others, since Twain saw Bartley as Samuel Langhorn Clemens. Others saw him more fittingly as Bret Harte, who had a history of drinking and unpaid debts and who, in Twain's loud opinion, had deserted his wife and children.[50] "I should be ashamed," Howells told his publisher, "to write a novel that did not distinctly mean something, or that did not show that I had felt strongly about it."[51] "Ah! if you knew what I have suffered from the unchallenged predominance of America's Bartley Hubbards," his new friend, George Washington Cable wrote, "you could understand the grateful delight with which I behold them with a ring in their nose at last!"[52]

As Cable discovered, Hubbard is a journalist without conscience, a clever plagiarist who ultimately dies at the hands of an irate reader. *A Modern Instance* illustrates Howells' mixed feelings about journalism, which friends like James thought brutalizing to perception and inimical to culture. More broadly it signals a new phase in Howells' awareness of the economic forces shaping both national ethics and individual lives. It is in this sense a precursor of an American novel like Frank Norris' *The Octopus* (1901) and also a worthy rival of George Gissing's *New Grub Street* (1891) and Émile Zola's *Germinal* (1885). The best comparison with Howells' work is perhaps Thomas Hardy's earlier *Return of the Native* (1878). Like Hardy's novel, Howells' defies simple plot summary. Its evocation of New England as a place of dark mysteries, no less than Hardy's Wessex, and the personality of its barely civilized heroine, driven by primitive compulsions, allow the novel to transcend its time and place. The story moves with an unusual rhythm as it chronicles the waste of lives not governed by standards of custom or habit. Owen Wister, whose cowboy hero in *The Virginian* endures in Westerns and film, remembered the distinctive quality of Howells' work. "Some novels are all plot and no characters. They are like unoccupied houses. . . . I read *A Modern Instance* in the early eighties. Until I reread it a while ago, I could have told you but obscurely of its incidents; whereas of Bartley Hubbard, and Marcia his wife, and her father Squire Gaylord, I could have given you a quite definite account."[53] The same would be true of Howells' best-known novel, *The Rise of Silas Lapham* (1885), which invites comparison with another of Hardy's novels, *The Mayor of Casterbridge* (1886), a parallel story of a crude man's rise, fall, and redemption.

A Modern Instance, whose title comes from Shakespeare's *As You Like It*, addresses the still-censored topics of female sexuality and marital failure. Howells presents Marcia as the product of her upbringing. She and her father spoil each other "as father and daughter are apt to do, when left to themselves. What was good in the child certainly received no harm from his indulgence; and what was naughty was after all not so very naughty. She was passionate, but she was generous; and if she showed a jealous temperament that must hereafter make her unhappy, for the time being it charmed and flattered her father to have her so fond of him that she could not endure any rivalry in his affection."[54] Howells had thought to call his book *A New Medea*, a title that would convey the depth of Marcia's passion. Caught in her own jealous webs, she destroys herself, along with Hubbard and an upper-class Bostonian named Ben Halleck who has long loved her. It seems unlikely that, once widowed, she will marry again. The last lines of the novel, however, speak to the prospect of another marriage—"Ah, I don't know! I don't know," Marcia says, making her own end, and the novel's, ambiguous.

A Modern Instance shocked readers by its open discussion of divorce, a scandalous topic that Howells appropriated from the popular press and dealt with as a common fact of "modern" life. Robert Louis Stevenson, who published *Treasure Island* in 1882, read Howells' treatment of divorce as a personal insult. Himself married to a divorced woman, Stevenson sent Howells an "unanswerable letter" and refused to receive him. It took him a dozen years to half admit that he had misunderstood the book and owed Howells an apology.[55]

Looking back in *Literature and Life*, Howells wrote that "a novelist needs experience and observation, not so much of others as of himself, for ultimately his characters will all come out of himself, and he will need to know motive and character with such thoroughness and accuracy as he can acquire only through his own heart. . . . Until he is well on toward forty, he will hardly have assimilated the material of a great novel."[56] With *A Modern Instance*, his books began to take on complexity, and his subsequent novels may have come "out of himself" in ways he never anticipated. Careers, however, rarely take clear trajectories. After the punishing analysis and unsentimental narrative of *A Modern Instance*, he took some backward steps.

Howells had begun *A Woman's Reason* in 1878, and by the fall of 1882 he spoke about the romance of an orphaned girl and her shipwrecked fiancé as still "reluctantly taking shape."[57] Except that he had a February deadline for magazine serialization, he treated this, his first main European project, as a busman's holiday. "I have written but a hundred pages of it in six weeks," he told Gosse in September, "and I have had such a good time that I have been unable to do so much even as kill a consumptive girl, or even make a lover homesick enough to start home from China and get wrecked on an atoll in the South Pacific: he is shamelessly hanging around Hong Kong."[58] Unsure how to read Howells' playfulness, Gosse replied with misplaced advice. "If you are really writing about Hong Kong, you had better let me send you some blue-books [governmental reports] lately published here, on the atrocious tyrannies of the local police, quite a Zolaesque study of the life in the low quarter of the town."[59] Howells answered that though he intended the character to be "well-principled" he might invent someone who visited the sordid parts of Hong Kong. Gosse's mention of Zola and "low quarters" did not prepare him for graphic accounts of squalor and sexual debauchery, and, according to Gosse, "he surprised me by giving no sign of having received this scabrous treasure." When Gosse pressed him, Howells admitted he had burned the offending material and put aside all thought of writing about Hong Kong.[60] Gosse had assumed that, like so many of his English friends, Howells distinguished between private license and public consumption. Whatever Howells' repugnance, he might have returned Gosse's "treasure" without moral injury.

For an apparent companion to *A Woman's Reason,* Howells envisioned a historical romance about a young ship's captain from Massachusetts disembarking in Venice. However strait-laced, he would be stirred by the love affairs awaiting him "in the capital of the dying republic."[61] The plot, Howells granted, remained hazy. How he squared this sort of narrative fluff with what might be called the sexual capitalism of a novel like *A Modern Instance*—a novel that pushed the boundaries of conventional decency and crossed into social and psychological territories that estranged readers and critics—he did not say. If Howells' muse sometimes erred on the side of chastity (for temperamental or economic reasons), the novels of this time emphasize how much his notions of *realism* spanned a range unknown to most novelists and unrecognized by later readers. They include the daring of *A Modern Instance* on the one hand and the domestic accuracy of a Jane Austen or Anthony Trollope on the other; but whether novels of manners or novels of social exploration, they avoid the urban misery of writers like Zola or the brothers Goncourt.[62] Courting a harsher but not necessarily a better muse, later realists reflected the license of less rigidly censored times.

You won't expect me to say anything about Venice, merely because I'm here, will you? The idea of being here is benumbing and silencing. I feel like the Wandering Jew, or the ghost of the Cardiff Giant. I used sometimes to dream of having come back, but nothing was ever so strange as this reality, for it isn't strange at all—so far as I'm able to express it.

—W. D. HOWELLS to Mark Twain, April 22, 1883

While still in Villeneuve, Howells considered and rejected an offer of a professorship in literature from Daniel C. Gilman, the president of Johns Hopkins University. The prompt came from Richard Watson Gilder, the genial editor who seemed to know everyone worth knowing and tried in various ways to further his friends' careers. Howells must have been tempted by Gilman's invitation. At least he asked for Osgood's and Lowell's guidance. Lowell once again weighed the pros and cons, suggesting that *if* Howells could retain his integrity as a writer, he *might* consider the job. (He said nothing about his own academic employment.) This reinforced Howells' misgivings not just about the demands of teaching and the loss of time to write, but also about money. Hjalmar Boyesen, he knew, earned a lavish $7,500 at Columbia, a third again as much as Gilman was offering—and he had a wealthy wife. Howells replied to Gilman, "I am afraid in the first place that you do not know how rich and various are my disqualifications for such a position as that you offer me. . . . I have a literary use of Spanish, French, German, and Italian, and I have some knowledge of the literature and the literary history of those languages; but I have not a *scholarly* acquaintance with them."[63]

For the time being, he left the possibility open. "I do feel strongly and deeply, the art of literature, and I believe I could make others feel its beauty and importance." He then went on to outline an enlightened philosophy of teaching. "I should begin by making each one tell me what he had read, in whatever language. Then I should inquire into his preferences and require the reason for them. When I had acquainted myself fully with the literary attainments and opinions of the class and come perfectly into *rapport* with them, I should want to see their work, to criticize it with them and correct—not in detail but 'by sample.' . . . I should seek at every step to make them partners in the enterprise, and not treat them as bottles to be filled with so much literary information."[64] In a time before English departments, Howells imagined himself introducing students to a broad course of reading unconstrained by nationality or academic specialty. In addition to teaching students to write fiction and poetry, he would have been a ranging commentator on literary culture, with an understanding of his work resembling that of John Dewey. Gilman wanted exactly the knowledge and skills Howells described. He renewed his offer, to be denied once again, before Howells left Europe. Howells in the end preferred his independence. Besides, he earned twice as much by writing as he could by teaching.

In December the family turned their "frost-bitten noses southward," exchanging the snows of Switzerland for the "mawkish tepidity" of Florence.[65] Elinor would revel in the sights, the art, and perhaps most of all the society she found in Florence. At first they had trouble adjusting. The "transformation from the tonic air of the Swiss mountains" brought a sense of lassitude so powerful that they scarcely left the hotel for the first two weeks, and Winny, "still half an invalid," lost more strength in the December damp.[66] That did not stop her, when she felt well, from dancing until two in the morning and exhausting herself again. Howells worried about Winny and begrudged his attendance at the social events they had avoided in Switzerland. "I was out every night or afternoon but one [he says of a typical week]; I find myself fatally well known, and I have a suspicion that my books have been at least heard of along with the British drumbeat." Still, it flattered him to think, as one German critic insisted, that his books were read by all young English-speaking Germans.[67]

Wherever Howells traveled, he stayed in touch with his father, who was now trying to map a new future. Against his son's advice, he had resigned the Toronto consulship and determined, in the self-punishing family tradition, to buy a farm in Virginia. Frustrated by what he saw as another false start, Howells allowed himself some rare sarcasm: "It looks to me very much like a repetition of the happy experiment at Eureka, with your increased years and Joe's invalidism [brought on by overwork] to contribute to its success."[68] William ignored his advice and, with the success his son predicted (and his own father had illustrated) purchased his farm.

William's new venture added to Howells' money worries and made his assorted writing projects more urgent. He went to Italy out of nostalgia and in the hope of rest and better health but also to gather materials for his proposed *Tuscan Cities,* which would appear serially in the *Century* with drawings by the popular illustrator Joseph Pennell. Overcoming Howells' reservations, Gilder had arranged for Pennell to accompany him on his travels. "I am expecting the artist Pennell every day," Howells wrote in late January 1883. On his arrival ten days later, Pennell described the meeting to his wife. "Got here. Howells is a *howling swell*—very impressive and also very jolly when you can get him alone, which isn't very often."[69] Both men had reservations about the collaboration. Instead of traveling with Pennell to Rome, as planned, Howells begged off. "The idea of the Colosseum makes me sick," he wrote, "and I am satisfied that the dome of the State House is good enough for me."[70] John accompanied Pennell, excited as the artist himself to see the Colosseum, the Vatican, and other attractions that left his father jaded but inspired the would-be architect.

If Howells grew impatient with sightseeing at the best of times, sightseeing with a stranger tested him more. He had always felt at home in artists' studios and with artists, and he enjoyed watching Quincy Ward or William Stillman, John La Farge or Augustus Saint-Gaudens at work. As Larkin Mead and his wife lived in Florence, he spent many hours relaxing in Larkin's studio. Pennell's studio had no quiet corner, indeed no walls. Collaboration with him required traipsing around cities, adding the burdens of sweat and sore feet to the constant negotiations between them. Pennell had accepted the advice of the art editor of the *Century* "to get fotografs of old masterpieces to be introduced as illustrations." Howells strongly objected. "*I don't want them,*" he wrote Gilder—or, for that matter, anything of old art or old approaches. On the other hand, he wanted to travel comfortably, which to Pennell meant expensively. Pennell wrote from Pisa that he was "off here with the 'most finished American novelist'—he'll finish me financially before long."[71]

The two disagreed about more than money and aesthetics. Each man assumed himself the expert and expected his own schedule to take precedence. Relieved when they actually came to like one another, Pennell added a large *but:* "When a man incidentally mentions that Dickens' work 'is trash' I feel like stopping the production of Am. novels." They managed to finish their tour on a cordial note. "This week," Pennell wrote from Pisa, "I have been running around with Howells—yesterday we started from here—drove across the country to Lucca. I am getting along very much better with him than I did at first—and if he wasn't going to Venice next week—I would probably fall desperately in love with him."[72] Whether or not Pennell's company or ways of looking helped Howells write a better book, *Tuscan Cities* must have satisfied them both. Pennell went on to provide illustrations for his later work, including a new edition of *Italian Journeys* in 1891—illustrations that reviewers called wonderful and wholly unrelated to the text.

With or without Pennell's company, but perhaps with his nudging, Howells imagined *Tuscan Cities* as a study in perspectives. He begins the book by describing his children as they look out at Florence from the hotel window. What the children are seeing for the first time, their parents view through the lens of their earlier memories. These different vantage points anticipate both the pattern and the underlying subject of his book. "I have often thought," he writes, "that we must get a false impression of the past by the laws governing perspective, in which the remoter objects are inevitably pressed together in their succession, and the spaces between are ignored." In a painting, he says, "these spaces are imagined; but in history, the objects, the events are what alone make their appeal, and there seems nothing else."[73] He, the writer, must bring back the past by avoiding "fine rhetoric," at times using "broken" accounts or "grizzly details" for the effect he creates.[74] He calls the main part of his book, on Florence itself, "A Florentine Mosaic," an "owning up," as he tells his readers, and a hint about his inventive writing.

Tuscan Cities is not a history but glimpses of history; not a guidebook but sectioned like a guidebook, and it works as a journal works, reflecting a range of moods and places. Bit by bit it pays tribute to Italy and to the political freedoms Italians have come to enjoy. In a hundred pages, Howells comments on religion, carnivals, architecture, art, the Florentine people themselves, christenings and funerals, the Italian theater, Dante, *and* the historic "rule by one man" that has left Italy a disadvantaged union. As a kind of sideshow, he pokes fun at British tourists. "The sentimentalist is very abundant in Italy," he writes, "and most commonly he is of our race and religion," and English. "The Englishman, so chary of his sensibilities at home, abandons himself to them abroad."[75]

In this first Italian travel book since *Italian Journeys,* Howells extends the method of *Venetian Life,* writing with even greater ease and humor and more apparent openness about his moods, opinions, and private reflections. "Is it possible," he asks, "that sometimes evil prevails by its superior force in the universe?" It is certainly possible, he makes clear, when people are badly governed. "True freedom is only a means to peace; and if such freedom as [people] have will not give them peace, then they must accept it from slavery."[76] For this and so much else, Florence (or Italy as a whole) serves as an object lesson in courage and right governance. Howells himself held *Tuscan Cities* in high esteem. If a reported comment is accurate, he said that "there is nowhere, to my knowledge, so compendious a sketch of all Florentine history as in my book."[77]

In early March the family went for a month to Siena. Howells called his account of their visit "Panforte di Siena," a joke about the pastry he never tried and its importance to an anonymous author whose guidebook he quotes. He loved Siena for its medieval and picturesque qualities, its cathedral and setting, and for its surrounding landscape. With all this "the cordial city" welcomed him, offering as a bonus "the frank and loyal friendship" of the John Hay family. Unable to meet except briefly in Florence, they reunited in Siena.

A writer and politician, Hay was the kind of man Howells might have become. He had known this fellow Ohioan from the days of his appointment to Venice and, as editor of the *Atlantic,* had sought whatever the author of *Castilian Days* could offer. Later he would encourage the massive "history" of Lincoln that Hay, with his ailing friend George Nicolay, finally brought to conclusion. A complex man, Hay showed different personalities to different friends. John Singer Sargent's 1903 portrait emphasizes his long white moustaches, shaggy beard, and a misplaced curl on his high brow that give a rakish or Mephistophelean cast to his face. In the company of the Henry Adamses and Clarence King, he was a witty poet and journalist, the husband of a wealthy woman whose father built railroad bridges, and the lover of Nannie Lodge, wife of Henry Cabot Lodge. To Howells, he was a valued writer and accomplished diplomat, though evidently not an intimate friend. As the anonymous author of a controversial antilabor novel, *The Bread-Winners,* Hay stood on the opposite side from Howells on almost every political and social issue. (That did not dissuade some readers from thinking that Howells wrote Hay's book.) Hay kept his confidences, about family, writing, and politics, and he always remained somewhat distant, sending letters from Washington or Cleveland that read as if they belonged in a diplomatic pouch. His discretion appealed to Presidents McKinley and Roosevelt, under both of whom he served as secretary of state.

Hay and Howells had fallen out briefly in 1877, when Howells wrote a column criticizing Hay's father-in-law, Asa Stone, for the collapse of a railroad bridge spanning the Ashtabula River Gorge. Either Hay set him straight or Howells chose to recant, admitting in another column that he had been unaware of all the circumstances—despite a court judgment finding the company negligent.[78] In November 1877, soon after the bridge disagreement, the Hays had invited Howells and Elinor to Cleveland for a performance of *Counterfeit Presentment.* Now they met to enjoy the sights, the food, and the wine of Tuscany.

Following their few weeks in Siena, the family returned to Florence, avoiding society so that Howells could write and indulge in "the proper business of sight-seeing." He found it an unsettling time, when his sense of the "Tuscan Cities" and Italy itself shifted from day to day. As in his Venetian years, he described being "torn between two homesicknesses: the longing for America, and the desire to stay in Italy."[79] To Thomas Perry he spoke of "turning over a good many books, and putting myself in rapport with Italy again." Then he added, "But I'm not sure it pays. After all, *we* have the country of the present and future."[80] He lost confidence in his book, felt at odds with the region and the country, and once again did an absolute turnabout. A few months later, he wrote: "Our hearts were all sick for Italy. Elinor and I have quite changed our minds about the Italians: we now think them not only very sympathetic and brilliant, but really and thoroughly good-hearted."[81] In this mood it was the Italians who could teach the Americans, and his own country he found wanting.

He had in a sense circled around Florence as if postponing the return to Venice. His sketches of places such as Fiesole come across less as sketches or "fragments" than afterthoughts, but not his account of leaving Florence.[82] "I looked again at the distant mountains, where they smoldered along the horizon: they were purple to their tips, and no ghost of snow glimmered under any fold of their mist. Our winter in Florence had come to an end."[83]

They moved on finally to what he hoped would be the climax of their journey, Venice—followed by ten days in Verona with his old "young" friend, Brunetta. If Florence had sometimes bored him, Venice proved a disaster. In the first place, he found it impossible to write there. James added to his difficulty: his piece on Venice in the November *Century* somehow preempted "doing" it again. Besides, Howells had reservations about re-treading hallowed ground. The city appealed and repelled, bringing back the nostalgia along with the disgust and delights he had forgotten. "Venice is shabbier and gayer and lovelier than ever," he wrote to Osgood. "There's a full moon to-night—But what's the use of trying to talk Venice to a man who's never been here?—When I first came out of the station on my arrival, I tho't I'd never been away. It's, inexplicably, inconceivably the same."[84] It struck him once more as a place of magic and magnificence and a sad, impoverished outpost, though now Italian rather than Austrian. Albeit crammed with strangers, crowds of English and Americans who remain nameless in his accounts, the city somehow felt empty. He did visit with Padre Giacomo of the Armenian Convent, who, "gray and fat" like the other monks, welcomed his children like a loving uncle.[85]

Giving up hope of writing, Howells accounted for the month in the city as a recuperative holiday for Winny. After "drooping in Florence," she recovered in "her native air as if by magic."[86] At "the first breath of the lagoons . . . [her] tortured nerves began to calm themselves. The motion which was rest, the rest which was motion, in the gliding, dreaming gondola, was the medicine which her eager spirit and fragile body needed; and the beauty of the city, inexhaustible, ineffable, utterly satisfied the craving of one born to the intensest love of beauty." It was as if "the mother city took pity on its child."[87] "She takes the deadly romantic view of Venice," Howells told Twain, "and doesn't hesitate to tell me that I did the place great injustice in my books. It is quite amusing. She thinks it is *all* beauty and gaiety; but for my part, the poor old place is forlorner and shabbier than ever. I don't think I began to see the misery of it when I lived here."[88]

Part of Howells' ambivalence about the city reflected his unending struggle to write its history. In *A Fearful Responsibility,* the character Ellmore tells his wife that "no one ever came back to finish a history of Venice," a confession of his own and his author's failure.[89] Howells had compelling reasons not to write a history. Since his own *Venetian Life,* dozens of works had appeared for the tourist trade, from Cook's and Baedeker's ever-present "handbooks" to "satchel-guides" to "pocket-book" guides to individual studies of Italy or Northern Italy or Venice yet again. In that crowded market Howells published *Tuscan Cities,* but he neither wrote a history of Venice nor ever entirely abandoned the idea. Years later he would negotiate with Henry Alden, his friend and editor at Harper's, about financing a year in Venice so that he could write the still-unborn book. Alden and the press proved willing, the author not.

As the Howells family said good-bye to Venice, Constance Fenimore Woolson, the writer and close friend of Henry James, saw them off. For Winny's autograph book Woolson wrote an affectionate note about the "beautiful old water-city," Winny's birthplace and her own adopted home. "This is my 'Xanadu,'" Woolson told her,—"But not for always; Xanadu never lasts, you know!" Still, she added, they might meet again at home.[90] "Xanadu never lasts." Or it lasts as a chimera: exhilarating, baffling, neither to be captured in historical records nor erased from memory. Their reunion was not to be. Woolson, whose story "Miss Grief" tells of a brilliant but unsuccessful writer, died in Italy from a fall through her apartment window. Whether it was accident or suicide, no one knew. The city that had been Woolson's home, that temporarily inspirited Winny, a child of the city, would become for her parents another reminder of heartbreak and loss.

There seems to be a mistake somewhere; perhaps it's mine in not making sure of passing a leisurely eternity with you and your friends.

—W. D. HOWELLS to Edmund Gosse, June 26, 1883

This year abroad was pivotal for Howells, who had begun a marathon decade of publishing and entered into two remarkable arrangements. In James Osgood he had found a wise if eccentric adviser, someone to consult about professorships as well as books and a trustworthy man of business. Osgood accepted the responsibilities of placing Howells' articles, arranging for reviews, negotiating contracts, and publishing the novels following their magazine serialization. His legendary charm only partly explains the trust he inspired in Howells. From his days as Howells' employer at the *Atlantic,* Osgood had paid him well, overlooked his mistakes of judgment—such as an unpopular series of articles by Oliver Wendell Holmes—and continued as his confidant. Their friendship survived setbacks through the 1870s, including the havoc of the Boston fire.[91] When Osgood died in England in 1892, Howells described him as being "as generous as he was adventurous; he had a mind quick to conceive and prompt to execute; he carried into business the whole sympathies of a poet and the ardor of an idealist. . . . A word from him was a pledge which he felt bound to fulfil."[92]

In letters to Osgood Howells tests his plans and reports on progress. He refers to project "number-one," or the looming "number-three," which resulted in *The Rise of Silas Lapham.* He speaks of "the strain of working out plots and characters amidst new and distracting scenes," while planning a string of books and articles that would strain anyone else merely to contemplate.[93] He wonders about Osgood's continued interest in a proposed magazine that Howells himself would edit; about the fate of articles he has sent for the *Century,* the status of "Niagara Revisited," and, as ever, about the "History of Venice," not now conceived as an exhaustive, scholarly work but rather as a popular book to make his publisher and himself a lot of money.

Through Osgood, Howells had entered into an agreement with the Scottish publisher David Douglas. Douglas was to receive manuscript copies of his new works, have them set in type, and apply for copyright. (An 1868 case made it possible for foreigners to secure copyright if their work first appeared in Britain.) The scheme served a number of purposes: it protected Howells' earnings, provided printing plates—still an author's responsibility—for

American publication, and enabled Douglas to issue handsome trade editions of his novels. Douglas also published smaller, cheaper, but well-bound volumes in his American Authors series, which prominently featured Howells.

More than arranging for the typesetting of books and the handling of copyright, Douglas offered an extensive selection of Howells' novels and did what he could to make them sell. He became, Howells said, one of his dearest friends. "English writers seem largely to suspect their publishers," he wrote in 1893. "I cannot say with how much reason, for my English publisher is Scotch, and I should be glad to be so true a man as I think him."[94] He liked Douglas enough to prefer his company in the late spring of 1883 to that of Andrew Carnegie, whose invitation to Skibo, Carnegie's Scottish estate, he declined. Except for *Venetian Life,* only *Suburban Sketches* and *The Undiscovered Country* had been published in England before Douglas accepted responsibility for all Howells' "literary property in Great Britain" and became the sole publisher of his works from 1882 until 1913.[95] He selected carefully for British readers, maintaining modest sales while publishing more of the early novels. Douglas inaugurated his American Authors series with eight books, all by Howells. Beginning with *A Woman's Reason,* he added *A Chance Acquaintance, A Counterfeit Presentment, Their Wedding Journey, The Lady of the Aroostook, Out of the Question, The Undiscovered Country,* and *A Fearful Responsibility.* Neither these nor later books became best sellers, though Douglas sold fourteen thousand copies of *A Chance Acquaintance* (in his cheaper edition) within three years of publication.

After leaving Scotland in August, Howells took his family to Hay-on-Wye, the Welsh market town where his father had been born. On this first of several visits, he found a brick mill that had belonged to his great-grandfather, Thomas Howells, and was still in operation. Another outbuilding had become a stable, while the third housed a printing office and bookstore. Having watched the local militia practice in one of the old mills, Howells complained to Aurelia, "Think of its Quaker origin!"[96] His great-grandfather's fortunes and his pride in his "Cymric," or Welsh, heritage were to grow with each visit to Hay-on-Wye. Writers tinker with time no less than clockmakers, which might suggest why Howells had his photograph taken beside a family clock that bears his surname on the dial.[97] In 1911, he told Aurelia that he had previously mistaken the size of one of the mills. It was much larger *and* five stories high. When Mildred, marveling at the lovely countryside, turned to him and said, "It is worthy of *us,* isn't it?" he did not object.[98]

From Wales the Howells family returned to London, where they were again taken up by writers and artists and publishers whom they met at Lowell's dinners in his honor or the Gosses' Sunday evenings. Howells owed the acquaintance of the Rossettis, George du Maurier, John Singer Sargent, Algernon Charles Swinburne, and Thomas Hardy to Gosse, who honored him with a final extravaganza at the Saville. On July 5, the family sailed from Liverpool on the *Parisian,* arriving eight days later in Quebec. "After Verona, Boston!" he wrote to his father. "What a contrast! But Boston it must be, and we all recognize that the right thing is the best."[99]

11

THE MAN OF BUSINESS

1883–1886

I found America changed even in the year I was gone. It had grown
more American, and I with my crimson opinions was scarcely more
than a dull purple in politics and religion.

—W. D. HOWELLS to Edmund Gosse, December 9, 1883

HOWELLS HAD BEEN HOME from England four months when England, in the person of Matthew Arnold, followed him across the
Atlantic. Arnold's 1883 trip, the first of two he made to the United States,
seemed a counterpart to Howells' English visit, though Howells had traveled to write, Arnold to lecture. Arriving as a literary lion, and met by Andrew Carnegie at the New York pier, he went on to a tiring but gratifying
reception, except for invasions by the American press. He spoke to large
audiences at two dollars a head in places as distant as Richmond, Chicago,
and Binghamton. The lectures he gave, with mixed success, seemed to him
the best he had written and the best medium for addressing questions of
democracy, culture, and literature. Henry James, a great admirer, had long
supported Arnold's impatience with English smugness; Howells welcomed
him as a fellow critic of American parochialism.

Or, rather, Howells welcomed him in spirit. When Arnold, with his wife
and daughter, arrived in Boston, Howells was out of town, working with

Twain on their gag-filled *Colonel Sellers as a Scientist.* Duty, or more likely curiosity, inspired Elinor to do the honors in his stead. Elinor "is greatly excited about having to call on Matthew Arnold alone," Howells told his father.[1] If it surprised Arnold to find a woman and a stranger at the door, he kept his silence, except to wonder about Howells' appreciation of Twain's humor. "He doesn't like *that* sort of thing?" "He likes Mr. Clemens very much," Elinor replied, "and he thinks him one of the greatest men he ever knew."[2] And so apparently would Arnold when he and Twain met at a Hartford reception. "Who—who in the world is that?" he asked Howells, staring at the peculiar red-haired figure across the room. "Oh that is Mark Twain," Howells told him, and for that night and the next Arnold could be found by Twain's side.[3] The infatuation was short-lived, for, after Arnold wrote a grudging review of General Grant's *Memoirs* (which Twain himself had published), Twain wrote a blistering rejoinder—his "sort of thing."[4]

Arnold made a peculiar impression on his American hosts. Known as a young man for his dandyism, and now as the model of English urbanity, he surprised those he met. Red-faced and "common" in appearance, he lacked the charm of Dickens or Thackeray or the flamboyance of Oscar Wilde, his popular forerunners on the American tour. Like Howells a quiet, undramatic performer, his voice barely carried in large auditoriums. Andrew Carnegie suggested elocution lessons, and Arnold suffered through a few. Delivery apart, he often misunderstood his audiences—at home and abroad—assuming they shared his own strong views. Just as Howells had irritated readers of the *Century,* Arnold provoked listeners in Boston, the city most inclined to welcome him.[5] With a member of Emerson's family attending, he offered what seemed off-the-cuff criticisms of Boston's prized author. Arnold's recitation of long, untranslated passages from ancient Greek sounded affected even to Bostonians. In the view of Walt Whitman, such a man, a veritable excess of "delicacy" and "prettiness," could never understand the United States, let alone appreciate the virtues of democracy.[6]

Howells, neither "too fervid an Emersonian" himself nor likely to agree with Whitman, disagreed with critics now and called the lecture he attended a success.[7] Howells wrote to Edmund Gosse that he liked Arnold. "I don't know whether he quite makes us out; he seems at times rather bewildered, and I don't wonder."[8] Given at times to what the French call *depaysment*— that queasiness of soul in a strange place—Howells sympathized with the "prophet of culture," and he may well have appreciated the irony of hearing his own attacks on Dickens and Thackeray repaid in trumps by the outspoken Englishman. Howells seems to have overlooked his own dismissal of English critics as the puppets of a decadent aristocracy, though on this point Arnold would have agreed—himself of course excepted.

In his third Boston lecture, Arnold made a point of praising Howells' depiction of New England life. His compliment may have been more than pro forma or belated politeness. Coming as they did from very different backgrounds (Arnold's father was headmaster at Rugby School, later a professor at Oxford, and Arnold himself was Oxford educated), the two nevertheless found common ground on a range of issues. Arnold too struggled with his "basis," earning his living as an inspector of schools. Like Howells, he had admired Heine in his youth and turned to other cultures in an effort to enrich his own. Arnold revered ancient Greece, modern France and Germany; Howells looked to France, Germany, Spain, and above all Italy. They shared an appreciation of Welsh traditions, a matter for each of family history and cultural principle, though Arnold saw "Celtic" traditions (and ancient Greek models) as antidotes to the unleavened English character. Each recognized the dynamic nature of civilization, the need to accommodate change without sacrificing whatever history had to teach.

They differed mainly in method and emphasis. Unlike Howells, Arnold preferred good criticism to any less-than-outstanding art, believing that English writers needed an intellectual discipline lacking since the Romantic poets (whom he nevertheless loved and imitated). He wrote primarily about literature of the past, seeking out "the best that has been thought and said," whereas Howells, for all his love of Dante or Cervantes, took a riskier measure of the literature of his age. More than Arnold's, his interests extended to painting, sculpture and architecture, as well as to emerging fields like psychology. Until the end he remained open-minded, no less curious about new technologies than people. When the two men met in 1883, Howells could look past Arnold's failings to see a kindred spirit: a man belonging to and temperamentally exiled from his own country.

I put all my sense into my novels—I keep none for myself.

—W. D. HOWELLS to James Parton, March 27, 1885

Returning home had proved more difficult than Howells anticipated. For a start, the house they rented at 4 Louisburg Square seemed almost jinxed. When, shortly after Arnold's departure from Boston, John contracted scarlet fever, Howells had to have the place fumigated with brimstone—this, he rightly complained, to destroy germs that Mildred might still get from any stranger on the streetcar. John's illness cost between three and four hundred dollars, enough to prompt his father to think about cutting expenses. Instead, in August 1884, the family made another "permanent," and expensive, move to a renovated house at 302 Beacon Street in Boston.

Among his new neighbors, Howells particularly prized Oliver Wendell Holmes. Years later, when friends planned to commemorate Holmes with a stone bench behind his house, Howells imagined passing through his back gate to beg for a place beside the divine shade.[9] Now he made his way through the gate for conversations with his friend just two doors away. He could not simply drop in: Holmes stuck to an unbending rule that all visitors, even the best of friends, had to be announced.

The Howells house had belonged to the family of George Santayana, the Spanish-born Harvard philosopher who also thought of himself as a Boston outsider. In 1872, the nine-year-old Santayana arrived in the United States knowing no English. In those days water still came up to Copley Square, and the neighborhood around his house consisted of half-built streets and vacant lots to the east. The house and its exact duplicate—three stories of brick with a mansard roof and an iron balcony running beneath the parlor windows—had been built on speculation. "The pair were a product of that 'producer's economy,' then beginning to prevail in America," Santayana later wrote, "which first creates articles and then attempts to create a demand for them; an economy that has flooded the country with breakfast foods, shaving soaps, poets, and professors of philosophy." He thought it the perfect house "for a rich spinster or for an ambitious young married couple."[10] To one interviewer the house on Beacon Street—with its light-colored carpets and massive oak sideboard, replete with crystal decanters—suited the ambitions of a wealthy banker.

As Santayana pointed out, an address on the water side of Beacon Street had social advantages. "Sometimes I feel it an extraordinary thing that I should have been able to buy a house on Beacon str.," Howells wrote to James, "but I built one on Concord Avenue of nearly the same cost when I had far less money to begin with. In those doubting days I used to go and look at the cellar they were digging, and ask myself, knowing that I had barely money to pay for the lot, '*Can* blood be got out of a turnip?' Now I know that some divine power loves turnips, and that somehow the blood will be got out of the particular turnip which I represent."[11] Eventually he would have an elevator installed and joke that Elinor rocketed up to the second floor, "leaving a brilliant trail of conversation behind her."[12] The large windows of Howells' study looked over to the Bunker Hill Monument and out on the Back Bay and Charles River, blanketed on stormy days with wild ducks. At other times he caught the raised voices of Harvard students rowing their skiffs and singing to the accompaniment of the guitar or mandolin. In the distant night sky the chimneys of the Somerville factories belched smoke like "giant torches."[13]

The factories, the passing seasons, the vanished voices reminded him of the changes in his life and the world around him. If, when Santayana resided in the Beacon Street house, Bostonians ranked a Back Bay sunset among the world's seven wonders, Howells from the vantage of his study was more skeptical. "The sun goes down over Cambridge with as much apparent interest as if he were a Harvard graduate," he wrote James, "and he spreads a glory over the Back Bay that is not to be equaled by the blush of a Boston Independent for such of us Republicans as are going to vote for Blaine."[14] He referred here to the scandal-ridden presidential election of 1884. James G. Blaine, secretary of state under Garfield and Harrison, could not defend himself convincingly against charges of graft. Grover Cleveland, his Democratic opponent, presented another sort of embarrassment after admitting that he had fathered an illegitimate child. Of the two, Howells chose Blaine, or rather he chose the platform of the party that had rewarded his family for loyal service. When Thomas Perry asked how he could justify the vote to his son, Howells responded: "I will tell John that I voted for a man *accused* of bribery, and that I would not vote for a man *guilty* of what society sends a woman to hell for. Politician for politician, self-seeker for self-seeker, I prefer a Republican to a Democrat."[15] Along with national Republican leaders—and other friends of Howells such as George W. Curtis and E. L. Godkin—Mark Twain turned Mugwump, one of those Republican defectors who supported Cleveland. Preferring licentiousness to graft, Twain delighted in the fuss over a bachelor's "private intercourse with a consenting widow."[16] Howells would have preferred to be spared a choice he knew to be a splitting of hairs. Though the Blaine-Cleveland controversy forms no part of his next novel, set in the 1870s, the questions it prompted about self-interest and public disclosure do.

He had come back to Boston ready to work, and not surprisingly he began a book about a man building a house on the water side of Beacon Street. "I shall be able to use all of my experiences, down to the quick," he told James. "Perhaps the novel may pay for the house."[17] By July he had littered his desk with pen wipers and papers that nearly obscured the new typewriter, rented for ten dollars a month. His first typewriter, from Twain, had been traded for a saddle. This "delightfully simple and manageable" machine worked so well that he allowed the company to use his "unsolicited testimony" for advertising. Later he proposed a script typeface to the Hammond typewriter manufacturers, who marketed it as the "W. D. Howells Special."[18] Typing allowed greater ease and saved his hand from cramping, without changing his routines of work.

Howells did not mention his new machine when he agreed to answer six questions about his writing process for a book on the "Methods of Authors."

1. Did he write during the day or at night? His response: "Daytime; forenoon."

2. Did he make an outline first? "Generally not—almost never."

3. Did he use stimulants such as wine, coffee, or tobacco? "No."

4. Did he have any particular habits at work? "None."

5. How many hours did he work at a time? "Two or three; sometimes four."

6. Did he ever force himself to work?

To the last question he gave a full Howells reply: "I am lazy, and always force myself more or less to work, keeping from it as long as I can invent any excuse. I often work when dull or heavy from a bad night, and find that the indisposition wears off. I rarely miss a day from any cause. After my early dinner I read, correct proof, walk about and pay visits. For a lazy man I am extremely industrious."[19]

Few writers have been so industrious or so prolific. In the 1880s Howells published nine novels (ten with the novella *A Fearful Responsibility*), quite apart from work writing for the stage and magazines. In 1885 alone he fulfilled in advance the terms of his Harper's contract with three "farces," *The Mouse-Trap, Five O'Clock Tea,* and *A Likely Story.*[20] He needed to work at this pace to afford the house on Beacon Street. "Ah! The expenses!" he told a friend in March. "I am on fire, and I *must boil.* But as yet I like the boiling—and somehow, somehow, I hope to be lifted off before I begin to burn the empty brain-pan. I have had a frightful year of work: since last March I have written one opera-libretto, one novel (Silas) five Italian papers, for the Century and two farces for Harper."[21] Whenever a project like *A Woman's Reason* dragged on unprofitably, he set it aside to pick it up later.

In May, to Twain, he admitted "worrying away at the start of a new story, which I haven't fairly got on its legs after a month's trying. And to-morrow I have to switch off and do a 'Study.' What a fool I was to undertake that!"[22] After listening to such lists for years, Norton would tell him: "I do not wonder that you are fagged with your constant writing. I used to look on the twenty one folio volumes, in double column, of the works of Albertus Magnus as a splendid monument to the leisure of the cloister. But you surpass him & leave him breathless behind you!"[23]

Howells, never at a loss for ideas himself, credited Elinor for providing his best. They might both have regretted one idea, a collection of Mildred's drawings of saints and madonnas published with his commentary. *A Little Girl among the Old Masters* (1883) earned the artist over one thousand dollars, which her proud father set aside for her education or dowry. Elinor saved and annotated the reviews. Critics who suggested that Mildred merely copied or reproduced paintings, rather than interpreted or imagined her own, sometimes earned two exclamation marks in the margins. She resented most the suggestions that Mr. Howells' little daughter might not be as simple and unconscious a child as he would have readers believe. Although a man who makes his own daughter a public figure can hardly blanch at the resulting publicity, he lamented the lack of taste in an advertisement that announced the new edition of "HOWELLS' *A Little Girl Among the Old Masters.*" Perhaps forgetting that he had felt the same about a notice of Winny's poetry, which also advertised her parentage, it surprised him that the book could be viewed as a form of exploitation. When a reviewer for the *New York Tribune* accused him of being a "showman" and Mildred "a dancing dog," he fired off a letter to the editor, his friend Whitelaw Reid. "An outrage was offered me in the house of my friend," he wrote from a particularly high horse. "You have to blame yourself in the past if your present attitude astonishes and hurts me." As soon as Reid apologized for the tone of the review, Howells relented, saying "good-bye to the whole matter!"[24]

He still enjoyed Edmund Gosse's vindication in the *Boston Daily Advertiser,* which covered everything the Howellses might have said themselves. "We *yelled* with joy," Howells wrote. "Since you have taken an interest in the little book, it seems due to you to say that if we had not known the child's unspoilableness we should not have ventured upon it. I don't think any one could be less conscious of it than she. At first she was very proud of having made a book—as a book, merely; but she never was in the least 'set up' with any one's praise of it, nor vain of her little skill, which we ourselves feel is probably an efflorescence of her childish spirit, with no sort of future before it. If it should come to anything it will not be through any prompting or petting of ours."[25] Gosse might have been tempted to add an exclamation point of his own.

Mildred's book provided an odd sideshow to other ventures, ranging from editing the biography series for James R. Osgood and the American Humor series with Twain to writing lyrics for an operetta.[26] Having had modest success with his songs in the past, Howells saw golden opportunities in musical theater, which offered a way to write less and earn more. When George Henschel, the first conductor of the Boston Symphony Orchestra, asked him to collaborate, he took his title *A Sea-Change; Or Love's Stowaway* from *The Tempest*. In the spirit of Gilbert and Sullivan, the heroine sings:

> I am a member of that Aristocracy,
> Wholly composed of the lovelier sex . . .
> In the heart of our New-World Democracy.[27]

Howells looked forward to the opening of the operetta at the Bijou Theater in May 1884, and boasted a little to Twain that he and Henschel would receive fifty dollars for each evening performance, twenty-five for matinees.[28] Before the first performance, however, the manager, boarding his yacht in the notoriously thick fog of Boston harbor, slipped and fractured his skull. A disappointed Howells summed up the situation for Henry James. With the man's death, he said, "our legal hold upon a potential fortune" evaporated.[29] A performance for invited guests in the Boston Museum on January 27, 1885, generated no further interest, maybe because Howells' stage directions called for too much pomp and circumstance, including "a big portion of the deck of an ocean steamship, but also an iceberg, big enough to be the habitation of the chorus, which must float alongside the vessel and be lashed to her."[30] The next year, he published the lyrics in *Harper's Weekly* for the sum of $650, probably more than he would have made from an average run of the play.

Love's Stowaway suggests the scope of Howells' writing for the theater. He translated *Sansone* and did the libretto for this "opera," or Broadway musical, but he found his gift to lie in the writing of farces. He prided himself on giving lengthy stage directions about the setting, situation, and at times the characters, a practice soon to be followed by George Bernard Shaw, who in fact admired Howells' plays. "With three weeks practice," Shaw wrote, "the American novelist could write the heads off the bunglers to whom our managers vainly appeal when they want a small bit of work to amuse the people who come at eight."[31] Howells called the stage directions his major contribution to the American theater, believing they created "a middle form between narrative and drama."[32] Later he decided that the last word belonged to the actors rather than the writer. From 1874 to 1911 he wrote or translated thirty-six plays and worked, without success, to adapt his own novels for the stage. *A Foregone Conclusion,* which the British dramatist and actor William Poel produced in 1884 as *Priest or Painter,* met with limited acclaim in England. Howells cut Poel's script, added dialogue, and wrote a whole new first act for a trial performance in 1886 at Madison Square Theater (the first in a series of "Author's Matinees"). The house was splendid, the applause incessant, and Howells left thinking the performance a triumph. "Without a dissenting voice," the newspapers pronounced the play bad.[33]

The collaborative nature of theater makes it the most fickle of arts and the most commercially risky. As Howells explains in *The Story of a Play,* "It's a compromise all the way through—a cursed spite from beginning to end."[34] Whether or not he was the best judge of his own work, he remained an astute commentator on the American theater. Lamenting the popularity of self-sacrificing heroines, jealous husbands, heroic highwaymen, and repentant prostitutes, he anticipated the focus of playwrights in the 1930s by urging contemporaries to approach social and psychological problems as regional writers "deal with the humble life of New York and New England."[35] He praised Henrik Ibsen's *Ghosts* in 1889 and defended it again in 1894 when others called it unclean and vicious. The United States would not have a truly national theater, Howells argued, until it embraced both the diversity and the facts of American life.

———

> Mr. Howells is beyond dispute a great artist. Slowly and by gradual stages even we Philistine English people are beginning with a grudging reluctance to perceive it.
>
> —"Current Criticism," *Critic,* October 17, 1885

Livy Clemens spoke for many readers when she said that *The Rise of Silas Lapham* (1885) surpassed anything Howells had previously written. More complex, more shaded, more humane, it marked—in Livy's mind—a new "moral" phase of his art.[36] "Moral" certainly applies to the novel's central dilemma: Lapham's increasing struggle to make an honest living and meet responsibilities to his family and himself. The questions that underlie *Silas Lapham* and the novels that follow reflect Howells' own shifting state of mind. His story chronicles the personal and ethical trials confronting a middle-aged man—a man about as old as Howells himself.

One of the first American novels to focus on business, *The Rise of Silas Lapham* introduces "a rude, common, unrefined" entrepreneur who holds out against temptation and, in the end, chooses "ruin rather than inflict it" on others.[37] The book came to life in Howells' Beacon Street study, and while it tells the story of a man, it is at the same time the story of a house, or houses. Having made a fortune with a formula for paint, Lapham moves his wife and two daughters, Irene and Penelope, from their homestead in rural Vermont to a comfortable but unfashionable Boston neighborhood. Chance brings the Laphams into contact with the Coreys, an old Boston family, whose only son wins the hearts of both sisters. His social ambitions stirred, Lapham contracts to build a mansion on the "swamp-side" of Beacon Street. The novel might have been called "The Education of Silas Lapham," for under the tutelage of Tom Corey, whom he takes into business, Lapham comes to understand what it means to be a "gentleman" in first a merely social, later a more honorable sense. Almost overnight the self-made millionaire finds himself short of cash—like his author when stock in the Chicago, Burlington, & Quincy Railroad fell thirteen points below its purchase price.[38] As the cost of Lapham's house nearly quadruples, technical changes in the paint business make his product less competitive. Hoping at first to raise cash by selling mills he has accepted as collateral, he finds his investment to be essentially worthless. He can sell the property if he lies about it, or his company if he hides recent losses, but either ploy requires a blurring of ethics he can no longer allow himself. His last resource, the uninsured house on Beacon Street, goes up in smoke, accidentally set on fire by Lapham himself.

Howells plays God to Lapham's Job. Lapham has little understanding of what has happened to him. Were it to be done over again, he tells the minister in whom he confides, he guesses he would do things the same way.[39] For all his rough groping for words, Lapham speaks eloquently about the force of individual conscience in a world that can be neither controlled nor comprehended. Perhaps because this is what Howells himself believed, he offers, through the character of Lapham's minister, a simple but profound formula for living. Given the choice, it is better for one person to suffer than three, the minister tells Lapham, who seeks his advice after Tom Corey proposes to Penelope instead of Irene, the prettier sister they had assumed he wanted. Howells calls the philosophy an "economy of pain," by which he means a containment, not an end, of heartache. The "tragic sense of life" that Howells understood as well as anyone has in Lapham a comic or burlesque as well as a commercial side. Men and women have to make their living, and the power of *Silas Lapham* comes in part from the braggart-businessman losing and finding again, then "rising" doggedly to his embrace of personal and financial loss. Howells no doubt appreciated in Lapham's struggle his own—and Twain's—unending and at times humorous business dealings, along with the houses that measured their success.

Much of the appeal of *Silas Lapham* centers on Penelope, its outspoken, dark-haired heroine. But it is Howells' even-handed portrayal of the Laphams and the Coreys that still intrigues—and perplexes—readers. As with Lapham's formula for paint, Howells creates his protagonist from a mix of elements: defensive, volatile, a man of generous impulses, he makes even his wife and daughters cringe. So too with the Coreys, whose taste and reticence he mixes with a destructive snobbery. Howells ends the novel with Lapham's return to his Vermont house and with Tom and Penelope's marriage. The young people plan to live in Mexico until Tom succeeds in making his fortune. This he does, and he and Penelope make a cameo appearance in a later novel, *The Minister's Charge.* By that time, Boston has learned to adjust to the large, democratizing changes their marriage represents.

Henry James compared *The Rise of Silas Lapham* with his own *The Bostonians* (1884), the tale of his native city in the years following the Civil War. James' novel caused a stir among Bostonians who thought they recognized Nathaniel Hawthorne's sister-in-law, Elizabeth Peabody, in his unflattering characterization of the scatterbrained Miss Birdseye. It was a pretty bad business, his brother William wrote, and another James, James Russell Lowell, agreed. James himself swore he had not intended the parody while admitting to seeing "the whole moral history of Boston . . . reflected in her displaced spectacles."[40] Howells' Boston comes into focus through similar details: the gradual removal of Bromfield Corey's dilettantish paintings from front rooms to back corners, his wife's elevation of Lapham from colonel to general. In comparison to *The Rise of Silas Lapham,* James wrote, *The Bostonians* appeared mere "sugar-cake." He may have conceded to Howells a greater craftsmanship in this novel, along with a depth of insight he had not seen before, a recognition that there are in human affairs no answers for moral conundrums and no escape from individual choice and conscience.[41]

Although Howells wrote many novels, his reputation rested for decades on *Silas Lapham*. Hippolyte Taine, the influential French critic, compared it to the work of Honoré de Balzac when recommending its publication. The *Century's* Roswell Smith estimated that more than a million people read the serialized version.[42] In the year after publication, Ticknor printed more than ten thousand copies.[43] In 1911, the novel became required reading in classes at Yale, Columbia, and Cornell.[44] In retrospect it is always difficult to gauge the impact of a book, even on individual readers. This book was different. *Silas Lapham* not only inspired future generations of readers and younger novelists; it also affected disciplines as remote as architectural design. Cass Gilbert, the architect of the Woolworth Building in New York, insisted that Howells did "more to cultivate good taste" in American architecture than any professional then living. "A single sentence in 'Silas Lapham' about [the ugliness of] *black walnut*," he wrote, "changed the entire trend of thought and made it possible for the architects of the time to stem the turbid tide of brown stone and black walnut so dear to the heart of the American millionaire"—and dear to the Howellses themselves in their house long ago on Sacramento Street.[45] *Silas Lapham* has continued to attract readers because, as Gilbert suggests, it offers them a measure, a way of testing their own standards against those of the Coreys and their cousins in all but name, the Laphams. A domestic drama on a larger scale, the novel addresses the process that turns people like the Laphams into people like the Coreys while showing how little separates any person from another. The ironic design of the book, its appeal to the best and worst tendencies in readers as they shift allegiances from one family to the other—not to mention the insiders' look at how the rich live—have made *Silas Lapham* one of the most enduring of American novels. An additional reason for its popularity is harder to pin down. Unlike *A Hazard of New Fortunes*, the novel seems as circumspect as a Jane Austen novel, its emphasis resting almost entirely on personal behavior. Though the setting of *Silas Lapham* is historical and its themes social, readers come back to the book, as Livy Clemens understood, to explore its moral universe.

Like the capitalist Silas Lapham, Howells wanted to make quick money. He saw in the novel what Twain saw in *The Gilded Age*, a potential windfall. Hoping to profit from a hit play, he showed a script to W. H. Crane, who thought it insufficiently dramatic without major rewriting. Still optimistic about the project in the late 1890s, Howells collaborated unsuccessfully with his playwright cousin, Paul Kester, and another man of the theater, Francis S. Drake. According to James A. Herne, a theater impresario of the time, the collaborative effort amounted to little more than a transcription of the novel. *Silas Lapham* did not reach the stage until 1919, when Lillian Sabine's altogether revamped version ran to lukewarm reviews for forty-seven performances at New York's Garrick Theater. Howells granted Sabine the film rights for two years. After that, they were to revert to Howells and his heirs. In 1934 his daughter Mildred would try to interest Fox Studios in a film adaptation. Though legal questions about who owned rights to the play may have sunk the project, people thought it perfect for the talents of Will Rogers.[46] In the end, neither *Silas Lapham* nor any of Howells' other novels became movies—an ironic legacy for a man who used dialogue brilliantly and proved an early and shrewd critic of silent "moving pictures." And that, of course, might explain the failure: Howells was in a sense all talk before the movies had any.

I am a coward and all kinds of a tacit liar—not because I don't love the truth, heaven knows, but because I'm afraid to tell it very often.

—W. D. HOWELLS to S. Weir Mitchell, October 20, 1885

As if he were not busy enough trying to juggle his novel and playwriting with another series of Italian essays and plans for Winny's debut, Howells worked to bring Edmund Gosse to the United States during the winter of 1884–85. He acted as Gosse's agent, counseling him on how much money he needed to earn to make his visit pay (several thousand dollars) and securing him an invitation to give the Lowell Institute lectures. Negotiating the lecture contract was, Howells wrote, "the most disagreeable [task] that I have had since being justly snubbed for poverty and obscurity."[47] It did not help that his snubber, Augustus Lowell, who ran the institute with the same authority as his factories in Lowell, Massachusetts, was a cousin of James Russell Lowell. (He also had three gifted children: a Harvard president, an Imagist poet, and the iconoclastic astronomer who "observed" water and remnants of civilization on the planet Mars.)

With the help of Richard Watson Gilder, Howells had arranged for Gosse to address private gatherings as well as student audiences at Johns Hopkins, Yale, and Harvard, where he lectured gratis to a crowd of six hundred. On the night of his arrival in the United States, he discovered a reporter camped outside his hotel door, a herald of the mania to come. Arriving at the Howellses' on December 1, Gosse and his wife, Nellie, learned that every ticket for his first lecture had been taken. People braved the weather, standing in line under dripping umbrellas to get a chance to hear him. The *Boston Gazette* reported that by 9:30 A.M. the line already circled the hall. "Several ladies had brought books to read, some found a camp chair to roost on, others entertained themselves by watching the people come and fall into line, a line that grew longer and longer until it doubled, and at length trebled round the great hall."[48] When Howells speaks of Boston as literary, he has in mind a scene like this, with a thousand people competing for seats at a lecture. The Gosses had never imagined, never mind experienced, such celebrity, which Howells tagged "the Gosse boom."[49] At his Harvard lecture, Gosse met the model for James' Miss Birdseye, the "transcendental" Elizabeth Peabody, in the flesh, complete, as he wrote, with "long silky white curls, soft pink complexion, enflamed eyes, [and] long trails of grey beard."[50] They found one another charming.

Not everything in Boston went so cordially. Augustus Lowell, hosting a dinner for the Gosses, invited various luminaries. One was Charles Eliot Norton, who held forth on the deterioration of London society. During his diatribe he "happened to refer to Alma-Tadema's wife as the daughter of a cocoa-vender, James Epps," ignorant that she was a niece rather than a daughter of the chocolate magnate and, more to the point, that Nellie Gosse was her sister. Norton, either not seeing or not reading Gosse's expression, mentioned the omnipresent advertisement for Epps' cocoa, which featured two lovely women symbolizing gratitude and comfort. "I do not know which one he married," Norton said, "'Grateful' or 'Comforting!'" Before Howells could divert the conversation, Gosse shot out: "He married 'Grateful'; I married 'Comforting' myself." Hearing the story, Henry James assured Norton's sister Grace that Gosse had taken "Charles's *faux pas* altogether too tragically."[51]

The Howellses themselves hosted a less strained reception on December 4. In the words of a reporter for the New York *Daily Tribune,* the guest list included "the best known people of Boston and Cambridge." Gosse's diary listed them as the actor Edwin Booth, Thomas Wentworth Higginson, Edward Everett Hale, Horace Scudder, the Aldriches, the historian Francis Parkman, and the statesman Henry Cabot Lodge.[52] Gosse particularly liked Oliver Wendell Holmes, with his "little boyish figure," bright eyes, and chuckle, and made a point of seeing him almost every day during his two-and-a-half-week stay.[53] "Dr. Holmes calls at 10," Gosse recorded. "Howells reads MS. of 'Silas Lapham.' E. E. Hale calls at 12, I visit Dr. Holmes and borrow his new 'Emerson.' After lunch, C. E. Norton calls, Francis Parkman, Bigelow, etc. Howells and I go up to office of the 'Atlantic Monthly.' Scudder and Garrison. Walk back. Talk on the passion of love. Lecture. Dr. Holmes."[54]

A week after the Howells reception on December 11, members of the Tavern Club honored Gosse at the studio of the painter Frederic Porter Vinter. Writing home at the end of his visit, Gosse spoke of having met more than six hundred people. "We have enjoyed—but I must not be reported to have said it—the greatest social success that any Englishman of letters has enjoyed since Thackeray lectured in Boston." Holmes himself—"the intellectual king of Boston"—assured him that no one had ever made such a conquest.[55] Gosse's welcome also paid tribute to the man who hosted him. When Gosse returned to London a richer man (by almost $2,500—about $40,000 today), he dined immediately with James, whose first question was, "How is Howells?" To some extent, Gosse's success in the United States proved his undoing in England. The book that came out of his lectures, *English Literature from Shakespeare to Pope,* met with a battery of criticism for its inaccuracies.

Much as Howells enjoyed Gosse's company and the success of his visit, he had problems to attend to, including his father's purchase of Rio Vista, the farm five miles west of Richmond, Virginia, which spread over a hundred acres. William's property included the house itself, a graceful structure with large French windows that opened out to the James River Valley, a second house suitable for a shop and storeroom, and a stable with carriage and sundry other sheds. Age had not dampened William's enthusiasms. Along with tending his extensive vineyard and orchards, he looked forward to raising fish to support his family, which now included a new son-in-law, John H. Mulholland. Vic had married in 1883 after securing Mulholland's promise to care for Henry. Her marriage prompted William to rewrite his will so that he could provide for Henry and Aurelia while giving Vic first refusal on the farm. He named Howells his executor.[56]

Distressed about his seventy-seven-year-old father's doing physical labor, Howells offered to pay for help and began sending a monthly stipend of twenty-five dollars, which he doubled after three years.[57] His sisters meanwhile did what they could to earn extra money. Always inventive—she had once designed a sewing needle with a larger eye for easy threading—Vic now joined with Aurelia to sell boxes of holly, cut with their father's one-handed grape shears. At Christmas, Howells received a cornucopia of evergreens. He could not refrain from giving advice with his thanks: another year, they should use bigger boxes, put in fewer, longer boughs, and add mistletoe. Had he thought again about the Epps cocoa advertisements, he might have pictured William's "grape gatherers" finding a market and his sisters posing as Plenitude and Sweetness.

At this moment Howells' own economic future lay in doubt. At the beginning of May 1885, James R. Osgood & Co., the source of his weekly salary, fell into receivership. Few could believe that someone like Osgood, "singularly fitted" for his work "both by instinct and by education," could suddenly fail when all of his individual enterprises succeeded.[58] After thirty years in publishing, Osgood, who had one hundred thousand dollars invested in projects that were not yet earning royalties, lacked, as Howells put it, "the qualities as well as the resources" to cope with fierce competition and a market flooded with cheap books.[59] Howells might have put a little of Osgood into Silas Lapham—as another character describes him. "I suppose that a hopeful temperament and fondness for round numbers have called him to set his figures beyond their actual worth. I don't say he's been dishonest about it, but he's had a loose way of reckoning his assets; he's reckoned his wealth on the basis of his capital, and some of his capital is borrowed."[60]

From England a shocked James sought Howells' advice; Osgood still owed him four thousand dollars for the serialization of *The Bostonians*. What could he do? William James then asked Howells "to tip" Harry "a line of information," or tell him, William, how to find out what was happening. A week later he asked again: "I suppose you know how Osgood's affairs are going. . . . Do you suppose it would lessen Harry's risks in any way if I were to put his interests into a lawyer's hands to look after?" Howells' silence, followed by his testament to Osgood's honesty, did little to reassure Henry James, who very much needed—and never received—the money owed to him.[61]

Because of Osgood's unexpected bankruptcy, Howells had to reassess his own career and the ways he made his money. He had raised his children to a standard of living he himself as a child had known only from books. "I must give my daughter her chance in this despicable world, where I'm so much better for having had none," he wrote an old friend; "I must get my boy through school and into college,—where I'm so much wiser for not having been. It's the pleasures and follies that we pay dearest for."[62] With Gosse's example in mind, he considered and rejected the possibility of lecturing. Twain still teased him about being a poor speaker, and Howells had his own doubts about keeping an audience's attention. When the two read at Madison Square Garden in late April 1885 to raise funds for the American Copyright League, Twain changed his tune. "Heiliger Gott! but it was a good reading," he wrote. "Far better than Cable could have done it—

which is not much of a compliment, but it started honestly *out* to be a compliment. It had simplicity, sincerity, & absence of artificiality, in place of Cable's self-complacency, sham feeling & labored artificiality. Sincerity *is* a great & valuable thing in front of an audience."[63] It incensed Twain that Cable used his wife's illness as an excuse not to participate in the benefit.[64] He conceded Cable's great intellect, "but in order to find room for this greatness in his pygmy carcase, God had to cramp his other qualities more than it was judicious."[65] Though Twain had a number of problems with Cable, the most galling may have been that described in James Pond's telltale reminiscences. On the lecture tour, Pond wrote, "Mr. Cable became a student of Mark and fell to aping him to such an extent as to make him appear ridiculous. He assumed Mark's drawl in his readings and it became almost a second nature to him to the extent that he was imitating Mark even in his conversation."[66] With no chance of attempting to imitate Twain's performances, Howells took his friend's mixed praise of his reading as a sign that he might succeed on the lecture circuit.

In the years following the Civil War, only a handful of writers earned a living from literature, and their success reflected the prosperity of the magazine industry. Depending on what James called his "maga-writing" for his income and reputation, Howells never freed himself from its demands. The larger part of his earnings came from the magazines, a fact that complicates his publishing history and our sense of his audience. Howells knew, as his newspaperman Bartley Hubbard illustrates, the way that writers and editors pander to the public and to their advertisers. He too had to please readers, yet he also had a measure of freedom in contracts that ensured his income. *A Modern Instance* eventually sold ten thousand volumes (not counting sales in England and Europe), which might seem modest until we also remember that it reached more than one hundred thousand potential readers through serialization in the *Century,* and maybe more assuming that two or more people read each issue.[67] Most people who knew Howells read him in the magazines, which reduced the need or incentive to buy his books. Magazine publication, which made Howells a household name—even, like Twain, a best-selling author—may suggest one reason why he took the modest sales of his books philosophically.

After the turn of the century, he grew more impatient and often shared concerns about low sales with his fellow sufferer, Henry James: "Of course one is more or less corrupted by the spectacle of the immense success around one, and it galls me that I should sell only as many thousands as the gilded youth of both sexes are selling hundreds of thousands, and largely as I believe for want of publicity—that is the new word for advertising."[68] In other moods he blamed himself, his public, or the times. His books sold well enough to make a handsome living, not enough to make him feel safe in an era without social security or guaranteed health care. Despite losing his salary of ten thousand dollars a year, Howells told friends that he would go back to Osgood if the man resumed business. That happened only in his fancy. Osgood went to work for Harper & Brothers in England, where he associated with the English avant-garde, published Oscar Wilde's *House of Pomegranates* under his own imprint, and died in 1892. A decade later, Howells dreamed that he and Osgood were to start their own publishing house, and "it seemed all right."[69]

Turning potential disaster into an opportunity, Howells made the most of being a free agent, playing one publisher off against another as he cast about for a new "basis." Negotiating with Roswell Smith, the owner of the *Century*, he prepared a list of questions and options:

I. Whether he is ready to monopolize me.

II. Whether he could put all that I write in *The Century*.

III. Could he leave me free in choice of subjects?

IV. That I could not go on under O[sgood]'s contract except for the stories stipulated for.

V. What percentage on books?

VI. Go abroad and write a history, when sick of stories.[70]

He felt that he could always fall back on Benjamin Ticknor, a man he had known since his 1860 trip to Boston and whom he trusted as Ticknor trusted him. Intending to acquire Osgood's company, Ticknor assured him he would be paid in full. Ticknor, knowing that Howells would likely sign with Harper's, still tried to persuade him to stay. He paid him a lump sum of $1,730.77 and guaranteed weekly payments on a scale of $7,500 a year, plus royalties.[71] In return, Howells agreed to supply six short stories, his Italian essays, *Tuscan Cities*, and books, including *Indian Summer* (1886), which had been Osgood's property.[72]

Because of Osgood and through the mediation of Charles Fairchild, his old Belmont landlord, Howells signed a contract with Harper & Brothers the following fall.[73] His relationship with Ticknor ended amicably, and in June of that year, with his income assured, Howells relaxed with his family in Great Barrington, Massachusetts, and other seaside towns. He went to Wells and Kennebunkport, Maine, and Old Orchard Beach, which he liked to call Old Orchard "Beast." August found him in Bethlehem, New Hampshire, where he attended a memorial service for Ulysses S. Grant, to whom the Howellses owed the extension of William's consulship. Howells reminded Twain that if General Grant "had not been there to neutralize us, I think we should have had my father turned out of his place and imprisoned for life. . . . I used to tremble when I thought of our success in that matter. Have we lost our cunning?"[74] Twain could count another success, no matter how qualified in Arnold's opinion. Before Grant died, he had secured the *Memoirs* for his own publishing company. Twain's intercession brought Grant's widow more than $420,000 in royalties. At the service, as Howells sat listening to people pump "song and praise" over Grant's memory, he kept thinking of the day he and Twain had dined with the general, not on caviar but on pork and beans.[75]

Howells had arrived at the age when, as he said, his memory spanned decades and played tricks. In March he had turned forty-eight. Though he felt younger than ever, his own daughters thought him elderly and verging on prosaic. Mark Twain spoke of their shared plight of lost youth, that "cloudy sense of . . . having been a prince, once, in some enchanted far-off land, & of being in exile now, & desolate."[76] Inspired by Winny's romantic view of Italy and his own mixed feelings, Howells had written his poignant comedy about youth and age, *Indian Summer*. Finished sixteen months earlier—before *Silas Lapham*—it began its serialization in the July 1885 issue of *Harper's Monthly*.

The romance between a middle-aged bachelor and a woman young enough to be his daughter made Twain laugh and cry and feel old and forlorn. Thomas Aldrich could not wait to read the installments to come. Nor could one Mrs. Meader, who wrote to beg advance sheets of the novel before she died. Her letter touched Howells. "I cannot tell you how sincerely and humbly grateful I am to be the means of lightening the moments of sickness to you, and this book of mine will always have a peculiar interest to me because it has interested you at this time." More skeptical, Henry Alden, James Osgood, and Henry Harper requested confirmation from the woman's doctor. Their suspicions of a hoax proved correct. Shamed by the sincerity of Howells' response, Mrs. Meader, also known as Helen Walter, wrote to apologize.[77] Howells later adapted the incident to bring would-be lovers together in his novel *Fennel and Rue* (1908).

Indian Summer may be Howells at his wittiest and wisest. Friends like

Twain, who tended to see themselves in the protagonist Theodore Colville, should have recognized the temperamental similarities between Colville and his author, though the well-knit plot of the story, which brings a retired editor of a Western newspaper back to Florence after twenty years, is of Howells' imagining. The tentative Colville, adrift in the city that had been the site of his great love, meets Lina Ridgely, the best friend of the woman who had rejected him. In the interim, Lina has become Mrs. Bowen, a widow with both a young daughter and a surrogate daughter, the impressionable, beautiful Imogene Graham of Buffalo, New York. For Imogene, Colville's long-ago affair marks him as a romantic figure, and she decides to redress the past by throwing herself into his arms. The ensuing engagement develops as one long misunderstanding, with Howells making fun of the innocence of Colville and the guile of his betrothed. Because of Imogene's abandon and her unjaded capacity for pleasure, Colville feels his age, and, more intensely, his losses; these include his estrangement from Mrs. Bowen and hers from Imogene. Colville cannot take what Imogene offers. Each of us lives "to himself in the world," he tells her. No one "could hope to enter into the life of another and complete it."[78] The novel comes to the first of a series of comic climaxes during the carnival, where the masked lovers are both unmasked. Colville marries Mrs. Bowen, who loved him in her youth, manages to love him still, and almost forgives him. Imogene, sadder and wiser and back in Buffalo, will apparently marry her previous suitor, a dull young minister.

For all its humor, *Indian Summer* captures the angst of growing older. When did it happen, Colville asks, this weakening of passion and direction? "What did he care for the Italians of to-day, or the history of the Florentines as expressed in their architectural monuments? It was the problems of the vast, tumultuous American life, which he had turned his back on, that really concerned him. . . . He was no longer young, that was true; but with an ache of old regret he felt that he had not yet lived his life, that his was a baffled destiny, an arrested fate."[79] The folly of his past and present behavior brings Colville to a reluctant understanding and a measured, if rueful, perspective on Florence. "What a history is written all over it, public and private! If you don't take it simply, like any other landscape, it becomes an oppression. It's well that tourists come to Italy so ignorant, and keep so. Otherwise they couldn't live to get home again: the past would crush them."[80] *Indian Summer* concludes on this bittersweet wisdom of middle age. Had James written it, Colville would have returned unmarried to the United States, leaving Mrs. Bowen and her daughter to drift through

Europe. Distinctly not James, and presenting a comic world, Howells allows Colville to claim his bride, albeit twenty years late, and a daughter too; and, as might be expected from an indulgent father, he lets Colville settle every dispute between mother and daughter in the daughter's favor.

The novel seems the more poignant in light of Howells' personal situation. In October 1885, he let the house on Beacon Street, which was to have been the setting of Winny's social triumph. "Poor Winny is too poorly to do any society in it," he wrote Gosse, "and without that her mother and I have no heart for it."[81] If their house did not go up in flames like Silas Lapham's, it came to remind them of loss and personal failure. Winny was then being treated by James Jackson Putnam, a Boston neurologist. In Putnam's opinion, her case posed no immediate danger, but he told her anxious parents that if her condition deteriorated, he would turn her over to the nation's best-known specialist, S. Weir Mitchell, Howells' friend and fellow novelist. The summer trips the family took in search of healthier air found their way into Howells' books; a visit to the fashionable resort of Campobello, at the Canadian border, for example, provided a setting for *April Hopes* (1888). No place they found did Winny any lasting good.

Treatments cost money, and Howells welcomed his contract with Harper & Brothers, effective October 16, 1885. For $3,000 a year, he agreed to write monthly columns for the Editor's Study. Harper's would pay him another $10,000 for a farce and for the serial rights to one novel. Harper's based his salary on the rate of $50 per thousand words in the *Monthly* and $30 in the *Weekly.* In line with common practice, Howells provided the plates of his books (usually from David Douglas in Edinburgh or Joe Howells in Jefferson), and Harper's paid royalties of 12.5 percent.[82] Although the financial pressures on Howells did not diminish, he still had the luxury of a steady salary.

This contract served as a template for his future dealings with Harper's: an agreed-upon number of contributions for a substantial annual salary, and royalties determined on the basis of the costs of distribution and the setting of type. In 1892, for instance, Howells negotiated royalties of 20 percent for the first five thousand copies of his novels and a very high 25 percent thereafter; his farces and travel literature typically earned less. "You'll have heard of my contract with Harper's," he wrote Gosse—who could scarcely have failed to.[83] New York papers reported his offers and counteroffers. He had become a newsworthy figure, and the public, he would later joke, cared about the pay of poets second only to their passions. Hamlin Garland remembered that Howells' *Modern Instance, Indian Summer, The*

Minister's Charge, and *Silas Lapham* struck readers as the most original and technically skilled writing America had known. People eagerly awaited their publication and debated their merits.

As Howells' fortunes waxed, his brother Sam's waned. Always a financial burden to the family, he had lost yet another place, and Howells did everything possible to find him a job while continuing to send money. In September 1886 he bought Sam the *Index,* a small newspaper in Madison, Ohio, not far from Ashtabula. "I didn't wish to do so, I'll confess," he wrote to his father, "but he was constantly asking me for money; I was paying his house-rent; and I thought I had better give him this chance at self support." He reckoned that the office would yield an annual income of $1,000 to $1,200 a year, which would increase Sam's weekly pay from $2 to $20. Sam promised to put his daughters to work in the office and make the paper a family concern on the order of the *Sentinel.* "I shall be glad if he keeps half of his promises, but you'll not be surprised to know that I have no faith in them or him."[84]

On the one hand, Howells felt that Sam had himself to blame; on the other, he wrestled with the endless puzzle of family responsibility and the unfairness of life. It seemed wrong, for instance, that beautiful, airy houses in Boston sat unoccupied while "thousands upon thousands of poor creatures" stifled in "wretched barracks," whole families crammed into one room.[85] His difficulty lay in deciding what could be changed and accepting what could not. To sort out issues or understand them rationally did not mean that he could live by his principles. But then, he could always write about them. From his Editor's Study column in *Harper's Monthly,* he sent letters to the world (to borrow Emily Dickinson's phrase) that explored and tested his social thinking and, in the years to come, won him as many enemies as friends.

Sometimes it has seemed to me that the crudest expression of any creative art is better than the finest comment upon it.

—w. d. howells, *Criticism and Fiction,* 1893

The Editor's Study came into being not because Howells wanted a forum but because his editor needed a column. In September 1885, Henry Alden, the senior editor at Harper's, asked him to consider a literary department for *Harper's Monthly* "corresponding to that which the Editor's Easy Chair has to the current social movements." Reluctantly, Howells wrote a pilot article. Alden responded with enthusiasm, declaring it just what he had in mind. "What impresses me most about it is that your subtlest analysis is not addressed to the acute & exceptional intellect but to the common sense."[86] This was exactly what Howells wanted, indeed what he lived by. Throughout his career he prided himself on writing about complex issues in ways that any intelligent reader could understand.

He agreed to take on the Editor's Study, which ran from January 1886 through March 1892, with the express stipulation that he could write whatever he wanted, regardless of editorial interests or the objections of advertisers. The column developed, like Howells' relationship with Alden, in ways unforeseen by both men. There came times when Alden had to use all his tact to persuade Howells not to appear to side with anarchists or infuriate God-fearing subscribers. Checking Howells' enthusiastic review of *Robert Elsmere,* Mrs. Humphry Ward's novel about religious doubts, Alden first urged, then insisted on, compliance. The magazine, he wrote, "is pledged not to offend any of its readers."[87] Henry Harper himself explained that readers might choose their books, but the magazine "is pledged against offense to any of its patrons," their ignorance notwithstanding.[88] Howells must have heard his own editor's voice speaking through Alden's cautions, but almost always he took his own course with his friend's blessing. The two grew close, as their later essays on each other testify, partly because they shared similar religious values—Alden wrote books about life after death and related topics—and tested those values through painful times.

From his editor's study, Howells told readers, he could look out upon "the confluent waters of the Hudson and the Charles, with expanses, in the middle distance, of the Mississippi, the Great Lakes, and the Golden Gate, and in the background the misty line of the Thames, with reaches of the remoter Seine, and glints of the Tiber's yellow tide."[89] In other words, from his real or imaginary perch he could see what distinguishes the arts of various times and nations and also what unifies them. He called his columns "a symposium of one." Ranging far beyond Alden's initial mandate, they provided a forum for commenting on literature, language, art, architecture, music, and politics.[90] A column that had been mainly literary at the outset became polemical, wide-ranging, and political, though with constant attention to recent books and issues of literary importance.

The actual writing of a column took Howells a day or two, far less time than its preparation. He told an interviewer that he worked from nine in the morning to one or two in the afternoon and then read "Russian books in French . . . Spanish books . . . Italian always . . . and every notable American and English book that comes out; they all go to the making of my 'Study' work."[91] Probably thousands of readers owed their knowledge of European as well as American literature to the breadth and sympathy of Howells' columns. Writing to Charles Warner, he predicted that the next age would look upon big novels as his looked upon Richardson's. Turgenev, with his small novels and "vast outlook," had set the standard for the future.[92] Undaunted by contradictions, he promoted the big ones just as enthusiastically—the novels of Dostoyevsky and Tolstoy. His support for these still-unknown or unpopular writers—along with Émile Zola and Henrik Ibsen—extended to individuals he thought to be overlooked. As a voice for the defense, he took up more than literary issues. Speaking out for Rose Quinn, a woman sentenced to death for drowning her baby, he prompted a discussion of the case that forced editors, critics, and the larger public to engage his arguments—and he in turn theirs.

Howells' combination of social and literary agendas underscores how indistinguishable the two had become to him by the late 1880s. In an 1888 essay on Matthew Arnold, written shortly after Arnold's death, he praises Arnold's contribution to literature and revisits the Englishman's reservations about American culture. "Mr. Arnold might have said with some truth," he writes, "that we have not even been equal to our political and economic opportunities; we cannot be particularly proud of our legislatures and administrations; the relations of capital and labor in our free democracy are about as full of violence as those in any European monarchy; we have wasted the public lands which we won largely by force and fraud, and we are the prey of many vast and corrupting monopolies . . . and if the future is still ours, the present is by no means without its danger and disgrace." He uses Arnold to argue his own political agenda just as he would use Tolstoy and others in times to come, but he agrees with and goes beyond Arnold in appreciating what Arnold and other contemporaries saw as the paradoxical creation of greatness in a democratic land. "A nation which has produced . . . Lincoln, Longfellow, Grant, Emerson, John Brown, Mrs. Stowe, Hawthorne, not to name many others eminent in art and science and finance . . . has subtly but surely done its work." However abused, America's premise of a "common humanity" yields an abundance of great individuals and the health of the nation itself.[93]

Howells' columns advanced the careers of a variety of American writers, many of them women. He had a long relationship with Sarah Orne Jewett, the Maine writer who became Annie Fields' companion after the death of James Fields. As Anne Elliot, Jewett began sending stories to the *Atlantic*. When she submitted her *Strangers and Wayfarers*, a collection of stories originally published in the magazine, Howells responded: "We all have a tender pleasure in your work, which there is no name for but love. I think *no* one has shown finer art in a way, than you, and that something which is so much better than art, besides. Your voice is like a thrush's in the din of all the literary noises that stun us so."[94] He advised Jewett not to make her narrator a "character of the alien sex," advice she passed on to Willa Cather after objecting to Jim Burden's story in *My Ántonia*.[95]

Howells' appreciation of Jewett and other regional writers, among them Hamlin Garland and the Tennessee writer Charles Egbert Craddock—who surprised him by turning out to be Mary Noailles Murfree—shows his uncommon openness to the styles of writing lumped under the general category of "regional." His prejudice in favor of writers who focus on a single place grows from his understanding of Nathaniel Hawthorne, who, he writes, could only be thought "provincial if we understand the word to mean someone who saw less of the world in New England than one sees in Europe, *not* if we think of it in terms encompassing mind and soul."[96]

Above all, Howells was an eclectic reader who entered completely into fictional worlds. His enthusiastic reviews created a canon of late-nineteenth-century literature. "Such an encomium from such a source!" Charles Chesnutt responded when Howells launched his career with a favorable review of *The Conjure Woman* in 1899.[97] The *Harper's* essays in both the Editor's Study and the Easy Chair, which he occupied after 1900, read like encapsulated literary histories—"Dostoyevski Discovered" (1886), "From Emerson to Tolstoi" (1888), and "Emily Dickinson Announced" (1891). Had Dickinson written to Howells instead of Thomas Wentworth Higginson she might well have been "discovered" in her lifetime. Howells understood that she wanted her poems read. His essay, half of which is quotation, lets the poems speak for themselves. Their singularity, compression, and piercing introspection (to use Howells' terms) are as "characteristic of our life as our business enterprise, our political turmoil, our demagogism, our millionairism. 'Listen!'"[98] The names of those he praised—or introduced to his readers—goes on: Paul Laurence Dunbar, Frank Norris, Stephen Crane, Edward Bellamy, George Washington Cable, Rose Terry Cooke, Mary Wilkins Freeman, Thomas Hardy, Bernard Shaw, Laurence Gronland, H. G. Wells, and William Morris. His topics included "the question of modern civilization" (1887), "sex in literature" (1880), the Dred Scott case (1891), "the rise of psychologism" (1903), "race-patriotism" (1902)—the end of Anglo-

Saxon empire and world union—and "international government" (1916). This partial list omits other topics he discussed, such as painting (he wrote about the Paris exhibition of American Impressionists in 1895) and, late in life, moving pictures.

Henry Alden once said that of all the writers he knew, Howells was "the most difficult to associate with any theory about writing," even the literary realism he championed. "Though so excellent a critic, he never makes a point of analyzing the writings of others; at least his analysis never comes eruptively to the surface—it is creative." Alden thought that Howells' arguments, often presented in the form of a dialogue, dealt as much with life as literature.[99] Accused of eccentricity and dogmatism, of favoring Continental literature over British literature, Howells became all the more dogged when the attacks became personal. Hamlin Garland decided that if he "had been a lifelong radical fighting conservative literary tastes from the outside, the 'Study' would not have been the bitter struggle that it was for him. . . . But Howells belonged to the accepted circle of American authors, he had personal ties with his critical enemies, he fought from within the stronghold; and this made all the difference, and should make quite a difference in our estimate of Howells as a man."[100]

Even when his columns for *Harper's* reached over two hundred thousand readers in the new century, Howells remained skeptical about the benefits of reviewing. This view of course had little bearing on his own practice. He knew firsthand that critics were highly subjective and that an author must rely on his or her own judgment. At the same time, writing, especially magazine writing, had to be a collaborative process to the extent that writers negotiated with editors and readers. He deleted, for example, a line in *Silas Lapham* about Jews bringing down real estate prices. To the person who objected, he wrote: "I have already struck it out of my book, and it will not reappear. In that passage I merely recognized to rebuke it, the existence of a feeling which civilized men should be ashamed of. But perhaps it is better not to recognize all the facts. Perhaps also you owe me an apology for making an unjust accusation. I leave that to you."[101] He got his apology.

When *Silas Lapham* appeared serially in the *Century*, Richard Watson Gilder, the editor, and Roswell Smith, the publisher, asked him to expunge a sentence that mentioned dynamite. "I know what your first impression will be likely . . . ," Smith wrote, "& that is simply to let it stand as it is— but when you have thought about it, twenty four hours I am sure you will come to our conclusion—It may be well enough to joke about taking possession of the houses of the rich, &c.—but blowing open the shutters with a charge of Dynamite—suggests nihilism, destructiveness—revenge— . . . think of the recent events in London & elsewhere abroad & in New York—I am sure it won't do—Then I fancy the Law might stop the magazine or make the Publisher trouble in England." Gilder put the same sentiment in dollars and cents: "The leap made this year in the Century's circulation—up to 210,000 & *still rising*—has thrown upon us, we cannot help feeling, a greater responsibility than ever, & we cannot help being on guard against any false step which may injure our prestige & influence."[102] The public had become frightened by any mention of dynamite since the publication of Johann Most's *Revolutionary War Science: A Little Handbook of Instruction in the Use and Preparation of Nitroglycerine, Dynamite, Gun-Cotton, Fulminating Mercury, Bombs, Fuses, Poisons, etc., etc.* (1885), which explained how to exterminate the bourgeoisie. Once again Howells complied.

Neither Smith nor Gilder needed to tell him about the power or the fickleness of readers. He ranked readers above critics for influence, both benign and otherwise, because they spoke with their pocketbooks. In his novel about publishing, *The World of Chance* (1893), he has a publisher explain that a work of literary art is either a "merchantable or unmerchantable commodity." "*No* one can tell whether a book will succeed or not; no one knows what makes a book succeed. . . . If I were to trust my own observation, I should say it was *luck*, pure and simple, and mostly bad luck."[103] Howells himself writes that criticism may do "some good we do not know of. It apparently does not affect the author directly, but it may reach him through the reader. . . . We doubt if it can do more than that; but if it can do that, we will admit that it may be the toad of adversity, ugly and venomous, from whose unpleasant brow he is to snatch the precious jewel of lasting fame."[104] That said, he would continue his columns for *Harper's* with the tenacity of his boyhood hero tilting at windmills.

"HEARTACHE AND HORROR"

1886–1890

I shall be fifty my next birthday, the 1st of March. I've heard people say that they are not conscious of growing older; but *I* am. I'm perfectly aware of the shrinking bounds. I don't plan so largely as I used, and without having lost hope, I don't have so much use for it as once. I feel my half century fully. Lord, how it's slipped away!

—W. D. HOWELLS to Henry James, December 25, 1886

ON THE LAST DAY OF MARCH 1887, in the thin, afternoon light, hundreds of people gathered at the Boston Museum to honor the memory of Henry Wadsworth Longfellow. There was not an empty seat in the theater. Oliver Wendell Holmes, Mark Twain, Julia Ward Howe, James Russell Lowell, and Howells had agreed to read. The proceeds would go toward a statue of the poet and landscaping for his Craigie House memorial. When the lights dimmed and the curtain opened, the audience saw the participants seated on sofas and chairs in an irregular semicircle. Howells sat as if at home, feet stretched far apart, hands hidden in the pockets of his gray trousers, head resting on the back of his chair. The urbane Charles Eliot Norton, serving as master of ceremonies, introduced Howells. In the twenty years since Norton had helped him to buy the house on Sacramento Street, Howells had become almost a household name.

Since January of the preceding year, Howells had been writing his Editor's Study column for *Harper's Monthly*, renewing his attacks on sentimental fiction and promoting a version of realism that his harshest critics considered a threat to public morality. In the audience he recognized many of the old Cambridge faces. Some had thought him overeager, as others now thought him downright dangerous. (Howells himself would say that people do not so much change as evolve.) Whether those gathered for the ceremony looked at Howells as a stranger or saw the outlines of his former self, the Longfellow tribute provided an opportunity for reacquaintance and introductions. Norton pointedly offered them a new Howells. Commending the tough but humane realist, the man he now honored as much for his ethics as his literary talents, he said, in closing, "I present to you the moral writer, the idealist, Howells."[1]

Within a few months Norton's remarks would seem bizarrely prescient, as Howells, acting on his principles, risked both reputation and livelihood in a cause that neither Norton nor any other friends agreed to support. Through his "half century" he had not shied away from controversy—writing, for example, about scandalous topics in *A Modern Instance*—though most of his quarrels involved what he regarded as parochial clashes, his fencing with British and American critics in the magazines. "It's fun, having one's open say again, and banging the babes of Romance about," he told Edmund Gosse in 1886. "It does my soul lots of good; and how every number [of *Harper's* with the Editor's Study] makes 'em dance! There hasn't been so much honest truth aired in this country since Columbus's second mate shouted 'Land, ho!' and Columbus retorted 'What a lie! It's clouds.'"[2] In these rare moments of self-satisfaction Howells presented himself as "something of a 'shining mark,'" the honest critic of literary folly.[3] Following the conviction and sentencing of the Haymarket anarchists, he would be put to a larger test, not simply of honesty and conscience but of every precept he stood for: equal justice, the sanctity of human life, and the security of his own family. Of Basil March in *A Hazard of New Fortunes* Howells later wrote: "He faced the fact, which no good man can front without terror, that he was risking the support of his family, and for a point of pride, of honour, which perhaps he had no right to consider in view of the possible adversity."[4]

The inaptly named Haymarket Riot—there was no riot—took place in Haymarket Square, Chicago, at the corner of Desplaines and Randolph Streets on May 4, 1886. It marked the culmination of two decades of social conflict and resulted in a trial that gripped the entire country. Chicago had long been a center for socialist and later "anarchist" groups who built on the experience of the Bread Riots in 1873 and played a major part in what grew from a railroad strike into a nationwide strike in 1877. However quickly put down by Federal troops, the 1877 strike led to hundreds of deaths and to the rise of groups that would form America's first labor unions. After the "monster strike" of 1879, the coming of better times—better harvests and business—temporarily lulled radical agitation. The economic depression of the early 1880s revived a sense of urgency among workers and apprehension among their employers, who promoted violent reprisals.

As Henry James suggests through the collaboration of philanthropists and revolutionaries in *The Princess Casamassima*, a novel published in the Haymarket year, anarchism was an international movement. Key figures such as Johann J. Most moved easily from Berlin to London, New York, and Chicago, speaking to eager gatherings. To whatever extent men like Most stirred their followers or advocated the throwing of bombs, international groups had little or nothing to do with the Haymarket events.[5] In cities like Chicago, local cells of mainly German immigrants and American-born militants tended to work independently. Armed groups staged marches through downtown districts, and clashes between police and demonstrators routinely followed. Radical newspapers, many in German, proclaimed a new order on the premise that the Vanderbilts and Goulds—and the local Pullmans and Marshall Fieldses—should divide their wealth among the poor. The gulf between a common worker's ninety cents a day and Andrew Carnegie's untold millions had to be bridged. In the year of the Haymarket trial Carnegie himself said, without a nod to widespread unemployment, "I defy any man to show that there is pauperism in the U.S."[6] Disillusioned with prospects for political acceptance or gradual reform, anarchists called for violent action or outright revolution. Howells could sympathize with both Johann Most and Andrew Carnegie (whom he once called "simple-hearted and quite unspoiled" for offering to pay off the national debt of Venezuela). Disapproving of Most's advocacy of violence, he nevertheless admired the man's pluck. In an Editor's Study column he wrote that "one might make Herr Most the hero of a labor-question romance with perfect impunity" and contrasted his courage with that of American novelists, very few of whom "have been forced into exile or led out to be shot."[7] Howells identified with the plight of underpaid workers and supported their aspirations for better lives; at the same time, he dreaded the outbreak of violent conflict.[8]

The Haymarket crisis began when the fledgling Federation of Organized

Trades and Labor Unions announced a May 1 strike in support of an eight-hour workday. The strike spread. At a May 3 meeting of workers near the McCormick Harvesting Machine Company, a man named August Spies addressed a crowd, which heckled, then fought with, scab workers more than it listened to Spies' harangue. With the arrival of the police, the strikers hurled rocks; the police responded with gunfire, as if practicing for what would follow. The next night, partly in response to a flyer distributed by Spies, partly to plan tactics for future protests, a group of anarchists called a meeting at the Haymarket, a site where as many as twenty thousand people could gather. Chicago's Mayor Harrison, who in spite of his later actions believed in the right to free assembly, ordered police to patrol nearby, at a safe distance from the meeting place, and to deploy only as a last—and unlikely—resort. The meeting started quietly, with a far smaller crowd than expected, and almost ended with the coming of rain. Many protesters had gone home by the time the police moved in to disperse what remained of the crowd. At that point, someone—never identified—threw a bomb into the police ranks. The police opened fire, killing their own men along with the civilians. In all, seven police officers and four civilians died; hundreds were wounded. Whether the police were under orders to break up the gathering or the police captain decided to act on his own, an otherwise harmless event came to a bloody climax.

The police arrested Spies and six other men, searched houses without warrants, and laid the groundwork for a horrific course of events. Of the indicted defendants—Albert Parsons, Michael Schwab, Samuel Fielden, George Engel, Adolph Fischer, Oscar Neebe, Louis Lingg, William Seliger, and Rudolph Schnaubelt—Seliger turned state's evidence to avoid prosecution, and Schnaubelt slipped out of Chicago, never to return. The most celebrated member of the group, an eloquent Texan named Albert Parsons, went into hiding following the riot. The rest were jailed to await their trial, which took place in July and August 1887.

From the outset, Howells followed reports of the Haymarket story and the trial. His version, which anticipated the findings of later historians, ran contrary to almost every contemporary editorial and every assumption about justice in the national press. He did not consider the process supervised by Judge Joseph Easton Gary a trial at all. As he saw it, Gary selected his own biased jury, silenced or overruled an able defense team, and found consistently for the prosecution. Among his questionable procedures was his decision to invite groups of society women, who sat next to him and chatted about the courtroom entertainment. Gary had support from Julius S. Grinnell, a canny and ambitious state's attorney as intent as Gary himself on using any available maneuver or tainted witness to condemn the defendants. Before their testimony collapsed, paid informants accounted for most of the "evidence" against the anarchists. William Perkins Black's defense team disproved each specific charge, to no avail. Gary instructed the jury that if the defendants had "conspired to overthrow law by force," whether in print or speech, regardless of specific orders or reference to individuals, or times, or events, they must be found guilty as accessories to murder.[9] A jury given no choice wanted none. The defendants were sentenced to death.

Howells pitied the defendants as victims of a judicial system gone awry.[10] His story of Haymarket includes the bold reappearance of Albert Parsons, who, encouraged by his wife and lawyer, turned himself over to the police rather than let his companions be tried without him. It involves the complicity of businessmen and police officers, police informers, and state's attorneys with the judge, who would proudly defend his actions by saying that the times warranted unusual, if necessary illegal, methods. The defendants' wives and children attended the trial to hear their husbands and fathers called "loathsome murderers," "organized assassins," and "rats to be driven back to their holes."[11] From the point of view of their opponents— the prosecution, the city government, the corporations, and the press— some of the defendants *were* potentially dangerous, even if innocent of the bombing charges. One of them made bombs, and most approved of using violence for political ends. Howells himself believed they should have been indicted for conspiracy. In a time of social turmoil, they faced a frightened and angry citizenry and determined officials who not only intended to teach a lesson about public safety (and the need to keep wages low) but violated the civil rights, indeed the lives, of innocent men in the cause of social order. The broad majority of Americans applauded their efforts and, spurred on by newspapers, demanded vengeance. Shortly before the executions, a cartoon in *Life* featured seven hooded figures on the gallows with the caption "Seven Up. A Game that will be Played in Chicago Next Month."[12]

Howells' life would have seemed far removed from the trial and appeals of anarchists in Chicago. In 1885, he had signed his contract with Harper's for ten thousand dollars a year (worth perhaps two hundred thousand today), and the next year turned down an offer of a professorship in foreign languages at Harvard. He enjoyed the privileges of property, investments, and servants, could reside and travel where he wanted (he now moved back and forth between Boston and New York), and might easily have deplored the injustice in Chicago from the comfort of his editor's study without making it a personal campaign. When he wrote to his father a few years later that he and Elinor, like Mark Twain and Livy, considered themselves "theoretical socialists, and practical aristocrats," he summed up much of his previous life.[13] On November 4, 1887, he wrote to Francis F. Browne, editor of the *Dial*: "For many weeks, for months, it [Haymarket] has not been for one hour out of my waking thoughts: it is the first thing when I wake up. It blackens my life. . . . I feel the horror and the shame of the crime which the law is about to commit against justice."[14] With Elinor's full support, the theoretical socialist became a practicing radical, not by arming himself or declaiming to crowds but by using the skill he knew best.

The "shocking travesty of justice," as one defense attorney labeled the Haymarket trial, had forced the defendants to reconsider their situation.[15] Though Parsons understood when he turned himself in that he might well be hanged, the defendants still hoped to establish their innocence on appeal. Anticipating that the decision of the Illinois Supreme Court would go against them, their lawyers turned to Leonard Swett, the former law partner of Abraham Lincoln, and Judge Roger A. Pryor, a prominent New York lawyer, to plead their case in the U.S. Supreme Court.

It was some months after the trial but before the appeals were exhausted that Howells weighed in to support the men whose activities he liked no more than their opinions and whose plight moved him as he had perhaps never been moved before. He wrote a private letter and a petition to the governor of Illinois, Richard J. Oglesby, urging clemency for the condemned men, and he asked George W. Curtis and John Greenleaf Whittier to cosign the petition. Curtis believed Howells wrong and told him so. Whittier, who not long before had asked Howells to write his biography, replied that, much as he opposed the death penalty—he was a practicing Quaker—he saw no reason to interfere with the law in individual cases. He had, as Howells knew, "interfered" in earlier situations. Now, calling himself "thy admirer and friend," he washed his hands of the matter.[16] The previous year, Whittier had told Annie Fields: "I see so much that needs to be done and said, that I am ashamed of my being only a looker on. But I dare say the world will go on without my meddling."[17] Howells might have quoted Whittier to Whittier on the issue of slavery: "My God! Can such things be!" Instead he wrote a diplomatic reply. "A letter from you would have great weight with [the Illinois governor]. I beseech you to write it, and do what one great and blameless man may to avert the cruellest wrong that ever threatened our fame as a nation."[18] Whether Whittier felt annoyed or disagreed with Howells' argument, he kept his silence—and Whittier's silences, according to Howells, spoke with eloquence.[19] Fair enough, until he broke his silence to let others know about his refusal to help. Not one of Howells' friends endorsed his protest—not Twain, Garland, Edward Everett Hale, Norton, Higginson, or even James Russell Lowell.

Howells felt driven to write Judge Pryor, a man he had met the year before, expressing thanks that he had agreed to lead the anarchists' defense and implicitly offering his services. "I have never believed them guilty of murder," he said, "and I do not think they were justly convicted."[20] Pryor wrote back to say that "in the whirlwind of passion which swept over Chicago," the anarchists had been denied "a fair and legal trial." He followed this reply with a request that Howells write a letter to the *New York Tribune*. A "temperate claim on behalf of the Anarchists . . . under the *imprimatur* of your name, cannot but be of wholesome and happy effect."[21] Howells agreed to write, then backed off, telling Pryor that his letter might harm himself without helping the cause.[22] Soon after, he met at Pryor's house a number of men opposed to the Haymarket judgments, among them the popular playwright, actor, and theater manager Steele MacKaye. He also found allies in two men of opposing politics but similar principles: Henry Demarest Lloyd, who had provided money to the defendants, and William Mackintire Salter, an outspoken Unitarian minister and a lecturer at the Chicago Ethical Society.[23] There were other pockets of support for the anarchists in the United States, and in the year after the trial an increasing number of people spoke against the events in Chicago. Samuel Gompers and fellow labor leaders, for example, held a mass meeting at New York's Cooper Union. Most Americans, including liberally minded artists and intellectuals, agreed with the verdicts or said nothing.

When his friend Curtis, now editing *Harper's Weekly*, committed the magazine against the anarchists, Howells doubtless saw a threat to his financial arrangement with the Harper brothers, who, like their editor, had been affected by the climate of fear.[24] Once again Henry Alden warned Howells about the possible consequences of any public statement breaching the terms of his Harper's contract. Howells stood his ground, and neither Alden nor Curtis let friendship interfere with their scruples—or with the Harpers' finances.

Perhaps only saints live consistently by principles, and, in fairness to Curtis or Alden, Whittier or Lowell, it must be said that Howells himself sometimes contradicted his own positions. In 1891 he entertained the political assassin and writer known as Stepniak before recommending him to Twain and getting him work with the New York *Sun*. "A Garibaldi-like adventurer" who supported Serbian insurgents against the Turks, as well as the failed Benevento uprising near Naples, Stepniak had, in the broad daylight of a Saint Petersburg street, casually approached the chief of the imperial secret police and shot him.[25] In an 1884 letter to Edmund Gosse about the notorious O'Donnell case in England, Howells had said that while "no man should be hung . . . that man was a cruel and pitiless assassin, and rightly suffered under the law."[26] A further irony with the O'Donnell incident grew out of American (mainly Irish-American) support for the condemned man; in the Haymarket case, the English protested bitterly against American injustice. William Morris, the socialist visionary, sought help for the anarchists, enlisting, among others, George Bernard Shaw. In France, too, a large number of left-leaning members of the Chamber of Deputies petitioned Governor Oglesby as Howells urged his friends and countrymen to do. Brand Whitlock, an Ohio state archivist who went on to become a novelist and a reform mayor of Toledo before his appointment as minister to Belgium during the First World War, remembered that of all the protesting authors around the world, no one seemed more forceful, no one braver, than Howells.[27]

Alone but no less sure in his isolation, Howells took action. When, on November 2, the United States Supreme Court denied the defendants' appeal, he discussed the matter with Elinor and sent his letter to Whitelaw Reid, the one editor he expected to publish it. "I don't sympathize one bit with it," Reid told him.[28] He nevertheless printed the letter, which appeared in the *New York Tribune* on November 6, 1887, and was reprinted, without permission, in the *Chicago Tribune*.

> As I have petitioned the Governor of Illinois to commute the death penalty of the Anarchists to imprisonment, and have also personally written him in their behalf, I ask your leave to express here the hope that those who are inclined to do either will not lose faith in themselves because the Supreme Court has denied the condemned a writ of error. That court simply affirmed the legality of the forms under which the Chicago court proceeded; it did not affirm the propriety of trying for murder men fairly indictable for conspiracy alone; and it by no means approved the principle of punishing them because of their frantic opinions, for a crime which they were not shown to have committed. The justice or injustice of their sentence was not before the highest tribunal of our law, and unhappily could not be got there. That question must remain for history, which judges the judgment of courts, to deal with; and I, for one, cannot doubt what the judgment of history will be.
>
> But the worst still is for a very few days reparable; the men sentenced to

death are still alive, and their lives may be finally saved through the clemency of the Governor, whose prerogative is now the supreme law in their case. I conjure all those who believe that it would be either injustice or impolicy to put them to death, to join in urging him by petition, by letter, through the press, and from the pulpit and the platform, to use his power, in the only direction where power can never be misused, for the mitigation of their punishment.

William Dean Howells[29]

By this time, tempered petitions for clemency had run in both the *New York Times* (signed by Howells' old friend Moncure Conway) and the *Chicago Tribune.* They reflected a slight shift in public opinion. Governor Oglesby responded to appeals for clemency by commuting to life imprisonment the sentences of two of the anarchists, Samuel Fielden and Michael Schwab. They and Oscar Neebe (who, without even a remote connection to the case, had received a fifteen-year sentence from Judge Gary) were freed in 1893 by Governor John P. Altgeld. Altgeld wrote a stinging censure of Gary and everyone connected with the trial. For his criticism he would be vilified and turned out of office at the next election.

Despite Howells' disagreement with the anarchists and his belief that justice mattered more than politics, he found himself, like Governor Altgeld later, demonized in the press. *The Tribune* itself made four separate attempts to distance the paper from the Howells letter it published.[30] Already widely attacked for his positions on literary realism, he felt battered by what he now read. On November 10, 1877, the night before the hangings of Parsons, Spies, Engel, and Fischer, Louis Lingg either killed himself by detonating an explosive cap in his mouth or died at the hands of police. "Miserable Lingg!" Howells wrote in his November 4 letter to Francis F. Browne, "I'm glad he's out of the story; but even with his death, it seems to me that humanity's judgment of the law begins. . . . So the evil will grow from violence to violence."[31] The next day, angry and distraught, he wrote a sardonic letter to the *Tribune,* a letter either he never sent or Whitelaw Reid refused to publish. With the five men dead, Howells might have seen the futility of any further letters or known that Reid would find this one too long and too raw.

I have borne with what patience I must, during the past fortnight, to be called by the Tribune, day after day imbecile and a bad citizen, with the others who desired mercy for the men killed yesterday at Chicago. . . .
I now ask you to have a little patience with me.

It seems, of course, almost a pity to mix a note of regret with the hymn of thanksgiving for blood going up from thousands of newspapers all over the land this morning; but I reflect that though I write amidst this joyful noise, my letter cannot reach the public before Monday at the earliest, and cannot therefore be regarded as an indecent interruption of the *Te Deum*.

He goes on to restate the crux of his argument, that men were put to death "*in the prime of the freest Republic the world has ever known, for their opinions' sake.* It is useless to deny this truth, to cover it up, to turn our backs upon it, to frown it down, or sneer it down. We have committed an atrocious and irreparable wrong. . . . I dread the Anarchy of the Courts," he writes, "but I have never been afraid of the prevalence of the dead anarchists' doctrine, because that must always remain to plain common sense unthinkable. . . . I have no doubt that Judge Gary will live long to enjoy the regard upon which he has already entered in his re-election."[32] Although Howells' prophecy, even his ironic prediction for Gary (who upbraided his critics for "childish whimpering"), came to pass, the nation swung little by little to share his view of the events.[33]

Much of the Haymarket rhetoric—whether the historical contexts cited by the anarchists, the racial aspersions cast by the prosecution, the incontinent ranting in newspapers, or the way that Howells wrote about the case—recalls the rhetoric of debate over slavery in pre–Civil War America. "I feel more than ever," Howells wrote to George W. Curtis, "that it was not a fair trial. . . . They are condemned to death upon a principle that would have sent every ardent anti-slavery man to the gallows."[34] Like anarchists and other labor groups, he saw parallels between slavery and the oppression of workers, in this case militant workers. To Howells the comparison carried direct, personal significance. Remembering John Brown's end, or perhaps reconsidering the risks his father had taken in the fight against slavery, he acknowledged a record of injustice that had to be met by vigorous opposition. His letters through these months must have pleased William, reminding him of his own commitment to a higher law. Howells wrote to his father shortly after the hangings, in November 1887: "I send you the *Tribune,* with my unavailing word for the Anarchists. All is over now, except the judgment that begins at once for every unjust and evil deed, and goes on forever."[35]

With his father and wife excepted, he seemed through these months scarcely to have had a sympathetic friend, let alone a generous critic. The reasons lay as much in his jeremiads about politics and literature as in his

Haymarket actions. It made sense for one derisive critic to ask: "Has our Boston friend followed Tolstoi so far as to have become a non-resistant?" Howells' lonely campaign had begun shortly after he discovered Tolstoy's social and religious writings in 1886. Certain books speak to people at particular times in their lives. As Cervantes had long ago brought him awareness of exotic worlds, Tolstoy now prodded Howells to rethink the world around him. "Whenever I open a page of Tolstoy's I am aware of the thrill and glory of wonder that filled me when I first read him. It is like the clasp of a great warm hand, with the beat of a friendly heart in it, the heart of a man who neither looks down upon his fellow man, nor up to him, but meets him on the common level of their humanity, and begins at once to live with him in the real things of his soul."[36]

He read *War and Peace* in January 1887, when consumed by the urgency of the Haymarket case and the loss of his sister Vic, who had died from malaria. As if parodying Tolstoy's message about tilling the field, his father had exchanged his farm in Virginia for another in Jefferson, Ohio, where Howells traveled to be with his family during Vic's last days. Mourning the sister whose husband had deserted her, he also mourned his own failings, made the more acute by Winny's erratic illness. Tolstoy, "the human being with whom [he found himself] in the greatest sympathy," seemed to speak directly to his situation and to the person he wanted to be: the idealist described by Charles Norton who, more self-consciously than ever, sought to live by his principles.[37]

The Russian aristocrat's pity for the poor and lowly, his abhorrence of violence and pride cast Howells down, exposing "the utter selfishness and insufficiency of my past life."[38] The effect resembled a conversion, with both the epiphany and the illumination experienced by his father and grandfather— or Saul on the road to Damascus. Civilization seemed "all wrong," and, in regard to labor, irrelevant. In the Editor's Study, he argued that people who worked for the social order and not merely for themselves served their "own highest spiritual destiny."[39] He read Tolstoy's parable *What Then Must We Do?* which came with a powerful reminder that his own prosperity depended on the exploitation of the labor and poverty of others. Tolstoy told him to live simply as Christ bade: "socially and politically, severally and collectively. There's no more to it," as Howells wrote a friend, "but Heaven knows that's enough, and hard enough."[40]

For Howells' contemporaries, Tolstoy represented in literature what the Haymarket defendants represented in politics. Un-American, anticapitalist, and dedicated to the principle of shared resources, he was anathema.

In 1888, a reviewer of *Annie Kilburn* would dismiss it as a stew of pernicious influences. "Tolstoi dashed with Anarchy might be said to be the most conspicuous flavors in the book."[41] The novel builds toward the Reverend Peck's plea for justice that in a "truly Christian State . . . all shall share alike, and want and luxury and killing toil and heartless indolence shall all cease together."[42] Hamlin Garland remembered that Howells' "outspoken defense of the 'new fiction' inflamed critical tempers on both sides of the Atlantic. Critics rose to challenge his arguments for realism, newspapers carried notices of his strange admiration for monsters like Zola and Tolstoi, speakers derided him from public platforms . . . [for] his shocking crusade."[43] Even a loyal friend like Thomas Bailey Aldrich thought him mad.

Profound as Tolstoy seemed, he troubled Howells. "His remedy is to go into the country, and share the labor of his peasants—to forego luxury and superfluity; but I don't exactly see how this helps except that it makes all poor alike, and saves one's self from remorse. It's a terrible question. How shall it ever be answered?"[44] He may well have remembered the dismal family experiment at Eureka Mills, which should have persuaded any sane person that a rural, utopian experiment offered little chance of physical happiness or spiritual gain. "To work for others, yes," he wrote Edward Everett Hale; "but to work with my hands, I'm not sure, seeing that I'm now fifty, awkward and fat. I worked ten years at a trade—printing—and thirty years I've worked at novelling. Shall I learn still another trade?"[45] He had seen at Eureka Mills how money governs even those who disavow it, and he remained too much a skeptic to accept Tolstoy's answers for Russian serfdom or czarist rule as applicable to American democratic capitalism. No less idealistic, his own ideas presupposed an educated, enlightened, and altruistic voting public. *Altruism,* a relatively new addition in the English lexicon, became his personal catchword because it spoke to the need for self-sacrifice and allowed for participation "by the people." He would return to this question in *The World of Chance* (1893), where the characters debate Tolstoy. "He's sold all he has in order to give to the poor," one character says, "but his wife manages the proceeds." When another objects, the speaker explains that practically he doesn't follow Tolstoy. "We shall never redeem the world by eschewing it. Society is not to be saved by self-outlawry. The body politic is to be healed politically."[46] The more Howells read Tolstoy, the more he found him naive. "I'm afraid Tolstoi doesn't value amusement enough in a world that seems to get wicked without it. I'm afraid also that this fear is a sneaking love of the world."[47]

To read Howells' letters, his appeals to one's better self and to honest dealings, is to appreciate the man in a fuller way. Without what he called the lost hopes of youth, it is unlikely he expected his unpopular views to prevail, and in a sense it may have been less the injustice of the Haymarket affair than the wounded lives that troubled him most. Here, too, he had a few supporters. The hanged victims were finally honored with a large memorial in Chicago's Waldheim Cemetery—a small consolation to the survivors. It mattered little that elected officials, newspaper reporters, and the general public came to denounce the anarchists' trial as mob justice; the lives of the men's families had, in almost every case, been ruined.

Howells' role in the Haymarket affair would not be forgotten. Shortly after the executions, he received a letter with enclosures from a woman in London. "I take the liberty of sending you the translations," she wrote, "because these Scandinavians grapple with the *real* problem of our day—the social problem, they are the true realists" and "because ever since you had the courage to sign the appeal demanding a new trial for the Anarchists, I have known you were not only a true artist and a great writer, but that even rarer thing, a brave and just man. All that you have written of late, and the way you speak of the 'unnecessary suffering' of the great mass of humanity tell me that you feel with the people." She introduced herself, saying that she and her husband, Dr. Edward Aveling, had lectured in the United States. "My father's name I am sure you know—Karl Marx."[48]

The letter that would have meant the most to Howells came from an old friend. "And now let me say something I have been wishing to say this great while," Lowell wrote.

> I have seen some of the unworthy slings at you in the papers of late. I know you will not feel them more than an honest man should. But I have indignantly felt them. You are one of the chief honors of our literature & your praises are dear to us all. You know I don't share some of your opinions or sympathize with some of your judgments, but I am not such an ass as not to like a man better for saying what *he* thinks & not what *I* think. Though I thought those Chicago ruffians well hanged, I specially honored your courage in saying what you did about them. You can't make me fonder of you, but I am here sure you will make me prouder of you.[49]

It was the apology of a Boston Brahmin, perhaps of Boston itself. For, as one reporter remarked, those who found Howells un-Bostonian should remember that his recent bout of philanthropy—in the cause of Chicago anarchists—made him most New Englandy.

On the anniversary of the hangings, Howells was honored in absentia in a hall hung in red and with pictures of the anarchists. He chose not to attend the Chicago memorial, as he told the organizers, not because he had changed his mind about the anarchists but because he had done and said all he could for the failed cause. In times to come, he supported a wide range of legal as well as socialist and working people's causes, just as he would support the rights—and writings—of African Americans. He would never be a consistent political thinker, yet as an essayist, above all as a novelist, he established himself as one of his country's most astute commentators.

America had been changed by Haymarket, and so too had Howells. The events did not of course make him a happier man or help him to deal with the personal calamities he faced; his life simply took a different direction. When we read about literary careers—or rather the lives of most writers— the trajectory often runs from youthful zeal in liberal causes to a quieter and safer old age. Robert Browning, who hated older writers' reneging and who reneged himself, spoke of his boyhood idol, Wordsworth, declining into the conservative "lost leader." Howells moved differently. In his later years he embraced or reverted to liberal causes, becoming more introspective, perhaps more deeply caring, more willing to take a stand and to stand alone. What he had fought against pushed him to look more sharply at the political and social world around him and to write accordingly. He would, for example, support the retrial of Maria Barberi, accused of murdering her abusive lover, as well as push for the passage of a charity tax to improve the lives of people like Barberi, the epileptic daughter of alcoholics.[50] Remembering the families of the Haymarket anarchists, he would denounce a prison system that condemned the innocent families of prisoners to poverty.

Without imitating Tolstoy's novels, Howells intensified his fictional treatment of actual wrongs. In February 1887 he and Elinor spent two days in Lowell, Massachusetts, touring the cotton and carpet mills as research for *Annie Kilburn*. They saw firsthand a new industrialism. Granting the workplaces to be humanely managed, he still believed the cost in misery too great a price to pay. In the novel, published in 1889, he showed how America's impoverished other half lived. "If a community was corrupt, if an age was immoral," he had written earlier, in *The Minister's Charge* (1886), "it was not because of the vicious, but the virtuous who fancied themselves indifferent spectators."[51]

Along with many of his contemporaries, Howells did not put hope in charity to solve problems unless it came from lived sympathy. The blundering of the upper-class Annie Kilburn makes this clear. "We people of leisure, or comparative leisure," she says, "have really nothing in common with you people who work with your hands for a living; and as we really can't be friends with you, we won't patronize you. We won't advise you, and we won't help you, but here's the money. If you fail, you fail; and if you succeed, you won't succeed by our aid and comfort."[52] The Reverend Peck lives by a Tolstoyan example, and in Tolstoyan paradox, refusing his daughter any comforts or education unavailable to the masses. "I am not sure I have the right to give advantages of any kind," he tells Miss Kilburn, "to lift her above the lot, the chance, of the least fortunate."[53] In *A Hazard of New Fortunes* and other later novels, Howells would also address the commercial rapacity, the breakdown of traditional values, and the capitalist greed he saw to be overwhelming his country. The most apt of his titles, *An Imperative Duty* (1892), speaks to his new commitments and the role he played, reluctantly but eloquently, during the Haymarket months. This was for Howells a trying period, one of the most trying in his life. He had begun to feel displaced, whether by time and circumstance or by his own convictions. Reading Tolstoy may have brought insight; it did not bring comfort. At fifty, Howells appreciated too clearly that most of his life lay behind him. Nor did he expect any longer to have the ambition or energy that had driven him before. While he kept his publisher after Haymarket and would go on to write much of his best fiction, he was "perfectly aware of the shrinking bounds." "One is so limp and helpless," he would write, "in the presence of the injustice which underlies society."[54]

The Haymarket futilities brought home to Howells a sense of responsibility for his family. In these months, when other lives mattered as much as or more than his own, he felt impotent to help the family he loved, including those in Jefferson who mourned a daughter and sister. At home Winny's misery persisted, and her symptoms baffled the best of doctors. What happened with Winny—what he did or did not do for her—would haunt him for the rest of his life.

Some day I should like to write the tragedy of a man trying to escape his circumstances. It would be funny.

—W. D. HOWELLS to William C. Howells, October 7, 1888

Clover Adams once quipped that "the insane asylum seems to be the goal of every good and conscientious Bostonian, babies and insanity the two leading topics. So and so has a baby. She becomes insane and goes to Somerville, baby grows up and promptly retires to Somerville."[55] Mrs. Adams knew whereof she wrote. Members of her family suffered from depression. She herself, inconsolable after the death of her father, would commit suicide.

Winny and Elinor had gone together not to Somerville but to nearby Arlington Heights, in search of cures for elusive ailments. Institutions for rest and healing were common, and Howells might have considered depression a fashionable indulgence had he not known the anguish firsthand or watched the changes it wrought in his daughter. Winny's health, which had taken them to Europe in 1882, held the entire family in thrall. From the age of sixteen, she had complained of general pain and fatigue. By her twenties, she could barely tolerate food or cold. Frustrated and powerless, Howells observed her with the guilty conviction that she sometimes exaggerated her symptoms. In Siena, the kitchen staff had waved their hands triumphantly and shouted, "Mangia, mangia!" (She's eating, she's eating!) as if Winny were a wounded bird tempted at last to take food. Knowing from experience the power an invalid can wield over friends and strangers, Howells remembered to Winny's disadvantage his own wrestling with hypochondria. In books like *April Hopes* (1888), *Ragged Lady* (1899), *Miss Bellard's Inspiration* (1905), and particularly *The Kentons* (1902), in which the feelings of a disappointed daughter necessitate family moves from Ohio to New York and New York to Europe, he explored the despotism of illness and its repercussions. He describes the husband in *Ragged Lady* as a man from whom "all initiative had been taken. . . . He had fallen into the mere follower of a woman guided only by her whims"; in *Miss Bellard's Inspiration,* the neurotic Mrs. Mevison deliberately wounds her husband; and in *The Kentons* the father cannot "keep down a certain resentment, senseless and cruel, as if the poor girl were somehow to blame for their exile."[56]

As a child Winny had enjoyed her illnesses, in the way children do, perhaps encouraged by the unfortunate example of her mother's near-chronic ailing. Winny "was overjoyed at being slightly sick one morning," Annie reported in 1867, when she assisted after Elinor's miscarriage, "so Will and I took both their breakfasts up to them, which they ate in bed."[57] According to Annie, they had almost to force Winny to get well. By adolescence, she had learned to work upon her parents' sympathy in ways that made them powerless to carry out plans for her benefit.[58] They had tried everything and its opposite, from stimulants and amusements to complete rest, yet Winny showed only brief flashes of vitality. Each new specialist offered a different diagnosis, including gastric or uterine troubles, maladies associated in those days with nervous exhaustion and hysteria. Howells feared that she would become a lifelong invalid, and so did Winny. "Who would lift for a moment the curtain of Fate?" she asked in an 1884 poem.

Surely not I. Let me think that the years ahead
Will easier seem in part for the years that are fled
To one who has learned in youth to forego and wait.[59]

Too sick beyond her twenty-fourth year to write at all, she still sketched beautiful and grotesque faces in the margins of her manuscripts. Often she could not bear to talk or think, and she struggled with the effects of her illness. "Don't expect anything of me," she sobbed one evening, "*don't* expect anything!"[60]

In 1887, the hope of a cure sent the family to Lake George (Elinor called their cottage "By George"), where they could follow Winny's progress at a sanatorium in Dansville, New York.[61] With every move or change of doctor, Winny appeared to recover, then fail again. Her fits of alternating strength and prostration told on the whole family, so that, even when helped by a nurse, Elinor remained exhausted. The arguments over eating, getting out of bed, and exercising became routine until one day Winny collapsed on the stairs. That, for Howells, stood as the defining moment, the beginning of a long decline.[62] With a child they loved for being "heavenly meek," patient, and wise now turning querulous and stubborn, Howells thanked the gods that the healthy Mildred seemed so docile.[63]

Because Winny's relationship with her parents had deteriorated, the Dansville doctors advised a separation. The respite would benefit everyone, Howells not least. Still lamenting Vic's squandered life, he worried about the effects of her death on his father's household. Henry had grown so uncontrollable that the family could not keep an attendant. With her own health problems, Aurelia lacked the strength to get Henry upstairs or keep him secured even when he was sedated. On more than one occasion Henry had injured William, and he could be expected to do worse. Howells dreamt about Henry's attacking him as he had attacked their father, in a manner he cryptically describes as "odious."[64] Like his fictional reporter Bartley Hubbard, he could well have imagined the sordid headlines: "Father and Sister of Famous Novelist Slain." "Unless you and Aurelia realize that from this time forth there is *no* safety for you but in keeping him *closely confined, locked up*—he will cause your death."[65] Howells believed his brother criminally insane, his daughter neurasthenic. Twenty years earlier he had escaped the domestic situation in Jefferson; now he found himself in a similar nightmare and, for all his experience, just as impotent.

With Winny ensconced at Dansville, the Howellses found a hotel in Niagara, not too far from Jefferson. They expected to remain there about three and a half months. "The only objection we have to the place is a queer one," Howells told Annie, "and I'm afraid you won't think it sincere. Elinor and I both no longer care for the world's life, and would like to be settled somewhere very humbly and simply, where we could be socially identified with the principles of progress and sympathy for the struggling mass." He expressed this wish after the execution of the anarchists, which he could not separate from his daughter's suffering. "The last two months have been full of heartache and horror for me," he explained, "on account of the civic murder" committed in Chicago. For that "atrocious piece of frenzy and cruelty . . . we must stand ashamed forever before history."[66]

In these months, Howells encountered the writings of the Danish-American philosopher Laurence Gronlund, a radical socialist whom he had heard lecture in Buffalo. Gronlund's argument for the greater distribution of wealth appealed to him as a practical complement to Tolstoy's Christian Socialism. Reviewing *Co-operative Commonwealth* in the April 1888 Editor's Study, he focused on the prospect of reconciling rights and duties, liberty and equality. Unconsciously he may have been making his own bargain with God, as if by living more according to Christ's teachings he might secure his daughter's recovery.

Though he and Elinor returned despondent and without Winny to New York City that March, when chill winds whipped around corners under lowering skies, the change lifted their spirits. Boston seemed to belong to a distant planet heavy with diminished dreams, while they found New York—at once foreign and aboundingly American—full of talented young life. Both parents and children felt better able to cope. As a temporary measure, Howells rented a four-room apartment in one of the vast "caravanseries . . . so common in New York,—ten stories high, and housing six hundred people."[67] There briefly he brought his "sad problem," as he called Winny, before setting off again to a villa surrounded by forty acres in Little Nahant, outside Boston, to get the benefits of sea air.[68]

For the moment, this experiment worked. When Winny began to eat a little without being forced, Howells blamed the sanatorium for encouraging in her the worst habits of invalidism. "We must break them up by force . . . an awful job," he told his father, adding that it had "its ludicrous as well as sorrowful side."[69] Still cautious, he believed the worst of her symptoms to be subsiding and planned to rent the Nahant house through October. In the meantime, he and Elinor spent six days in New York looking at nearly a hundred flats and houses—a discouraging odyssey repeated by his fictional couple the Marches in the first hundred pages of *A Hazard of New Fortunes*. Of the Marches, he writes: "They varied their day by taking a coupé, by renouncing advertisement, and by reverting to agents. . . . They looked at three thousand and four thousand dollar apartments, and rejected them for one reason or another which had nothing to do with the rent."[70] Like the Marches, he and Elinor considered unfurnished houses, with and without steam heat or elevator, furnished houses filled with knickknacks from foreign travels, and untold rooms and flats and suites until they felt dazed. "It's wearing, sickening business," he wrote his father around the time he decided on a two-floor apartment on Seventeenth Street, overlooking Livingston Place, "and I watch my money flow as a stuck pig its life-stream. It's horrible to spend so much but I seem bound to it hand and foot. How I envy your simple, quiet righteous life!"[71]

Barely a month passed before he and Elinor were forced to make their most important and, as it turned out, most disastrous decision. They placed Winny under the care of S. Weir Mitchell at his clinic in Philadelphia. Mitchell, the nation's most prominent women's doctor, seemed their last hope. If he failed to cure her, they had nowhere else to turn. Her weight had shrunk to fifty-nine pounds. Her treatment would cost two thousand dollars—an enormous sum at a time when the average family of four lived for a year on less than half that amount. But to Howells, who had few illusions about a cure, the choice lay between Mitchell's clinic and Winny's sure slide into dementia and death. Elinor consented with misgivings.

Howells had known Mitchell since the *Atlantic* days, when the two corresponded about Mitchell's poems and stories. His writing appealed to Howells for its combination of mystical, realistic, and scientific strains. He saw in Mitchell another Oliver Wendell Holmes, a bookish physician whose medical office resembled a gentleman's library. Mitchell's literary reputation rests today on his historical novel *Hugh Wynne, Free Quaker* and on *Autobiography of a Quack* (1899), a picaresque tale about a physician cum con artist, an expert in vegetable remedies and electromagnetic treatments. Gaunt and bearded, the charismatic Mitchell reminded contemporaries of Uncle Sam. The most famous neurologist of his day, he had earned his reputation by bringing about astonishing cures. Howells would have known that he coaxed Thomas Wentworth Higginson's wife to health after eighteen months of total invalidism.

Mitchell's patients were primarily wealthy women between the ages of twenty and thirty who were underweight, nervous, anemic, enervated, and sometimes addicted to medicines and opiates. He described his typical patient as someone alarmed by an unopened letter, prone to irritability, and defeated by daily tasks. "She can no longer sit still and sew or read," Mitchell wrote in *Doctor and Patient.* "Conversation no longer interests, or it even troubles her. Noises, especially sudden noises, startle her, and the cries and laughter of children have become distresses of which she is ashamed, of which she complains, or not, as her nature weak or enduring. . . . Her sense of moral proportion becomes impaired. Trifles grow large to her. . . . The telegram or any cause of emotion sets her shaking. She cries for no cause."[72] Insisting that patients cooperate in their treatment and essentially relearn how to live, he held them responsible for their illnesses; he took credit for the cures.

Winny Howells might have been the prototype for Mitchell's neurasthenic. Three years before he had offered to treat her with the "mind-cure" he made famous in the United States and England. "If you want at any time to send Miss Howells to me," he wrote in 1885, "I can so arrange things as to make the expenses comparatively small, & without real loss to anyone. . . . Lastly let me assure you of the real pleasure it would give me to serve in any way & at all times. I am on *tap always.*"[73] Tempted then, Howells described the cure to his father as "rest, utter and profound, without the torturing stress to any sort of exertion or responsibility."[74] Just as important, the regimen included massive amounts of rich and fatty foods, together with daily massage. Howells had no sense of Mitchell's arrogance, or how his love of celebrity led him to invent stories of his own magnificence. Today these stories would have him—a pull-yourself-up-by-your-bootstraps Freud—defending his license to practice medicine. Once, leaving the room of a patient who refused to get out of bed, he reportedly told the medical students waiting outside that she would soon follow. "I set her bed on fire," he said. He took another for a long carriage ride, stopped the carriage, and then told her to alight and walk home. Still another he threatened with rape, stripping to his underpants before she dragged herself from her sickroom.[75] The same man would later dismiss one of Freud's psychoanalytical books as filth. Charlotte Perkins Gilman, an author who for many years suffered from melancholia, felt certain Mitchell's rest cure drove her to the border of insanity. After sending Mitchell a copy of *The Yellow Wall-*

paper (1913), a direct attack on his practices, she claimed that he changed his mind, at least about women reading and writing during their cure. If she had done so, she declared, she had not lived in vain.

Writing twenty years after Winny's death, Gilman obviously knew the same doctor involved in the same practices, and her response seems to have paralleled Winny's. But few people in an era when doctors treated women generically could separate the doctor from his reputation. To Howells, desperate for help, Mitchell obviously seemed "the best and wisest and kindest" of the many specialists he had unsuccessfully consulted. His respect for Mitchell as a writer added to his confidence. "The old wizard" assured him that everything that could be done would be done, though Winny's case was complicated by the girl's hypochondriacal illusions and obstinacy in believing her symptoms physical rather than mental. Mitchell assumed that her hysteria would lessen once her body and brain had been properly nourished, and he intended to feed her with or without her consent. "It has already come to a tussle of wills," Howells wrote his father, "and he believes that as soon as she finds that he is absolutely unyielding, she will give in."[76]

That appeared to be the case in January 1889. Mitchell reported that Winny had gained twelve pounds. She now weighed seventy-one pounds, with every promise of gaining more. By the end of January, she had gained another three, and while she still had "to be forced along the path to health" by Mitchell's firm hand, Howells applauded. "There is none of the Dansville sentimentality in the business; she would instantly take advantage of that."[77] After she put on another five pounds, Mitchell thought it time for her to begin exercising. As he explained in *Fat and Blood* (1877), a woman is "to be made to walk, with no regard to her aches," and to persist until she is no longer fatigued.[78] Granting that Winny had spoiled her nervous system with long habits of self-indulgence, Mitchell felt sure that her youth and his knowledge would save her.

Winny did not survive the next stage of treatment. She died on March 2, 1889, at Merchantville, a country retreat. The coroner attributed her death to heart failure. To the last, Winny had insisted—contrary to Mitchell's opinion—that she was not improving. If her condition resulted from a congenital defect or a childhood disease such as measles, whooping cough, or scarlet fever (or the doses of arsenic used to treat them) rather than what might be called a twentieth-century disease like anorexia, she had, nevertheless, been misdiagnosed and mistreated.[79] The combination of vigorous exercise and a diet of fatty foods can themselves trigger a heart attack in someone who has been underweight for several years. Tormented by what he had brought about, Howells had to grant that her pain had been as great as she said. How could he—and Mitchell—have been so wrong, or Winny so right? He found it intolerable that he had added homesickness to her other suffering: "We were denied the sad consolation of bidding her good bye. She had been dead five hours when we heard, and while we still thought her on the way to recovery. It is hard to bear."[80]

"Winifred died at Philadelphia this night," Howells wrote his old friend and fellow *Atlantic* editor, Horace Scudder, "and I have to beg of your friendship something which we are helpless to do ourselves."[81] Himself a father, and surrogate uncle to the Howells girls, Scudder accepted the sad task of receiving Winny's remains and seeing to her service and burial. Friends gathered a few days later at the First Church of Cambridge, where Winny had attended Sunday school and now lay in a casket covered with flowers. Henry James sent his condolences. Of Winny's woes, he wrote that "they were untalkable—& I know they were for you a perpetual fountain of pain. When a man loses a loved child everything that is most tender in him must be infinitely lacerated: yet I hope there is a sort of joy for both of you in the complete extinction of so much suffering—to be young & gentle & do no harm, & only to pay for it as if it were a crime—I *do* thank heaven, my dear Howells, both for your wife & yourself that *that* is over."[82] Sarah Orne Jewett, reminded of all they had hoped for Winny, quoted from a poem by Thomas Bailey Aldrich:

The subtle hurt that nature feels when a
blossoming bough is broken.[83]

Howells could not bear it. Three years later, Mark Twain would write a concerned Mrs. Fairchild, at Belmont, "Oh, I know! I know! But there is no help; nothing will ever cheer Howells up again; his heart is buried in Winnie's grave."[84] He could not anticipate that he too would lose a daughter. Several years after Susy died from spinal meningitis, Twain wrote to Howells: "About the last time I saw you I described to you the culminating disaster in a book I was going to write (& will yet, when the stroke is further away)—a man's dead daughter brought to him when he had been through all other possible misfortunes—& I said it couldn't be done as it ought to be done except by a man who had lived it—it must be written with the blood out of a man's heart. I could not know, then, how soon I was to be made competent. I have thought of it many a time since. If you were here I think we could cry down each other's necks, as in your dream. For we *are* a pair of old derelicts drifting around, now, with some of our passengers gone & the sunniness of the others in (total) eclipse."[85] Howells responded immediately: "Two days ago came the beautiful picture of your Susie with her heavenly face and her eyes of angel innocence. They affect me as the eyes of Winny sometimes did: with the error and the wrong that every man's life seems to include. I am afraid to look in them, and think of what I am."[86] If Howells blamed himself for thinking Winny a hypochondriac like her father, Twain regretted being overbearing with his willful, passionate, and adored daughter. At least he managed to console himself by thinking her suffering brief, "not lingering & awful like Winny Howells's. The beautiful fabric of Susy's mind did not crumble to slow ruin, its light was not smothered in slow darkness, but passed swiftly out in a disordered splendor. These are mercies. They will help us to bear what has befallen."[87]

In their separate ways, the Howellses bore what they had to. Elinor left for New York immediately with John and Mildred; he stayed to see his daughter laid in the Cambridge Cemetery. From New York, he wrote Scudder a brave note of thanks. He expressed his surprise at finding his family well, "and in one of those cheerful moods which express the inability of life to accept the fact of death. We have had our tears, our moments of insupportable heaviness, but we have begun to live on, and I suppose we shall live into some consciousness of the fact that now seems so incredible. I wrote as usual, Pilla went to her drawing, and my wife busied herself with her many cares. It must be best to do so; at any rate it is the best we can do."[88] Howells wanted to believe Winny freed from pain, from whatever is "cruel and clumsy and uncouth in life." Yet "never to hear, never to see, never to touch, till time shall be no more! How can I bear that? And that is what I must bear."[89] He could realize her loss but not consent to it, and she returned to him in dreams in which he caught glimpses of her childish self obscured by the sad phantom she became.

Much as he might have wished to talk about his agony with Mark Twain, he dared not leave Elinor, now bitterly inconsolable and, with the onset of a difficult menopause, destined to be ill all winter. Though she depended upon him "almost momently," she also blamed him and, perhaps more hurtfully, blamed herself for allowing him to make the last decisions about Winny's treatment.[90] Howells told his father that she bore Winny's loss bravely and generously, considering her reservations about Mitchell. He and Elinor could not get away from their endless thoughts of Winny's anguish, and they dared not acknowledge what they read in the other's sorrow. Better the long years of her illness than this cold, sham comfort. "Oh Annie,

Annie!" he wrote his sister. "How hard it is to remember the least unkindness now, when to remember the love I showed her is almost torture."[91] Adding to this guilt, he was forced to a new understanding of what his father had endured in refusing to institutionalize *his* afflicted child, and in burying Johnny, a quarter of a century before.

Howells remained confident that Mitchell had done all he could for Winny, indeed that he had suffered almost as much as they. "No turn of thanks," he would write to him in 1908, nine years after Winny's death, "could bear you my gratitude, which is shared and doubled by the feeling of my wife. You have been part of our life and our death. If she could forget that, she would not be the unforgetting mother she is, and we are in nothing more united than our share of your wish to do everything for us when it was too late to do anything."[92] Despite this reassurance, Mitchell would tell Howells that Winny's "great eloquent eyes now & then stare at me of a sudden." And perhaps with reason.[93] There are curious circumstances surrounding the records of Winny's treatment. The Philadelphia Orthopaedic Hospital and Infirmary for Nervous Diseases has, in the first place, no record of her being a patient. They list "Miss A. [illegible middle initial] Howell, age 22," as a patient diagnosed with neurasthenia on July 8, 1889, who improved enough to be discharged after a month (August 5, 1889). According to the 1890 annual report, the hospital had 59 neurasthenic patients the previous year, 16 of whom were cured, 19 improved, and 11 unchanged or worse. None supposedly died, at least not at the sanatorium itself. To add to the mystery, Mitchell's case studies from 1889 and 1890 are missing. The record itself is incomplete, and no one will ever likely know the story of Winny's last days. We do know that they brought strain to the marriage and gnawed at both Howells and Elinor until their own deaths. It pained Howells that Elinor felt everything too intensely. His recital of her mood swings and withdrawal from a shared social life speaks to unending personal anguish.

For the first two years after her death, Winny—like Mary Howells before her—returned to Howells in his dreams. In one, he held her cheeks between his hands and cried. In another he found her standing in her mother's room wearing the gray dressing grown she often wore. Elinor said, "Here's Winny," and when he held her close and long, she said, "Then you *do* love me?" "O, *love* you!" he choked, and that was all. One night after Howells rose and went to his study to contemplate a photograph of Winny, he dreamed that she had returned to them. He and Elinor were sitting at a small table in a hotel, and Mildred and Winny entered.

"Why here's Winny! [he said to Elinor] Don't you see? It's Winny!" She was dressed in dark blue, which she sometimes wore, and she was girlish and slender, but looked strong; . . . I knew that it was her spirit, and I began at once with what is so much in my mind about her. . . . "Are you happy there, Winny?" I asked. "Yes," she said. "At first I was lonesome, and cried." Then she laughed and said, as if joking at the form of the verb she used, "but I haven't *weeped* since." I was holding her hand, glad of its warmth and strength after so much sorrowful sense as I used to have of her sickness; and now I looked very earnestly into her face and said, "Is it interesting there?" . . . She answered, "Yes," in a way as if she would like to explain. "But not like here?" I went on. "No," she said, and . . . then the dream changed. She and Pilla were sitting on a window sill, somewhere. I introduced some young man to Winny. "This my daughter who is dead; this is her spirit." She slightly acknowledged the introduction, as if there were nothing strange in the affair; and then we were going up hill, as if to our house at Belmont, and I put my hand on her waist behind, to help her, and said, "I don't suppose you need that now." "No," she said "I am well," or something like that; and then the dream ended.[94]

Whatever solace he found in such dreams soon vanished, leaving him to take stock of his life. Over the next few months he felt so anxious about himself that he made an inventory not only of guilt and sorrow, but of tangible financial assets. His four insurance policies amounted to something like $28,450; the house on Concord Avenue in Cambridge rented for $800, with a value approaching $12,000 of the $15,000 he had put into it; and he had deposits of $11,000 in the New England Trust Company, along with the stocks worth roughly $6,000. "All this," he told John, now a student at Harvard, should realize $57,450 and yield an income of nearly $3,000, added to book royalties of $1,500. From his estate he wished his father to be paid $300 a year, that sum to continue to Aurelia for Henry's care after his father's death.[95] In the turmoil of his daughter's dying, there had to be some kind of reckoning.

As a memorial tribute to Winny, Howells collected her poems, together with a sketch of her life, into a little book that he had printed for private distribution. The last poem she wrote reads:

She had been used to write these rhymes like this;
. . . .
Till like a spider lost in her own web,
She suddenly stopped, and ceased to rhyme at all.[96]

Fourteen years after Winny's death, Howells wrote to Annie while visiting Horace Scudder's widow in Cambridge. "It is scarcely three minutes from here to the house on Concord Avenue, which Elinor and I built forty years ago to live in always. It is sad, but it isn't so terrible as you think, and Cambridge is not so ghostly. Life can never be what it was, yet it is still life, and I am old and forget much more than I dared hope I could."[97] He got on, he liked to say, because he hung on. In 1900, he published "Father and Mother, A Mystery," a one-act play about a grieving couple whose love conjures the healing spirit of their daughter. "We have had our glimpse of life beyond the veil," the father tells his wife; "As every one who sorrows somehow has. The world is not so hollow as it was. There still is meaning in the universe."[98]

WORDS AND DEEDS

1890–1894

Words, words, words! How to make them things, deeds . . . with me
they only breed more words.

—W. D. HOWELLS to Edward Everett Hale, October 28, 1888

D URING THE LAST YEAR OF HIS DAUGHTER'S LIFE, Howells managed to write the opening chapters of *A Hazard of New Fortunes*. In
moments of grief he stared out at the towers of Saint George's Church above
the trees of Stuyvesant Square, from the same address (330 East Seventeenth
Street) he gives to his characters, Basil and Isabel March. "I was in my fifty-
second year," he remembered, "and in the prime, such as it was, of my powers," but also "at a moment of great psychological import."[1] The first installment of *A Hazard of New Fortunes* appeared the day after Winny died. Its
title conveys Howells' sense of the forces, both benign and menacing, in a
world beyond his control. Slowly, almost stealthily, he felt, they had defeated him. The novel addresses his deepening sense of the unreality of his
own life and that of the American middle class.[2] "America is so big and the
life here has so many sides," he would tell an interviewer in 1898, that no
writer could synthesize it.[3]

His conviction that chance or accident determined lives overlapped with
his rising apprehension about a nation hungry for wealth. Howells sees New

York, the great mercenary city, filled with buyers and sellers: artists hawking illustrations, women seeking husbands, and would-be saints pursuing martyrdom. Featuring the now-middle-aged Marches of *Their Wedding Journey,* the novel speaks to the afflictions of growing older, when children have left home (at least in spirit), and long-married couples prefer peace to honesty. The plot has obvious autobiographical echoes, for, having spent the years since his marriage working for a Boston insurance company, Basil March, like W. D. Howells, gets a chance to begin again—as the editor of a new magazine called *Every Other Week.*

In the Marches' search for an apartment to rent, they learn about the wealthy who can afford a view of Central Park and the poor who stare out at brick walls and polluting chimneys. Although readers, and Howells himself, have made fun of his devoting a fifth of the novel to the couple's search for a place to live, the passage underscores the moral drifting, displacement, and consumerism in a city that doubled its population each decade and housed its wealthy in the great boxes that came to be called apartment houses. Against their wills, the Marches accept a capitalist standard they previously scorned. Before Basil throws up his hands and takes a furnished apartment Isabel has rejected, they read, interpret, and even speak the copy of advertisements.[4] At the end of the novel, they live like cliff dwellers above his office at the magazine—another sign, as Howells makes clear, of the unhealthy alliance between commercial necessity and familial values.

Howells uses the magazine, which is to be run along the lines of a cooperative, as a microcosm of both the nation and its representative city. The magazine brings together people who would in most circumstances never meet: its owner, a natural gas millionaire named Dryfoos; Beaton, a decadent artist, who toys with Dryfoos' daughter Christine; Lindau, an old socialist who first introduced Basil to the poetry of Heine; Fulkerson, an editor rather like James Fields; Margaret Vance, a society woman who becomes a nun; and of course the thousands of unnamed persons who pack the streets and commercial houses and keep the city running. March must mediate between Dryfoos and Lindau and Dryfoos and his son, Conrad, for whom Dryfoos thought to buy the magazine. Each of these characters occupies a different position on a scale ranging from pure selfishness to altruism. How much can one person take, Lindau asks, without robbing another? Howells' climax, a streetcar strike based on the one that paralyzed New York in 1889, ends with Conrad's death from a stray bullet. Suppliants to fortune, his characters are defenseless against its whims.

At one point contemplating the world he lives in, Basil March thinks, like his author, of a "play of energies as free and planless as those that force the forest from the soil to the sky." The "Godless" universe seems devoid of purpose, and March acknowledges his own inescapable participation in the disorder, if only because "individual selfishness" drives him to put the needs of his family first. At first such recognitions provoke a "vague discomfort"; gradually they come to shape his world, as Howells records March's hesitations, stumbles, and headlong plunges into the lives of others.[5] The word *March* suggests the opposite of Basil's journey through life but seems a complement to the narrative of *Their Wedding Journey,* which is driven by trains and steamboats. Here the couple march to a different plot in a radically changed world. If by the novel's end Basil arrives at some awareness of the forces that hinder civilization and make a misery of human existence, he remains mostly an observer with no solution, except for an eccentric flash of courage shown in his refusal to fire his old friend Lindau. The moment brings no comfort, no answers, no strength of purpose. Providence will determine whether he can fashion a better future from thousands of such moments, or whether small acts of conscience and kindness *might* mitigate the tragedy of people pushing, pulling, lying, stealing, and cheating their way through life. More than one hundred years later, Howells' bold and unbending novel has lost none of its resonance.

A Hazard of New Fortunes appeared in book form at the beginning of 1890. By then the Howells family, after little more than a year in New York, had retreated to Cambridge. "It is a great relief to be settled again," Howells told his father in a letter otherwise heavy with sorrow. "Don't be depressed by my letter," he added as a postscript, "I must write from a mood, but we have many brighter moods."[6] Mildred had missed her childhood friends, and they wanted to be nearer John, now a junior at Harvard. They leased a large old house overlooking Fresh Pond, a temporary haven among fields and market gardens twenty minutes from Harvard Square.

When Howells looked back after twenty years to the time of his novel, he remembered a more promising situation than he or Basil March experienced in 1890. The rich, he wrote, "seemed not so much to despise the poor, the poor did not so hopelessly repine." The realization of the dreams of Henry George, Edward Bellamy, and "the generous visionaries of the past, seemed not impossibly far off."[7] Howells might have been thinking of George's electrifying but unsuccessful campaign to become mayor of New York City in 1887. The author of *Progress and Poverty,* George had campaigned against Tammany Hall, monopolies, and Mrs. Astor, the symbol of unearned wealth, with the slogan "Honest labor against thieving landlords and politicians—the land belongs to the people!"[8] Visiting George in 1892, Howells approved the simplicity of his surroundings and his choice of books: George and his wife were reading aloud *A Hazard of New Fortunes* to their ailing daughter.

Howells may also have recalled the groundswell of altruism he associated with the rise of the Populist party, its 1892 platform driven by reformers who supported the founding of the American Federation of Labor (1886) and advocated public ownership of corporations. In a letter to his father of November 1892, he called the Republican party "a lie in defamation of its past. It promises nothing in the way of economic or social reform, and it is only less corrupt than the scoundrelly democracy. The only live and honest party is the People's Party." He looked forward, he said, "to the decay of both the old parties, and the growth of a new one that will mean true equality and real freedom."[9] If he recalled that the Populist party won in excess of a million votes, he overlooked more ominous developments. In the year *A Hazard of New Fortunes* appeared, U.S. soldiers massacred two hundred Sioux at Wounded Knee; Andrew Carnegie published *The Gospel of Wealth;* the United States Post Office prohibited the mailing of Leo Tolstoy's *Kreutzer Sonata* on grounds of obscenity; and Jacob Riis' *How the Other Half Lives* shocked middle-class readers by reporting that 1 percent of Americans owned more than the rest of the population combined.

Then, too, positive as the passage of the Sherman Antitrust Act may have appeared in 1890, the Homestead Strike two years later turned public sentiment against strikers and effectively prevented the organization of steelworkers until after the First World War. Named for the Carnegie steel mill at Homestead, Pennsylvania, the strike began on July 6, 1892, when union and nonunion workers whose contracts had expired united to keep scabs from entering the mill. Three hundred Pinkerton detectives, hired to break the strike, opened fire on striking workers after someone fired a gun. The strikers retaliated in kind. The battle, which lasted eleven hours, ended when the Pinkertons surrendered. Three detectives died; seven workers were wounded. Order was restored six days later with the arrival of the National Guard. The company retaliated by evicting workers from company-owned housing and issuing complaints against individuals, who had to post repeated bail and fight costly court cases. On November 17, day laborers and mechanics voted to return to work. "It is hard, in our sympathy with the working class, to remember that the men are playing a lawless part, and that they must be made to give up the Carnegie property," Howells wrote his father. Though he applauded the end of "Pinkertonism," he thought the trouble would last as long as competition lasted. The strikes themselves were symptoms, not cures. Indeed, he thought both sides lost, especially those caught in the middle. "One must pity those poor wretches of detectives, too; how shockingly they were used after their surrender. I come back to my old conviction, that every drop of blood shed for a good cause helps to make a bad cause."[10] Contradicting himself—or as usual seeing another side—he speculated that it might have been better for the detectives to shoot down the unarmed strikers and given them the power of martyrdom.

Howells' ambivalence extended to Carnegie, whom he had first met at a Delmonico luncheon in February 1892. Shortly afterward, he asked Carnegie to write an article on steelmaking and—tongue in cheek or not—to call it "The Poetry of a Pound of Steel."[11] Much as he deplored Carnegie's excessive wealth and exploitation of workers, he pitied the man, whom he thought unpretentious, because he carried the responsibilities of money and power. Howells approved the endowment of libraries across the nation as an honest reflection of the man and the counterpart to the cold-hearted overseer of the Homestead mill. Describing Carnegie to his father as having "a sort of queer pig-face, shrewd and humorous and set," a man who "laid down the law" and told stories of his native Scotland, he added: "Somehow I liked him. Still, I would rather not be one of his hands."[12]

No Carnegie himself, Howells in 1890 tallied his net worth at $60,000; in 1892 it rose to $68,000; in 1894 to $84,000; and in 1897 to $93,000.[13] (The equivalent of $93,000 in today's dollars would be about $2,000,000.) Howells received income from his property and other investments; then, too, Harper & Brothers had done well for him, and he for Harper's. *A Hazard of New Fortunes,* for example, sold twenty thousand copies the first year—far more than his books during the 1880s. The paradox of enjoying his own ample means in the face of widespread social injustice made more disturbing what Howells saw as the widening gap between the rich and the poor. "We Americans," he wrote, "are yet so far lost in the dark ages as to suppose that there is freedom where the caprice of one citizen can interfere with the comfort or pleasure of the rest."[14]

Along with reformers such as Edward Everett Hale and Julia Ward Howe, he attended the Nationalist Club in Boston, just one of many groups inspired by Edward Bellamy's utopian romance *Looking Backward* (1888), which even a doubter like Mark Twain called "the latest and best of all the Bibles."[15] (Its success would encourage imitators, Howells among them, to write their own utopian fiction.) Oddly enough, Nationalism represented for its supporters a form of international socialism. Bellamy said he chose the name because the average person associated socialists with godlessness, the red flag, and sexual license.[16] In Boston, the organization drew support from aging abolitionists like Thomas Wentworth Higginson, who accompanied Howells to the founding meeting. Some, like Hale, who sat on the boards of social and charitable organizations, had become institutions themselves. A Unitarian minister and great-nephew of the Revolutionary War hero, Hale achieved fame for his Civil War book *A Man without a Country* (1863) and for a motto to a short story, "Ten Times One Is Ten," which went: "Look up and not down, look forward and not back, look out and not in, and lend a hand." The lines grew so popular that Lend-a-Hand Clubs and Look-Up Legions spread nationwide and helped Hale to his appointment, in 1902, as chaplain of the United States Senate.

Howells understood that most men and women live their lives by appealing to higher truths while contradicting them at every step. The Nationalist Club of Boston, which tended to preach to the converted, shared the drawbacks of less high-minded groups. Other founding members agreed and applauded Hale's hope that once before he died he "might be a member of a body that had no by-laws to squabble over."[17] Howells increased the applause with his feet, kicking his heels against the wooden box he sat on. The ironies of membership were not lost on Higginson, who called the Nationalist movement a "statue with feet of clay and limbs of iron and a forehead of brass . . . with a cigar in its lips and a wine glass in its right hand."[18] The *Atlantic* feuds behind them, he and Howells agreed about the futility of well-meaning organizations as about the decay of American politics.

In 1888, Howells had written to Henry James that "after fifty years of optimistic content with 'civilization' and its ability to come out all right in the end, I now abhor it, and feel that it is coming out all wrong . . . unless it bases itself anew on a real equality. Meantime, I wear a fur-lined overcoat, and live in all the luxury my money can buy."[19] The "theoretical socialist" could at least be honest about the way he lived. Hamlin Garland, indebted as much to Howells as to the socialist Henry George, labeled Howells a "communist." It frustrated Garland that he could never get Howells to appreciate what he believed to be their sharp political differences. "He was fixed upon some communistic reform," Garland remembered, "whilst I was perfectly clear that land monopoly was the fundamental cause of poverty and must be destroyed first and all."[20] For Howells nothing appeared so straightforward. What Garland reduced to simple alternatives, he understood as multiple and overlapping viewpoints. He came closer to a later writer like John Dos Passos, famous for his cinematic composition of New York in *Manhattan Transfer*, than to a younger contemporary like Garland. To both Howells and Dos Passos, the basic condition of human existence remained monotonously the same: men and women struggling against the institutions they had themselves created. In a country infected with the "virus of commercialism," no institution could be independent, and that included the arts, which, as the title of Howells' 1893 essay suggests, make a man of letters into a man of business.[21] At his most bitter—cynics might say his most prescient—he predicted that the "adman" might become "the supreme artist of the twentieth century."[22] He kept his sense of humor, however, granting George Harris & Sons of Chicago permission to put his face on a cigar box.[23]

He had been drawn to Edward Bellamy (who returned his admiration) because Bellamy admitted to writing *Looking Backward* out of selfishness. Bellamy "had come to think of our hopeless conditions suddenly, one day, in looking at his own children, and reflecting that he could not place them beyond the chance of want by any industry or forecast or providence," and that this was true for every parent.[24] Howells the realist saw Bellamy's novel as "pure romance" and liked it no less for that.[25] After Bellamy's death, he tried to help the man's widow by proposing a stage production of *Looking Backward*.

Our feelings are not at our bidding.

    —W. D. HOWELLS, "The Shadow of a Dream," 1890

Eight months after Winny's death, Howells informed his father from Cambridge that he was about to relocate again, this time from a house they had subleased on Mount Auburn Street to an apartment on Boston's Commonwealth Avenue, where the family lived for the next two years. He would have preferred New York or to settle in the country and (he half-joked) raise English violets and chickens, but he felt either choice would be unfair to the children. Mildred, needing some deliverance from sadness, threw herself into the social whirl they had both dreaded and eagerly anticipated with Winny's coming out. By coincidence, Mildred's debut took place on Winny's birthday, December 17, 1890.[26] John accompanied Mildred to Saturday evening dances, where—according to his father—he made it his business "to look after the plain and neglected girls."[27]

Unable to render his loss of Winny understandable or to rethink life without her, Howells spoke of living "from moment to moment: to write, to read, to eat, above all to sleep and forget."[28] Forgetting was something he simply could not do. Where was she? Would he see her again? Such questions filled his waking and dreaming hours. "I believe in nothing, though I am afraid of everything," he wrote a friend. "I do not always feel sure that I shall live again, but when I wake at night the room seems dense with spirits."[29] In one dream, offered freedom or death as a prisoner on the gallows, he chose death. "It's only a momentary wrench, and then I shall be with *her*."[30] Awake, he feared nothing more than meeting Winny.

Ten years before Freud's *Interpretation of Dreams*, Howells speculated about the dream world being amoral and dreamers not accountable for their subconscious thoughts. He wrote of his dreams to family and friends, including S. Weir Mitchell, and he turned them, like so much of his experience, to fictional account. In the same year that *A Hazard of New Fortunes* appeared, he published *The Shadow of a Dream* (1890), a book almost exclusively psychological in focus. In this novel a husband has died, and his wife and best friend plan to marry; but, shamed by their knowledge of the dead man's deluded sense, in fact his dream, that they were lovers, they cannot come together. What makes the story "occult"—as one reviewer called it—is the nether land in which mere suggestion, a fantasy not one's own, becomes reality.

From the time of his mother's death a decade before, Howells had devoted much of his thinking to such issues. "O God, if there is a god, save my soul, if I have a soul." The Victorian witticism about religious uncertainty speaks to Howells' own doubts in these years. Now confiding more in his father and equating his life directly with William's, he saw that living coherently, let alone like Christ, remained impossible, even for such a man as Tolstoy. On matters of right living and social justice father and son stood on common ground not just because they agreed in principle but because neither believed that the political sphere—any more than the professional or social—could be separated from the spiritual. "We have been parted, domestically, for 35 years," he wrote to William, "but the letters have held us constantly together, as I think few fathers and sons of our ages have continued. May we have all eternity together!"[31] He read Swedenborg again and attended several churches, including the First Spiritual Temple and the Church of the Carpenter, a mission of the Episcopal Church with ties to the Society of Christian Socialists. He felt especially moved in an African American Methodist Church, where, sounding like Harriet Beecher Stowe, he described the congregation as kind and "lowly," humbled like himself.[32] Yet even his moments of resignation brought bitter awareness. Others did "good" because they loved, he confided in Charles Norton, he because he hated.[33]

Boston's Church of the Carpenter seemed an attractive institution, blending English and American Christian Socialism with ethical and spiritual principles and high hopes for a better society. Its leader, William Dwight Porter Bliss, also read and agreed with Howells' guides, Gronlund and Bellamy, and believed in an unspecified relationship between religion and altruistic politics. Writing to Edward Everett Hale about *Annie Kilburn* in 1888, Howells admitted: "I solve nothing, except what was solved eighteen centuries ago. The most that I can do is perhaps to set a few people thinking; for as yet I haven't got to doing anything, myself."[34] Much as he wanted to improve conditions for his children and hoped to make his life and his fiction *matter*, he found peace of mind in neither the Church of the Carpenter nor any of the faiths, social philosophies, or institutions he explored.

He does not mention Søren Kierkegaard, the skeptical Danish thinker who wrote long, unresolvable dialogues with himself—one aptly titled *Either-Or*—but he shared Kierkegaard's spiritual longings and impatience with facile creeds. There were of course thousands of other skeptical seekers after spiritual solace. Close to home, William James' personal odyssey culminated in his *Varieties of Religious Experience* (1902). Although Howells' novels almost overlap with those of Henry James, he had much in common with William, not just as religious thinker but as the author of *The Principles of Psychology* (1890), which Howells called poetic and "distinctly human."[35] Each a sympathetic reader of the other's books, William appreciated Howells' clear writing as a corrective to Henry's impenetrability, while Howells praised William's ease with complex subjects and the sense of humor that played through his writing. Both were fascinated with questions of truth and reality that could be "carved"—to use James' word—in different ways. Few topics escaped the attention of either man.[36] James might have cited himself or Howells in the case studies of "neurasthenic" suffering and spiritual questing he portrayed so sympathetically.

Believing, he said, that only "an arrogant ass" would "dabble with things beyond him," Howells himself dabbled with supernatural states in books such as *Questionable Shapes* (1903) and *Between the Dark and the Daylight* (1907). "I *must* meddle with them," he wrote Howard Pyle (known by generations of children for his illustrations of Robin Hood), "both in my own defective conduct and in the imagined lives of others."[37] The year after this letter, in 1891, he attended a meeting of the Psychical Research Society to hear people trade ghost stories. He also participated in a séance held in a Concord, Massachusetts, farmhouse. The scene belonged in a Howells novel like *The Undiscovered Country*. A middle-aged, obviously prosperous gentleman holds hands in a circle with a rural medium and other hopefuls while the frigid February air seeps through the walls. In the hush of expectation, Howells reported to his father, the house shook and "the table lifted and banged with blows as from a hammer. . . . It all sounds absurd when you tell it; but I was badly rattled at the time, and I don't want to see any more of the performance."[38] Howells attended the séance with Robertson James, the younger brother of Henry and William; here, too, William would have been an appropriate companion.

In addition to his *Shadow of a Dream*, Howells published another sort of "dream-story" in 1890. A memoir of his years in Hamilton, *A Boy's Town* recalls Thomas Hughes' *Tom Brown's School Days* or Thomas Bailey Aldrich's *Story of a Bad Boy*, not to mention Twain's *Tom Sawyer*, earlier books for boys that Howells had reviewed. It delighted him to discover how much he remembered of his childhood, and how clearly. "It makes me think that my strongest faculty, after all, may have been an art of seeing and hearing everything. I am sure I c'd not invent half as many things, thoughts, ideas, as I can remember."[39] Writing almost coyly about children in the 1840s, he targets *A Boy's Town* for those now "who read *Harper's Young People*," children who do everything differently and remain essentially the same.

Howells found that regardless of vivid memories, he could not recover the essence of his boyhood. The experiences might live again, yet their meaning eluded him. It is through fiction, not through memoirs, he wrote, that inner lives can best be expressed. His admission, both ironic and shrewd, points to the challenge he felt as a creator of fictional worlds and a writer of autobiographies. In *A Boy's Town* he shrugs off first-person storytelling by speaking of "my boy," a construction suggesting the distance and methods of fiction writing rather than the personal intimacy of autobiography. "I shall call this boy, my boy," he explains; "but I hope he might have been almost anybody's boy; and I mean him sometimes for a boy in general, as well as a boy in particular."[40] Because the older narrator defines his younger self through family, history, and the boys with whom he grows up, his account offers an almost generic boy. To make an unlikely pairing of authors and books, *A Boy's Town* stands with *The Education of Henry Adams* (privately printed in 1907) among the few American autobiographies told in the third person. Adams' bitter self-analysis—written more than twenty years after his wife's suicide in 1885—reads nothing like Howells' book. It is filled with outrage and personal recriminations, doubts and depression. Yet both autobiographies convey profound regret, Adams' lamenting an unfulfilled life, Howells' a past that might have been and a daughter he has lost. Each of his books from this period—*A Boy's Town, The Shadow of a Dream, An Imperative Duty,* and the work in progress that became *The Quality of Mercy, A Story of Contemporary American Life* (1892)—comments at least obliquely on Winny's death.

In *An Imperative Duty* (1892), the story of Rhoda Aldgate, a woman who discovers her African heritage, Howells addresses the controversial issue of "passing," or exchanging one racial identity for another. Rhoda's passing as white moves beyond social or racial complexities to philosophical and scientific questions about free will and genetics. Just as Howells expected his own hypochondria to assert itself in the next generation, Rhoda's aunt waits to see if any sinister, atavistic tendencies will emerge in her niece. When she learns the history of her birth, Rhoda indignantly blames her aunt for letting her deceive herself "and every one else."[41] As early as 1860, Howells had endorsed interracial marriage, and *An Imperative Duty* provides a model for what his contemporaries called "absorption," or the mingling of separate races into one race. At the novel's end, a nerve specialist named Olney marries Rhoda and whisks her off to Italy, where, coming full circle, she is accepted as a native. To the dismay of recent critics, Howells' ending presents racial identity as if it were an illness to be cured.

Like W. E. B. Du Bois, Howells believed prejudice toward African Americans to be a result of slavery and therefore the product of social rather than inherited characteristics. Du Bois would praise Howells on the occasion of his seventy-fifth birthday for facing, in *An Imperative Duty,* "our national foolishness and shuffling and evasion." As Du Bois saw it, "Here was a white girl engaged to a white man who discovers herself to be 'black.' The problem looms before her as tremendous, awful. The world wavers. She peers beyond the veil and shudders and then—tells her story frankly, marries her man, and goes her way as thousands of others have done and are doing."[42] The novel drew protests—not mainly from African Americans, whom, in a moment of anger, the self-loathing Rhoda describes as "burlesques of humanity, worse than apes"—but from the Irish, stereotyped again as slovenly and servile.[43] Readers of the serial installments attributed to the author Olney's negative comments about the Irish, which, by an odd logic, Howells had intended to bolster the standing of African Americans. He cut the offending passages from the published book. Following the serial publication of *An Imperative Duty,* the African American writer Frances Harper published *Iola Leroy* (1892), the story of a woman who learns that her mother had been her father's property. Along with books like Anna Dickinson's *What Answer?* (1869), *An Imperative Duty* helped to create a market for fiction, especially African American fiction, presenting characters of "mixed blood."[44]

Howells had struggled with the question of duty from his days in Jefferson. By the late 1880s, it had become for him the overriding question. He had trouble finishing his next novel, *The Quality of Mercy,* probably because it concerns an inadequate father, an embezzler who flees to Canada and leaves his daughter to deal with creditors. He knew that his difficulties reflected his state of mind. "I feel sometimes like simply running away from it," he told Twain.[45] One month shy of his fifty-fourth birthday in February 1891, he was exhausted and suffering from pains in his legs and feet. *The Quality of Mercy* turned out to be a surprising success, capturing the interest of readers who had followed similar cases of millionaire defaulters in the newspapers; but its author once again needed a "basis." Harper's showed no inclination to extend his contract beyond 1891, until—it may have been coincidental—they learned that McClure's wanted him to edit a highbrow illustrated monthly.[46] Then, alluding to Basil March's imperious publisher in *A Hazard of New Fortunes,* the Harpers apologized for "the Dryfoos-*père* aspect" of their behavior. "Would it be proper for us to inquire, in strict confidence, as to the nature of the engagements you have in contemplation for '92, & whether or not they would be likely to interfere with the continuance of the *Study* for that year?"[47] Henry Alden played mediator, agreeing to Howells' continuing the column but complaining about its failure to interest more readers. They came to agreement, and Howells' last Editor's Study appeared in March 1892. With no apparent ill will on either side, Harper's continued to publish Howells' books, and he agreed to write later columns.

A secure income mattered more than ever to Howells because he wanted to free his father from worries about money. Looking at his accounts that January (as he always did at the new year), he reckoned that he had advanced William about $2,400, which he did not want charged against Aurelia's inheritance but would accept against other heirs to his father's estate. Since 1885, he had been sending his father and sister a monthly allowance, in addition to money for incidentals, medications, and emergencies. This sum did not include what he sent Sam, who, to his chagrin, gave up the *Index* but dishonestly collected rent on the building. "I am troubled, as I always am, after I part with you," Howells would write his father in June 1892, "for fear I have been indelicate with you about money matters. You are so refined and considerate yourself, that I seem by contrast, vulgar and brutal. I hope I did nothing to wound you, or to add to the difficulty you feel in letting me help you. I am sure that so far as you and Aurelia are concerned it is a pleasure as well as a duty, and first a pleasure."[48] Howells' income, which might have appeared enormous to outsiders, depended on his health, the whims of editors and fashion, and to some extent the stock market. The previous year, six thousand shares of railroad stock he owned had dropped in value from slightly over a dollar to twenty-four cents. He recovered some of this investment by turning the story of his loss into a *Harper's* column.

John's graduation from Harvard, in June 1891, brought his father a mix of joy and sad reminders, which he shared in a long meditation with his own father.

> It will be interesting to see whether he [John] is an improvement on the rest of us. I am not satisfied with this part of my doing, any more than the rest. The whole of life seems unreal and unfair; but what I try to teach the children is to be ready for the change that *must* come in favor of truth and justice, and not to oppose it. Of course the world still looks beautiful to them; they cannot see it as I do; but I hope they can see the right. In the meantime Elinor and I live along like our neighbors; only, we have a bad conscience. Sometimes, however, the whole affair goes to pieces in my apprehension, and I feel as if I had no more authority to judge myself or to try to do this or that, than any other expression of the Infinite Life,—say a tree, or a field of wheat, or a horse. The only proof I have that I ought to do right is that I suffer for my selfishness; and perhaps this is enough. I dare say God can take care of all the rest. I wish I could once leave it to him.[49]

Concerns about money, health, family, the pressure to produce and meet deadlines—these and memories of Winny help to explain a decision that most of Howells' friends found unthinkable. As the year 1892 began, he bade his farewells in Boston and, reversing his switch from the *Nation* to the *Atlantic* a quarter century before, accepted a position with New York's *Cosmopolitan*. Perhaps justifying the decision to William, he said simply: "There is more for me to see and learn there."[50]

We [artists] ought to feel the tie that binds us to all the toilers of the shop and field, not as a galling chain, but as a mystic bond.

—W. D. HOWELLS, "The Man of Letters as a Man of Business," 1893

Howells' move to the *Cosmopolitan* made news. "Mr. Howells has come to stand for the most vital and progressive principle in American literature," a contemporary reporter wrote, "and to have him assume editorial charge of a magazine means a great deal to the conservative as well as to the more radical wing of our literary public." Another saw his choice of the *Cosmopolitan* as a second revolution, a shot to be heard around the world.[51] By 1886 half the major publishing houses could be found in New York City, which came to stand for whatever was "splendidly and sordidly commercial," in publishing as in everything else.[52] The city's magazines dwarfed the *Atlantic Monthly,* with its small circulation and smaller profits, and drew the scorn of New York editors who could demand high advertising rates because they reached hundreds of thousands of readers.

This was the place and potential audience Howells acquired with the magazine. He planned to coax the *Cosmopolitan*'s contributors and readers to a higher standard.[53] Most writers with literary pretensions preferred to publish elsewhere—until, that is, they learned the rate of pay. John Brisben Walker had bought the magazine in 1889 when its circulation hovered at an anemic 16,000. By 1892 it had reached 250,000; by 1894 400,000.[54] Decidedly not highbrow, the magazine featured light fiction, household hints, and socially conscious articles bearing titles like "On Earth Peace, Good Will towards Men." Charles Eliot Norton warned that Howells would "have work to lift 'the Cosmopolitan' out of the atmosphere in which it has flourished—, an atmosphere in which there has been a large mingling of the noxious oxide gas of second-rate vulgarity."[55] Yet the aim of both the owner and Howells resembled that of the founders of the *Atlantic* or the *North American.* They dreamed, in Howells' words, of doing "something for humanity as well as the humanities." A man of "strong socialist tendencies," Walker had already hired political activists such as Edward Everett Hale and Brander Matthews, who shared his and Howells' politics.[56] Walker had asked (in an editorial praising *A Hazard of New Fortunes*) what it was that gave Howells "his broad hold on the American Public." "Is it not his sympathy with human failings, even while holding them up to ridicule? . . . Is he not sorry alike for the struggles of the poor for bread, and of the vulgar rich for social advancement? And if he is a socialist, why, then, the good God made us all socialists."[57] Walker imagined his new editor as a dazzling popularizer who could speak to and inspire the next generation.[58]

According to a contemporary report, Howells wrote to Walker after reading an address Walker had given at the Catholic University in Washington, DC. A convert to Catholicism, Walker challenged the Church to distribute its wealth. "The letter led to a meeting, the meeting to a discussion of business, the discussion to a proposal" in early December 1891, and the proposal to a job.[59] Howells told his father that the work would either rejuvenate or kill him. "The best thing about it is Mr. Walker's infatuation with his bargain; yet it is terrible, in a way, to have a man so satisfied with you."[60] He would have done well to remember Basil March's reservations about Fulkerson, the editor in *A Hazard of New Fortunes.* Seduced by Walker's promises, he anticipated the luxury of rewriting, concentrating on quality rather than quantity, and finishing his books before they began serialization. When James wailed, "Why (let me not be odious!) are you hanging again round your neck the chain & emblem of bondage?" Howells might have answered that Walker had made him an offer he could not refuse.[61] Agreeing to write exclusively for the *Cosmopolitan,* he promised to supply, for fifteen thousand dollars a year, one long story of sixty thousand words or the equivalent in shorter pieces. The question was, what sort of job had he been offered? Did he go to the magazine as editor, literary editor, or associate editor? Had Walker promised Howells the power he had enjoyed with the *Atlantic,* or did he imagine it? So much about his brief tenure and his relations with Walker remains vague at best. To begin with, on March 30, he signed a five-year contract with Harper's that took effect on April 1 and gave *them* first consideration of all novels, stories, and other writings to appear in book form. Even the question of when he began the *Cosmopolitan* job has been a matter of guesswork. In all likelihood, however, he began his editorship in May 1892, after substantial work on that month's issue, and he joined the magazine believing he would have freedoms that in fact did not materialize.

Walker prepared the way for Howells' arrival with journalistic aplomb. The cover of the February 1892 issue of the magazine featured a full-page picture of Howells with the announcement that on March 1 (actually May 1), he and Walker would share editorial control. An essay by Howells' old Cambridge friend and adviser to Walker, Hjalmar Boyesen, completed the "advertisement" of "Mr. Howells and His Work." In the interim, Howells began lining up contributors: Henry James, Hamlin Garland, Sarah Orne

Jewett, Edward Everett Hale, and Brander Matthews. His inaugural May issue carried a large portrait of James Lowell, with his poem "The Nobler Lover" on the opposite page. Lowell had died the summer before, and Howells intended the issue partly as a tribute.

With Lowell's death, an era might be said to have ended and a sad procession begun. John Greenleaf Whittier died the year Howells went to work for Walker, Oliver Wendell Holmes two years later (in 1894), and Harriet Beecher Stowe two years after that. With his Boston friends aging or dying, Howells embraced New York as the city of the future, the world city full of youth, energy, and human drama. New York had its crime and sensational journalism and—as ever—its notorious fires, its graft, corruption, and Tammany politics, its great new bridge arching across to Brooklyn, and its Central Park, into which he could escape as if to the countryside. Roaming its streets with the wonder, anxiety, and exhilaration of a young man, he came to know multiple New Yorks: one was home to literary men and old friends such as Edmund Stedman, Richard Stoddard, and Richard Watson Gilder, another to architects like his brother-in-law William Mead and Mead's partners Charles McKim and Stanford White, whom he met at the Century Club.

Because Howells spent so much time in New York, and enjoyed good friends there, his transition had begun years before. At the Stoddards, among the bric-à-brac and easy chairs, the paintings by Eastman and Bierstadt, the first editions that had once belonged to Keats and Byron, the autographs of Burns, Cowper, and Dickens, not to mention locks of hair from Milton and Washington, Howells might have felt he had never left Boston—so much did this room resemble Thomas Bailey Aldrich's study on Mount Vernon Street. In every house he saw familiar signs. The Gilders owned a chimney-piece by Stanford White and a Donatello cast selected by their mutual friend, Augustus Saint-Gaudens.[62] On the evenings of the Stedmans' and Stoddards' and Gilders' "at-homes," which the Howellses did not emulate, he could meet poets and playwrights, foreign dignitaries, actors, and musicians.

Like Howells himself, friends who began as journalists and poets had made their fortunes, married, and raised their children in semi-Bohemian comfort. Many lived part of their lives abroad and shared, like Howells or Norton or James, an international circle of acquaintance. Each had a reputation for hospitality, though Stedman drew the line at Oscar Wilde, who came to him with letters from Lowell and Holmes. It made him angry, he told Edmund Gosse, to see the "display made by certain classes of our 'society'" doing homage "to the knee-buckles and hose of this youth apostle."

Not without his own affectations, Stedman posed theatrically, his hand pressed to the back of his head to relieve pain from overwork. One friend suspected that he enjoyed the idea of having a serious condition, as if petty illnesses favored petty men.[63] Ever the diplomat, Gosse applauded Stedman's "noble social courage."[64] New Yorkers applauded his integrity. After his son's unwise investments brought about the liquidation of his firm in August 1882, Stedman paid every debt and within two years reclaimed his seat on the stock exchange. Five hundred colleagues lined up to shake his hand. If Howells found him something of a complainer, he did not forget Stedman's long-ago kindness to a young poet from Ohio who appeared in Washington to lobby for a consulship.[65]

Howells respected and had great affection for Gilder, one of New York's busiest and most civic-minded men. As a young man, Gilder had fought in an artillery unit at Gettysburg. Now he served as the director of various municipal and charitable boards, including the Tenement House Commission, the Kindergarten Association, and a City and Suburban Homes Company to provide wage-earners with affordable housing.[66] Sympathizing as he did with Gilder's desire to foster a greater freedom in literature, Howells parodied his gentility in *The World of Chance,* in which a young writer is advised to be bold, but not too bold—a little dig at Gilder for not accepting his submissions outright.[67]

The unliterary may not have known these men, or seen them merely as "celebrities," yet Americans far from New York could recite Stedman's poetry or tell of his vow to learn "how more stupid men made a living" gambling on Wall Street. Gilder's story was the story of *Scribner's,* which published Howells' *A Modern Instance, The Rise of Silas Lapham, A Woman's Reason,* and *The Minister's Charge,* and then that of the *Century,* which *Scribner's* became.[68] New Yorkers recognized Gilder as the man with the moustache turning white long before his brown hair had grayed. Readers of the "life and letters" memorials published by the daughters of these writers found it intriguing that Richard Stoddard sometimes uttered nothing but monosyllables for hours, whereas Henry Alden, an unassuming man, lectured his guests on his favorite subject of metaphysics long after they would have normally retired for bed, though not before they had fallen asleep.

A more recent friend than Stoddard or Gilder, Alden was not only a philosopher but the distinguished editor Howells admired—and negotiated with—at Harper's. He wrote some of the most heart-wrenching letters Howells ever received about his wife's various operations for breast cancer, the hoped-for cures, and the inevitable recurrences. With his compliments to Alden's wife, Howells sent suggestions about the latest electromagnetic treatment, and when he visited her, at her request—she had heard so much of him through his letters to her husband—she felt as if the "King" had come bearing blessings.[69] The aspirations of youth, the pain of intervening years, shared losses and tragedies, and above all, perhaps, familiarity— these bound Howells ever more closely to friends of his own generation.

In their time, and to aspiring writers like Hamlin Garland, Howells and his friends stood for "high thinking."[70] Today, the names of men like Stedman, Gilder, and Alden mean little or nothing to most readers. There were problems even in Howells' day. Laurence Hutton, an acclaimed and long-forgotten drama critic, told a comic version of introducing George Washington Cable to an audience in Hartford, Connecticut. "The original idea was that Mr. William Dean Howells of New York was to introduce Mr. Cable of New Orleans . . . when it occurred to the Committee that Mr. Howells was himself a stranger to Hartford and did not know Hartford, nor did Hartford know him. So Mr. Thomas Bailey Aldrich, of Boston, was brought from Boston to introduce Mr. Howells of New York, who was to introduce Mr. Cable of New Orleans. But some one was necessary to introduce Mr. Aldrich of Boston, so Mr. Gilder of New York was asked to introduce Mr. Aldrich of Boston, who was . . ." and so on.[71] The anecdote highlights the problem of speaking about people who, while literary giants to many of their contemporaries, have slipped out of any collective memory. Howells himself fell from far greater fame to relative obscurity. It bothered him that strangers who had never read his books wanted to collect his signature as if it were a postage stamp to be traded among collectors. He jested about giving his name only to those who could prove "by intelligent comment" that they had read one of his books. "If they can inclose a bookseller's certificate that they have bought the book, their case will be very much strengthened. . . . I will never 'add a sentiment' except in the case of applicants who can give proof that they have read all my books, now some thirty or forty in number."[72]

That said, Howells understood and honored the impulse which first brought the young Hamlin Garland to his door in the summer of 1887. "There is really no harm in seeking the presence of a famous man," he wrote in *Literary Friends and Acquaintance*. "There are bores everywhere, but [an established writer] is likelier to find them in the wonted figures of society than in those young people, or old people, who come to him in the love of what he has done."[73] The Howellses had retreated to a grand resort in Auburndale, Massachusetts, when Garland arrived bearing a letter of introduction from a mutual friend, Edward Clement, editor of the *Boston Transcript*. It had taken Garland several walks around the block before he summoned the nerve to enter the hotel, and when he asked for Mr. Howells, the clerk looked at his long sideburns, broad-brimmed hat, worn coat, and plaid tie before announcing that Mr. Howells was dining. Not knowing the time reserved for afternoon calls, Garland had assumed that everyone had their midday meal between twelve and one. Nonetheless, he persisted, and the letter from Clement went from hand to hand until it arrived at Howells' table. When word came back that the visitor should wait, Garland found himself escorted to a small, formal sitting room.

Howells came in a few minutes later. Garland remembered not so much the man's appearance as the feeling of being regarded so thoroughly, with such penetration, that he had no secrets. "Won't you be seated?" the older man said, his impassive face breaking into a warm smile, his hand pointing to one of the gilded chairs next to a sofa. Almost instantly at ease, Garland began pouring forth his theories. Howells asked his opinion about a story he intended to write—it became *The Shadow of a Dream*—and Garland, with new confidence, urged against it, preferring the "realistic" vein of novels such as *A Modern Instance* and *Silas Lapham*. Howells considered his advice seriously, credited his arguments, and afterward walked him to the station. As Garland waited for his train, he experienced an epiphany that recalls Howells' own journey as a young man to Boston. The years of Garland's apprenticeship had ended; Howells had accepted him. Writing in tribute after Howells' death, Garland would say that he had lost a spiritual guide and arbiter, that no death except his father's had affected him so deeply.[74]

The anecdote indicates Howells' impact on the next generation as well as the charm that brought new talent to his publishers. He could connect with people few others tolerated, among them the notorious Lafcadio Hearn. Hearn had slipped in and out of New York City by way of Philadelphia and the French West Indies. From his apprentice days as a journalist in Cincinnati, he had become an essayist and translator of French literature (his version of de Maupassant's "String of Pearls" still appears in anthologies) and a student of ethnic cultures, especially Creole New Orleans and Caribbean French. The writer of travel books and two exotic novels, he had already taken a fortuitous interest in things Japanese. Hearn began to publish in the *Atlantic* and *Harper's Monthly*, but he was, as usual, lonely, angry, and broke.

Soon after Hearn arrived in New York, Henry Harper invited him to attend a dinner at the Union League Club, and Harper asked his editor (and

Hearn's), Henry Alden, to make sure that he attended. Those familiar with Hearn realized that while he might accept an invitation to a dinner party, he would arrive shivering with fear, often to run away before the door opened. This time, though angry with Alden for refusing another advance, Hearn trusted him enough to go inside—not without Alden grabbing his seldom-worn, or likely borrowed, dinner jacket and tugging him past the coatroom and lounge into the banquet room. Seated at table, Hearn hunched over and nibbled like a man alone. Howells noticed the strange, half-blind and extremely short man he had met on the way in and asked Henry Harper about him. On hearing Hearn's name, "Howells jumped up"—those are Harper's words—"went round to Hearn and apologized for not recognizing him. There was only one Lafcadio Hearn, he said, and he was so pleased to meet him that he wanted to shake his hand again."[75] It isn't hard to picture this encounter: the well-fed and heavyset Howells, walking deliberately with his head thrust forward, perhaps touching his broad moustache, and bending over the starved figure. Turning aside to hide his blind eye, Hearn would have whispered a response. Howells knew how to soothe feelings and to flatter. Hearn, who longed for attention as much as he hated it, actually began to talk as the evening went on, and he found that others listened. Familiar with Howells' work and reputation—who was not?—he had belittled in print everything Howells stood for, especially a literary realism that rejected notions of genius. Hearn's opinions had no effect on Howells' generosity. At this one meeting, an otherwise mundane dinner party, he gave Lafcadio Hearn a rare taste of sympathy and recognition, possibly the last he enjoyed before leaving, a few months later, to live the rest of his short life in Meiji Japan.

Howells returned to Boston in February 1892 for a concert in Cambridge's Appleton Chapel honoring Lowell's birthday. The sense of ghosts gathering, of walking here hand in hand with Winny, the loss of Lowell, the misery of his and others' lives—all threatened to overwhelm him that day. He coped by nearly falling asleep. He imagined Lowell laughing from above, his old self before the last months of pain. After the concert he wrote to another Cambridge mentor some of what he might have said to Lowell himself. "I had a most lovely visit with you," he told Norton, "and came away warmed through and through by the sense of my love for you, which seemed almost like your love for me. I hope it is partly so; these things get mixed in our dream of existence, and one hardly knows his emotion from his friend's."[76]

Four months later he must have questioned his decision to leave Boston, for at the end of June he and the *Cosmopolitan* parted ways. The reasons for the breakup remain unclear. People have cited Walker's unwillingness to share control and the difference in his and Howells' styles. As someone with ties to the magazine recalled, "Mr. Walker had curious methods of work. . . . In the first place, he insisted that everyone in his employ—no matter who he was—should be at his desk not later than eight o'clock in the morning. . . . There was a legend to the effect that once, when William Dean Howells was editor of the *Cosmopolitan,* he found a note upon his desk one morning, requesting that he report for duty at the unconscionable hour."[77] Howells may well have found the job more confining than liberating, or Walker too capricious to be trustworthy, though miraculously the two stayed friends. Walker himself probably had second thoughts about tinkering with a moneymaking formula when he could contract separately for Howells' magazine contributions, including *A Traveler from Altruria* (1894), which he published as a series of "letters" from November 1892 to October 1893.

Howells conceived the letters, as he would his Easy Chair columns for *Harper's Monthly,* as dramatic dialogues between an "Altrurian" traveler, Homos, and representative Americans, including a banker, Mr. Bullion, and a popular novelist, Mr. Twelvemough, otherwise W. D. Howells in a satiric self-portrait. The conversations between Twelvemough and Homos—another ill-assorted pair of Siamese twins—highlight the conundrum at the heart of Howells' own life: the obligation any person owes another. His argument with himself reflects his argument with America. As Mr. Twelvemough, the author of *Airs and Graces,* explains, he cannot make himself understood to the Altrurian, whose logic topples everything he has been taught to believe about the democratic workings of his country.

The two talk at odds about a society at odds: an America without equality, without common regard for others, without religious principle, but proudly in search of wealth so abundant and privately hoarded that it makes vassals of other citizens. Homos, whose native land combines the qualities of Christian charity with Greek culture, has read the American Declaration of Independence and is surprised to learn that the country it defined has long forgotten its basic principles. His questions about the practice of tipping—unheard of in Altruria, where every citizen is truly equal—has the effect of silencing even so loquacious a man as Twelvemough:

"Have you any ranks or classes?"

"Well, not exactly, in the English sense. Our ranks and classes, such as we have, are what I may call voluntary."

"Oh, I understand. I suppose that from time to time certain ones among you feel the need of serving, and ask leave of the commonwealth to subordinate themselves to the rest of the state, and perform all the lowlier offices in it. Such persons must be held in peculiar honor. Is it something like that?"

"Well, no, I can't say it's quite like that. In fact, I think I'd better let you trust to your own observation of our life."

"But I'm sure," said the Altrurian, with a simplicity so fine that it was a long time before I could believe it quite real, "that I shall approach it so much more intelligently with a little instruction from you. You say that your social divisions are voluntary. But do I understand that those who serve among you do not wish to do so?"

"Well, I don't suppose they would serve if they could help it," I replied.

"Surely," said the Altrurian with a look of horror, "you don't mean that they are slaves!"[78]

Howells would apologize to his readers for not bringing his "romances" to a definite conclusion, suggesting that the alien nature of Altrurian civilization made that impossible.

For some old friends, the Altrurian letters underscored how much of an iconoclast Howells had become. Horace Scudder, a normally diffident man, complained that Howells' literary proselytizing made him intolerant of "worshippers of false gods" and overly generous to true believers.[79] Henry James spoke for many in wishing him to pontificate less and "novel" more. As early as 1887, James had said that Howells should "content himself with writing the novel as he thinks it should be and not talking about it; he does the one so much better than the other."[80] If still a novelist, Howells had extended the range of his writing beyond what either James or himself could have predicted a few years before. His letter in the *Tribune* on the fate of the anarchists, his columns, and his experiments with new kinds of fiction speak to a broadening literary career. His relationship with the *Cosmopolitan* marked a giant step away from Boston respectability and toward a more open populism. At this time politics drove his writing, for which he sought an audience (in the words of the Declaration of Independence) "of the people."

Howells called the books that grew out of his *Cosmopolitan* essays—*A Traveler from Altruria* and *Through the Eye of the Needle*—romances in the sense that they looked toward an idealized future that readers themselves could make reality. The Altrurian romances highlight the complicated ways in which his books and other writings reach across genres, as if part of a larger conversation. Henry Alden described the Easy Chair columns as "preserving the separate mask of each interlocutor as carefully as if he were writing a novel of dramatic characterization."[81] The same applies conversely to his novels, in which arguments about life or literature grow from the talk of specific characters in familiar situations. From the early *Venetian Life* or *Suburban Sketches* to the hallucinatory scenes of *The Undiscovered Country* or the rambling opening of *A Hazard of New Fortunes,* Howells took technical risks. Yet perhaps his greatest gift to writers who followed him was to show how fiction, "realistic fiction," could take almost any shape. In 1904, he would tell an interviewer that "realism makes all things its province, the uncommon as well as the every-day affairs of human existence."[82]

In years to come, Eugene O'Neill would borrow the background of *A Modern Instance* for his "Grecian" tragedies of American life; and Jessie Fauset would adapt his ideas about the social construction of race for *Plum Bun,* her novel of passing. To think of Howells only as a "literary" man or "a man of letters" diminishes the scope of his interests and his work. Henry James seems the model of a writer living most fully in his books, Mark Twain the nineteenth-century example of popularity and influence. Howells matches them in his own way. Through his columns, essays and articles, political biographies, children's stories, travel books, fiction, and poetry, he participated in nearly every public debate of his day. If he sometimes called the essayist the enemy of the novelist and vice versa, he could not finally decide in favor of one or the other. Their opposition kept him honest. Alden thought him the author most like his books: "you cannot classify him," he wrote. "You cannot set him down as a socialist or a democrat— he takes no label, and least of all a literary label."[83]

After his break with Walker and the *Cosmopolitan,* Howells tried to interest the publishing firm of Appleton in an *Atlantic*-style magazine. They finally declined. Except during an occasional row on a nearby pond, he found it difficult to get away from his old money cares. "Perhaps I am not reasonable," he told Aurelia. "I think I write too much, but I can't write less, and meet my expenses. I dare say it will be easier sometime."[84] He would take on the New York scene in his next two novels, *The Coast of Bohemia* (1892), a send-up of artistic pretensions, and *The World of Chance* (1893), his biting study of American publishing. As for money, he should not have worried; in 1893, the year the stock market crashed and one-third of all American railroads went bankrupt, he earned from his writing almost thirty thousand dollars. To give a relative sense of his income, Harper's in 1905 would publish a reference book for young and inexperienced housewives called *Family Living on $500 a Year.*

In October 1893, Howells told Norton, "I am getting my old books about me again, out of the boxes where they have been shut up for five years. Most of them are pangs, wounds from the past, with its manifold associations, and its power to hurt. What a grotesque notion, that anyone should be willing to live his life over again."[85] But, in a sense, he *was* willing, if not to relive his life, at least to pick up and start again. The Adirondacks, Saratoga, and Intervale, New Hampshire, would be succeeded by Lakewood, Auburndale, Sunapee, Magnolia, Far Rockaway, Kennebunkport, York, and Kittery Point, the names like way stations on his own railroad. To that list should be added Chicago, where, in 1893, he discovered a model of America's future.

I view the fair as the outcome of a socialistic impulse, which it really was.

—W. D. HOWELLS to William C. Howells, October 15, 1893

Over twenty million people, nearly a quarter of the population of the United States in 1893, paid fifty cents apiece to visit the Columbian Exposition. More than a thousand acres along Lake Michigan had been transformed into the White City to celebrate Columbus' discovery of America four hundred years before. Terraced parks, boulevards, and canals fanned out from its central colonnaded buildings, illuminated by the sun or by thousands of those late-century wonders, electric lights.

Howells and Mildred attended the exposition after a visit to Jefferson. It was the largest event of its kind ever held, dwarfing even England's Great Exhibition of 1851. Like other sightseers they traveled on a moving sidewalk, rode the Ferris wheel (fifty cents for two revolutions), tasted the exotic new delicacy called grapefruit, and saw champagne frozen into sherbet. They took an evening boat ride on the lagoon and ate in old Vienna. Strolling through the Women's Building, past a manuscript of *Jane Eyre,* murals by Mary Cassatt, costumes from around the world, and a facsimile of the 1879 law allowing women to plead cases before the U.S. Supreme Court, they also saw a facsimile of Mildred, who had modeled for Lucia Fairchild's painted panel "The Women of Plymouth." Howells could tell Elinor that the 400,000-square-foot Agricultural Building designed by his

Howells in the 1870s, when he was editor of the *Atlantic Monthly*. Courtesy Howells Memorial, Kittery Point, Maine.

John, Mildred, and
Winny. Courtesy
Herrick Memorial
Library, Alfred
University.

Howells' elegant
study in the
Concord Avenue
house. Courtesy
Houghton Library,
Harvard University.

A modern photograph of Redtop, the Belmont house. From here, Howells said, they could see to Europe. Courtesy Houghton Library, Harvard University.

Henry James. Sketch by John Singer Sargent. Clifton Waller Barrett Library, University of Virginia.

William James,
1887. Courtesy
Houghton Library,
Harvard University.

Charles Eliot Norton.

Rutherford B. Hayes around the time of the Howellses' stay at the White House. Courtesy Rutherford B. Hayes Presidential Center.

Howells looking "forward to the fatness of the future." Courtesy Herrick Memorial Library, Alfred University.

Howells and Twain, bad boys caught on camera. Courtesy the Mark Twain Project, The Bancroft Library.

Howells, theoretical socialist and practicing aristocrat. Courtesy Houghton Library, Harvard University.

Mildred Howells. Courtesy Herrick Memorial Library, Alfred University.

Sam Howells. Courtesy Herrick Memorial Library, Alfred University.

Hamlin Garland in the Klondike. Courtesy Miami University.

William Dean Howells, "America's Greatest Living Novelist." Courtesy *Success Magazine,* 1898.

"The Great Novelist Caught in an Unconventional Pose." *Literary Digest,* 1920.

The author at work. Courtesy William White Howells.

Elinor and Mildred, 1895. Courtesy Houghton Library, Harvard University.

Howells and his grandsons, Billy and Johnny, around the time of his eightieth birthday. Courtesy Herrick Memorial Library, Alfred University.

Howells in his Kittery Point study. Courtesy Houghton Library, Harvard University.

brother-in-law's firm, McKim, Mead, and White, outdid all the others in Beaux Arts style. It housed what visitors might expect—animals, machines, tools, even weather stations—and also the unexpected: a map of the United States made entirely of pickles and two models of the Liberty Bell, one fashioned from wheat, oats, and rye, the other from oranges. Canada displayed a 22,000-pound "Monster Cheese," and the Schlitz Brewery had a much-frequented booth. Howells faulted only the brightly colored gondolas and their more brightly dressed boatmen speckling the canal. In Venice, gondoliers dressed as plainly as American cab drivers, and the gondolas were black, with maybe a bit of gold in the decoration; no one had the bad taste to paint them red and green.[86] He did not care that red and green were the national colors of Italy.

The scale of the exposition and the number of exhibits—over a hundred devoted to tobacco alone—overwhelmed them. As the guests first of Hjalmar Boyesen's brother, a successful lawyer, and then of the director of works at the Exhibition grounds, Daniel H. Burnham, they spent nearly two weeks in Chicago. Howells and Mildred dutifully walked the vast fairground and honored their old and new homes by attending a reception at the Massachusetts House and a dinner for Japanese Shinto priests given by the New York Commission.

Howells wrote of his experiences in letters for the *Cosmopolitan,* which eventually became *A Traveler from Altruria.* For him as for his Altrurian, Homos, the fair, with its own systems of sewerage and transportation, its police force and governing bodies, represented a perfect marriage between industry and the arts. Businessmen and entrepreneurs had put themselves in the hands of artists and, as Howells saw it, set aside their struggle for profit to work here for peace. If not Altruria, this was Edward Bellamy's utopian vision of the country's enormous resources, natural and manufactured, enriching the lives of every citizen. At a dinner in March 1893 for the fair's director, Richard Watson Gilder had offered a toast "to the White City. . . . Say not, 'Greece is no more!' . . . Her white-winged soul sinks on the New World's breast."[87] With Charles Norton, Charles Dudley Warner, Frederick Law Olmsted, his brothers-in-law Larkin and William Mead, John La Farge, and Augustus Saint-Gaudens, Howells raised his glass to celebrate the unselfish cooperation of those visionaries who offered the country a new standard for civic behavior. The exposition that opened the following month became a model for the City Beautiful movement and for city planning across America.

In 1907, when Howells wrote his introduction to *Through the Eye of the*

Needle, the sequel to *A Traveler from Altruria,* he would emphasize how far Americans had come since Homos' first visit. He pointed to the endowment of public institutions, improvements in housing and the environment, the downfall of monopolies, the fostering of the arts, and a growing love of literature. In the months after his visit to Chicago, as he reflected on his country's civilization, he focused less on art or literature and more on the creative process, the intangible factors that inspired the White City and promised what humanity *might* achieve. Like his Altrurian, Homos, he looked in from the outside at a culture both familiar and strange.

Not everyone viewed the fair from Howells' and Gilder's perspective. Henry Adams, for one, saw technological advances, notably the dynamo used to propel machinery in the Hall of Engineering, as symbols of an age in which raw power would obliterate the beliefs that had inspired people for centuries. He marveled that a city as young and commercial as Chicago found an ideal in ancient Greece. Like the dynamo of the earlier Paris Exhibition, this one defied understanding but seemed no less an ill omen. In the short term, certainly, history proved Adams right. Five days after the fair opened on May 1, the stock market collapsed and the worst depression in the country's history began. The next year, Frederick Jackson Turner addressed members of the American Historical Society, who chose the setting of the exposition for their annual meeting. Predicting dramatic changes in the organization and psychology of the nation, Turner announced the closing of the American frontier.

Howells needed no reason to travel, but the fair's combination of Old World beauty and New World technology may have prompted his desire for another glimpse of Europe the following summer. Wherever they lived, Elinor and Howells escaped somewhere for the summer months. In 1894, they went for the first time in different directions, she vacationing with her sister Mary in Saratoga, he and Mildred sailing together for Europe. Father and daughter arrived in Paris on June 13, eager to see John, now a student at the École des Beaux Arts.

John took his father and sister to his apartment and introduced them to his neighbor, James McNeill Whistler, the expatriate American artist notorious for his biting wit and propensity to sue. Once, when John Ruskin described his *Black and Gold—The Falling Rocket* (1877) as a pot of paint flung with Cockney impudence in the public's face, Whistler had taken him to court and won a farthing in damages. The next year Howells would worry that Mildred, who posed for Whistler in London and was a friend of his sister-in-law, might be called to testify in another suit, this one involving

Lord and Lady Eden, whose portrait Whistler had refused to deliver and actually defaced. Howells wanted his son to whisk Mildred away from wherever the case might be tried.[88] It was in Whistler's garden that Howells gave Sturgis Bigelow, a friend of Henry James, the advice that inspired James' *The Ambassadors*. "It doesn't so much matter what you do—but live," Howells told him. "I haven't done so—and now I'm old. . . . You have time. . . . Live!"[89] James modeled his protagonist Lambert Strether, the middle-aged editor of a New England literary journal, on Howells. Contemplating Strether, he would write (with or without irony): "I can't make him a novelist—too like W.D.H. . . . But I want him 'intellectual,' I want him *fine,* clever, literary almost."[90] He could not resist the "almost." In James' novel, Strether travels to Paris to rescue a friend's son, Chad Newsome, from Madame de Vionnet, his married lover, who represents the allure of European culture. Strether comes to learn, as Howells himself told James, that living in Europe makes America seem "thin, so thin." For the first time, he "got the notion of something denser on the other side."[91] Though Strether urges the young man to remain with his mistress, in short to live, he himself returns to America and a lonely, diminished existence.

Unlike his fictional counterpart, Howells had little opportunity to taste Parisian life or even spend time with John. The day after their arrival he received the news that his father had suffered a stroke. Two weeks later, he was called home. Kate Wiggin, the author of *Rebecca of Sunnybrook Farm,* volunteered to look after Mildred, and on July 1 Howells began his return journey. He almost cried when he saw his daughter "wave her tiger-lily hand." "You are a brave girl," he told her, "and I respect you quite as much as I love you, and *how* much I love you!"[92] He still managed to remind her to pay their full share of expenses for a planned trip with friends that afternoon. She was approaching her twenty-second birthday, John his twenty-fifth. Howells gave his son a father's caution, the opposite of his advice to Sturgis Bigelow. John should not allow the "poison of Europe" to seep into his soul. "You must look out for that. They live more fully than we do. Life here [in America] is still for the future,—it is a land of Emersons—and I like a little present moment in mine. When I think of the Whistler garden!"[93]

Howells arrived in Jefferson on July 11 to find his father looking surprisingly well and in good spirits, though worried about how Aurelia would cope after his death. In 1883, housebound for much of the year with colic and rheumatism, he had written his brother Joseph that, should Henry outlive him, "his sister will have the whole care of him. . . . I feel I cannot part with him to go [to] an asylum. When that becomes an alternative that I cannot avert, I will meet it as I shall death, leaving it all to the affections of those to whose care he falls."[94] The stroke affected William's speech without any interruption of his joking, which may have included fun about the champagne Howells sent regularly—for medicinal purposes. Unable to move the muscles on his left side, William seemed unlikely to walk or even stand again. He did, however, recover enough to be "on foot," and Howells left for Magnolia, Massachusetts, confident about his progress.[95]

William died on August 28. "You know what a strange summer I had, between Europe and America," Howells wrote Charles Norton. "I got home in time to have a good fortnight with my dear old father, a month before he died; but he died, and so the first chapter of being is closed for me. I can go back with him to my childhood no more. It has aged me as nothing else could have done."[96] Howells found comfort in William's last words, an apparent reference to his wife, Mary: "Mother! Mother! Mother!"[97] As he finished the final section and prepared his father's autobiography for publication, he brooded about what he might have done to make William's death easier or his life more pleasant. He quoted one of William's favorite remarks, that youth was "the time to *believe,* age . . . the time to *trust,*" and he could at least be sure that his father had trusted him.[98] In this spirit, he wrote Joe that he had a curious longing to go back to Jefferson rather than remain in the East, and he quoted loosely Oliver Goldsmith's lines from "The Deserted Village":

And as the hare whom horse and hounds pursue
Pants to the spot from whence at first it flew—[99]

Much as he honored his father's memory, and the past they shared, he made brief visits to Ohio but could not go home again.

PERIPATETIC
1895–1899

> You still giggle? I do, but more and more sadly. Death has come into the world since I saw you, and it is not so merry here below as it used to be.
>
> —W. D. HOWELLS to Edmund Gosse, September 22, 1895

THE EVER-PRESENT SORROW of his daughter's death and the passing of his father, which aged him as if overnight, ended what Howells called "the first chapter." He was, as he said, "of the generation next to death," a realization that both terrified and liberated him.[1] In a poem called "From Generation to Generation" and collected in *Stops of Various Quills* (1895), he wrote:

> We have not to consent or to refuse,
> It is not ours to choose:
> We come because we must,
> We know not by what law, if unjust or if just.
> The doom is on us, as it is on you,
> That nothing can undo.[2]

In the same year that this book of poems appeared, Howells worked at a snail's pace on *The Landlord at Lion's Head,* hampered by illnesses that united against him or followed one another in dispiriting succession. Lameness, indigestion, long spells of dizziness and headaches—each seemed a painful symptom of his state of mind. They climaxed in the spring of 1896 with a gallstone attack that had Elinor sending for the doctor at 2 A.M. The prescribed treatment was a shot of morphine, beef tea, and his era's equivalent of Pepto-Bismol.

Weary from great loss and feeling old as he approached sixty, Howells could still rebound, whereas Elinor, struggling bravely with her own ailments, kept to the house and found any social activity a burden. As she withdrew, Howells increasingly made a companion of Mildred, whom he accompanied to the season's round of teas and dances. Friends now invited Mildred to occasions they knew Elinor would not or could not attend. Howells worried about his daughter's future, and in his characteristic way he let her know about his ambivalence without addressing it directly. He told her about a dream. "You were asked over to stay with Queen Victoria, and I found you having rather a dull time with her. I asked you what you had been invited for, and you said, 'To marry the son of Prince Henry of Battenberg, rather a highly dissipated young person.' I asked, 'Why not come away with me?' and you said if you didn't marry him Lady Arabella Villiers (?) would. I urged that this was not a reason for staying, and you said, 'Well, you would wait and see what he was like.' It was all very circumstantial."[3] And no doubt troubling.

Being the daughter of W. D. Howells had its liabilities and advantages. Mildred lived with the burden of making up for Winny's loss, proving herself reliable and cheerful in a role Howells knew to be unfair and felt powerless to alter. What he had said about the prospect of John's marrying applied even more to his daughter. "'It ain't all 'oney and it ain't all jam,'" he told Annie, anticipating her own son's marriage, "this giving your boy away to a strange girl, it doesn't matter how pretty she is; and the longer you have had the boy the less 'oney and jam there is."[4] He expected his daughter to marry and encouraged her to pursue a career. Whereas Mark Twain recoiled at the idea of a writer's life for his daughters, Howells told Mildred—already the author of poems and dramatic comedies—"literature *is* the life I would have chosen for *you,* and I am more than satisfied."[5] When he got stuck or tangled in words and read his work aloud to Mildred, she offered few specific suggestions (what daughter of a famous father would dare?) but seemed to him to speak for youth. With her encouragement he brought *The Landlord at Lion's Head* to a conclusion.

The closer relationship between father and daughter reflected various family shifts after William Cooper Howells' death. Alternating between regret and relief, Howells would start with anxiety about sending money or prescriptions or writing the Sunday letter to his father, then recall that William had died, that he need "not be harassed about him ever again."[6] As often happens, new responsibilities found a way to replace the old. Because he contributed to his siblings' financial support, Howells assumed—and they accorded him—the respect that goes to family patriarchs. He had long ago adopted a paternal tone with his siblings, and, to echo Vic's lament, there were times when even Joe did not relish being William Dean Howells' brother. Probably relieved to lay some of the burden at his brother's door, Joe had more than he could manage supporting his immediate family. He had one son who worked at the *Sentinel* and another who was a professional harpist and eventually joined a minstrel troupe. Howells assured Joe that his son's choice—if "not exactly" what one might expect from a Howells— should be seen as "an honorable calling, and much better than cheating somebody in trade."[7] When, after his health broke down in the 1890s, Joe lobbied for a consulship in the British West Indies, his brother's intervention helped to make that possible.

Aurelia's dependence unavoidably complicated her relationship with both brothers. She seemed to have the bearing or sense of honor of a previous era, and though she exasperated Howells, he could never be angry with her beyond the writing of one, irritated paragraph. Continuing his Sunday letters home, he addressed them now and until his death to Aurelia, often including colored portraits cut from newspapers for Henry's amusement. He knew that he could be autocratic, and it bothered him that she feared upsetting him. "Don't be downcast because I urge certain things upon you," he told her, "I do it from my concern for you, and if some times my will seems hard, you must take my deed."[8] There were limits to his sympathy—chiefly because he could do little to change the situation—and Aurelia felt his displeasure when she ignored his advice. Once, after she replaced an alcoholic servant with another who brought an illegitimate daughter, he wrote: "Your household is a queer one, but I think that your consciousness of doing a poor fallen creature good must be a great consolation to you. I don't sentimentalize such people, they rather give me the creeps; but life has taught me to judge all sin, as we call it, leniently, and I think sinners who have been *found out* are specially to be treated mercifully."[9] From a distance, Howells' assessments no doubt seemed clear enough, but Aurelia, who suffered as maid and nurse to her own family, found no lasting solutions. She had one small mercy: Henry's behavior improved for a time after his father's death, as it had after his mother's.

Sam and his "slatternly" daughters presented a different set of problems. It irked Howells to give a grown, able-bodied man an allowance, either as simple charity or with the pretense of making Sam self-sufficient. Sam knew no shame, and in Howells' mind neither did his daughters. He was appalled to learn that they had pawned their jewelry and sent one sister to Cleveland "on the *chance* of her getting married there." Sam actually scolded him for not supplying the fare.[10] Howells had "such a creepy feeling" about his brother's family that he hated to connect himself with them or face his own guilt. "I am afraid that I have wounded his soft heart by my neglect," he told Aurelia, who favored Sam. "He is not to blame for them; I do not know that they are to blame themselves for being so vulgar; I don't know that vulgarity is bad; I don't know but I am vulgar myself."[11] He did know that scolding or complaining about an elderly scapegrace accomplished nothing—and that he could not stop. When Sam worked briefly for Joe in 1896, Howells wanted to know his salary so that he could deduct it from the seven dollars a week he had been contributing. Four months later Sam dunned him for ten dollars to apply for a clerkship in the post office. Next he asked Howells to set him up in business selling eyeglasses to African Americans in what appeared to be a "squalid" con.[12] From a brother who preferred begging to working, no news was good news. Unlike Twain, Howells did not find his brother an irresistible subject for comedy.

Annie remained the one sibling he did not worry about, and if her career at times complicated their relationship, it also provided a bond. She had modest success placing articles in magazines such as *McClure's* and *Harper's Bazar*, which printed Henry James' recipes for the speech and manners of American women as well as those for foolproof puddings. Howells helped her find a publisher for her children's books, *On Grandfather's Farm* and *The Farm's Little People* (1897), which he thought perfect pictures of childhood. The children she had in mind when writing these books had by this time grown up. Vevie, the little girl who accompanied Howells and Elinor up the Saint Lawrence River in 1882, and her brother Howells were probably his favorite niece and nephew. He had also grown fond of their father, Achille Fréchette, with whom he corresponded regularly and respected as one of the finest men he knew.

Books are an ungrateful generation.

—W. D. HOWELLS to Charles Eliot Norton, June 14, 1866

Sorrow had changed Howells' understanding of life and its truths, as well as the limits of his internal censor. With novels that combine the panoramic scope of *A Hazard of New Fortunes* and the concentrated character-building of *A Modern Instance* or *The Rise of Silas Lapham,* he presented a more complex portrait of human experience and psychology, almost remaking himself as a writer. "I think I have ended an epoch of my literary life," he had written after finishing *The Coast of Bohemia* (1893). "I doubt if I shall ever write another story in which mating and marrying plays an important part. I am too old for it, and it does not interest me."[13] Had he said that marriage plots no longer interested him in the same way, or that he felt free to treat relationships in terms of once-forbidden topics, he would have been more accurate. In *The Coast of Bohemia* he hints at lesbian love; in *An Open-Eyed Conspiracy* (1897) he examines the lies that couples create about themselves and their spouses. *The Landlord at Lion's Head* (1897) takes a different course. The story of a selfish man driven by appetites, this proved to be one of Howells' most naturalistic and troubling novels.

In previous books as unlike as *Indian Summer* and *A Modern Instance*—in which Marcia stoops to kiss the doorknob Bartley has touched—Howells addressed erotic as well as social aspects of behavior and implied their connections. He went as far as his editor allowed in the couplings and uncouplings of *April Hopes* (1888), and though his contracts with Harper's had the standard clause prohibiting anything of "a scandalous or libellous character," he tested their limits with his portrait of Thomas Jefferson Durgin in *The Landlord at Lion's Head*.[14] Jeff Durgin is a virile provincial who dreams of turning the family farm into a pricey summer resort. The transformation of the inn parallels the changes in Durgin as he goes off to Harvard to join the middle classes he once served. In the process, he betrays his childhood sweetheart, toys with an upper-class woman as sexually careless as himself, and finally marries a vapid beauty whose family has previously snubbed him. Durgin dominates the novel, "as imperative and importunate" as the Great Stone Face, the mountaintop lion's head that casts his family's farm in shadow.[15]

Though seven years separate this novel from *The Son of Royal Langbrith* (1904), both work from the inside out, which is to say that the plot or sequence of events emanates from the depths of character. At the same time, a novel that contains aspects of determinism leaves the formation of character an open mystery, and neither the rugged setting nor the vagaries of class account for Durgin's ruthless hedonism. As with *Silas Lapham,* it seems almost incidental that his personal life reflects the upheavals in American society. Howells' characters have entered a pragmatic world where reality becomes what they need or interpret it to be. "You think the truth itself, merely as truth, has no claim upon our recognition," a character in *Langbrith* says. "What is truth?" another asks. Does it not include every circumstance, "every extenuation in motive and temperament"?[16]

In *The Landlord at Lion's Head,* Howells embeds these questions in the landscape itself. "If you looked at the mountain from the west, the line of the summit was wandering and uncertain, like that of most mountain-tops; but seen from the east, the mass of granite showing above the dense forests of the lower slope had the form of a sleeping lion."[17] This, the first sentence of the novel, suggests the counterworlds of Edith Wharton's *Summer* and the grim profundity of Robert Frost's "Out! Out!" (Howells praised the work of both writers.) The reader enters the landscape through the voice of an omniscient narrator, whose tone gives it the quality, almost the sublimity, of druidical ruins, and then through the eye of a painter named Westover. Westover's ability to see the landscape both personally and pictorially captures Howells' understanding of the artist's double perspective.

The portrait of Westover belongs in a gallery of similar portraits, beginning with his discussion of Italian painters in *Venetian Life* and extending through novels such as *A Foregone Conclusion, Indian Summer, A Hazard of New Fortunes,* and *The Coast of Bohemia.* One of the last pieces he wrote, "Eighty Years and After," brings him full circle, opening with an anecdote about the Venetian painter Titian. Howells' fictional painters—rogues and charlatans like *Hazard's* Angus Beaton as well as steady men like Westover or *Indian Summer's* Inglehart boys, modeled after the Frankenstein brothers he met at Niagara—belong to his running discussion of art from the decades following the Civil War through the First World War. In *A Foregone Conclusion,* the inventor-priest Don Ippolito "doubles" as a painter who copies masterpieces—"saints of either sex, ascensions, assumptions, martyrdoms and what not"—and then colors them "after his own fancy." His counterpart, the artist and consul Ferris, wants to present the essence of Venice through what he omits from his paintings. "Suppose I made a picture of this very bit," he tells Florida Vervain, "ourselves in the foreground looking at the garden over there where the amusing Vandal of an owner had just had his statues painted white: would our friends at home understand it? A whole history must be left unexpressed." The author himself leaves *which* history vague. Does he mean the "wicked past" read in vine-covered villas or the present Venice that people at home know only through mass reproductions and sentimental fiction?[18]

Howells returns to the subject of composition in *The Coast of Bohemia*, in which the painter Ludlow cannot decide on a title for a picture of "a slim, shadowy and uncertain young girl" among hollyhocks.[19] Should he call it "Hollyhocks" or "Girls," since the hollyhocks themselves suggest the figure of a girl? Howells' attention to the integrity in sculpture or painting in, for example, *Annie Kilburn* and *The Son of Royal Langbrith,* reflects his thinking about the form and content of his own fiction. The intensely visual descriptions of landscape that begin novels like *A Modern Instance* or *The Landlord at Lion's Head* recall the intimate yet immense spaces of John Singer Sargent's Italian vistas or Winslow Homer's seascapes with human figures or his scenes of rural New England, and the connection is not likely coincidental. Howells studied the work of artists throughout his life and applied what knowledge he could use for the writing of novels.

Friends and foes alike considered Howells the preeminent writer of his time. In 1895 he had begun contributing a regular column to *Harper's Weekly* called Life and Letters, which appeared until 1898. That year he also published the memoir *My Literary Passions* and the remarkable *Stops of Various Quills,* a collection of poems that, like some of his novels, recalls the work of Thomas Hardy. Hardy pushed his own bleak vision to the extreme in *Jude the Obscure* (1896); after the novel's negative reception he turned away from novel writing and back to poetry. With this collection Howells did the same, albeit temporarily. Despite its somber tone, *Stops of Various Quills* received sympathetic reviews, and so did his other new work. The editors of the *Ladies' Home Journal* felt that in buying the rights to *The Coast of Bohemia* and *My Literary Passions* they had monopolized the services of the country's most important, if not most celebrated, author.[20] Cyrus Curtis paid Howells $10,000 for the *Literary Passions* memoir and claimed to have spent another $50,000 advertising the book. "We are investing in a trade-mark," he argued, that "will all come back in time."[21] "The wolf will have to gnaw through contracts for $30,000," Howells assured Mildred, "before it reaches the door."[22] No matter that the president of the U.S. Senate denounced him for furthering the socialistic theories of Leo Tolstoy, Howells' reputation among his readers—including Tolstoy himself—stood for literary excellence.

As with any career spanning many decades, Howells' describes a long trajectory—a rise to possibly unmatched eminence and a decline to near obscurity in the years before and after his death in 1920. Of course, at any given point he found people touting or disparaging his work, and he faced like any writer the vagaries of the marketplace. By the 1890s competition from British authors made it increasingly difficult to place his stories. Howells considered the "foothold" at *Harper's* a godsend to the extent that it freed him from peddling his wares, though at times he doubted that even Harper's had his interests at heart.[23] In 1891, he had strongly objected when they wanted to pay less under a new contract than he thought he deserved.[24] All three of the books he published in 1896—*A Parting and a Meeting, The Day of Their Wedding,* and *Impressions and Experiences*—sold relatively poorly, received mixed reviews, and indicated to many readers a falling-off. When the *Cincinnati Medical Journal* admitted pirating "A Masterpiece of Diplomacy," two years before, he had wisely accepted compensation in the form of advertising rather than cash.

The publisher George Mifflin warned Elizabeth Stuart Phelps (author of the best-selling *Story of Avis*) about imitating Howells' "rolling stone policy," by which he meant hard bargaining for less saleable writings.

> His books now simply don't sell, and he finds doors once so hospitably open now closed to him. I may say to you in strictest confidence that we recently had the offer of bringing together all his books for a final 'definitive' Edition, which had it been made and sold by the methods we had in mind should have brought him in a permanent and steady income; but we declined the offer . . . and this because owing to his methods, he has written himself out, has so scattered his works that he has killed the goose so to speak that "laid the golden egg!" He . . . saw his interest in "the highest bid" policy, and the results in his case have been quite disastrous to his permanent place in literature and I believe also to his personal happiness.[25]

Mifflin's argument failed to convince Phelps, who had read her Howells, especially *The World of Chance,* which castigates publishers' pandering to the lowest tastes for the highest profits.

> Life has settled into a sort of vague expectation with us, and we wait from steamer to steamer for the children's letters. I am always working, either at the story I have in hand, or at something for the magazines.
>
> —W. D. HOWELLS to Aurelia H. Howells, October 13, 1895

In 1896, after looking for another convenient summer escape, Howells found a twelve-room house in Far Rockaway, Long Island, a year-round community that in summer attracted thousands of beachgoers seeking relief from city heat. "When Elinor and I came to think seriously of the country we found ourselves too old and timid to face its loneliness," he explained to Aurelia.[26] Just forty-five minutes by train from New York, Far Rockaway offered an attractive compromise. The quaint village reminded him of Nahant and its proximity to Boston. Their new, old-fashioned, verandahed house, "shingled to the ground," sat half a mile from the beach resort and the same distance from the bay, where he and Elinor intended to keep a boat. They never fully took possession. Packing and unpacking exhausted Elinor, and instead of the sea air's working its usual magic, she grew worse. Before tasting the first home-grown melon, they fled to the Fabyan House at the base of Mount Washington, in the White Mountains of New Hampshire. Ten days later, they returned to Far Rockaway with Elinor much improved. By October, after a new round of "nervous fever," they had moved into the Hotel Albert in New York City and left the Far Rockaway house to renters.

Concerns about health propelled them the next summer to Europe. They went to Carlsbad, Bohemia, in July 1897, where Howells sought a cure for recurrent attacks of gallstones and colic. In hopes that a dose of mountain heights and sulfur baths would ease his pain and frazzled nerves, he committed himself to rise at six o'clock, "walk to the spring, and drink three glasses of dish-water, 15 minutes apart."[27] Every day he strolled for two to three hours, and twice a week he soaked for fifteen minutes in one of the hot springs. Because rumors already circulated about war with Spain, he and Elinor decided against a Spanish tour in the spring. After Carlsbad, the parents and Mildred met John in Nuremberg, toured with him, then visited Würzburg and went on to Weimar (once the home of Goethe and the cultural center of Germany), Berlin, and Düsseldorf (because of Heine). They were glad to leave behind what Howells called "the military stiffness of Germany."[28] Toward the end of their surprisingly vigorous travel, they celebrated Mildred's twenty-fifth birthday in Holland, visited Paris, and that same September stopped in London so that Howells could spend a few days with Henry James.[29]

The reunion proved bittersweet. Only the other day, Howells had been thirty-one, James twenty-five. When they met at the station, James found his friend slimmer and fitter, the white hair thinner on his large, Napoleonic head but the blue eyes no less intense. Howells worried about a stouter,

balder James, his face stiffened into a Roman mask. Elinor left them to themselves, and in the morning they walked as in times past, enveloped in "the
soft lap, & under the motherly apron, of the dear old muffling fog." James
had grown "needlessly but deeply discouraged" about his work.[30] Felt more
than seen, Howells lumbered by his side, as if James exhaled his insecuri-
ties unheard into the dank air. He told James he needed only a different
strategy for marketing his work and reassured him about sympathetic readers in the United States. On his return home, Howells translated words into
deeds, successfully recommending *The Awkward Age* to *Harper's Weekly,*
which began publication in October 1898. "You were wholly right," James
acknowledged, "as to the fee . . . ($3000) is exactly what would have been
the form of *my* golden dream. . . . What is more to the point is that you
will never know at how psychological a moment you appeared to me the
other day. . . . I felt myself, somehow perishing in my pride or rotting un-
gathered, like an old maid against the wall & on her lonely bench. Well,
I'm *not* an old maid (for the blessed trade) quite yet. And you *were* Don
Quixote."[31]

His immediate problem was not to find a publisher for James but to get
Elinor and himself and their many bags home. Returning to New York on
November 6, he wrote Twain that "neither of us was very well, and we lost
courage and came home; that is *I* lost courage first, as mostly happens in
these cases, and then she did."[32] In her enjoyment of Europe, Elinor had
overextended herself and arrived in New York spent. Europe made them
feel old, if not incompetent, which she could hardly bear, and her collapse
meant that they were forced to postpone housekeeping and take rented
rooms at the Westminster Hotel. After two weeks, they retreated to their
old apartment house, the Dalhousie, overlooking Central Park. John in the
meantime had returned from Paris. He and Isaac Newton Phelps Stokes, a
Harvard classmate and fellow graduate of the École des Beaux Arts, began
their twenty-three-year partnership with a commission for the University
Settlement building.

Howells wrote to Aurelia in December about their difficult homecoming. "You see we have got back to the old place, but as yet we are only eating and sleeping in it. We shall gradually take shape in it, and then, I hope,
forget it."[33] Life, he told her, no longer interested him as it once had, but
here, too, he came to prove himself wrong. At about this time he dreamed
of his father. The two of them attended a circus and watched mechanical
figures perform instead of human beings. They had stopped climbing a stair-
case to wait for William to catch his breath when a real boy came by and

threw something over William's shoulders to keep him warm. Howells told the boy that his father was ninety-three years old. William, asking the boy if he would like to know the year he was born, opened his watch case to show 1807 inscribed on the face. The boy read the date as 1897. "Just one year and a half old!" he said.[34] William had been given another beginning, and Howells too, without fully realizing it. "We have had to think too much of *where* we were," he wrote, "and have not thought enough *what* we were for twenty years past, or ever since we left Cambridge."[35] He would in the coming year take stock of himself and the nation, reaching out to a new generation of writers, lecturing to distant audiences, and protesting America's war with Spain.

From the day he first heard his father's retelling of *Don Quixote*, Howells had loved Spain and Spanish literature. He remembered the sensuous feel of books ordered from the international publisher Baudry, in Paris. Wrapped in saffron-colored paper, they had a look and smell as sensuous as a pretty woman. He had taught himself Spanish to read his beloved Cervantes and gone on to introduce readers of his columns and reviews to the work of modern writers such as Armando Palacio Valdés and Vicente Blasco Ibáñez. He told American writers they shared with Spanish counterparts an affinity for the comic and should read the old picaresque stories that Spaniards invented and told so well.

America's war with Spain struck Howells as wrong on every count, "a wicked, wanton thing."[36] Unlike the majority of his compatriots, including both Mark Twain and Elinor, whom he jokingly called "a Jingo," he saw no justification for "freeing" Cuba from Spanish rule. Twain, on the other hand, sympathized with Cuban freedom fighters, if not with America's annexation of the Philippines.[37] Opponents like Howells argued that this war went against everything the Constitution stood for. To make bad policy worse, the public received untrustworthy information in what Howells saw as a campaign of propaganda, as if hundreds of his own Bartley Hubbards—those who manufacture rather than report the news—had sprung to life.

The "Newspaper War," as it came to be called, used sensational coverage to whip up public sentiment after Spain's suppression of the revolt in 1895. William Randolph Hearst's *New York Journal* and Joseph Pulitzer's *World* carried stories—many of them true—about butchered nuns, mass executions, and children starving in camps where they were to be protected from rebels. Reporters in 1898 speculated that war had claimed a quarter of Cuba's population. Howells knew both Pulitzer and Hearst, the one lacking respect for "American traditions," the other the epitome of bad journalism. When Hearst presided over the Anti-Imperialist League in 1890—the year Howells began serving as vice president—Charles Norton had the satisfaction of resigning in protest.[38] The February 16 sinking of the *Maine,* at anchor in the Havana harbor, drove the press to clamor for intervention. Few Americans doubted the outcome. On April 25, the United States declared war on Spain. Howells, like many of his countrymen, worried about retaliation. He told Aurelia that Far Rockaway might be safe enough, but he could not rent his house when people feared bombardment from the sea. "However it turns out," he predicted, poor men "will pay for it with their blood and money," and fortunes will be made from "the horrors of the battle fields."[39] People as unlike as Theodore Roosevelt and George Santayana found such alarms naively moralistic. For Santayana, war with Spain announced that the country accepted its legitimate "part in the history of the world."[40] Every nation had an obligation to pursue its separate interests.

In addition to protesting the war by signing petitions, Howells later joined organizations dedicated to Filipino independence.[41] In 1901 he would write Aurelia: "I see a great deal of Mark Twain nowadays, and we have high good times denouncing everything. We agree perfectly about the Boer war and the Filipino war, and war generally. Then, we are old fellows, and it is pleasant to find the world so much worse than it was when we were young."[42] He and Twain had much to denounce. They united in contempt for King Leopold, whose personal ownership of the Belgian Congo remained largely unchallenged long after the African American George Washington Williams' scathing report (and his "Open Letter" to Leopold) and fictional exposés like Joseph Conrad's *Heart of Darkness* revealed the brutality of Belgian rule. Revolted as he was by such injustices, Howells cared more about his own country's flagging standards of liberty, law, and plain humanity. Twain put this more directly: "The United States," he wrote, "had gone to hell."[43]

Clinging to a belief in the power of fiction to change the world, Howells wrote an antiwar story called "Editha," in which a young woman blithely sends her fiancé off to fight. This polemic stands apart from the ironic civility of the Altrurian letters. As Editha presents herself to the dead man's grieving mother, the mother tells her she has no right to mourn the man she has killed. The exchange troubles Editha until she persuades herself of the mother's vulgarity relative to her own patriotic nobility. At the time when many readers interpreted Rudyard Kipling's phrase "the white man's burden" as a moral imperative and used words like *honor* and *duty* to justify colonial wars, Howells took a critical stance. The sardonic view in

"Editha" points toward the so-called lost generation's rejection of empty words and bankrupt ideals. The war itself came with a personal "note of warning."[44] Howells worried that his nephew, Joe Jr., would enlist. "If the poor fellow could only calm down to helping his father in the office!"[45] Joe Jr. did leave for Puerto Rico, but, unlike Editha's reluctant young man, came back unharmed.

Spending the summer of 1898 in Maine, Howells observed Spanish prisoners of war interned at the Portsmouth Naval Prison. He considered them, like American soldiers, "the innocents" in a guilty war. One young man, or boy, tried to smile and could not because his cheek had been half chopped off by a machete. In fact, Howells saw nothing in the prisoners but "a sort of cheerful purpose to live up to that military ideal of duty which is so much nobler than the civil ideal of self-interest."[46] He left hoping that duty might someday become a "civil ideal" uniting people across the globe. Fed up with the United States, which had become home to "almost the meanest and the wickedest" people on earth, he dreamed of the socialist New Zealand in the utopian way his grandfather had dreamed of Ohio. "If I were young," he wrote Aurelia, "I should cast my lot with them."[47]

I should have preferred . . . the millennium much simpler, much more independent of modern inventions, modern conveniences, modern facilities. It seemed to me that in an ideal condition (the only condition finally worth having) we should get on without most of these things, which are but sorry patches on the rags of an outworn civilization.

—W. D. HOWELLS on Edward Bellamy's *Looking Backward,* 1898

As Howells approached the turn of the century, he cast his lot not with New Zealanders or Altrurians but with younger writers at home. Hamlin Garland's anecdote about the meeting in the Auburndale resort highlights Howells' importance to the generation after his, and also theirs to him. Just as he gave men like Garland or the younger Harold Frederic confidence in their power, they challenged him personally and professionally. Frederic, who called Howells the "chief of American novelists," believed himself a disciple of the man who portrayed ordinary lives in a contemporary world. He visited Howells in 1888 to express his indebtedness and later asked Garland to pass on "messages of admiration, gratitude, and fealty." It troubled him that Howells did not respond to his *Damnation of Theron Ware* in 1896, even when asked for his opinion. "I always wanted to know how Theron Ware struck him, but he would never tell me."[48] On Garland's suggestion, Stephen Crane had sent Howells a copy of *Maggie: Girl of the Streets* in 1893. Howells kept his silence, and Crane, too, wrote in disappointment: "I must decide then that you think it a wretched thing?"[49] Howells assured him he did not. *Maggie* remained his favorite among Crane's novels; *The Red Badge of Courage* seemed to him less authentic because too removed from lived experience.

Crane's bad health and usually impoverished life, not to mention his seedy roommates and trouble with the New York police, might have kept the two apart. However, these were incidentals to Howells, who liked the handsome young man with the permanently raised eyebrows—and accepted that he could never come to know him. He wrote the widowed Cora Crane in 1900 that "a man of power before he comes to full expression is hard to understand; it is doubtful if he is quite in the secret himself."[50] He recognized Crane's talent and supported and encouraged him. Crane, for his part, thanked God that he could genuinely admire Howells' work instead of "being indelibly indebted to the Chump in Art or even to the Semi-Chump in Art."[51] At the urging of Howells and Garland, and for the sake of accurate reporting, Crane slept in a flophouse and joined a breadline.[52] He inscribed a copy of *The Red Badge of Courage* (1895) "To W. D. Howells, this small belated book as a token of the veneration and gratitude of Stephen Crane for many things he has learned of the common man, and, above all, for a certain re-adjustment of his point of view notoriously concluded some time in 1892."[53] When Crane—who considered his own writer's creed identical with Howells'—interviewed the older man for the *New York Times,* he kept the identities of the speakers vague, as if either might have spoken for the other.[54]

With Crane and other friends or by himself, Howells roamed New York's ethnic neighborhoods. He watched laborers and shopkeepers, bridge workers and policemen at their tasks. In the same years, the president of the Police Commission, Theodore Roosevelt, made his rounds, led by the social activist Jacob Riis. By 1890, New York was home to over 300,000 immigrants from Ireland, 54,000 from Italy, and 380,000 from Germany. In a cellar on the East Side, Howells glimpsed a bed with sheets and blankets piled on it. From "out of this hole, as if she had been a rat, scared from it by the light, a young girl came, rubbing her eyes and vaguely smiling" before vanishing again upstairs.[55] A "week's sojourn" in the Bowery, he writes in *Impressions and Experiences,* "with no more hope of a better lot than they could have, would make anarchists of the best people in the city."[56] What he saw came close to embittering him, as his almost Brechtian "Heredity" suggests:

What swollen paunch you are doomed to bear
Your gluttonous grandsire used to wear;
That tongue, at once so light and dull,
Wagged in your grandam's empty skull;
That leering of the sensual eye
Your father, when he came to die,
Left yours alone; and that cheap flirt,
Your mother, gave you from the dirt
The simper which she used upon
So many men ere he was won.

In the same year that Howells published *Stops of Various Quills*—the book he thought came closest to expressing his "poetic consciousness"—Crane published *The Black Riders,* a volume of experimental poetry that probes the outer world of social responsibility and an inner world of somber revelation.[57]

Writers like Crane, Abraham Cahan, and Paul Laurence Dunbar not only took as gospel the arguments Howells made for "realism"; they legitimized new directions for his fiction in the nineties. Nothing shows the success of his efforts better than their radically differing applications of his principles. Emerson called for an "American" poet, Howells for men and women who wrote from their own hard-won truths. Crane's imaginative reconstruction of history and the hallucinatory visions of his poems, Cahan's mix of Russian and Talmudic fables with Marxist theory, and Dunbar's use of dialect were all for Howells natural extensions of his own realism. Since changing realities demanded corresponding fictions, he welcomed what ambitious young writers had to say. After reading a short story by Cahan, he left him a note at a local café: "I would like to have the pleasure of being acquainted with you." Cahan remembered that Howells lived in a comfortable, old-fashioned house next to Stuyvesant Park. On the way, he could feel his heart beating. "I am going to Howells!" he echoed Garland. "I felt both young and old, humble and proud—an American sense of having arrived."[58]

Cahan's experience recalls that of Howells as a "bashful boy from Ohio" overawed by the Fields' house—and its beautiful mistress.[59] "You Marxists always talk about economic interests as the foundation of all that is done in the world," Howells told Cahan. "I'll tell you something—a man and his wife have the same economic interests. For that reason, Mrs. Howells has a great interest in all that I write. And if something doesn't please her, she rips it to shreds mercilessly."[60] Howells, who practiced his German by reading Yiddish newspapers (Cahan edited the *Arbeiter Zeitung* for the United Hebrew Trades), helped to find Cahan a publisher and a title for *Yekl: A Story of the New York Ghetto,* originally called "Yankel the Yankee." After Howells reviewed the novel, along with Crane's *George's Mother,* Cahan woke to find reporters at his door. Several years later (the Howellses had since moved to Fifty-ninth Street), Cahan looked back affectionately on his visit to Stuyvesant Square.

> In his [Howells'] house everything looked aristocratic in the American manner. The scent of spiritual nobility was in the air. Mrs. Howells had a tactful and hospitable formality. When her hands were not busy, she held them folded across her chest as if she were cold.
>
> At the table she said (among other things) that in Berlin she had noticed a thin American woman wearing a little shawl. "She sat stiffly and hugged herself under her shawl," Mrs. Howells mimicked the motions, "and immediately I knew she was from Boston. Only a Bostonian could sit like that with a shawl. It turned out that I was right."
>
> Saying this Mrs. Howells looked exactly like the Bostonian lady she was describing.[61]

Although Dunbar knew Howells first through a friend's recital of his poems, the two met when the older man reviewed *Majors and Minors* in *Harper's Weekly* (June 27, 1896), then recommended Dunbar to James Pond and invited him to Far Rockaway. Dunbar remembered opening the gate and seeing a small man with white hair running toward him, grabbing his hands, and crying: "This is Paul Dunbar!" As he left, Howells insisted on lending him his own overcoat to wear back to the city. If it disturbed him that Dunbar saw his gesture as unusual, nevertheless both men were glad to have met. "I have been entirely overwhelmed by the attention directed to me by Mr. Howell's article," Dunbar told a friend. "Imagine, if you please, an obscure young man plodding on without discipline in his own slow way, suddenly brought to the notice of so many people. Imagine a slender mail of perhaps two or four letters a day suddenly inflated to sixty five. . . . Then imagine an exceedingly nervous temperament subjected to this & decide for yourself as to the result."[62]

Howells wrote an introduction to Dunbar's *Lyrics of the Lowly,* prophesying the power of art to end racial hostility and prejudice.[63] The poems gave, as W. E. B. Du Bois quoted Howells as saying, "the final proofs that God had made one blood of all nations of men. I thought his [Dunbar's] merits positive and not comparative; and I held that if his black poems had been written by a white man, I should not have found them less admirable. I accepted them as an evidence of the essential unity of the human race, which does not think or feel black in one and white in another, but humanly all."[64] However, in repeating Howells' words, Du Bois omits a key statement. "There is a precious difference of temperament between the races which it would be a great pity ever to lose," Howells wrote, "and . . . this is best preserved and most charmingly suggested by Mr. Dunbar in those pieces of his where he studies the moods and traits of his race in their own accents of English."[65] Dunbar came to rue this endorsement.[66] Following Howells' lead, other editors judged the dialect poems—just a fraction of his work—the most "authentic."[67] Dunbar found it difficult to find a home for his other poems, a consequence that Howells could not have predicted and did his best to avoid.

Charles Chesnutt and William Braithwaite had better luck with Howells' sponsorship. Braithwaite enjoyed a sympathetic audience for his volume of poetry, *The House of the Falling Leaves* (1908), and Chesnutt became the first African American author to earn a living from his writing. Howells corresponded with him about possible projects for Harper's. Of Chesnutt's characters, he wrote:

> They are like us because they are of one blood by more than a half, or three quarters, or nine tenths. It is not, in such cases, their negro blood that characterizes them; but it is their negro blood that excludes them. . . . With Mr. Booker Washington the first American orator of our time, fresh upon the time of Frederick Douglass; with Mr. Dunbar among the truest of our poets; with Mr. Tanner, a black American, among the only three Americans from whom the French government ever bought a picture, Mr. Chesnutt may well be willing to own his color.[68]

Braithwaite returned the compliments in reviews, while Chesnutt felt slighted by Howells' muted criticism of *The Marrow of Tradition,* an exposé of white racism. In an otherwise positive notice, Howells regretted the book's bitter tone but recognized its source in a long history of prejudice and violence. Anyone who reads Chesnutt's book, he says, would see "a portent of the sort of negro equality against which no series of hangings and burnings will finally avail."[69] "Good Lord!" he told a friend, "How such a negro must hate us."[70] Miffed or not, Chesnutt would continue to invoke Howells' name for purposes of self-advertising. With few available venues like the Colored Co-operative Publishing Company available, African American writers had a difficult time reaching a broad audience. Booker T. Washington became a best-selling author only after Doubleday, Page & Company republished his autobiography *Outlook* with the dramatic title *Up from Slavery.*

Younger writers did not necessarily return Howells' courtesy. Frank Norris he respected and reviewed without meeting frequently. Calling *The Octopus* and *McTeague,* which he offered to read in manuscript, great books, Howells entertained Norris in dinner jacket and lounging slippers on the day they discussed *McTeague.* Norris, who hailed Howells as the father of a new generation of literature, later faulted him for wanting to ignore the sensational aspects of life. Since Howells wrote a favorable review of *McTeague*—a naturalistic tale of lust, greed, madness, and murder—Norris' criticism seems as cranky as it is ungenerous. Still, finding life in New York uncongenial, Norris asked Howells for advice about returning to San Francisco. Howells told him that a literary man could write wherever he felt comfortable. Unlike the younger Howells, who had ignored James Lowell's advice about living in the West, Norris went home.[71]

Theodore Dreiser, a fellow Midwesterner, newspaperman, and fan of Howells' *Their Wedding Journey,* sought him out, only to dismiss him as the wrong stuff. In 1898, Dreiser published "How He Climbed Fame's Ladder," an interview with Howells that in all likelihood never took place. The substance of his and Howells' imaginary conversation comes from other interviews and from *My Literary Passions,* published three years earlier. The Howells who emerges from Dreiser's portrait has a bit of *An American Tragedy*'s Clyde Griffiths in him; a man driven by the social and material rewards of literature. "The man of business" certainly existed, but Dreiser— intent on fame and success—remakes Howells in his own image. If, on the other hand, he considered the interview a flattering calling card, it failed. Howells either did not see or chose to ignore it. Dreiser, as brash as he could be abject, followed this interview with another, titled "The Real Howells." Damning with praise, it begins by describing this "nobleman of literature" as greater than his work and greater than his reputation, which "far outweighs his achievements."[72] Howells ignored this interview, too, and less understandably remained silent about both *Sister Carrie* (1900), the great novel to follow, and its suppression. In 1902, he sent on to Aurelia a curious letter from Dreiser, praising his memorial essay on Longfellow. "If the common ground is to be credited with the flowering out of such minds as yours," Dreiser wrote, near suicide after *Sister Carrie* sold only five hundred copies, "I shall not be disturbed to return to the dust. There is enough in the thought to explain the wonder of the night, the sparkle of the waters—the thrill of tender feeling that runs abroad in the odours and murmers and sighs. Buried Howells and Hardys and Tolstoys shall explain it for me."[73] Howells never hinted that he knew, let alone had been interviewed by, Dreiser, who wished to honor him while he was "still above ground." He found Dreiser's letter laughable yet "very appealing, somehow, and genuine."[74] Dreiser would become increasingly critical of Howells, and to some extent he had a legitimate grievance. On the grounds that he had not read *The "Genius,"* Howells refused (along with Ellen Glasgow and Hamlin Garland) to add his signature to those of his peers who protested its suppression. He still considered Dreiser's story of a grieving widower, "The Lost Phoebe," to be unmatched and included it near the end of his life in *The Great Modern American Short Stories* (1920).[75]

To Ellen Glasgow as to Dreiser, Howells belonged to a previous era of critics and novelists. Glasgow remembered her first visit to the Authors Club in 1898, where she met the men "who would soon become, by self-election, the Forty Immortals of the American Academy. They were important, and they knew it, but they were also as affable as royalty; and no one who valued manners could help liking them. Life had been easy for them, and literature had been easier. They had created both the literature of America and the literary renown that embalmed it. They constituted the only critical judgment as well as the only material for criticism. . . . They were elderly, but they were not yet mature."[76] So wrote the South's staunchest realist, a woman who made the protagonist of her first novel, *The Descendant* (1897), a bastard—but who herself "valued manners," courted for favorable reviews the critics she mocked, and owed her extremely comfortable life to her brother's charity. Glasgow blamed men like Howells for the mediocrity of American literature, which focused, in Howells' own ironic phrase, on the "smiling aspects of life." Although she did not grasp the irony, in March 1898 she and Howells would find themselves allied when the Authors Club debated a resolution in support of Émile Zola. "I was astonished at the opposition," Howells wrote Garland after the motion was tabled, "for I feel strongly that Zola's trial was an outrage and his punishment an infamy. . . . But what is the use?"[77]

It is labor, always labor, novel-writing.

—W. D. HOWELLS, interview, 1886

Howells the lecturer remained a self-conscious understudy to the self-confident writer. Despite the modest success of his Harvard and Lowell Institute lectures, and the long practice he had from hundreds of public speaking assignments, lecturing came hard. Knowing his work, people expected more from him than he could easily give, and his every slip or mishap made news in the next day's paper. There had been, in 1895, the episode of his clubbing a bat that flew into the hall during a reading. Of course, Howells told his sister, an Irishman had delivered the actual blow while he stood by, perplexed at the commotion. Gossip about celebrities sold papers, and the image of the pacifist author turned slayer proved too tempting. Even Elinor found herself quoted. One scrap of gossip led to another. According to *Munsey's Magazine,* which obviously missed her joke, she had no idea that her husband had exposed her to the world as Mrs. March. "An acquaintance asked her the other day what she thought of the series of farces in which she has been drawn as the inconsequent married woman. 'I haven't read them,' Mrs. Howells said carelessly. 'I never have time to read what Mr. Howells writes.'"[78] There is no record of her opinion about a proposed lecture tour, but Howells, remembering Mark Twain's lucrative speaking tour with Cable, thought he might test the waters.

He first consulted James Burton Pond, the lecturers' impresario, in 1896. Pond was the type of man Howells would normally have found vulgar, in the sense that he held nothing sacred that drew a crowd. He did have the virtues of having grown up poor, in Wisconsin, and having fought with John Brown in Kansas. After an apprenticeship in a print shop, Pond joined another abolitionist, James Redpath, whose firm became synonymous with the lyceum system that provided entertainment and education to people nationwide. Capitalizing on base curiosity and anti-Mormon sentiment, Pond began his impresario's career by arranging a speaking tour for Ann Eliza Young, Brigham Young's estranged wife and the author of a memoir titled *Wife Number Nineteen.* Young tantalized her audiences with stories about Mormon polygamy. In her first season, she earned Pond over twenty thousand dollars. Pond went on to open his own agency in New York City, from which he arranged tours for people as diverse as Twain and Cable ("the twins of genius"), the poet James Whitcomb Riley, the soon-to-be-notorious

Henry Ward Beecher ("the other man" in the notorious Tilton divorce), and Arthur Conan Doyle, the creator of Sherlock Holmes.[79]

Now Pond, who had little admiration for Howells' books, approached Howells at the urging of Mark Twain. Pond claimed, with his usual understatement, to have used his "persuasive eloquence on him more than on any other American author."[80] Tempted, though not eager to lecture unless he could match his income from writing, Howells wondered what he might reasonably demand. He proposed that Pond arrange twenty-five to thirty talks at $150, each within five hours' distance from New York City.[81] For $200 each he would go as far west as Pittsburgh. To put his terms in perspective, Anna Dickinson, the now-forgotten abolitionist writer, received $400 performing (her critics said histrionically) to packed audiences in the 1870s, and Twain paid the flamboyant Cable, who charmed audiences by singing Louisiana folk songs, $450 a week plus expenses.[82]

Howells doubted his own talents and his stamina. Twain had traveled ten thousand miles, visiting seventy cities in four months, and hankering "for those fleshpots whose savor lingered on his palate and filled his nostrils after his withdrawal from the platform."[83] A consummate showman, Twain played cat-and-mouse with his audiences. He would halt in mid-sentence and rummage in his pockets for a handkerchief to wipe his brow, then seem to lose his train of thought, begin again, stumble, hesitate, recover his last thought, hitch himself up, and look intently at the audience as he deadpanned his punch line. Sometimes audiences were slow to get the joke until a few uncertain claps spurred the applause to deafening levels. What appeared to be spontaneous Twain had scripted, memorized, and practiced hundreds of times, down to the last gesture. "It was his custom," Howells explained in *My Mark Twain,* "always to think out his speeches, mentally wording them, and then memorizing them by a peculiar system of mnemonics which he had invented."[84] In the manner of ancient rhetoricians' "artificial memory," he set an imaginary dinner table and used spoons, salt cellars, and butter plates as prompts for individual passages he wanted to recall. Twain knew that the staged asides and hesitancies, the embarrassments and misplaced emphases, endeared him to his listeners.[85] Not even the greatest actor, he liked to say, could dazzle an audience reading from a script. That was, however, exactly what his less confident friend intended to do.

Howells began his trial performances in 1898, lecturing about ideal commonwealths and reading passages from his novels. In a letter from Jefferson in March, he told Elinor: "I have had a *famous* time, all round." At Oswego,

New York, it delighted him to find that the State Normal School used *A Traveler from Altruria* as a textbook.[86] (When the writer and reformer Upton Sinclair later asked to use sections of the Altrurian letters for "an anthology of dangerous thinking," Howells responded, "I like to be remembered as a dangerous thinker.")[87] The successful end of the mini-tour, at the Williamsport Seminary in Pennsylvania, made him think that for the right amount he might be willing to join the lecture circuit after all.

He nevertheless played hard to get. When Pond urged a longer tour, he hesitated, already wary of the physical cost of performance and travel. The continued negotiations irritated both men. Pond began to hint about Howells' greed, and Howells took offense. "I did not like your asking me if I cared only to get money out of lecturing, and implying that I did not care to give my readers the pleasure or profit of hearing me. I *do* want to get the money, all of it that I can, but I like to keep my affairs and my enjoyments separate."[88] In the end, he agreed to twenty-five lectures that would take him to seven states.[89] His contract, requiring up to three lectures a week, freed Howells from any obligation to reimburse Pond in case of illness.[90] Despite second thoughts about the wisdom of the project and Pond's reliability, he worked on his lectures over the summer at Kittery Point, Maine. He looked to Twain for reassurance, adding that Garland thought his lecture "The Man of Letters as a Man of Business" the best he had heard. Then again, Garland had not heard Twain at the podium.[91] Twain praised Pond for corralling Howells, "a most sinful man" whom he had always known "God would send to the platform if he didn't behave."[92]

Howells visited Jefferson before his round of lectures. Joe went with him to Ypsilanti, the first stop on his tour, by way of Detroit. The brothers intended the journey across Lake Michigan to be a vacation as well as a time for catching up. As usual, Howells recorded his impressions for Elinor: the price of dinner in the train station (seventy-five cents), the view of Cleveland at night ("a thunderstorm for smoky blackness, shot with electric lights"), the itinerary of the conductor, the name of the saloon where he filled his flask before boarding the boat ("The Last Chance"), and the people he met. Hearing the "r" in Westerners' speech made him feel at home in a way he had not anticipated. Everywhere he listened to debates about President McKinley's chances of reelection. Everywhere, too, he met people he had not seen in years, including friends from Columbus or someone who knew So-and-so, like the man whose wife came from Brattleboro and remembered (or had heard about) the Meads. The charm of these small-world coincidences would pale with each mile, as would his estimate of the West's being "up-to-date," but for now Howells enjoyed his whitefish in the morning, his Scotch at night, and the company of his older brother.[93]

His opening performance in Ypsilanti on October 19 went well despite first-night jitters and difficulty making himself heard. As Twain predicted, Howells did many things wrong, yet with the one exception, when he spoke to "450 refrigerators," he pleased his audiences.[94] It did not seem to matter that he stumbled or read directly from a manuscript, sometimes for two hours, or stood behind a podium. In the words of one surprised reporter, "the small-sized, deep-chested man, whose splendid head [and more splendid white moustaches] peeped over the reading desk . . . somehow managed early to put himself on excellent terms with his audience! . . . Is it any wonder men love Howells?"[95]

Shepherded by a young colleague of Pond's named Chizzola, Howells traveled by train from Ypsilanti to Evanston, Chicago, Grinnell, Des Moines, Lincoln, Marion, Topeka, Emporia, Ottumwa, Detroit, Columbus, Cincinnati, and finally Hamilton. The pace proved both exhilarating and grueling. He watched the changing landscape and noted, for example, the shorn wheatfields of Illinois, speckled with pigs and cattle, giving way to oak woodlands as he crossed the Iowa River. Hundreds paid a dollar, sometimes two in bigger cities, to hear him speak of Tolstoy as the modern master or of "novel-writing and novel-reading." People from outlying areas traveled miles to such lectures, which served of course as diversion but also as schooling or a link with broader culture. They went eager to meet the man billed as "The Greatest Living Author in America"—indeed, as one newspaper announced, the man who wrote *Daisy Miller*. Most startling about Howells' effect on the communities he visited was the discussion he generated during and after his stay. Reporters summarized or wrote rebuttals to his arguments for literary realism. They made lists of great novelists and novels and tried to evaluate Howells' own contributions. He set the public thinking about questions that today are largely banished to college literature classes.

No less than Twain, Howells learned to savor the adulation. From Chicago, where old friends welcomed him, he wrote Elinor that she missed seeing her "poor old little weary Pokey being lionized. The ladies fairly billowed upon me, wave after wave of them."[96] He entered into the spirit of things, as when he gave a professor of palmistry permission to photograph his hand. Hamlin Garland brought his fiancée to meet his mentor and later noted that Howells found her pleasing. In a city known for the stench of its stockyards, Howells donned formal attire to address three hundred members of the Twentieth Century Club. They came to the house of Harlow Higinbotham, president of the Columbian Exposition, where Howells had no difficulty making his every syllable heard in a private theater decorated with palms and roses. He met a different set at Jane Addams' Hull House, located among tenement buildings overflowing with immigrants from Czechoslovakia, Italy, Ireland, Poland, and Russia. Inspired by Tolstoy's "futile efforts to relieve the unspeakable distress and want in the Moscow winter of 1881," she had taken to heart "his inevitable conviction that only he who literally shares his own shelter and food with the needy, can claim to have served them."[97] Addams asked Howells to write a morally uplifting play to open at Hull House's big new auditorium. He professed to like the idea but never wrote the play.

As his Chicago itinerary suggests, Howells spoke to a cross section of Americans, not all of whom approved his performance or his politics. One Chicago cartoon depicted him as Howells might, at one time, have depicted James Russell Lowell: patting the head of a youngster who holds a book entitled "Us Folks Out West: A Book Written by a Mere Boy." "Keep on Writing, My Son," Howells reassures him. "Even If They Do Make Fun of You in the East."[98] Now he was the poor boy turned general and statesman revealing himself to the people.

Howells' notoriety from the Haymarket affair and his recent statements about America's role in the Philippines probably swelled attendance for his Chicago lectures. Before leaving the city, he made a point of calling on John Altgeld, the governor whose career had ended with his pardon of the anarchists and criticism of the Illinois courts. The press either overlooked or did not know about the meeting, perhaps more interested in recent events. At the beginning of his tour Howells volunteered his opinions about imperialism, attacking the British role in Africa and his government's in the Pacific, but by the end he did his best to avoid politics.

Following Chicago, he went to Grinnell—his "first glimpse of the real West"—then to Drake University in Iowa, and Nebraska and Kansas.[99] "Nebraska and Kansas are poor, *poor*," he wrote Elinor from Marion. If students paid ten cents for a show they took that sum "out of their stomachs or off their backs."[100] It disturbed him that in a town where there seemed hardly to be a dollar, six women scoured the streets trying to peddle tickets to his lecture. Howells did not want to take their money, except to meet expenses. He had entered Hamlin Garland's fictional country, a land where two hundred fifty cattle could drown in a hail- and rainstorm that lasted twenty minutes, where no one would give a chaw of tobacco for an acre of land. Though he found receptive audiences in Emporia and liked Topeka, the West began to seem too big, too hard, and too demanding. He wrote Pond not to book him anywhere else.

He could not sleep without drugs or bear the strain of being constantly with people, no matter how considerate. In each town, he held court for several hours, receiving visitors and giving interviews. The sightseeing, receptions before and after his performance—and the luncheons and dinners where the guest of honor sang for his supper—left him feeling exhausted, nervous, and dyspeptic. "I dont want to disappoint people. . . . It is the *kindness* . . . that kills. I *cannot* refuse people's hospitality, and it is simply disastrous."[101] He missed his family and they missed him. Mildred, who handled his correspondence, sent him a poem called "Lines written by a Young Lady to her Father, a Celebrity, on the Occasion of his Absence in the West":

> Like the drops within the Ocean
> Like the Sands upon the Shore
> Postmen in Perpetual motion
> Bring me letters by the score.
>
> Letters bring from every nation
> Letters framed to sap the mind
> Till I wish in desperation
> You were back, or I were blind.[102]

With the tour nearing its end, Howells became more irritable and less trusting. He asked Pond for a weekly reckoning of expenses and refused to have Chizzola's salary charged against the account. Chizzola was Pond's employee, and he would no sooner pay him than pay Pond himself. His irritation had something to do with his scheduled return to Ohio, which still brought anxieties, though he looked forward to seeing Elinor's cousin Laura and her husband, John Grant Mitchell, in Columbus.

The Mitchells met him at the station and took him to their home on East Broad Street, where two hundred guests had the pleasure of shaking his hand. So many years had passed since he first met Elinor and shared those winter walks and the dances at the old Starling Medical College. He spent only two days playing the city's native son before moving on to Cincinnati to see John Piatt—and help raise money for the Presbyterian Hospital. Because he stayed over in Cincinnati from a Wednesday to a Sunday, Howells had time to attend a reception hosted by Elinor's old friend and teacher, Clara Nourse, and to have his head examined by a doctor of phrenology. The doctor pronounced him, among other things, home-loving, gentle, patient, modest, and diligent. Apart from a cure for sore memories, he needed nothing but a little rest before Hamilton, the last stop on his tour.

He had not seen his "Boy's Town" in over forty years. Stepping off the train on Sunday morning, he almost immediately spied an old playfellow, George T. Earhart, now sporting a heavy moustache and a cigar. Earhart offered him a seat in his buggy and deposited him at the corner of Front Street and Buckeye, home to his uncle Henry. The first dentist in Hamilton to use chloroform, Henry Howells still practiced. People described him as "a small man, with long white hair and courtly, old-school manners"— not unlike his famous nephew.[103] That afternoon Earhart took Howells on a tour of Hamilton from Prospect Hill across the Black Street Bridge and north to the Butler County Fairgrounds, where they found one of their favorite childhood swimming holes, then back near the center of town to the remodeled brick building on the northeast corner of Third and Court Streets that had once been home to William Cooper Howells' *Intelligencer.* On the second floor, accessible only by outside steps from Third Street, Howells had learned compositing. Though his family's first house on Second and Dayton no longer existed, and a bank had replaced their last house on Falconer, Hamilton felt familiar. He paused before the City Building on South Water Street, looking in vain for his old school, and remembered with photographic precision the phantoms of Smith's pork house and Jones' wagon factory.

As he entered the high school auditorium to make his informal address, three hundred students rose to greet him. They shouted as he approached the podium and gave the school's "Chautauqua salute." Then a courteous silence fell. "Young ladies and gentlemen," Howells began,

> I suppose you have little idea how much I am afraid of you. The most
> incredible thing to me as I again visit Hamilton is the sight now before
> me. I went to school in the old South district, the teacher of which
> was old Mr. Ferris and all the boys were in great terror of him because
> he whipped so severely—however, we liked him very much. Very little
> of Hamilton that I knew now remains. Familiar faces are gone. Houses
> in which I lived are now passed away. But I think that if I were a boy
> or a girl I would be quite glad to live in Hamilton. The woods in which
> I rambled are gone. But then I must not ramble on. I do not know when
> I will see you again but do not wait for that, but come and see me. Good-
> bye, good-bye.[104]

That afternoon every citizen of Hamilton was invited to a reception for him at the home of the Cullens on Dayton Street. People came from surrounding towns—Franklin, Trenton, Oxford, Middleton, and College Hill—and stood in line to meet the town's famous author. At 7:30, he presented his lecture, a combination of his talk on the writing and reading of novels interspersed with personal recollections. He called it "My Life since I Left Hamilton." The next day he boarded a train for New York City, where he greeted his wife on Thanksgiving eve, ate the "young" turkey he had particularly requested, and slept for almost twenty-four hours. Quite apart from his head feeling sprained, his stomach discombobulated, and his heart taxed, he had also made only half as much money as Pond promised.

Twenty-one years after Howells' lecture tour, Booth Tarkington remembered his coming "to a midland city where a nervous young writer, just beginning to publish, had been appointed his local courier or guide, to take him to the dinner given for him and to see the church where he was to speak." Howells talked to him in "a kind, sad voice, a little pityingly amused" about the injury done by critics. "Ah," he said, "you'll find they can still hurt you long after their power to please you is gone!" Tarkington could not imagine his guest vulnerable. Everyone he knew, especially the best and the most intelligent people, he writes, read Howells, so much so that one of Tarkington's friends found it incredible that she had never met him. All her life, whenever anything interested her a great deal, she had paused to ask: "What would Mr. Howells think of that? . . . It is he who is responsible for whatever I have in the way of a mind."[105]

Whether or not people liked what Mr. Howells thought, many had begun to think their lives "the warp and woof of all that he has wrought."[106] As one critic wrote in 1899, "We breathe Howells—most of us. He is part of our literary heritage."[107] Howells himself was perhaps most deeply touched by the simple courtesy of Rudyard Kipling, who saw his difficulties with a new pair of overshoes and got down on one knee to put them on for him: "He said he always did it for his father."[108] In retrospect, Howells sometimes thought his years between fifty and sixty the best. Having worked hard and mastered his trade, he enjoyed relative prosperity; life had its quieter pleasures, with death less fearsome than before.[109] He could face the new century with equanimity but not, he told Pond, a second lecture tour.

15

KITTERY POINT
1900–1905

I should not mind being old, so much, if I always had the young, sure grip of myself. What I hate is this dreamy fumbling about my own identity, in which I detect myself at odd times. It seems sometimes as if it were somebody else, and I sometimes wish it were. But it will have to go on, and I must get what help I can out of the fact that it always *has* gone on.

—W. D. HOWELLS to Thomas Bailey Aldrich, July 3, 1902

THROUGHOUT HIS LIFE and increasingly with age, Howells reflected on the times he had lived through, on his own aging, and on things past and future, whether the vanished years of childhood or what he called, echoing Shakespeare, "the undiscovered country," the afterlife he hoped for and feared. If time, at least human time, involves perception more than the ticking of the clock or the counting of years, Howells listened and counted more than most. "How is it that great pieces of luck fall to us?" he once wrote. "The clock strikes twelve as it strikes two, and with no more premonition."[1] For Howells, clock time, and, to use his own word, "existential" time mixed with the workings of memory and his notions of personal identity, as a novel like *Indian Summer* or an autobiography like *Years of My Youth* can illustrate. He broods about the bond between memory and place as intensely as his younger contemporaries, Marcel Proust and Virginia Woolf.

Few people would associate Howells, the accepted model of American realism, with a British modernist like Virginia Woolf. It was Woolf who made the whimsical declaration that human nature changed in 1910. By the opening of the new century Howells, a pioneer himself, already felt left behind, and Woolf had scarcely begun. But however out of step historically or different they might have been as novelists, both Howells and Woolf dwelled on the paradoxical nature of time, its intensely subjective flashes, which Woolf called "moments of being," and its other passages, too banal to remember. Perhaps nothing illustrates their recapturing of time so much as houses, those images of self and memory that for both writers presented an almost human face.

Howells imagined houses both as bulwarks against time and as empty, disappointing memorials. He could not bear to drive by the house on Concord Avenue with its sad associations; neither could he stop himself from visiting the old neighborhood. The Quaker meeting house in Stuyvesant Square brought back memories of William, who had urged him to attend it, and Saint George's Church evoked Winny—as nearly everything did—because she had loved to glimpse its towers through the trees. For reasons hard to pin down, he had grown to resent the Belmont house. The family and friends, like their landlords, the Fairchilds, had watched it take shape week by week, and every nook and cranny spoke of Elinor, who first sketched it with her brother Will. As Redtop grew, the house on Concord Avenue—an "expense," a "hindrance"—lost its hold. Howells never bought Redtop outright, partly because he could not sell the house on Concord Avenue, partly because it no longer suited. Something unspecified but as palpable as Silas Lapham's empty show house or the ghost in "His Apparition" (1903) drove them out.

The Howellses' unending quest for the perfect house led them in the spring of 1900 to Cape Ann, near Gloucester, Massachusetts. A place they found in Annisquam delighted them so much they took an option for a longer lease. It seemed ideal for seven or eight quiet months of the year and allowed a few months for apartment living in New York. "I can hardly make you understand what it is like," Howells wrote to Aurelia. "But if you will imagine a house on the corner of a 25 acre hill of red pines, looking out over a pretty village to the sea, which puts into a wooded cove at its feet, that is where we live." The house had "everything that a reasonable person could ask," including fruit and linden trees planted by its German-born previous owner. It offered a combination of accessibility to Boston and New York (by boat), and a comforting distance. Above all, it suited the author. "I have a big room to work in, and I expect to do a lot of writing."[2]

"I can understand your hunger for New England, in these later years," he wrote to Henry James. The rugged, bleak charms of Cape Ann "were irresistible," the vistas magnificent, the ways of the local people deeply satisfying.[3] Rural New England struck him as both another country and another world. In Annisquam the Howellses kept apart from the other summer residents, "rather an arid lot"; and for Mildred, separated from friends and the likelihood of meeting eligible young men, they thought the isolation unfair.[4] In the fall they were back in New York, the next summer in York Harbor, Maine. Annisquam joined Redtop on their roster of once irresistible, now discarded places. Howells knew that his restless search, whether for a permanent house or a summer escape, had its comic side. In a piece included in *Literature and Life,* he told about a family—unmistakably his own—"of the sort whose combined ideal for their summer outing was summed-up in the simple desire for society and solitude, mountain-air and sea-bathing." A part of that large, pitiable class of people with the means to flee the city but uncertain about where to go, they spend an entire summer crisscrossing the Northeast, victims of "chance" as much as "choice." In mock pity, he explains that the plight of such people will not be evident to the lucky souls insolvent enough to spend their summers at home.[5]

Whether or not people have the means to escape, no one has the means to ward off illness or bad luck or disappointment, and Howells' wry assessment of his and Elinor's peregrinations recalls bitter seasons in the family's past. The summer spent dashing to and around New York State for Winny's health held a world of choice and chance beyond sea bathing or mountain air without helping a suffering child. Now, too, there were practical reasons for Howells' change of place. After a summer diminished by the deaths of friends like Stephen Crane and Charles Dudley Warner, combined with problems writing and trying to place *The Kentons* (1902)—his first novel not to be serialized—he fixed again on issues of economic security.

He had learned shortly after the end of his lecture tour about the default of Harper & Brothers. Their solid reputation and the enormous sales of books like George Du Maurier's *Trilby* in the mid-nineties had not kept the company solvent. "I no more dreamt of their failing," Howells wrote to Aurelia, "than of the U.S. government failing."[6] When Samuel S. McClure agreed to take over the firm and Howells received his overdue money, he concluded that it probably did not matter who was in charge. Besides,

McClure assured him that everything would go on as before.[7] The crisis had "cost him half a night's sleep" and almost made him forget "the shame of the Philippine war." After McClure himself failed to raise the necessary capital and the company fell into a brief receivership, Colonel George P. Harvey, owner of the *North American Review,* took over. At a time when publishers like Appleton went under, Harper's, with the new management and financial backing, somehow prevailed. Happy to have his own problems resolved, Howells still worried about less fortunate friends, including the Harper brothers themselves.

He agreed in September 1900 to a contract similar to the one he had signed in 1885 (after Osgood's default), which assured him ten thousand dollars a year. The exclusive provisions gave Harper's the rights to everything he wrote, with a minimum each year of one novel and a farce. Beginning in December 1900, he would take over the Editor's Easy Chair in *Harper's Monthly,* a forum similar to the Editor's Study and running concurrently. Over the next two years he also contributed monthly articles to the *North American Review.* In the years to come he used the Easy Chair as he had the Study, for literary and political commentary, for helping friends or letting off a little steam, though he saw the two columns as quite distinct. Recalling the "strenuous days" of the Editor's Study, he promised (with tongue in cheek) "no stormy reverberations from that sulphurous past, no echoes of that fierce intolerance, that tempestuous propaganda which left the apostle without a friend or follower in the aesthetic world."[8] From his seat in what Howells called his "Uneasy Chair," he took on an astounding range of topics: love and marriage, drugs and guns, travel and automobiles, life after death or on other planets, the supposed death of poetry, the vote for women, revenge, capital punishment, the function of art in society, and the virtues of a new art, the moving picture. His discussions of New York City, which every year he found denser and dirtier and wrote about with affectionate irony, perhaps set an example for Harold Ross' *New Yorker* column, Talk of the Town. In a dialogue with "a good citizen," the "we" of the Easy Chair asks: "But what *were* you aiming at? The fact that New York is a bad place? Well, we knew that already. It is dangerous, but you cannot deny it's amusing."[9]

During the period of his earlier contract with Harper's, the firm cautioned against ringing any "little bell," a hint not to stir up trouble with his political opinions. Howells both did and did not comply. He had written forcefully about the Haymarket events but chose other venues than the Editor's Study, a compromise that allowed the firm to keep a favorite writer and Howells to express his convictions. Otherwise he gave himself an open forum in the Editor's Study, whether to extol Tolstoy's Christian Socialism or fault his own country for betraying its ideals. He would do the same with the Editor's Easy Chair, advocating a federal income tax, subsidies to farmers, pensions for working men and women, and, in times to come, land grants for World War I veterans.

The arrangement with Harper's served both publisher and author well. In the early years of the century, when he spoke of failed energy, aging into "self doubt," or indifference to what had been his passions, Howells often referred to himself in the past tense.[10] It annoyed him that younger writers sold in the hundreds of thousands relative to his few thousands. "The fact is," he said, "that in *my* palmiest days, my novels sold very moderately."[11] While overly diffident, or forgetful of magazine sales, he was right about absolute numbers. Less popular English authors than Du Maurier—who sold books by the millions—enjoyed success beyond anything he ever realized. H. G. Wells and Arthur Conan Doyle had enviable sales, as did Americans like Twain, who signed his own agreement with Harper's in 1900. (Harper's, after publishing Wells' *War of the Worlds,* bumped his *Love and Mr. Lewisham* to serialize one of Howells' novels, though Wells, like Twain, outsold Howells and could demand more money.)[12] Twain got a guaranteed five-year contract of twenty-five thousand dollars a year, two and a half times what Howells negotiated. Yet Howells still had an edge. Today, when he has been dropped even from many academic anthologies, people forget his renown a century ago. A *Harper's* poll asking readers to name the ten best American writers ranked Mark Twain second to William Dean Howells.[13] (Neither Twain nor Howells had a New York apartment house named for them, as Henry James did.)

Howells' worries about money and readers never interrupted his generosity toward old friends like Twain or James or the young writers who sought his help. He had continued to support Stephen Crane until Crane's early death. When Crane went to say good-bye before sailing for England for the last time, Howells found him restless. "Even then," he told his widow, when they were "getting at each other less than ever," he felt Crane's power. America had not "produced a more distinctive and vital talent."[14] Three months after his condolence letter to Cora Crane, Howells wrote another to Susan Warner. Much as the years had swept them apart, he told her, Warner and he had recovered their former intimacy on the few occasions they could meet. (Warner had taken over the Editor's Study in 1892.) It especially touched Howells that the critic of the Gilded Age died in the tenement home of an African American man he had been mentoring, "among the poor, humble people to whom and to whose race so much of his thought and heart had been given."[15]

Howells' connections with young writers fulfilled a clause in his Harper's contract obliging him to solicit and advise on manuscripts. To Edith Wharton, who had yet to publish a full-length novel, he wrote in praise of the short stories he had read. "I have been tempted to write you and tell you of your old editor's—perhaps your first editor's?—very great pleasure in them." Howells had published one of Wharton's early poems, sent on to him by Longfellow. "But with the years come misgivings; we are not sure that our praise is wanted; in your case I knew that mine was not needed; and I should not now perhaps be offering your charming talent my recognition if I had not Business to back me."[16] The letter hints at the awkwardness of his role and, possibly, at doubts about his own career. With Hamlin Garland, he was more blunt, advising him about everything from approaching publishers to the use of punctuation in play scripts. At the same time, he tried to fend off requests to provide blurbs for his books. "A fellow who stands as strong upon his legs as you, wanting a hand from a dotard like me! I think the public would say, 'Who is this pothering fool who introduces a book of Garland's to us?'"[17] He relied on Garland for a description of a house raising when working on *New Leaf Mills* (1913) and for help in finding a bow and "very *blunt*" arrow for one of his grandsons. By accepting the position of agent and senior editor with Harper's, Howells once more secured his income and compromised his independence. The work "chopped up" his time, while the daily writing and the glut of new projects wearied him.[18]

"An aged man is but a paltry thing," William Butler Yeats wrote with stoic irony, expressing what Howells himself had felt for decades. At sixty-three, with an invalid wife, his parents and eldest child dead, his son often working elsewhere, and Mildred nursing a sore throat in places like Bermuda, he checked a tendency toward crankiness. "As I grow older," he told Aurelia, "the world seems much wickeder . . . perhaps it is just my circle of observation that has worked and deepened."[19] He had long ago dismissed the Republican party as "the party of industrial slavery." Good men had voted for McKinley, he wrote in 1896, "but so did every bad and corrupting element in our political and financial life."[20] At the opening of the new century, he may, as he felt, have lost some of his passion, but he was no less troubled or vocal. The change came not in his convictions but in the sense of his position in the world.

Through the previous decade he had sympathized with the Boer republics of South Africa against the British. Believing the Boer War to be nothing more than imperialist thieving, he did not comment on the Boers' own seizure of territory or mistreatment of African tribes. When Winston Churchill, still a young and politically ambitious war correspondent, made plans for an American visit to sell books and, under James Pond's auspices, to lecture on "The War in South Africa as I Saw It," Pond listed Howells among the welcoming celebrities. Exasperated by this "invitation" in the form of announcement, Howells sent off a terse note.

My dear Major:
I would not for anything take a platform seat, or any seat, at a lecture celebrating the British invasion of the South African Republics. I might make this stronger, but I hope it is clear enough.[21]

Twain responded to his invitation with more craft. He attended Pond's gala reception at the Waldorf Astoria, introduced Churchill, and made his feelings known. "Mr. Churchill and I do not agree on the righteousness of the South African war," he said and spelled out why. Acknowledging America and England's special relationship, he managed to end on both a gracious and a biting note. England and the United States "have always been kin," he said: "kin in blood, kin in religion, kin in representative government, kin in ideals, kin in just and lofty purposes; and now we are kin in sin, the harmony is complete, the blend is perfect, like Mr. Churchill himself, whom I now have the honor to present to you."[22] At Howells' instigation, Twain published an anti-imperialistic article in the *North American Review* (February 1901) addressed "To the Person Sitting in the Darkness."

Like Twain, Howells had an acute sense of what he saw to be British *and* American mischief. "Evil" is the word he increasingly used, mainly to characterize American foreign policy. He saw his nation turning away from broader freedom and democracy in a grab for world power. That did not mean he necessarily disliked people who thought differently—Theodore Roosevelt, for example, or Roosevelt's secretary of state, his own good friend John Hay, who unofficially supported the British side in the Boer War, pushed for the "open door" policy for China, and, almost as bad in Howells' view, seized the land that allowed construction of the Panama Canal. He would quote Hay's sense of having no choice on complicated issues. "I do not know where we are to come the delayed cropper," Hay had written. "But it will come. At least we are spared the infamy of an alliance with Germany. I would rather, I think, be the dupe of China than the chum of the Kaiser." Howells said of Hay that "he was beyond poets and novelists a diviner of men, their greatness or meanness, and this instinct compelled him to the love of Lincoln."[23] Much as E. M. Forster did, Howells made a continued effort to separate loyalty to his country from personal friendship and to put loyalty to friends first.

His relationship with Roosevelt cut several ways. He knew Roosevelt personally from the 1880s, had written favorable reviews of books like *The Winning of the West,* and had invited Roosevelt's contributions when editing the *Cosmopolitan.* On his part, Roosevelt valued the reviews and the letters of support, and he admired Howells' writings, particularly *A Boy's Town,* which reminded him of his own childhood. But while, like many contemporaries, Roosevelt ranked Howells as the country's first novelist, on topics other than writing the two had running, sometimes testy arguments. Howells decried Roosevelt's elitism, what he saw as the racially biased advocacy of large families, and above all his readiness to use military aggression. Roosevelt associated Howells with dangerous politics and, in private conversation, reportedly blamed him for a share in the McKinley assassination. "Hearst and Altgeld, and to an only less degree, Tolstoi and the feeble apostles of Tolstoi, like . . . William Dean Howells, who united in petitions for the pardon of anarchists, have a heavy part in the burden of responsibility for crimes of this kind."[24] During and for a time after the Spanish-American War, the two stood wholly apart. Howells called Roosevelt "a good, strong clean man, but a man who did more than any other to bring on the war, and now wants us to have a big army and navy, and go in for imperialism."[25] He condemned Roosevelt's militarism while honoring his war on corporate monopolies and the untaxed and irresponsible men who ran them. An environmentalist who protested the destruction of New Hampshire's forests, Howells applauded Roosevelt's effort to preserve American wilderness by creating the national parks. He was fond of Roosevelt as a person and felt comfortable approaching him about favors for Sam, in the government printing office, and Joe, a stalwart Republican, who sought a consulship in a warm climate.

As an older man Howells carefully watched his own behavior, as if wrestling with his conscience. Sometimes he would stop in mid-thought or mid-sentence to correct himself. Regretting a damning review he had written in 1901 of an academic survey of American literature, he decided that it didn't do to let one's self go. Thirteen years later, he apologized to the author, Barrett Wendell, for the "abominable spirit" of his review. "Your behavior to me since, as often as we have met, has made me wish to tell you that I was, when too late, immediately sorry for what I had done, and have always been ashamed."[26] For Howells as for Sigmund Freud, the question of personal control had larger implications. "The savage lurks so close to the surface in every man," Howells had written in *Tuscan Cities*, "that a constant watch must be kept upon the passions and impulses, or he leaps out in his war-paint, and the poor integument of civilization that held him is flung aside."[27] Except on issues like crooked politics, he kept both civility and civilization in mind. Speaking out, he rarely indulged the luxury of blaming others for what he accepted as innate frailties of human beings. Almost every comment about his own decisions suggests he held to the Swedenborgian principle that evil breeds evil, so that if a person has made evil his good and good his evil, he has created his own hell—no matter how hellish the world around him.

When, in the fall of 1900, Howells suffered from a temporary but painful loss of fingernails (possibly caused by a fungus), he made the best of things in a letter to Aurelia, who now received a large share of his confidences. For all his complaints, he said—at the end of a string of them—he felt he had nothing to complain about. Among the blessings, he was happy to see so much of Mark Twain. Just two years later he would write to Norton that "The man I most have to say with is Mark Twain, but we seldom meet, for he lives up the river where he can see the steam-boats passing, and he is kept closely at home by what now seems the hopeless case of his wife. It has changed the poor old fellow, but when he can break away, almost the best talk in the world is left in him."[28] Letters had to suffice, and those to Twain remained witty, affectionate, at times madcap, as when he described his dream about showing up at Twain's house in the middle of the night and being turned away like a thief. Occasionally, with quiet appeals for his company, he chided his friend for not reading an essay he had sent or pretending to have misplaced an invitation. More often he joked, and in language like Twain's. "Now you're sick, I've a great mind to have it out with you about Jane Austen. If you say much more I'll come out and read 'Pride and Prejudice' to you."[29]

In these years Howells' moods changed quickly, melancholy giving way to apology or tenderness, reflective nostalgia to regret. "It is a beautiful [February] morning," he wrote Aurelia in 1901, "and I wish I could walk out with you and the poor silent father-boy, and look at the quiet fields of snow, and the woods blackening up from them. How impatient I used to be with that beauty, in my longing to be out in the world! Now it is all past; I have got what I wanted, and I wish I had kept what I had."[30] He remembered small incidents from the past such as their collecting beechnuts on the Jefferson fairgrounds. In March, he found the quiet of Bermuda restorative. "Not a trolley, not a steam car; nothing louder than the telephone."[31]

I think I could deal with the present, bad and bothering as it is, if it were not for visions of the past in which I appear to be mostly running about, full of sound and fury signifying nothing.

—W. D. HOWELLS to Thomas Bailey Aldrich, July 3, 1902

The search for quiet drew Howells back to southern Maine and to the summer life he came to love there. In 1901, the family picked York Harbor, a wealthy community with imposing houses overlooking sea cliffs, where Howells would buy his last summer house. In the spring of 1902, they bought a property in Kittery Point, a forty-minute trolley ride from York. Of all their houses, they may have loved the one at Kittery Point most. John, having a particular attachment to the house, would inherit it, and Elinor, who in Howells' words "grannied her flowers," enjoyed there some of her best health.[32] Howells once called the house ugly, his improvements failures, but perhaps less to criticize than to ward off pride or bad luck. Mostly he thought of the place as the measure of any other. For extra space upstairs, the house had a Mansard roof—once as popular as it was pretentious, he would write in *Hither and Thither in Germany* (1920). He arranged for an existing stable to be moved for a large library—his "barnbrary," he called it—with stalls converted into bookshelves and a "superfluity" of his own books.[33] "Just now," he told William James, who had written to praise *The Kentons*, "the stable has rested on its journey from the street corner to the east of the house, where I am going to turn it into a study, and is trying to look into our bay-window; to move a building was about all that remained for me to do; and it is such an American experience!"[34]

The house stood—as it stands today—back from the granite shore with vistas across the Portsmouth Harbor to the Atlantic and Gerrish Island, on land green and wooded at the mouth of Chauncey Creek. The old village of New Castle and the town of Portsmouth stretch along the southern coast. From their backyard, the Howells could look across to the shore where the American Impressionist Edward Tarbell painted his friends, family, and garden. The sweep of Portsmouth Harbor was, to Howells, like a grander Grand

Canal, a place where ships sometimes foundered, fog crept in from the ocean, and naval gunships, veterans of the Spanish war, rode gray and menacing to the shipyard.

Perhaps all houses seem like castles, whether on the coast of Maine or "the coast of Bohemia." Even his city cooperative, in the handsome artists' complex on West Fifty-seventh Street, would offer a haven from the noise and scrambling of city life. He set parts of his utopian novels in New York, where, as in Edward Bellamy's *Looking Backward,* intelligent people talk in comfortable sitting rooms about justice and equality. Before New York, Cambridge had offered its own cultural utopia of musicians, historians, scientists, writers, and painters. Each of Howells' summer residences, Belmont included, began as a utopian retreat to a place where he could write and the family could recover their health and cultivate their garden. Planting remained a spring rite. "We have taken our cottage at Kittery Point, and I am going down to begin a garden as soon as the spring opens."[35] John—with a green thumb like his father's—arrived first in succeeding years to plant as early as the erratic weather allowed.

On clear days, Howells counted the hundreds of yachts dotting the harbor and tallied the expense. Some of these vessels "cost at least $1000 per week to run" and required crews of thirty to forty men.[36] Soon after buying the property, he reported "a wonderful morning of summer sun and wind, with a sea that sparkles and dances in both. They say we are at the end of our yachting season, but two very handsome big yachts are lying off our shore this morning, and what is somehow pleasanter to the eye a great, black, empty coal barge, high out of the water." Looking out at the barges, the yachts, and the dredges, he could be as transported as he had been, literally, when a young man in Venice. Like Venice, the Maine coast could also bring on an unaccountable homesickness. "There is something in the landscapes we knew when young," he told Aurelia, "that no beauty makes up for in those we see later." At once looking out and looking back, he felt a "rebellious heartache," a reminder of that chronic sense of loss.[37]

At Kittery Point, Howells lived close to three major hotels, with yet a fourth on Gerrish Island, and two majestic hotels, the Wentworth in New Castle and the Rockingham in Portsmouth. By boats, trains, and carriages, summer visitors crowded to the Portsmouth-Kittery seacoast as they did to nearby York. Here the theoretical socialist could indulge aristocratic habits in a beautiful if not exactly rustic world. When he arrived for the season in southern Maine, he encountered other "birds of summer" making their flights to popular resorts. A more fastidious Edith Wharton faulted hotel life for its "promiscuity," whereas Howells claimed to hate "hotelling" but clearly relished its impersonality and freedom from responsibility. At Kittery Point he got his share of hotel life without staying in a hotel. Private and enviably set as it was, his house might have been mistaken for an attractive annex to not too distant hotel grounds. Guests sauntered along walkways nearby and visited with the Howells family, who joined in the hotel's entertainments.

The idea that strangers came and went or met and courted amidst the rocks, sand, and gulls, or in the music rooms of grand hotels, appealed to Howells for several reasons, not least because it provided grist for his novelistic mill. Beginning with *Their Wedding Journey,* he had habitually turned travels into novels. A visit with Elinor and a bored Mildred to Saratoga in 1897 materialized as *An Open-Eyed Conspiracy,* while *The Landlord at Lion's Head* (1897), with its frank treatment of sexuality within and between different social classes, shows the opportunities available in fancy watering places. Communities in *Annie Kilburn* (1889) and *The Son of Royal Langbrith* (1904) must adjust to the visitors that swell their summer populations.

With *The Son of Royal Langbrith,* the story of a town and its leading family, Howells returned to the elemental New England setting and themes of *A Modern Instance.* Originally called "Mother and Son," this story of a son who ignorantly worships his monstrous father and prevents his mother's remarriage has the overtones of Greek tragedy. Though the disclosure of the truth prevents the son from imitating his father, the town never learns about Royal Langbrith's misdeeds. The moment his memory passes into official town history with the dedication of a votive tablet, his reputation suffers "a kind of discoloration. . . . Nobody could say whether he was really the saint and sage that he was reputed, and of what nobody can say, the contrary can be affirmed without contention."[38] Howells knew that every town has its reprobate, that the generations sacrifice each other out of mistaken love and jealousy and fear, and that lies, as much as truth, have their personal and public uses. For all its Hawthornesque innuendos, *The Son of Royal Langbrith,* like the earlier *Landlord at Lion's Head,* escapes the deterministic underpinnings of its plot. Sons do not necessarily have to pay for the iniquities of their fathers, and the past need not determine the future. Royal Langbrith's son will live to become a good husband, father, and citizen. The sheer mobility of American life seemed to Howells to have undermined the notions of collective memory for this town, perhaps for most towns. Across the country he had witnessed the "masses" becoming the "classes," the restlessness and aspirations driving the rest of the country as they drove himself. It amused him that many in the nautical crowd at Kittery Point's Champernowne Hotel came from places as removed as small-town Ohio.

Notwithstanding the tourists and the grand hotels, Howells saw a social gulf between Kittery Point and nearby York, which struck him as beautiful in its own way: a place with cottages "dropped, as near the ocean as may be," and with the attractions of a "reading room," concerts, and a mix of modern convenience and long history.[39] In 1902 he helped Twain and other summer residents raise funds for restoring the Old York Jail, which dated to colonial times. He thought Kittery Point more pleasant because less spoiled. The village itself kept the sense of a village. It was not, as he said, "untainted by summer cottages," but, with its fishing harbor and the naval yard close by, it pleased him to think that Kittery Point still had its "sea-legs."[40] From his own house he could look up the road to the William Pepperrell property, of which his own had been a tiny slice. In his day America's richest man, Sir William had led troops to take Louisburg from the French and had himself been stripped of wealth during the Revolution. His eighteenth-century mansion now stood as a grand, weather-beaten testimony to a living past, as did the Congregational church across the road, a true New England structure—compact, simple, and "wrapped" in clapboards—where Howells read a sermon in the form of a passage from his second Altrurian romance.

The outer world came in various guises to Kittery, and Howells watched the parade. In the article he published about Spanish prisoners housed at the Portsmouth Navy Yard, he imagined himself looking at the shore through the eyes of a captive.

> It was beautiful, I had to own, even in my quality of exile and prisoner. The meadows and the orchards came down to the water, or, where the wandering line of the land was broken and lifted in black fronts of rock, they crept to the edge of the cliff and peered over it. A summer hotel stretched its verandas along a lovely level; everywhere in clovery hollows and on breezy knolls were gray old farm-houses and summer cottages— like weather-beaten birds' nests, and like freshly painted marten-boxes; but all of a cold New England neatness which made me homesick for my malodorous Spanish fishing-village, shambling down in stony lanes to the warm tides of my native seas.[41]

In this piece for *Harper's Weekly*, Howells finds a characteristically new perspective, a way of seeing the magnificent vista through the eyes of lonely and exiled soldiers. As in his early Niagara pieces or *Tuscan Cities*, he forces his middle-class readers to look clearly at what they take for granted, and to look with compassion on the dispossessed. He adds again a personal irony about the coziness of his own summer place and his self-indulgence. "The drawback," he told Aurelia, "is the old feeling of selfishness that I have been enjoying all this while so many cannot. Really, the misery of the world seems to take unfair advantage of prosperity."[42]

At Kittery Point he renewed his friendship with Sarah Orne Jewett, who lived most of the year with Annie Fields in Boston but returned in the summer to her family home in South Berwick, a few miles north. Having no telephone, Jewett could only be reached by placing a call to her neighbors in the general store. Periodically Howells would call ahead and make the trip by trolley. He brought Henry James to see her in 1905, and his sister Annie in 1909, shortly before Jewett's death. In earlier years he had advised Jewett to write about what she knew, about Maine and its people, which she did so well in *Deephaven* and *The Country of the Pointed Firs*. "You got an uncommon feeling for *talk*," he had told her in 1873, "I *hear* your people."[43] In "an age which has no Jane Austen of its own," he honored Jewett as America's best equivalent.[44]

The return each summer to Kittery Point brought memories of Annie Fields' and Jewett's friend Celia Thaxter. His own friendship with Thaxter, who had died in 1894, went back to 1860, the year he first came to New England. Belonging to the world he dreamed of entering, she appeared as fine, frank, and finished as her poetry. "She was a most beautiful creature," he reminisced, "still very young, with a slender figure, and an exquisite perfection of feature." Thaxter embodied another aspect of New England, keeping to what Howells called "her native field," where she had made "those sea-beaten rocks to blossom. Something strangely full and bright came to her verse from the mystical environment of the ocean, like the luxury of leaf and tint that it gave the narrower flower-plots of her native isles."[45] With the painter Childe Hassam and other friends of Thaxter, Howells had visited Appledore—formerly Hogg Island—and seen her at work in the family hotel, now defunct.

In his passion for southern Maine, Howells perhaps thought himself an adopted outsider, a little less Western, a little more Down-Eastern, as comfortable in New England as Henry James in old England. Though living in Maine just a few months a year, he came to regard the house on Kittery Point as his home, New York his place of work. However much he loved Maine, Howells responded in the fall of each year to "a steady pull of the heart cityward." As the hotels emptied and the maples paid their last brilliant tribute to the end of the season, he began to "sniff the asphalt," "the roar of the street" calling to him as "the voice of the sea" waned.[46] He returned to another life, mainly in New York but with trips to Atlantic City for Elinor's health, to the Great Lakes when John took a trip to Yellowstone, and in 1904 to Italy and England. "So we go back to New York," he wrote in 1901, "our refuge, our ugly exile."[47]

New York for Howells and Elinor had long involved a routine exchanging of houses, which meant, between 1900 and 1902, they moved from 40 West Fifty-ninth Street to 115 East Sixteenth Street to 38 East Seventy-third Street to 48 West Fifty-ninth Street, then back to 40 West Fifty-ninth Street and back again to 48 West Fifty-ninth Street. In a shadow version of their domestic moves, Howells bought houses for investment. When they took the Kittery Point house, they traded the Far Rockaway property, to good advantage, and bought a townhouse on West Eighty-second Street.

The return to life in New York always brought a decline in Elinor's health. "She begins to droop when she is shut up in our hot rooms after the open air life of the summer," Howells wrote to Annie Fields in 1903.[48] With Elinor often "past doing anything," the Howellses "kept moving," finding first one, then another lodging that seemed to promise relief.[49] Howells asked Vevie Fréchette, when she studied art in the city, to come visit: for her aunt, the climb to Vevie's fourth-floor apartment would be like scaling the Matterhorn.

Mainly because of Elinor's condition, they were unable or disinclined to entertain, probably both. But in March 1902, Howells determined on what he called the "first entertainment I have given any friends of mine since our early days in the Beacon Street house." He intended the occasion to repay Colonel Harvey, of Harper & Brothers, for past kindnesses. This would be a men's get-together, with Twain, as usual, the featured entertainment. When it turned out that Twain had gone yachting, the party took place without him and seemed to Howells a success. The guest list suggests the range of his connections and the tenacity with which he kept them. "Quincy Ward, my old friend the sculptor; Janvier, the story-writer; John La Farge, the painter; Crowninshield, an old friend, painter and poet; Harry Harper, and Rutgers Marshall, a psychologist and architect, all Century Club men. The talk was great, as good almost as I used to hear in Cambridge, without the New England stiffness, and they sat *from half past one till ten minutes past six!* They said this broke the record. I wish Joe could have been there."[50]

Although Howells' long-planned Mississippi voyage with Twain never took place, he managed a similar trip with Joe in 1902, down the Ohio. For the Editor's Easy Chair he described the two of them as "light-hearted youngsters of sixty-five and seventy setting out on their journey in fulfillment of a long-cherished dream" to "rehabilitate" the past. The echoes in this article of his youthful journey to Saint Louis must have been self-conscious. The landscape he watches along the river banks has been spoiled by "pitiless industrialism," yet the farms remain, and the people, so different from Easterners, with serious faces and eager purpose, strike him as unchanged. Howells once more finds himself in the heartland of America, accompanied by the brother who shared his boyhood experiences—like the episode near Eureka Mills when the two interrupted their journey home to rest in a moonlit clearing. Years later, writing his fictional version of those times in *New Leaf Mills,* Howells would ask Joe to read the manuscript, in a gesture of friendship and nostalgia. Before making the Ohio voyage, Howells had described himself as "tired out."[51] On his return he wrote Mildred, "I had a glorious trip on the Ohio—a thousand miles—and I have come home restored to my sleep, and feeling fine. . . . I sat on the hurricane deck or in the pilot house every minute I was not eating or sleeping, and purred away with the pilots or Uncle Joe, who went with me, and looked after me as if I were sick."[52] With Joe again his big brother, he had enjoyed the convalescent's luxury of doing nothing.

Quite irrespective of the rightness of England or the wrongness of America . . . each is in fact inevitably right in its way.

—W. D. HOWELLS to Charles Eliot Norton, June 11, 1905

Howells seemed always to set off for Europe sick or recovering from sickness and "worn down" from writing. Ailing again in the spring of 1904, though with Elinor's health worse than his own, he planned a trip to England and Italy for himself and Mildred. Elinor would stay behind unless or until she felt well enough to join them. Father and daughter sailed in early March on the German liner *Moltke,* named for the general who had long before prepared plans for Germany's 1914 invasion of France. They landed on March 9 in Plymouth, the port from which Sir Francis Drake had sailed to fight the invading Spanish Armada over three centuries before.

Having grown more forgiving of the English and more interested in English history, Howells intended this trip for the making of English travel books. Supported by his editor, Frederick Duneka, he arranged a limited leave from Harper's, which allowed him to write *London Films* (1905) and *Certain Delightful English Towns* (1906), along with a third book, *Seven English Cities* (1909), that drew later from the same material. Wasting no time, Howells began gathering material aboard the *Moltke* and proceeded like a court stenographer. His observations went first into impressionistic letters to Elinor, who might have wished for something a bit more personal. An early letter, about Plymouth, ends:

> Quaint hillside streets, with old over-hung houses. House where the King stayed? (Charles I? II? William III? Please look up.) We expect to leave for Exeter at 10:30 tomorrow A.M.
> *Keep all these scribbles for notes.* Pale dull sky, with a moment of heat at noon: weather very warm last week.
> *Love to John.*
> *"Papa"*[53]

Howells' new infatuation with things English coincided with dismay about readers and critics at home. His *Letters Home* (1903), which presents various correspondents writing about the same or overlapping events in their private "conversations," received tepid praise at best in the United States. The British, on the other hand, paid him handsome compliments. "Thank you, and thank Mrs. Strachey too," he wrote John St. Loe Strachey, cousin of Lytton Strachey and editor of the influential *Spectator,* "for being so good to my poor 'Letters Home' which has shivered about without a friend here since it came out. Perhaps a friend or two; but it has had no success." He quipped that American readers declined his fidelity to life "with thanks."[54] In England praise came from newspapers and magazines, and from Oxford University, which was to award him an honorary doctorate.

Since May 1898, he had been contributing an occasional column to *Literature,* a joint venture between the London *Times* and Harper & Brothers and a forerunner of the *Times Literary Supplement.* Early the next year, his comments began appearing weekly, ranging over topics from Canadian literature to Yiddish poetry and the influence on the American novel of Thorstein Veblen's social and economic inquiries into the "leisure class." The *Literature* pieces secured Howells a new international audience and authority that may have appealed to the dons at Oxford. Elinor sailed in June, in time to witness the Oxford ceremony, which her husband described as something of an anticlimax. He had only to listen to his "own eulogy in

Latin, then climb some steps to shake the hand of the Chancellor," who greeted him in Latin and motioned him to a seat. Lunch in All Souls College followed the "degreeing," then dinner in Christ Church College.[55] Maybe prompted by the Oxford ceremony, Western Reserve University awarded him a doctor of law degree that year, and Columbia conferred "all possible honors" the following June.[56]

In the next decade, Howells would amend his earlier remarks about British icons like Charles Dickens, whom he now ranked with Cervantes, Molière, Swift, and Twain. "Dickens even surpassed Mark Twain in characterizing and coloring the speech of his time," he wrote in 1913. "We who read Dickens in his heyday not only read him, we talked him."[57] Three years later, he applauded two British comedies—*Hobson's Choice* and *The Quinneys*—for being "better in texture than our own dramatic things."[58] Regularly in his *Harper's Weekly* columns he brought contemporary English writers to the notice of American readers, among them the urban novelist Israel Zangwill, the spiritual autobiographer William Hale White, and Virginia Woolf's whipping boy, Arnold Bennett.

Howells saw Jane Austen as a literary compatriot and would not have gone to England without a visit to Bath, where he joked about spying Catherine Morland and Henry Tilney, the lovers in *Northanger Abbey*, as living people. On the way to Bath, he and Mildred passed through Lyme Regis and other settings of Austen's novels, which felt to both father and daughter like ancestral places, so many Hays-on-Wye. In Bath, as he writes in *Certain Delightful English Towns*, they stayed in a hotel not far from where "the divine, the only Jane Austen herself had lived."[59]

Mark Twain, who in earlier days might have laughed at Howells' infatuation, struggled at this time through his long agony over Livy's health and their search for relief abroad. Howells had written in April from London to recommend a doctor and to say how deeply he felt for them both. The letter he received from Twain in June still came as a shock. Livy had died on June 5. "I bent over her & looked in her face, & I think I spoke," Twain wrote, "—I was surprised and troubled that she did not notice me. Then we understood, & our hearts broke. How poor we are today!" He wanted Howells to know that in her "worn old Testament," he found "a dear & gentle letter from you, dated Far Rockaway, Sept. 13, 1896, about our poor Susy's death."[60] The news "wrung his heart," Howells said. He could say nothing nor even pretend to ease the suffering.[61]

Livy's death drove home the wastefulness of inflicting pain on others. He spoke at this time of donning corrective lenses, by which he meant seeing others and his own behavior in a more generous light. This may have led to his new appreciation for traditions that in the past he would have dismissed out of hand. When he visited Sutton Court, the Somerset estate of John Strachey's brother, he promised Strachey that "you may be sure that I shall see it with eyes unhardened by any prejudices against primogeniture, and with a tenderness that your love for it has taught me to feel. In a world which, to an old Tolstoyan manqué (Tolstoy himself is a Tolstoyan manqué) like myself seems altogether wrong I cannot select particular objects of reform."[62] Liking and admiring Strachey, he was more ready to be open, as he says, and at the same time he took pleasure in the silent beauty of the old estates, in their history, and to some extent their values. He tried to explain his feelings to a man sure to understand, the Anglophile Charles Norton. "The impression of England on me was so great as to be almost pulverizing. . . . I shall never be able, in what I write, to impart the sense of this, and I see much pity in my having gone out of my American way to be crushed. I was fitted to my groove, and contentedly slipping on in it to the end. Now, I find myself so much at odds with what I used to be that I do not know what sort of re-beginning to make."[63] If Italy, where the Howellses wintered in San Remo, brought no similar readjustments, Howells continued his "re-beginnings" when he came home. Of course he remained stuck, as anyone might, in some of his grooves.

Arriving in New York by April 17, the Howellses went directly to Kittery Point for the summer. From there he tried to appease Annie, who felt slighted by his not visiting Joe. The year of travel had left him feeling "broken up" and fumbling. He needed to get back to work and earn his salary. Together he and Elinor were a "hapless pair of do-nothings." As Annie knew (she knew better), he seldom went from home, "and when I do," he wrote, "I go on business disguised as pleasure."[64]

Peace Envoys' Meeting Is Likely to Be Held at Hotel Wentworth, New Castle. Russian and Japanese Envoys to Confer in This Locality. Washington Dispatch Calls for Local Information.

Portsmouth (NH) *Herald,* July 7, 1905

Anticipating the town's moment in history, the Portsmouth *Herald* asserted that "some one ought to see to it that [the delegates] are supplied with the books of Miss (Sarah Orne) Jewett and T. B. Aldrich that will aid them to appreciate the spirit of the place."[65] (Howells apparently did not measure up as a local author.) The "delegates" from the two warring powers, Japan and Russia, would, through an unlikely chain of circumstances, arrive in the quiet New Hampshire town to play their part in what many saw as the great event of the new century.

An international power for little more than a decade, Japan had routed the Chinese in battles that only a Japanophile like Lafcadio Hearn believed they could win. The Russians, who had been pushing toward the Pacific for three centuries, had the reputation of being perhaps the most powerful European nation, while Japan had barely built its battleships. In recent years, the Russians had broken treaties and moved steadily into both Manchuria and Korea, threatening Japan and capturing Port Arthur, a long-coveted outlet for trade and a linchpin for naval dominance. In the wake of the division of China and the Boxer Rebellion that followed, the Russians took advantage of their opportunities. They ignored Japanese protests and British warnings along with words of caution from their own statesmen, notably Sergius Witte, the minister of finance fired by Czar Nicholas II for his brusque honesty and opposition to war with Japan.

In February 1904 Japanese forces slipped into Russian-controlled waters and destroyed the Russian fleet at Port Arthur. Climaxing in the aptly named battle of Mukden, Russian advances ended in a dust storm and retreat. Undeterred, the czar sent his Baltic fleet halfway around the world to be sunk in the Straits of Tsushima in "the greatest sea-battle since Trafalgar."[66] Despite his semireligious belief in Russian impregnability, the Czar recognized the risks of continued war, and so did the Japanese. Japan turned to Theodore Roosevelt, a known supporter who had been nudging them to seek peace. Roosevelt responded immediately, and in August 1905, Sergius Witte brought the Russian delegation, Foreign Minister Komura the Japanese, to the Portsmouth Naval Shipyard, about a mile from Howells' house.

Mark Twain may have been right in thinking Portsmouth a *very* dull town, accessible if at all by uncomfortable trains. Howells himself, who spoke of "the dear old town," chose not to buy a house there because he found it too quiet. Sleepy or not, Portsmouth sprang to life that summer. In late July, engineers widening the harbor dynamited Henderson's Point on the Piscataqua River—to that date the largest man-made explosion in history. Thousands of people watched and more heard as a quarter million tons of rock blasted into the air. Serendipitous as it was, the explosion announced the importance of the coming conference. The state governor, town officials, federal agents, local businessmen, ladies' societies, bands, school-children, and the national guard turned Portsmouth into a festive host city.

While playing no active part in the conference, Howells—who appears with dignitaries in the extant photographs—had a reporter's access to the public meetings and covered the conference for *Harper's Weekly*. His observations range across politics, international manners, the evils of colonialism, and the pageantry itself.

> The day when the commissioners came in to Kittery harbor in their three American ships, looming whitely out of the white fog which had delayed them twenty-four hours, was a day which contributed everything meteorology could do to the dignity of their approach. Up they came, the beautiful ships in their majestic succession, out of the milky horizon, past the Isles of Shoals, and on between the red tower of Whaleback Light and the white tower of Fort Constitution, and swam swiftly and then slowly toward us as if they were going to mount our own meadow.[67]

The elegant Wentworth-by-the-Sea Hotel, located in adjacent New Castle, hosted the two delegations and many of the hundreds of reporters, who, like today's paparazzi, chased negotiators by carriage or boat, photographing every gathering and reporting every scrap of gossip. The town of Portsmouth organized parades and grand dinners, and the estate of a late beer baron, rather than the New Hampshire or United States government, paid the costs of the negotiators' accommodations.

After welcoming the delegates at his summer house at Oyster Bay, New York, Roosevelt did not attend the conference, though he kept in close touch through daily briefings. Had Howells' good friend John Hay not died on July 1, he might have represented the president at the international event. "World attention" focused on the spectacle of an Asian country negotiating with a Western power on equal terms, and Howells had a front-row seat.[68]

He complained in *Harper's Weekly* that he "was sorry when in the streets of Portsmouth our people cheered the bowing and smiling Japanese and failed to cheer equally the bowing and smiling Russians."[69] He shared the Russian response to the Japanese as "five-foot, hundred pound, little brown mysteries," more secretive than the Russians and less interested in the kind of public relations that Witte handled so skillfully.[70] He might have remembered his own height, which approximated that of the Japanese diplomats. The shrewd and soft-spoken Komura—a graduate of Harvard Law School who could quote Emerson or Tennyson by the hour—stood five feet two. Witte towered over Howells and the Japanese delegates by more than a foot. To Aurelia, Howells described a breakfast where Count Witte gave him reasons for preferring the Russians. "On Tuesday Pilla and I went to the breakfast given by the admiral to the Jap and Russian peace commissioners at the Navy Yard. It was a very easy, pleasant affair. The Russians were the most interesting. Witte, the chief of them, brought Pilla her breakfast, and his secretary said everyone knew my name in Russia, but I think I could probably find a few scores of millions to whom it would be strange."[71] If no more "fair" in appearance than the Japanese, the Russians seemed to Howells "more our kind"—the more so when they praised his books and fame abroad. Still, he considered Russia no better than Japan for its rapacity and autocratic (in Japan's case oligarchic) politics.

The events of the conference seem from this distance almost perfunctory, in that both sides needed to make peace and arrived in Portsmouth ready to compromise. Russia knew before the opening protocols that they would have to abandon Port Arthur and give up much of Manchuria— not to the Chinese or Koreans, of course, but to the Japanese. On their side, most of the Japanese leaders understood that they would not get indemnities for their losses in war and would have to cede the island of Sakhalin. Komura told Witte that he spoke like a victor intent on spoils. Witte replied unhesitatingly: "There are no victors here, and, therefore, no defeated."[72] The Japanese swallowed the indemnity claim and agreed to a division of Sakhalin. There remained the naming of the treaty, a topic debated throughout the negotiations by members of the press and politicians. Howells had written that the "Peace of Portsmouth" did not sound "so bad" but he preferred "the Peace of Kittery." Witte had the last word. He wrote to thank Roosevelt for his "humane efforts upon peace" and for making possible "the Treaty of Portsmouth, N.H."[73]

As an ironic footnote to the Portsmouth Conference, two hated rivals ultimately became allies, shifting the balance of power in the Far East. Thinking in terms of global politics and his own prestige, Roosevelt proclaimed the agreement good for the Japanese, good for the Russians, and bully good for him too.[74] Howells thought differently. He concluded a *Harper's Weekly* piece with a personal if unprophetic wish. "The truth is I am a Korean sympathizer, and have been from the beginning of the war, and so far from being concerned whether Russia or Japan shall come out of the peace negotiations in possession of that placid empire, I have the single wish that it may emerge from the dispute a free and independent Korean republic, perhaps of the type which we are going, a hundred years hence, to set up for the Filipinos."[75] His misgivings anticipate the coming international struggles for "racial superiority" and "national destiny." To think of Portsmouth, New Hampshire (or Kittery, Maine), as a focal point for East-West struggles or to remember the "Treaty of Portsmouth" emerging in that small New England community suggests how, to use Howells' ready word, "chance" plays its part in historic events. Roosevelt might have picked a dozen other towns, possibly with a different outcome. Portsmouth turned out to be a good choice. Roosevelt won national support as well as the Nobel Prize (in 1906) for his peacemaking efforts.

The intersection of private lives with public events is the stuff of history as well as of biography. At the peace conference, Howells spoke about the officer in charge of the base who entertained them. "The Admiral's name is Mead, and though he is now a Kentuckian, his people come from Connecticut, and Elinor scents a kinsman in him."[76] They discovered him to be a distant relative; yet the point here is that Howells met him and was involved, if not with the business of the peace conference, certainly with its principal actors. As in his boyhood Ohio, he witnessed great issues being decided. His father advanced the political career of James Garfield. He himself remembered the exit of the Wyandot Indians when the U.S. government forced them from Ohio into Kansas. John Brown's family, who considered the Howellses friends, visited before and after the Harpers Ferry raid. Howells lived in Venice the year before the expulsion of the Austrians and the city's final unification with Italy. He participated from a distance, yet directly and courageously, in the Haymarket affair. In a small way Howells had helped Lincoln's candidacy for president, and he repeated the favor for Rutherford B. Hayes, who repaid his efforts by sending James Lowell as ambassador to England—where Howells would meet Gladstone and other British dignitaries. What he did not experience directly in his long life, he read and wrote about, be it the Spanish-American War or the Boer War. And in 1905 he watched from a kind of box seat the end of the conflict between Japan and Russia, the negotiations for which took place, to change the metaphor, in his own backyard.

His month as *Harper's* witness in Portsmouth brought a minor pause from all but journalistic writing. When he looked back he judged the summer a failure, and, in a list of woes to Hamlin Garland, spoke of shirking his work, "feeling tired in my brain, physically tired, for many weeks."[77] He experienced that daunting between-times, between-novels numbness that makes writers think they have no more work in them. One cause of his low spirits might have been Henry James' visit in June. After an absence of twenty years, James had decided to return to the United States to see family and friends. He felt driven, he told Howells, "pathetically and tragically," by a fervor of nostalgia.[78] Before he grew too old, he wanted to feel America, to taste its air, to loll on a hillside in the manner of his youth. To finance his trip, he hoped to garner the kinds of material details, including how Americans ate their eggs and how they now spoke, that readers of travel literature expected. Howells had seen James in England and in the meantime had helped plan his American tour, which extended as far as Los Angeles and resulted in his cantankerous work *The American Scene.*

Astute friends predicted James would hate everything he saw in the United States. Morose and very stout ("filled out from head to foot, in a sort of chamfered squareness"), he also proved an uneasy guest at Kittery Point.[79] According to Elinor, who loved his novels, he had as a young man been tragic and beautiful; now he was simply tragic. He came for two days in the hottest weather and worst of moods. Elinor thought the house too informal for him to feel comfortable. "He is very fussy and has quite an elegant house, with a walled garden and five servants in Rye. . . . He thinks so much of *things.* But his family was always traveling when he was young, and he has told us how much he hated it. So this is the result."[80] Howells felt glad to see him go. "I am not sure that he ought to have come, but it was inevitable. Still, when you are past sixty, I say, Stay put." When James visited Edith Wharton in Lenox, Massachusetts, and complained of the heat, she ministered to him with fresh oranges and buckets of ice for his swollen feet.

From the sanctity of James' own Lamb House, the visit to Kittery Point appeared less gloomy. "I find a beautiful summer here," James wrote Elinor, "& the sense of the return to private life & the resumption of literary labour most sustaining. But all the things I didn't say to Howells, while I was with you, still whirl about the room like importunate bats—tormenting me overmuch. Tell him, please, that I love his new London chapters [in *Certain Delightful English Towns*] & wish they wd. go on & on. Also please that I love *him* & constantly hang about him." He mentions with pleasure the visit he and Howells had made to Sarah Orne Jewett. Teasing his hosts about being "Accessories to Portsmouth drama," he can at most claim to have "*almost* seen the Wentworth Hotel . . . & the Navy Yard, & the rest of the Scene of Action." Like Howells, he is thankful to be home, "the Pilgrim at rest."[81]

James had once called Howells "the most peripatetic man" he knew, by which he may have meant the uncountable houses his friend inhabited or the places he visited—or perhaps, with a little irony, the long walks they had taken together.[82] In all senses Howells *was* peripatetic. From the days he embarked on his uncles' paddleboats to follow the Ohio and Mississippi rivers and visit cities as far apart as Cincinnati and Saint Louis, he longed to be elsewhere and often moved on as soon as he arrived. Now he wanted a quiet routine, allowing himself the trolley ride to South Berwick or York Harbor, but content to enjoy his summer garden and, until the end of the season, "stay put." Kittery Point meant to him what the town of Rye meant to Henry James.

When Howells thought about this summer, he found consolation in the family's having been "much together," with Elinor in remarkably better health, and though John had gone briefly to Colorado—also for his health—Howells himself had recovered from a spring ailment. Nature reflected his shift in mood. Whereas men had exploded unprecedented tons of dynamite before the peace conference, Nature played the *finale.* "We are in the midst of a tremendous southeasterly storm," he told Aurelia, "and it is splendid in its way. With the making of peace between Russia and Japan, the elements seem to have gone to war. We had an earthquake, last week, and fumes of sulphur came up on the beaches, with some blaze."[83] Fireworks and international upheavals at a standstill, he went back to work.

16

GREATER LOSSES
1906–1910

Tomorrow I shall be 69, but I do not seem to care. I did not start the affair, and I have not been consulted about it at any step. I was born to be afraid of dying, but not of getting old.

—W. D. HOWELLS to Mark Twain, February 28, 1906

HOWELLS BEGAN THE YEAR 1906 in a nostalgic mood. Mark Twain's secretary rang with a question: When had Twain "*raised hell* about Emerson and Longfellow"?[1] The question and visit that followed brought back the "old time of long talks," when their children had been youngsters and he and Twain confident about the future, full of plans. John was now thirty-seven, a practicing architect, and Mildred thirty-three, a poet and artist. It touched Howells that his children had grown to be "such good comrades" and that John, to whom he turned increasingly for advice, liked to spend his evenings at home playing the mandolin or reading with the family.

He thought of his own brothers and sisters, especially of Joe, who, despite poor health, had begun another career at seventy-three. More than forty years before, Howells had gone to Venice as a United States consul; now Joe had won a consular appointment to Turks Island, a dot of land in the Caribbean held by Jamaica. Hoping mostly to escape Ohio winters, Joe traveled to his new home in search of a warm climate. Howells worried that he might be bored by a community where the entertainments were limited to a reading room, a library, three churches, and the weekly arrival of ships delivering mail and supplies. To keep Joe active, Howells pushed him to write, especially letters to his brother. "Is the color line very closely drawn? What church do you go to?" he asked. "Don't be afraid that I shall not be interested in the smallest details."[2] Joe may well have regretted taking his brother at his word. Howells lectured him, as he had their father, about everything from lapses in grammar to what he owed his office. When Joe admitted to his embarrassment at ceremonial dinners, Howells told him he *must* get on his feet and say a few words. It was his job. He cautioned Joe to curb his criticism of the American government in his columns for the *Sentinel*, which could lose him the $1,500 salary. A year later, when Joe began to find the island too confining, Howells suggested thinking of it as a sanatorium. Wasn't his present situation "better than running into zero weather at Jefferson, or arguing with a farmer against stopping his paper, or stoking the engine"?[3] Joe leaned toward the merits of selling the *Sentinel* until Howells did the math. Even assuming that Joe could trust the person who bought the paper, he would not earn anything approaching his present income. The paper cleared $1,200 a year *and* supported the son who now ran it.[4] Joe, in Howells' phrase, decided to stay put.

Impatiently as he responded to Aurelia, Howells more often worried about his lack of sympathy or felt humbled by the woman who continued to care for their deranged and dangerous brother. "Judge me not as I judge myself, O Lord!" he wrote in a poem called "Conscience" (in *Stops of Various Quills*).

Show me some mercy, or I may not live:
Let the good in me go without reward;
Forgive the evil I must not forgive!"

Partly for Aurelia's sake, he made a point, when attending a congressional hearing on copyright law in December 1906, of visiting Sam, the black sheep. Sam had grown "enormously fat," while his wife, Florence, suffering from stomach cancer, looked as thin as a "sick bird." They lived from hand to mouth, Sam's salary at the government printing office having been reduced by half for incompetence and sloth.[5] Howells presumed once more on his acquaintance with the president. At first showing a willingness to help, Roosevelt soon heard the reports from Sam's fellow workers. Little remained for Howells to do except cross his fingers. "Sam is always slow unless he has to ask something," he wrote Joe; "then he is very prompt; and his silence now may mean that things are not going unfavorably with him."[6]

It struck him as odd that Sam's character had remained unchanged while the man himself had aged like his older brothers. Ten years before, a man delivering a watermelon had described Howells to their cook as a "little old gentleman, in gray clothes, rather chunky." Elinor laughed until Howells told her that someone had asked the cook whether "the old lady had come in yet?"[7] He did not feel as comfortable as he once had in New York, which he saw as a young person's city. It took strenuous effort to meet the simplest needs. "It is a great chaos of life that rather frightens me," he told Aurelia after he and Elinor had navigated their way around a flood from a burst main on Fifth Avenue. Since they had first moved there the city had grown forests of buildings that blotted out the sky. Yesterday there had been country beyond them. Now automobiles packed Fifth Avenue so closely "that you could walk to and fro on their tops more safely than you can cross the street among them." He complained about the construction of the Grand Central Tunnel that produced stifling dirt and din.[8] In one mood he thought that if only he suffered less in Boston's winters, he would go back there to live; in another mood, he knew that Boston would never do. He could more easily deal with broken water lines than with the chaos of regret, which went beyond the memories of his daughter. Whenever he went to Cambridge he saw his dead contemporaries in the faces of their children.

Winters in New York proving no more salubrious than those in Boston, they escaped in February to Atlantic City. In later years Howells preferred Georgia and Saint Augustine, Florida. Mildred went to Bermuda, where she met old friends from the United States and abroad and busied herself with writing, sketching, and the perpetual round of picnics and dances. Atlantic City seemed far enough to Elinor, who felt she could manage the short train ride from New York. She and Howells played tourists, strolling on the boardwalk, sitting for hours at a time in the weak winter sun, and occasionally attending an evening vaudeville show or having their fortunes told. The Saint Charles Hotel offered relative anonymity; no one felt obliged to let Howells know which of his books had or had not pleased. He wrote Charles Norton that during their six-week stay they had not seen "one distinguished figure or striking face" among the "decent average." In earlier years, he would have rejoiced for his "poor literature's sake; but now, though I still see all things as before, I no longer make note of them, voluntarily or involuntarily. What interests me in this fact is that it is unexpected. . . .

I had not supposed that nature would intimate in this way that it was time for me to close up business."[9] Having expected to gather material to the end, he found that he had stored up enough to last a lifetime.

There came times when he felt himself more ancestral than individual. He had taken to wearing his father's glasses for reading, and, catching a familiar face in the mirror, he paused, waiting for his own to emerge. Fascinated as ever by the riddles of the self, he wondered what makes an individual uniquely himself or herself. Once again he pondered issues of remembering and forgetting as they bear on human identity. In "Sleep and Forgetting," he wrote about a girl who loses her memory but "keeps her personality intact," her story reflecting the mystery both of human consciousness and possible consciousness after death.[10] Do people recall their former selves? Will they recognize those they loved? His speculation suggests Plato's myth reversed: not people coming into life and forgetting what they knew, but the prospect of losing life without the knowledge of having lived and loved. Citing nerves, Elinor begged off listening to "Sleep and Forgetting."

The day before his sixty-ninth birthday, Howells wrote Twain that sometimes "in these latter days I *realize* that I shall die, hitherto having regarded it as problematical, and the sense of it is awful. I do not see how so many people stand it. That is nonsense, but the notion does not present itself conceivably. My wife does not let me discuss these ideas with her, and so I keep them for my own edification. When my father was 87 he once said to me that the night before he had thought it all out, and now he was satisfied. Perhaps each has to come to some such settlement with himself." Age had its advantages, he wrote, and if "old men were not so ridiculous," he could stand being one. "But they *are* ridiculous, and they are ugly."[11] Twain expressed surprise that Howells tried to pass himself off for sixty-nine. "I have known him longer than that. I am sorry to see a man trying to appear so young."[12]

Increasingly drawn to psychology, both his own and the studies of William James (among others), he urged Mark Twain to send him pages from his still-unfinished autobiography. Twain obliged with an episode about the prodigal Orion who, arriving unannounced in Hannibal and intent on surprising his family the next morning, had climbed into his old bed. Waking up, he discovered his family's house rented to a doctor and himself in bed with two of the doctor's elderly sisters. Howells applauded Twain's effort. Not only had he—and Orion—gone where no autobiographer had gone before; he was "nakeder than Adam and Eve put together,

GREATER LOSSES, 1906–1910
384

and truer than sin. But—but—but—," he ended, "you really *mustn't* let Orion have got into the bed. I know he did, but—."[13] He demanded the next 578 pages.

Having returned to New York in March and settled into yet another hotel, this time the Regent at Broadway and Seventieth with a view of the Hudson, Howells prepared for a visit from H. G. Wells. Wells had entertained him and Mildred at Sandgate in 1904, and Howells had admired the house, looking out on the English Channel, that his host had built with his own hands. Wells liked to think of himself as belonging to no class, which delighted Howells.[14] That did not stop his describing Wells as "a little cockney man, but of a brave spirit, who is socialistic in his expectations of the future, and boldly owns to having been a dry goods clerk in his past."[15] Of all the English novelists he met, he liked Wells best. Each man respected the other's work. Wells praised *The Undiscovered Country,* and Howells returned the compliment by noting the "extraordinary breadth" of *Love and Mr. Lewisham.*[16] Taking Wells' visit to New York as an opportunity, Howells decided to host a lunch for "the man from Mars and other malign planets."[17] Twain dined with them, along with Twain's friend Joseph Twichell and the painter Francis D. Millet, who would soon die on the *Titanic.* If table talk turned to common friends like Henry James, Wells and Twain might have found themselves allied. In 1915 Wells was to write a Twainlike parody of James, burlesquing his theories of the novel. He compared a James novel to "a church lit but without a congregation to distract you, with every light and line focused on the high altar."[18] Before Wells returned to England, Howells gave him a memento: seeds for black Mexican sweet corn and crookneck squash, which, if cooked as Howells specified—stewed and dressed with cream—would be as "tender as a maiden's feelings."[19]

Wells left before they disagreed about Maxim Gorky, the Russian novelist who came to New York in April, hoping to win financial support for the cause of Russian democracy. Twain organized the visit. With Howells at his side, he announced a dinner "to offer Gorky the literary hospitality of the country. . . . We want to do it in proper style, and will have authors not only from New York, but from Chicago, and we may have some literary geniuses from Indiana, where I believe they breed 'em."[20] The visit began with something like a mass celebration. Reporters thronged to see Gorky as he drove through the streets and enjoyed the sights of New York. He particularly liked Grant's tomb and lunch at the Saint Regis Hotel, where he explored the kitchen and wine cellars. "What a marvelous country!" he said, with people "so happy, so conscious of their rights."

With the New York *World*'s announcement that "Gorky Brings Actress Here as Mme. Gorky," the mutual goodwill collapsed. Except for a few independent souls like John Dewey, no one cared that Gorky had separated from his wife long ago or that Russians considered the actress, Mme. Andreyeva, to be his common-law wife. Gorky and Mme. Andreyeva found themselves unceremoniously evicted from their New York hotel and unwelcome in any other. Even Howells and Twain withdrew their support. Twain said that "the ink was wasted" defending Gorky because "laws can be evaded and punishment escaped, but an openly transgressed custom brings sure punishment."[21] Howells laughed about himself and Twain having "a lively time about the Russian novelist and revolutionist" who had "been put out of 3 hotels with the lady who was not his wife." He caught himself and added: "I feel sorry for him; he has suffered enough in his own country. . . . He is a simple soul and a great writer, but he cannot do impossible things."[22]

From England, Wells pronounced Gorky's treatment shameful. "He had come—the Russian peasant in person, out of a terrific confusion of bloodshed, squalor, injustice—to tell America, the land of light and achieved freedom, of all these evil things. . . . And to him she had shown herself no more than the luminous hive of multitudes of base and busy, greedy and childish little men."[23] Americans who had been able to accept the charming assassin Stepniak balked at Mme. Andreyeva. Gorky had been, in Wells' opinion, dined, lunched, photographed, and lynched.

After Wells' visit, Howells—vowing once again to give up politics—looked forward to "gardening and loafing" at Kittery Point.[24] Not all was quiet there. In a great storm, a schooner had smashed against the rocks in Piscataqua Bay, taking Howells' dock with it. The local disaster shrank into perspective on April 18, 1906, when the great earthquake devastated San Francisco and spread fires that burned for days. Five hundred people died. "You have lived through the great Civil War and the detestable Spanish ones," Howells wrote Norton, "but has your experience of life anything in it like this awful San Francisco earthquake?" Reassured by John that the city could be rebuilt, the skeptical father felt shaken, as if he had lived through the calamity himself. It festered in his imagination, a symbol of "all the appallingness of historical disaster."[25]

He had, as he told Joe, begun to grow absentminded as well as irritable about a world that intruded on his peace or buffeted him like the recent storm. At the beginning of 1907 he found himself at odds with Norton over a commemorative address he had agreed to give for Longfellow. Norton wanted the talk to be intimate and anecdotal, whereas Howells preferred something less personal, less troubling, about Longfellow's contribution to American poetry. Norton had the better argument. "When I said two or three months ago that I was delighted that you were going to speak of Longfellow's art, it never occurred to me that you would treat it abstractly." Cambridge, he assured him, "cherishes the memory of the years when you were Longfellow's neighbor, & he & you were friends. You are part of the best Cambridge tradition, & it will not do for you to come as if you were a stranger & a critic of the poet & not one of ourselves."[26] Unfortunately, Howells did feel like a stranger, and he found it difficult to confront the sadness of the past. He swung between the desire to recapture his earlier life—in his autobiographies—and the need to keep busy in an intrusive present. Things that would have been easy for him a few years ago, he told Norton, he now resented as burdens. Maybe annoyed by Norton's calling him a critic, he capitulated, without his usual graciousness; and Norton, with unusual humility, thanked him. Later Howells admitted that Norton had been right and blamed his resistance on "nervous exhaustion" rather than on the distress of commemorating dead friends.[27] Norton and Twain, "so strangely contrasted," had remained the friends he valued most.[28]

In the end, Howells missed the Longfellow commemoration on February 27, 1907, kept away by an attack of flu. Bliss Perry, another *Atlantic* editor, read the essay for him. Alice Longfellow thanked Howells by sending him a bust of Milton that had belonged first to the orator Charles Sumner, then to her father. Its inscription reads "Given to Longfellow / by Charles Sumner / Given to W. D. Howells, 1907 / by Alice Longfellow."[29] Norton took advantage of his absence "to turn a little of the celebration" his friend's way, reminding people that in just two days Howells would turn seventy.

In an ironic twist to his plea that Howells take a more public role, Norton himself resigned from the new Academy of Arts and Letters, over which Howells presided. Originally an honorary group within the National Institute of Arts and Letters, the academy consisted of thirty members chosen by elaborate balloting. A small minority shared Norton's impatience with institutions they regarded as celebrating mediocrity. William James declined to join because he did not approve of the Academy's elitism ("we are in and you are out"). Besides, "other families might think the Jameses' influence too rank and strong." He presumably did not know that his "younger and shallower and vainer brother" had voted twice against his inclusion.[30] Howells, who had been elected on the first balloting, perhaps thought of the Academy as an open meritocracy, though he shared William

James' objection to elitism. In 1917, he would lobby to admit someone who had not published in the past twenty years. "Does a man cease to be an author because he no longer prints?" he asked Hamlin Garland. "I would have every man who has done good things . . . welcomed [underlined three times]."[31] His public visibility, his renown as a novelist and critic, and above all his tact made him the ideal cultural ambassador and president of the academy. He had never stopped advising the public and the governing powers on literature and the arts—the self-appointed role of the academy.

For his seventieth birthday Howells' publishers wanted to honor him with a formal dinner. Illness allowed him to beg off. To Joe he wrote: "I don't know how you feel in your age, but perhaps from our scrambling and impermanent life, things do not seem so settled as they did. . . . I rattle [my work] off at a great rate, but it does not delight me as it used . . . though now and then a little paper seems just as good as anything I ever did."[32] Many readers would have agreed with this assessment. A sign of the public esteem he enjoyed can be seen in a March 1 birthday greeting on the front page of the New York *Sun*. "Please, WILLIAM DEAN HOWELLS, do not look askance if this merely secular entity presumes to make a humbler proffer of its respect and honor; and if your indulgence will permit, of its sincere affection."[33]

If his pattern of incessant work had been set too long ago for him to change now, it gave the comfort of habit. In December he could congratulate himself on the serialization of a collaborative novel aptly titled *The Whole Family*. Borrowing Twain's idea for a book jointly authored by several writers, he had imagined a story spanning three generations. He assigned himself the first chapter, told by the father. Other writers included Elizabeth Stuart Phelps (the Married Daughter), Henry James (the Son-in-Law), and Mary Wilkins Freeman (the Old-Maid Aunt).[34] The plan called for each author to write a chapter, picking up where the previous chapter left off. Freeman almost killed the project by making the old-maid aunt a femme fatale who steals the daughter's fiancé. James enjoyed his chapter so much that he volunteered to finish the book himself, lest succeeding authors ruin his work.

Returning to the courting and marriage plots of *A Foregone Conclusion* or *A Chance Acquaintance*, Howells wanted the book to suggest that any marriage concerns the *whole* family, a topic long on his mind.[35] A few years earlier, Mildred had become engaged to the botanist David Fairchild. Soon after she confided in him, Howells wrote, "That was a great talk we had in the woods. I now think of you as my equal; but you may not think that is much. I also love you dearly, and I am keeping faith with you about the Bird in the bush."[36] To his disappointment, the engagement lasted only three months. Marriage to an international horticulturist meant a great deal of travel or lengthy separations, and Mildred may have worried about leaving her parents for extended periods. If her story about an engaged couple "Turn and Turn About" bears any connection to her own situation, there had been other problems: her need to be right, his to dominate.[37] Initially Howells thought Mildred's behavior "whimsical," not to say irresponsible. Annie's daughter Vevie reported: "He says there is nothing against Mr. F., that she simply changed her mind. I think they feel pretty badly about it, & although of course he did not say so, I think he is provoked at Pilla. He wanted you to know, but said not to mention it to others—just to say that everything was indefinite, if you are asked."[38]

In *Indian Summer* Howells had looked at such matters more philosophically. "A broken engagement *may* be a bad thing in some cases," the minister, Mr. Waters, explains, "but I am inclined to think that it is the very best thing that could happen in most cases where it happens. The evil is done long before; the broken engagement is merely sanative, and so far beneficent."[39] In *A Hazard of New Fortunes,* Basil March goes further: "Why shouldn't we rejoice as much at a nonmarriage as a marriage? When we consider the enormous risks people take in linking their lives together after not half so much thought as goes to an ordinary horse trade, I think we ought to be glad whenever they don't do it. . . . It's offered in fiction as the highest premium for virtue, courage, beauty, learning, and saving human life. We all know it isn't. We know that in reality, marriage is dogcheap, and anybody can have it for the asking—if he keeps asking enough people."[40] Mildred must have heard her father express similar views, and of course she did not need her father's books to know that a cause for celebration in fiction can be harder to bear in life. As a proponent of women's rights, she may have had more general doubts about marriage. John, whom Elinor could still treat like a "small boy" at forty, had shown no inclination to marry either.[41] Howells concluded that both his children would probably remain single.

John proved him wrong. His surprised parents learned—as they prepared to sail for Italy—that he had become engaged to Abby White, a woman eleven years his junior. "A dark beauty, very slim, and about Pilla's height," in Howells' words, Abby was "wonderfully New Yorky, but very intelligent." Her father, Horace White, owned the New York *Evening Post,* which might explain her disposition "to overrate her fatherinlaw's literature."[42] The couple, who had known each other since the previous winter, wanted an early wedding. Howells, with mixed feelings about the changes in all their lives, took pleasure in John's having "some one in his life closer than we can come." In a letter to Aurelia, he called Abby's family respectable and she herself "amiable and good."[43] Her father told Elinor how much he loved John, which Howells said went pretty far for a political economist.[44]

The wedding took place on December 15, 1907, in the chapel John had designed for Columbia University. "The bride and groom bore themselves with great dignity," Howells reported, "and the two families looked on with entire complacency. No one else was present except Abby's old nurse and maid, our colored Charles, a creature built of mauve velvet; the wife of the Bishop Coadjutor who married the pair; John's partner and his wife, two girl friends of Abby's, and Mary Mead. Then the two families went to the bride's late home and gorged themselves, at the wedding breakfast."[45] Annie sent the newlyweds a gift of lace, Aurelia swords that had belonged to her brother Johnny, for whom John was named. Her gesture deeply touched John; he remembered gazing at their crossed blades on the wall of his grandfather's library. Pleased himself, Howells, who had just increased Aurelia's allowance for the winter, sent checks for January and February with a little extra for Christmas.

When I was here before I was only 27; now at 70, I cannot stand up against the wonder that I then took so lightly on the shield of my youth. One should be a cat, here, and have nine lives, at least. If I were, I would give one of them to have you here with me.

—W. D. HOWELLS to Charles Eliot Norton, February 3, 1908

The Howellses celebrated the new year with their delayed trip to Europe, financed by travel letters (paying a hundred dollars apiece) brokered by Harper's to the New York *Sun*. The basis of *Roman Holidays and Others* (1908), the articles follow the travelers from Madeira to Gibraltar, Naples, Genoa, and Rome, where Howells and Elinor had not been in forty-five years. Understandably nostalgic, they sought out their old lodgings at 5 via del Gambero. The street had not changed. Howells stood staring at the house and at the window from which he half expected his younger self to wave. "Who was I, and what was I doing there?" he wondered. "Was I waiting, hanging idly about, to see the Armenian archbishop coming to carry my other self in his red coach to the Sistine Chapel, where we were to hear Pius IX. say mass? I could not tell my proud young double that we were one, and that I was going in the archbishop's red coach as well; he would never have believed it of my gray hairs and sunken figure." He could not ask the man he had been what became of the grocer who used to sell him eggs and oranges and with whom he discussed the weather. The street, the house, the absent grocer made the past both present and dreamlike. "Where really was I? At the window up there, or leaning against the apse of the church opposite? What church was it, anyway? I never knew; I never asked. Why should I insist upon a common identity with a man of twenty-seven to whom my threescore and ten could only bring perplexity, to say the least, and very likely vexation?"[46] Instead of the hoped-for renewal, he left with a sense of disorder.

Because Mildred came down with "the grippe," and Elinor, after her initial excitement, flagged—probably overwhelmed, like her husband, by the passing of years—they were able to do little sightseeing. "But thank goodness," Howells told Aurelia, "I was well enough to go and see the great Norwegian Bjørnstjerne Bjørnson (author of *Arne, The Fishermaiden,* etc.) whom I knew 25 years ago in America" and with whom he had kept in touch. A giant of a man, he recognized Howells at once, and met him "with both hands out, and 'My dear, dear Howells!'"[47] Despite the pleasures and duties— among them a private audience with King Victor Emmanuel to discuss American politics—Howells decided this would be his and Elinor's last trip abroad. Neither new doctors nor a diet of koumiss (fermented mares' milk prescribed for neurasthenics) did the trick. "She is one who looks back," he explained two summers before (forgetting that he himself routinely looked back), "and gains a good deal of discouragement by comparing what she is now with what she was a few years ago, and thinking how she then did things she now does no longer. She is very gloomy at times, and then as gay as ever, but Pilla and I unite in cheering her up when she is down-hearted, and with the change from summer to fall, and then from country to town she will be kept along."[48] Her condition had not improved during their travels. She is "really a very broken person," he wrote home, "and I cannot stand the nervous strain of arriving and departing, except at home, where I know every possible rope."[49] He found himself enraged by little things that should not have mattered, like Aurelia's putting a two-cent stamp on a letter she knew required six.

They stayed in Europe through June 1908, the month his brother Henry died. Aurelia was desolate, and Howells helped the only way he could, by trying to plan for her future. She should live with Annie, or even with Sam's family, he thought, to ease the drain on his own purse. Aurelia, despite her fondness for Sam, dreaded living in his house, and Annie for the moment could not take her. And on and on "round the mulberry bush."[50] The matter ended by default when Aurelia managed a week at Kittery Point before returning to Ottawa to stay with Annie. The problem of Sam did not go away. Appalled that his brother would entertain a marriage proposal from "a widow of forty, with 'bronze gold hair,'" and threatening never to send him another penny, Howells pronounced Sam as unfit for marriage as for work.[51] "I find," he wrote Joe, "that in Columbus in 1859 I was worrying over Sam, as I am worrying over him now at K. P. . . . The whole business of family ties is very curious. He is the sort of man I would last have chosen for a brother, but somehow I can't unchoose him."[52]

From Kittery Point Howells commuted to New York to check on the progress of his twelve-room "studio-apartment" at 130 West Fifty-seventh Street (not far from the old Carnegie Hall and the Art Students League). In a neighborhood already known as an artists' enclave, the building represented a new phase for Howells and for New York in general. Designed by Pollard and Steinam and conceived as a cooperative for artists, it played a role in inducing wealthy New Yorkers to accept apartment living. The building consisted of "an inter-locking scheme of duplex apartments and smaller two- and three-room simplex apartments for rental." It put a premium on light and air, which the owners preferred to "tawdry decoration."[53] Then and now, only well-to-do artists—a Childe Hassam or a Woody Allen—could afford the address. Elegant and spacious, the building offered double studios in each apartment. Howells made his—27 feet long and 22 feet high—into a library. When Mildred assumed responsibility for selecting the wallpapers, her mother, after a summer of painful dentistry, objected to one: "The peacock paper sets my teeth on edge—in spite of Whistler's peacock room example. It looks so painty," she wrote. "Get any paper but peacock. I am so sick of peacock. All New York is in peacock."[54] Perhaps they each remembered the real peacock Howells' parents had sent the children in Cambridge. All these years afterward, Mildred still lived with her parents, and John and his family came to occupy a second-floor apartment in the same building.

That fall Howells returned to a novel that would become *The Vacation of the Kelwyns* (1920). He had put it aside over a decade before, partly because Elinor, who loved *The Undiscovered Country*, had objected to his making use of the Shakers again; it seemed to violate the hospitality they had received during their 1875 stay in Shirley, Massachusetts. Although he vacillated, sending and then recalling parts of the manuscript, Howells deferred to his wife's feelings and withheld the novel during his lifetime. She "had 'absolute pitch' in matters of that sort," he would tell S. Weir Mitchell; "she *could* not fail, and she loved me too much to spare me."[55] To the ailing Charles Norton he mentioned a change in his attitude—from dramatic to contemplative—toward his characters. "In the ten or fifteen years since I began the story I have grown another man."[56]

This would be the last letter he wrote to his old friend. Norton died on October 11, 1908, a little over a week after receiving Howells' letter. The last time the old friends had visited, Howells found him alone in his Cambridge house, "forlorn and very old and broken. It was a sadder time than I have ever had with him," he told James, despite Norton's plucking "up the courage to talk of old times."[57] On the day of the funeral, Sarah Orne Jewett saw but did not get a chance to speak to Howells. Later she wrote that his presence had cheered her. Looking "immensely unfriended," he still made her aware of a "new spring coming" from life's "attachment and affection."[58]

When every few months seemed to bring bad news, Howells faced a disagreeable assignment. His friend and successor at the *Atlantic,* Thomas Bailey Aldrich, had died shortly after the Longfellow memorial, and Lilian Aldrich, the widow, expected Howells' presence at a ceremony in Portsmouth. She had bought her husband's boyhood home, the setting of *The Story of a Bad Boy,* and presented it to the city as a memorial. Twelve hundred people received invitations to the 1908 dedication. Nothing would excuse Howells' absence except his own death. Influenza had kept him, an honorary pallbearer, from the funeral, and he had declined to write a commemorative essay for *Harper's Weekly.* So many of his friends had died that he had begun to feel like a professional "epitapher."

Having agreed to a prominent part in the dedication service, Howells looked forward to seeing his much-alive friend, Mark Twain, who introduced another problem. Twain detested Lilian Aldrich—a "vanity-devoured, detestable woman," and it was anyone's guess how he might behave at the ceremony. "For the protection of the reader," Twain wrote in his *Autobiography,* "I must confess that I am perhaps prejudiced. It is possible that I would never be able to see anything creditable in anything Mrs. Aldrich might do. I conceived an aversion for her the first time I ever saw her."[59] The winter night when Aldrich first brought Twain to his home had been brutally cold, and she, taking Boston's most sought-after guest for a drunkard, refused him even a cup of tea. As Bret Harte could have told her, to injure

Twain was to make an unforgiving enemy.[60] Twain found it hard to decide what he disliked more about her: the false affection or the social climbing. In the difficult days when his finances had collapsed and the average citizen read accounts of Twain's debits and credits in the daily papers, she bragged to him about her wealth. As for travel, first-class accommodations barely improved on steerage; only a suite on the promenade deck would do. She did not care what Worth, the Paris designer, charged for new gowns as long as he saved her the tedious fittings. Twain especially resented the time when she evicted him from her elegant guest quarters to accommodate an ex-governor's marriageable daughter. Even that paled on the day of the dedication, when he watched fellow passengers from Boston—who thought that, as custom demanded, Mrs. Aldrich had paid for their transportation—grope for fares they could ill afford. For Twain, the incident exposed the "undeodorized" Mrs. Aldrich, "and not a whiff of her missing. Here she was, rich, getting all the glory inseparable from the act of indulging in the imposing grandeur of a special train . . . and then stepping aside and leaving her sixty hard-worked bread-winners to pay the bill for her."[61]

Relishing the farce of Mrs. Aldrich's museum, Twain speculated that one person in ten thousand might enter such a place in Boston or New York, but, given the sleepiness of Portsmouth and the discomforts of the train ride, people would have to be paid to view Aldrich's relics. Aside from Lilian Aldrich's own failings, her husband had never been "widely known; his books never attained to a wide circulation; his prose was diffuse, self-conscious and barren of distinction in the matter of style; his fame as a writer of prose is not considerable; his fame as a writer of verse is also very limited." Twain admired Aldrich himself. "When it came to making fun of folly, a silliness, a windy pretense, a wild absurdity, Aldrich the brilliant, Aldrich the sarcastic, Aldrich the merciless, was a master," except, to be sure, in his own home, where he had been mastered by a grasping, snobbish wife who played to his vanity.[62]

Silently kicking and screaming, Twain and Howells appeared dutifully in the Portsmouth Music Hall (Twain, who hated opera, renamed it "the Opera House"), where literary friends of the dead man and curious locals joined the state governor and the mayor. The stage had been decorated with evergreens; orchids and a wreath of laurels adorned the speaker's desk, on loan from the Authors Club. Nearby a small sofa held the collective bulk of Twain and Howells, sitting like impish, elderly versions of Tom Sawyer and Huck Finn. Trapped in the stifling auditorium, they were once again bad boys making the most of absurdity. Howells loved every bit of Twain's iconoclasm, while Twain egged on Howells by his sighs and glances and whispered jokes. Afterward Twain described an interminable string of poets "crawling" to and from the desk, where they bored everyone else to death by reading from prepared texts. Twain remembered Howells' performance as "fine" and brief and "felicitously worded," which meant better than most but more of the same. The "mortuary festival," he wrote, "was devilish; it was hard to endure; there were two sweltering hours of it, but I would not have missed it for twice the heat and exhaustion and Boston and Maine travel it cost, and the cinders I swallowed." He coped with Aldrich's death and the other unspeakable ones with fury and humor. It only added to the fun to imagine Aldrich, the original "bad boy," listening to his own obituaries.[63]

Howells paid dutiful homage (no more, in fact, than Twain) and reverently viewed the odds and ends beatifying Tom Aldrich the child, the schoolboy, and the poet. With others of the select throng, he and Twain shuffled from room to room to admire their friend's first watch and last yacht, his scarf pins, pipes, and pens, a tea caddy that had belonged to Byron, and a flask from Longfellow. Twain probably hoped to spy something of his own so that he could unmask the widow for a thief. Both laughed at the pomp and pretension. Howells wrote to Mildred that he had finished with his "Mrs. Aldriching," a term he felt no need to explain.

While there is nothing like Twain's passion, outrage, or unruly laughter in Howells' account of the Aldrich event, he had the same consciousness of endings and probably felt the same unspoken reminder of a Twain or a Howells memorial in the not-so-distant future. When Emerson died in 1882, Aldrich had said that it was "like having the front rank shot down! We, whatever our stature, stand next."[64]

You have lost a father. Shall I dare tell you of the desolation of an old man who has lost a friend, and finds himself alone in the great world which has now wholly perished around?

— W. D. HOWELLS to Clara Clemens, April 22, 1910

Howells valued the "courage to talk of old times," which he had shared with Norton and still shared with Twain. Twain wanted to read the letters he had written to Howells as a young man before turning them over to his biographer, Albert Paine. Howells warned him that some might remind him of the time when "this night was blackest with you," adding: "*I* can't read them. But I know that *you* can, because you have the best courage of any man, and because as the years pass we like to renew our grief for the lost, which is all we have left of them, and like to feel our hearts bleed again. We pretend otherwise, but this is the truth, and it is strange enough." Another's suffering wrings our heart, he wrote, but we manage to bear our own.[65] Both men bowed to what they could neither bear nor avoid.

Howells and Elinor moved into their elegant cooperative in the second week of January 1909. "It promises well, and the process is in a way rejuvenating." At the new year, he told Norton's daughter Sally that he and Elinor were beginning again in their "72nd year the tale so often told in our lives, of housekeeping in a new place."[66] Nothing made him feel older, or younger, than the birth of a grandson that November—"a beautiful boy, with long eyes, a pretty mouth and forehead, the shapeliest dear little head, covered with as much hair as I have got left, but as dark as mine is white. I can't tell you what a joy he is to granny and me. I suppose his mother and father like him too, but that is mere nature."[67] "Billy" would become a prefix in Howells' lexicon. He went for "Billy-walks" in the morning and had "Billy-talks" when he read to the child at night. On his birthday, the three-month-old Billy "sent" him a card. Howells responded: "It is very sweet of you to send that birthday card, where we are walking toward the sunset together. It is a lovely sunset, but sad, and the night is beyond it. Hold fast to my hand, dear little boy, and keep me with you as long as you can. Some day, I hope not too late, you will know how I love you."[68] How could he not? One of Billy's first memories was of his parents' apartment on Fifty-seventh Street, where he heard someone singing the same three notes over and over and over again. The boy's quaint sayings and his fascination with grandfather's typewriter—along with submarines, dinosaurs, and anatomy (he became a Harvard anthropologist), his circus tricks, love of nature, his rivalries with the brother two years his junior, and his love of books—gave his grandfather, who marveled at the conundrums of blood and families, his greatest joy. Of this grandson he would write: "He is a most interesting child; a little wilful, but good at heart . . . our family tradition is unbroken in him; . . . He was not much struck by there being a King Howell (in Brittany), but he thinks I am a very great man."[69] Howells would leave Billy the gold watch that he and Elinor had bought long ago with earnings from his guidebook to Venice.

For all their ailments (he with colic, she with a broken collarbone), Howells managed to think Elinor and himself pretty young for "oldlings"— young enough for him to contemplate another European trip.[70] With hopes of a cure and plans for a new book, he and Mildred sailed on the *President Grant* for Germany. After a stopover at Leipzig, they arrived in Carlsbad on August 16, 1909. As he repeated the regimen that had helped him a dozen years before, Elinor was to remain at Kittery Point with her sister Mary. From Carlsbad, Howells gossiped to Henry James about a divorced princess who wanted the Vatican to annul her first marriage; to Twain about surgeons recommending that he be pried open with cutlasses; and to both about hipless hussies who exposed so much breast and abdomen that, with so little to conceal, he was sure "they *must* be good."[71] He and Mildred left after three weeks for London and Cholderton, a village near Salisbury, where Elinor had asked them to do some genealogizing.

They returned to New York on October 4 to find Elinor in bed. During their absence and without their knowledge, she had undergone an operation for swollen glands, a condition she had lived with for several decades. When she broke her collarbone the year before, Howells could think only of her sickness, which "filled" his life.[72] His distress probably contributed to her decision to keep the operation secret. Mary Mead made the deception possible by mailing letters to Howells from Kittery Point. In hindsight, given Elinor's frailty and the risks of anesthesia, it seems astounding that any doctor consented to operate. The physical shock to her system had left her, already a nervous woman, close to collapse. Howells wrote Aurelia that Elinor could not use "the arm of her poor wounded side without fancying that she brings on pain. I believe it is really rheumatism, but with the active life she has always led it is in any case a great trial to her. All she can do is to read the papers and talk."[73] In the evenings, they read aloud James' novel *The Tragic Muse.* "My wife no longer cares for many things that used to occupy her," he told James: "*hohheits* [nobility] of all nations, special characters in history, the genealogy of both our families." Well, what *do* you care for? he asked her. Her answer disarmed him. "Well, James, and his way of doing things—and you." She was entranced by *The Tragic Muse,* which he read to her in tiny sections, and hated to reach the end. "Where," she asked, "shall we find anything like it?"[74]

Elinor had long been reclusive. She would perch on the stairs eavesdropping on conversations below, or, if Howells and Mildred attended an event she herself could not attend, she made them describe it in such detail that they often relished the narrative more than the occasion itself. During the summer of 1907 she had improved and was, as Howells said, "like a girl in her early sixties."[75] That year she lived for the morning and evening papers, which carried accounts of Harry Thaw's trial for the murder of Stanford White—her brother's partner in the architectural firm. White had seduced Evelyn Nesbitt, Thaw's showgirl wife. "You may not know it," Howells had told Joe, "but she is really conducting the Thaw trial. . . . She calls all the women concerned by their first names, and she knows just what Jerome and Delmas [the attorneys] are at."[76] Now almost nothing held her attention except James' novels. After *The Tragic Muse, The Bostonians* transported them to those "dear yet terrible" years of their Cambridge life, sparing Elinor for brief moments the distress of her suffering.[77]

Through these same months, Howells seemed to nurse James from afar, reaching out to a man in physical distress and grieving for failures made tangible in the New York edition of his novels, from which his first royalty payment totaled $212.[78] In Howells' opinion, a man of sixty-eight should not and could not rewrite the books he had written at thirty-eight. "Still," he concluded, "he is our best in so many ways that we must always own him so."[79] Gout, angina pectoris, nervousness, stomach and gum problems—these ailments drove James from Lamb House in the summer of 1910 to the baths at Bad Nauheim and on to Zurich, Lucerne, and Geneva. Five years before, he had appeared pathetic in his solitude, "with only the strange unpleasant shades of his own creation for his companions."[80] He had since lost hope. Howells offered the one comfort he could: faith in the greatness of his friend's work. *The Bostonians* ranked as "one of the masterpieces of all fiction. Closely woven, deep, subtle, reaching out into worlds that I did not imagine you knew, and avouching you citizen of the American Cosmos, it is such a novel as the like hasn't been done in our time."[81] Though putting on a brave face for James, he would have agreed with him that 1910 had to be one of "the bitterest, *poisonest* winters" of his life. James' brother William died that fall, and, by a numbing coincidence, Elinor's brother Larkin and her sister Mary died in the same year.

Mark Twain had escaped to Bermuda for his own precarious health. In January, with death much on his mind, Howells found a way to tell Twain how much he meant to him. Alluding to his 1904 honorary degree from Oxford, he wrote: "I shall feel it honor enough, if they put on my tombstone, 'He was born in the same Century and general Section of middle western Country with Dr. S. L. Clemens, Oxon., and had his Degree three Years before him through a Mistake of the University.'"[82] Twain gave this letter to his biographer. "I reckon," he wrote, "this spontaneous outburst from the first critic of the day is good to keep, aint it, Paine?"[83] Twain lived only three more months. He managed to make the journey back to Stormfield, where he died on April 21. "When Clemens died I felt *desolate,* as I never had before; he had been such a world-full friend."[84] Two days later, Howells attended the funeral at New York's Brick Church and accepted the task of writing the memorial essay that became *My Mark Twain* (1910).

Because Twain died first, it fell to Howells to chronicle the friendship—and to sort it out. This would not be for him the chore of the Aldrich memorial, with its "Mrs. Aldriching," or another obituary notice spun out by the "standard epitapher." He wanted it to be as honest as Twain deserved, though he did compromise in a small way. He agreed to delete a reference to Twain's overimbibing after his editor pointed out that half the newspapers in the country would make it a headline and Howells its sponsor. "One may say that he has been a thief, a defaulter, dishonest in every way, worthless, a murderer perhaps," but not a drunk, which was all anyone would remember.[85] Howells saw the wisdom and took the advice.

Few memoirs match the affection—or the majesty—of *My Mark Twain*. Writing as Elinor fought for her life, Howells ended his book with a paean to his friend, or rather a dirge, his personal loss touching on the loss of those he loved and what he had forgotten or mourned in himself. Lamenting that words cannot say enough, that it is vain to "try to give a notion of the intensity with which he pierced to the heart of life, and the breadth of vision with which he compassed the whole world," he describes with sorrow their too-few meetings toward the end of Twain's life, then the image of the man lying in his coffin:

> I looked a moment at the face I knew so well; and it was patient with the patience I had so often seen in it; something of a puzzle, a great silent dignity, an assent to what must be from the depths of a nature whose tragical seriousness broke in the laughter which the unwise took for the whole of him. Emerson, Longfellow, Lowell, Holmes—I knew them all and all the rest of our sages, poets, seers, critics, humorists; they were all like one another and like other literary men; but Clemens was sole, incomparable, the Lincoln of our literature.[86]

In this glowing peroration, with its ring of an older rhetoric, Howells makes his claim for Twain both as his own dearest friend and, if not the greatest American, one who shared that honor with the emancipator of slaves. Always fascinated by faces, he sees in Twain's lifeless features what he calls "the Mystery that makes a man and then leaves him to make himself."[87] The phrase "great silent dignity" defines for him Twain's singularity and separates *his* "Mark Twain" from "all the rest." Even as Longfellow and Lowell and the other giants of his youth seem to merge with one another, Twain stands apart, in death as in life and in his friend's remembering.

The book has been called a great "tall tale" that exaggerates the intimacy between the two men and distorts Howells' more complicated responses to Twain. The exaggeration may be there, reflecting his difficulty doing justice to Twain and to their friendship as he coped with his own great pain. Like Clara Clemens remembering the unstoppable laughter when the two men met, Howells struggles with the emotions of memory. It may also be that *My Mark Twain* betrays a distance between the two that his writing seeks to minimize.[88] Not even he could say with confidence how close they had been or how much closer they might have become. Yet Howells confronts these questions and more. Fully aware that no friendship survives unflawed— or can be explained to others—he speaks about the tests of loyalty and affection underlying any relationship, the "mystery" that brings together and separates people, or prevents, sometimes physically, sometimes in spirit, the intimacy Montaigne describes and mourns in his essay "Of Friendship."

It may be true that when people protest too much, we become wary, even of a soul-searching Montaigne. But the language of love, its terms, freedoms, and taboos change with time and custom. At the least, Howells' tribute gives the lie to his reputation for temperamental coolness, which obviously did not extend to family or friendships. *My Mark Twain* is a meditative work, its subject both a record of friendship and a measuring of his own life. When he looks back on Twain "with an old man's falterings and uncertainties," he veers for a moment from his usual pattern of seeing the best in others and announcing the worst in himself.[89] About Livy Clemens he proudly writes: "She trusted me, I can say with a satisfaction few things now give me, to be her husband's true and cordial advisor, and I was so. I believe I never failed him in this part, though in so many of our enterprises and projects I was false as water through my temperamental love of backing out of any undertaking."[90] The inveterate autobiographer comes to terms with unfinished business, weighing the paradoxes of love and separation, laughter and suffering. In acknowledging Twain as the greater man, he offers a double assessment of his friend and himself—an assessment, of course, that Twain would have rejected. He makes clear that his own end will not shake the earth like the passing of his friend. There have been great spirits on the earth, but just the one, the "sole, incomparable" Mark Twain.

As president of the Academy of Arts and Letters, Howells also bore the responsibility of organizing the Twain memorial service. He hoped to secure well-known speakers representative of different aspects of Twain's life and career: George Ade, an Indiana humorist known for his use of racy vernacular; Booker T. Washington, to represent "a race which Clemens meant well by"; James Whitcomb Riley, "who would sing of him divinely"; and Joseph A. Choate, a reformer who shared Twain's politics.[91] He considered and rejected asking Theodore Roosevelt, reasoning that the former president's energy proved exhausting to anyone over forty, and his dominant personality would cast Twain's in shadow. Besides, Twain had disliked his politics and spoken publicly against them. Thirty-five hundred people attended the event, with a thousand more lined up outside. Presiding over the "nightmare" event had "a killing effect," he told Joe, in that already "deathful year!"[92]

I realize that I have no *home* on earth, now. . . . I suppose it was so with father, for many years, though as he lived nearer and nearer to mother, he was more at peace.

—W. D. HOWELLS to Aurelia H. Howells, November 12, 1911

In February 1910, Elinor began taking morphine for her worsening neuritis. The morphine clouded her mind and slowed down her bodily functions, as her doctors must have known it would. Expenses associated with her care (two nurses, with a doctor visiting night and morning) drove Howells to ask Harper's for an increase in salary, which they immediately granted. At first accepting $1,500 for the essays that became *My Mark Twain,* he later returned it, thinking that he had held up the firm for extra payment. "I never could say what a God-send it was to me when Colonel Harvey offered me the job which I have held so much on my own terms."[93]

March brought a sad birthday, though he felt slightly cheered by the thought that Elinor, who could sit in a wheelchair for a few minutes a day, seemed to be improving. In this period of "deceitful respite," they laughed about his wish to die first.[94] Meanwhile he asked his brothers and sisters for memories of their lives at Eureka Mills, to be used in his novel *New Leaf Mills.* Whether in letters to friends or in this novel based largely on his mother's life, Howells' writing through these months reads like one long epitaph. Asked to give a historian of the Western Reserve some facts about his mother, Howells wrote, "I could not wish to have had another sort of mother; I do not believe there was a better woman. It is more than thirty years since she died, but I still dream of her among the living who visit me in sleep, and I dream of her often."[95] As Elinor, in a mist of morphine, lay confined to bed, his work on the Twain memoir and *New Leaf Mills* brought a little relief. "If we do not work, we die; at least I do," he told a friend.[96]

On May 8, Howells sat down to write his sisters Aurelia and Annie:

> I telegraphed last night. You will know how I feel.
>
> Last Sunday was her birthday, and when I told her she smiled. She smiled a day or two later when I told her something about Billy; she loved him so; but after that first brightening on her birthday, there was after 24 hours, only a peaceful oblivion, which last night at ten minutes to eight became the peace everlasting.
>
> Pity me.
>
> *Your aff'te brother*
> *Will*[97]

Five days later he wrote: "It is over, and what is left of our life must again begin. Elinor lies beside Winny in the Cambridge cemetery."[98] "Boston is a beautiful town and Cambridge a wonder of leaves and grass—but with graves under them everywhere."[99] Such sorrow had been happening since the world began, and nothing alleviated it.[100] He wished that he could expect to meet Elinor in some future place, but "she believed in none," he said, "and how can I?"[101]

In the days following Elinor's death, life seemed a "succession of shocks," above all describing his "experiences to her as if she were still alive," then realizing again that she was gone. "What I am sure of," he wrote Joe in echo of their father, "is that it will all be arranged without consulting me, as my birth was, and her death. . . . I long to sleep and forget myself, I cannot truly say that an eternal sleep would be an evil; only, it seems to me that it would not be fair from the creator to his creature. But then again I submit."[102]

With Elinor in mind, he and Mildred thought they might like to try living in Cambridge for a part of each year, at the Concord Avenue house. They had not realized what the change would involve. The house appeared "dreadful in its ghostliness and ghastliness," and the two trolley lines that now ran by would have made sleep impossible, even if Howells had not already suffered from insomnia.[103] Instead Mildred left her father in Boston, looked after by Annie and Aurelia, before going to Kittery Point to ready the house for everyone's arrival. Howells could not bear to see Elinor's things, and Mildred promised to store them away. Annie and Aurelia were to have a vacation while father and daughter went to England and Wales. John and Abby—the Johnabbies or Jabbies, as Howells called his son and daughter-in-law—had gone to Rome and planned to join them for a fortnight in the Welsh countryside.

Howells arrived in London via Liverpool on June 23. As James closed up Lamb House and prepared to sail to the United States with his brother and sister-in-law, they saw much of one another. To James, Howells admitted that he tried "to be decent, to be humble, to be grateful, and to say that if I must lose my wife it is all that the world can still give in keeping such a daughter as mine. I am ashamed to have her devote herself so to me, but I cannot help it, and I hope she will get some joy and distraction from our being here."[104] He saw old friends like Edmund Gosse and the archaeologist Charles Waldstein; literary men such as James M. Barrie and John Galsworthy; politicians, including the socialist labor leader John Burns and the prime minister, David Lloyd George, whose wife's grandmother was a Howell and possibly a relative.

The spelling of "Howells" continued to amuse the family. That fall, Howells teased Joe—in the spirit in which Lowell had once teased him—for thinking he might have written James Howell's *Familiar Letters.*

> That volume of Howell's (not Howells') Letters was something which I wrote mainly in the Fleet Prison in London about the first third of the 17th century. I had then been with Charles I, when he was Prince of Wales, in Spain where he courted the Spanish Infanta, and I had written delightful letters home from there and afterwards from Venice. I was then known as James Howell; nearly three centuries later, when I had become W. D. Howells, I wrote other delightful letters from Venice. How have you managed to keep yourself ignorant of all this for nearly eighty years? *I* knew about it when I was only seventeen.[105]

Before leaving London, Howells visited the Swedenborg Society, where he saw two tracts his father had written and took pleasure in the fact that each had sold over fifteen thousand copies. He and Mildred joined John and Abby in Tunbridge Wells, Kent, and all four went on to Stratford-on-Avon for "Shakespearings." After touring Scotland and Wales, they sailed back on September 24 from Liverpool.

The return brought no feeling of homecoming. Howells could not live in the apartment Elinor had made her own, and in October he leased it, moving into a hotel.[106] "I suppose Elinor's death has broken my life in two," he wrote Joe in December 1910. "I keep on mechanically at the old things, but the joy is gone out of them. I start to tell her of something, and then I stop! Otherwise there are long times when I forget what has happened."[107] To James, five months later: "I am really very cheerful, and happy as ever in my work. With my children I always talk gayly of their mother, not purposely, but because her life and mine was mostly a life of pleasure in the droll and amusing things. . . . The pang is no longer a sense of hopeless loss, but of wonder that I did not make more of her keenly humorous criticism of all that we knew in common."[108] There were times, he told Joe, in August, "when a man can go to nobody but his wife to tell the things that weigh on him."[109] He pitied his friend James, who had neither wife nor children and had lost the solace of work.

Two words summed up his own coping: "I write."[110] The hardest passage he wrote, in *Years of My Youth,* concerned Elinor. Shown a draft, John objected that it seemed scant tribute to her or her contribution to his father's career. She had, as Howells himself told Grace Norton, made a religion of his ambition. Taken aback by his son's reproach, he tried to explain the dilemma to Elinor's cousin, Laura Mitchell. "In his memoir my father barely noted the fact in regard to my mother, but they were most tenderly and beautifully attached, and from my own widowerhood, I know that he was always thinking of her. If I indulged my feeling, I would not say anything; that part of me is inexpressible."[111] He intended the revised passage to convey by omission the love he felt and the depth of his loss. He speaks about the dances he and Elinor attended in the magical winter when they first met, almost half a century before. "I can only be sure that they summed up the raptures of the time, which was the most memorable of my whole life; for now I met her who was to be my wife. We were married the next year, and she became with her unerring artistic taste and conscience my constant impulse toward reality and sincerity in my work. She was the first to blame and the first to praise, as she was the first to read what I wrote. Forty-seven years we were together here, and then she died."[112]

RECONSIDERATIONS

1911–1917

The nakedness of humanity under its clothes must be sensible to the painter or he will not be able to render the figure, even if it is no more part of the drama than a table or a chair.

—W. D. HOWELLS, Editor's Easy Chair, March 1911

DESPITE BEING MENTIONED HIMSELF as a candidate for the 1911 Nobel Prize in literature, Howells readily agreed to Edith Wharton's appeal that he lead the American effort on behalf of Henry James. The prize of thirty-seven thousand dollars would secure James' independence, and no one deserved it more. Their plan required absolute secrecy. If they failed and James found out, he would be humiliated. Howells' first tactic involved the American Academy's sending a petition of support to the Swedish Academy. The membership demurred. Endorsement of any single member for a foreign honor struck them as improper. Their compromise, a letter signed by individual members, resulted in a mere list of names and, in Howells' opinion, hurt rather than helped James' nomination. He considered resigning his presidency.

Edmund Gosse, who knew several members of the Nobel Committee, had begun the campaign for James in England, with doubts, however, about his chances. Hardly known in Sweden, where American literature ranked as a colonial sideshow, James also seemed to Gosse too retiring. Someone like Rudyard Kipling, winner of the 1907 prize, had stamped his personality on the world's consciousness and in a sense demanded the committee's attention. When the 1911 prize went to the Belgian writer Maurice Maeterlinck, Gosse had the small consolation of being right.

It was not until 1930 that an American writer—Sinclair Lewis—received the Nobel Prize. James might have turned in his grave when Lewis used his acceptance speech to accuse William Dean Howells of exerting a genteel and paralyzing stranglehold on American taste. Lewis had taken offense at Howells' criticism of *The Trail of the Hawk*—a book he stopped reading, picked up again, and, as he told Lewis, *hoped* to finish. Wharton told Lewis to reread Howells, who had made possible his own *Main Street* and *Arrowsmith,* not to mention his Nobel Prize. For a time Lewis must have agreed in spirit, or hedged his bets.[1] He had paid homage by visiting Howells one winter in Saint Augustine, Florida.

After the failure of the Nobel plan, the "wild woman" or "angel of devastation," as James called Wharton, began a new campaign. A month before James' seventieth birthday in April 1913, she sent a "private and confidential" letter to thirty-one American friends—including Henry Adams, S. Weir Mitchell, George Vanderbilt, Charles Scribner, and Howells—proposing that together they should donate "a sum of money (not less than $5,000) for the purchase of a gift, the choice of which would be left to him."[2] When an appalled Henry James got wind of the plan, he ordered her with unusual directness to stop. Wharton blamed Howells:

> It was apparently Mr. Howells who betrayed our confidence, & revealed the plan to Mrs Wm James, who cabled to H.J. that I was 'raising a fund' for his support—apparently giving the impression that I was collecting money to pay his debts or buy him an annuity! He lost his head completely, & cabled to her to put a stop to the plan at once. . . . It always interests me to see the sense of honour of such hyperscrupulous persons as Mr. Howells & Mrs Wm James display itself in its full beauty! The spectacle is profoundly edifying.[3]

As her later reprimand of Lewis suggests, Wharton forgave Howells, though she allowed herself occasional witticisms at his expense. To a friend who could not visit, she would write: "I do feel, you know, that your reasons for *not* coming to see me are a little like those which prevent the elderly married couple in a Howells novel of 450 pages from telling the young girl in their charge that they have heard that the young man who is 'attentive' to her once drove another girl to a quilting party."[4] James certainly bore no grudge against Howells, who evidently never learned of Wharton's pique.

James had returned to the United States in August 1910 with his sister-in-law and brother and stayed on that fall after William James' death. Before returning to England, he spent the first week of July 1911 with Howells in Maine. Once again the heat was unbearable, and both men were lonely. Howells had implored Thomas Perry, recently back from Europe, to spend time with him, promising meats, drinks, and smokes. Perry could cheer him up. Now he had to cheer or try to cheer James.

Bad as he felt about James' visit, Howells looked forward to seeing him and would see him soon again in England. Unable to find a house to rent in York Harbor, Maine, he and Mildred opted for Europe and sailed from Boston on July 25, 1911. They landed in southern Wales and traveled, by way of Pembroke, to Llandrindod Wells. Here, too, it was blisteringly hot, with travel made difficult by a rail strike. Howells, suffering from yet another "very strange" ailment, hoped the Welsh spa would cure him. He wanted to be in the best possible health when he arrived in Spain.

For more than half a century he had dreamed of visiting Cervantes' homeland. The novelist Armando Palacio Valdés arranged to welcome him, and Howells, determined to speak with Valdés in Spanish, had prepared himself by engaging a tutor. When he and Valdés met in Madrid on October 11, they settled on the compromise of their letter writing, his host speaking Spanish, Howells Italian. Valdés surprised him by being, if not an Altrurian, then a blue-eyed, white-haired Asturian, which Howells described as "a species of Spanish New Englander, as from Brattleboro', Vt." Madrid itself turned out, in Jamesian parlance, to be "the real thing, the thing 'as advertised.'" Howells thought the people grave to the point of appearing "Bostonianly" reproving. "You know I love all Latins, for their hollow courtesy and the rest; but the Spaniards will not let you love them as the Italians do; they are not simpaticé, and Pilla frankly hates them—all except our dear novelist Palacio Valdés for whom our whole family has had a devotion for many years."[5]

Howells had reviewed and promoted the work of Valdés as early as 1886. At the time of the Spanish American War, he had written for the British publication *Literature*: "If by any effect of advancing civility we could have treated with Spain for . . . her three novelists Pérez Galdós, Emilia Pardo Bazán, and Armando Palacio Valdés, I, for one American, should have been much more content than I am with Cuba, Puerto Rico, and the Philippines." In fact, the peace commissioners at Paris would have done well paying "Spain $20,000,000 for the last novelist alone." High stakes aside, he himself was ready to trade various American novelists and a poet or two for Valdés.[6] Kind and courteous as Howells and Mildred found Valdés, who escorted them to landscapes described in his novels, Cervantes proved their favorite guide. Mildred remembered stopping at Valladolid "to revere the house of Cervantes" and making "the long journey from Madrid to Cordova slowly and inconveniently by day, that we might see the plains of La Mancha . . . my father could not spare an inch."[7] As always, he intended his experiences to yield a book, this one to be *Familiar Spanish Travels* (1913)—an echo of James Howell's *Familiar Letters*.

From Spain, Howells sent his languishing brother Joe medications and advice, such as baking his cold hands in a lamp-heated box. Back in New York by early December, Howells consulted a doctor, who thought Joe could safely remain abroad until spring. Meanwhile, Joe's wife Eliza begged Howells to come to Turks Island. "I am now an old man," he replied; "I have constant work to do, and I must regard my immediate family. I say all this because I hate to seem selfish. There is no one in the world after my children and Billy so near and dear to me as Joe, and it hurts me deeply to say that under the circumstances I cannot come to you."[8] He made arrangements for Joe's son Willy to bring his father to the United States if necessary and agreed to pay for any modifications to Willy's home in Auburndale, Florida. Entreating his brother to keep up his courage and look facts in the face, he wrote: "You are old and you are sick; Eliza is not so young or so well as she once was, and your place is naturally with your children. This is a hard saying to one who has been so helpful to himself and others as you have always been, but I cannot soften it."[9] He did not want his brother to think of Turks Island as a life sentence. "When you want to leave, leave; and I will meet you in Brooklyn with a taxicab and a fur coat, and tumble you into a warm bed in a steam-heated room with beef steaks and baked potatoes and hot coffee."[10] In February Howells made good on his promise before sending Joe and Eliza on to Florida.

Howells turned seventy-five on March 1, 1912. At the request of New York's superintendent of libraries, he wrote a greeting to be read to children in every public school. "While I would wish you to love America most because it is your home, I would have you love the whole world and think of all the people in it as your countrymen. You will hear people more foolish than wicked say, 'Our country, right or wrong,' but that is a false patriotism and bad Americanism. When our country is wrong she is worse than other countries when they are wrong, for she has more light than other countries, and we somehow ought to make her feel that we are sorry and ashamed for her."[11]

Whether or not Howells had the plight of African Americans in mind here, the occasion of his birthday prompted W. E. B. Du Bois to publish a letter in the *Boston Transcript,* praising his treatment of race in *An Imperative Duty,* his support of Paul Laurence Dunbar and Charles Chesnutt, and his backing of the NAACP, founded in 1909. Du Bois wrote:

> When, on the centenary of Lincoln's birth, a band of earnest men said: We must finish the work of Negro emancipation and break the spiritual bonds that still enslave this people, William Dean Howells was among the first to sign the call. From this call came the National Association for the Advancement of Colored People and the "Crisis Magazine."
>
> For such reasons, America regardless of race and America, all inclusive mother of all races, hastens to honor the man whose hand, and brain has given his land the truest and deepest affection.[12]

On March 2, four hundred guests assembled to honor Howells at Sherry's restaurant on Park Avenue, where Colonel George Harvey of Harper's hosted the dinner. President Taft sat conspicuously on Harvey's left, Howells on his right. Tributes preceded the courses. After Harvey's welcome, Taft jokingly commended political patronage for having sent Howells to Italy and given readers *Venetian Life.* (*He* got the title right.) Dressed in an outmoded cutaway coat and striped trousers, an actor impersonated Howells' own Silas Lapham. Thomas Hardy, H. G. Wells, Anne Thackeray Ritchie, Arnold Bennett, Mrs. Humphry Ward, Arthur Conan Doyle, J. M. Barrie, S. Weir Mitchell, Julian Hawthorne, George W. Cable, Hamlin Garland, and of course Henry James sent their congratulations. Writing to Aurelia about the event, Howells said: "The bitter is thinking how many are not here. . . . But I was pretty unconscious, and the melted butter seemed to be poured over some one else."[13]

Pleased as he was by the more than two hundred letters of congratulations, he was particularly moved by James', which appeared in the *North American Review* (April 1912) as "A Letter to Mr. Howells." James acknowledged that neither Daisy Miller nor Isabel Archer would have come to life without his friend's example. He emphasized Howells' "grasp" of American life. "You knew and felt these things better than I. You had learned them earlier and more intimately . . . stroke by stroke and book by book your work was to become for this exquisite notation of our whole democratic light and shade and give and take in the highest degree *documentary,* so that none other, through all your fine long season, could approach it in value and amplitude . . . [with] a method so easy and so natural, so marked with the personal element of your humor and the play, not less personal, of your sympathy." He wished "to put on record" his "sense of that unfailing, testifying truth" that would keep his friend "from ever being neglected."[14] James' loving tribute is the more poignant for being written at a time when both men knew their reputations to be sagging.

Howells told James he would remember his words when waking at night to self-recriminations. He thought of his own books in a less exalted way:

"Dr. Breen's Practice"—A good piece of work, *I* thought.

"Venetian Life"—The book that made friends with fortune for me.

"A Chance Acquaintance"—The book that made me most friends.

"The Undiscovered Country"—My wife's favorite.

"Indian Summer"—The one I *like* best.

"A Modern Instance"—The strongest.

"Suburban Sketches"—First studies to American Life.

"Their Wedding Journey"—My first attempt to mingle fiction and travel—fiction got the best of it.[15]

The birthday celebration at the elegant Sherry's could not have ended without a speech from Howells himself. He deliberately named luminaries he had known: Hawthorne, Emerson, Whitman, Longfellow, Holmes, Whittier, Bancroft, Motley, Lowell, Bryant, Julia Ward Howe, Artemus Ward, Francis Parkman, and John Fiske. We must honor the lives of such men and women, he said, while recognizing they belonged to another era. "Literature, which was once limited to the cloister, the school, has become more and more of the forum and the market-place. But it is actuated now by as high and noble motives as ever it was in the history of the world. . . . If we have no single name so sovereign as these names I have cited . . . let us remember their limitations and consider the potentiality of the artists who now are and are to be."[16] In the audience sat a cross section of American writers facing their own unpredictable futures: Willa Cather, James Branch Cabell, Margaret Deland, Ellen Glasgow, Mary Austin, Zane Grey, Hutchins Hapgood, Ida Tarbell, and Emily Post. Howells had wanted his brother to be there, but Joe had been too frail to attend.

Joe Howells died on August 10, 1912. The previous September Howells had told him: "I don't believe it'll be known before the judgment who's a failure or who's a success; and I suppose a great many people will be astonished at that time at the estimate put upon different earthly careers. In the meanwhile, if you persuaded me that you were not what is best to be, you would destroy one of my ideals and prevent me forever from bragging of 'my brother Joe,' as I like to do when there's any question of goodness and self-sacrifice."[17] For his grave Joe had requested the stone on which he composed the type for the *Hamilton Intelligencer,* the *Dayton Transcript,* and the *Ashtabula Sentinel.* Howells wrote the epitaph:

To the Memory of Joseph Alexander Howells:
Printer, and then Editor,
He imposed in pages on this stone,
Which he desired should mark
His final resting place,
The types of the Ashtabula Sentinel
From 1851 to 1905.

Howells thought that people ought to have several lives, "not so many as a cat," yet enough "to correct the mistakes of one in another."[18] Whatever disagreements or rivalry there had been between brothers, they had respected and loved one another. Howells knew from childhood that Joe had guarded him against pride and pomposity, laughing about his boyhood diaries, keeping him honest. "As my poor brother used to say of my work," he told his editor, "it is as natural as the toothache."[19] He wished that Joe had lived to read *New Leaf Mills,* which drew on their shared remembering.

———————

Sometimes I think I am left aside by the rush of the new tide, but I take myself by the collar, and ask, "Here! Haven't you had your share?" and so try to behave.

—W. D. HOWELLS to Hamlin Garland, December 19, 1913

Howells wrote his letter to Garland following a year of painful readjustment, not just to his own place in the literary pantheon but to his assessment of himself. He felt compelled to set his proverbial house in order, and for Howells that also meant real houses. In February 1912 he finally let the

Cambridge property go. Built forty years before, it had been the house he and Elinor had planned to live in always. The next February he boarded with Grace Scudder, the widow of his *Atlantic* associate, Horace Scudder, and the friend he had turned to after Winny's death. It took just three minutes to walk from the Scudders' to 3 Concord Avenue. "It is sad, but it isn't so terrible as you would think, and Cambridge is not so ghostly," he wrote Annie in Lausanne, Switzerland.[20] Against his advice, the Fréchettes had retired to Lausanne, taking Aurelia with them. With the people he cared for scattered and "home" nothing more than a shifting idea, he came to accept that "if we live we must die, and if we outlive we must lose."[21]

In 1912, the year he sold the Concord Avenue house, Mildred had a serious breakdown. Too sick to leave her bed, she took many months to recover and six years later still described herself as a "shakey reed."[22] As soon as she regained some strength, they moved back to New York City, where a nurse attended her. The doctor permitted Howells to visit only a few minutes a day, "better not at all." Saddened by the thought that he must in some way be part of her problem, he found the nights "dreadful."[23] Two and a half grains of veronal helped him through the worst times. "The first effect next day is as creative as that of morphine," he told his old friend S. Weir Mitchell, "the second, the sleep of the just."[24]

Though little is known about Mildred's illness, it coincided with unhappiness, or perhaps depression about her life. Before her fortieth birthday in 1911, she had written a poem for *Harper's Monthly* titled "Unsatisfied":

Like some sad child sent supperless to bed
Unsatisfied I sleep among the dead,
For at the feast of Life I sat all day
And saw the shadowy shapes that serve it lay
Before each waiting guest beside me there
Little or great, his own allotted share.
All day I watched them with a patient smile
Telling myself that in a little while
Surely the Host my empty plate would see
And send some portion of the feast to me.
None came; and smiling still lest men might say
I left unfilled—starving I came away.[25]

It was not that Mildred lacked successes. She published in reputable magazines and exhibited her watercolors in Paris. With John's assistance she designed a whist calendar, and with a teacher friend named Mary Burt wrote and illustrated a book for children, *The Literary Primer,* which appeared in 1901. At one time she contemplated an illustrated volume of her poetry. Despite her achievements, however, she had much in common with her father's sisters. She too had lived with a disabled sibling for whom she felt responsible. Elinor recorded her daughter's creating a private world in loneliness and separation: "Today she was saying [about her doll, Hop Sing] 'Poor itt fellow he has only a sister his father & mother died before he was born.' . . . It is shocking though to hear her going through the catechism to him. 'Who made you, Hop Sing?' 'God.' She would not let him see a Japanese tea set the other day, because she said it would make him homesick."[26]

Mildred grew up to assume the daily responsibilities that would have fallen to Elinor had she been well. With the pattern of her devotion set by Winny's death and Elinor's invalidism, she spent long stretches of her life caring for her parents. "It's a terrible mistake," she told her Aunt Annie, "to let one's family discover that one can do things."[27] The hurt cut both ways. What father could bear to read a poem by his daughter titled "Unsatisfied," especially if he also remembered another daughter's lines about learning to forgo and wait?[28] Long before, after the birth of one of Hamlin Garland's daughters, Howells had written: "Children alone render us a reason for being, and they make it richly worthwhile. I have been passionately happy in mine; and if I could have kept them from sorrow, I should count the sorrow from them all gain."[29]

If, as Mildred admitted, she stopped reading what her father wrote in his later years "because he no longer read her poems," both must have felt a diminishing of their intimacy.[30] It would have been difficult for Mildred to confront her father; he blamed himself, and, in blaming, became defensive. He recommended that she read Julia Ward Howe's life of Margaret Fuller, whose father would make him "fade into mere gossamer as a burden."[31] Mildred's frequent travels, particularly her winter sojourns in Bermuda, granted her some respite, even independence, though she relied on her father's resources and enjoyed the attention his reputation brought her. Trapped by good intentions, vanity, habit, and comfort, she lived as Howells' daughter, later the angel at his grave. Like Edmund Stedman's daughter, Mildred would edit her father's letters and protect his literary property from marauding scholars. The winter of 1913 she spent recuperating in Pomfret Center, Connecticut. Howells had persuaded her not to go to Bermuda because her absence made him "homesick."

He had never comfortably lived alone. In Mildred's absence he stayed for short periods with John and his family. By 1912, finding Kittery Point, like the New York cooperative, too evocative of Elinor, he moved to York Harbor, leaving the Kittery Point house to John and Abby. Howells thought of calling his red-shingled "cottage," surrounded by shagbark hickories, Hickory Trees or Tyn-y-Coed, the Welsh for House in the Woods; he decided on Shagbark. It apparently did not disturb him much to return to the same house that he and Elinor had rented eleven summers before.

In July 1913 Howells and Mildred, now in better health, took yet another tour of England. When they came back in early September, the transition to York Harbor did not go as easily as expected. John had contracted a mild case of typhoid fever. A disease that lasted, according to Howells, three weeks in romantic fiction, it ran closer to three months in real life. With Abby nursing John in New York, the children went to live with their aunt and grandfather. But, thanks in part to Thomas Perry, a frequent visitor at Kittery Point and now at York Harbor, Howells came to feel at home in Shagbark. He had even gone to see the Perrys in their Hancock, New Hampshire, retreat, where Lilla Perry, an accomplished artist, painted his portrait. Perry—a descendant of Commodore Perry, who took the "black ships" to Tokyo Bay and opened Japan to Western trade—entered wholly into the spirit of the seacoast. After dinner, in the mellow haze of cigar smoke and coastal fog, Howells would read his latest column, for which he sought Perry's advice, or an early novel that now seemed to him the work of another man.

Howells had Perry to thank for his friendship with Helen Choate Bell, an elderly York Harbor neighbor and fellow Cantabrigian known in her youth for her beauty, always for her wit and support of the arts. He had been too shy to invite her to dinner, but, once persuaded, found her unalarming. Mildred liked her, too, and acquaintance deepened into friendship. By all accounts, "Helen Bell was a great talker, and, like Dr. Johnson, a great friend," with "a thundering great heart" and an endless store of humor. Her father's family came from Hogg Island, the renamed Appledore, of the Isles of Shoals. If their descendants inherited barely "enough to buy their next dinner and a pair of cowhide boots," they had learned to love nature on those stern New England rocks.[32]

Widowed and childless, Bell had a penchant for cats, things French, music, and literature. In 1914, Howells wrote Annie Fields that he and Mildred saw Mrs. Bell "every other day" and that "she lives every other house from us, and our lights look at one another after dark, and we run the same risks of being motored down by day."[33] The rise to Mrs. Bell's house he called Beacon Hill. "It affects my legs in the same way as that bad eminence," he told Perry, alluding both to the steep streets of the neighborhood in Boston and Satan's throne in *Paradise Lost.*[34] When the writer Stuart P. Sherman criticized Henry James for being too refined and out of touch with American life, Howells felt it "a blessing to have Mrs. Bell so near."[35] She saw the world as Howells did, and in times of crisis, such as Mildred's getting blood poisoning, "it is Mrs. Bell who mostly keeps us alive."[36] "What a wonder she is!" he told Perry. "She has just lent me Eckermann *[Conversations with Goethe],* which I had not read yet."[37] Three years before, he had listed his own reading as "Tacitus his annals, Bjornson's plays, R. Browning's The Ring and the Book, Gilbert's opera texts, Tennyson's poems, Ade's sketches, Cellini's autobiog., Stephen's Travels (4 vols.) etc. Also Herrick's capital new novel, Clark's Field."[38] Howells' tribute to the unnamed Helen Bell in "Eighty Years and After" (1919) recalls his earlier praise for Livy Clemens.

> I should like to touch here, but barely touch, the thought of the dear
> and lovely lady which has all this time been in the back of my mind as a
> supreme proof of the highest praise that could be given to an aging woman.
> She was of the finest modernity in her love of the best things in literature
> and life, and could no more err in taste than in truth or the beauty which
> is one with it. She is gone now, who was so lately here in such perfection
> of mind and soul that it seems as if she could never have left us who were
> privileged to share the bounty of her wisdom and grace.[39]

Every few months brought another closing. In 1915, "Dame" Annie Fields died, as did John Piatt, the friend of his youth, who late in life resorted to selling the autographs of his friends, Howells included, and had to depend on charity from the Authors Club. The news of Annie Fields' death came hard. She was, he wrote Mildred, "the last of the world I came into at Boston, for Mrs. Bell was not in it for years later. It was to Mrs. Fields's liking me, Lowell insisted, that I owed my place on the Atlantic. Yes, I am glad we went to see her last summer; I wish I had gone oftener to see her in Boston; but we cannot treat people as if we expected them to die."[40] He seemed to be living life in retrospect, in part because he worked each day on his autobiography, *Years of My Youth,* prompting his memory by rereading old letters and journals and trying to date key incidents of his life. Having grown up near the western frontier of Ohio, he looked back, from just a few decades later, to a boyhood no longer imaginable to contemporary readers for whom the frontier had already come to mean Oregon or California or even a lost dream in American history. And when he wrote about meetings with Holmes, Emerson, or Lowell, it was with the unflinching awareness not only that these writers had disappeared as completely as the literary worlds of Concord and Boston but that his time, too, had passed.

He struggled with what to leave out of the memoir and what to remember to put in. "I always supposed my life in Columbus was most brilliant and joyous," he wrote to John, "but I can't seem to prove it, or that it was even important. I find largely that Tolstoy was right when in trying to furnish reminiscences for his biographer he declared that remembering was Hell: with the little brave and good you recall so much bad and base. However, I shall push on and get it all down, and then cut, cut, cut, until I make myself a respectable figure."[41] He was not above a little showing off. He felt flattered by Tolstoy's remark about bringing together three men he admired—Henry Demarest Lloyd, the author of *Wealth against Commonwealth;* Henry George, the political economist; and William Dean Howells. "Pretty good for a little novelist, what, from the greatest that ever lived?"[42] Howells wanted John to pass the story on to his son Billy.

"Why, man, you don't suppose I *want* to live hereafter? Do you think I'm anxious to have it all over again, or *any* of it?"

—W. D. HOWELLS, "A Difficult Case," 1900

Each of us, as Howells had written in *A Hazard of New Fortunes,* has the making of several characters, with one or another emerging at different times and places.[43] As a young man playing the dutiful son, the flirt, the flatterer, the lover, the journalist, and the businessman, he had watched himself, alert to what he called his "pestilent and unlucky disposition to oblige."[44] Success, or time, brought sharper self-scrutiny along with a reluctance to pretend.

When Sam visited him in York Harbor in the fall of 1914, their physical similarities had led Howells to speculate how easily he might have resembled his brother in temperament, "if some dynamite" had not somehow got into him.[45] Finding Sam more intelligent than he remembered, if pathetically proper, old, and heavy, he could imagine how people wearied of life's immutabilities. "The fear of death, of ceasing to be, continues after the love of living has lessened. That is partly the effect of the absences," he told Aurelia, "which have replaced the familiar presences."[46] He continued to support Sam and Aurelia and also helped the next year to keep Sam's daughter and her ailing husband from want.[47] Though his brother rarely acknowledged his help, Howells felt kindlier toward him—and himself— than he had in years.

The humility of old age had much to do with his awareness of the enigmas of life and whatever lay beyond, as well as of his declining powers, dependence on the children, and sometimes strained relationships with people he would once have charmed. He had recurrent tiffs with his editor at Harper's, Frederick Duneka, who did not hesitate to ask him for cuts or revisions or even a better column at a stage of life when topics came less readily to mind. Used to more deference from editors like Henry Alden, he began to sound defensive about his work and at times boastful. One day he might tell Aurelia, then traveling through Italy, to read *his* books ("there are no books like them for Italy") or that "if I regard quantity, without regarding quality, what I have done is really immense, and if people care to remember me, the future must be amazed at the amount of my production."[48]

Nothing captures better Howells' sense of his life or the state of his reputation in this period than the failure of his handsome library edition. The thirty-five-volume edition he had planned with Colonel Harvey in 1909 was to have included illustrations, indexes, a bibliography, and prefaces. Even as he took pleasure in the preparations, he knew he risked imitating James, whose New York Edition had done so badly.[49] The negotiations got as far as the details of design. Howells pushed for dark, rich, sober cloth in another color than James' maroon, with the title lettered directly on the cloth rather than printed on a paper label. Harvey thought they might incorporate a sprig of peach blossoms, Howells' favorite flower (along with orchids). The project fell through because Houghton Mifflin would not relinquish copyright on the early books that still made money and because Mifflin still resented Howells for selling his books to the highest bidder. Harper's went ahead in 1911 with a first installment of six olive-green volumes: *My Literary Passions, Criticism and Fiction, The Landlord at Lion's Head, A Hazard of New Fortunes, London Films and Certain Delightful English Towns,* and *Literary Friends and Acquaintance* (which included *My Mark Twain*). No further volumes appeared. The Howells edition met the same fate as the James edition and led to the same disheartening realization that his books had lost their broad appeal.

During the summer of 1914 in York Harbor, Howells took up *The Leatherwood God* (1916), a story he had toyed with for years. He wrote Aurelia that he wished he had some more cheerful theme than this "strange episode" in

Ohio history of religious charlatanism and bigamy, but Joseph C. Dylks and his followers would not let him be.[50] He had first read about Dylks when reviewing the *Ohio Valley Historical Series* for the *Atlantic* in 1871, and he included an account of the false prophet in his volume for young people, *Stories of Ohio* (1896). Howells thought of the book not only as his last great novel but also as a belated homage to his father, who had been intrigued by the topic, and to Joe, who had urged him on.[51]

Dylks suggests Howells' version of Hawthorne's shadowy figure in the clearing or Twain's "mysterious stranger."[52] Dressed in a black frock coat and beaver hat, with dark hair hanging to his shoulders—not quite cloven-footed, though snorting like a horse—he appears at a camp meeting in the isolated hamlet of Leatherwood. The opening lines of the novel give a sense of history bordering on fable: "Already in the third decade of the nineteenth century, the settlers in the valley of Leatherwood Creek had opened the primeval forest to their fields of corn and tobacco on the fertile slopes and rich bottomlands." A plant growing along the banks of the river lent its name to the town, and the town passed on the name "to the man who came and went there in mystery and obloquy, and remained lastingly famed in the annals of the region as the Leatherwood God."[53] In a community where camp meetings provide the chief entertainment and outlet for sexual energies, the excitement of Dylks' arrival wins him converts. No one except his former brother-in-law and the wife he deserted recognizes this former neighbor thought to be dead. His presence splits the community into believers and nonbelievers as husbands and wives, parents and children, brothers, and neighbors fight over the question of his divinity. Dylks convinces the faithful to come with him to the New Jerusalem (in fact Philadelphia), where they will live in houses built of diamonds. When he drowns on the trek, he leaves his wife free to live with her second husband, father to her new baby and to the son Dylks had abandoned as an infant. Garland optimistically thought *The Leatherwood God* might be made into a movie—Howells said "picturized"—but nothing came of it.[54] Sinclair Lewis' *Elmer Gantry,* which recalls *The Leatherwood God,* was adapted for the screen and starred Burt Lancaster and Jean Simmons.

Howells' novel emphasizes the dangers of fanaticism in any form. While his letters to friends and family suggest how much his fiction reflected his own aching desire to believe, he could not make the necessary leap of faith. He distrusted the irrational. "Somewhere, tucked away in us, is the longing to know whether we will live again," an atheist lawyer in *The Leatherwood God* explains to a Cambridge visitor, "and the hope that we'll live happy. I've got fun out of that fact in a community where I've had the reputation of an infidel for fifty years; but all along I've felt it in myself."[55] People want, perhaps need, to be deceived. The best in them draws them toward an ideal they have always heard and read about. To Elinor's cousin Laura, who lost a daughter, the "non-believer" Howells recommended Swedenborg's *Heaven and Hell* "as a stupendous piece of imagination if not as revelation." Admitting that he did not accept it himself, he still marveled at "the realistic circumstantiality of his account of the spirit after its arrival in the other world." He credited Aurelia's belief that the spirit world would be a glorified earth, "and our friends will be waiting within, and we shall live very much as we do here, only perfectly instead of imperfectly."[56]

The Leatherwood God has any number of biographical echoes, from John Mulholland's desertion of Victoria Howells to William Cooper Howells' memory of religious factions coming to blows in Mt. Pleasant, Ohio, to Howells' knowledge of the charismatic John Humphrey Noyes and his interest in the Mormon leaders Joseph Smith and Brigham Young. A kind of dystopian counter to his Altrurian letters, the novel reflects ominous developments in Western civilization. He finished it as war ravaged Europe and cut off his sisters, niece, and brother-in-law from home.[57]

The Leatherwood God explores what happens when people longing for illusory wholeness and seeking something greater than themselves fall victim to a diabolic character. Like Thomas Mann in *Tonio Kröger,* Howells had political leaders in mind. He found the equivalent of his Leatherwood God in Germany's Kaiser Wilhelm II. After war broke out it shamed him that the United States did not take a stand against German aggression, the beginnings of which he had observed on his 1897 trip to Carlsbad. In *Their Silver Wedding Journey* (1899), Howells' aging alter ego, Basil March, notes the endless statuary dedicated to German military heroes. In Düsseldorf he interprets the neglect of Heinrich Heine as a sign of anti-Semitism. There "would always be the question," March says, "whether the Jew-born Heine had even a step-fatherland in the Germany he loved so tenderly and mocked so pitilessly."[58] If in 1897 Howells had seen an analogy between Germans' treatment of Jews and Americans' treatment of blacks, he now thought Germany itself the most inhuman and savage of nations, its ruler the incarnation of evil. "I suppose if the Germans won," he wrote Perry in 1914, "God would still rule,—but under the Kaiser! What a loathsome beast, with his piety, the K. is!"[59]

The First World War challenged Howells' every principle. Having protested every war but the Civil War, and thought it improper for the Academy of Arts and Sciences to dismiss Germany's contribution to the arts, he now despised the Germans and resented the opposition to the war by German Americans.[60] To his mind, President Wilson's letter protesting the sinking of the *Lusitania* had at least one effect: it made "German-Americans quiet down or else declare their loyalty. They are worse than the home-Germans," he told his sister, "for those cannot help being what they are. But here there is no despotism to make Germans slaves or friends of their national slavery."[61] Despite his pacifist leanings, he believed war necessary unless Germany was "to rule the world."[62] When he imagined the horror that awaited young soldiers committed to "mutual butchery," he tried to remember "that this war was sent for the salvation of the world, and the destruction of despotism and deviltry."[63]

Like Henry James and Edith Wharton—indeed like most of the anti-German world—he saw World War I as an assault on civilization and wanted to help in any way possible. Under his presidency, the Academy invited the French dramatist Eugène Brieux to speak in 1914. Brieux represented for many Americans his government's defense of humanity.[64] The Academy also sent one hundred thousand dollars to Italy, along with more than a hundred ambulances, presented in the names of American poets. Howells' best service came, as always, from his writing. Not averse to propaganda in the right cause, he wrote a poem for the *North American Review* (November 1916) that ends with harsh speeches from the ghosts of the sunken *Lusitania* and a short story called "A Case of Metaphantasmia" in *Off Duty* (1919), a volume intended specifically for soldiers and sailors.[65] He also contributed to *The Book of the Homeless* (1916), a humanitarian fund-raising effort edited by Edith Wharton with James' help, which included a musical score by Igor Stravinsky; artwork by Max Beerbohm, Jacques-Émile Blanche, John Singer Sargent, Claude Monet, and Walter Gay; and pieces by James, Wharton, John Galsworthy, Joseph Conrad, Rupert Brooke, Paul Claudel, Jean Claudel, Thomas Hardy, and W. B. Yeats.[66]

After having offered his poem "The Little Children," Howells had second thoughts, believing it too crude, too useless. James protested. "'Tear it up' forsooth, my dear Howells! I would as soon tear up—in fact much sooner—every existing page of every member of my own past procession of masterpieces."[67] Howells revised and allowed publication of the poem:

"Suffer little children to come unto me,"
Christ bade, and answering with infernal glee,
Take them!" the arch-fiend scoffed; and from the tottering walls

Of their wrecked homes, and from the cattle's stalls,
And the dogs' kennels, and the cold
Of the waste fields, and from the hapless hold
Of their dead mother's arms, famished and bare,
And maimed by shot and shell,
The master-spirit of hell
Caught them all up, and through the shuddering air
Of the hope-forsaken world
The little ones he hurled;
Mocking that Pity in his pitiless might—
The Anti-Christ of Schrecklichkeit.[68]

Just as the war made him rethink his attitude toward Germany, it forced a reconsideration of his prejudice against the Irish, whose role in the war disturbed him. Irish nationalists seized the moment on Easter Monday 1916 to proclaim independence from Great Britain. In the street fighting that followed, more than five hundred people died, including a hundred British soldiers. The insurrection ended with the surrender and execution of rebel leaders, those William Butler Yeats commemorates in "Easter 1916." Not since the execution of the Chicago anarchists had Howells been so exercised. He sent off a letter to the editor of the *Evening Post*. "Nothing more lamentable in the course of the war now raging has come to pass than this act of bloody vengeance by the British Government. . . . The shooting of the Irish insurrectionists is too much like the shooting of prisoners of war, too much like taking a leaf from the German classic of Schrecklichkeit; and in giving way to her vengeance, England has roused the moral sense of mankind against her."[69]

Any thought of England or English politics brought Henry James painfully to mind. Having for years defended his friend against the sin of literary absenteeism, he had to bear James' decision to renounce American citizenship. To James, recovering from a stroke, he wrote: "Though I have written so seldom to you, you may be sure that no event or circumstance of your life has been unnoted by me, and especially none in this *dies irae,* when you have been moved and stirred so deeply. I am much older than you, and I shall soon be in my eightieth year; but I have always somehow looked to you as my senior in so many important things." James had "greatly and nobly lived for brave as well as beautiful things," Howells said in reference to his becoming a British subject, "and your name and fame are dear to all who honor such things."[70] James died in February 1916, the month of the German attack on Verdun and three months before the Somme, when England suffered sixty thousand casualties on the first day of battle. Howells regretted that his friend had not lived to learn the outcome of the war.

Within a week of James' death, Frederick Duneka approached Howells about a commemorative essay on James. He liked the idea: "No one knew James as I did from the first, and . . . I will write for you such a paper as I wrote about Longfellow, about Lowell, about Holmes." Or, he might have added, about Twain.[71] He felt so enthusiastic about the assignment that he apologized for the "bouncing" tone of his acceptance, until, that is, he realized Duneka wanted the essay immediately. "Oh! oh! Oh! / Oh! oh! oh! / How *could* you ask it?"[72] When Duneka refused to pay him the $2,500 he hoped for, he explained that his price reflected not only market value (Harper's had paid $1,500 for "My Mark Twain") but also the measure of strain it cost him. With the return of grief and remembering, he put the essay aside.

By 1915, Howells had only limited obligations to Harper's. That year the company had been reorganized under the auspices of J. P. Morgan & Co., and, after consulting with John, he had decided to retain the Easy Chair, for $5,000 per year, while leaving himself free to market other work elsewhere. For Mildred he figured his net annual income to be about $14,000 (perhaps $275,000 today), which included royalties on old books ($1,500), rents ($4,500 after losses of about $5,000), stocks, bonds, interest, and dividends. "On this," he told her, "we could live handsomely."[73] The new situation suited Howells, who felt that Duneka had been too busy to push his interests. His idea for a story about a group of retirees living in Saint Augustine had been rejected out of hand. Neither his honorary degree from Princeton in 1912 nor his gold medal from the National Institute of Arts and Letters for fiction in 1915 served to protect him from the whims of editors or the market. "I have no criticism to make of this adverse judgment," he told Duneka; "but I feel that my sort of fiction is no longer desired at Franklin Square, and I think I should be free to offer it elsewhere without having to explain that it has failed of liking there. [He had promised them first refusal.] The present condition seems hampering to both sides, for I do not suppose that the Harper editors like to refuse any more than I like to be refused."[74] *Century* paid him five thousand dollars for the serialization of *The Leatherwood God* and another thousand-dollar advance against book sales at a royalty rate of 20 percent.

Besides postponing the James tribute in the summer of 1916, Howells wrote little else, and what he managed to write he disliked. Nearing his eightieth birthday, he did not suppose that anyone could feel as dog tired as he did. "Age is a cruel thing," he wrote, thinking that his back had begun to bend like his father's, "but I have had a good time and I still have—at times, and when I get fairly launched on my novel I dare say I shall be quite young again."[75]

Mr. Howells may be what people call "old," but he does not write old.

Boston Transcript, March 1, 1917

The invitation announced in capitals "A MEETING [ACTUALLY A DINNER] IN HONOR OF WILLIAM DEAN HOWELLS WHO IS EIGHTY YEARS OLD THIS MONTH, AT THE NATIONAL ARTS CLUB, 15 GRAMERCY PARK, WEDNESDAY, MARCH 21ST, 1917; AT EIGHT-THIRTY O'CLOCK." Hamlin Garland, the farm boy who had thought himself Howells' adopted son, was to preside as chairman of the Joint Committee of Literary Arts, a group that included, in consideration of the range of Howells' activities, the presidents of the Authors' League of America, the Society of American Dramatists, the Authors Club, the Poetry Society of America, the National Arts Club, the MacDowell Club of New York City, and the Pen and Brush Club.

Guests congregated that evening in the mansion once owned by Samuel Tilden, the New York governor who had won the popular vote in the 1876 presidential election before losing the electoral college vote to Howells' friend and Elinor's cousin, Rutherford B. Hayes. In 1906 the National Arts Club had acquired the house—a magnificent example of period Gothic, with elaborate carvings and stained-glass windows—and added a thirteen-story building divided into artists' studios and studies. People chatted in the music and billiard rooms or wandered through the glass-domed library (now a bar open to the public) before settling in for an evening of Howells. The program began with a welcome from Garland and readings from Howells' prose and verse, including three of his poems set to music by the composer Edward MacDowell: "Folksong," "Through the Meadow," and "The Sea." The entertainment climaxed with a performance of Howells' "The Register," a play set in different apartments whose occupants eavesdrop on one another through the heating system.

Howells had tried to persuade Garland to squelch the tribute. "I ought to accomplish that anniversary in peace and quietness, not only for my own sake but that of my long-suffering public," he wrote. "Let the rest be my part of literary history; everything of personal effect has been fully said."[76] Obviously Garland thought otherwise. Friends present and absent offered their congratulations, which Howells referred to as "obituary testimonials."[77] The Kentucky writer John Lane Allen reminded Howells that he might have been born in *his* home state except for the interference of the Ohio River. One artist promised a portrait of Howells' head, "not a Cubist work," she assured him. (Howells wanted to know why people thought he had a big head when "the average hat of the dining room hat rack" came down over his ears.)[78] John Luther Long, who wrote the short story that became the basis for Puccini's *Madame Butterfly,* confessed that he had once purloined a few pages from Howells.

The moment had arrived for Howells to rise and address his well-wishers, to humbly bow and make them feel as if the evening had been a celebration for them rather than for him—as in a way it had. Howells himself had decided not to appear. Though he could legitimately attribute his absence to distance and ill health, he had, by staying away, delivered a gentle snub to premature farewells. Besides, like his friend and mentor, James Lowell, he disliked feasts of self-congratulation, his eightieth birthday not excepted. From Augusta, one of a string of stops in Georgia that winter, he wrote that ten or twenty years hence he hoped to commemorate the birthday of some other octogenarian. His gratitude would remain "life-long," he said, "if not so long as the arts in which we are all, young and old, brethren."[79]

His letter contained a request, perhaps a reminder. For some years now it had become a rite of passage for younger writers to disown his influence. Gertrude Atherton, the glamorous, self-promoting romancer, publicly wished that Howells had never been born. Maybe worse, some younger writers, on the basis of isolated statements in *Criticism and Fiction,* had come to identify him with prudery. From early letters to his brother Johnny or his burning of the "scabrous" materials from Edmund Gosse, Howells had certainly struggled with issues of morality and literature. But while he found the women's page of most newspapers unfit reading for girls (or anyone else), his cautions did not extend to works of guilty passion such as *Anna Karenina* and *Madame Bovary* and *Tess of the D'Urbervilles.* He could not, he said, name "any great modern novel which has not been distinctly moral in effect."[80] Howells, who referred to his contemporaries as literary ghosts, knew his own fate well enough. He and Elinor had tried to prepare themselves for the time when his books no longer sold or, as Henry James put it, for the ravages of "hungry generations" ready to gobble up their elders.[81] The year Howells turned eighty, H. L. Mencken asked if anyone still read him.

Shortly after the birthday celebration, Howells received two different but related books, a sumptuous collection of birthday greetings from Harper & Brothers, bound in red leather, and the first book of criticism devoted solely to his work. He responded graciously to the contributors of the birthday book: "You know without my saying it how I value such a recognition. It is something I might have imagined in some hour of vain-glory when I had my work before me, and I might then have taken it all for praise of myself, but now when I have done my best I must hope and believe that it is to me beyond any reckoning of mine."[82] As for the other book, Alexander Harvey's *William Dean Howells: A Study of the Achievement of a Literary Artist,* it seemed another disturbing way of looking at himself in a mirror. "I saw some one of my name and work powerfully reflected," he wrote, "and being possessed with the doubt whether it was really I. . . . It is perhaps the kind of thing that I might well have coveted on coming back from the dead half a hundred years hence."[83]

Howells did not know what to make of a commentary that extravagantly praised and then scorned him as "the leader of a sissy school of literature."[84] He understood, as his protagonist in *The Son of Royal Langbrith* explains, "that each generation exists to itself, and is so full of its own events that those of the past cannot be livingly transmitted to it; that it divinely refuses the burden which elder sins or sorrows would lay upon it, and that it must do this perhaps as a condition of bearing its own."[85] However ridiculous he thought the aging authors who whooped "it up over their forgotten books," he did not deny himself a small protest.[86] He saw in his own writing little to blame on the one hand and little to praise on the other. When he met Harvey, he was surprised to find him "not the callow ass's colt" he had pictured, "but a staid old horse of fifty."[87]

A few days after playing truant from his birthday party, Howells accepted an invitation from an African American school in Savannah, Georgia, where he was feted by faculty and staff. A contemporary newspaper account described a much smaller man than people expected strolling with the school principal into the dining room and taking his place among the teachers. Around them sat several hundred quiet children trying not to be caught staring. With the teachers, Howells talked of suffrage and federal appointments, paintings and movies. To the one antisuffragist in the group, he described the first big suffrage parade in New York City, in which his sister

Aurelia had marched and Charlotte Perkins Gilman had spoken with passionate conviction. As he began to listen more than he talked, schoolgirl waitresses served him a second helping of what he praised as the best scalloped oysters he had ever tasted. Everything at the school seemed to delight him, from the centerpiece of wildflowers to the menu cards the children had made and decorated with fresh violets. The cards bore lines from Paul Laurence Dunbar and his own *Through the Eye of the Needle*. One person remembered him leaning forward to sniff the violets fastened to his card before appropriating them for his buttonhole. After lunch he was driven through groves of ancient oaks dripping with moss to the Georgia State Industrial College. The president of the college greeted him and told how refugees from the slave ship *Wanderer* had sought shelter on this spot and of the Scotsman who had left an endowment for the college. Following a tour and talk about books, Howells retired to his hotel. "I don't want to go in a bit," he told his host, "and yet I suppose I must. . . . I've had a beautiful time."[88] If he chose dinner in the Georgia school over Sherry's in New York, he allowed himself the right of an eighty-year-old man to do occasionally what he likes.

In the last months of World War I, Howells sent a letter to the head of the Associated Press in Rome. He did not want Italians to believe the German slander that Americans cared nothing for them. Please tell them, he asked, "from an old American author whose literary life began with 'Venetian Life' that he has never known any American who does not love Italy with patriotic fervor and is not proud to claim fellowship with her sons in the ideal Republic which unites all the children of liberty." Italy's cause is *our* cause, he stressed. "I lived through the last four years of Austrians at Venice, and it is the great sorrow of my old age that I see them again on the shores of the Lagoon while it is my strongest hope that I shall live to see them driven from them forever."[89] Widely circulated, his "May-day" letter (May 1, 1918) reached thousands of Italians. "I can't fire a long-range gun into the air, without launching more punk," he wrote his son John. "I don't say that my letter isn't partly punk."[90]

On August 4, 1918, all the bells in Kittery rang to mark an Allied victory at the second battle of the Marne and the defeat of the German advance. The day before, Howells had visited Longfellow's house in Portland, Maine. "I remembered seeing the house 55 years ago, when I first saw the sea, here," he wrote Aurelia. "I was 23 then and now I am 81! But of course I couldn't stay 23, and I am very well, and very happy for an old man."[91] When World War I ended in November 1918, Howells wrote his daughter-in-law, son, and son's sons that they would remember this glorious event, "the greatest thing in the history of mankind," to tell another generation how they felt. He would have preferred to celebrate with them in New York, but it seemed fitting to be in Boston, where the long battle for freedom had begun.[92] The king of Belgium wished to bestow on him the Broad Ribbon of the Order of Leopold II in appreciation of his support of liberty. Howells acknowledged the honor, and refused: kingly prizes seemed improper for the citizen of a republic.

EIGHTY YEARS AND AFTER

1918–1920

> I have long looked forward to settling for life. Now at times I have to
> recognize that there is very little of this life to be settled for, and that
> I ought to be settling myself for the next, if I wish to be settled at all.
>
> —W. D. HOWELLS to William C. Howells, February 19, 1893

H OWELLS ADMIRED the great Renaissance and Venetian painter
Titian, who died at ninety-nine and worked to the last.[1] Except that
he lived a shorter life, so too did Howells. At eighty-one, he accepted a
commission to write an introduction to a new edition of Charles Jarvis'
translation of *Don Quixote* (1923). Making the book available to readers was
a labor of love. Rereading Cervantes awakened the ghost of his younger
self through half-remembered lines or, as he suggests in "Eighty Years and
After," through a half-remembered life.

He had set himself remembering in the autobiographical *Years of My
Youth* in 1916, and he contemplated a sequel titled "Years of My Middle
Life." As always, he made newsprint out of episodes in his past, publishing with John's illustrations an article on historic Saint Augustine and ru-
minating on the wonders of old age. In "Eighty Years and After," he talks
about the cooling of the passions, the failing of memory and energy, and,
most poignantly, the loneliness of old age. He had for any of them "no rem-

edy to suggest, unless it is the rather mechanical device of cultivating the acquaintance of the young. But then the young are so often dull, too, and they cumber one with kindness, more than the old; you do not see *us* helping the old on with their overcoats." Best is to have been "born of a copious generation, with lots of brothers and sisters, and no end of cousins." No doubt thinking of Sam he admits that relatives can be afflictions, especially when they are no fitter for "the kingdom of heaven in their pecuniary circumstances than for the best society of a democratic republic."[2]

Writing as if he speaks to a roomful of seniors, Howells alludes to the dreams that haunt them without talking specifically of his own. Privately he described his dreams to friends and to Mildred. "Last night I had one of my lost-ones dreams," he wrote in 1918. "It was to arrange a second marriage between her [Elinor] and myself! The only second marriage I could imagine for myself. . . . The master-spirit seemed to be an ancient Briton whose name I forget. Mamma arranged getting a motor, which turned into a motor bus full of people to take us through the slush, to the hotel where we were to be married, but forgot the trunks, and we exchanged reproaches. All very realistic and probable."[3] He marvels that the strangeness of old age has brought an even stranger benefit. As a boy he used to pray that he might not die during the night and go to hell for his sins; since his loss of faith in the 1870s and 1880s, he has been free of the fear of damnation, though not of dying. "All along the line of living, from the moment of birth when we first catch our breath and cry out in terror of life, death has set his signals, beckoning us the way which we must go. . . . All the men born of women must die in a destined course; every man of eighty and after must die as certainly as the newborn babe, or often sooner."[4] Without damnation, without hope of salvation, death becomes a merciless though at least simple fact of nature.

In the intervals between his conscious now and the "merciless morrow," Howells lived as he had invariably lived, as fully as possible. He bought a Ford motorcar—instead of a Daimler like Edith Wharton—to commute from York Harbor to Kittery Point. He moved back and forth between Savannah and Saint Augustine, New York and Boston. "I have been seriously considering Boston *versus* New York," he had written in 1915, possibly for the hundredth time. "Three lunches have rather sickened me of the Century, where too many hail me on being so hearty, and wish to clasp me to their shirtfronts. . . . I should say now, a hotel ap't in B., with a month here, for theatres, and two in the South. . . . But, there! I talk as if I were to live forever!"[5] He wrote through the morning and spent the afternoons going for a ride, "grandsonning," or indulging in his new pleasure, the movies.

Motion pictures (still silent), which he regarded as a younger sister to pantomime and vaudeville, intrigued him. Sitting in the cool darkness of the theater, he could hear the audience badgering the villain or encouraging the hero. Howells dismissed critics who denounced these theaters as dens of iniquity. Yet the popularity of movies, their ability to inspire, assuage, or shape public sentiment, struck him with the symbolic force that the Industrial Dynamo struck Henry Adams. As early as 1912, he worried about the commercial and political uses of the movies, and, being Howells, he also imagined movie theaters as classrooms where students could view medical procedures or stroll through an Italian market. In a 1919 Easy Chair column about Arctic explorers using movies to instruct "the Eskimos in the facts of our civilization," he concluded that

> the students of our life would see us flinging ourselves in the saddle, and disappearing in the clouds of desert-dust from our flight or pursuit; or in the riot of ballrooms, which are also barrooms, wildly embraced, with our hats and spurs on, by bare-necked ladies of advanced vampire species . . . [and] in its Eastern episodes the Eskimo would be invited to see us reveling amidst the splendor of our palaces on the Riverside Drive while the skilled burglar ascends or descends by the drain-pipe outside and leans over to peer at our revelry through the casements, and marks his intended loot on our persons.[6]

According to Howells, the filmmaker, like the novelist, owes his or her audience something beyond the surface glitter of life. He speculated about the way in which a "flick," a series of flicks, or a flashing scene creates a different kind of narrative or "graphic history"—and perhaps a new verisimilitude. In his seventies and eighties, cinema inspired him to revisit the whole vexed question of realism. What is the relationship between lived reality and the reality presented in film? he asked. How do flickering images, the product of an editor's selection and arrangement, create meaning and emotion?

Though not always with the same fervor, he still read widely. Books brought him new friends in younger writers like Booth Tarkington, who passed his summers in not-too-distant Kennebunkport. When Thomas Perry had visited in September 1914, Howells invited Tarkington, who had called earlier and found no one home, to meet him. In January 1915 Howells sent a New Year's greeting to praise Tarkington's novel *The Turmoil,* then running in *Harper's Monthly.* "I tremble a little for you," he wrote. "Now you must go on and be of the greatest, or you must retreat and be of the most popular as you have always been."[7] After publication of *The Magnificent Ambersons* (1918), Tarkington's saga of a Midwestern family that Orson Welles made into an acclaimed film, Howells called it "very touching, and tragic, tragic."[8]

Tarkington once mistook a compliment for reproof and wrote to Howells: "It is strange: we think we are aware of your lesson, taking advantage of what you showed us—and then, suddenly perhaps, we get a cold glimpse of what we have done; and we see it smeared with those infernal old stencils! You long ago showed us how ridiculous they are—and we understood—and yet some devil slides them under our hands when we work."[9] Howells not only continued to support younger writers personally; he also published their work in his edition of *The Great Modern American Stories* (1920). Fulfilling the promise of its title, the book included pieces by Mark Twain, Bret Harte, Mary Wilkins Freeman, George Washington Cable, Joel Chandler Harris, Henry James, Ambrose Bierce, Edith Wharton, Theodore Dreiser, Sarah Orne Jewett, and Charlotte Perkins Gilman. Howells proved no less clairvoyant about the direction of poetry, welcoming books by Amy Lowell, Edgar Lee Masters, Conrad Aiken, James Oppenheim, Edwin Arlington Robinson, Vachel Lindsay, and Robert Frost, who returned the compliment—after Howells' death—by praising *his* poetry.

As Howells reached out to writers of past and present generations, he attended to his friend and favorite, Henry James. Once again he picked up the tribute he had contemplated and dropped in the weeks following his friend's death. "Never was a great writer so vulgarly hooted at and rejected by his own people," he wrote Thomas Perry from Savannah in January 1920. "Some time I may blow out about it all."[10] The fragment of the essay he left—"The American James"—begins with their meeting, the walks they took, and the family suppers at Sacramento Street, where James, eating next to nothing, read to his young hosts as they sat around the patent airtight stove in the parlor. More ambivalent is his partial draft of an essay on James' letters, edited by Percy Lubbock, for the Editor's Easy Chair, in which he tries to come to terms with the "oddity" of James' personality and what Howells still strove to understand, the anomaly of James' rejection of American citizenship. Howells' heavily edited manuscripts, the qualifying and amending of his own opinions, suggest the difficulty he had facing his subject. He needed to see James, whom he thought French by temperament and schooling, as "never anything but American."[11] Any other conclusion somehow negated his understanding of the past.

In April, laid low with the influenza that struck millions after the war, Howells received Edwin Markham's new book of poetry, *Gates of Paradise*. "With equal admiration and affection," Markham dedicated his poems "to that lover of justice and brotherhood who has had all the courage to take unprofitable risks—to that writer who wears the greatest honour and bears the greatest name in our contemporary letters—to William Dean Howells." Howells responded that despite "four months of bedridden helplessness . . . I must, I *must*, try to tell you how deeply your words and your book have touched me. I thank, I thank you, I thank you, I thank you. I wish there were words besides these hard little dry words; but such as they are, here they are."[12]

It was the last letter he wrote. Shortly after midnight on May 11, with his children by his side, Howells died in his sleep. He had come three weeks before from Savannah to an apartment at the Saint Hubert Hotel, just doors from his old home at 140 West Fifty-seventh Street. Mildred wrote her aunts: "My father died, very peacefully in his sleep, after he had lain unconscious for nearly a week, and quite free from pain. It was hard to let him go without a word, but blessed that he had no terror or consciousness of the change which he had always dreaded. He would have loved dearly to see you both, but we didn't know how to manage it without alarming him, and we tried to keep everything as normal as we could."[13] He had requested that his body be cremated and his ashes taken to Cambridge.

"What is death?" he had asked and had not been able to answer, except to talk of love. "The best of existence, the home and the children, proceed from it; without it there can be no death and the rending of the dearest ties and the anguish of grief come from love too; the grave as well as the home awaits it."[14] Whatever little we may know, he wrote, "We know that somewhere there is love, the love that welcomed us here, the love that draws us together in our pairing that our children may live, the love in our children which shall see that their fathers and mothers do not die before their time even if their time shall be delayed till eighty and after."[15] Howells speaks here to his belief in the immortality that memory, and memory alone, confers. He imagined generations of Howellses telling the story of the day World War I came to its bittersweet end; of his grandchildren and their grandchildren taking pride in the family's rich history—the three consuls, the editors and architects and advisers to presidents, and his own astonishing career—as in due course they have.

In his effort to prompt or test memory, to commemorate his own past and the lives of parents and siblings, he once returned to Eureka Mills. The son of the present-day miller acted as his guide, following him about and answering questions as best he could. "The epoch of our possession was as remote and as unstoried to him as that of the Mound-Builders," Howells wrote in a draft of *Years of My Youth.*

> A small-frame house, exactly the size and shape of our log-cabin, occupied its site, and he had never even heard that any other house had ever stood there. The "new house," shingled and weather-boarded with black-walnut, had bleached to a silvery gray, and had no longer a trace of its rich brown. He let me go into it, and wander about at will. It was very little, and the small rooms were very low. It was plastered now; it was even papered; but it was not so fine as it used to be. I asked him if there was a graveyard on top of the hill, and he said, yes; an old one; and we went up together to look at it, with stones all fallen, or sunked away, and no memory of the simple, harmless man and his little children whom I had seen laid there, going down with each into the dust, in terror, and desolation of spirit. . . . The boy at my elbow could not make out why the gray-mustached, middle-aged man should care.[16]

If, for the moment, Howells had the sense of imposing on his listener, he believed that someday the boy to whom he spoke would seem as distant to *his* youth as Howells to his. Just possibly he would remember the day and feel for the man wanting to see the house that he too had lived in and to honor the graves of his playmates, dead so many years.

Howells sympathized with the boy who had chores to do or games to play. "When I attempted to tell him that I had once been a boy of his age there, and that this place had been my home, the boy of whom I have here written so freely seemed so much less a part of me than the boy to whom I spoke, that, upon the whole, I had rather a sense of imposing on my listener." Why should this boy care, after all? Why should any of us care about other lives? The answer had long been plain to Howells: because people matter. He stood by this one certainty, not just in his opposition to the Haymarket executions or those of the Irish insurgents, but each day in his life as son, husband, father, friend, and writer. He wrote about the commonplace doings of ordinary people, of the conflict between private citizens and their governments, of historical movements and market forces, of men and women in and out of love, and finally of death itself. His books, at least ten of which stand with the best in American literature, his editorships and influence, the men and women he knew and loved—these also matter.

He could not understand why someone as gifted as his friend Clarence

King would prefer mapping and mining to the writing of fiction. Whether Howells himself began writing because it was all he knew or for the fame it might bring, he continued for the work itself. Through times when he hated it, when pain and sorrow overwhelmed him, he kept on, long after he might have stopped, because he found the world around him perennially as full of life as of books to be written. He gave us his own epitaph when he spoke of working like the pilot on a Mississippi steamboat who reads the landmarks and steers as he must to the end.

ABBREVIATIONS

Alfred	Herrick Memorial Library, Alfred University.
Amherst	William Rutherford Mead (AC 1867) and Olga Kilyeni Mead Papers (Box 1, Folder 14), Archives and Special Collections, Amherst College Library.
Bancroft	The Bancroft Library, University of California, Berkeley.
Columbia	Butler Library, Columbia University.
Houghton	Howells collection, Houghton Library, Harvard University: bMS Am 1743.1 (120), bMS Am 1784.6 (4), bMS Am 1784.9 (39), bMS Am 1784.13 (11), bMS Am 1784.7 (5), bMS Am 1784 (6), bMS Am 1784.1 (17), (19), (67), (72), (78), bMS Am 1784 (597), bMS Am 1784 (301), bMS Am 1784 (79), bMS Am 1784 (87), bMS Am 1784.1 (10), bMS Am 1784.1 (73), bMS Am 1784 (62). Quoted by permission of the Houghton Library.
Huntington	Huntington Library, San Marino, CA. Quoted by permission of the Huntington Library.
Life in Letters	Mildred Howells, *Life in Letters of William Dean Howells,* 2 volumes (Garden City, NY: Doubleday, Doran, 1928).
Life in Ohio	William C. Howells, *Recollections of Life in Ohio from 1813 to 1840* (Gainesville, FL: Scholars' Facsimiles & Reprints, 1963).
SL	*Selected Letters of William Dean Howells,* 6 volumes, edited and annotated by George Arms et al.; textual editors Don L. Cook et al. (Boston: Twayne, 1879–1983).
Twain-Howells Letters	*Mark Twain–Howells Letters: The Correspondence of Samuel L. Clemens and William Dean Howells, 1872–1910,* 2 volumes, ed. Henry Nash Smith and William M. Gibson (Cambridge, MA: Harvard University Press, 1960).

University of Pennsylvania	Charles Patterson Van Pelt Library, University of Pennsylvania.
USC	Edward L. Doheny Memorial Library, University of Southern California.
"Venetian Diary"	Diary covering roughly the first year and a half of Howells' stay in Venice; Houghton Library manuscript.
Virginia	William Dean Howells Collection, Clifton Waller Barrett Library, Special Collections, University of Virginia Library.
WDH	William Dean Howells.
Years	William Dean Howells, *Years of My Youth and Three Essays,* ed. David J. Nordloh (Bloomington: Indiana University Press, 1975).

NOTES

PREFACE

1. Mark Twain, *Life on the Mississippi,* intro. James M. Cox (New York: Penguin, 1984), 286.

2. WDH, *Literary Friends and Acquaintance: A Personal Retrospect of American Authorship,* ed. David F. Hiatt and Edwin H. Cady (Bloomington: Indiana University Press, 1968), 7.

3. Thomas Wentworth Higginson, *Short Studies of American Authors* (Boston: Lee & Shepard, 1880), 36–37.

4. WDH to Homer Saint-Gaudens, *Reminiscences of Augustus Saint-Gaudens* (New York: Century, 1913), 2: 61–62. See also *SL,* 6: 138 n2.

5. WDH, introduction to *Life in Ohio,* vii.

6. Mark Twain to Thomas Bailey Aldrich (and his wife), 21 December 1901, *Twain-Howells Letters,* 2: 723.

7. Mark Twain to WDH, 14 March 1904, *Twain-Howells Letters,* 2: 782; WDH to Twain, 14 February 1904, *SL,* 5: 77–78.

CHAPTER ONE

1. WDH to Elinor M. Howells, 3 June 1871, *SL,* 1: 372–73.

2. WDH to Elinor M. Howells, 3 June 1871, *SL,* 1: 373.

3. WDH to Elinor M. Howells, 3 June 1871, *SL,* 1: 371.

4. WDH to Elinor M. Howells, 7 June 1871 (Houghton).

5. WDH to Elinor M. Howells, 4 June 1871 (Houghton).

6. James A. Garfield to Victoria M. Howells, 9 February 1871 (Alfred).

7. WDH, *Years,* 176.

8. WDH to Elinor M. Howells, 7 June 1871 (Houghton), quoting Keats.

9. The magazine was called *Harper's New Monthly* until 1900, when its name became *Harper's Monthly.* In 1925 it became known as *Harper's.*

10. WDH to Annie T. and Aurelia H. Howells, 13 November 1859, *SL,* 1: 50.

11. For this anecdote, see Calvin Dill Wilson and David Bruce Fitzgerald, "A Day in Howells's 'Boy's Town,'" *New England Magazine* 36 (1907): 297.

12. WDH to Elinor M. Howells, 7 June 1871 (Houghton).

13. William C. Howells, *Life in Ohio,* 47.

14. William C. Howells, untitled manuscript on personal conduct, 35 (Alfred).

15. WDH to Aurelia H. Howells, 30 December 1905, *SL,* 5: 145.

16. WDH to Joseph A. Howells, 29 May 1911, *SL,* 5: 356–57.

17. WDH to Aurelia H. Howells, 16 August 1874, *SL,* 2: 65.

18. Francis P. Weisenburger, *The Passing of the Frontier: 1825–1850,* in *The History of the State of Ohio,* ed. Carl Wittke (Columbus: Ohio State Archaeological and Historical Society, 1900–1938), 3: 4.

19. U.S. Bureau of the Census, *Seventh Census of the United States,* 1850 (Washington, DC: Government Printing Office, 1852), xciv.

20. William C. Howells, *Life in Ohio,* 166.

21. Frank Luther Mott, *A History of American Magazines, 1741–1850* (Cambridge, MA: Harvard University Press, 1930), 1: 341.

22. For information on Mary Dean, see Rodney D. Olsen, *Dancing in Chains: The Youth of William Dean Howells* (New York: New York University Press, 1991), 22–26.

23. WDH, *Years,* 25.

24. WDH, *Years,* 25.

25. Mary D. Howells to Victoria M. Howells, 29? October [1856–57] (Alfred). The date is written as "Thursday Oct I do not know but guess 29th."

26. Mary D. Howells to Aurelia H. Howells, 9 December [1860?] (Alfred).

27. William C. Howells, "Women's Sphere &c," *Dayton Transcript,* 17 January 1850, quoted in Olsen, *Dancing in Chains,* 138.

28. Mary D. Howells to Victoria M. Howells, 29 October [ca. 1856]; quoted in Olsen, *Dancing in Chains,* 129.

29. WDH, *Years,* 20.

30. WDH to Aurelia Howells, 10 September 1905, *SL,* 5: 134–35.

31. WDH, *Years,* 50–51.

32. WDH to Joseph A. Howells, 29 May 1911, *SL,* 5: 356–57.

33. William worked for the *Belmont Chronicle,* the *National Historian,* the *Repository,* and *Webster's Spelling Book* (at $1.50 a day, his highest wage yet), as well as the *Scioto Gazette.*

34. WDH, *Years,* 14. They lived in Hamilton from late February 1840 to May 1849.

35. See WDH, *A Boy's Town* (New York: Harper & Brothers, 1890), 28–32.

36. WDH, *Years,* 31.

37. WDH, *Years,* 21.

38. WDH, *A Boy's Town,* 12.

39. See Edwin H. Cady, *The Road to Realism: The Early Years 1837–1885 of William Dean Howells* (Syracuse, NY: Syracuse University Press, 1956), 16.

40. *The Intelligencer,* 7 December 1848, 1.

41. Quoted in Lester L. Riley, "William Dean Howells as a Boy in Dayton," *High School Times* 16 (October 1896): 7.

42. WDH, *Years,* 35.

43. WDH, *Years,* 31–32.

44. WDH, *A Boy's Town,* 242–43.

45. WDH to Joseph A. Howells, 11 December 1910, *SL,* 5: 338; WDH to Joseph A. Howells, 9 January 1911 (Houghton).

46. *Dayton Transcript,* 22 April 1850, cited in Olsen, *Dancing in Chains,* 40.

47. WDH, *New Leaf Mills* (New York: Harper & Brothers, 1913), 26. For background on Eureka Mills, see William Baker, "Howells: The Heritage of Eureka Mills," *Old Northwest* 9 (Fall 1983): 225–65.

48. WDH, *Years,* 38.

49. WDH, *New Leaf Mills,* 51.

50. WDH, *Years,* 24.

51. Alexander Dean to William C. Howells, 3 November 1857 (Alfred).

52. WDH, *A Boy's Town,* 9.

53. See WDH, *Years,* 51.

CHAPTER TWO

1. WDH, *Years,* 58.

2. WDH, *Years,* 78.

3. WDH, *Years,* 78.

4. WDH, *My Literary Passions: Criticism and Fiction* (New York: Harper & Brothers, 1895), 11.

5. WDH, *My Literary Passions,* 36.

6. WDH, *Impressions and Experiences* (New York: Harper & Brothers, 1909), 25.

7. WDH, "'The Real Diary of a Boy': Howells in Ohio, 1852–1853," ed. Thomas Wortham, *Old Northwest* 10 (1984): 21–22.

8. WDH, *Years,* 63.

9. WDH, *The Early Prose Writings of William Dean Howells, 1853–1861,* ed. Thomas Wortham (Athens: Ohio University Press, 1990), 197.

10. Quoted in Edwin H. Cady, *The Road to Realism: The Early Years 1837–1885 of William Dean Howells* (Syracuse, NY: Syracuse University Press, 1956), 45.

11. WDH, "The Real Diary," 20.

12. Undated newspaper clipping (Houghton).

13. WDH, "The Real Diary," 19–20.

14. WDH, "The Real Diary," 38 n58.

15. WDH, *Years,* 110.

16. WDH to William C. French, 25 July 1852, *SL,* 1: 6.

17. WDH, "The Real Diary," 32.

18. WDH, *Stories of Ohio* (New York: American Book Co., 1897), 259.

19. *Ashtabula Sentinel,* January 8, 1853. See Edwin H. Cady, "William Dean

Howells and the Ashtabula Sentinel," *Ohio State Archaeological and Historical Quarterly* 53 (January/March 1944): 40, 41.

20. In 1850, the sole name of Joshua R. Giddings appeared on the front page; in 1852 and 1853 it was replaced by Fassett and William Cooper Howells, then by J. L. Oliver and Co. In 1854, Joe purchased Oliver's interest in the office, and the *Sentinel* appeared under the firm name of J. A. Howells & Co.

21. WDH, *Years,* 92.

22. WDH, "Conclusion," *Life in Ohio,* 202.

23. WDH to Dune Dean, 9 September 1857, *SL,* 1: 11.

24. WDH to Aurelia H. Howells, 12 May 1895, *SL,* 4: 105.

25. See John W. Crowley, "Dating Howells' Adolescent Breakdown," *Old Northwest* 8 (Spring 1982): 13–22. Also see Cady, *Road to Realism,* 55. Cady settles on 1856 for several reasons: Howells published nothing between 3 April 1856 and 6 January 1857, and he associated his illness with the summer he read Tennyson. As early as 1854, however, his uncle Thomas, the physician, had recommended a water cure for similar symptoms. See Rodney D. Olsen, *Dancing in Chains: The Youth of William Dean Howells* (New York: New York University Press, 1991), 73, 298 n49.

26. *Intelligencer,* 13 August 1841.

27. WDH, *Years,* 79.

28. For a psychoanalytical commentary on related conditions, see Silvano Arieti, *The Parnas* (New York: Basic Books, 1979), 156–58.

29. WDH, *Years,* 80

30. WDH, *My Literary Passions,* 68.

31. WDH, *My Literary Passions,* 113.

32. See Aurelia H. Howells to WDH, 14 June 1915 (Alfred).

33. WDH, *Years,* 99.

34. William C. Howells, untitled manuscript on "character," 12 (Alfred).

35. WDH, *My Literary Passions,* 114–15.

36. WDH, *Early Prose Writings,* 45.

37. Annie Howells Fréchette, "William Dean Howells," *Canadian Bookman* 2 (July 1920): 11.

38. WDH, *Years,* 25.

39. WDH, *Years,* 55.

40. WDH, *Years,* 36.

41. Victoria M. Howells, diary, 30 March 1871 (Alfred).

42. Leon Edel, *Henry James: A Life* (New York: Harper & Row, 1985), 568.

43. WDH, *Years,* 81.

44. WDH to Victoria M. Howells, 2 January 1859, *SL,* 1: 21.

45. William C. Howells, 6 January 1887 (Alfred), quoted in Polly H. Howells, "Mildred Howells as the Father's Daughter," *Harvard Library Bulletin* 5 (Spring 1994): 25.

46. William C. Howells to Joseph Howells, 24 October 1888 (Huntington).

47. Victoria M. Howells, diary, 30 March 1871 (Alfred), quoted in Polly H. Howells, "Mildred Howells," 24 n44.

48. Joseph A. Howells to WDH, 14 July 1903 (Houghton); WDH to Annie Fréchette, 23 October 1891 (Houghton).

49. WDH, *The Undiscovered Country* (Boston: Houghton Mifflin, 1880), 291.

50. Cady, *Road to Realism,* 44.

51. WDH, *A Hazard of New Fortunes,* introduction by Everett Carter; notes to the text and text established by David J. Nordloh (Bloomington: Indiana University Press, 1993), 190.

52. WDH, *Years,* 118.

53. WDH, *Years,* 121–22.

54. WDH, *Years,* 122.

55. WDH, *Years,* 123.

56. WDH to Joseph A. Howells, 10 April 1857, *SL,* 1: 8.

57. Henry Adams, *The Education of Henry Adams,* ed. Ira B. Nadel (New York: Oxford University Press, 1999), 179.

58. WDH, *Years,* 153.

59. WDH to Victoria M. Howells, 27 October 1857, *SL,* 1: 13.

60. WDH to Victoria M. Howells, 27 October 1857, *SL,* 1: 14.

61. WDH to Harvey and Jane Green, 30 November 1857, *SL,* 1: 15.

62. WDH to Dune Dean, 9 September 1857, *SL,* 1: 11.

63. WDH, *Years,* 90–91.

64. WDH, *Early Prose Writings,* 102.

65. *Ashtabula Sentinel,* 17 November 1853.

66. WDH to Dune Dean, 9 September 1857, *SL,* 1: 10.

67. WDH, *Years,* 13.

68. WDH, *Early Prose Writings,* 105.

69. WDH, "The Man of Letters as a Man of Business," *Literature and Life* (New York: Harper & Brothers, 1902), 35.

70. WDH to Victoria M. Howells, 24 August 1859 (Houghton).

71. WDH to Victoria M. Howells, 2 January 1859, *SL,* 1: 22.

72. WDH to Oliver W. Holmes Jr., 24 February 1861, *SL,* 1: 74.

73. WDH, *Years,* 129.

74. WDH, *Years,* 127.

75. WDH, *Early Prose Writings,* 140.

76. WDH, *Years,* 132.

77. "Journal for Vic," 25 April and 1 May 1859, *SL,* 1: 33, 34.

78. WDH to Victoria M. Howells, 25 April and 1 May 1859, *SL,* 1: 33.

79. WDH, *Years,* 145.

80. WDH to Mary D. Howells, 24 May 1859, *SL,* 1: 38–39.

81. WDH to Mary D. Howells, 24 May 1859, *SL,* 1: 38.

82. WDH, *Years,* 168.

83. WDH, *My Literary Passions,* 98.

84. "Journal for Vic," 16–22 May 1859, *SL,* 1: 36.

85. WDH to John J. Piatt, 10 September 1859, *SL,* 1: 41.

CHAPTER THREE

1. WDH to William C. Howells, 26 October 1859, *SL,* 1: 47; WDH to William C. Howells, 20 October 1859, *SL,* 1: 49 n7.

2. Francis P. Weisenburger, *The Passing of the Frontier: 1825–1850,* in *The History of the State of Ohio,* ed. Carl Wittke (Columbus: Ohio State Archaeological and Historical Society, 1900–1938), 3: 475.

3. WDH to William C. Howells, 6 November 1859, *SL,* 1: 49.

4. WDH to William C. Howells, 6 November 1859, *SL,* 1: 48–49.

5. William C. Howells, *Ashtabula Sentinel,* 27 October 1859.

6. *Ashtabula Sentinel,* 10 November 1859. For reaction to Brown's execution, see Eugene Roseboom, *The Civil War Era, 1850–1873,* in *A History of the State of Ohio,* ed. Carl Wittke (Columbus: Ohio State Archaeological and Historical Society, 1944), 4: 358.

7. WDH, *The Early Prose Writings of William Dean Howells, 1853–1861,* ed. Thomas Wortham (Athens: Ohio University Press, 1990), 145.

8. Edwin H. Cady, *The Road to Realism: The Early Years 1837–1885 of William Dean Howells* (Syracuse, NY: Syracuse University Press, 1956), 45.

9. Edwin H. Cady, *Young Howells and John Brown: Episodes in a Radical Education* (Columbus: Ohio State University Press, 1985), 51, 52.

10. John Brown Jr. to WDH, 28 January 1874 (Houghton).

11. WDH to Aurelia H. Howells, 5 March 1861 (Houghton).

12. WDH, "The Pilot's Story," *Atlantic Monthly* 6 (September 1860): 323–25; reprinted in Cady, *Young Howells and John Brown,* 74–79.

13. WDH to William C. Howells, 21 April 1860, *SL,* 1: 54–55.

14. WDH, *Stories of Ohio* (New York: American Book Co., 1897), 226–27.

15. See Cady, *Young Howells and John Brown,* 72; and Robert Price, "The Road to Boston: 1860 Travel Correspondence of William Dean Howells," *Ohio History* 80 (1971): 85–154.

16. Mark Arnold-Foster, "The Incredible Cruelty of the Teutons," *The World War* (New York: American Academy of Arts and Science, 1919), 20.

17. WDH to John J. Piatt, 22 September 1859, *SL,* 1: 44.

18. WDH to John J. Piatt, 5 October 1859, *SL,* 1: 46.

19. See Robert Price, "Young Howells Drafts a 'Life' for Lincoln," *Ohio History* 76 (1976): 232–46.

20. WDH, *Years,* 174–75.

21. WDH, *The Lives and Speeches of Abraham Lincoln and Hannibal Hamlin* (Columbus, OH: Follett, Foster, 1860), 40, 50–51.

22. WDH, *Lincoln*, 94.

23. WDH, "Niagara, First and Last," in *W. D. Howells, Mark Twain, Prof. Nathaniel S. Shaler, and Others, The Niagara Book* (New York: Doubleday, Page, 1901), 255, 259–60.

24. WDH to Brander Matthews, 6 September 1898 (Columbia). Quoted in WDH, *The Kentons,* introduction and notes to the text by George C. Carrington Jr.; text established by Carrington and Ronald Gottesman (Bloomington: Indiana University Press, 1971), xiii.

25. WDH, *Literature and Life* (New York: Harper & Brothers, 1902), iii.

26. Henry James, "The American Scene," *Collected Travel Writings: Great Britain and America,* ed. Richard Howard (New York: Library of America, 1993), 495.

27. James R. Lowell to WDH, 22 September 1869, *Letters of James Russell Lowell,* ed. Charles Eliot Norton (New York: Harper & Brothers, 1894), 2: 44.

28. WDH, *The Minister's Charge, or The Apprenticeship of Lemuel Barker,* introduction and notes to the text by Howard M. Munford; text established by David J. Nordloh and David Kleinman (Bloomington: Indiana University Press, 1978), 3. For a shrewd discussion of Lowell's influence on Howells' politics, see George Arms, "The Literary Background of Howells's Social Criticism," *American Literature* 14 (November 1942): 260–76.

29. Edward Waldo Emerson, *The Early Years of the Saturday Club, 1855–1870* (Freeport, NY: Books for Libraries Press, 1967), 156.

30. Oliver Wendell Holmes, "At the Saturday Club," *The Atlantic Monthly* 54 (July 1884): 68–71.

31. WDH, *Literary Friends and Acquaintance: A Personal Retrospect of American Authorship,* ed. David F. Hiatt and Edwin H. Cady (Bloomington: Indiana University Press, 1968), 40.

32. WDH, *Literary Friends and Acquaintance,* 36.

33. Harriet Prescott Spofford, *A Little Book of Friends* (Boston: Little, Brown, 1916), 6.

34. Spofford, *A Little Book of Friends,* 16–17.

35. W. S. Tryon, *Parnassus Corner: A Life of James T. Fields, Publisher to the Victorians* (Boston: Houghton Mifflin Co., 1963), 297–98.

36. Spofford, *A Little Book of Friends,* 7.

37. Henry James, "Mr. and Mrs. Fields," *Atlantic Monthly* 116 (July 1915): 30. Also see *Literary Criticism: Essays on Literature, American Writers, and English Writers,* ed. Leon Edel (New York: Library of America, 1984), 1: 170.

38. Van Wyck Brooks, *New England: Indian Summer, 1865–1915* (New York: E. P. Dutton, 1940), 375.

39. James R. Lowell to Nathaniel Hawthorne, August 1860, *Letters of James Russell Lowell,* 1: 305–6.

40. WDH, *Years,* 51.

41. WDH, *Literary Friends and Acquaintance,* 58.

42. See WDH, *Literary Friends and Acquaintance,* 61.

43. See Roy Morris Jr., *The Better Angel: Walt Whitman in the Civil War* (New York: Oxford University Press, 2000), 19. Also see Howells' description of him in *Literary Friends and Acquaintance,* 66–67.

44. See Jerome Loving, *Walt Whitman: The Song of Himself* (Berkeley: University of California Press, 1999), 235. Loving notes that William Winter, a regular at Pfaff's, claimed that Howells had never visited the restaurant and saloon.

45. WDH, *Literary Friends and Acquaintance,* 64.

46. WDH, *Literary Friends and Acquaintance,* 67.

47. WDH, *Early Prose Writings,* 180.

48. WDH, *Early Prose Writings,* 152.

49. See Loving, *Walt Whitman,* 304–5.

50. WDH, *Early Prose Writings,* 179.

51. WDH, *Early Prose Writings,* 181.

52. WDH, *Early Prose Writings,* 181.

53. WDH to Edmund C. Stedman, 5 December 1866, *SL,* 1: 271.

54. WDH, *Literary Friends and Acquaintance,* 68.

55. WDH to James T. Fields, 22 August 1860, *SL,* 1: 58.

56. James R. Lowell to WDH, 1 December 1860, *SL,* 1: 61 n4. Also see James R. Lowell to WDH, 1 December 1860, *Letters of James Russell Lowell,* 1: 306–7.

57. WDH to James R. Lowell, 14 December 1860, *SL,* 1: 68.

58. WDH, *Literary Friends and Acquaintance,* 70.

59. WDH to Victoria M. Howells, 24 March 1861, *SL,* 1: 76.

60. WDH, *Early Prose Writings,* 255, 308. For an analysis of the novella, see John W. Crowley, *The Black Heart's Truth: The Early Career of W. D. Howells* (Chapel Hill: University of North Carolina Press, 1985), 45–50.

61. James Russell Lowell to WDH, Cambridge, Monday (Houghton).

62. Scholars have differed about the date of Elinor and Howells' first meeting. Edwin Cady and Ginette de B. Merrill remain the most reliable on the chronology of their relationship. The family letters and diaries make clear that their courtship occurred in the winter of 1860–61. See Merrill, "The Meeting of Elinor Gertrude Mead and Will Howells and Their Courtship," *Old Northwest* 8 (Spring 1982): 23–47.

63. WDH, *Stories of Ohio,* 246.

64. Rutherford B. Hayes to Laura Platt, ca. 20 September 1858, in *Diary and Letters of Rutherford Birchard Hayes,* ed. Charles Richard Williams (Columbus: Ohio State Archaeological and Historical Society, 1922), 1: 531–32.

65. Larkin G. Mead to John R. Miller, 7 November 1847, *John Humphrey*

Noyes, The Putney Community, ed. George Wallingford Noyes (Oneida, NY, n.p.: 1931), 296.

66. WDH to William C. Howells, 15 March 1863, *Life in Letters,* 1: 64.

67. *Twain-Howells Letters,* 2: 658–59.

68. WDH, *A Hazard of New Fortunes,* introduction by Everett Carter; notes to the text and text established by David J. Nordloh (Bloomington: Indiana University Press, 1993), 25–26.

69. WDH, *Years,* 192.

70. WDH, "Venetian Diary," *If Not Literature: Letters of Elinor Mead Howells,* ed. Ginette de B. Merrill and George Arms (Columbus: Ohio State University Press, 1988), 10. The volume includes excerpts from the diaries Elinor and Howells kept in Venice.

71. WDH, *Years,* 150.

72. Marian (Clover) Adams to Robert William Hooper, 20 February 1881, *The Letters of Mrs. Henry Adams, 1865–1883,* ed. Ward Thorn (Boston: Little, Brown, 1936), 268.

73. Isabella Carter to Aurelia H. Howells, 3 May 1863; Merrill, "The Meeting of Elinor and Will," 46 n21.

74. WDH to Victoria M. Howells, 24 March 1861, *SL,* 1: 76.

75. WDH to Mary D. Howells, 5 May 1861, *Life in Letters,* 1: 34.

76. See Charles Edward Crane, *Winter in Vermont* (New York: Alfred A. Knopf, 1941), 57.

77. Larkin Mead to Elinor Mead, November 1855 (Amherst).

78. Larkin Mead to Mary Mead, 20 September 1855 (Amherst).

79. Larkin Mead to Mary Mead, n.d. (Amherst).

80. Larkin Mead to Elinor Mead, 7 September 1855 (Amherst).

81. WDH to Edmund C. Stedman, 16 August 1863, *Life in Letters,* 1: 72.

82. WDH, *The Story of a Play* (New York: Harper & Brothers, 1898), 35.

83. WDH to Mary D. Howells, 26 May 1861, *SL,* 1: 79.

84. WDH, *Years,* 403.

85. WDH to Victoria M. Howells, 21 April 1861, *SL,* 1: 77.

86. WDH, *A Fearful Responsibility and Other Stories* (Boston: James R. Osgood, 1884), 3.

87. WDH to John G. Nicolay, 13 March 1861, *SL,* 1: 74–75.

88. Joshua R. Giddings to W. H. Seward, 24 June 1861; petition to Lincoln, 12 March 1861, National Archives and Records Administration.

89. Moncure Conway to W. H. Seward 14 March 1860, National Archives and Records Administration.

90. Petition to Lincoln, 12 March 1861, National Archives and Records Administration.

91. WDH to John G. Nicolay, 18 June 1861, *SL,* 1: 81 n1.

92. WDH to John Hay, 24 June 1861, *SL,* 1: 80.

93. WDH, *Years,* 204.
94. WDH to Mrs. Samuel M. Smith (Susan), 28 September 1861, *SL,* 1: 84.
95. WDH to Mrs. Samuel M. Smith, 28 September 1861, *SL,* 1: 84.
96. WDH, "Overland to Venice," *Years,* 220.
97. WDH to Mrs. Samuel M. Smith, 28 September 1861, *SL,* 1: 84.

CHAPTER FOUR

1. WDH, "Overland to Venice," *Years,* 209–10.
2. WDH, "Overland to Venice," 209.
3. WDH, "Overland to Venice," 210.
4. WDH to William C. Howells family, 7 December 1861, *SL,* 1: 99.
5. WDH to Victoria M. Howells, 18 January 1862, *SL,* 1: 103.
6. WDH, "Overland to Venice," 218.
7. WDH, "Overland to Venice," 220–21.
8. WDH to William C. Howells family, 7 December 1861, *SL,* 1: 99. He had learned some of this language from earlier travelers to Italy, such as Goethe in *Italian Journeys* and Longfellow in *Outre-Mer: A Pilgrimage beyond the Sea* (1835).
9. WDH, *Venetian Life* (New York: Houghton Mifflin, 1907), 1 :24. The Indiana edition of *Venetian Life* is not yet available. The 1907 edition (published in both one-volume and two-volume formats and reissued in 1908) was the last of Howells' expanded texts. It remains, however, less widely available than the 1891 edition, which includes all but the "Venice Revisited" chapter and a prefatory "To the Reader." We have cited the 1891 version except as noted. See William M. Gibson and George Arms, *A Bibliography of William Dean Howells* (New York: New York Public Library, 1948).
10. Among the countless studies of Venetian history and culture, see Derek Harry Hearder, *Italy: A Short History* (Cambridge: Cambridge University Press, 1990); Paul Ginsborg, *Daniele Manin and the Revolution of 1848* (Cambridge: Cambridge University Press, 1979); Derek Beales, *England and Italy, 1859–60* (London: Thomas Nelson, 1961), along with nineteenth-century studies by Augustus J. C. Hare, Margaret Oliphant, Henry James, and the eminent English historian John Richard Green.
11. WDH, *Venetian Life,* 1: 27.
12. WDH, "Venetian Diary," 17.
13. WDH, "Venetian Diary," 24.
14. "WDH, Recent Literature," *Atlantic Monthly* 29 (May 1872): 278.
15. WDH to Annie T. Howells, 19 December 1861, *SL,* 1: 100–101.
16. WDH, *Venetian Life,* 2: 20–21.
17. WDH to John J. Piatt, 27 January 1862, *SL,* 1: 106–8.
18. WDH to Victoria M. Howells, 26 April 1862, *SL,* 1: 114.

19. WDH, "Venetian Diary," 46.

20. WDH to William C. Howells, undated but late June or early July 1862 (Houghton).

21. WDH, "Venetian Diary," 37.

22. WDH, "Venetian Diary," 4.

23. WDH to William C. Howells, 7 March 1862, *Life in Letters* 1: 53.

24. "Letter of the Secretary of State, Transmitting a Report on the Commercial Relations of the United States with Foreign Nations, for the year ending September 30, 1864" (Washington, DC: Government Printing Office, 1865), 462.

25. WDH, *Years,* 385.

26. WDH, *Years,* 201.

27. See *SL,* 1: 88 n1. See also *Years,* 209.

28. WDH, "Venetian Diary," 2.

29. WDH, "Venetian Diary," 54.

30. WDH to James R. Lowell, 21 August 1864, *SL,* 1: 194.

31. James Woodress, *Howells and Italy* (Durham, NC: Duke University Press, 1952), 21. This book is invaluable for any reader of Howells.

32. WDH, "Venetian Diary," 50.

33. WDH, "Venetian Diary," 51.

34. WDH, "Homesick"; quoted in Ginette de B. Merrill, "The Meeting of Elinor Gertrude Mead and Will Howells and Their Courtship," *Old Northwest* 8 (Spring 1982): 37.

35. WDH, "Venetian Diary," 56.

36. WDH, "Venetian Diary," 38.

37. WDH, "Venetian Diary," 53.

38. WDH, "An Old Venetian Friend," *Years,* 225–26.

39. WDH, "Venetian Diary," 36.

40. WDH, *Venetian Life,* 1: 59.

41. WDH, "A Young Venetian Friend," *Years,* 239.

42. WDH, *Venetian Life,* 2: 191; "A Young Venetian Friend," 240.

43. WDH, "A Young Venetian Friend," 247.

44. *Venetian Life,* 1: 248. See Woodress, *Howells and Italy,* 157–62, on Padre Giacomo and Howells' novels, especially *A Foregone Conclusion.*

45. WDH, "Venetian Diary," 15.

46. WDH, "Venetian Diary," 29.

47. WDH to Richard Hildreth, 22 December 1862, quoted in Merrill, "The Meeting of Elinor and Will," 36.

48. WDH, 7 January 1862, "Venetian Diary," 16.

49. Elinor M. Howells to Lucy Webb Hayes, 17 May 1863, *If Not Literature: Letters of Elinor Mead Howells,* ed. Ginette de B. Merrill and George Arms (Columbus: Ohio State University Press, 1988), 29.

50. WDH to William C. Howells, 22 July 1862, *SL,* 1: 119–20.

51. WDH to William C. Howells, 28 August 1862, *SL*, 1: 123.

52. WDH to Mary D. Howells, 3 August 1862 (Houghton).

53. WDH, "I Talk of Dreams," *Impressions and Experiences* (New York: Harper & Brothers, 1909), 93.

54. William C. Howells to James M. Comly, 19 December 1862; quoted in *If Not Literature,* 12 n3.

55. WDH to Larkin G. Mead Sr., 24 December 1862, *SL*, 1: 132.

56. Ernest Samuels, *Henry Adams* (Cambridge, MA: Harvard University Press, 1989), 58.

57. Henry Adams to John Hay, 24 September 1883, *The Letters of Henry Adams* (Cambridge, MA: Harvard University Press, 1982), 2: 512–13.

58. Elinor M. Howells to Lucy Webb Hayes, 17 May 1863, *If Not Literature,* 30.

59. Elinor M. Howells to William C. Howells, 4 January 1863, *If Not Literature,* 18.

60. Elinor M. Howells to William C. Howells, 4 January 1863, *If Not Literature,* 18; Elinor M. Howells, pocket diary, 24 March 1863, *If Not Literature,* 22.

61. WDH to William C. Howells, 15 March 1863, *Life in Letters,* 1: 64–65. See Rudolf and Clara Kirk, "Howells's Guidebook to Venice," *American Literature* 33 (May 1961): 221–24.

62. WDH to William C. and Mary D. Howells, 17 December 1863, *SL*, 1: 171.

63. Elinor M. Howells, "Venetian Diary," *If Not Literature,* 49–50.

64. Elinor M. Howells, "Venetian Diary," *If Not Literature,* 46.

65. WDH, *Venetian Life,* 1: 156.

66. Quoted in *If Not Literature,* 46 n1.

67. WDH to Mary D. Howells, 26 October 1864 (Houghton).

68. WDH to Mary D. Howells, 28 October 1864, *SL*, 1: 203.

69. Elinor M. Howells to Lucy Webb Hayes, 17 May 1863, *If Not Literature,* 29–30.

70. WDH, *Venetian Life,* 1: 128.

71. Elinor M. Howells to Victoria M. Howells, 17 June 1863, *If Not Literature,* 34.

72. WDH, *Venetian Life,* 1: 132.

73. WDH, *Venetian Life,* 1: 132.

74. WDH to Aurelia H. Howells, 14 January 1861, *SL*, 6: 170–71.

75. WDH, "Venetian Diary," 60.

76. Elinor M. Howells, "Venetian Diary," *If Not Literature,* 36.

77. Elinor M. Howells, "Venetian Diary," *If Not Literature,* 41.

78. Elinor M. Howells to Aurelia H. Howells, 15 May 1863, *If Not Literature,* 26.

79. See James Woodress, "*Venetian Life:* The Background, Composition, Publication, and Reception," *Old Northwest* 8 (1982): 55.

80. WDH to Moncure D. Conway, 22 August 1863, *SL,* 1: 155.

81. Elinor M. Howells, "Venetian Diary," *If Not Literature,* 42 n9.

82. WDH, *Years,* 199–200.

83. WDH to Mary D. Howells, 3 August 1862 (Houghton).

84. WDH, "The Battle in the Clouds," MS #5651 (Virginia).

85. Salmon P. Chase to WDH, 25 August 1863 (Houghton).

86. WDH to Samuel D. Howells, 19 May 1864, *SL,* 1: 189

87. WDH to Mary D. Howells, 3 August 1862 (Houghton).

88. WDH to Samuel D. Howells, 21 September 1864 (Houghton).

89. WDH to Mary D. Howells, 18 June 1863, *SL,* 1: 154.

90. WDH to Joseph A. Howells, *Life in Letters,* 1: 73.

91. WDH, "John Butler Howells" (Alfred).

92. WDH to Moncure D. Conway, 24 March 1863, *SL,* 1: 145.

93. Frank Luther Mott, *A History of American Magazines, 1741–1850* (Cambridge, MA: Harvard University Press, 1930), 3: 258.

94. WDH, *Venetian Life,* 1: 9–10.

95. WDH, *Venetian Life,* 2: 259.

96. Brenda Murphy, *A Realist in the American Theatre* (Athens: Ohio University Press, 1992), 3.

97. WDH, *Venetian Life,* 2: 180–81.

98. Henry James, *Transatlantic Sketches* (Boston: J. R. Osgood, 1875), 86.

99. WDH, *Venetian Life,* 2: 165.

100. Henry James, review of *Italian Journeys, North American Review* (January 1868), in *Literary Reviews and Essays,* ed. Albert Mordell (New Haven, CT: College and University Press, 1957), 199.

101. Journal of Annie T. Howells (Alfred).

102. WDH to W. H. Seward, 1 May 1865 (MS in National Archive); cited in Woodress, *Howells and Italy,* 47.

103. John L. Motley to WDH, 10 June 1865 (Houghton).

104. WDH, *Venetian Life,* 2: 283.

CHAPTER FIVE

1. Elinor M. Howells, "Venetian Diary," 19 December 1864, quoted in *SL,* 1: 204–5 n1.

2. WDH to Aurelia H. Howells, 21 July 1915, *SL,* 6: 83.

3. Thomas Wentworth Higginson, *Old Cambridge* (New York: Macmillan, 1900), 184.

4. WDH [review of De Forest's *Miss Ravenel*], *Selected Literary Criticism,* ed. Ulrich Halfmann, Christoph J. Lohmann, Don L. Cook, David J. Nordloh, Donald Pizer, and Ronald Gottesman (Bloomington: Indiana University Press, 1993), 1: 96.

5. Ellen Glasgow, *A Certain Measure: An Interpretation of Prose Fiction* (New York: Harcourt, Brace and Co., 1943), 12.

6. WDH to William C. Howells, 25 August 1854, *SL,* 1: 197.

7. WDH, *A Chance Acquaintance,* introduction and notes to the text by Jonathan Thomas and David J. Nordloh; text established by Ronald Gottesman, Nordloh, and Thomas (Bloomington: Indiana University Press, 1971), 71.

8. "Real Conversations, I. A Dialogue between William Dean Howells and Hjalmar Hjorth Boyesen," *Interviews with William Dean Howells,* ed. Ulrich Halfmann, *American Literary Realism,* special issue, 6 (Fall 1973): 308.

9. WDH, *Literary Friends and Acquaintance: A Personal Retrospect of American Authorship,* ed. David F. Hiatt and Edwin H. Cady (Bloomington: Indiana University Press, 1968), 105.

10. WDH, *A Modern Instance,* introduction and notes by George N. Bennett (Bloomington: Indiana University Press, 1977), 51.

11. William C. Howells, unpublished manuscript on "character," 35 (Alfred).

12. WDH, "A Personal Retrospect of James Russell Lowell," *Scribner's Magazine* 22 (September 1900): 363.

13. WDH to James R. Lowell, 19 August 1865, *SL,* 1: 224.

14. See Rita K. Gollin, *Annie Adams Fields, Woman of Letters* (Amherst: University of Massachusetts Press, 2002), 35–36.

15. Quoted in Bertram Wyatt-Brown, "Anatomy of a Murder," *New York Review of Books* (24 October 2002): 24. Also see Edward Steers Jr., *Blood on the Moon: The Assassination of Abraham Lincoln* (Lexington: University Press of Kentucky, 2002); and James L. Swanson and Daniel R. Weinberg Jr., *Lincoln's Assassins: Their Trial and Execution* (New York: Arena, 2002).

16. WDH to Elinor M. Howells, 23 September 1865, *SL,* 1: 231.

17. Joseph Richards, first publisher of the *Nation;* quoted in E. L. Doctorow, *The Nation, 1865–1900* (New York: Thunder's Mouth Press, 1990), xi.

18. James J. Storrow Jr., "Publisher's Foreword," *The Nation,* 100th anniversary issue (20 September 1965): 17.

19. WDH to Elinor M. Howells, 17 November 1865, *SL,* 1: 237.

20. Elinor M. Howells to Miss Przemysl, 26 November 1865, *If Not Literature: Letters of Elinor Mead Howells,* ed. Ginette de B. Merrill and George Arms (Columbus: Ohio State University Press, 1988), 90.

21. James R. Lowell to WDH, 17 October 1865 (Houghton), quoted in *SL,* 1: 233 n4.

22. WDH to William C. Howells, 7 May 1871, *SL,* 1: 370.

23. WDH, unsigned review, "Two Men," *Nation* 1 (26 October 1865): 537–38; also see WDH, *Literary Friends and Acquaintance,* 87.

24. WDH, *Literary Friends and Acquaintance,* 111.

25. James T. Fields to WDH, 11 January 1866, *SL,* 1: 247 n1.

26. WDH to William C. Howells, 8 February 1866, *SL,* 1: 250.

27. Elinor M. Howells to William C. Howells, 23 January 1866, *If Not Literature*, 93.

28. Norton's brother-in-law William S. Bullard, a partner in a firm of East India merchants, lent Howells most of the money to buy the house.

29. Edward Waldo Emerson, *The Early Years of the Saturday Club, 1855–1870* (Freeport, NY: Books for Libraries Press, 1967), 75.

30. Edith Wharton, *A Backward Glance* (New York: Charles Scribner's Sons, 1964), 154, 155.

31. On the relationship, see, for example, Clara M. Kirk, "Toward a Theory of Art: A Dialogue between W. D. Howells and C. E. Norton," *New England Quarterly* 36 (1963): 291–319; and Kermit Vanderbilt's response, "Howells and Norton: Some Frustrations of the Biographer," *New England Quarterly* 37 (March 1964): 84–89.

32. John Ruskin, quoted in Kermit Vanderbilt, *Charles Eliot Norton: Apostle of Culture in a Democracy* (Cambridge, MA: Harvard University Press, 1959).

33. WDH to Charles Eliot Norton, 4 July 1880; quoted in Kirk, "Toward a Theory of Art," 310.

34. Quoted in Richard Cary, "William Dean Howells to Thomas Sergeant Perry," *Colby Library Quarterly* 8 (December 1968): 160.

35. WDH to Charles Eliot Norton, 25 May 1866, *SL*, 1: 253.

36. Elinor M. Howells to Aurelia H. Howells, 22 August [1866], *If Not Literature*, 106.

37. Elinor M. Howells to Aurelia H. Howells, 28 May 1866, *If Not Literature*, 99.

38. WDH to Charles Eliot Norton, 25 May 1866, *If Not Literature*, 102 n1.

39. Elinor M. Howells to William C. Howells, 4 February 1866, *If Not Literature*, 95.

40. James Russell Lowell to WDH, 18 May 1869 (Houghton).

41. Diary of Annie Fields, quoted in *If Not Literature*, 106–7 n3.

42. WDH, "Venetian Diary," 2.

43. WDH to William C. Howells, 5 September 1869, *SL*, 1: 338.

44. Laurence Hutton, *Talks in a Library with Laurence Hutton* (New York: G. P. Putnam's Sons, 1905), 416–17, 370–71.

45. Elinor M. Howells to Aurelia H. Howells, 28 May 1866, *If Not Literature*, 98–99.

46. WDH to Charles Eliot Norton, 29 August 1868, *SL*, 1: 298.

47. Thomas Wentworth Higginson began building his house on Buckingham Street in 1880.

48. WDH, *Literary Friends and Acquaintance*, 131; see also Higginson, *Old Cambridge*, 15.

49. See Van Wyck Brooks, *New England: Indian Summer, 1865–1915* (New York: E. P. Dutton, 1940), which relies on Howells' *Literary Friends and Ac-*

quaintance. See also Brooks' study *Howells, His Life and World* (New York: Dutton, 1959).

50. Richard Henry Stoddard, *Recollections, Personal and Literary* (New York: A. S. Barnes, 1903), 275.

51. WDH, *Literary Friends and Acquaintance,* 194.

52. WDH, "The American James," *Life in Letters,* 2: 398. Also see *Letters, Fictions, Lives: Henry James and William Dean Howells,* ed. Michael Anesko (New York: Oxford University Press, 1997), 471–72, which includes a transcription of the MS in the Houghton Library.

53. Wharton, *A Backward Glance,* 178–79.

54. WDH to Edmund C. Stedman, 5 December 1866, *SL,* 1: 271.

55. Henry James, "Mr. and Mrs. James T. Fields," *Literary Criticism,* 1: 170.

56. Houghton MS; Anesko, *Letters, Fictions, Lives,* 472.

57. WDH to Henry James, 26 June 1869, *SL,* 1: 331.

58. Henry James to WDH, 22 June 1873, in Anesko, *Letters, Fictions, Lives,* 83.

59. Anesko, *Letters, Fictions, Lives,* 471.

60. Anesko, *Letters, Fictions, Lives,* 471.

61. Henry Wadsworth Longfellow to WDH, 25 August 1866, *The Letters of Henry Wadsworth Longfellow,* ed. Andrew Hilen (Cambridge, MA: Harvard University Press, 1972), 4: 74.

62. Bayard Taylor to WDH, 26 August 1866, *SL,* 1: 266–67 n3.

63. WDH to James M. Comly, 8 July 1866, *SL,* 1: 263–64.

64. WDH to Charles Eliot Norton, 14 June 1866, *SL,* 1: 258–59.

65. WDH to Melancthon M. Hurd, 13 August 1866, *SL,* 1: 265.

66. Mark Twain, "William Dean Howells," in *Mark Twain: Collected Tales, Sketches, Speeches, and Essays, 1891–1910,* ed. Louis J. Budd (New York: Library of America, 1992), 2: 722.

67. WDH, *Literary Friends and Acquaintance,* 251.

68. James R. Lowell to WDH, 12 May 1869 (Houghton).

69. Henry Adams, *The Education of Henry Adams,* ed. Ira B. Nadel (New York: Oxford University Press, 1999), 257.

70. Henry James to Henry James Sr., 10 May [1869], *Henry James, Selected Letters,* ed. Leon Edel (Cambridge, MA: Harvard University Press, 1987), 1: 36.

71. See Henry James to Thomas S. Perry, 20 September and 15 August 1867, in Edel, *Henry James, Selected Letters,* 1: 77, 72.

72. WDH, *Suburban Sketches* (Boston: Houghton, Mifflin, 1888), 71.

73. WDH, *Suburban Sketches,* 65–66.

74. WDH to William C. Howells, 12 September 1869 (Houghton).

75. WDH, *Suburban Sketches,* 172, 191.

76. Review of *Suburban Sketches, Overland Monthly* (April 1871): 368.

77. WDH to Annie T. Howells, 15 December 1867, *SL,* 1: 290.

78. See Thomas Wentworth Higginson, *Cheerful Yesterdays* (Boston: Houghton Mifflin, 1898), 167.

79. See Vanderbilt, *Charles Eliot Norton,* 90, 264 n64.

80. M. A. DeWolfe Howe, *The Atlantic Monthly and Its Makers* (Westport, CT: Greenwood Press, 1971), 33. See also Martin Green, *The Problem of Boston* (New York: W. W. Norton, 1966), 115–18.

81. For a discussion of the *Atlantic's* early editors and its place in American (and Boston) intellectual life, see Ellery Sedgwick, *The Atlantic Monthly, 1857–1909: Yankee Humanism at High Tide and Ebb* (Amherst: University of Massachusetts Press, 1994).

82. WDH, *Literary Friends and Acquaintance,* 358.

83. James C. Austin, *Fields of the Atlantic Monthly: Letters to an Editor, 1861–1870* (San Marino, CA: The Huntington Library, 1953), 152.

84. WDH, "Professor Barrett Wendell's Notions of American Literature," Selected *Literary Criticism,* 3: 62.

85. WDH to William C. Howells, 7 November 1869 (Houghton).

86. WDH to Annie T. Howells, 3 February 1873 (Houghton); quoted in Edwin H. Cady, *The Road to Realism: The Early Years 1837–1885 of William Dean Howells* (Syracuse, NY: Syracuse University Press, 1956), 133.

87. WDH to Belton O. Townsend, 19 December 187, *SL,* 2: 83.

88. Austin, *Fields of the Atlantic Monthly,* 145.

CHAPTER SIX

1. Annie T. Howells, "To all at home," edited, typed transcript of her letters (Alfred).

2. Annie T. Howells to William C. Howells, 17 March 1867 (Alfred).

3. WDH to Annie T. Howells, 18 June 1867, in *If Not Literature: Letters of Elinor Mead Howells,* ed. Ginette de B. Merrill and George Arms (Columbus: Ohio State University Press, 1988), 112 n6.

4. Elinor M. Howells to Mary D. Howells, [5 May? 1867], *If Not Literature,* 108–9.

5. Typed manuscript of letters of Annie T. Howells, entry for 2 February 1867 (Alfred).

6. Typed manuscript of letters of Annie T. Howells, entry for 18 February 1867 (Alfred).

7. Typed manuscript of letters of Annie T. Howells, entry for 18 February 1867 (Alfred).

8. Victoria M. Howells, 23? February 1870 (Alfred). Included among the James Garfield Papers.

9. Annie T. Howells, diary, entry for 30 March 1867 (Alfred).

10. WDH to Annie T. Howells, 26 September 1867, *SL,* 1: 285–86.

11. John Spencer Clark to WDH, 5 February 1868, *SL,* 1: 293.

12. WDH to William C. Howells family, 6 March 1868, *SL,* 1: 292.

13. WDH to Charles Eliot Norton, 29 August 1868, *SL,* 1: 297.

14. WDH to James M. Comly, 20 October 1868, *SL,* 1: 302–3.

15. WDH to Aurelia H. Howells, 11 March 1895 (Houghton).

16. WDH to Aurelia H. Howells, 1 March 1907 (Houghton).

17. WDH to William C. Howells, 17 January 1869, *SL,* 1: 311.

18. See WDH to William C. Howells, 2 May 1869, *SL,* 1: 325.

19. WDH to James T. Fields, 24 August 1869, *SL,* 1: 336.

20. WDH to Elinor M. Howells, 18 June 1869 (Houghton); 25 June 1869, *If Not Literature,* 128.

21. WDH to William C. Howells, 11 July 1869 (Houghton).

22. WDH to William C. Howells, 26 December 1869, *SL,* 1: 349–50.

23. WDH to James T. Fields, 24 August 1869, *SL,* 1: 334.

24. *Life and Letters of Harriet Beecher Stowe,* ed. Annie Fields (Cambridge, MA: Riverside Press, 1897), 322.

25. James C. Austin, *Fields of the Atlantic Monthly: Letters to an Editor, 1861–1870* (San Marino, CA: The Huntington Library, 1953), 294.

26. Austin, *Fields of the Atlantic Monthly,* 293.

27. WDH to John B. Howells, 1 June 1863, *SL,* 1: 151–52.

28. WDH, *My Literary Passions,* 15.

29. WDH to William C. Howells, 22 September 1869, *SL,* 1: 339–40.

30. See Louis Menand, *The Metaphysical Club* (New York: Farrar, Straus and Giroux, 2001), 203. See also Virginia Harlow, *Thomas Sergeant Perry: A Biography* (Durham, NC: Duke University Press, 1950), 46–47; and M. A. DeWolfe Howe, *Later Years of the Saturday Club, 1870–1920* (Freeport, NY: Books for Library Presses, 1968), 69–77.

31. WDH to Aurelia H. Howells, 7 July 1901, *SL,* 4: 269.

32. WDH to William C. Howells, 25 April 1869 (Houghton). A similar passage occurs in *Suburban Sketches.* In an expurgated passage from *The Rise of Silas Lapham,* the protagonist explains that though it's cruel and people should be ashamed, the price of real estate falls once Jews move into the neighborhood. See George Arms and William M. Gibson, "Silas Lapham, 'Daisy Miller,' and the Jews," *New England Quarterly* 16 (March 1943): 118–22.

33. WDH to Hjalmar Boyesen, 6 September 1872, 28 October 1873 (Virginia).

34. Elinor M. Howells to the Howells family, [20 November 1870], *If Not Literature,* 132.

35. Henry James to Grace Norton, 20 May 1870, *Henry James, Selected Letters,* ed. Leon Edel (Cambridge, MA: Harvard University Press, 1987), 1: 38.

36. WDH, Editor's Easy Chair, *Harper's Monthly* 108 (December 1903): 154.

37. Elinor M. Howells to Victoria and Aurelia H. Howells, [17 March 1871], *If Not Literature,* 137.

38. Elinor M. Howells to Victoria and Aurelia H. Howells, [17 March 1871], *If Not Literature,* 138.

39. WDH to William C. Howells, 26 February 1871 (Houghton).

40. Elinor M. Howells to Victoria and Aurelia H. Howells, [17 March 1871], *If Not Literature,* 138.

41. John Fiske to Ethel Fiske, 2 March 1871, *The Letters of John Fiske,* ed. Ethel Fiske (New York: Macmillan, 1940), 200, quoted in *If Not Literature,* 142.

42. Gary Scharnhorst, "W. D. Howells and Bret Harte: The Star System in Nineteenth-Century American Literature," *Essays in Arts and Science 25* (October 1996): 104.

43. Ellen B. Ballou, *The Building of the House: Houghton Mifflin's Formative Years* (Boston: Houghton Mifflin Co., 1970), 207.

44. WDH to William C. Howells, 12 March 1871 (Houghton).

45. WDH to William C. Howells, 27 November 1870, *SL,* 1: 360.

46. WDH to John S. Hart, 2 July 1871, *SL,* 1: 375.

47. WDH, "Recollections of an *Atlantic* Editorship," *Atlantic Monthly* 100 (November 1907): 594.

48. Ballou, *The Building of the House,* 94.

49. Carl J. Weber, *The Rise and Fall of James Ripley Osgood* (Waterville, ME: Colby College Press, 1959), 66.

50. Clara Marburg Kirk, *W. D. Howells and Art in His Time* (New Brunswick, NJ: Rutgers University Press, 1965), 76–77.

51. WDH, "Recollections of an *Atlantic* Editorship," 595.

52. Ellery Sedgwick, *The Atlantic Monthly, 1857–1909: Yankee Humanism at High Tide and Ebb* (Amherst: University of Massachusetts Press, 1994), 125.

53. See John J. McCusker, "How Much Is That in Real Money? A Historical Price Index for Use as a Deflator of Money Values in the Economy of the U.S.," *Proceedings of the American Antiquarian Society* 101, part 2 (Worcester, MA: AAS, 1992): 332.

54. Elinor M. Howells to Annie T. Howells, 23 November 1871, *If Not Literature,* 144.

55. See M. A. DeWolfe Howe, *The Atlantic Monthly and Its Makers* (Westport, CT: Greenwood Press, 1971), 33.

56. Thomas Wentworth Higginson to WDH, 30 September 1871, *SL,* 1: 402.

57. Annie T. Fields, *Memories of a Hostess* (Boston: *Atlantic Monthly* Press, 1922), 80.

58. Henry James to Charles Eliot Norton, 9 August 1871, in *Henry James Letters,* ed. Leon Edel (Cambridge, MA: Harvard University Press, 1974–1984), 1: 262.

59. Henry James to James T. Fields, 15 November 1870, in Edel, *Henry James Letters,* 1: 249. See Michael Anesko's fine discussion in "A Season in Cambridge," 11–22.

60. Howells memorabilia, newspaper clippings (Alfred).

61. Annie T. Howells to WDH, 17 October 1877 (Alfred).

62. Warren S. Tryon, *Parnassus Corner: A Life of James T. Fields* (Boston: Houghton Mifflin Co., 1963), 85.

63. Austin, *Fields of the Atlantic Monthly,* 32.

64. James Russell Lowell to WDH, 19 January 1890 (Houghton).

65. *Thomas Wentworth Higginson, Short Studies of American Authors* (Boston: Lee & Shepard, 1880), 32.

66. WDH to Edmund C. Stedman, 12 December 1876, *SL,* 2: 141.

67. WDH to Mark Twain, 10 October 1876, *Twain-Howells Letters,* 1: 156–57.

68. Ellery Sedgwick, *The Atlantic Monthly, 1857–1909: Yankee Humanism at High Tide and Ebb* (Amherst: University of Massachusetts Press, 1994), 38.

69. Frank Luther Mott, *A History of American Magazines, 1741–1850* (Cambridge, MA: Harvard University Press, 1930),3: 6; 4: 717. Also see Sedgwick, *The Atlantic Monthly,* 127.

70. Burt G. Wilder, "Time Works Wonders," *Atlantic Monthly* 25 (March 1870): 321.

71. WDH, *The Lady of the Aroostook* (Boston: Houghton, Osgood, 1877), 90.

72. WDH, *"Literary Criticism," Selected Literary Criticism,* ed. Ulrich Halfmann, Christoph J. Lohmann, Don L. Cook, David J. Nordloh, Donald Pizer, and Ronald Gottesman (Bloomington: Indiana University Press, 1993), 1: 60

73. *Atlantic Monthly* 25 (April 1870): 512.

74. Unsigned review, *Atlantic Monthly* 26 (July 1870): 128.

75. WDH, "Professor Barrett Wendell's Notions of American Literature," *Selected Literary Criticism* 3: 50.

76. WDH, "[Literature and Its Professors]," *Selected Literary Criticism,* 1: 98–99.

77. WDH to Henry James, 6 March 1870, *SL,* 1: 354.

78. WDH, unsigned review, "Bjørnson's Tales," *Atlantic Monthly* 25 (April 1870): 505.

79. WDH to William C. Howells, 5 December 1880, *SL,* 2: 270.

80. See Sedgwick, *The Atlantic Monthly,* 120. Under Fields, the *Atlantic* allotted four or five pages to notices of books. By the end of his tenure, Howells had increased this allowance to twelve or fourteen pages. Literary articles, inclusive of reviews, rose from around five per year in the mid-1860s to around seventy by the time he left the magazine.

81. WDH, "[Turgenev's Novel of Russian Life]," *Atlantic Monthly,* February 1873, *Selected Literary Criticism,* 1: 207.

82. WDH, "[Turgenev's Study of Character]," *Atlantic Monthly,* September 1873, *Selected Literary Criticism,* 1: 219. Also see *W. D. Howells as Critic,* ed. Edwin H. Cady (London: Routledge & Kegan Paul, 1973), 45.

83. Ivan Turgenev to WDH, 28 October 1874, *SL,* 2: 70. American critics

thought that Howells sometimes kept too close to reality. See Franklin Smith, "An Hour with Mr. Howells," *Interviews with William Dean Howells,* ed. Ulrich Halfmann, *American Literary Realism,* special issue, 6 (Fall 1973): 298.

84. WDH, review of *The Story of a Bad Boy, Atlantic Monthly* 25 (January 1870): 124.

85. WDH, "Recollections of an Atlantic Editorship," 595.

86. WDH to George Bainton, 8 January 1888, *SL,* 3: 213.

87. Carl Van Vechten, *Peter Whiffle, His Life and Works* (New York: Alfred A. Knopf, 1922), 183.

88. See Ivan Turgenev to WDH, 28 October 1874, *SL,* 2: 79. Howells sent a copy of his novel to Turgenev.

89. WDH to Ralph Keeler, 23 September 1871; quoted in introduction to *Their Wedding Journey,* ed. John K. Reeves (Bloomington: Indiana University Press, 1968), xiv.

CHAPTER SEVEN

1. WDH, *My Mark Twain* (New York: Harper & Brothers, 1910), 4.

2. WDH, "Mark Twain's *The Innocents Abroad,*" *Atlantic Monthly* 24 (December 1869): 764–66; quotations from 765, 766.

3. See WDH, "Mark Twain," *Century Magazine* 24 (September 1882): 780.

4. WDH, *My Mark Twain,* 35.

5. WDH, "The Truthfulness of Mark Twain's Fiction," *Harper's Monthly* (May 1887), *Selected Literary Criticism,* ed. Ulrich Halfmann, Christoph J. Lohmann, Don L. Cook, David J. Nordloh, Donald Pizer, and Ronald Gottesman (Bloomington: Indiana University Press, 1993), 2: 49–50.

6. 1886 interview, "The Home of Fiction," *Interviews with William Dean Howells,* ed. Ulrich Halfmann, *American Literary Realism,* special issue, 6 (Fall 1973): 284.

7. WDH, *My Mark Twain,* 17: "Of all the literary men I have known he was the most unliterary in his make and manner."

8. Ernest Hemingway, *Green Hills of Africa* (New York: Scribner's, 1935), 22.

9. WDH, *My Mark Twain,* 101. See John Crowley, "The Sacerdotal Cult and the Sealskin Coat: W. D. Howells in *My Mark Twain,*" *English Language Notes* 11 (June 1974): 287. Crowley says that the whole of Howells' tribute "may be regarded as a tall-tale of sorts" and as a sign of Howells' "divided feelings" or "tension" in his portrayal of Twain. It seems just as likely that his high praise of Twain reflects the generosity of someone aware of his own achievements and free to honor the qualities in another man. The same might be said of his unstinting praise for Henry James.

10. WDH, *My Mark Twain,* 4.

11. See James M. Cox, *Mark Twain: The Fate of Humor* (Princeton: Princeton University Press, 1966), and Lewis Leary's shrewd commentary, "On Writing about Writers: Mark Twain and Howells," *Southern Review* 4 (1968): 551–57.

12. Cited in *Mark Twain: Collected Tales, Sketches, Speeches, & Essays, 1891–1910* (New York: Library of America, 1992), 964.

13. WDH to Mark Twain, 16 February 1875, *Twain-Howells Letters,* 1: 66.

14. Clara Clemens, *My Father: Mark Twain* (New York: Harper, 1931), 43; quoted in Kenneth E. Eble's fine article, "Howells and Twain: Being and Staying Friends," *Old Northwest* 10 (Spring 1984): 103.

15. Mark Twain, "William Dean Howells," *Harper's Monthly* (July 1906); *Mark Twain: Collected Tales,* 727.

16. WDH, *My Mark Twain,* 9.

17. WDH to Thomas Bailey Aldrich, 8 December 1901, *SL,* 4: 275.

18. WDH, *Literary Friends and Acquaintance: A Personal Retrospect of American Authorship,* ed. David F. Hiatt and Edwin H. Cady (Bloomington: Indiana University Press, 1968), 231–33. Howells wrote an affectionate article on Keeler in the *Atlantic* 33 (March 1874). See Philip Graham, "Ralph Keeler, Journalism's Mystery," *Journalism Quarterly* 40 (Winter 1963): 45–52.

19. Twain's inscription is dated Hartford, 1877 (Houghton).

20. WDH to James M. Comly, 21 March 1874, *SL,* 2: 56.

21. WDH, *My Mark Twain,* 13.

22. WDH, *My Mark Twain,* 10–11.

23. WDH to William C. Howells, 15 November 1891 (Houghton).

24. WDH, *Their Wedding Journey,* ed. John K. Reeves (Bloomington: Indiana University Press, 1968), 28–29.

25. Mark Twain to WDH, [14 December 1874], *Twain-Howells Letters,* 1: 54. Smith and Gibson note that this is the first of the letters between Twain and Howells to be typed.

26. WDH to Mark Twain, 24 January 1875, *Twain-Howells Letters,* 1: 61.

27. WDH to Mark Twain, 10 January 1875, *Twain-Howells Letters,* 1: 57.

28. WDH to Mark Twain, 28 February 1875, *SL,* 2: 91.

29. WDH to Mark Twain, 8 June 1876, *Twain-Howells Letters,* 1: 141.

30. WDH to Mark Twain, 16 January 1876, *Twain-Howells Letters,* 1: 120.

31. Mark Twain, *The Autobiography of Mark Twain,* ed. Charles Neider (New York: Harper & Brothers, 1959), 203.

32. Twain, *Autobiography,* 213.

33. Mark Twain to Olivia Langdon, 1 March [1869], *Love Letters of Mark Twain,* ed. Dixon Wecter (New York: Harper, 1949), 76.

34. Virginia Harlow, *Thomas Sergeant Perry: A Biography* (Durham, NC: Duke University Press, 1950), 209.

35. WDH, *My Mark Twain,* 49.

36. WDH to Mark Twain, 23 October 1898, *Twain-Howells Letters,* 2: 680–81.

37. WDH to Mark Twain, 21 November 1875, *Twain-Howells Letters,* 1: 110–11.

38. WDH to Mark Twain, 11 July 1874, *SL,* 2: 63.

39. For an excellent account of Howells' evolving views of realism on the stage, see Brenda Murphy, *A Realist in the American Theatre* (Athens: Ohio University Press, 1992), 1–18. For specific information about Lawrence Barrett and his relationship to Howells, see the introduction to *Staging Howells: Plays and Correspondence with Lawrence Barrett,* ed. George Arms, Mary Bess Whidden, and Gary Scharnhorst (Albuquerque: University of New Mexico Press, 1994), xv–xxii. The editors recovered correspondence between the actor and playwright previously thought lost or destroyed.

40. Lawrence Barrett to WDH, 9 June 1875, in Arms, Whidden, and Scharnhorst, *Staging Howells,* 3.

41. Arms, Whidden, and Scharnhorst, *Staging Howells,* 5–6 n.

42. Arms, Whidden, and Scharnhorst, *Staging Howells,* 3–4 n.

43. Arms, Whidden, and Scharnhorst, *Staging Howells,* 8. Also see Walter J. Meserve, ed., *The Complete Plays of W. D. Howells* (New York: New York University Press, 1960), xxiii–xxv, 1. Howells' first translation was of Ippolito D'Aste's *Sansone.*

44. Meserve, *Complete Plays,* 70.

45. WDH to William C. Howells, 3 April 1878; quoted in Meserve, *Complete Plays,* 71.

46. Booth Tarkington, "Mr. Howells," *Harper's Monthly* 141 (August 1920): 348.

47. WDH to Mark Twain, 2 June 1878, *SL,* 2: 199.

48. Mark Twain to WDH, 15 September 1879, *Twain-Howells Letters,* 1: 269.

49. See Mark Twain to WDH, 21 January 1879, *Twain-Howells Letters,* 1: 246.

50. Bret Harte to Mark Twain, 1 March 1877; quoted in *Twain-Howells Letters,* 1: 186 n3.

51. See *Twain-Howells Letters,* 1: 186 n3.

52. WDH to Rutherford B. Hayes, 9 April 1878, *SL,* 2: 194–95.

53. Mark Twain to WDH, 27 June 1878, *Twain-Howells Letters,* 1: 235.

54. Mark Twain to WDH, 5 September 1881, *Twain-Howells Letters,* 1: 372.

55. WDH to Edmund Gosse, 8 December 1883, *SL,* 3: 86. For information about the writing of the play and the authors' negotiation, see Meserve, *Complete Plays,* 205–8.

56. Meserve, *Complete Plays,* 207. See *Twain-Howells Letters,* 1: 452 n3.

57. WDH, *My Mark Twain,* 26.

58. WDH to Mark Twain, 11 May 1886, *Twain-Howells Letters,* 2: 558. Also see 559 n1.

59. WDH, *The Undiscovered Country* (Boston: Houghton Mifflin, 1880), 321.

60. WDH to Mark Twain, 7 February 1890, *Twain-Howells Letters,* 2: 630.

61. WDH, *My Mark Twain,* 24. Among other accounts of this failed enterprise, see Walter Meserve's "Colonel Sellers as Scientist: A Play by S. L. Clemens and W. D. Howells," *Modern Drama* 1 (December 1958): 151–56.

62. WDH to John Hay, 18 March 1882, *SL,* 3: 13.

63. WDH to Mark Twain, 13 December 1880, *Twain-Howells Letters,* 1: 338.

64. WDH, *Century Magazine,* September 1882, in *My Mark Twain,* 141.

65. Twain, *Autobiography,* 363.

66. WDH, *My Mark Twain,* 181.

67. WDH, *My Mark Twain,* 47–48.

68. Mark Twain to WDH, 30 January [1879], *Twain-Howells Letters,* 1: 248.

69. Mark Twain to WDH, 19 October [1875], *Twain-Howells Letters,* 1: 106–7.

70. Quoted from Patricia O'Toole, *The Five of Hearts* (New York: Clarkson Potter, 1990), 86.

71. Whitelaw Reid to WDH, 17 April 1872, *SL,* 1: 395 n1.

72. Mark Twain to WDH, 18 January 1876, *Twain-Howells Letters,* 1: 121.

73. See *Twain-Howells Letters,* 2: 482–83, 494 n2, 494–95, 497, 499, 500.

74. Mark Twain to WDH, 27 October [1875], *Twain-Howells Letters,* 1: 108; WDH to Mark Twain, 9 October 1909, *Twain-Howells Letters,* 2: 707.

75. Mark Twain to WDH, in 22 September 1889, *Twain-Howells Letters,* 2: 613.

76. Mark Twain to WDH, 22 August [1874], *Twain-Howells Letters,* 1: 21.

77. Mark Twain to WDH, 27 June [1878], *Twain-Howells Letters,* 1: 237.

78. WDH to Mark Twain, 23 October 1898, *Twain-Howells Letters,* 2: 680; Mark Twain to WDH, 30 December 1898–[3 January 1899], 2: 684.

79. Mark Twain to WDH, 21 July 1885, *Twain-Howells Letters,* 2: 533.

80. Mark Twain to WDH, 21 July 1885, *Twain-Howells Letters,* 2: 534.

81. Mark Twain, "William Dean Howells," *Mark Twain: Collected Tales,* 722.

82. WDH to Mark Twain, 14 February 1904, *SL,* 5: 77–78.

83. WDH, *My Mark Twain,* 30.

84. WDH, *My Mark Twain,* 34.

85. WDH, *My Mark Twain,* 40–41.

86. WDH, *My Mark Twain,* 53.

87. Cable defended himself in a letter to the editor of the *Herald,* 14 May 1885. See Arlin Turner, *George W. Cable: A Biography* (Durham, NC: Duke University Press, 1956), 211–12.

88. Ellen B. Ballou, *The Building of the House: Houghton Mifflin's Formative Years* (Boston: Houghton Mifflin, 1970), 395.

89. Meserve, *Complete Plays*, xxiv.

90. WDH to Mark Twain, 28 May 1880, *Life in Letters*, 1: 287.

91. WDH, *My Mark Twain*, 42.

92. WDH, *My Mark Twain*, 29.

93. See Eble, "Howells and Twain," 91–106.

94. WDH to Mark Twain, 5 August 1876, *Twain-Howells Letters*, 1: 142.

95. Mark Twain to WDH, 9 August 1876, *Twain-Howells Letters*, 1: 143.

96. WDH, Editor's Easy Chair, *Harper's Monthly* 108 (December 1903): 156.

97. Twain, "William Dean Howells," *Mark Twain: Collected Tales*, 730.

98. See Karen Lystra, *Dangerous Intimacy: The Untold Story of Mark Twain's Final Years* (Berkeley: University of California Press, 2004), 219, 220.

99. WDH to Mark Twain, 15 October 1901, *Twain-Howells Letters*, 2: 730.

100. WDH to Mark Twain, 16 October 1901, *Twain-Howells Letters*, 2: 731.

101. *Life in Letters*, 2: 147.

CHAPTER EIGHT

1. WDH to James M. Comly, 22 October 1871, *SL*, 1: 380.

2. See John Updike, "Howells as Anti-Novelist," *New Yorker* 63 (13 July 1987): 78–88. As Updike puts it, "In defiance of novelistic convention, which asked for elaborate plots, for heroes and crises," Howells' stories seem to tell themselves.

3. WDH to James R. Osgood, 1 April 1871, *SL*, 1: 367.

4. WDH, *Their Wedding Journey*, ed. John K. Reeves (Bloomington: Indiana University Press, 1968), 55.

5. WDH, *Their Wedding Journey*, 14.

6. WDH, *The Lady of the Aroostook* (Boston: Houghton, Osgood, 1877), 52.

7. Ernest Samuels, *Henry Adams* (Cambridge, MA: Harvard University Press, 1989), 96–97.

8. Ellis Parker Butler, "Tributes to William Dean Howells on the Occasion of his 80th Birthday" (Houghton).

9. WDH, "Eighty Years and After," *SL*, 6: 158.

10. WDH to Ben W. Lacy, 6 February 1874, *SL*, 2: 54 n1.

11. WDH to William C. Howells, 8 April 1872, *SL*, 1: 394.

12. WDH to William C. Howells, 20 April 1873, *SL*, 2: 24.

13. WDH, *A Chance Acquaintance*, introduction and notes to the text by Jonathan Thomas and David J. Nordloh; text established by Ronald Gottesman, Nordloh, and Thomas (Bloomington: Indiana University Press, 1971), 81.

14. WDH, *A Chance Acquaintance*, 111.

15. WDH to William C. Howells, 9 April 1871 (Houghton).

16. WDH to Annie T. Howells, 6 March 1873, *SL*, 2: 16.

17. WDH to William C. Howells, 5 February 1873, *SL*, 2: 13–14.

18. WDH to William C. Howells, 16 February 1873 (Houghton).

19. James Doyle, *Annie Howells and Achille Fréchette* (Toronto: University of Toronto Press, 1979), 37.

20. Annie Howells to Aurelia H. Howells, 30 September 1872 (Alfred).

21. Victoria M. Howells, diary, 19 April [year missing] (Alfred); quoted in Polly H. Howells, "Mildred Howells as the Father's Daughter," *Harvard Library Bulletin* 5 (Spring 1994): 25–26. Hinton was a cousin.

22. Victoria M. Howells to WDH, 14 December 1875 (Alfred).

23. See Victoria M. Howells to Annie Fréchette, 5 March 1882 (Alfred).

24. WDH to William C. Howells, 28 January 1872, *SL,* 1: 390.

25. E. L. Godkin to Charles Eliot Norton, 6 May 1871, *Life and Letters of Edwin Lawrence Godkin,* ed. Rollo Ogden (Westport, CT: Greenwood Press, 1972, c. 1907), 2: 307; quoted in Van Wyck Brooks, *Howells, His Life and World* (New York: Dutton, 1959), 65.

26. WDH to William C. Howells, 14 May 1873 (Houghton).

27. WDH to William C. Howells, 22 September 1872, *SL,* 1: 401.

28. WDH to Joseph A. Howells, 8 September 1872, *SL,* 1: 400.

29. "Some Sayings & Doings of Winnie & Johnny Howells" (Houghton); quoted in *If Not Literature: Letters of Elinor Mead Howells,* ed. Ginette de B. Merrill and George Arms (Columbus: Ohio State University Press, 1988), xxxii.

30. WDH, *Their Wedding Journey,* 183.

31. Autograph book of Winifred Howells: Mark Twain, December 1879; Henry Wadsworth Longfellow, 13 August 1878 (Houghton).

32. WDH to William C. Howells, 21 August 1881 (Houghton).

33. WDH to Henry James, 26 June 1869, *SL,* 1: 331.

34. Elinor M. Howells to Victoria M. Howells, 8 February [1872], *If Not Literature,* 149.

35. WDH to William C. Howells, 6 April 1873, *Life in Letters,* 1: 178.

36. He wrote three books on New England architecture, including *The Architectural Heritage of the Piscataqua,* which deals mainly with houses in Portsmouth, New Hampshire.

37. WDH, *Christmas Every Day and Other Stories* (New York: Harper & Brothers, 1892), 22.

38. WDH, "The Pumpkin Glory," *Christmas Every Day,* 71.

39. WDH, "The Pony Engine and the Pacific Express," *Christmas Every Day,* 51.

40. "Some Sayings & Doings of Winnie & Johnny Howells" (Houghton); quoted in *If Not Literature,* xxxiii.

41. George Santayana, *Persons and Places: The Background of My Life* (New York: Charles Scribner's Sons, 1944), 72.

42. See Ellen B. Ballou, *The Building of the House: Houghton Mifflin's Formative Years* (Boston: Houghton Mifflin, 1970), 200.

43. WDH to William C. Howells, 16 February 1873 (Houghton).

44. WDH to Henry James, 26 August 1873, *SL*, 2: 34.

45. WDH to Annie T. Howells, 21 October 1873, *SL*, 2: 37.

46. Elinor M. Howells to Annie T. Howells, 9 July [1872], *If Not Literature,* 154.

47. WDH to Joseph A. Howells, 6 August 1874 (Houghton). Howells wrote:

I wish to goodness, father would stick to the English language in his letters to the Sentinel. That heading *Choses du Quebec* means nothing and is ungrammatical besides. Couldn't you just head the letters, "Letters from Quebec," and then apologize to father about it on the ground that the readers don't understand French? (It's lucky for him they don't!)

48. WDH to William C. Howells, 9 July 1874, *SL*, 2: 62.

49. Victoria M. Howells to WDH, 26 October 1875 (Alfred).

50. Joseph A. Howells to William C. Howells, 4 September 1880 (Alfred).

51. See Joseph A. Howells to Annie T. Howells, 24 March 1874; 1 December 1873 (Alfred).

52. The vagaries of magazine and book publishing are unclear even in the chronicles of the presses and the biographies of the people involved. The shifting associations led to partnerships between Osgood and Houghton, which meant Hurd and Houghton and Houghton and Mifflin until Osgood had his own independent company, which failed in May 1885.

53. WDH to James M. Comly, 12 December 1873, *SL*, 2: 43.

54. *A Foregone Conclusion* carries a publication date of 1875. Postdating allowed a book published late in the previous year to still appear a new book in the next.

55. The novel appeared on 3 December 1874, in its final month of serial publication in the *Atlantic.*

56. WDH to Charles Eliot Norton, 12 December 1874, *Life in Letters,* 1: 198.

57. Edmund C. Stedman to WDH, 7 December 1874, *SL*, 2: 81 n1.

58. WDH to Clarence C. Stedman, 8 December 1874, *SL*, 2: 80.

59. Mark Twain to WDH, 22 August [1878], *Twain-Howells Letters,* 1: 21.

60. Henry James, review of *A Foregone Conclusion, Nation* 20 (7 January 1875); *Letters, Fictions, Lives: Henry James and William Dean Howells,* ed. Michael Anesko (New York: Oxford University Press, 1997), 98, 100. See Henry James to WDH, 19 October 1886, in Anesko, *Letters, Fictions, Lives,* 256. James would worry about appearing "too mutual & reciprocal."

61. WDH to William C. Howells, 9 January 1875, *SL*, 2: 88.

62. WDH to the editor of the *Evening Transcript,* 18 December 1874, *SL*, 2: 84.

63. WDH to William C. Howells, 9 January 1875, *SL*, 2: 88.

64. "The Whittier Dinner," *The Boston Daily Globe,* 18 December 1877.

65. *The Critic* 4 (28 November 1885): 253.

66. *Twain-Howells Letters,* 1: 212 n1. Also see "The Whittier Dinner" and WDH, *My Mark Twain* (New York: Harper & Brothers, 1910), 60.

67. WDH, *My Mark Twain,* 59–60.

68. WDH to Mark Twain, 27 September [1878], *Twain-Howells Letters,* 1: 239.

69. WDH, *My Mark Twain,* 63.

70. WDH to William C. Howells, 22 December 1877, *SL,* 2: 183.

71. Charles Eliot Norton to James Russell Lowell, 6 February 1874, *The Letters of Charles Eliot Norton,* ed. Sara Norton and M. A. DeWolfe Howe (Boston: Houghton Mifflin, 1913), 2: 33.

72. Henry James to Grace Norton, 27 November 1871, *Henry James Letters,* ed. Leon Edel (Cambridge: Harvard University Press, 1974–1984), 1: 264.

73. George P. Lathrop to WDH, 1 September 1877, *SL,* 2: 214 n5.

74. Letter of 5 October 1876, *The Collected Letters of George Gissing,* ed. Paul F. Mattheisen, Arthur C. Young, and Pierre Coustillas (Athens: Ohio University Press, 1990), 1: 47.

75. Elinor M. Howells to Annie T. Howells, [late February–early March 1876], *If Not Literature,* 169–70.

76. See Aurelia Howells, diary, 31 December 1876 (Huntington).

77. Annie T. Howells to Elinor M. Howells, "Fri., the 5th," [1876] (Alfred); quoted in Doyle, *Annie Howells,* 50.

78. Elinor M. Howells to Victoria M. Howells, 16 September 1876, *If Not Literature,* 173.

79. WDH to William C. Howells, 12 November 1876, *SL,* 2: 141.

80. Louis J. Budd, "Howells, the *Atlantic Monthly,* and Republicanism," *American Literature* 24 (May 1952): 140. We have drawn on Budd's essay for this section.

81. WDH to Rutherford B. Hayes, 18 June 1876; Rutherford B. Hayes to WDH, 27 June 1876, *SL,* 2: 131 n3.

82. WDH to Rutherford B. Hayes, 20 July 1876, *SL,* 2: 131–32.

83. WDH to Rutherford B. Hayes, 7 September 1876, *SL,* 2: 137.

84. Charles Eliot Norton to WDH, 21 September 1876, *SL,* 2: 140 n1.

85. WDH, Rutherford B. Hayes (Boston: H. O. Houghton and Co., 1876), 195.

86. Victoria M. Howells to WDH, 26 December 1876 (Alfred).

87. WDH to James R. Osgood, 18 March 1877, *SL,* 2: 159.

88. WDH to William C. Howells, 2 September 1877, *SL,* 2: 173.

CHAPTER NINE

1. WDH to William C. Howells, 6 January 1878, *SL,* 2: 186.

2. Elinor M. Howells to Miss Webster, 20 January 1876, *If Not Literature:*

Letters of Elinor Mead Howells, ed. Ginette de B. Merrill and George Arms (Columbus: Ohio State University Press, 1988), 167.

3. WDH to William C. Howells, 28 November 1880 (Houghton).

4. WDH to Annie T. Howells, 18 February 1877, *SL,* 2: 157.

5. WDH to William C. Howells, 22 April 1877, *SL,* 2: 164–65.

6. Quoted in Samuel G. White, *The Houses of McKim, Mead, and White* (New York: Rizzoli, 1988), 10, our source for much of the preceding paragraph.

7. See among others, White, *The Houses of McKim, Mead, and White,* 9–14.

8. WDH, *Annie Kilburn,* in *Novels, 1886–1888,* ed. Don L. Cook (New York: Library of America, 1989), 711.

9. Elinor M. Howells to William Mead, 16 October 1877 (Amherst).

10. Ginette de B. Merrill, "Redtop and the Belmont Years of W. D. Howells and His Family," *Harvard Library Bulletin,* 28 (January 1980): 37.

11. Myers Co. Builders, "Account of Extras on W D Howells House" (Amherst).

12. Merrill, "Redtop and the Belmont *Years,*" 39.

13. WDH to James Russell Lowell, 22 June 1879; WDH to S. P. Langley, 18 May 1879, quoted in Merrill, "Redtop and the Belmont *Years,*" 39.

14. WDH, "Buying a Horse," *Atlantic Monthly* (June 1879): 741–51.

15. Elinor M. Howells to William Mead, 21 January 1878 (Amherst).

16. See Ginette de B. Merrill, "More on Howells in Belmont: A Letter to the Transcript and 'A Perfect Success,'" *Harvard Library Bulletin* 28 (April 1980): 171–74. The story first appeared in *Childhood Appeal,* 17 December 1880.

17. Merrill, "Redtop and the Belmont *Years,*" 45–46.

18. WDH, *The Lady of the Aroostook* (Boston: Houghton, Osgood, 1877), 115.

19. WDH, *The Lady of the Aroostook,* 70–71.

20. WDH, *The Lady of the Aroostook,* 70–71.

21. Henry James to WDH, 22 July 1879, quoted in *Letters, Fictions, Lives: Henry James and William Dean Howells,* ed. Michael Anesko (New York: Oxford University Press, 1997), 137.

22. WDH to William C. Howells, 6 January 1878, *SL,* 2: 186. Howells thought about sending the children to a New Church school in Waltham. In the end, Winny attended Mr. Justin E. Gales' Young Ladies' School, and John Miss Sarah H. Page's.

23. WDH, *A Chance Acquaintance,* introduction and notes to the text by Jonathan Thomas and David J. Nordloh; text established by Ronald Gottesman, Nordloh, and Thomas (Bloomington: Indiana University Press, 1971), 91.

24. WDH to William C. Howells, 21 July 1878, *SL,* 2: 203; and WDH to James Russell Lowell, 22 June 1879, *SL,* 2: 230.

25. WDH, *The Undiscovered Country* (Boston: Houghton Mifflin, 1880), 251.

26. Oliver Wendell Holmes to WDH, 14 December 1879, in John Torrey Morse, *Life and Letters of Oliver Wendell Holmes* (Boston: Houghton, Mifflin, 1896), 2: 44.

27. WDH to William C. Howells, 4 May 1879, *SL,* 2: 227.

28. WDH, *The Undiscovered Country,* 161.

29. WDH, *The Undiscovered Country,* 224.

30. Henry James to WDH, 20 July 1880, in Anesko, *Letters, Fictions, Lives,* 152.

31. Ellen B. Ballou, *The Building of the House: Houghton Mifflin's Formative Years* (Boston: Houghton Mifflin, 1970), 270.

32. WDH to William C. Howells, 17 October 1880, *SL,* 2: 268.

33. WDH to William C. Howells, 29 February 1880, *SL,* 2: 244.

34. Polly H. Howells, "Mildred Howells as the Father's Daughter," *Harvard Library Bulletin* 5 (Spring 1994): 12.

35. Elinor M. Howells to the Howells family, 13 July [1879], *If Not Literature,* 219.

36. Elinor M. Howells to Annie Fréchette, 8 November [1879], *If Not Literature,* 223.

37. Quoted in Rodney D. Olsen, *Dancing in Chains: The Youth of William Dean Howells* (New York: New York University Press, 1991), 56.

38. WDH, *The Undiscovered Country,* 323.

39. WDH to William C. Howells, 21 July 1878, *SL,* 2: 203.

40. WDH to Horace E. Scudder, 8 February 1881, *SL,* 2: 274.

41. See WDH to William C. Howells, 13 February 1881, *SL,* 2: 275.

42. WDH to William C. Howells, 2 May 1880, *SL,* 2: 251.

43. Patricia O'Toole, *The Five of Hearts* (New York: Clarkson Potter, 1990), 70.

44. Marian (Clover) Adams to Robert William Hooper, 20 February 1881, *The Letters of Mrs. Henry Adams, 1865–1883,* ed. Ward Thorn (Boston: Little, Brown, 1936), 269.

45. Marian Adams to Robert William Hooper, 23 January 1881, *The Letters of Mrs. Henry Adams,* 260.

46. Quoted in Ari Hoogenboom, *The Presidency of Rutherford B. Hayes* (Lawrence: University Press of Kansas, 1988), 208–9.

47. WDH to William C. Howells, 17 July 1881 (Houghton), partly quoted in *SL,* 2: 289 n3.

48. WDH to William C. Howells, 22 September 1881 (Houghton).

49. WDH to William C. Howells, 23 October 1881, *SL,* 2: 299.

50. WDH to William C. Howells, 25 March 1882, *SL,* 3: 15.

51. WDH to Charles D. Warner, 2 April 1882, *SL,* 3: 16.

52. WDH to Charles D. Warner, 2 April 1882, *SL,* 3: 16.

53. WDH to Charles D. Warner, 2 April 1882, *SL,* 3: 16.

54. Quoted in *The Letters of Henry James,* ed. Percy Lubbock (New York: Charles Scribner's Sons, 1920), 1: 89.

55. WDH to William H. Bishop, 21 March 1880, *SL,* 2: 246.

56. WDH, *A Foregone Conclusion,* in *Novels, 1875–1886,* ed. Edwin H. Cady (New York: Library of America, 1982), 14.

57. Henry James, *Daisy Miller,* in *Daisy Miller: A Study; An International Episode; Four Meetings* (London: Macmillan, 1879), 17–19.

58. WDH, *The Lady of the Aroostook,* 125–26.

59. Henry James, *The Portrait of a Lady,* in *Novels, 1881–1886* (New York: Library of America, 1985), 397. We are indebted to Anesko for this example (*Letters, Fictions, Lives,* 42). Anesko traces these writers' indebtedness to each other throughout his fine book. See, for example, 37–46.

60. Henry James, *The Portrait of a Lady,* in *Novels, 1881–1886,* 193.

61. Henry James, *The Bostonians,* in *Novels, 1881–1886,* 803.

62. WDH, *A Foregone Conclusion,* in *Novels, 1875–1886,* 1.

63. WDH, *The Rise of Silas Lapham,* in *Novels, 1875–1886,* 861.

64. Henry James to WDH, 7 April 1879, in Anesko, *Letters, Fictions, Lives,* 132–33.

65. WDH, review of *A Passionate Pilgrim and Other Tales, Atlantic Monthly* 35 (April 1875); Anesko, *Letters, Fictions, Lives,* 107.

66. WDH to Henry James, 25 December 1886, in Anesko, *Letters, Fictions, Lives,* 260.

CHAPTER TEN

1. WDH to Victoria M. Howells, 21 July 1882, *SL,* 3: 22.

2. WDH to Victoria M. Howells, 21 July 1882, *SL,* 3: 21–22.

3. WDH to William C. Howells, 31 July [1882], *SL,* 3: 23.

4. Quoted in *SL,* 3: 24 n1.

5. WDH to Mark Twain, 1 September 1882, *SL,* 3: 27.

6. WDH, *Certain Delightful English Towns* (New York: Harper & Brothers, 1906), 1.

7. *The Athenaeum* 2864 (16 September 1882): 372.

8. Patricia O'Toole, *The Five of Hearts* (New York: Clarkson Potter, 1990), 110–11.

9. See Thomas Wentworth Higginson, *Old Cambridge* (New York: Macmillan, 1900), 192. Higginson writes of Lowell that "his Americanism was the dominant passion of his life, that and not poetry nor letters nor even those friendships and affections which were to him as the air he breathed."

10. WDH to William C. Howells, 21 June 1883, *SL,* 3: 69.

11. Elinor M. Howells to William C. Howells, [30 August–1 September 1882], *If Not Literature: Letters of Elinor Mead Howells,* ed. Ginette de B. Merrill and

George Arms (Columbus: Ohio State University Press, 1988), 244–45. See also Laurence Hutton, *Talks in a Library with Laurence Hutton* (New York: G. P. Putnam's Sons, 1905), 364.

12. Elinor M. Howells to William C. Howells, [30 August–1 September 1882], *If Not Literature,* 244–45.

13. Elinor M. Howells to Victoria M. Howells, 31 August 1882, *If Not Literature,* 246.

14. WDH to William C. Howells, 21 June 1883, *SL,* 3: 69.

15. WDH to Charles Eliot Norton, 14 September 1882, *SL,* 3: 31–32.

16. See Clara Marburg Kirk, *W. D. Howells and Art in His Time* (New Brunswick, NJ: Rutgers University Press, 1965), 181–82.

17. Quotations from Christopher Wood, *Victorian Painting* (Boston: Little, Brown, 1999), 268–70.

18. Ann Thwaite, *Edmund Gosse: A Literary Landscape 1849–1928* (London: Secker & Warburg, 1984), 226.

19. Henry James to WDH, 29 September 1888, *SL,* 3: 232 n3.

20. WDH to Edmund Gosse, 1 August 1882, in Edmund Gosse, *Transatlantic Dialogue: Selected American Correspondence,* ed. Paul F. Mattheisen and Michael Millgate (Austin: University of Texas Press, 1965), 93.

21. Edmund Gosse to Edward C. Stedman, 21 August 1882, *Transatlantic Dialogue,* 95.

22. Edmund Gosse to WDH, 30 August 1882, *Transatlantic Dialogue,* 97.

23. Quoted in Thwaite, *Edmund Gosse,* 84.

24. WDH to Edmund Gosse, 26 August 1882, *Transatlantic Dialogue,* 96.

25. Edmund Gosse to WDH, 30 August 1882, *Transatlantic Dialogue,* 97.

26. Thwaite, *Edmund Gosse,* 194.

27. For a "homosocial" reading of Howells' relationship with Charles Stoddard, see John W. Crowley, "Howells, Stoddard, and Male Homosocial Attachment," *The Mask of Fiction* (Amherst: University of Massachusetts Press, 1989), 56–82.

28. Quoted in Olev Fryckstedt, *In Quest of America: A Study of Howells' Early Development as a Novelist* (Cambridge, MA: Harvard University Press, 1958), 18.

29. "Novels of the Week," *Athenaeum* 2867 (7 October 1882): 460.

30. WDH, *Their Wedding Journey,* ed. John K. Reeves (Bloomington: Indiana University Press, 1968), 43.

31. WDH to William C. Howells, 11 September 1881, *SL,* 2: 296.

32. Michael Anesko, ed., *Letters, Fictions, Lives: Henry James and William Dean Howells* (New York: Oxford University Press, 1997), 230, 234.

33. See Anesko, *Letters, Fictions, Lives,* 237 n9.

34. Anesko, *Letters, Fictions, Lives,* 237.

35. George Moore, *Confessions of a Young Man* (Montreal: McGill–Queen's University Press, 1972), 152.

36. [Margaret Oliphant], "American Literature in England," *Blackwood's Magazine* 133 (January 1883): 144.

37. WDH to Edmund Gosse, 16 November 1882, *Transatlantic Dialogue,* 104.

38. WDH, *Early Prose Writings,* 205.

39. See Scott Bennett, "David Douglas and the British Publication of W. D. Howells' Works," *Studies in Bibliography* 25 (1972): 121; and Leon Edel and Dan H. Laurence, with James Rambeau, *A Bibliography of Henry James,* 3rd rev. ed. (New York: Oxford University Press, 1982); cited in Anesko, *Letters, Fictions, Lives,* 57 n43.

40. Review of *A Hazard of New Fortunes, Spectator* 64 (8 March 1890): 342–43.

41. Anesko, *Letters, Fictions, Lives,* 235–38.

42. Edmund Gosse to WDH, 8 November 1882, *Transatlantic Dialogue,* 102.

43. Edmund Gosse to WDH, 14 November 1882, *Transatlantic Dialogue,* 103.

44. WDH to Edmund Gosse, 16 November 1882, *Transatlantic Dialogue,* 104–5.

45. WDH, Life and Letters, *Harper's Weekly* 40 (4 January 1896): 7, cited in Anesko, *Letters, Fictions, Lives,* 301 n8.

46. WDH to Henry James, 4 October 1882, *SL,* 3: 34.

47. WDH to Charles Dudley Warner, 3 September 1881, *SL,* 2: 295.

48. WDH to Achille Fréchette, 16 November 1886, *SL,* 3: 168.

49. WDH to Brander Matthews, 22 July 1911, *Life in Letters,* 2: 301.

50. Gary Scharnhorst, "W. D. Howells and Bret Harte: The Star System in Nineteenth-Century American Literature," *Essays in Arts and Science* 25 (October 1996): 103–10.

51. WDH to James R. Osgood, 18 February 1881, *A Modern Instance,* xxx.

52. George Washington Cable to WDH, 27 January 1883 (Houghton).

53. Owen Wister, "William Dean Howells," *Atlantic* 160 (December 1937): 704.

54. WDH, *A Modern Instance,* introduction and notes by George N. Bennett (Bloomington: Indiana University Press, 1977), 89.

55. See WDH to Robert Louis Stevenson, 13 September 1893, *SL,* 5: 49. For responses to Howells' subject, see Kenneth S. Lynn, *William Dean Howells: An American Life* (New York: Harcourt Brace Jovanovich, 1971), 267.

56. WDH, *Literature and Life* (New York: Harper & Brothers, 1902), 29–30.

57. WDH to Henry James, 4 October 1882, *SL,* 3: 35.

58. WDH to Edmund Gosse, 9 September 1882, *Transatlantic Dialogue,* 98.

59. Edmund Gosse to WDH, 12 October 1882, *Transatlantic Dialogue,* 100.

60. Edmund Gosse, "The Passing of William Dean Howells," *Littel's Living Age* 306 (10 July 1920): 99.

61. WDH to James R. Osgood, 16 October 1882, *SL,* 3: 36–37.

62. See WDH, "Émile Zola," *North American Review* 175 (November 1902); *W. D. Howells as Critic,* ed. Edwin H. Cady (London: Routledge & Kegan Paul, 1973), 389. To use his own distinction, he stayed closer to Daudet than to Zola, whose books he described as often indecent but never immoral.

63. WDH to Daniel C. Gilman, 3 December 1882, *SL,* 3: 45.

64. WDH to Daniel C. Gilman, 3 December 1882, *SL,* 3: 45.

65. WDH to Edmund W. Gosse, 16 November 1882, *SL,* 3: 41.

66. WDH to William C. Howells, 28 January 1883; WDH to William C. Howells, 5 February 1883, *SL,* 3: 50; 52.

67. WDH to William C. Howells, 28 January 1883, *SL,* 3: 51.

68. WDH to William C. Howells, 1 April 1883, *SL,* 3: 58–59 n3.

69. Elizabeth Robins Pennell, *Life and Letters of Joseph Pennell* (Boston: Little, Brown, 1929), 2: 82.

70. WDH to Charles D. Warner, 4 March 1883, *SL,* 3: 56.

71. Pennell, *Life and Letters,* 2: 84–85.

72. Pennell, *Life and Letters,* 2: 85.

73. WDH, *Tuscan Cities* (Boston and New York: Ticknor, 1884), 42.

74. WDH, *Tuscan Cities,* 55, 126.

75. WDH, *Tuscan Cities,* 14.

76. WDH, *Tuscan Cities,* 74–75.

77. Preface, *Florence in Art and Literature* (Philadelphia: Booklovers Library, 1901), quoted in James Woodress, *Howells and Italy* (Durham, NC: Duke University Press, 1952), 181.

78. See O'Toole, *The Five of Hearts,* 58–59.

79. WDH to Edmund W. Gosse, 3 April 1883, *SL,* 3: 59.

80. WDH to Thomas S. Perry, 13 March 1883, *SL,* 3: 57.

81. WDH to William C. Howells, 3 June 1883, *SL,* 3: 67.

82. WDH to James R. Osgood, 9 February 1883, *SL,* 3: 52.

83. WDH, *Tuscan Cities,* 122.

84. WDH to James R. Osgood, 20 April 1883, *SL,* 3: 62–63.

85. WDH to James R. Osgood, 20 April 1883, *SL,* 3: 63.

86. WDH to Mark Twain, 22 April 1883, *SL,* 3: 65.

87. WDH, *Winifred Howells,* privately printed (1891), 4.

88. WDH to Mark Twain, 22 April 1883, *SL,* 3: 65.

89. WDH, *A Fearful Responsibility* (Boston: James R. Osgood and Co., 1884), 145.

90. Autograph book of Winifred Howells, C. F. Woolson, Venice, 11 May 1883 (Houghton).

91. Carl Jefferson, *The Rise and Fall of James Ripley Osgood* (Waterville, ME: Colby College Press, 1959), 133.

92. WDH, "James R. Osgood," *Harper's Weekly* (3 September 1892): 858.

93. WDH to James R. Osgood, 16 December 1882, *SL,* 3: 47.

94. WDH, *Literature and Life,* 17.

95. We have drawn information for this and most of the following passages from Scott Bennett's splendid article, "David Douglas and the British Publication of W. D. Howells' Works," *Studies in Bibliography* 25 (1972): 107–24.

96. WDH to Aurelia H. Howells, 15 August 1911, *SL,* 5: 363 n8.

97. David J. Nordloh, "Notes to the Text," *Years,* 259. Howells identifies the clockmaker as George Howells, his father's great-uncle. See *Life in Letters,* 2: 176.

98. WDH to Aurelia H. Howells, 15 August 1911 (Houghton).

99. WDH to William C. Howells, 3 June 1883, *SL,* 3: 67.

CHAPTER ELEVEN

1. WDH to William C. Howells, 11 November 1883, *If Not Literature: Letters of Elinor Mead Howells,* ed. Ginette de B. Merrill and George Arms (Columbus: Ohio State University Press, 1988), 258 n2.

2. WDH, *Literary Friends and Acquaintance: A Personal Retrospect of American Authorship,* ed. David F. Hiatt and Edwin H. Cady (Bloomington: Indiana University Press, 1968), 272–73.

3. WDH, *My Mark Twain* (New York: Harper & Brothers, 1910), 28.

4. See John Y. Simon, ed., *General Grant by Matthew Arnold, with a Rejoinder by Mark Twain* (Carbondale, IL: Southern Illinois University Press), 1966.

5. See chapter 12 of Lionel Trilling, *Matthew Arnold* (New York: World Publishing, 1955).

6. Horace Traubel, *With Walt Whitman in Camden* (New York: Mitchell, Kennerly, 1914), 3: 400. See also John Henry Raleigh, *Matthew Arnold and American Culture* (Berkeley: University of California Press, 1957).

7. WDH to Edmund W. Gosse, 9 December 1883, *Transatlantic Dialogue: Selected American Correspondence of Edmund Gosse,* ed. Paul F. Mattheisen and Michael Millgate (Austin: University of Texas Press, 1965), 125.

8. WDH to Edmund W. Gosse, 9 December 1883, *SL,* 3: 85–86.

9. WDH to Annie Fields, 3 May 1913, *SL,* 6: 36.

10. George Santayana, *Persons and Places: The Background of My Life* (New York: Charles Scribner's Sons, 1944), 141–43.

11. WDH to Henry James, 22 August 1884, *Letters, Fictions, Lives: Henry James and William Dean Howells,* ed. Michael Anesko (New York: Oxford University Press, 1997), 246.

12. WDH to Annie Fréchette, 14 September 1884, partially quoted in *If Not Literature,* xxiv.

13. "Mr. Howells in Beacon Street, Boston," *Critic* 6 (27 November 1886): 259–61, partially quoted in Clara Marburg Kirk, *W. D. Howells and Art in His Time* (New Brunswick, NJ: Rutgers University Press, 1965), 109.

14. WDH to Henry James, 22 August 1884, in Anesko, *Letters, Fictions, Lives,* 246.

15. WDH to Thomas S. Perry, 15 August 1884, *SL,* 3: 108.

16. Mark Twain to WDH, 31 August 1884, *Twain-Howells Letters,* 2: 501.

17. WDH to Henry James, 22 August 1884, in Anesko, *Letters, Fictions, Lives,* 246.

18. See WDH to William C. Howells, 6 April 1890, *SL,* 3: 278, and *Twain-Howells Letters,* 2: 639 n2.

19. WDH to Hugo Erichsen, 20 June 1884, *SL,* 3: 102–3.

20. Walter J. Meserve, ed., *The Complete Plays of W. D. Howells* (New York: New York University Press, 1960), xxviii.

21. WDH to James Parton, 27 March 1885, *SL,* 3: 119.

22. WDH to Mark Twain, 23 May 1886, *SL,* 3: 154–55.

23. WDH to Charles Eliot Norton, 28 January 1904, *SL,* 5: 75 n3.

24. See *SL,* 3: 84–85 n1; also WDH to Whitelaw Reid, 27 November 1883, *SL,* 3: 84.

25. WDH to Edmund W. Gosse, 2 January 1883, *SL,* 3: 87. As the editors note, the letter is misdated and should read 1884.

26. Twain paid Howells $2,500 for his work, later published as *Mark Twain's Library of Humor* in 1887. See *SL,* 3: 137 n1.

27. Meserve, *Complete Plays,* 278.

28. WDH to Mark Twain, 10 May 1884, *Twain-Howells Letters,* 2: 486.

29. WDH to Henry James, 22 August 1884, in Anesko, *Letters, Fictions, Lives,* 247.

30. Meserve, *Complete Plays,* 269–70.

31. George Bernard Shaw, "Told You So," in *Critical Essays on W. D. Howells, 1866–1920,* ed. Edwin H. Cady and Norma W. Cady (Boston: G. K. Hall, 1983), 175–76.

32. William Dean Howells to John Hay, 22 February 1877, *John Hay–Howells Letters: The Correspondence of John Milton Hay and William Dean Howells, 1861–1903* (Boston: Twayne, 1980), 24.

33. WDH to William C. Howells, 21 November 1886 (Houghton), quoted in Meserve, *Complete Plays,* 314.

34. WDH, *The Story of a Play* (New York: Harper & Brothers, 1898), 78.

35. Brenda Murphy, introduction, *A Realist in the American Theater* (Athens: Ohio University Press, 1992), 3.

36. *Twain-Howells Letters,* 531 n1.

37. WDH to Richard W. Gilder, 31 July 1884, *SL,* 4: 103.

38. WDH to Mark Twain, 2 July 1884, *Twain-Howells Letters,* 2: 494. Howells turned his loss, which he attributed to a strike that turned violent, into a *Harper's Weekly* column, "Was There Nothing to Arbitrate?" (21 April 1888).

39. WDH, *The Rise of Silas Lapham*, introduction and notes by Walter J. Meserve (Bloomington: Indiana University Press, 1971), 365.

40. Leon Edel, *Henry James: A Life* (New York: Harper & Row, 1985), 311.

41. Henry James to Grace Norton, 9 December [1885], *Henry James Letters*, ed. Leon Edel (Cambridge, MA: Harvard University Press, 1974–1984), 3: 106. *The Rise of Silas Lapham* met with generally favorable reviews. "Future historians will find more of value in his fiction, than in our histories," one critic wrote; another commented that the novel was "almost a new species of work" (Clayton L. Eichelberger, *Published Comment on William Dean Howells through 1920: A Research Bibliography* [Boston: G. K. Hall, 1976], 54–55). Dissenters complained about the second half of the novel, Lapham's confused business arrangements, and the pert characterization of Penelope.

42. Meserve, "Introduction," *The Rise of Silas Lapham*, xxiv.

43. David J. Nordloh, "Textual Commentary," *The Rise of Silas Lapham*, 374.

44. Meserve, "Introduction," *The Rise of Silas Lapham*, xxviii.

45. Cass Gilbert to WDH, 10 March 1917, "Tributes to William Dean Howells on the Occasion of his 80th Birthday by His Fellow Craftsmen" (Houghton).

46. For a history of the stage production of *Silas Lapham*, see Meserve, *Complete Plays*, 481–83.

47. WDH to Edmund Gosse, 9 December 1883, *SL*, 3: 85.

48. "Edmund W. Gosse: How Boston Goes to Lectures," *Boston Gazette*, 13 December 1884, taken from clipping in Rutgers University library; quoted in *Transatlantic Dialogue*, 11.

49. WDH to Edmund Gosse, 9 March 1885, *SL*, 3: 117.

50. Quoted in *Transatlantic Dialogue*, 12–13.

51. Ann Thwaite, *Edmund Gosse*, 252–73. Also see Clara Kirk and Rudolf Kirk, "Letters to an 'Enchanted Guest': W. D. Howells to Edmund Gosse," *Journal of the Rutgers University Library* 22 (June 1959): 17 n43.

52. Cited in Kirk and Kirk, "Letters to an 'Enchanted Guest,'" 13; *Transatlantic Dialogue*, 13.

53. Quoted in *Transatlantic Dialogue*, 12.

54. *Transatlantic Dialogue*, 14.

55. *Transatlantic Dialogue*, 14.

56. Under the will, each of the children (Joseph, William, Victoria, Samuel, Aurelia, Annie, and Henry) were to receive $250. Howells got the rest of the property to manage for Henry and Aurelia during their joint lives, or as long as Aurelia remained unmarried. Otherwise William's estate went to Henry until his death, and after that it was to be divided equally among all other living children or their descendants. If Henry died before Aurelia, she was to inherit his share. Victoria got first refusal on the farm, and a codicil named Joe as Henry's trustee and gave Vic William's personal property in lieu of an original $2,000 bequest.

57. See WDH to Aurelia H. Howells, 12 June 1885, *SL,* 3: 124.

58. WDH, *Literary Friends and Acquaintance,* 105.

59. WDH, *Literary Friends and Acquaintance,* 105. See also Eugene Exman, *The House of Harper: One Hundred Fifty Years of Publishing* (New York: Harper & Row, 1967), 161.

60. WDH, *The Rise of Silas Lapham,* 300–301.

61. Anesko, *Letters, Fictions, Lives,* 183.

62. WDH to James Parton, 27 March 1885, *SL,* 3: 119–20.

63. Mark Twain to WDH, 5 May 1885, *Twain-Howells Letters,* 2: 527.

64. See Arlin Turner, *George W. Cable: A Biography* (Durham, NC: Duke University Press, 1956), 212.

65. Mark Twain to WDH, 5 May 1885, *SL,* 3: 121 n2.

66. James Pond, manuscript of "Eccentricities of Genius" (Virginia).

67. Robert L. Hough, *The Quiet Rebel: William Dean Howells as Social Commentator* (Lincoln: University of Nebraska Press, 1959), 110–11.

68. WDH to Henry James, 15 July 1900, *SL,* 4: 241.

69. Carl Jefferson, *The Rise and Fall of James Ripley Osgood* (Waterville, ME: Colby College Press, 1959), 267.

70. Questions noted down to put to Mr. Roswell Smith, in expectation of a conditional offer from him, Monday evening, 11 May [18]85 (Houghton), quoted in Anesko, *Letters, Fictions, Lives,* 212 n37.

71. See *SL,* 3: 129–30 n2.

72. For details of the contract, see *SL,* 3: 123 n3.

73. WDH to Joseph W. Harper Jr., 13 March 1885, *SL,* 3: 119.

74. WDH to Mark Twain, 18 April 1882, *Twain-Howells Letters,* 1: 402–3.

75. WDH to Mark Twain, 9 August 1885, *SL,* 3: 127.

76. Mark Twain to WDH, 21 July 1885, *Twain-Howells Letters,* 2: 533–34.

77. See WDH to Helen Walter, 18 November 1885, *SL,* 3: 134–35.

78. WDH, *Indian Summer,* introduction and notes to the text by Scott Bennett; text established by Bennett and David J. Nordloh (Bloomington: Indiana University Press, 1971), 54–55, 198.

79. WDH, *Indian Summer,* 66.

80. WDH, *Indian Summer,* 242.

81. WDH to Edmund Gosse, 26 October 1885, *SL,* 3: 132.

82. See archives of Harper & Brothers, 1817–1914, Chadwyck-Healy/Somerset House, series 1 (Columbia University); also Eugene Exman, *The House of Harper,* 153–54; and *SL,* 3: 131 n1.

83. WDH to Edmund Gosse, 26 October 1885, *SL,* 3: 133.

84. WDH to William C. Howells, 19 September 1886, *SL,* 3: 164.

85. WDH to William C. Howells, 10 August 1884, *SL,* 3: 105.

86. Henry Alden to WDH, 9 September 1885 (Houghton).

87. Henry Alden to WDH, 31 August 1888 (Houghton).

88. J. Henry Harper, *The House of Harper: A Century of Publishing in Franklin Square* (New York: Harper & Brothers, 1912), 620.

89. WDH, *Harper's Monthly*, 72 (January 1886): 325; *Editor's Study*, ed. James W. Simpson (Troy, NY: Whitson Publishing, 1993), 1.

90. WDH, Editor's Study, *Harper's Monthly*, 72 (January 1886): 325.

91. *The New York Times* (4 August 1886): 4; quoted in Simpson, *Editor's Study*, xxviii–xxix.

92. WDH to Charles D. Warner, 1 April 1877, *SL,* 2: 160.

93. Edwin H. Cady, ed., *W. D. Howells as Critic* (London: Routledge & Kegan Paul, 1973), 140–42.

94. WDH to Sarah Orne Jewett, 1 February 1891, *SL,* 3: 305.

95. WDH to Sarah Orne Jewett, 10 June 1876, *SL,* 2: 130 and 130 n2.

96. WDH, review of *Hawthorne, Atlantic Monthly* 45 (February 1880): 282–85; Anesko, *Letters, Fictions, Lives,* 143.

97. Charles Chesnutt, "Post-Bellum—Pre-Harlem," *The Crisis* 40 (June 1931): 194.

98. WDH, [Emily Dickinson's Poems], *Literary Criticism* (January 1891), 2: 165.

99. Henry Mills Alden, "William Dean Howells," *The Bookman* 49 (July 1919): 553–54.

100. Hamlin Garland, *Roadside Meetings* (New York: Macmillan, 1930) 197.

101. WDH to Cyrus L. Sulzberger, 17 July 1885, *SL,* 3: 124–25. See David J. Nordloh, "Textual Commentary," *The Rise of Silas Lapham,* 383–84.

102. Nordloh, "Textual Commentary," *The Rise of Silas Lapham,* 385–86.

103. WDH, *The World of Chance* (New York: Harper & Brothers, 1893), 71.

104. Cady, *W. D. Howells as Critic,* 110.

CHAPTER TWELVE

1. *Boston Transcript,* 1 April 1887, cited in *SL,* 3: 186 n1.

2. WDH to Edmund W. Gosse, 24 January 1886, *SL,* 3: 152.

3. WDH to William C. Howells, 27 February 1887, *SL,* 3: 184.

4. WDH, *A Hazard of New Fortunes,* introduction by Everett Carter; notes to the text and text established by David J. Nordloh (Bloomington: Indiana University Press, 1993), 353.

5. Paul Avrich, *The Haymarket Tragedy* (Princeton: Princeton University Press, 1984), 89. For much of the Haymarket background we have drawn from Avrich's fine study. See also Henry David, *The History of the Haymarket Affair* (New York: Farrar & Rinehart, 1936).

6. Quoted in Sender Garlin, *William Dean Howells and the Haymarket Era* (American Institute for Marxist Studies, 1979), 14.

7. WDH, *Editor's Study, Harper's Monthly,* September 1886, quoted in David, *The History of the Haymarket Affair,* 530–31.

8. WDH to Charles Eliot Norton, 6 April 1903, *SL,* 5: 50.

9. Quoted in Avrich, *The Haymarket Tragedy,* 277.

10. Among the various accounts of Howells and Haymarket, see Edwin H. Cady, *The Road to Realism: The Early Years 1837–1885 of William Dean Howells* (Syracuse, NY: Syracuse University Press, 1956), chapter 3; *SL,* 3, for 1886–87; Everett Carter, "The Haymarket Affair in Literature," *American Quarterly* 2 (Fall 1950): 270–78; and Clara Kirk and Rudolf Kirk, "William Dean Howells, George William Curtis, and the 'Haymarket Affair,'" *American Literature* 40 (January 1969): 487–98.

11. Quoted in Avrich, *The Haymarket Tragedy,* 268.

12. Quoted in *SL,* 3: 205 n5.

13. WDH to William C. Howells, 2 February 1890, *SL,* 3: 271.

14. WDH to Francis F. Browne, 4 November 1887, in J. W. Ward, "Another Howells Anarchist Letter," *American Literature* 22 (1951): 489–90. The letter appeared in the *Chicago Tribune,* 8 November 1887, without Howells' permission.

15. Robert Morss Lovett, *All Our Years: The Autobiography of Robert Morss Lovett* (New York: Viking, 1948), 55.

16. John Greenleaf Whittier to WDH, 21 September 1887, *The Letters of John Greenleaf Whittier,* ed. John B. Pickard (Cambridge, MA: Harvard University Press, 1975), 3: 538.

17. John Greenleaf Whittier to Annie Fields, 31 July 1886 (Huntington).

18. WDH to John Greenleaf Whittier, 1 November 1887, *SL,* 3: 198.

19. Harriet Earhart Monroe, "Statesman and Novelist: A Talk between Senator Ingalls and Mr. Howells," *Interviews with William Dean Howells,* ed. Ulrich Halfmann, *American Literary Realism,* special issue, 6 (Fall 1973): 286.

20. WDH to Roger A. Pryor, 25 September 1887, *SL,* 3: 197.

21. Roger A. Pryor to WDH, 3 October 1887, *Life in Letters,* 1: 394.

22. See *SL,* 3: 198 n2; Cady, *The Road to Realism,* 70–71.

23. See *SL,* 3: 199 n1.

24. See *SL,* 3: 194 n2.

25. James W. Hulse, *Revolutionists in London: A Study of Five Unorthodox Socialists* (Oxford: Clarendon Press, 1970), 8. See WDH to Mark Twain, 11 April 1891, *Twain-Howells Letters,* 2: 643.

26. WDH to Edmund Gosse, 2 January 1884, *Transatlantic Dialogue,* 128.

27. Brand Whitlock, *Forty Years of It* (New York: D. Appleton, 1920), 72.

28. Whitelaw Reid to WDH, 8 November 1887, *SL,* 3: 200 n1.

29. WDH to the editor of the *New York Tribune,* 6 November 1887, *SL,* 3: 199.

30. *New York Tribune,* 22 October; 6, 8, 11 November 1887. See *SL,* 3: 205 n2.

31. WDH to Francis F. Browne, 11 November 1887, *SL,* 3: 200.

32. WDH to the editor of the *New York Tribune,* 12 November 1887, *SL,* 3: 201–4.

33. See *SL,* 3: 205 n15.

34. WDH to George Curtis, 10 August 1887, *SL,* 3: 194 n1.

35. WDH to William C. Howells, 13 November 1887, *SL,* 3: 206.

36. WDH, "From Master and Man by Leo Tolstoy," *Prefaces to Contemporaries,* ed. George Arms, William M. Gibson, and Frederic C. Marston Jr. (Gainesville, FL: Scholars' Facsimiles and Reprints, 1957), 41.

37. WDH, "Lyof Tolstoi," *Harper's Weekly* 31 (23 April 1887): 299–300, cited in Louis Budd's excellent "Howells' Debt to Tolstoi," *American Slavic and East European Review* 9 (December 1950): 293.

38. WDH to Edward Everett Hale, 28 June 1887, *SL,* 3: 189.

39. WDH, August 1886, in *Editor's Study,* ed. James W. Simpson (Troy, NY: Whitson, 1993), 38.

40. WDH to Thomas W. Higginson, 28 September 1888, *SL,* 3: 230.

41. Review of *Annie Kilburn, New York Tribune* (23 December 1888): 16.

42. WDH, *Annie Kilburn, Novels, 1886–1888,* ed. Don L. Cook (New York: Library of America, 1989), 804.

43. Hamlin Garland, *Roadside Meetings* (New York: Macmillan, 1930), 197.

44. WDH to William C. Howells, 17 April 1887, *SL,* 3: 186.

45. WDH to Edward Everett Hale, 28 June 1887, *SL,* 3: 189.

46. WDH, *The World of Chance* (New York: Harper & Brothers, 1893), 91.

47. WDH to Edward Everett Hale, 28 June 1887, *SL,* 3: 189.

48. Undated letter transcribed in Garlin, *William Dean Howells and the Haymarket Era,* 38.

49. James R. Lowell to WDH, 16 January 1890 (Houghton).

50. "Marie Barberi's Story," *New York Times* (26 November 1896): 2: 9. Barberi's name is also given as Barbella.

51. WDH, *The Minister's Charge, or The Apprenticeship of Lemuel Barker,* introduction and notes to the text by Howard M. Munford; text established by David J. Nordloh and David Kleinman (Bloomington: Indiana University Press, 1978), 341.

52. WDH, *Annie Kilburn,* 861–62.

53. WDH, *Annie Kilburn,* 796.

54. WDH to Henry James, 25 December 1886, *SL,* 3: 176.

55. Marian Hooper to R. W. Hooper, 26 January 1879, quoted in Ernest Samuels, *Henry Adams* (Cambridge: Harvard University Press, 1989), 200.

56. WDH, *Ragged Lady* (New York: Harper & Brothers, 1908), 28; *The Kentons,* introduction and notes to the text by George C. Carrington Jr.; text established by Carrington and Ronald Gottesman (Bloomington: Indiana University Press, 1971), 14.

57. Ginette de B. Merrill, "Two Howells Collections," *Resources for American Literary Study* 11 (Spring 1981): 10.

58. WDH to William C. Howells, November 1888 (Houghton).

59. WDH, *Winifred Howells,* privately printed (1891), 15.

60. WDH, *Winifred Howells,* 10.

61. WDH to Charles Eliot Norton, 14 July 1897, *SL,* 3: 191.

62. WDH to Sam Howells, 31 March 1889 (Alfred).

63. WDH, *Winifred Howells,* 4.

64. WDH to William C. Howells, 13 February 1887 (Houghton).

65. WDH to William C. Howells, 19 March 1888 (Houghton).

66. WDH to Annie Fréchette, 18 November 1887, *SL,* 3: 207.

67. WDH to William C. Howells, 29 April 1888, *SL,* 3: 225.

68. WDH to Thomas S. Perry, 14 April 1888, *SL,* 3: 223; and to William C. Howells, 1 April 1888, *SL,* 3: 221.

69. WDH to William C. Howells, 8 July 1888, *SL,* 3: 226.

70. WDH, *A Hazard of New Fortunes,* 64.

71. WDH to William C. Howells, 7 October 1888, *SL,* 3: 230 n1.

72. S. Weir Mitchell, *Doctor and Patient* (New York: Arno Press & *The New York Times,* 1972), 118–19.

73. S. Weir Mitchell to WDH [response to Howells' letter of 20 October 1885], n.d. (University of Pennsylvania).

74. WDH to William C. Howells, 25 November 1888, *SL,* 3: 235 n1.

75. Anna Robeson Burr, *Weir Mitchell, His Life and Letters* (New York: Duffield & Co., 1929), 184.

76. WDH to William C. Howells, 2 December 1888, *SL,* 3: 235 n1.

77. WDH to William C. Howells, 6 January 1889, *SL,* 3: 243 n4.

78. S. Weir Mitchell, *Fat and Blood: An Essay on the Treatment of Certain Forms of Neurasthenia and Hysteria* (Philadelphia: J. B. Lippincott, 1907), 38.

79. For this interpretation of Winny's illness, see John W. Crowley, "Winifred Howells and the Economy of Pain," *The Mask of Fiction* (Amherst: University of Massachusetts Press, 1989), 83–114.

80. WDH to Samuel D. Howells, 31 March 1899 (Alfred).

81. WDH to Horace Scudder, 3 March 1889 (Houghton); see *SL,* 3: 246 n3.

82. Henry James to WDH, 20 March 1889, *SL,* 3: 251 n2.

83. Sarah Orne Jewett to WDH, 22 May 1889 (Houghton).

84. Mark Twain to Elisabeth Fairchild, 8 March 1892 (Virginia).

85. Mark Twain to WDH, 22 January 1898, *Twain-Howells Letters,* 2: 670.

86. WDH to Mark Twain, 9 January 1898, *Twain-Howells Letters,* 2: 667.

87. Mark Twain to Livy Clemens, 19 August 1896, *Twain-Howells Letters,* 2: 664 n1.

88. WDH to Horace E. Scudder, 11 March 1889, *Life in Letters,* 1: 422.

89. WDH to Edward Everett Hale, 5 April 1889, *Life in Letters,* 1: 425.

90. WDH to Mark Twain, 21 July 1889, *Life in Letters,* 1: 427.

91. WDH to Annie Fréchette, 3 April 1889 (Houghton).

92. WDH to S. Weir Mitchell, 30 October 1908, *SL,* 5: 261. Mitchell dedi-

cated *The Red City* to Howells, "in payment of a debt to a master of fiction and to a friend of many years."

93. S. Weir Mitchell to WDH, 29 February 1891 (University of Pennsylvania).

94. WDH to William C. Howells, 30 March 1890, *If Not Literature: Letters of Elinor Mead Howells,* ed. Ginette de B. Merrill and George Arms (Columbus: Ohio State University Press, 1988), 266–68.

95. WDH to John M. Howells, 15 June 1889, *SL,* 3: 254.

96. WDH, *Winifred Howells,* 25.

97. WDH to Annie Fréchette, 17 January 1913, *SL,* 6: 27.

98. WDH, "Father and Mother, A Mystery," *Harper's New Monthly Magazine* 100 (May 1900): 874.

CHAPTER THIRTEEN

1. WDH, *A Hazard of New Fortunes,* introduction by Everett Carter; notes to the text and text established by David J. Nordloh (Bloomington: Indiana University Press, 1993), 4.

2. See Amy Kaplan, *The Social Construction of American Realism* (Chicago: University of Chicago Press, 1988), 9. Kaplan argues that realists like Howells "engage in an enormous act of construction to organize, re-form, and control the social world," which makes it both static and "tentative" (10). See also Donald E. Pease, "Introduction," *New Essays on The Rise of Silas Lapham,* ed. Donald E. Pease (Cambridge: Oxford University Press, 1991), 1–28.

3. "As Howells Sees Fiction," *Interviews with William Dean Howells,* ed. Ulrich Halfmann, *American Literary Realism* 6 (Fall 1973): 335.

4. See Adam Gopnik, "A Hazard of No Fortune," *The New Yorker* (21 and 28 February 2000): 186.

5. WDH, *A Hazard of New Fortunes,* 184.

6. WDH to William C. Howells, 26 May 1889, *SL,* 3: 252.

7. WDH, *A Hazard of New Fortunes,* 4.

8. Edwin G. Burrows and Mike Wallace, *Gotham: A History of New York City to 1898* (New York: Oxford University Press, 1999), 1105.

9. WDH to William C. Howells, 6 November 1892, *SL,* 4: 29; WDH to William C. Howells, 9 November 1890, *Life in Letters,* 2: 8–9.

10. WDH to William C. Howells, 10 July 1892 (Houghton).

11. WDH to Andrew Carnegie, 26 February 1892, *SL,* 4: 15.

12. WDH to William C. Howells, 7 February 1892, *SL,* 4: 12.

13. Edwin H. Cady, *The Realist at War: The Mature Years, 1885–1920, of William Dean Howells* (Syracuse, NY: Syracuse University Press, 1958), 192.

14. WDH, *Impressions and Experiences* (New York: Harper & Brothers, 1909), 207.

15. *Twain-Howells Letters,* 2: 579.

16. Edward Bellamy to WDH, 17 June 1888, published in Joseph Schiffman, "Mutual Indebtedness: Unpublished Letters of Edward Bellamy to William Dean Howells," *Harvard Library Bulletin* 12 (Autumn 1958): 370.

17. Quoted in Thomas Peyser, *Utopia and Cosmopolis: Globalization in the Era of American Literary Realism* (Durham, NC: Duke University Press, 1998), 96.

18. Thomas W. Higginson, "Edward Bellamy's Nationalism," *The Magnificent Activist: The Writings of Thomas Wentworth Higginson (1823–1911),* ed. Howard N. Meyer (New York: Da Capo Press, 2000), 388.

19. WDH to Henry James, 10 October 1888, *Letters, Fictions, Lives: Henry James and William Dean Howells,* ed. Michael Anesko (New York: Oxford University Press, 1997), 271. See Gregory L. Crider, "William Dean Howells and the Gilded Age: Socialist in a Fur-Lined Overcoat," *Ohio History* 88 (Autumn 1979): 416.

20. Hamlin Garland, *Roadside Meetings* (New York: Macmillan, 1930), 63–64.

21. WDH, *A Hazard of New Fortunes,* 173.

22. WDH, *Literature and Life* (New York: Harper & Brothers, 1902), 271.

23. Thomas Peyser, *Utopia and Cosmopolis,* 134.

24. WDH, "Edward Bellamy," *W. D. Howells as Critic,* ed. Edwin H. Cady (London: Routledge & Kegan Paul, 1973), 285.

25. Editor's Study, *Harper's Monthly* (June 1888): 140–41.

26. Polly H. Howells, "Mildred Howells as the Father's Daughter," *Harvard Library Bulletin* 5 (Spring 1994): 17.

27. WDH to Aurelia H. Howells, 5 January 1890, *SL,* 3: 270.

28. WDH to William C. Howells, 24 November 1889, *SL,* 3: 262.

29. WDH to Howard Pyle, 22 December 1890, *SL,* 3: 299.

30. WDH to Aurelia H. Howells, 5 January 1890, *SL,* 3: 270.

31. WDH to William C. Howells, 19 April 1892 (Houghton).

32. See Clara Kirk and Rudolf Kirk, "Howells and the Church of the Carpenter," *New England Quarterly* 32 (June 1959): 185–206.

33. WDH to Charles Eliot Norton, 25 December 1889, *SL,* 3: 265.

34. WDH to Edward Everett Hale, 30 August 1888, *SL,* 3: 229.

35. WDH, [William James and Hjalmar Boyesen], *Literary Criticism* 2 (July 1891): 174.

36. See H. S. Thayer, "Introduction," in William James, *Pragmatism* (Cambridge, MA: Harvard University Press, 1975), xiii–xiv.

37. WDH to Howard Pyle, 13 April 1890, quoted in *The Shadow of a Dream and An Imperative Duty,* introduction and notes to the text by Martha Banta; text established by Banta, Ronald Gottesman, and David J. Nordloh (Bloomington: Indiana University Press, 1970), xvii.

38. WDH to William C. Howells, 15 February 1891, *SL,* 3: 307.

39. WDH to William C. Howells, 9 February 1890, *SL,* 3: 274.

40. WDH, *A Boy's Town* (New York: Harper & Brothers, 1890), 1–2.

41. WDH, "An Imperative Duty," in *The Shadow of a Dream and An Imperative Duty,* 50.

42. W. E. B. Dubois, "As a Friend of the Colored Man," *Boston Transcript* (24 February 1912), part 3: 2.

43. WDH, "An Imperative Duty," 58.

44. Howells was the first of three *Atlantic* editors who wrote novels dealing with race, the others being Bliss Perry with *The Plated City* (1895) and Walter Hines Page with *The Autobiography of Nicholas Worth* (1921).

45. WDH to Mark Twain, 19 May 1891, *Twain-Howells Letters,* 2: 644.

46. See Cady, *The Realist at War,* 163–64.

47. Harper's to WDH, 14 April 1890, *SL,* 3: 279 n1.

48. WDH to William C. Howells, 15 June 1892, *SL,* 4: 20.

49. WDH to William C. Howells, 14 June 1891, *SL,* 3: 314.

50. WDH to William C. Howells, 18 October 1891, *SL,* 3: 321.

51. Quoted in Clara Marburg Kirk, *W. D. Howells, Traveler from Altruria* (New Brunswick, NJ: Rutgers University Press, 1962), 54 n8, 62.

52. See WDH, *Literature and Life,* 222, 179.

53. "Editor" may be misleading; it is certainly inadequate to describe his never-quite-defined position with the *Cosmopolitan.* "Major contributor and literary director" would all make as much sense, with "figurehead" close behind.

54. D. M. Rein, "Howells and the *Cosmopolitan,*" *American Literature* 21 (March 1949): 49.

55. Charles Eliot Norton to WDH, 19 December 1891 (Houghton).

56. See WDH to Charles Eliot Norton, 12 December 1891, *SL,* 3: 327; WDH to William C. Howells, 13 December 1891, *SL,* 3: 328.

57. *The Cosmopolitan* (March 1890), quoted in Kirk, *W. D. Howells, Traveler from Altruria,* 43.

58. See Henry Alden to WDH, 14 September 1888 (Houghton); quoted in Kirk, *W. D. Howells, Traveler from Altruria,* 19.

59. Quoted in Rein, "Howells and the *Cosmopolitan,*" 51.

60. WDH to William C. Howells, 20 December 1891, *Life in Letters,* 2: 20.

61. Henry James to WDH, 12 December 1891, in Anesko, *Letters, Fictions, Lives,* 287.

62. *Letters of Richard Watson Gilder,* ed. Rosamond Gilder (Boston: Houghton Mifflin, 1916), 181.

63. Paul F. Mattheisen and Michael Millgate, eds., *Transatlantic Dialogue: Selected American Correspondence of Edmund Gosse* (Austin: University of Texas Press, 1965), 88–89.

64. *Transatlantic Dialogue,* 121 n1.

65. See *Life and Letters of Edmund Clarence Stedman,* ed. Laura Stedman and George H. Gould (New York: Moffat, Yard, 1910), 249.

66. See Arthur Johns, *The Best Years of the Century* (Urbana: University of Illinois Press, 1981), 215–16.

67. Quoted in Johns, *The Best Years of the Century,* 157.

68. See Johns, *The Best Years of the Century,* 24.

69. Henry Alden to WDH, 29 January 1890 (Houghton).

70. Hamlin Garland, *Roadside Meetings,* 338.

71. Laurence Hutton, *Talks in a Library with Laurence Hutton* (New York: G. P. Putnam's Sons, 1905), 416–17.

72. Edward Bok, *The Americanization of Edward Bok* (New York: Charles Scribner's Sons, 1921), 212.

73. WDH, *Literary Friends and Acquaintance: A Personal Retrospect of American Authorship,* ed. David F. Hiatt and Edwin H. Cady (Bloomington: Indiana University Press, 1968), 32.

74. Hamlin Garland, *My Friendly Contemporaries* (New York: Macmillan, 1932), 295.

75. See Elizabeth Stevenson, *Lafcadio Hearn* (New York: Macmillan, 1961), 186–87.

76. WDH to Charles Eliot Norton, 28 February 1892, *SL,* 4: 17.

77. Rein, "Howells and the *Cosmopolitan,*" 55.

78. WDH, *The Altrurian Romances,* introduction and notes to the text by Clara Kirk and Rudolf Kirk; text established by Scott Bennett (Bloomington: Indiana University Press, 1968), 14.

79. H. E. Scudder, Review of William Dean Howells' *Criticism and Fiction, Atlantic Monthly* 68 (October 1891): 567.

80. Henry James to Robert Louis Stevenson, 1 October 1887, *Henry James Letters,* ed. Leon Edel (Cambridge, MA: Harvard University Press, 1974–84), 3: 205.

81. Henry Mills Alden, "William Dean Howells," *The Bookman* 49 (July 1919): 553–54.

82. A. Schade van Westrum, "Mr. Howells on Love and Literature," *Interviews with William Dean Howells,* ed. Ulrich Halfmann, *American Literary Realism,* special issue, 6 (Fall 1973): 352.

83. Henry Mills Alden, "Recollections of a Fellow Editor," *The Book News Monthly* 26 (June 1908): 731.

84. WDH to Aurelia H. Howells, 21 October 1892, *SL,* 4: 26 n2.

85. WDH to Charles Eliot Norton, 16 October 1892, *SL,* 4: 25.

86. "Mr. Howells Sees the Fair," *The Sun* (22 October 1893).

87. Kirk, *W. D. Howells, Traveler from Altruria,* 101.

88. WDH to Mildred Howells, 14 July 1895 (Houghton).

89. Henry James, 31 October 1895, *The Complete Notebooks of Henry James,* ed. Leon Edel and Lyall H. Powers (New York: Oxford University Press, 1987), 141.

90. Henry James, 31 October 1895, *Complete Notebooks,* 141.

91. WDH to Henry James, 21 August 1894, *SL,* 4: 75.

92. WDH to Mildred Howells, 1 July 1894, *SL,* 4: 70.

93. WDH to John M. Howells, 27 July 1894, *Life in Letters,* 2: 52.

94. William C. Howells to Joseph Howells, 6–25 March 1893 (Huntington).

95. WDH to Henry James, 21 August 1894, *SL,* 4: 74.

96. WDH to Charles Eliot Norton, 25 October 1894, *SL,* 4: 78.

97. William C. Howells' Memorabilia and Lists (Alfred).

98. WDH to John Goddard, 16 September 1894, *SL,* 4: 77.

99. WDH to Joseph A. Howells, 15 September 1894, *SL,* 4: 76.

CHAPTER FOURTEEN

1. WDH to Charles Eliot Norton, 25 October 1894, *SL,* 4: 78.

2. WDH, "From Generation to Generation," *Harper's Monthly* 86 (March 1893): 549, published in *Stops of Various Quills* (New York: Harper, 1896).

3. WDH to Mildred Howells, 1 August 1895, *SL,* 4: 108.

4. WDH to Aurelia H. Howells [and Annie Howells], 8 December 1907 (Houghton).

5. WDH to Mildred Howells, 15 March 1907 (Houghton).

6. WDH to Aurelia H. Howells, 15 September 1895, *SL,* 4: 113.

7. WDH to Joseph A. Howells, 21 June 1906, *SL,* 5: 162 n3.

8. WDH to Aurelia H. Howells, 4 November 1894 (Houghton).

9. WDH to Aurelia H. Howells, 12 January 1896, *SL,* 4: 120. Minnie and her daughter Hazel would live with Aurelia from 1896 to 1901.

10. WDH to Aurelia H. Howells, 29 December 1895, *SL,* 4: 118.

11. WDH to Aurelia H. Howells, 30 January 1898, *SL,* 4: 163.

12. WDH to Aurelia H. Howells, 23 June 1907 (Houghton).

13. WDH to Charles Eliot Norton, 11 December 1892, *SL,* 4: 32 n2.

14. Harper & Brothers contract, 23 February 1892, Harper & Brothers Archives, Rare Book and Manuscript Library, Columbia University.

15. WDH, *The Landlord at Lion's Head* (New York: Dover Publications, 1983), 1.

16. WDH, *The Son of Royal Langbrith,* introduction and notes by David Burrows; text established by Burrows, Ronald Gottesman, and David J. Nordloh (Bloomington: Indiana University Press, 1969), 158.

17. WDH, *The Landlord at Lion's Head,* 1.

18. WDH, *A Foregone Conclusion,* in *Novels, 1875–1886,* ed. Edwin H. Cady (New York: The Library of America, 1982), 32–33, 67. See James L. Dean, *Howells' Travels toward Art* (Albuquerque: University of New Mexico Press, 1970).

19. WDH, *The Coast of Bohemia* (New York: Harper & Brothers, 1899), 335.

20. See Edward Bok, *The Americanization of Edward Bok* (New York: Charles Scribner's Sons, 1921), 191.

21. Bok, *The Americanization of Edward Bok,* 202.

22. WDH to Mildred Howells, 24 June 1895 (Houghton).

23. WDH to Aurelia H. Howells, 21 April 1895, *SL,* 4: 103.

24. Because Howells had completed the manuscript of *The Quality of Mercy* before he signed his new contract, Harper's wanted to pay him according to the royalty rate (10 percent) stipulated in his old contract. Howells asked for and received the new rate (20 percent) on all copies except the paper edition.

25. George Mifflin to Elizabeth Stuart Phelps, July 1897, *SL,* 4: 140 n1.

26. WDH to Aurelia H. Howells, 19 January 1896, *SL,* 4: 122.

27. WDH to Aurelia H. Howells, 25 July 1897, *SL,* 4: 155.

28. WDH to Aurelia H. Howells, 26 September 1897, *SL,* 4: 158.

29. WDH to Charles Eliot Norton, 27 December 1897, *SL,* 4: 161.

30. Henry James to WDH, 28 January 1898, *Letters, Fictions, Lives: Henry James and William Dean Howells,* ed. Michael Anesko (New York: Oxford University Press, 1997), 305.

31. Henry James to WDH, 27 November 1897, in Anesko, *Letters, Fictions, Lives,* 304.

32. WDH to Mark Twain, 9 January 1898, *Twain-Howells Letters,* 2: 667.

33. WDH to Aurelia H. Howells, 12 December 1897, *SL,* 4: 160.

34. WDH to Aurelia H. Howells, 19 June 1898, *SL,* 4: 177.

35. WDH to Aurelia H. Howells, 12 December 1897, *SL,* 4: 160.

36. WDH to Aurelia H. Howells, 19 June 1898, *SL,* 4: 178.

37. WDH to Mark Twain, 2 August 1898, *Twain-Howells Letters,* 2: 673.

38. WDH to Aurelia H. Howells, 29 December 1895, *SL,* 4: 118–19; Charles Eliot Norton to WDH, 12 December 1900 (Houghton).

39. WDH to Aurelia H. Howells, 17 April 1898, *SL,* 4: 170.

40. George Santayana, *Persons and Places: The Background of My Life* (New York: Charles Scribner's Sons, 1944), 2: 166–70.

41. See Jim Zwick, "William Dean Howells and the Anti-Imperialist League," *Mark Twain Journal* 32 (Spring 1994): 25–26. Howells belonged to the Philippine Independence Committee and served as vice president of the Filipino Progress Association. See also Cherrie L. Soper, "Howells, Santayana and the Spanish American War," *La Chispa '85, Selected Proceedings,* ed. Gilbert Paolini (New Orleans: Tulane University, 1985), 325–31.

42. WDH to Aurelia H. Howells, 24 February 1901, *Life in Letters,* 2: 142. For Twain and Howells on imperialism, see William M. Gibson, "Mark Twain and Howells: Anti-Imperialists," *New England Quarterly* 20 (December 1947): 435–70.

43. Quoted in Gibson, "Mark Twain and Howells," 466, 468.

44. "Opinions of W. D. Howells," *New York Sun,* 30 April 1899.

45. WDH to Aurelia H. Howells, 17 April 1898, *SL,* 4: 171.

46. WDH to Aurelia H. Howells, 24 July 1898, *SL,* 4: 180; WDH, "Spanish Prisoners of War," *Literature and Life* (New York: Harper & Brothers, 1902), 151.

47. WDH to Aurelia H. Howells, 15 May 1898, *SL,* 4: 175.

48. Harold Frederic to Hamlin Garland, 12 May 1897. This and the letters quoted above are cited in Everett Carter's fine introduction to Frederic's *The Damnation of Theron Ware* (Cambridge, MA: Harvard University Press, 1960), xi–xii.

49. Stephen Crane to WDH, 28 March 1893, *Stephen Crane: Letters,* ed. L. Gilkes and R. W. Stallman (London: P. Owen, 1960), 16.

50. WDH to Cora Crane, 29 July 1900, *SL,* 4: 248.

51. Stephen Crane to WDH, 15 August [1896], *Correspondence of Stephen Crane,* ed. Stanley Wetheim and Paul Sorrentino (New York: Columbia University Press, 1988), 245.

52. See Larzer Ziff's unmatched study, *The American 1890s: Life and Times of a Lost Generation* (New York: Viking, 1966), 187.

53. Stephen Crane, *Correspondence,* 247.

54. See *The Sullivan County Sketches of Stephen Crane,* ed. Melvin Shoberlin (Syracuse, NY: Syracuse University Press, 1949), 19. Also see Stephen Crane to WDH, 1 January [1894], *Life in Letters,* 2: 42.

55. WDH, *Impressions and Experiences* (New York: Harper & Brothers, 1909), 133.

56. WDH, *Impressions and Experiences,* 139.

57. WDH to Edmund C. Stedman, 13 September 1899, *SL,* 4: 213.

58. Rudolf Kirk and Clara M. Kirk, "Abraham Cahan and William Dean Howells," *American Jewish Historical Quarterly* 52 (September 1962): 29–30.

59. WDH to Annie Fields, 13 August 1911 (Huntington).

60. Abraham Cahan, "Bleter fun mein Leben," *Autobiography* (New York: n.p., 1926–1931), 4: 34–36, quoted in Kirk and Kirk, "Cahan and Howells," 33.

61. Quoted in Kirk and Kirk, "Cahan and Howells," 33.

62. Paul Laurence Dunbar to Lucy Giddons Morse, 30 October 1896 (Bancroft). James B. Pond arranged the meeting.

63. William Dean Howells, "Introduction," *The Life and Works of Paul Laurence Dunbar* (Nashville, TN: Winston-Derek, 1992), 15. See also Life and Letters, *Harper's Weekly* 40 (27 June 1896): 630; and Elsa Nettels, *Language, Race, and Social Class in Howells's America* (Lexington: University Press of Kentucky, 1988), 81.

64. W. E. B. Dubois, "As a Friend of the Colored Man," *Boston Transcript* (24 February 1912), 3: 2.

65. WDH, "Introduction," *Life and Works of Paul Laurence Dunbar,* 13–14.

66. For a discussion of Howells and Dunbar, see Nettels, *Language, Race, and Social Class,* 80–86; Clare R. Goldfarb, "The Questions of William Dean How-

ells's Racism," *Ball State University Forum* 12 (1971): 22–24; and James B. Stronks, "Paul Laurence Dunbar and William Dean Howells," *Ohio Historical Quarterly* 67 (April 1958): 95–108.

67. See William L. Andrews, "William Dean Howells and Charles W. Chesnutt: Criticism and Race Fiction in the Age of Booker T. Washington," *American Literature* 48 (November 1976): 327–39. See also Houston A. Baker, *The Journey Back: Issues in Black Literature and Criticism* (Chicago: University of Chicago Press, 1980), 158.

68. WDH, "Mr. Charles W. Chesnutt's Stories," *Atlantic Monthly* 85 (May 1900): 699–701.

69. WDH, "A Psychological Counter-Current in Recent Fiction," *North American Review* 173 (1901): 882–83. See Joseph R. McElrath Jr., "W. D. Howells and Race: Charles W. Chesnutt's Disappointment of the Dean," *Nineteenth-Century Literature* 51 (March 1997): 474–99.

70. WDH to Henry Blake Fuller, 10 November 1901, *SL*, 4: 274.

71. See Franklin Walker, *Frank Norris: A Biography* (New York: Russell & Russell, 1963), 209.

72. Theodore Dreiser, "The Real Howells," *Interviews with William Dean Howells*, ed. Ulrich Halfmann, *American Literary Realism*, special issue, 6 (Fall 1973): 347.

73. Theodore Dreiser to WDH, 14 May 1902, *SL*, 5: 28 n3.

74. WDH to Aurelia H. Howells, 24 May 1902, *SL*, 5: 27.

75. See WDH, *Prefaces to Contemporaries*, ed. George Arms, William M. Gibson, and Frederic C. Marston Jr. (Gainesville, FL: Scholars' Facsimiles and Reprints, 1957), 198.

76. Ellen Glasgow, *The Woman Within* (New York: Harcourt, Brace), 139–40.

77. WDH to Hamlin Garland, 18 March 1898 (USC).

78. "Mr. Howell's Model," *Munsey's Magazine* 11 (May 1894): 217.

79. James Pond, Eccentricities of Genius (New York: G. W. Dillingham, 1900), 231.

80. James Pond, *Eccentricities of Genius*, 333.

81. WDH to James B. Pond, 20 September 1896, *SL*, 4: 133 n1.

82. Arlin Turner, *Mark Twain and George W. Cable: The Record of a Literary Friendship* (East Lansing: Michigan State University, 1960), 44, 117. See Pond, *Eccentricities of Genius*, 231. Pond remembers the sum as six hundred dollars.

83. WDH, *My Mark Twain* (New York: Harper & Brothers, 1910), 53.

84. WDH, *My Mark Twain*, 50.

85. Mark Twain, *Autobiography of Mark Twain*, ed. Charles Neider (New York: Harper & Brothers, 1959), 181.

86. WDH to Elinor M. Howells, 27 March 1898, *SL*, 4: 147.

87. WDH to Frederick A. Duneka, 21 January 1915, *SL*, 6: 71.

88. WDH to James B. Pond, 4 June 1899 (Virginia).

89. WDH to Mark Twain, 11 June 1899, *Twain-Howells Letters*, 2: 700. See Thomas Wortham, "W. D. Howells' 1899 Midwest Lecture Tour: What the Letters Tell," *American Literary Realism* 11 (1978): 265–74. As Wortham writes, Howells cut his tour short, giving twenty lectures in all.

90. WDH to James B. Pond, 6 June 1899, *SL,* 5: 206 n2.

91. WDH to Mark Twain, 11 June 1899, *Twain-Howells Letters,* 2: 700.

92. Pond, *Eccentricities of Genius,* 334.

93. WDH to Elinor M. Howells, 18–19 October 1899, *SL,* 4: 214.

94. WDH to Elinor M. Howells, 29 October 1899, *SL,* 4: 219.

95. Quoted in Robert Rowlette, "William D. Howells' 1899 Midwest Lecture Tour," *American Literary Realism* 9 (1976): 18.

96. WDH to Elinor M. Howells, 24–25 October 1899, *SL,* 4: 216.

97. Jane Addams, *Twenty Years at Hull House* (New York: Macmillan, 1910), 260.

98. Rowlette, "William D. Howells' Lecture Tour," 130.

99. WDH to James B. Pond, 30 October 1899; quoted in *SL,* 4: 220 n3.

100. WDH to Elinor M. Howells, 6 November 1899, *SL,* 4: 222.

101. WDH to James B. Pond, 10 November 1899, *SL,* 4: 225.

102. Polly H. Howells, "Mildred Howells as the Father's Daughter," *Harvard Library Bulletin* 5 (Spring 1994): 20.

103. Quoted in Rowlette, "William D. Howells' Lecture Tour," 164 n106.

104. Rowlette, "William D. Howells' Lecture Tour," 151–52.

105. Booth Tarkington, "Mr. Howells," *Harper's Magazine* 141 (August 1920): 347.

106. Gerald Stanley Lee, "Mr. Howells on the Platform," *Critic* 35 (November 1899): 1030.

107. Lee, "Mr. Howells on the Platform," 1030.

108. WDH to Aurelia H. Howells, 26 February 1899, *Life in Letters,* 2: 100.

109. WDH, "Eighty Years and After," *SL,* 6: 160.

CHAPTER FIFTEEN

1. WDH, "Spanish Prisoners of War," *Literature and Life* (New York: Harper & Brothers, 1902), 148.

2. WDH to Aurelia H. Howells, 17 June 1900, *SL,* 4: 238.

3. WDH to Henry James, 15 July 1900, *SL,* 4: 241–42. See also WDH, "From New York into New England" (1898), *Literature and Life,* 228–39.

4. WDH to Henry James, 15 July 1900, *SL,* 4: 242.

5. WDH, "The Problem of the Summer," *Harper's Weekly* (11 July 1896), in *Literature and Life,* 217. The same volume includes "Confessions of a Summer Colonist" (*Atlantic Monthly,* December 1898).

6. WDH to Aurelia H. Howells, 28 January 1900, *SL,* 4: 229.

7. WDH to Henry James, 10 September 1899, *SL,* 4: 211.

8. WDH, *Harper's Monthly* 122 (May 1911): 122.

9. WDH, *Harper's Monthly* 124 (October 1911): 796–99.

10. WDH to Charles Eliot Norton, 6 April 1902, *SL,* 5: 22.

11. WDH to Aurelia H. Howells, 11 May 1902, *SL,* 5: 26.

12. For Howells' financial arrangements with *Harper's,* see Eugene Exman, *The House of Harper: One Hundred Fifty Years of Publishing* (New York: Harper & Row, 1967), 153–62.

13. Exman, *The House of Harper,* 178. The popular humorist John Kendrick Bangs conducted the poll sometime after 1898, when he and Howells did various "chores" for the *Harper's* magazines.

14. WDH to Cora Crane, 29 July 1900, *SL,* 4: 248.

15. WDH to Susan L. Warner, 29 October 1900, *SL,* 4: 251.

16. WDH to Edith Wharton, 29 October 1900, *SL,* 4: 252.

17. WDH to Hamlin Garland, 23 August 1893 (USC).

18. WDH to Aurelia H. Howells, 24 October 1900, *SL,* 4: 250.

19. WDH to Aurelia H. Howells, 25 June 1899 (Houghton).

20. WDH to Aurelia H. Howells, 7 November 1896 (Houghton); *SL,* 5: 133 n3.

21. WDH to James B. Pond, 5 December 1900, *SL,* 4: 256.

22. Mark Twain, "Introducing Winston S. Churchill," *Collected Tales, Sketches, Speeches, and Essays, 1891–1910* (New York: Library of America, 1992), 454–55.

23. WDH, quoting William Roscoe Thayer's *Life of John Hay,* Editor's Easy Chair, *Harper's Monthly* 132 (January 1916): 311.

24. Theodore Roosevelt to Henry Cabot Lodge, 9 December 1901, *Letters,* 3: 142. Cited in William M. Gibson, *Theodore Roosevelt among the Humorists: W. D. Howells, Mark Twain, and Mr. Dooley* (Knoxville: University of Tennessee Press, 1980), 15. We have relied on Gibson's fine study for much of this discussion.

25. WDH to Mark Twain, 23 October 1898, *Twain-Howells Letters,* 2: 682.

26. WDH to Barrett Wendell, 11 September 1914, *SL,* 6: 60–61.

27. WDH, *Tuscan Cities* (Boston and New York: Ticknor, 1884), 43.

28. WDH to Charles Eliot Norton, 6 April 1903, *SL,* 5: 51.

29. WDH to Mark Twain, 1 May 1903, *SL,* 5: 56.

30. WDH to Aurelia H. Howells, 24 February 1901, *SL,* 4: 258.

31. WDH to Aurelia H. Howells, 17 March 1901, *SL,* 4: 259.

32. WDH to Aurelia H. Howells, 3 August 1902 (Houghton).

33. WDH to Sir George Trevelyan, 24 May 1905, *SL,* 5: 121–22.

34. WDH to William James, 7 October 1902, *SL,* 5: 35.

35. WDH to Aurelia H. Howells, 30 March 1902, *SL,* 5: 20.

36. WDH to Aurelia H. Howells, 3 August 1903 (Houghton).

37. WDH to Aurelia H. Howells, 17 August 1902, *SL*, 5: 34.

38. WDH, *The Son of Royal Langbrith,* introduction and notes by David Burrows; text established by Burrows, Ronald Gottesman, and David J. Nordloh (Bloomington: Indiana University Press, 1969), 270.

39. WDH, "Confessions of a Summer Colonist," 48.

40. WDH, "Staccato Notes of a Vanished Summer," *Literature and Life,* 256.

41. WDH, "Spanish Prisoners," 142–43.

42. WDH to Aurelia H. Howells, 22 July 1902 (Houghton).

43. WDH to Sarah Orne Jewett, 21 May 1873 (Houghton).

44. WDH, "Certain of the Chicago School of Fiction," *North American Review* (May 1903), cited in *SL*, 5: 65 n3.

45. WDH, *Literary Friends and Acquaintance: A Personal Retrospect of American Authorship,* ed. David F. Hiatt and Edwin H. Cady (Bloomington: Indiana University Press, 1968), 107.

46. WDH, "Confessions of a Summer Colonist," 60, 62.

47. WDH to Charles Eliot Norton, 22 September 1901, *SL*, 4: 272.

48. WDH to Annie Fields, 23 February 1903, *SL*, 5: 48.

49. WDH to Aurelia H. Howells, 16 June 1901, *SL*, 4: 266.

50. WDH to Aurelia H. Howells, 30 March 1902, *SL*, 5: 20–21.

51. WDH to Thomas B. Aldrich, 5 March 1902, *SL*, 5: 16.

52. WDH to Mildred Howells, 17 March 1902, *SL*, 5: 17 n4.

53. WDH to Elinor M. Howells, 13 and 14 March 1904, *SL*, 5: 84.

54. WDH to John St. Loe Strachey, 14 February 1904, *SL*, 5: 79.

55. WDH to Aurelia H. Howells and Annie Fréchette, 26 June 1904, *SL*, 5: 106–7.

56. WDH to Aurelia H. Howells, 18 June 1905, *SL*, 5: 124–25 n2.

57. WDH, *Harper's Monthly* 126 (January 1913): 310.

58. WDH, *Harper's Monthly* 132 (March 1916): 634.

59. WDH, *Certain Delightful English Towns* (New York: Harper & Brothers, 1906), 44.

60. Mark Twain to WDH, 6 June 1904, *Twain-Howells Letters*, 2: 785.

61. WDH to Mark Twain, 7 June 1904, *SL*, 5: 104.

62. WDH to John St. Loe Strachey, 24 March 1904, *SL*, 5: 90.

63. WDH to Charles Eliot Norton, 11 June 1905, *SL*, 5: 123.

64. WDH to Annie Fréchette, 11 June 1905, *SL*, 5: 124.

65. Portsmouth (NH) *Herald,* 7 July 1905 (Aldrich Papers, Strawbery Banke Museum, Portsmouth, NH).

66. See Robert K. Massie, *Nicholas and Alexandra* (London: Folio Society, 2002), 94.

67. WDH, "The Peacemakers at Portsmouth," *Harper's Weekly* 26 (August 1905): 1225.

68. The phrase comes from Don L. Cook's fine lecture and pamphlet, "William Dean Howells: The Kittery Years" (William Dean Howells Memorial Committee: Kittery Point, Maine, 1991).

69. WDH, "The Peacemakers at Portsmouth," 1225.

70. WDH to David Douglas, 20 August 1905, *SL,* 5: 128.

71. WDH to Aurelia H. Howells, 13 August 1905, *SL,* 5: 129 n6.

72. *Memoirs of Count Witte;* quoted in Peter E. Randall, *There Are No Victors Here! A Local Perspective on the Treaty of Portsmouth* (Portsmouth, NH: Portsmouth Marine Society, 1983), 51.

73. Randall, *There Are No Victors,* 51–52.

74. See Kathleen Dalton, *Theodore Rex* (New York: Random House, 2001), 414.

75. WDH, *Harper's Weekly* 49 (August 1905): 1244.

76. WDH to Aurelia H. Howells, 13 August 1905, *SL,* 5: 129 n6.

77. WDH to Hamlin Garland, 20 August 1905, *SL,* 5: 130.

78. Leon Edel, *Henry James: A Life* (New York: Harper & Row, 1985), 588. Biographical information is taken from Edel as well as from Fred Kaplan, *Henry James: The Imagination of Genius* (New York: William Morrow, 1992).

79. WDH to Elinor M. Howells, 24 and 25 March 1904, *SL,* 5: 92.

80. Elinor M. Howells to Lucy E. Keeler, 7 February 1905, *If Not Literature: Letters of Elinor Mead Howells,* ed. Ginette de B. Merrill and George Arms (Columbus: Ohio State University Press, 1988), 300–301.

81. Henry James to Elinor M. Howells, 14 August 1905, *If Not Literature,* 298.

82. Quoted in Cook, "William Dean Howells," 1.

83. WDH to Aurelia H. Howells, 3 September 1905, *SL,* 5: 131.

CHAPTER SIXTEEN

1. See WDH to Joseph A. Howells, 4 January 1906, *SL,* 5: 157.

2. WDH to Joseph A. Howells, 4 January 1906, *SL,* 5: 157.

3. WDH to Joseph A. Howells, 25 November 1906, *SL,* 5: 197.

4. WDH to Joseph A. Howells, 20 April 1906, *SL,* 5: 174.

5. WDH to Aurelia H. Howells, 9 December 1906, *SL,* 5: 202 n2.

6. WDH to Joseph A. Howells, 5 September 1906, *SL,* 5: 193–94 n1.

7. WDH to Aurelia H. Howells, 10 June 1896 (Houghton).

8. WDH, Editor's Easy Chair, *Harper's Monthly* 128 (February 1914): 472–73.

9. WDH to Charles Eliot Norton, 11 March 1906, *SL,* 5: 167.

10. WDH to Aurelia H. Howells, 18 February 1906, *SL,* 5: 161 n3.

11. WDH to Mark Twain, 28 February 1906, *SL,* 5: 166.

12. Mark Twain speaking of WDH (as "the head of American literature"), 4 March 1906. Cited in *Twain-Howells Letters,* 2: 802 n1.

13. WDH to Mark Twain, 8 April 1906, *SL,* 5: 169.

14. WDH to Elinor M. Howells, 13 May 1904, *SL,* 5: 100.

15. WDH to Aurelia H. Howells, 8 April 1906, *SL,* 5: 170.

16. WDH to H. G. Wells, 24 June 1904, *SL,* 5: 105.

17. WDH to Mark Twain, 6 April 1906, *Twain-Howells Letters,* 2: 803.

18. See Leon Edel, *Henry James: A Life* (New York: Harper & Row, 1985), 700–702.

19. WDH to H. G. Wells, 19 May 1906, *SL,* 5: 178.

20. "Maxim Gorky Visits the Tomb of Grant," *New York Times* (13 April 1906): 2: 3.

21. Mark Twain, "The Gorky Incident" (1906) in *Mark Twain: Collected Tales, Sketches, Speeches, and Essays, 1891–1910* (New York: Library of America, 1992), 720.

22. WDH to Joseph A. Howells, 16 April 1906, *SL,* 5: 171.

23. H. G. Wells, "The Future in America: A Search after Realities," *Harper's Weekly* 8 (September 1906): 1284.

24. WDH to Joseph A. Howells, 16 April 1906, *SL,* 5: 171.

25. WDH to Charles Eliot Norton, 22 April 1906, *SL,* 5: 175 n5.

26. Charles Eliot Norton to WDH, 31 January 1907, partly quoted in *SL,* 5: 206 n1.

27. WDH to Charles Eliot Norton, 13 October 1907, *SL,* 5: 232.

28. WDH to Charles Eliot Norton, 27 June 1906, *SL,* 5: 186.

29. See *SL,* 5: 212 n2.

30. R. W. B. Lewis, "The Founders' Story," *A Century of Arts and Letters,* ed. John Updike (New York: Columbia University Press, 1998), 19–21.

31. WDH to Hamlin Garland, 23 July 1917 (USC).

32. WDH to Joseph A. Howells, 13 March 1907, *SL,* 5: 216–17.

33. Quoted in *SL,* 5: 217 n7.

34. See Alfred Bendixen, "Introduction," *The Whole Family: A Novel by Twelve Authors* (New York: Ungar Publishing Co., 1987), xi, xxxv. Harper's Bazar carried the novel from December 1907 to November 1908. See also June Howard, *Publishing the Family* (Durham, NC: Duke University Press, 2001). See also "Henry James and the Bazar Letters," in *Howells and James: A Double Billing,* ed. Leon Edel and Lyall H. Powers (New York: New York Public Library, 1958), 27–55.

35. WDH to Elizabeth Jordan, 4 June 1906, *SL,* 5: 180 n3.

36. WDH to Mildred Howells, 13 July 1902 (Houghton).

37. Mildred Howells, "Turn and Turn About," *Harper's New Monthly Magazine* 99 (1899): 980–81.

38. Quoted in Polly H. Howells, "Mildred Howells as the Father's Daughter," *Harvard Library Bulletin* 5 (Spring 1994): 21.

39. WDH, *Indian Summer,* introduction and notes to the text by Scott Bennett; text established by Bennett and David J. Nordloh (Bloomington: Indiana University Press, 1971), 269.

40. WDH, *A Hazard of New Fortunes,* introduction by Everett Carter; notes to the text and text established by David J. Nordloh (Bloomington: Indiana University Press, 1993), 479.

41. WDH to Joseph A. Howells, 13 March 1907, *SL,* 5: 217.

42. WDH to Henry James, 2 August 1908, *SL,* 5: 253.

43. WDH to Aurelia H. Howells, 22 November 1907, *SL,* 5: 235.

44. WDH to Aurelia H. Howells, 28 November 1907 (Houghton).

45. WDH to Aurelia H. Howells, 22 December 1907, *Life in Letters,* 2: 246–47.

46. WDH, *Roman Holidays and Others* (New York: Harper & Brothers, 1908), 123–24.

47. WDH to Aurelia H. Howells, 15 February 1908, *SL,* 5: 245.

48. WDH to Aurelia H. Howells, 26 August 1906 (Houghton).

49. WDH to Aurelia H. Howells, 26 April 1908 (Houghton).

50. WDH to Joseph A. Howells, 24 September 1908, *SL,* 5: 257.

51. WDH to Aurelia H. Howells, 28 October 1908, *SL,* 5: 293 n5.

52. WDH to Joseph A. Howells, 4 July 1909, *SL,* 5: 279.

53. Elizabeth Hawes, *New York, New York: How the Apartment House Transformed the Life of the City (1869–1930)* (New York: Alfred A. Knopf, 1993), 169.

54. Elinor M. Howells to Mildred Howells, 21 November 1908, *SL,* 5: 263 n2.

55. WDH to S. Weir Mitchell, 9 February 1911, *SL,* 5: 346.

56. WDH to Charles Eliot Norton, 11 October 1908, *SL,* 5: 259.

57. WDH to Henry James, 2 August 1908, *SL,* 5: 253.

58. Sarah Orne Jewett to WDH, 23 October [1909] (Houghton).

59. Mark Twain, *The Autobiography of Mark Twain,* ed. Charles Neider (New York: Harper & Brothers, 1959), 358, 359.

60. James Pond, *Eccentricities of Genius* (New York: G. W. Dillingham, 1900), 197.

61. Twain, *Autobiography,* 364.

62. Twain, *Autobiography,* 358.

63. Twain, *Autobiography,* 367.

64. WDH to Edmund C. Stedman, 28 April 1882 (Houghton).

65. WDH to Mark Twain, 12 March 1909, *SL,* 5: 270.

66. WDH to Sara Norton, 31 January 1909, *SL,* 5: 266.

67. WDH to Annie Fréchette, 6 December 1908, *SL,* 5: 265.

68. WDH to William W. Howells, 1 March 1909, *SL,* 5: 268.

69. WDH to Aurelia H. Howells and Annie Fréchette, 7 April 1917 (Houghton).

70. WDH to Elinor M. Howells, 24 March 1909, *SL,* 5: 272.

71. WDH to Henry James, 20 August 1909, *SL,* 5: 283; WDH to Mark Twain, 25 August 1909, *SL,* 5: 284.

72. WDH to "Dear Girls," 27 March 1910 (Houghton).

73. WDH to Aurelia H. Howells, 25 November 1909, *SL,* 5: 292.

74. WDH to Henry James, 25 December 1909, *SL,* 5: 294.

75. WDH to Mildred Howells, 27 August 1907 (Houghton).

76. WDH to Joseph A. Howells, 13 March 1907, *SL,* 5: 217. Howells speculated that Thaw had been brought up to believe he could buy anything with money, and in the end he was released after being committed to a mental institution.

77. WDH to Henry James, 1 February 1910, *SL,* 5: 307.

78. Edel, *Henry James: A Life,* 662.

79. WDH to Charles Eliot Norton, 12 April 1908, *SL,* 5: 247.

80. Charles Eliot Norton to WDH, 19 October 1905 (Houghton).

81. WDH to Henry James, 1 February 1910, *SL,* 5: 307.

82. WDH to Mark Twain, 18 January 1910, *SL,* 5: 306.

83. WDH to Mark Twain, 18 January 1910, *SL,* 5: 307 n2.

84. WDH to Joseph H. Twichell, July 1910, *SL,* 5: 326.

85. Frederick A. Duneka to WDH, 28 April 1910, archive of American Antiquarian Society, Worcester, MA.

86. WDH, *My Mark Twain,* 101–2.

87. WDH, *My Mark Twain,* 100.

88. See, for example, Kenneth E. Eble's fine essay, "Howells and Twain: Being and Staying Friends," *Old Northwest* 10 (Spring 1984): 101.

89. WDH, *My Mark Twain,* 49.

90. WDH, *My Mark Twain,* 47.

91. WDH to Frederick A. Duneka, 1 June 1910, *SL,* 5: 319. The actual speakers were Van Dyke, Cable, Choate, and Twichell; Joseph G. Cannon, the congressman from Illinois and Speaker of the House when Twain and Howells testified about copyright in 1906; Champ (Joseph B.) Clark, congressman from Missouri and Speaker of the House in 1911; and Colonel Henry Watterson, editor of the Louisville *Courier-Journal.*

92. WDH to Henry James, 7 January 1911, *SL,* 5: 341; WDH to Joseph A. Howells, 25 November 1910, *SL,* 5: 336.

93. WDH to Frederick A. Duneka, 19 December 1910, *SL,* 5: 338–39.

94. WDH to Grace Norton, 13 May 1910, *If Not Literature: Letters of Elinor Mead Howells,* ed. Ginette de B. Merrill and George Arms (Columbus: Ohio State University Press, 1988), 307.

95. WDH to Harriet T. Upton, 9 March 1910, *SL,* 5: 312–13.

96. WDH to Elizabeth Stuart Phelps Ward, 9 November 1909, *SL,* 5: 319 n2.

97. WDH to Aurelia H. Howells and Annie Fréchette, 8 May 1910, *SL,* 5: 318.

98. WDH to Aurelia H. Howells and Annie Fréchette, 13 May 1910, *SL,* 5: 318.

99. WDH to Henry James, 9 June 1910, *SL,* 5: 322.

100. WDH to William James, 8 June 1910, *SL,* 5: 320.

101. WDH to William James, 8 June 1910, *SL,* 5: 321.

102. WDH to Joseph A. Howells, 9 June 1910, *SL*, 5: 321–22.

103. WDH to Henry James, 1 July 1910, *SL*, 5: 323.

104. WDH to Henry James, 2 July 1910, *SL*, 5: 323.

105. WDH to Joseph A. Howells, 25 November 1910, *SL*, 5: 335–36.

106. WDH to Joseph A. Howells, 5 July 1910, *SL*, 5: 325.

107. WDH to Joseph A. Howells, 11 December 1910, *SL*, 5: 337.

108. WDH to Henry James, 19 May 1911, *SL*, 5: 353.

109. WDH to Joseph A. Howells, 18 August 1911, *SL*, 5: 362–63.

110. WDH to Henry James, 19 May 1911, *SL*, 5: 354.

111. WDH to Laura Mitchell, 9 February 1914, *SL*, 6: 50.

112. WDH, *Years,* 194.

CHAPTER SEVENTEEN

1. Edith Wharton to Sinclair Lewis, 9 February 1931, in Ellen Phillips Du-Press, "Wharton, Lewis and the Nobel Prize Address," *American Literature* 56 (May 1984): 265. Also see John W. Crowley, *The Dean of American Letters* (Amherst: University of Massachusetts Press, 1999), 81.

2. Edith Wharton, March 1913, *Collected Letters,* ed. R. W. B. Lewis and Nancy Lewis (New York: Charles Scribner's Sons, 1988), 286.

3. Edith Wharton to Sara Norton, 12 April 1913, *Collected Letters,* 293–94.

4. Edith Wharton to Gaillard Lapsley, 10 January 1916, *Collected Letters,* 369.

5. WDH to Henry James, 15 October 1911, *SL*, 5: 369–70.

6. WDH, "A Charming Spanish Novel," *Literature* 18 (12 May 1899): 409.

7. Mildred Howells, introduction to *Don Quixote,* ed. William Dean Howells, trans. Charles Jarvis (New York: Harper & Brothers, 1923), xiii–xv.

8. WDH to Eliza W. Howells, 9 December 1911, *SL*, 5: 376.

9. WDH to Joseph A. Howells, 17 December 1911, *SL*, 5: 377 n4.

10. WDH to Joseph A. Howells, 19 January 1912, *SL*, 6: 11.

11. WDH, "William Dean Howells," *North American Review* 212 (July 1920): 5.

12. W. E. B. Du Bois, tribute to Howells, *Boston Transcript* 3 (24 February 1912): 2. See also Calvin Kytle, "The Story of the NAACP," *Coronet* 40 (August 1956): 140–46.

13. WDH to Aurelia H. Howells, 18 March 1912 (Houghton).

14. Henry James, "A Letter to Mr. Howells," *Letters, Fictions, Lives: Henry James and William Dean Howells,* ed. Michael Anesko (New York: Oxford University Press, 1997), 452.

15. WDH, *Literary News,* October 1897; *The Book Buyer,* July 1897 (USC).

16. WDH, "William Dean Howells," 9.

17. WDH to Joseph A. Howells, 8 September 1912, Rutherford B. Hayes Library, Fremont, OH.

18. WDH to Frederick A. Duneka, 28 February 1918, *SL,* 6: 127.

19. WDH to Frederick A. Duneka, 17 November 1912, *SL,* 6: 25.

20. WDH to Annie Fréchette, 17 January 1913, *SL,* 6: 27.

21. WDH to Hamlin Garland, 19 December 1913, *SL,* 6: 44.

22. Polly H. Howells, "Mildred Howells as the Father's Daughter," *Harvard Library Bulletin* 5 (Spring 1994): 10.

23. WDH to Frederick A. Duneka, 10 December 1912, *SL,* 6: 26.

24. WDH to S. Weir Mitchell, 22 November 1913, *SL,* 6: 43.

25. Mildred Howells, "Unsatisfied," *Harper's Monthly* 123 (June 1911): 49, quoted in Polly H. Howells, "Mildred Howells," 28.

26. Polly H. Howells, "Mildred Howells," 15.

27. Mildred Howells to Annie Fréchette, 29 August 1901 (Alfred), quoted in Polly H. Howells, "Mildred Howells," 25.

28. WDH, *Winifred Howells,* privately printed [1890], 15.

29. WDH to Hamlin Garland, 26 July 1903, *SL,* 5: 59.

30. Polly H. Howells, "Mildred Howells," 21.

31. WDH to Mildred Howells, 3 May 1913 (Houghton), quoted in "Mildred Howells," 24.

32. Paulina C. Drown, *Mrs. Bell* (Boston, 1931), 3, 4, 77.

33. WDH to Annie Fields, 15 June 1914, *SL,* 6: 56.

34. WDH to Thomas S. Perry, 23 June 1914, *SL,* 6: 58.

35. WDH to Thomas S. Perry, 12 July 1914, *SL,* 6: 59.

36. WDH to Thomas S. Perry, 24 July 1915, *SL,* 6: 84.

37. WDH to Thomas S. Perry, 23 August 1917, *SL,* 6: 121.

38. WDH to Thomas S. Perry, 23 June 1914, *SL,* 6: 58.

39. WDH, "Eighty Years and After," *SL,* 6: 166.

40. WDH to Mildred Howells, 6 January 1915, *SL,* 6: 69.

41. WDH to John M. Howells, 12 January 1914, *SL,* 6: 46. See *Years,* 3.

42. WDH to John M. Howells, 13 May 1912, *Life in Letters,* 2: 322.

43. WDH, *A Hazard of New Fortunes,* introduction by Everett Carter; notes to the text and text established by David J. Nordloh (Bloomington: Indiana University Press, 1993), 318–19.

44. WDH to Moncure Conway, 26 January 1864, *SL,* 1: 175.

45. WDH to Annie Fréchette, 13 September 1914, *SL,* 6: 61.

46. WDH to Aurelia H. Howells, 4 July 1916, *SL,* 6: 99.

47. See WDH to Aurelia H. Howells, 23 December 1914 (Houghton).

48. WDH to Aurelia H. Howells, 12 May 1914, *SL,* 6: 54; 21 June 1914, *SL,* 6: 57.

49. See WDH to Frederick A. Duneka, 19 June 1909, *SL,* 5: 277.

50. WDH to Aurelia H. Howells, 21 June 1914, *SL,* 6: 57. The novel was serialized in *Century* from April through November 1916.

51. WDH to Annie Fréchette, 13 September 1914, *SL,* 6: 62.

52. See WDH, Editor's Easy Chair, *Harper's Monthly* 134 (February 1917): 442. Of Twain, he wrote: "The old tenderness for suffering, the old indignation with wrong is there . . . but the laughter has died out of it all."

53. WDH, *The Leatherwood God,* introduction and notes to the text by Eugene Pattison; text established by David J. Nordloh, with James P. Elliott and Robert D. Schildgen (Bloomington: Indiana University Press, 1976), 3.

54. See WDH to Hamlin Garland, 17 July 1916 (USC); partly quoted in *SL,* 6: 103 n1.

55. WDH, *The Leatherwood God,* 156–57.

56. WDH to Laura Mitchell, 9 February 1914, *SL,* 6: 50.

57. See Annie Howells to Paul Kester, 2 September 1917, quoted in James Doyle, *Annie Howells and Achille Fréchette* (Toronto: University of Toronto Press, 1979), 108.

58. WDH, *Their Silver Wedding Journey* (New York: Harper & Brothers, 1909), 451.

59. WDH to Thomas S. Perry, 23 September 1914, *SL,* 6: 63 n5.

60. See WDH to board of directors of American Academy of Arts and Letters, 22 August 1918, *SL,* 6: 139.

61. WDH to Aurelia H. Howells, 23 May 1915, *SL,* 6: 77.

62. WDH to Aurelia H. Howells, 13 June 1917, *SL,* 6: 115.

63. WDH to Aurelia H. Howells, 12 May 1918 and 4 May 1918 (Houghton).

64. WDH to Robert U. Underwood, 8 November 1914, *SL,* 6: 65.

65. Howells later regretted the tone of his poem, which he attributed to the times. See Howells to Van Wyck Brooks, 5 August 1918, Van Pelt Library, University of Pennsylvania.

66. For background on *The Book of the Homeless,* see Alan Price, *End of the Age of Innocence: Edith Wharton and the First World War* (New York: Macmillan, 1996), 60–69, 77–79, 202–3 n11. Howells also contributed "War Stops Literature" to *Literature in the Making,* presented by Joyce Kilmer (Harper & Brothers, 1917).

67. Henry James to WDH, 20 August 1915, in Anesko, *Letters, Fictions, Lives,* 462.

68. WDH, "The Little Children," *The Book of the Homeless,* ed. Edith Wharton (New York: Charles Scribner's Sons, 1916), 17.

69. WDH to editor of the *Evening Post,* 6 May 1916, *SL,* 6: 96–97.

70. WDH to Henry James, 26 January 1916, *SL,* 6: 90.

71. WDH to Frederick A. Duneka, 7 March 1916, *SL,* 6: 92–93.

72. WDH to Frederick A. Duneka, 17 March 1916, *SL,* 6: 93.

73. WDH to Mildred Howells, 2 November 1915, *SL,* 6: 86.

74. WDH to Frederick A. Duneka, 19 November 1916, *SL,* 6: 107.

75. WDH to Thomas S. Perry, 13 October 1916, *SL,* 6: 104–5.

76. WDH to Hamlin Garland 12 October 1916 (USC).

77. WDH to Hamlin Garland, 7 April 1917, *SL*, 6: 113–14 n1.

78. WDH to Hamlin Garland, 22 July 1917 (USC).

79. WDH to Hamlin Garland, 18 March 1917, *SL*, 6: 113.

80. WDH, "Novel-Writing and Novel-Reading: An Impersonal Explanation," 1899, *Selected Literary Criticism*, ed. Ulrich Halfmann, Christoph J. Lohmann, Don L. Cook, David J. Nordloh, Donald Pizer, and Ronald Gottesman (Bloomington: Indiana University Press, 1993), 3: 228.

81. Henry James to Sara Norton Darwin, 11 September 1907, *Henry James Letters*, ed. Leon Edel (Cambridge, MA: Harvard University Press, 1974–84), 4: 504 n1.

82. WDH to Hamlin Garland, 9 November 1917 (USC); also see WDH to Garland, 7 September 1917 (USC).

83. WDH to William Griffith, 19 August 1917, *SL*, 6: 119.

84. See Alexander Harvey, *William Dean Howells: A Study of the Achievement of a Literary Artist* (New York: B. W. Huebsch, 1917), 180.

85. WDH, *The Son of Royal Langbrith,* introduction and notes by David Burrows; text established by Burrows, Ronald Gottesman, and David J. Nordloh (Bloomington: Indiana University Press, 1969), 110.

86. WDH to Thomas S. Perry, 22 November 1903, *SL*, 5: 68.

87. WDH to Thomas S. Perry, 7 December 1917, *SL*, 6: 123 n2.

88. Jane Judge, "Howells in Savannah," *The Springfield Sunday Republican,* 25 March 1917 (Alfred).

89. WDH to Salvatore Coetesi, 1 May 1918, *SL*, 6: 130.

90. WDH to John M. Howells, 1 May 1918, *SL*, 6: 130 n1.

91. WDH to Aurelia H. Howells, 4 August 1918 (Houghton).

92. See WDH to the John M. Howells family, 7 November 1918, *SL*, 6: 142.

CHAPTER EIGHTEEN

1. WDH, "Eighty Years and After," *SL*, 6: 162.

2. WDH, "Eighty Years and After," *SL*, 6: 164–65.

3. WDH to Mildred Howells, 14 July 1918 (Houghton).

4. WDH, "Eighty Years and After," *SL*, 6: 167.

5. WDH to Mildred Howells, [November ?] 1915 (Houghton).

6. WDH, Editor's Easy Chair, *Harper's Monthly* 139 (October 1919): 765.

7. WDH to Booth Tarkington, 9 January 1915, *SL*, 6: 70.

8. WDH to Booth Tarkington, 20 August 1919, *SL*, 6: 146.

9. Booth Tarkington to WDH, 28 August 1919, *SL*, 6: 146 n2.

10. WDH to Thomas S. Perry, 22 January 1920, *SL*, 6: 152.

11. WDH, "The American James," *Letters, Fictions, Lives: Henry James and*

William Dean Howells, ed. Michael Anesko (New York: Oxford University Press, 1997), 473; and Editor's Easy Chair [The Letters of Henry James], in Anesko, *Letters, Fictions, Lives,* 469.

12. WDH to Edwin Markham, 20 April 1920, *SL,* 6: 154–55.

13. Mildred Howells to Annie Fréchette and Aurelia H. Howells, 15 May 1920 (Alfred).

14. WDH, "Eighty Years and After," *SL,* 6: 158.

15. WDH, "Eighty Years and After," *SL,* 6: 167.

16. WDH, *Years,* 364–65. Howells made the trip to Eureka Mills in 1881.

INDEX

Adams, Brook, 133

Adams, Henry, 36, 65, 73, 112, 113, 195, 213–14, 242, 326, 406, 430; on Cambridge, 117; *Democracy*, 30; *The Education of Henry Adams*, 133, 310–11; and WDH, 85, 218; and journalism, 35, 36; on literature, 133, 145; review of *Their Wedding Journey, 176*

Adams, John, 122

Adams, Marion Hooper (Mrs. H. A., "Clover"), 65, 176, 213–14, 242, 290

Addams, Jane, 352

Ade, George, 401, 415

Africa (ship), 85

The African Liberator, 9

Aiken, Conrad, 431

Agassiz, Jean L. R., 112, 113, 121

Alcott, Louisa M., 181

Alden, Henry M., 244, 266, 281, 312, 323, 417; and Editor's Study, 269–74; and wife's illness, 317–18

Alden (Mrs. H. M.), 318

Aldrich, Lilian (Mrs. T. B. A.), 136, 261, 266, 393–95, 399

Aldrich, Thomas B., xvi, 58, 142, 153, 170, 224, 296, 316, 356, 365, 374; edits *Atlantic*, 213, 216; edits *Every Saturday*, 142, 153; friendship with WDH, 124, 261, 286; memorial for, 393–95, 399; *Story of a Bad Boy*, 310, 393

Allen, James L., 424

Alma-Tadema, Lawrence, 226–27, 261

Altgelt, John P., 283, 352, 363

American Academy of Arts and Letters, 134, 147, 347, 387–88, 400, 419–20

American Impressionists, 226

Amherst College, 62

Anderson, Sherwood: *Winesburg, Ohio*, 25

Andreyeva, Mme., 386

Appleton & Co., 323, 359

Appomattox, 100

Arnold, Benedict, 44

Arnold, Matthew, 248–50, 271

Arthur, Chester, 216

Ashcroft, Ralph, 172

Ashtabula Sentinel, 22–25, 34–36, 38, 49, 116, 124, 269, 331, 411; edited by William Cooper Howells, 3, 21–25, 32, 36, 440n20; party affiliations of, 24; and the anti-slavery movement, 45–46

Asia (ship), 100

Associated Press, 35, 426

Astor, William W., 200

Athenaeum (London), 224, 229, 233

Atkins, Elisha, 202

Atlantic Monthly, 62, 79, 215, 224, 261–62, 314, 319, 382, 417; and Thomas B. Aldrich, ed., 393; circulation, 133, 142; Contributors Club, 142; dinners of: 1874, 189; for Whittier (1877), 189–92; and James T. Fields, ed., 54, 58, 61, 70, 91, 111, 112, 113, 115, 122–23, 131, 138–40, 160, 189, 195, 209, 272, 415; and Bret Harte, 135–37; history of, 121–23; WDH as asst. editor of, 103–24, 130–34; WDH as editor of, xiv, 1, 4, 138–47, 159, 173, 193, 198, 199, 208, 212, 217, 229, 245, 293, 313; and James R. Lowell, ed., 69, 70, 121–23, 139, 140, 189; and Bliss Perry, ed., 387; publishes WDH, 42, 46, 56, 59, 71; and the Republican Party, 195–97; sale of, 187; and Harriet Beecher Stowe, 121, 131–33; and Mark Twain, 148–49; and *Venetian Life, 91*

Atherton, Gertrude, 424

499

Austen, Jane, 206, 237, 259, 369; *Northanger Abbey,* 373; *Pride and Prejudice,* 364
Austin, Mary H., 410
Authors Club, 347, 394, 415, 423
Authors' League of America, 423
Aveling, Eleanor M., 287

Babb, Edmund B., 33–34
Baedeker's guides, 75, 244
Balzac, Honoré de, 164, 206, 259
Bancroft, George, 410
Barberi, Maria, 288
Barnum, P. T., 11
Barrett, Lawrence, 160–61, 202
Barrie, James M., 403, 409
Baudry (publishing house), 339
Bazán, Emilia Pardo, 407
Beecher, Henry W., 349
Beerbohm, Max, 420
Bell, Helen C., 414–15
Bellamy, Edward, 272, 303, 305–6, 309, 325; *Looking Backward,* 197, 305–7, 341, 366
Bellini, Giovanni, 76
Belmont, MA, 206–7
Bennett, Arnold, 373, 409
Bettina (nurse in Venice), 90
Bierce, Ambrose, 101, 431
Bierstadt, Albert, 316
Bigelow, Sturgis, 327
Bigelow, William B., 202
Bismark, Otto von, 79
Bjørnson, Bjørnstjerne, 144–45, 391, 414; *Arne,* 391; *The Fisher-maiden,* 391; *The Happy Boy,* 144
Black, William P., 279
Blackwood's Magazine, 231
Blanche, Jacques-Emile, 420
Blaine, James, G., 252
Bliss, William D. P., 309
Blondin, Charles, 51
Boer War, 340, 362, 378
Booth, Edwin, 202, 224, 261
Boston, MA, xiii, xvi, 53, 109–10, 112–20, 189, 193, 261, 269, 402
Boston Courier, 48

Boston Daily Advertiser, 254; and "Letters from Venice," 91, 103, 106
Boston Daily Globe, 190
Boston, fires of, 1872, 183–84; and 1879, 210
Boston Gazette, 261
Boston Museum, 255, 275
Boston Transcript, 35, 189, 318, 409, 423
Bowers, David, 26, 27
Boxer Rebellion, 375
Boyesen, Hjalmar, 135, 145, 200, 238; *Gunnar,* 135; "Mister Howells and His Work," 315
Brady, Matthew, 35, 102
Braithwaite, William S., 345–46; *The House of the Falling Leaves,* 345
Brattleboro, VT, 61–62, 70, 104
Brieux, Eugène, 420
Bronté, Charlotte: *Jane Eyre,* 32, 188, 201
Bronté sisters, 35; *The Tenant of Wildfell Hall,* 32; *Wuthering Heights,* 32
Brook Farm, 134
Brooke, Rupert, 420
Brooks, Van Wyck, 113; *New England: Indian Summer;* 113; *The Ordeal of Mark Twain,* 156
Brown, Harrison B., 71, 72, 78, 79
Brown, Henry K., 66, 67, 71, 120
Brown, John, 5, 43–47, 108, 109, 229, 271, 284, 348, 378; death of, 45; and Harpers Ferry Raid, 43–47; and Howells family, 44–46; WDH on, 44–47
Brown, John Jr., 9–10, 43–47
Brown, Thomas, 22
Browne, Francis F., 280, 283
Browning, Robert, 288; *The Ring and the Book,* 415
Brunetta, Eugenio, 81–82, 86, 243
Bryant, William C., 410
Bull, Ole, 55, 155
Burbank, Alfred P., 163
Burne-Jones, Edward C., 225–26
Burnham, Daniel H., 325
Burns, John, 403
Burns, Robert, 9, 316
Burt, Mary, 412–13; *The Literary Primer* (with M. Howells), 413

Byron, Lady Annabel, 45, 131
Byron, Lord George G., 131–33, 316, 395

Cabel, James B., 410
Cable, George W., 235, 272, 318, 409, 431;
    The Grandissimes, 216; and lecture
    tours, 170, 263, 264, 348–49;
Cabot, James E., 121
Cahan, Abraham, 343–44; Arbeiter
    Zeitung, ed. of, 344; Yekl: A Story
    of the New York Ghetto, 344
Cambridge (riverboat), 38
Cambridge University, 225
Campbell, Alexander, 8
Carey, Alice, 56
Carlsbad, Bohemia (Czechoslavakia), 337,
    419
Carnegie, Andrew, xiii, 119, 246, 248,
    249, 277, 304–5; Gospel of Wealth,
    304
Carpenter, B. O., 8
Carter, Isabella E. ("Belle"), 61, 64–66, 83
Cather, Willa, My Ántonia, 272, 410
Catholicism, 8
Cellini, Benvenuto, 415
Century Club, 370, 429
Century Magazine (formerly Scribner's),
    143, 221, 230–33, 239–40, 243, 245,
    249, 253, 265; and Richard W. Gilder,
    317; WDH publishes in, 221, 230–33,
    239–40, 243, 245, 249, 253; serializes
    A Modern Instance, 265; serializes The
    Rise of Silas Lapham, 274; Cervantes,
    Miguel de, 24, 193, 224, 250, 285, 373,
    407–8; and Don Quixote, 20, 338–39,
    428
Chase, Salmon P., 40, 43, 48, 61, 69, 92
Chase, Kate, 40
Chaucer, Geoffrey, 132
Chesnutt, Charles, xiv, 345–46, 409; The
    Conjure Woman, 272; The Marrow
    of Tradition, 345
Chicago Tribune, 35, 282, 283
Child, Francis J., 116, 127, 135, 191
Chinese Exclusion Act, 214
Chizzola, Maurice, 351, 353
Choate, Joseph A., 401

Church of the Carpenter, 308–9
Church, Frederic, 90, 226
Churchill, Winston, 362
Cincinnati Commercial, 33, 216
Cincinnati Gazette, 33–34, 36, 37, 50–59,
    107
City of Glasgow (ship), 73, 223
Civil War, xiii, 3, 8, 59–60, 70, 100–103,
    105, 141, 165, 188, 225, 334, 386, 419;
    Antietam, 92; Bull Run, first battle
    of, 70; Chickamauga, 3; Gettysburg,
    3, 35, 93; Richmond, 93, 98; Shiloh, 3,
    35; Vicksburg, 93; WDH's comments
    on, 68, 70–1, 91–93
Clapp, Henry, 56–58
Claudel, Jean, 420
Claudel, Paul, 420
Clay, Henry, 13–14, 23
Clemens, Clara L., 152, 395, 400
Clemens, Olivia L. (Mrs. S. L. C., "Livy"),
    149–50, 217, 256, 259, 280; compared
    with Elinor, 153–54; death of, 373;
    health of, 155–56; WDH on, 154, 400
Clemens, Orion, 150, 161, 384–85
Clemens, Samuel L. See Mark Twain
Clemens, Susy, 156, 296–97
Clement, Edward, 319
Cleveland, Grover, 233, 252
Cleveland Herald, 37
The Club, 133, 153
Coggeshall, William T.: Poets and Poetry
    of the West, 47, 59
Colored Co-operative Publishing Co., 346
Columbia University, 238, 259, 390
Columbian Exposition, Chicago, 102,
    324–26, 352
Columbus, OH, 19–20, 30–33, 61–63; and
    Underground Railroad, 43
Comly, James M., 104, 116, 174, 187, 189
Conrad, Joseph, xvi, 39, 420; Heart of
    Darkness, 340
Conway Moncure D., 69, 78, 91 224, 225,
    283
Cook, Thomas, 95, 244
Cooke, Henry D., 39–40
Cooke, Rose T., 272
Cooper, James F., 113

Copeland, Ada, 224
Coppoc, Barclay, 46, 47
Copyright League, 263
Cornell University, 259
The Cosmopolitan, 313–16, 321, 322, 323, 325, 363, 481n53
Courant (Hartford), 152
Cowper, William, 9, 316
Crane, Hart, 153
Crane, Cora (Mrs. S. C.), 342, 360
Crane, Stephen, 102, 167, 272, 358; *The Black Riders,* 343; friendship with WDH, 342–43, 360; *George's Mother,* 344; *Maggie: Girl of the Streets,* 342; *The Red Badge of Courage,* 101, 342
Crane, W. H., 259
The Crisis, 409
Crowninshield, Francis W., 370
Curtis, Benjamin R., 195
Curtis, George W., 35, 40, 252; and Haymarket anarchists, 280, 281, 284; *The Howardji in Syria,* 56; *Lotus Eating,* 56

da Benvenuti, Marietta (Mrs. L. Mead, Jr.), 80
Daly, Augustin, 171
Dana, Richard H., and the *North American Review,* 112, 121
Dana, Richard H. (son), 112, 127; *Two Years Before the Mast,* 113
Dana, Mrs. R. H., 208
Dante Alighieri, 216, 241, 250; *Divine Comedy,* 86; *Inferno,* 113
Dante Club, 113–14
Darwin, Charles R., 114, 121, 225; *Origin of Species,* 225
Darwin, Francis, 225
Daudet, Alphonse, 230
Davis, Rebecca H., 55; *Life in the Iron Mills,* 147
Dayton Transcript, 14–15, 18, 411
Dean, Alexander (WDH's uncle), 17
Dean, Samuel (WDH's uncle), 38
De Forest, John: *Miss Ravenel's Conversion,* 101, 102
Deland, Margaret, 410
Democratic Party, 24, 37, 40, 252

Dennison, William, 69
De Quincey, Thomas, 27
Dewey, John, 239, 386
Dickens, Charles, 14, 89, 108, 122, 128, 226, 316; and *David Copperfield,* 73; WDH on, 229–30, 240, 249, 373; on Harriet B. Stowe, 132
Dickinson, Anna, 349; *What Answer?* 312
Dickinson, Emily, 122, 176, 269, 272
Disciples of Christ, 8, 318
Dos Passos, John, 306–7; *Manhattan Transfer,* 307
Dostoyevski, Feodor M., 145, 271, 272
Doubleday, Page & Co., 346
Douglas, David, 268; and American Authors series, 246; publisher of WDH in Great Britain, 245–56
Douglass, Frederick, 346
Doyle, Arthur Conan 349, 360, 409
Drake, Sir Francis, 371
Drake, Francis S., 259
Dred Scott case, 195, 272
Dreiser, Theodore, 4, 346–47, 431; *An American Tragedy,* 346; *The Genius,* 347; "How He Climbed Fame's Ladder," 346; "The Lost Phoebe," 347; "The Real Howells," 346; *Sister Carrie,* 346–47
Du Bois, W. E. B., 311; on WDH, 345, 409
Dubufe, Claude M., 14–15
Du Maurier, George, 360; *Trilby,* 209, 247, 358
Dunbar, Paul L., xiv, 167, 272, 343–45, 409, 426; *Lyrics of the Lowly,* 344; *Majors and Minors,* 344
Duneka, Frederick A., 372, 417
Duveneck, Frank, 226
Dylks, Joseph C., 6, 418

Eakins, Thomas, 226
Earhart, George T., 354
Eastlake, Charles, 185
Eastlake, Charles L., 185
Eastman, Seth, 316
Echoes of Harper's Ferry, 46
Edison, Thomas A., 163, 214

Editor's Easy Chair (*Harper's Monthly*), 40, 321, 323, 430, 431

Electric Observer and Workingman's Advocate, 9

Eliot, Charles W., 124

Eliot, George, 37, 123, 144, 168, 230

Eliot, T. S., 144

Emmanuel, King Victor, 66, 391

Emerson, Ralph W., xv, 11–12, 17, 21, 46, 54, 249, 343; and *Atlantic,* 113, 121, 122, 139, 191, 381; death of, 113; on James R. Lowell, 108–9; and WDH, xiii, 56–58, 91, 271, 272, 399, 410; and the Saturday Club, 187

Engel, George, 278, 283

Epps, James, 261

Eureka Mills, OH, 15–18, 24, 29, 62, 207, 432–33

Evans, F. W.: "Autobiography of a Shaker," 209

Evening Post (New York), 389, 421

Every Saturday (Chicago), 136, 142, 153

Examiner (London), review of *Venetian Life,* 115

Fairchild, Charles W., 216, 265, 357

Fairchild, David, 388–89

Fairchild, Lucia, 324

Falier, Casa (Venice), 88–89, 94

Faliero, Marino, 94

Fauset, Jesse, *Plum Bun,* 323

Fielding, Henry, 230

Fielding, Samuel, 278, 283

Fields, Annie A., 55, 131, 140, 280, 370, 412; on WDH and Elinor, 104, 111–12, 120, 122; and Sarah Orne Jewett, 271, 369; *Life and Letters of Harriet Beecher Stowe,* 133

Fields, James T., 54, 111, 112, 113, 115, 131, 160, 195, 272; described, 122; as editor of *Atlantic Monthly,* 58, 61, 70, 91, 111, 112, 113, 115, 122, 189, 104, 107, 122–23, 131, 138–140, 148–49, 189, 209

Fields, Osgood & Co., 136

Fischer, Adolph, 278, 283

Fiske, John, 114, 133–34, 136, 410; *Myth*

and Mythmakers (dedicated to WDH), 134

Flaubert, Gustave: *Madame Bovary,* 424

Follett, Foster & Co., 47–49

Forster, E. M., 363

Fortuny, Mariano, 224, 227

Frankenstein, Godfrey, 50–51, 226, 334

Frankenstein, John, 50–51, 226, 334

Franklin, Benjamin, 20, 150

Fréchette, Achille, 194, 223, 332

Fréchette, Anne T. *See* Howells, Anne T., "Annie"

Fréchette, L. de P. R. W. C. Howells (Annie's son), 185–86

Fréchette, Marie A. ("Vevie"), 222, 332, 370, 389

Frederic, Harold: *The Damnation of Theron Ware,* 341–42

Frederic Wilhelm (German Kaiser), 419

Freeman, Mary W., 206, 272, 388, 431

Freud, Sigmund, 294, 364; *Interpretation of Dreams,* 308

Frith, William P., 226

Frost, Robert, 334, 431; *"Out! Out!"* 334

Froude, James A., *Caesar,* 212

Fugitive Slave Act, 40, 44

Fuller, George, 202

Fuller, Henry B., 114

Fullerton, Artemis T., 39

Galaxy (New York), 194

Galdos, Perez, 407

Galsworthy, John, 403, 420

Garfield, James A., 2–4, 195–96, 214, 252, 378; and Howells family, 69, 127, 139, 213

Garland, Hamlin, 6, 163, 268–69, 272, 315, 346–47, 352, 378, 411; friendship with WDH, 318–19, 341–42, 343, 351, 409, 413, 418; WDH on, 361; on WDH, 273, 286, 306, 319, 350, 409, 418, 423–24, 425; and politics, 281, 306

Garibaldi, Giuseppe, 78

Garner, Margaret, 43

Garrison, William L., 194, 262

Gary, Horace, 195

Gary, Joseph E., 278–79, 283, 284

Gay, Walter, 420

George, Henry, 303–4, 416; *Progress and Poverty,* 303

Georgia State Industrial School, 425–26

Giddings, Joshua R., 30, 40, 43, 45, 47, 68–69

Gilbert, Cass, 259

Gilbert and Sullivan, 255

Gilbert, William S., 415

Gilder, Richard W., 156, 227, 238, 260, 273–74; and *Century,* 316–18; and Columbian Exposition, 325, 326; editorial standards of, 157; and *Tuscan Cities,* 240

Giles Female Academy, 20

Gilman, Charlotte P., 294–95, 426, 431; *The Yellow Wallpaper,* 294–95

Gilman, Daniel C., 238–39

Giovanna (Venetian housemaid), 89–90, 118

Giustiniani, Palazzo (Venice), 90

Gissing, George, 193–94, 231; *New Grub Street,* 193, 235; *The Odd Women,* 193

Gladstone, William E., 224, 378

Glasgow, Ellen, 347, 410; *The Battle-Ground,* 101–2; *The Descendant,* 347 *The Gleaner,* 8

Godkin, Edwin L., 106–6, 124, 180, 252

Goethe, Johann W. von, 39, 337

Goldoni, Carlo, 86, 96

Goldsmith, Oliver, *The Deserted Village,* 328

Gompers, Samuel, 281

Goncourt Brothers, 237

Gorky, Maxim, 385–86

Gosse, Sir Edmund W., 227–30, 247, 316–17, 403, 424; and *Century Magazine,* 227; *English Literature from Shakespeare to Pope,* 262; *Father and Son,* 228; and friendship with WDH, 227–30, 254–55; and Henry James, 227, 405–6; lecture tour in U.S., 229, 260–62; letters to and from WDH, 228–29, 245, 249, 268, 276, 282, 329; "Motto for an American Critic," 233

Gosse, Nellie (Mrs. E. W. G), 260

Gosse, Philip H., *The Omphalos,* 228

Grant, Ulysses S., 5, 35, 39, 78, 92, 195–96, 266, 271; and William C. Howells, 185, 216; and Winifred Howells, 182; and Twain, 149, 249, 266

Gray, Asa, 121

Great Eastern (ship), 73

Greeley, Horace, 35, 123

Green, Harvey, 101

Green, John R., 225

Grey, Zane, 410

Grimm Brothers, 134

Grinnell, Julius S., 278–79

Gronlund, Laurence, 197, 272, 292, 309; *Co-operative Commonweath,* 292

Guiccioli, Countess Teresa, 131

Hale, Charles, 91

Hale, Edward E., 91, 261, 281, 286, 301, 309, 314, 316; *A Man without a Country,* 306; and Nationalists, 304–6

Hamilton Intelligencer, 11–13, 26, 354, 411

Hammond, Charles, 33

Hancock, John, 112

Hapgood, Hutchins, 410

Hardy, Thomas, xiv, 231, 247, 272, 347, 409, 420; *Jude the Obscure,* 335; *The Mayor of Casterbridge,* 236; *Return of the Native,* 235; *Tess of the D'Urbervilles,* 424

Harper, Frances, *Iola Leroy,* 312

Harper, Henry, 266, 270, 281, 319–20, 370

Harper, Joseph H., 281

Harper & Brothers, 4, 171, 244, 253, 269, 305, 318, 345, 370, 390, 417, 425; and WDH's contracts with, 205, 265, 268, 279, 312, 333, 336, 359–61, 372, 401

Harper's Bazaar, 332

Harpers Ferry raid, 24, 378

Harper's Monthly, 56, 121, 141, 168, 223, 266, 269, 276, 319, 430; and *Atlantic,* 142–43, 147; WDH as columnist for, xiv; 40, 168, 268–74, 359–60, 405, 430, 431

Harper's Weekly, 233, 255, 268, 281, 338, 344, 360, 373, 376–78, 393; WDH's articles on Portsmouth Peace Conference, 376; WDH's Life and Letters, 335

Howells, Anne (WDH's grandmother), 5

Howells, Anne T. (WDH's sister), 11, 25, 90, 93, 98, 180, 369, 392; and *Atlantic,* 140–41; and John Brown, Jr., 46; and *A Chance Acquaintance,* 178–79, 194; *The Farm's Little People,* 332; *On Grandfather's Farm,* 332; on John Howells' death, 94; and Winifred Howells, 290; letters to and from WDH, 124, 139, 292, 297–98, 300, 402; and Longfellow, 126, 127; marriage of, 194, 202; *Popular Sayings from Old Iberia* (with Premio Real), 185; relationship with WDH, 128, 178–79, 185–86, 194, 332, 374; *Reuben Dale,* 194; and World War I, 412, 413; as writer, 32, 128, 140–41, 142, 178–79, 185–86, 194, 222–23, 332

Howells, Aurelia H. (WDH's sister), 11, 65, 90, 179, 180, 185, 381, 401, 419; anti-slavery sentiments of, 46, 98; as caretaker of brother Henry, 31–32, 194, 291, 299, 327, 331–32, 391–92; described, 42; Elinor's sketches of, 197–98; finances of, 262, 313, 390; letters to and from WDH, xiii, 7, 25, 26, 31, 129, 134, 246, 323, 336, 337, 338, 340, 341, 357–58, 364, 366, 369, 377, 380, 383, 391, 397, 401, 402, 412, 416, 417, 417, 427; and Sam Howells, 382, 392; and suffrage, 425–26

Howells, Elinor M. ("EGM," Mrs. W. D. H.), 77, 107, 108, 136, 170, 180, 249, 412, 414, 419, 423, 424; as artist, 66–67, 125, 182, 197–98, 200, 205, 226, 392–93; and her children: 87, 110, 181–82, 211–12, 204, 254–55, 293, 297; in Columbus, 61–63; death of, 401–2, 403, 429; described, 61–62, 153–54, 175, 251–52, 344; family in Brattleboro, Vermont, 61–63, 104; health of, 91, 126, 127–28, 180–81, 184, 214–15, 217, 290, 337–38, 365, 370, 371, 380, 391, 392, 397–98, 399, 413; on WDH, 106, 348; and Howells family, 82, 105; and Henry James, 379; letters to and from WDH, 2, 324,

349, 351, 352, 372; and politics, 280, 282, 408–9; and Redtop, 203–4; relationship with WDH, 2, 85, 61–68, 70–71, 80, 83–85, 189, 298; travels in Europe, 86–99, 243, 326, 332, 367, 383–84, 390; and the Twains, 63, 150

Howells, Eliza (Mrs. J. A. H., WDH's sister-in-law), 408

Howells, Henry (WDH's uncle), 354

Howells, Henry (WDH's brother), 11, 29, 65, 150, 180, 194, 262, 331; death of, 391; described, 31, 42, 201; medical condition, 31, 184, 291–92, 327–28

Howells, Israel (WDH's uncle), 15–17, 26

Howells, John B. (WDH's brother), 11, 298, 424; and Civil War, 68; death of, 94, 101; described, 37, 42, 344

Howells, John M. (WDH's son), 128–29, 181, 200, 204, 299, 303, 313, 330, 370, 380, 390, 416, 426–27; career of, 240, 386, 428; and family, 211, 307, 326–27, 337, 392, 403, 412–14; and health, 184, 250–51; and Kittery Point house, 365–66; marriage of, 389–90

Howells, Joseph (WDH's grandfather), 5–7, 12, 27

Howells, Joseph, Jr. (WDH's uncle), 10, 16, 327

Howells, Joseph A. (WDH's brother), 20, 29, 42, 192, 268, 374; and the *Ashtabula Sentinel,* 23, 27–28, 32, 37, 84, 102, 186–87, 332; and son, William Dean Howells, 34, 408; and Civil War songbook, 107; consul at Turks's Island, 331, 363, 381–82, 408; death of, 411; on Henry Howells, 31; and WDH, 10, 18, 22, 27–28, 41; illnesses of, 239, 408, 410–11; letters to and from WDH, 328, 383, 386, 388, 392, 398, 401, 403, 404; travels with WDH, 250–51, 350, 370–71; and trustee of Wilberforce University, 93; on Twain, 173; visits WDH, 126, 127

Howells, Mary D. (WDH's mother), 93, 94, 125; on John Brown, Jr., 9–10; death of, 31, 129; described, 9–10, 14, 18, 23, 42, 71; family background, 9;

illness and depression of, 29; marriage to William C. Howells, 9–12, 14, 17–18; relationship with children, 10–11, 41–42, 65

Howells, Mildred, "Pilla" (WDH's daughter), 246, 335, 361, 377, 383, 432; childhood of, 181, 204, 251, 291; engagement of, 388–89; and family, 211, 307, 330–32, 392; on father and Mark Twain, 173; on father's death, 303; health of, 391, 412–14; and WDH's fiction, 260, 330; letters to and from, 94, 371, 395, 415, 429; "Lines Written by a Young Lady to Her Father," 353; *The Literary Primer* (with Mary Burt), 413; *A Little Girl among the Old Masters* (with WDH), 254–55; travels with WDH, 246, 324, 326–27, 337, 367, 371–74, 391, 397, 403, 407–8, 414; 'Turn and Turn About," 389; as writer, 202, 412–14; *"Unsatisfied,"* 412

Howells, Samuel (WDH's brother), 11, 2 3, 92, 150, 197, 382–83, 392; as Civil War soldier, 68, 84, 93, 94, 101; dependence on WDH, 269, 313, 332, 363; visits WDH in Maine, 416–17

Howells, Thomas (WDH's great grandfather), 7, 246

Howells, Victoria, (WDH's sister, "Vic"), 11, 23, 29, 89, 101, 127, 197, 331; as caretaker for brother Henry, 31–32, 65, 94, 194; in Columbus, OH, 30–32; and conflict with Joe Howells (brother), 186–87; death of, 31; friendship and conflicts with WDH, 30–31, 128, 179; WDH on, 291; letters to and from WDH, 34, 36, 37, 41, 68, 73, 83, 222; marriage of, 262, 419; as writer, 30–31, 179–80

Howells, William C. (WDH's father), xv; 1, 94, 136, 175, 180, 223, 384, 403, 417, 419, 423; and the *Ashtabula Sentinel*, 3, 21–25, 32, 36, 440n20; and anti-slavery movement, 13–14, 284; and John Brown, 45–46; as consul at Quebec, 186; as consul at Toronto, 197, 216, 222, 239; and *Dayton Tran-*

script, 14–16; death, 328, 330, 473n56; and Eureka Mills, 16–18, 19; family background, 5–7; as father and husband, 10–18, 29, 31, 65, 84, 85; and friendship with James Garfield, 3–4, 42; and *The Gleaner,* 8–9; and *Hamilton Intelligencer,* 11–13, 26, 354, 411; homestead visit with WDH, 1–4; WDH on, xv, 7, 15, 222, 308, 338–39, 463n52; illnesses of, 11, 327–28; inventions of, 93, 157; as legislative reporter, 20; letters to and from WDH, 42, 44, 45, 137, 180, 190, 205, 212, 223,247, 289 313, 323, 428; and Ohio politics, 8, 13–14, 93; *Recollections of Life in Ohio,* 5–7, 130, 228; and religion, 8, 12; and *The Retina,,* 12–13; and Rio Vista farm, 262–3, 285; and *Scioto Gazette,* 8; and will of, 262, 312

Howells, William Dean
—and Anti-Imperialist League, 340, 484n41
—and art, 14–15, 50–51, 76, 86–87, 225–27, 239–41, 273
—and *Atlantic Monthly:* assistant editor of, 107–8, 133–34; editor of, 138–47, 189, 192
—and autobiography, xiii, xv, xvii, 1, 22, 97, 137–38, 168, 400
—and biography, xiii, xv–xvi, xvii
—birth and boyhood, of 11–18
—and Boston and Cambridge, 112–20, 189, 193, 199, 200–201, 206–8, 218
—and Byron, 131–33
—and the Centennial, 169–70
—and Chicago anarchists, xv, 226, 276–89, 421
—as Chispa (pseud.), 52
—on Civil War, 68, 70–1, 91–93
—and the Club, 133, 53
—and collaboration with Twain, 160–64
—consulship in Venice: 1, 70–71, 74–99
—and copyright, 170–71, 232, 245, 263, 382
—courtship with Elinor Mead, 61–68, 70–71, 80, 83–85, 189

Howells, William Dean (continued)
—and criticism, 106, 123–24, 143–47,
166–68, 230–32, 270–74, 276, 430,
416n80, 470n62
—and culture, xiv, 123–24, 249–50, 271
—death of, 432
—and domestic life, 25, 42, 63, 111–12,
118–20, 125–26, 155, 298, 331, 401–2,
404
—dreams of, 84, 129, 184, 298–99, 308,
330, 338–39, 429
—on economics, 110, 269
—as editor of Cosmopolitan, 481n53
—education of, 20–21, 24, 37, 237–38
—on England and the English, 221,
222–33, 241, 256
—and father, 129, 331, 384, 423
—finances of: 77, 90, 184, 255, 258, 263,
265, 268, 299, 205, 312–13, 323–24,
335; Atlantic income, 120, 128, 139,
215; contract with Cosmopolitan, 315;
with Harper & Bros., 265, 268, 279,
205, 312, 333, 336, 359–61, 372, 401;
and James R. Osgood & Co., 212–13;
and James B. Pond, 349–50
—and foreign languages, 20, 37, 71, 138,
238, 339
—on genius, 4–5, 145
—as Genug (pseud.), 37
—and Germans, 33, 419–21
—and Harper's Monthly: Easy Chair,
359–60, 405, 430, 431; editor of, 1, 4,
138–47, 208, 212, 217; Editor's Study,
168, 269–74, 359–60
—health of: 156, 184, 200–201, 215–17,
330, 337, 364, 407; boyhood crises,
15, 25–33, 37, 42, 128, 440n25
—honorary degrees, 124, 173, 214, 233,
372–73, 398
—and journalism: 25, 34, 102–4, 234–
45, 264; as journalist, 30, 32–36, 38–
41, 376
—Jeffersonian letters, 32
—as lecturer, 263: Harvard, 124, 348;
Lowell Institute, 135, 348; and the
Irish, 117–18, 134, 421; and Midwest
tours, 348–55

—library edition of, 417
—on marriage, 2, 67, 154, 176–77, 330, 389
—methods of writing, 1, 10, 21–22, 115,
129, 146, 146–47, 150–51, 158, 174–75,
177, 200, 205, 252–54, 270–72, 323
—and movies, xvi, 430; and the Nation,
105–7
—on New England, 52–53, 272; on
New York, 47, 316, 383
—as novelist, 4–5, 32, 57–59, 175–78,
218–20, 236–37, 264–65, 323, 333–35,
374, 417–19, 424–25
—as parent, 110, 199–202, 204–5,
465n22, 182–3, 413–14
—as poet, 42, 56–58, 91, 146, 329, 335,
343, 383, 420–21
—politics of, 248, 377–78; Homestead
strike, 304–5; and imperialism, 339–
41, 362–63; and Nationalist Club,
305–6; Pinkertonism, 304–5; and
Populist party, 304; Republican party,
38, 40, 195–97, 252, 304, 361; and
socialism, 292, 324; as Will Narlie
(pseud.), 22
—and race relations, 51, 110, 165, 167,
272, 289, 311–12, 343–45, 349, 409,
426
—and realism, 119, 132, 145, 218, 230–
31, 237, 271, 273, 461n2
—and religion: 5, 129–30, 308–10, 313,
417–19; and Swedenborgianism, 3,
12–13, 26–27, 403
—and reputation, 360, 417, 424–24
—residences of: Annisquam, MA, 357–
58; Ashtabula, OH, 22–23; Belmont,
MA, "Redtop," 199, 208, 213, 215,
216, 357, 366; Boston, 216, 250–
52, 257, 268; Dayton, OH, 14–15;
Eureka Mills, OH, 15–18, 24, 29,
62, 207, 371; Far Rockaway, 337,
340; Hamilton, OH; 11–14, 354;
Jefferson, OH, 23–27, 34–38; Cambridge, MA, 108, 134, 135, 181, 184–
85, 199, 205, 216, 259. 299, 300, 357,
402, 412, 452n28; Cincinnati, OH,
34; Columbus, OH, 30–33; Florence,
Italy, 239–41, 243; Kittery Point, ME,

James, Henry Sr., 26, 30, 112, 113, 122, 129–30; *The Secret of Swedenborg,* 124

James, Robertson, 310

James, William, 113, 133, 258, 263, 384, 398, 407; and American Academy of Arts and Letters, 387–88; described, 127; and WDH, 309–10, 365; and history, 134; *Principles of Psychology,* 309; *Varieties of Religious Experience,* 210, 309

Janvier, Thomas A., 370

Jarvis, Charles, 20, 428

Jefferson, Thomas, 44

Jesus Christ, 285, 292, 308

Jewett, Sarah O., 181, 206, 315–16, 369, 374, 379, 393, 431; *Country of the Pointed Firs,* 369; *Deephaven,* 369; WDH on, 369; on Winifred Howells' death, 296; mentored by WDH, 167, 271–72; *Strangers and Wayfarers,* 272; Johns Hopkins University, 124, 238–39, 260

Johnson, Andrew, 30, 40

Johnson, Chief of Six Nations, 182

Jones, S. R., 9

Joyce, James, 14

Keats, John, 316

Keeler, Ralph, 147; *Vagabond Adventures,* 153

Kester, Paul, 259

Kierkegaard, Søren: *Either-Or,* 309

Kilenyi, Olga, 80

King, Clarence, 224, 242, 433–44; *Mountaineering in the Sierra Nevada,* 224

Kingsley, Charles, 185

Kipling, Rudyard, 85–86, 340, 355, 406

Kittery Point, Maine, xvi, 365–70, 386, 392, 413–14

Komura, Jutaro, 375–77

Kossuth, Lajos, 19–20

Kügler, Franz T.: *Kügler's Italian Art,* 86

Ladies Home Journal, 335

LaFarge, John, 113, 240, 325, 370

Lamb, Charles, 53

Langdon, Jervis, 155

Lathrop, George, 193

Lawrence, D. H., 10

Lecky, W. E. H.: *History of European Morals,* 123

Lee, Robert E., 100

Leigh, Augusta, 131

Leopold II (King of Belgium), 340

Lewis, Sinclair, 406; *Arrowsmith,* 406; *Elmer Gantry,* 418; *Main Street,* 406; *The Trail of the Hawk,* 406

Limbeck, Otto, 37

Lincoln, Abraham, 4, 35, 90, 109, 271, 280, 363; administration of, 40, 68–69, 74, 79; assassination of, 98; on *Atlantic,* 141, 195; WDH's biography of, xiii, 48–50, 68, 378; WDH compares Twain to, 399; WDH fails to meet, 61

Lincoln–Douglas debates, 48

Lindsay, Vachel, 431

Lingg, Louis, 278, 283

Literary World (Boston), 185

Literature (London), 372

Livingstone, David, 35

Lloyd, Henry D., 281, 416

Lloyd George, David, 403

Lodge, Henry C., 242, 261

Lodge, Nannie (Mrs. H. C. L.), 242

London, Jack, 102

Long, John L., 424

Longfellow, Alice, 387

Longfellow, Henry W., 54, 79, 395, 426; and *Atlantic,* 121, 122, 132, 139, 361; death of, 216; described, 112, 113; "Evangeline," 82; *Hiawatha,* 52; and *The Inferno,* 113; and Annie Howells, 126, 127; and WDH, xv, 52, 113, 114, 130, 189, 399, 410; and Winifred Howells, 182; on Harpers Ferry, 44; memorial for, 275–6, 386–87; *The Spanish Student,* 52; on *Venetian Life,* 115–16; and Whittier dinner, 191

Lowell, Amy, 431

Lowell, Augustus, 260, 261

Lowell Institute, 260

Lowell, James R., 55, 58, 106, 118, 138, 167, 352, 381, 424; advises WDH, 61, 104, 105, 106, 130–33, 238, 346; and

Müller, Adalbert: *Venice: Her Art-Treasures and Historical Associations,* trans. WDH, 86
Munsey's Magazine, 348
Murfree, Mary N. (Charles Egbert Craddock), 272

NAACP, 409
Napoleon III, 75
Nation, 154, 188, 313; WDH's writing for, 34, 105–8; Minor Topics column, 106
National Arts Club, 423
National Institute of Arts and Letters, 387, 422
Neebe, Oscar E., 278, 283
Nesbitt, Evelyn, 398
New York Journal, 339
New York Post, 48
New York Times, 35, 105, 283, 342
New York Tribune, 35, 185, 254, 261, 281, 322
Niagara Falls, 50–51
Nicholas II (Czar of Russia), 375
Nicolay, J. George, 68–70, 79, 242
Nillson, Christine, 55
Nobel Prize for Literature, 405–6
Norris, Frank, 272, 346; *McTeague,* 346; *The Octopus,* 235, 346
North American Review, 103, 104, 112, 121, 188, 359, 362, 420; publishes WDH's essays, 106, 359
Norton, Charles E., 109, 153, 180, 189; and Anti-Imperialist League, 340; and Ashfield, 212; Ashfield Readers (planned with WDH), 109; and *Atlantic,* 121–22, 190, 195; and the Club, 134; cofounder of *The Nation,* 106; coeditor of *North American Review,* 103, 122; and culture, 113, 138, 261, 325; death of, 393; described 109–10; and Haymarket, 281; helps WDH family, 108, 225; WDH on, 110, 320, 364, 393; on WDH, 193, 254, 275–76, 285, 314; letters to and from WDH, 128, 188, 189, 309, 324, 328, 333, 371, 374, 383–84, 386, 390; and

Longfellow memorials, 275–76, 386–87; on *Venetian Life,* 116
Norton, Grace, 404
Norton, Sarah, 117, 396
Nourse, Clara, 353
Noyes, John H., 2, 61–62, 419

Oglesby, Richard J., 280, 283
Ohio, xvii; demographics, 60; history of, 8
Ohio Farmer, 22
Ohio State Anti-Slavery Society, 24
Ohio State Journal, 20, 22, 47–49, 59, 104; WDH news editor of, 39–40, 41
Oliphant, Margaret, 231
Oneida Community, 2, 61–62
O'Neill, Eugene, 323
Oppenheim, James, 431
Osgood, James R., 131, 174, 208, 255; advises WDH, 139, 175, 238; and *Atlantic,* 187, 199; described, 138–9, 245; finances of, 184, 265; and *Indian Summer* hoax, 266; and *A Modern Instance,* 234
Osgood, James R. & Co., 212–13, 263
Overland Monthly, 119
Owen, Robert D., 9
Owen, Wilfred, 92
Oxford University, 233, 250

Page, Walter H.,
Paine, Albert, 395–96
Panic of 1837, 11
Parisian (ship), 223, 247
Parker House, xiii, 53–54, 184
Parker, Theodore, 44, 126, 261
Parkman, Francis, 123, 134, 410
Parsons, Albert R., 278, 279, 280, 283
Parton, James, 250
Peabody, Elizabeth P., 258, 261
Pen and Brush Club, 423
Pennell, Joseph, 87, 239–41
Pepperrell, Sir William, 368
Perry, Bliss, 387
Perry, Lilla (Mrs. T. S.), 414
Perry, Matthew C., 95
Perry, Thomas. S., 113, 133, 177, 252, 407, 430; as *Atlantic* reviewer, 144–45; on

Washington, Booker T. 345–46, 401; *Up from Slavery,* 346
Washington, George, 7, 11, 44, 112, 316
Welles, Orson, 431
Wells, Herbert G., 272, 360, 385–86, 409; on Henry James, 385; *Love and Mr. Lewisham,* 360, 385; *War of the Worlds,* 360
Wendell, Barrett, 363–64
Western Reserve, 52
Wharton, Edith, 4, 41, 206, 361, 366–67, 379, 429, 431; *The Book of the Homeless,* ed., 420–21; and WDH, 406–7; and Henry James, 114–15, 405–6; describes Charles E. Norton, 109; *Summer,* 334
Whig party, 13–14, 23–24
Whistler, James M., 326–27
White, Stanford, 66, 202–3, 316, 397–98
White, William H., 373
Whitlock, Brand, 282
Whitman, Walt, 147, 232; on Matthew Arnold, 249; *Drum-Taps,* 101; WDH on, 47, 57–58; *Leaves of Grass,* 57, 67, 101; *Specimen Days,* 101
Whittier, John G., 46, 54, 122, 139, 316; and *Atlantic* birthday dinner, 190; and the Chicago anarchists, 280–81; *Who's Who in America,* 55

Wiggin, Kate D.: *Rebecca of Sunnybrook Farm,* 327
Wilde, Oscar, 122, 229, 249, 316; *House of Pomegranates,* 265
Wilhelm II (Kaiser of Germany), 227, 419
Williams, George W., 340
Williams, James E., 24
Wilson, Woodrow, 420
Wister, Owen: *The Virginian,* 235
Witte, Sergius Y., 375–77
Woolf, Virginia, 177, 224, 357, 373
Woolson, Constance F.: *Miss Grief,* 244
Wordsworth, William, 205, 288
World (London), 231
World (New York), 68, 339, 386
World War I, xiii, 92, 304, 334, 419–21, 426–27, 432
Wounded Knee, 304

Yale University, 214, 259, 260
Yeats, William B., 361, 420; "Easter 1916," 421
Young, Brigham, 348, 419

Young, Ann E.: *Wife Number Nineteen,* 348
Youth Companion, 210

Zola, Emile, xiv, 206, 230; *Germinal,* 235, 237, 271, 347

INDEX OF
HOWELLS' WORKS

DESIGNER
Victoria Kuskowski

COMPOSITOR
Integrated Composition Systems

TEXT
11.25/13.5 Adobe Garamond

DISPLAY
Engravers LH Bold, Adobe Garamond

PRINTER AND BINDER
Friesens Corporation